COMPLETE WORKS OF
TACITUS

MODERN LIBRARY COLLEGE EDITIONS

COMPLETE WORKS OF
TACITUS

The Annals · The History ·
The Life of Cnaeus Julius Agricola · Germany
and Its Tribes · A Dialogue on Oratory

TRANSLATED FROM THE LATIN BY
Alfred John Church AND *William Jackson Brodribb*

EDITED, WITH AN INTRODUCTION, BY
Moses Hadas

THE MODERN LIBRARY · *New York*

THE MODERN LIBRARY
is published by Random House, Inc.

Manufactured in the United States of America

PREFACE

Tacitus is the most difficult of the ancient prose authors to translate, and yet none has been rendered into modern languages more frequently. By 1837 there were 393 versions of the whole or part of his works into Italian, French, German, and English, and there have been hundreds more since, into every civilized tongue. But it is not *embarras de richesse* which makes a choice for fresh presentation to a wide audience difficult: considerations of accuracy, dignity, consistency, and completeness render one or another of the available versions undesirable. That in which Tacitus is most familiar to English readers is Arthur Murphy's, first published in 1793; Murphy's wordiness alone, aside from other faults, should disqualify him. For the 118 Latin words in the first chapter of the *Annals* he requires over 300 English words. Church and Brodribb bring the number down to 196, and in so doing are much more faithful to their original. Their version, in the judgment of the present editor, is the best available in English for the whole of Tacitus. Alterations in the text of Tacitus have been so slight despite the assiduity of text-critics, and Church and Brodribb's own taste and scholarship so sound that it has been thought best to print their version as it left their hands. The arrangement of the works in this volume follows what seems to be a logical order; adherence to the order of composition would result only in profitless confusion. Latin place names and coinage may bother the reader. For the former a Glossary with modern equivalents is provided at the end of the volume; for the latter a very rough approximation is a penny for the *as,* twenty cents for the *denarius,* and five cents for the *sestertius,* which is the most common denomination.

There are a number of annotated editions of the works of Tacitus whose introductions and commentaries will be found useful even by the student with no Latin. The standard editions of the various works in English are those of Furneaux, Gudeman, Spooner, and Anderson. The fullest modern account of the period involved is to be found in the tenth and eleventh volumes of the *Cambridge Ancient History* (1934 and 1936). Of various works of criticism Gaston Boissier's *Tacitus* (English translation, 1906) may be specially recommended.

M. H.

Columbia University
January, 1942

CONTENTS

vii

CONTENTS

INTRODUCTION

The apparent insensitivity of the Romans to their greatest historian is an exasperating accident of our faulty tradition or a melancholy commentary upon their civilization. Until the end of the fourth century when Ammianus Marcellinus, an Antiochene Greek, undertook to write a continuation of Tacitus' histories no writer other than his own friend Pliny makes mention of him. It is true that the Emperor Tacitus (275-276 A.D.) is reported, not improbably though the authority is dubious, to have ordered that ten copies of his putative ancestor's works be made annually and that these be deposited in various libraries. In any case the story would indicate that Tacitus had fallen into oblivion; and it is in fact only through a single mutilated manuscript that Tacitus' greatest work has survived the Middle Ages.

The Younger Pliny was associated with Tacitus in important legal pleading and has left us eleven letters addressed to him. These and a single inscription from Asia Minor are the only evidence for Tacitus' life and works we possess outside those works themselves. We know neither the place nor the date of his birth, though it has been suggested that he came from the North of Italy, and Pliny, who was born in 62 A.D., addresses him as somewhat his senior. This combined with the calculation of the probable age at which he held certain offices would give 55 A.D. or somewhat later for Tacitus' birth year. The best manuscript gives his name as *Publius* Cornelius Tacitus, but we cannot be sure of his given name, for other manuscripts give it as *Gaius* Cornelius Tacitus. The decidedly aristocratic bias in his works and the fashionable rhetorical education of which he speaks in his *Dialogue on Oratory* would suggest that his family possessed means and position; his marriage to the daughter of Agricola, governor of Britain, in 78 would point in the same direction. When Agricola died in 93 Tacitus tells us he had been absent from Rome for four years; the natural assumption is that he was engaged in some form of provincial administration, perhaps in Germany. This would suit what he tells us at the beginning of his *Histories:* "I would not deny that my elevation was begun by Vespasian, augmented by Titus, and still further advanced by Domitian." From Pliny again we learn that Tacitus as consul under Nerva in 97 pronounced the funeral oration for Verginius Rufus, one of the most admirable characters of his day. Three years later, in association with Pliny, Tacitus won an important case for the Africans against their oppressive governor, Marius Priscus. The inscription mentioned above indicates that Tacitus was governor of Asia Minor under Trajan, probably in 112. The latest event alluded to in Tacitus' extant writings is a reference in the second book of the *Annals* to the extension of the Empire to the Persian Gulf. This took place in 116, and Tacitus may have died at any subsequent date that will allow time for the completion of the remaining books of the *Annals.*

Of his works the oldest is probably the *Dialogue on Oratory.* The authenticity of this treatise has been doubted from time to time, chiefly on the ground of its stylistic divergence from the other writings. Its neo-Ciceronian style, markedly unlike that of his other works, has led some to date it not long after the dramatic date of the *Dialogue,* which is 75 A.D. But at the beginning of the *Dialogue* Tacitus states that he is reporting a conversation he overheard as a young man, and at the beginning of the Agricola, written in 98, he deprecates his inexperience in writing; and these considerations have led some scholars to move the date far forward. No other Latin dialogue (and we have many, from Cicero and Seneca) approaches Tacitus' in dramatic verisimilitude, and it would seem reasonable to suppose that even after Tacitus had developed his own unique style he could still represent older rhetoricians in a medium appropriate to them.

This golden booklet, as it has been styled since the Renascence, deals with much of perennial interest: with vocational and humanistic education, with dilettantism and scholarship, with philosophy as a guide in life, with the loss of individual responsibility as the price of good government. The subject of the inquiry is the change in oratory since Cicero's day. The change in educational ideals and in the conditions of life are mentioned as contributory causes; but the factor which overshadows all others is the change in political life. Only the Republic could make oratory vital, for only in the Republic did oratory serve a necessary function in the body politic.

The *Agricola,* written in 98, is a laudatory biography of the author's father-in-law, who had had a successful military and administrative career in Britain and had then fallen under the displeasure of Domitian. The early chapters tell of Agricola's career to his appointment as governor, and then give an account of Britain and its relations to Rome. The two strands are then combined, until Agricola's recall by the Emperor Domitian. Much is made of Agricola's exemplary conduct while he was the object of the Emperor's jealousy. The biography continues with an account of its hero's last illness and death, and closes with an address to the survivors. This epilogue is one of the finest passages in Latin and one of the best condolences in any literature. It is true that the life is eulogy rather than history, and that the eulogy might be applicable not to its subject alone but to any virtuous Roman. But for us, as for Tacitus' first readers, it is important to know that a good Roman could live through Domitian's Terror without becoming either an accessory to the Emperor's crimes or his compliant tool, "that great men can exist even under evil rulers" (*posse etiam sub malis principibus magnos viros esse*).

The fullest form of the title of the *Germania,* also written in 98, is *On the Origin, Geography, Institutions, and Tribes of the Germans,* and this indicates the book's character. It is a geographic and ethnologic treatise, artistic in form and scientific by contemporary standards. It has become a sort of ethnologic Bible for the Germans, and is studied in modern Germany more than any other ancient book. The early chapters deal with the public and private usages of the Germans in general, and then we have a more or less systematic account of the various tribes, with individual characteristics and other information given incidentally. The twenty-odd pages of this treatise constitute the most exhaustive and valuable work of its character preserved to us from antiquity. More than six hundred items of information are recorded, of a credibility, to be sure, varying with that of Tacitus' sources. The sources were undoubtedly the best available, and included eye-witness accounts as well as written material, and Tacitus was a conscientious workman; but it is as absurd to credit Tacitus with the ideals of nineteenth-century scholarship as it is to despise the work as uninformed journalism. The latter was the view of the great Mommsen, and is certainly as wide of the mark as is Gibbon's praise of the work as the result of "accurate observation and diligent inquiries."

It is a temptation to which many have succumbed to look upon the *Germania* as a sort of Utopia, a conscious idealization of a primitive and unspoiled people calculated to chasten and reform the decadent Romans. This view is justified in the degree that a strong moralizing strain runs through all Tacitus' work. It has been wittily remarked that no one in Tacitus is good except Agricola and the Germans. But the fact is that too many unlovely traits are reported of the Germans along with the idealization to justify making moral improvement the main end of the book.

We come now to the specifically historical works. Of these we know there were thirty books, and it is now generally assumed that there were twelve of the *Histories* and eighteen of the *Annals*. Mention should be made of the alternative theory current until recently which gave the *Histories* and the *Annals* fourteen and sixteen books respectively. The *Histories* covered the period from 69, the year of the four Emperors, to the death of Domitian in 96. Only the first four books and a fragment of the fifth have been preserved. The extant portion includes the melodramatic events of 69 and most of 70. The work was written and published during the reign of Trajan; more precise dating is impossible. The only title given in the manuscript of Tacitus' greatest work is *From the Death of Deified Augustus,* but the customary

Annals is justified on other grounds. This work covered the period from the death of Augustus in 14 A.D. to that of Nero in 68. The extant portion includes the first four books, a fragment of the fifth, most of the sixth (the first part is missing), and books eleven to sixteen, with the beginning of the eleventh and the end of the sixteenth missing. These extant books cover the reign of Tiberius (14-37), the latter seven years of Claudius (47-54), and the first twelve years of Nero (54-66). We have noted above that a passage in the second book indicates that it was written about 116. The *Annals* and *Histories* together covered the period from 14 to 96. In *Annals* 3.24 Tacitus promises a work on the reign of Augustus if life should permit, and in *Histories* 1.1 he reserves for his old age a study of the reigns of Nerva and Trajan. It may be significant of Tacitus' interests that the eighty-two years which his history covers included the frightful half of the period he proposed to deal with (and for this half it is, indeed, our best source), and that he did not find time for the happy reigns at either end of the span; the usual assumption is, of course, that Tacitus did not live to complete these projected works.

An account of Tacitus' career must be meagre, but fuller knowledge would, after all, be useful only insofar as it might contribute to a fuller understanding of his work; and here we are not so badly off, for his books show vividly what manner of man he was. No other ancient author has so impregnated his works with his own personality. It is easy enough to see what Tacitus thought of the world in which he lived, what his convictions and his prejudices were. The illustration and enforcement of certain convictions seem to him to be, in fact, the prime purpose in the writing of history. "This I regard as history's highest function," he writes (*Annals* 3.65), "to let no worthy action be uncommemorated, and to hold out the reprobation of posterity as a terror to evil words and deeds." His moralizing intent is made even clearer in another passage (*Annals* 4.33): "There must be good in carefully noting and recording this period, for it is but few who have the foresight to distinguish right from wrong or what is sound from what is hurtful. while most men learn virtue from the fortunes of others. Still, though this is instructive, it gives very little pleasure."

But no desire to give pleasure will persuade Tacitus to lower the dignity of his work. At several points he expresses regret that his incidents are so mean and his personalities so petty compared with the grander events and figures of the Republic, and he refuses to compromise what dignity his theme possesses by spicing his account with what is merely titivating. "I think it unbecoming the task I have undertaken," he writes (*Histories* 2.50), "to collect fabulous marvels and to entertain with fiction the tastes of my readers." A form such entertainment might take is glanced at in *Annals* 13.31: "One might fill volumes with the praise of the foundations and timber work on which Nero piled the immense amphitheatre in the Field of Mars. But we have learned that it suits the dignity of the Roman people to reserve history for great achievements, and to leave such details to the city's daily register."

It is the moralizing intent which explains and is served by Tacitus' interest in people. Broad principles, large movements, even great achievements move him not for their own sake but because they tell us about the people who were responsible for them. *"Tacite a introduit l'homme dans l'histoire,"* writes a French critic, *"c'est l'homme, c'est l'humanité qu'il raconte en racontant Rome et les Romains."* And not humanity in general but individual humans. Always Tacitus strives to penetrate into the thoughts and motives of the actors in his drama. It is Tacitus' skill in delineating characters, particularly intense and theatrical Roman characters, that is apt to strike the reader as his outstanding achievement. Macaulay has put the case well: "In the delineation of character Tacitus is unrivalled among historians and has very few superiors among dramatists and novelists. By the delineation of character we do not mean the practice of drawing up epigrammatic catalogues of good and bad qualities, and appending them to the names of eminent men. No writer, indeed, has done this more skilfully than Tacitus; but this is not his peculiar glory. All the persons who occupy a large space in his works have an individuality of character which seems to pervade all their words and actions. We know them as if we had lived with them."

"Very few superiors among dramatists and novelists." One recalls Aristotle's distinction between the poet (which would include the dramatist and novelist) and the historian, and his insistence that the poet is the more philosophical because his picture carries the conviction of general validity and is universally true (*Poetics* 1451b). Aristotle's historian, on the other hand, however accurate his transcription of particular events, remains only the reporter of particular events, which may in fact be freakish occurrences of highly improbable possibilities. The philosopher prefers probable impossibilities. Here a comparison with Tacitus' greatest Greek and greatest Latin predecessor is illuminating. Thucydides is interested in the actual and probable behavior not of individual men but of men in general, living in society. He does tell us a good deal about such men as Pericles, Alcibiades, Nicias, it is true, but the details he gives are such as the reader must possess in order to understand the course of the Peloponnesian War, which is Thucydides' main concern. For details of Pericles' relations with Aspasia or Alcibiades' lisp we must go to Plutarch, who is so far indifferent to political considerations that he represents the Peloponnesian War as having been started by Pericles in order to cover a scandal arising out of a private quarrel. Livy tells us much about the great Romans of the Republic, but his object, like that of Augustus in lining his Forum with their statues, was to create a gallery of heroes for the patriotic devotion of his contemporaries. All or almost all are idealized. In the period of the Second Punic War, for example, Fabius Cunctator, Marcellus, and Scipio Africanus are practically beatified, and the reverses of that war are blamed upon two scapegoats, Flaminius and Varro. We could guess, and modern historians have demonstrated, that the one group are not the saints they are pictured and the other not the villains. Tacitus' characters, unlike Thucydides', are there for their own sake, but they are there to be understood, not merely to be praised or condemned. And if Tacitus' bias goes far in the direction of pessimism we need but to look about us, alas, to be convinced that he is nearer the truth than is his contemporary Plutarch, who lived not in Rome but in a provincial Greek town, and who *chose* the men whose lives he wished to examine.

Something like this must have been in Gibbon's mind when he said of Tacitus that he was the "first of historians who applied the science of philosophy to the study of facts." For in philosophy in the ordinary sense Tacitus does not appear to advantage. It is in fact impossible to extract *a* philosophy from his writings. His *Weltanschauung* has been criticized as immature and full of irreconcilable contradictions. Following the tradition of Polybius he explains events by natural causes, and when natural causes fail he invokes accident or Fortune. But Tacitus refers events to transcendent causes also; he speaks of the gods, their grace and their wrath. He speaks of Inexorable Fate and Absolute Necessity, and then of chance, which makes a jest of prosperity and doubles the tragedy of suffering. It may be only a rhetorical striving for point that results in such odd combinations of the immanent and transcendent in explaining events: Varus succumbs to destiny and the strength of Arminius (*Annals* 1.55); a famine is averted by the grace of God and a mild Winter (*Annals* 12.43). The fact of the matter is that Tacitus is no more a closet philosopher than a research historian. He is a practical man, really less confused in relating life to theory than such Stoics as Seneca and even the Younger Cato; he is interested in events and not in speculation. It may be significant that he practically avoids the word *philosophia* and uses the homelier Latin term *sapientia* instead. Those expressions in his works which may be combined to prove his philosophic naïveté are part of a cultured vocabulary, and show only that Tacitus was neither a misologist nor interested in creating a neat and necessarily impracticable system.

Two other characteristics of Tacitus' work which are likely to distress the modern historian may be mentioned. One is the attribution to his characters of speeches which they cannot have delivered (an inscription discovered at Lyons in 1528 gives part of an actual speech of Claudius which Tacitus reports only in brief outline but quite differently in *Annals* 11.24), and the other is the manifest inaccuracy of his battle accounts. As for the speeches, they had become a fixture in history since Thucydides, and as in Thucydides they are frequently the most convenient way of setting forth a situation or a point of view. A discourse dramatically suited to events is more effective than exposition, and if effectiveness and intelligibility are desiderata, why reproduce a speech which is less effective and intelligible than one the writer can supply? Ancient historians are always more artists than scientists and could regard only as a fetish the sanctity we attach to inverted commas. Such a fictive speech as the British chieftain is made to deliver in the *Agricola,* for example, almost certainly sets forth the grounds for native opposition much better than any native could set them forth.

As for the battle description which follows this speech, it seems to have been lifted almost bodily from Sallust's description of a battle which had been fought in Africa two centuries before. Mommsen called Tacitus the most unmilitary of historians (which is unfair to Livy), and even Gibbon says his military history is more remarkable for elegance than perspicuity. When Tacitus describes a battle we are made to feel at least that strenuous and significant action took place; as for details, he follows the practice of the later historians generally, who seem to have resorted to commonplace books for such embellishments. All the naval battles in the later historians, for example, bear so pronounced a family resemblance that one is almost forced to the conclusion that Dio Cassius and the others resorted to the same file, under the folder marked "Sea Battles." Indeed, contemporary criticism would condemn a writer who refused to borrow from his predecessor as eccentric, and was prepared to tolerate a much larger volume of borrowing than can be charged to Tacitus.

If descriptions of battles are mere rhetoric, if speeches are fanciful, if motives are ascribed to characters when it cannot be known what their motives were, one may well ask how trustworthy the resultant history is. A modern historian guilty of such faults would surely lose all credit. But in the Roman concept the historian was never thought of as a researcher but primarily as a literary man, and his function not as the propagation of sound learning so much as the inculcation of salutary doctrine. The most highly regarded historian in Tacitus' day was Livy, who had lived a century earlier, and Livy's attitude to fact was much more cavalier than Tacitus'. Livy's professed aim was edification; he wished to make his degenerate contemporaries aware of the grand achievements and majestic personalities of their past, to the end that they might glory in the name of Rome and justify the responsibility of their noble heritage. Tacitus' program is not very different. He recognizes, to be sure, that the glory of the remote past is gone forever, but he is profoundly concerned that the degradation of the immediate past shall not be repeated. With allowance made for rhetorical embellishment customary in his day, and within the limits of distortion which his own views of morality and politics make inevitable, Tacitus never consciously sacrifices historical truth. He consulted good sources, memoirs, biographies, and official records, and he frequently implies that he had more than one source before him. He requested information of those in position to know, as we learn from a reply of Pliny to such a request. He exercises critical judgment in questioning the value of a biased account (*Annals* 13.20). Both knowledge and impartiality are recognized as prerequisites for the historian's task in the first chapter of the *Histories*. "The truthfulness of history," he writes, "has been impaired in many ways; at first through men's ignorance of public affairs, which were now wholly strange to them, then through their passion for flattery, or, on the other hand, their hatred of their masters." Similarly at the beginning of the *Annals* he insists that he is writing "without either bitterness or partiality."

For an authoritative opinion on the historical validity of Tacitus' writings we can do no better than turn to the sober *Cambridge Ancient History* (10.872, 1934): "Though he occasionally appears to group events more with a view to literary effect than to strict sequence in time, it would be difficult to produce an instance when he has deliberately misstated or falsified facts, and easy to cite passages when he carefully rejects and passes over versions and rumours which suit his book better, but which he eschews. His portrait of the slow degeneration of Tiberius or Claudius is severe, but with his preconceptions, and on the evidence before him he could not write otherwise: he depicted Tiberius as he does because the evidence before him all pointed that way. Modern research tends ultimately not so much to prove Tacitus false or malignant, but rather to illustrate and stress aspects of the history of the Empire in which Tacitus was not interested. Thus it comes about that the facts he reports are usually accurate enough and rarely refuted by modern discoveries, but his interpretation must often be challenged. . . . The trend of present-day scholarship is towards the recognition of his integrity and essential greatness." It is hard to imagine how bare and distorted our picture of Tacitus' period would be without Tacitus; all that has been written upon it since is either a dim reflection of his insight or a lifeless extract from his writings.

But Tacitus could see only through his own lenses, which were strongly colored, and it is a testimonial to his effectiveness that he has infected the world's view of the period with which he deals with the same tint. Tacitus was an aristocrat with a nostalgic admiration for the Republic and contempt for a populace and a nobility alike corrupted by slavery. Domitian's terror had touched his own circle and his own family. His is not history written by a white-smocked laboratory technician. His emotions are not relegated to such times as he may remove the smock and step out of his workroom. That is why he paints Tiberius too black and Germanicus too white, that is why he can carry his readers in the torrent of his own convictions.

Those critics who complain that Tacitus' philosophy cannot be reduced to a neat system are unhappy also because he does not provide a revolutionary program for restoring the Republic he so admired. He may be regarded as pusillanimous or prudential, according to the reader's disposition. A speech put into the mouth of Eprius Marcellus may fairly be cited for Tacitus' own point of view (*Histories* 4.8): "I do not forget the times in which I have been born, or the form of government which our fathers and grandfathers established. I may regard with admiration an earlier period, but I acquiesce in the present, and while I pray for good Em-

perors, I can endure whomsoever we may have." Tyranny is
galling, but the objections to it are not social or humani-
tarian. Indeed, Tacitus' attitude to the lower classes of society is very wide of the democratic (or Stoic) ideal. Slaves
cannot be credited with normal human sensibilities, the
blood of gladiators is characterized as worthless, and foreigners are regularly the object of distrust and loathing.
When he reports that four thousand freedmen infected with
Egyptian and Jewish "superstitions" were expelled to Sardinia he adds that the loss would be slight if they succumbed
to the unhealthy climate of that island (*Annals* 2.85). From
the point of view of general security and comfort, it is the
excess of these commodities rather than their lack which distresses Tacitus. He puts a good case for oppressed provincials, but it is inefficient and greedy administration he objects to rather than the principle of empire. He rejoices in
the Empire, in fact, and justifies it on the ground of the
white man's burden. He realizes that empire is no longer
possible without an emperor, and only desires that the emperor be virtuous. Caesarism's vice is not physical or eco-
nomic oppression but spiritual degradation. The elimination
of the power of the aristocracy is for Tacitus the source of
corruption in society, of cringing nobles and upstart freedmen, of degradation at home and humiliation abroad. It
would have been interesting to see how Tacitus would have
treated the Caesarism of the "good" emperors whose history
he promised but never wrote. Perhaps lack of time was not
the only reason they were never written.

If Tacitus is artist as well as historian it remains to glance
at some of his artistic devices. The masterly characteriza-
tions of which we have spoken are achieved with remarkable
economy of detail. He never indulges, as Suetonius does, in
scandalous gossip for its own sake. His sketches are rendered
in bold strokes, his effects are obtained by the use of light
and shadow which bring out the essentials. If this technique
results in theatricality it is but the characteristic of the age.
The grand Romans all stalk about on a stage, like the lurid
figures in Seneca's tragedies; their grandeur and their intensity are always on parade, they are always conscious of

their public and their public's expectations. Is it natural for an old woman confronted by the assassins her son has sent to point to her womb and say "Strike here"? Theatrical to the highest degree and to the highest degree effective are such sequences (and they are many in number) as those which tell of Messalina's mock marriage in the eleventh book of the *Annals*, or of the events leading to Nero's murder of his mother in the fourteenth. Their effect is stunning, as theatre if not as life; no ancient dramatist approaches the decor and the direction.

Such scenes are not the only things in Tacitus which suggest the dramatist's art. Using identical materials different authors achieve the most diverse effects by selecting and grouping their details. In Tacitus the details chosen are frequently such as will produce horror; then occasionally amusing episodes or instances of ordinary humanity are inserted, very like the relaxing interludes with which Shakespeare relieves and points up tragic tension. After the storm and stress of the Piso conspiracy at the end of *Annals* 15, for example, we have the hoax of Dido's buried treasure at the beginning of Book 16. Ostensibly the annalistic form is followed, but the apparently chronological order conceals a subtle art of arrangement. Traditional and obvious connections are disregarded, and fresh and illuminating associations are substituted. Again the criterion is not political clarification but dramatic effectiveness.

Effective scenes are one requirement of the dramatic art, another is effective lines. In Seneca characters exchange single-line tags for pages, each compact and pointed, each eminently quotable. No paragraph in Tacitus is without its pregnant epigram embodying some acute observation or comment. Here the English reader is put at a serious disadvantage, for only rarely does the sharp point carry over in translation. Of one of the best known, *solitudinem faciunt pacem appellant*, only half the effectiveness is lost, for the translation requires only double the number of Latin words, "They make a wilderness and call it peace." It is to be expected that the loss in effectiveness is usually greater. In the case of the concise epigrams at least explanation is possible, but for Tacitus' style as a whole description to one who has

not read the Latin is as difficult as describing peppermint to
a man who has never tasted it. The style is unique and un-
mistakable. The ordinary word, the ordinary construction,
the ordinary arrangement are studiously avoided. The balance, the parallelism, the flow characteristic of Cicero or
Livy are eschewed. The only rule is that Tacitus will say a
thing differently than you expected and more concisely. The
effect is frequently that of sombre and full-toned organ music played staccato. By modern standards of style Tacitus is
labored, even precious; but Latin style, and particularly the
the Latin style of the Silver Age, must be judged by a different standard, for it never attempted to approximate the
spoken language. Yet in his straining to avoid the common-
place in diction Tacitus goes far even for Silver Latin. He
not only avoids "brothels" by saying (*Histories* 2.93) *in-
honesta dictu,* "places unseemly to mention," but he calls
spades "implements for digging earth and cutting turf"
(*Annals* 1.65). For death fifty different circumlocutions have
been counted in Tacitus.

Tacitus had to wait until the Italian Renascence for proper
appreciation. From the fifth century to the fifteenth he is
mentioned not more than two or three times. Early in the
latter century Niccolo Niccoli was in possession of the manuscript which is our sole authority for the *Histories* and the
second half of the *Annals,* and Poggio was working hard to
obtain the minor works; in 1455 Enoch of Ascoli brought
them from Germany in a manuscript which is apparently the
father of all our existing manuscripts of these works. In
1509 the manuscript which is our sole source for the first
part of the *Annals* was discovered at Corbey. Immediately
all writers on political subjects began to quarry from Tacitus. Machiavelli, as might be expected, quotes him, in the
Discourses and the *Florentine History,* and Montaigne
(3.8) remarks how applicable Tacitus is to his own France.
French interest in Tacitus was very marked. He was translated several times and very frequently echoed. D'Aubigné,
for example, says of Henry IV, *"digne du royaume s'il n'eût
point régné,"* a version, at the usual rate of expansion, of
imperii capax nisi imperasset. Tacitus figures large in French
political disputations. Saumaise considers him a champion

of absolutism, and is warmly refuted by John Milton. Montesquieu had a high regard for Tacitus and consciously strove to model himself after the man of whom he wrote: "Tacitus abridged everything because he saw everything." Voltaire finds him a republican, and Desmoulins in the *Vieux Cordelier* discourses on despotism from a text in Tacitus. Napoleon complains of Tacitus' vilification of the emperors and offers to correct "inaccuracies" in his work.

Dramatists and novelists have found Tacitus a no less fruitful source. Corneille has an *Otho*, Racine a *Britannicus*, Ben Jonson a *Sejanus*, Alfieri an *Octavia*, and Chénier a *Tiberius*; there are a dozen plays on Nero. Sinkiewicz' *Quo Vadis* and such contemporary novelists as Feuchtwanger in his Josephus stories and Robert Graves in his Claudius series have long sections which are but adaptations of Tacitus. Contemporary history also, aside from contemporary literature, shows increasingly long sections which are but adaptations of Tacitus, and Tacitus has a profounder claim on the attention of the modern reader than the mere satisfaction of antiquarian curiosity. Tacitus always helped men understand themselves and their history, but not for a hundred years have his lessons been as pertinent as they are today. Along with his great Greek model Thucydides, Tacitus provides an agreeable channel whereby the best historical insight and experience of the ancient world are made available for our own enlightenment. **M. H.**

CHRONOLOGY

Names of ruling emperors are printed in capitals; items of literary interest, including events in the career of Tacitus, in italics.

14 Death of AUGUSTUS and succession of TIBERIUS. Agrippa Postumus executed. Powers of comitia transferred to Senate. Military mutinies in Pannonia and Germany.

15 Campaign against Arminius.

16 Germanicus advances to the Elbe but is recalled, and the attempt to extend the Roman frontier is abandoned.

17 Triumph of Germanicus, who goes to the East. Rising of Tacfarinas in Africa. Cappadocia and Commagene annexed. *Death of Ovid and Livy.*

19 Germanicus in Egypt; dies in Syria.

20 Piso, charged with treason and with death of Germanicus, commits suicide.

23 Sejanus concentrates Praetorians in camp at city walls.

26 Sejanus quarrels with Agrippina. Tiberius leaves Rome to settle at Capri. Pontius Pilate procurator of Judaea.

33 Financial crisis. Drusus, son of Germanicus, executed. Death of the elder Agrippina.

37 TIBERIUS dies, succeeded by GAIUS (CALIGULA). Birth of Nero.

41 GAIUS murdered, CLAUDIUS made emperor. *Seneca exiled.*

43 Successful expedition to Britain.

48 Death of Messalina and her paramour.

49 CLAUDIUS marries Agrippina. *Seneca recalled to become tutor to Domitius (Nero); central period of his literary activity.*

50 CLAUDIUS adopts Domitius (hereafter Nero).

54 CLAUDIUS poisoned. NERO succeeds.

55 *Birth of Tacitus.*

59 Murder of Agrippina.

61 Uprising under Boadicea in Britain; suppressed by Paullinus, and Boadicea commits suicide.

62 Octavia divorced and murdered; NERO marries Poppaea.

64 Great fire at Rome.

65 Conspiracy of Piso, for which, among others, *Seneca* and *Lucan* suffer death.

66 Many executions, including that of *Petronius.*

68 NERO killed, GALBA succeeds.

69 OTHO, VITELLIUS, VESPASIAN successively made emperor.

70 Titus takes Jerusalem. Uprising in Gaul and Germany under Civilis. *Quintilian fills one of professorships instituted by Vespasian.*

75 *Tacitus studies under Aper and Secundus.*

78 *Tacitus marries Agricola's daughter;* Agricola to Britain.

79 Death of VESPASIAN, accession of TITUS. Destruction of Pompeii. *Death of Pliny the Elder.*

81 Death of TITUS, accession of DOMITIAN. *Tacitus' Dialogus composed about this time.*

85 Agricola recalled. Many executions.

88 *Tacitus praetor. Plutarch in Rome about this time.*

89-93 *Tacitus absent from Rome, probably as Propraetor of province (Belgium ?). Death of Valerius Flaccus.*

96 Murder of DOMITIAN; NERVA elected by Senate. *Death of Statius.*

98 Death of NERVA, accession of TRAJAN. *Tacitus consul. Publication of* Agricola *and* Germania.

100 *Younger Pliny consul. Tacitus prosecutes M. Priscus.*

101 *Death of Silius and Martial.*

112 *Tacitus Proconsul of Asia.* Histories *completed some time before.*

113 *Death of Younger Pliny.*

116 *Publication of Tacitus'* Annals, *and of first book of Juvenal.*

117 Death of TRAJAN, accession of HADRIAN.

FAMILY CONNECTIONS OF THE JULIO-CLAUDIAN EMPERORS

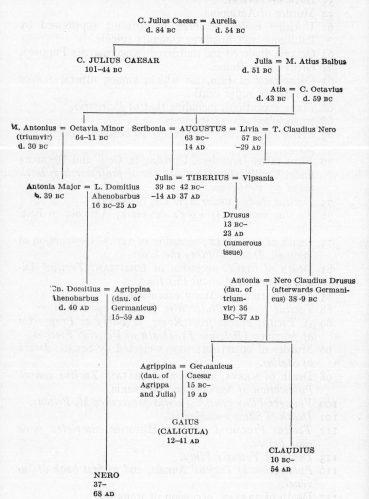

C. Julius Caesar = Aurelia
d. 84 BC   d. 54 BC

C. JULIUS CAESAR
101–44 BC

Julia = M. Atius Balbus
d. 51 BC

Atia = C. Octavius
d. 43 BC   d. 59 BC

M. Antonius = Octavia Minor   Scribonia = AUGUSTUS = Livia = T. Claudius Nero
(triumvir)   64–11 BC   63 BC–   57 BC
d. 30 BC   14 AD   –29 AD

Antonia Major = L. Domitius   Julia = TIBERIUS = Vipsania
b. 39 BC   Ahenobarbus   39 BC 42 BC–
         16 BC–25 AD   –14 AD 37 AD

Drusus
13 BC–
23 AD
(numerous
issue)

Cn. Domitius = Agrippina   Antonia = Nero Claudius Drusus
Ahenobarbus   (dau. of   (dau. of   (afterwards Germani-
d. 40 AD   Germanicus)   trium-   cus) 38–9 BC
         15–59 AD   vir) 36
                 BC–37 AD

Agrippina = Germanicus
(dau. of   Caesar
Agrippa   15 BC–
and Julia)   19 AD

GAIUS
(CALIGULA)
12–41 AD

CLAUDIUS
10 BC–
54 AD

NERO
37–
68 AD

THE ANNALS

THE ANNALS

BOOK I

A.D. 14, 15

1. ROME at the beginning was ruled by kings. Freedom and the consulship were established by Lucius Brutus. Dictatorships were held for a temporary crisis. The power of the decemvirs did not last beyond two years, nor was the consular jurisdiction of the military tribunes of long duration. The despotisms of Cinna and Sulla were brief; the rule of Pompeius and of Crassus soon yielded before Cæsar; the arms of Lepidus and Antonius before Augustus; who, when the world was wearied by civil strife, subjected it to empire under the title of "Prince." But the successes and reverses of the old Roman people have been recorded by famous historians; and fine intellects were not wanting to describe the times of Augustus, till growing sycophancy scared them away. The histories of Tiberius, Caius, Claudius, and Nero, while they were in power, were falsified through terror, and after their death were written under the irritation of a recent hatred. Hence my purpose is to relate a few facts about Augustus—more particularly his last acts, then the reign of Tiberius, and all which follows, without either bitterness or partiality, from any motives to which I am far removed.

2. When after the destruction of Brutus and Cassius there was no longer any army of the Commonwealth, when Pompeius was crushed in Sicily, and when, with Lepidus pushed aside and Antonius slain, even the Julian faction had only Cæsar left to lead it, then, dropping the title of triumvir, and giving out that he was a Consul, and was satisfied with a tribune's authority for the protection of the people, Augustus

3

won over the soldiers with gifts, the populace with cheap
corn, and all men with the sweets of repose, and so grew
greater by degrees, while he concentrated in himself the
functions of the Senate, the magistrates, and the laws. He
was wholly unopposed, for the boldest spirits had fallen in
battle, or in the proscription, while the remaining nobles, the
readier they were to be slaves, were raised the higher by
wealth and promotion, so that, aggrandised by revolution,
they preferred the safety of the present to the dangerous
past. Nor did the provinces dislike that condition of affairs,
for they distrusted the government of the Senate and the
people, because of the rivalries between the leading men and
the rapacity of the officials, while the protection of the laws
was unavailing, as they were continually deranged by violence, intrigue, and finally by corruption.

3. Augustus meanwhile, as supports to his despotism,
raised to the pontificate and curule ædileship Claudius Marcellus, his sister's son, while a mere stripling, and Marcus
Agrippa, of humble birth, a good soldier, and one who had
shared his victory, to two consecutive consulships, and as
Marcellus soon afterwards died, he also accepted him as his
son-in-law. Tiberius Nero and Claudius Drusus, his stepsons,
he honoured with imperial titles, although his own family
was as yet undiminished. For he had admitted the children of
Agrippa, Caius and Lucius, into the house of the Cæsars;
and before they had yet laid aside the dress of boyhood he
had most fervently desired, with an outward show of reluctance, that they should be entitled "princes of the youth,"
and be consuls-elect. When Agrippa died, and Lucius Cæsar
as he was on his way to our armies in Spain, and Caius while
returning from Armenia, still suffering from a wound, were
prematurely cut off by destiny, or by their step-mother
Livia's treachery, Drusus too having long been dead, Nero
remained alone of the stepsons, and in him everything tended
to centre. He was adopted as a son, as a colleague in empire
and a partner in the tribunitian power, and paraded through
all the armies, no longer through his mother's secret intrigues, but at her open suggestion. For she had gained such
a hold on the aged Augustus that he drove out as an exile
into the island of Planasia, his only grandson, Agrippa Pos-

tumus, who, though devoid of worthy qualities, and having only the brute courage of physical strength, had not been convicted of any gross offence. And yet Augustus had appointed Germanicus, Drusus's offspring, to the command of eight legions on the Rhine, and required Tiberius to adopt him, although Tiberius had a son, now a young man, in his house; but he did it that he might have several safeguards to rest on. He had no war at the time on his hands except against the Germans, which was rather to wipe out the disgrace of the loss of Quintilius Varus and his army than out of an ambition to extend the empire, or for any adequate recompense. At home all was tranquil, and there were magistrates with the same titles; there was a younger generation, sprung up since the victory of Actium, and even many of the older men had been born during the civil wars. How few were left who had seen the republic!

4. Thus the State had been revolutionised, and there was not a vestige left of the old sound morality. Stript of equality, all looked up to the commands of a sovereign without the least apprehension for the present, while Augustus in the vigour of life, could maintain his own position, that of his house, and the general tranquillity. When in advanced old age, he was worn out by a sickly frame, and the end was near and new prospects opened, a few spoke in vain of the blessings of freedom, but most people dreaded and some longed for war. The popular gossip of the large majority fastened itself variously on their future masters. "Agrippa was savage, and had been exasperated by insult, and neither from age nor experience in affairs was equal to so great a burden. Tiberius Nero was of mature years, and had established his fame in war, but he had the old arrogance inbred in the Claudian family, and many symptoms of a cruel temper, though they were repressed, now and then broke out. He had also from earliest infancy been reared in an imperial house; consulships and triumphs had been heaped on him in his younger days; even in the years which, on the pretext of seclusion he spent in exile at Rhodes, he had had no thoughts but of wrath, hypocrisy, and secret sensuality. There was his mother too with a woman's caprice. They must, it seemed, be subject to a female and to two striplings besides, who

for a while would burden, and some day rend asunder the State."

5. While these and like topics were discussed, the infirmities of Augustus increased, and some suspected guilt on his wife's part. For a rumour had gone abroad that a few months before he had sailed to Planasia on a visit to Agrippa, with the knowledge of some chosen friends, and with one companion, Fabius Maximus; that many tears were shed on both sides, with expressions of affection, and that thus there was a hope of the young man being restored to the home of his grandfather. This, it was said, Maximus had divulged to his wife Marcia, she again to Livia. All was known to Cæsar, and when Maximus soon afterwards died, by a death some thought to be self-inflicted, there were heard at his funeral wailings from Marcia, in which she reproached herself for having been the cause of her husband's destruction. Whatever the fact was, Tiberius as he was just entering Illyria was summoned home by an urgent letter from his mother, and it has not been thoroughly ascertained whether at the city of Nola he found Augustus still breathing or quite lifeless. For Livia had surrounded the house and its approaches with a strict watch, and favourable bulletins were published from time to time, till, provision having been made for the demands of the crisis, one and the same report told men that Augustus was dead and that Tiberius Nero was master of the State.

6. The first crime of the new reign was the murder of Postumus Agrippa. Though he was surprised and unarmed, a centurion of the firmest resolution despatched him with difficulty. Tiberius gave no explanation of the matter to the Senate; he pretended that there were directions from his father ordering the tribune in charge of the prisoner not to delay the slaughter of Agrippa, whenever he should himself have breathed his last. Beyond a doubt, Augustus had often complained of the young man's character, and had thus succeeded in obtaining the sanction of a decree of the Senate for his banishment. But he never was hard-hearted enough to destroy any of his kinsfolk, nor was it credible that death was to be the sentence of the grandson in order that the stepson might feel secure. It was more probable that Tiberius

and Livia, the one from fear, the other from a stepmother's enmity, hurried on the destruction of a youth whom they suspected and hated. When the centurion reported, according to military custom, that he had executed the command, Tiberius replied that he had not given the command, and that the act must be justified to the Senate.

As soon as Sallustius Crispus who shared the secret (he had, in fact, sent the written order to the tribune) knew this, fearing that the charge would be shifted on himself, and that his peril would be the same whether he uttered fiction or truth, he advised Livia not to divulge the secrets of her house or the counsels of friends, or any services performed by the soldiers, nor to let Tiberius weaken the strength of imperial power by referring everything to the Senate, for "the condition," he said, "of holding empire is that an account cannot be balanced unless it be rendered to one person."

7. Meanwhile at Rome people plunged into slavery—consuls, senators, knights. The higher a man's rank, the more eager his hypocrisy, and his looks the more carefully studied, so as neither to betray joy at the decease of one emperor nor sorrow at the rise of another, while he mingled delight and lamentations with his flattery. Sextus Pompeius and Sextus Apuleius, the consuls, were the first to swear allegiance to Tiberius Cæsar, and in their presence the oath was taken by Seius Strabo and Caius Turranius, respectively the commander of the prætorian cohorts and the superintendent of the corn supplies. Then the Senate, the soldiers and the people did the same. For Tiberius would inaugurate everything with the consuls, as though the ancient constitution remained, and he hesitated about being emperor. Even the proclamation by which he summoned the senators to their chamber, he issued merely with the title of Tribune, which he had received under Augustus. The wording of the proclamation was brief, and in a very modest tone. "He would," it said, "provide for the honours due to his father, and not leave the lifeless body, and this was the only public duty he now claimed."

As soon, however, as Augustus was dead, he had given the watchword to the prætorian cohorts, as commander-in-chief

He had the guard under arms, with all the other adjuncts of a court; soldiers attended him to the forum; soldiers went with him to the Senate House. He sent letters to the different armies, as though supreme power was now his, and showed hesitation only when he spoke in the Senate. His chief motive was fear that Germanicus, who had at his disposal so many legions, such vast auxiliary forces of the allies, and such wonderful popularity, might prefer the possession to the expectation of empire. He looked also at public opinion, wishing to have the credit of having been called and elected by the State rather than of having crept into power through the intrigues of a wife and a dotard's adoption. It was subsequently understood that he assumed a wavering attitude, to test likewise the temper of the nobles. For he would twist a word or a look into a crime and treasure it up in his memory.

8. On the first day of the Senate he allowed nothing to be discussed but the funeral of Augustus, whose will, which was brought in by the Vestal Virgins, named as his heirs Tiberius and Livia. The latter was to be admitted into the Julian family with the name of Augusta; next in expectation were the grand and great-grandchildren. In the third place, he had named the chief men of the State, most of whom he hated, simply out of ostentation and to win credit with posterity. His legacies were not beyond the scale of a private citizen, except a bequest of forty-three million five hundred thousand sesterces "to the people and populace of Rome," of one thousand to every prætorian soldier, and of three hundred to every man in the legionary cohorts composed of Roman citizens.

Next followed a deliberation about funeral honours. Of these the most imposing were thought fitting. The procession was to be conducted through "the gate of triumph," on the motion of Gallus Asinius; the titles of the laws passed, the names of the nations conquered by Augustus were to be borne in front, on that of Lucius Arruntius. Messala Valerius further proposed that the oath of allegiance to Tiberius should be yearly renewed, and when Tiberius asked him whether it was at *his* bidding that he had brought forward this motion, he replied that he had proposed it spontaneously, and that in whatever concerned the State he would use only his own discretion, even at the risk of offending. This was the only style of adulation which yet remained. The Senators unanimously exclaimed that the body ought to be borne on their shoulders to the funeral pile. The emperor left the point to them with disdainful moderation, and he then admonished the people by a proclamation not to indulge in that tumultuous enthusiasm which had distracted the funeral of the Divine Julius, or express a wish that Augustus should be burnt in the Forum instead of in his appointed resting-place in the Campus Martius.

On the day of the funeral soldiers stood round as a guard, amid much ridicule from those who had either themselves witnessed or who had heard from their parents of the famous day when slavery was still something fresh, and freedom had been resought in vain, when the slaying of Cæsar, the Dictator, seemed to some the vilest, to others, the most glorious of deeds. "Now," they said, "an aged sovereign, whose power had lasted long, who had provided his heirs with abundant means to coerce the State, requires forsooth the defence of soldiers that his burial may be undisturbed."

9. Then followed much talk about Augustus himself, and many expressed an idle wonder that the same day marked the beginning of his assumption of empire and the close of his life, and, again, that he had ended his days at Nola in the same house and room as his father Octavius. People extolled too the number of his consulships, in which he had equalled Valerius Corvus and Caius Marius combined, the continuance for thirty-seven years of the tribunitian power, the title of Imperator twenty-one times earned, and his other honours which had been either frequently repeated or were wholly new. Sensible men, however, spoke variously of his life with praise and censure. Some said "that dutiful feeling towards a father, and the necessities of the State in which laws had then no place, drove him into civil war, which can neither be planned nor conducted on any right principles. He had often yielded to Antonius, while he was taking vengeance on his father's murderers, often also to Lepidus. When the latter sank into feeble dotage and the former had been ruined by his profligacy, the only remedy for his distracted

country was the rule of a single man. Yet the State had been organized under the name neither of a kingdom nor a dictatorship, but under that of a prince. The ocean and remote rivers were the boundaries of the empire; the legions, provinces, fleets, all things were linked together; there was law for the citizens; there was respect shown to the allies. The capital had been embellished on a grand scale; only in a few instances had he resorted to force, simply to secure general tranquillity."

10. It was said, on the other hand, "that filial duty and State necessity were merely assumed as a mask. It was really from a lust of sovereignty that he had excited the veterans by bribery, had, when a young man and a subject, raised an army, tampered with the Consul's legions, and feigned an attachment to the faction of Pompeius. Then, when by a decree of the Senate he had usurped the high functions and authority of Prætor, when Hirtius and Pansa were slain— whether they were destroyed by the enemy, or Pansa by poison infused into a wound, Hirtius by his own soldiers and Cæsar's treacherous machinations—he at once possessed himself of both their armies, wrested the consulate from a reluctant Senate, and turned against the State the arms with which he had been intrusted against Antonius. Citizens were proscribed, lands divided, without so much as the approval of those who executed these deeds. Even granting that the deaths of Cassius and of the Bruti were sacrifices to a hereditary enmity (though duty requires us to waive private feuds for the sake of the public welfare), still Pompeius had been deluded by the phantom of peace, and Lepidus by the mask of friendship. Subsequently, Antonius had been lured on by the treaties of Tarentum and Brundisium, and by his marriage with the sister, and paid by his death the penalty of a treacherous alliance. No doubt, there was peace after all this, but it was a peace stained with blood; there were the disasters of Lollius and Varus, the murders at Rome of the Varros, Egnatii, and Juli."

The domestic life too of Augustus was not spared. "Nero's wife had been taken from him, and there had been the farce of consulting the pontiffs, whether, with a child conceived and not yet born, she could properly marry. There were the excesses of Quintus Tedius and Vedius Pollio; last of all, there was Livia, terrible to the State as a mother, terrible to the house of the Cæsars as a stepmother. No honour was left for the gods, when Augustus chose to be himself worshipped with temples and statues, like those of the deities, and with flamens and priests. He had not even adopted Tiberius as his successor out of affection or any regard to the State, but, having thoroughly seen his arrogant and savage temper, he had sought glory for himself by a contrast of extreme wickedness." For, in fact, Augustus, a few years before, when he was a second time asking from the Senate the tribunitian power for Tiberius, though his speech was complimentary, had thrown out certain hints as to his manners, style, and habits of life, which he meant as reproaches, while he seemed to excuse. However, when his obsequies had been duly performed, a temple with a religious ritual was decreed him.

11. After this all prayers were addressed to Tiberius. He, on his part, urged various considerations, the greatness of the empire, his distrust of himself. "Only," he said, "the intellect of the Divine Augustus was equal to such a burden. Called as he had been by him to share his anxieties, he had learnt by experience how exposed to fortune's caprices was the task of universal rule. Consequently, in a state which had the support of so many great men, they should not put everything on one man, as many, by uniting their efforts would more easily discharge public functions." There was more grand sentiment than good faith in such words. Tiberius's language even in matters which he did not care to conceal, either from nature or habit, was always hesitating and obscure, and now that he was struggling to hide his feelings completely, it was all the more involved in uncertainty and doubt. The Senators, however, whose only fear was lest they might seem to understand him, burst into complaints, tears, and prayers. They raised their hands to the gods, to the statue of Augustus, and to the knees of Tiberius, when he ordered a document to be produced and read. This contained a description of the resources of the State, of the number of citizens and allies under arms, of the fleets, subject kingdoms, provinces, taxes, direct and indirect, necessary ex·

penses and customary bounties. All these details Augustus
had written with his own hand, and had added a counsel,
that the empire should be confined to its present limits, either
from fear or out of jealousy.

12. Meantime, while the Senate stooped to the most abject
supplication, Tiberius happened to say that although he was
not equal to the whole burden of the State, yet he would
undertake the charge of whatever part of it might be intrusted to him. Thereupon Asinius Gallus said, "I ask you,
Cæsar, what part of the State you wish to have intrusted
to you?" Confounded by the sudden inquiry he was silent
for a few moments; then, recovering his presence of mind,
he replied that it would by no means become his modesty
to choose or to avoid in a case where he would prefer to be
wholly excused. Then Gallus again, who had inferred anger
from his looks, said that the question had not been asked
with the intention of dividing what could not be separated,
but to convince him by his own admission that the body of
the State was one, and must be directed by a single mind.
He further spoke in praise of Augustus, and reminded Tiberius himself of his victories, and of his admirable deeds
for many years as a civilian. Still, he did not thereby soften
the emperor's resentment, for he had long been detested
from an impression that, as he had married Vipsania, daughter of Marcus Agrippa, who had once been the wife of
Tiberius, he aspired to be more than a citizen, and kept up
the arrogant tone of his father, Asinius Pollio.

13. Next, Lucius Arruntius, who differed but little from
the speech of Gallus, gave like offence, though Tiberius had
no old grudge against him, but simply mistrusted him, because he was rich and daring, had brilliant accomplishments,
and corresponding popularity. For Augustus, when in his last
conversations he was discussing who would refuse the highest
place, though sufficiently capable, who would aspire to it
without being equal to it, and who would unite both the ability and ambition, had described Marcus Lepidus as able but
contemptuously indifferent, Gallus Asinius as ambitious and
incapable, Lucius Arruntius as not unworthy of it, and,
should the chance be given him, sure to make the venture.
About the two first there is a general agreement, but instead

of Arruntius some have mentioned Cneius Piso, and all these men, except Lepidus, were soon afterwards destroyed by various charges through the contrivance of Tiberius. Quintus Haterius too and Mamercus Scaurus ruffled his suspicious temper, Haterius by having said—"How long, Cæsar, will you suffer the State to be without a head?" Scaurus by the remark that there was a hope that the Senate's prayers would not be fruitless, seeing that he had not used his right as Tribune to negative the motion of the Consuls. Tiberius instantly broke out into invective against Haterius; Scaurus, with whom he was far more deeply displeased, he passed over in silence. Wearied at last by the assembly's clamorous importunity and the urgent demands of individual Senators, he gave way by degrees, not admitting that he undertook empire, but yet ceasing to refuse it and to be entreated. It is known that Haterius having entered the palace to ask pardon, and thrown himself at the knees of Tiberius as he was walking, was almost killed by the soldiers, because Tiberius fell forward, accidentally or from being entangled by the suppliant's hands. Yet the peril of so great a man did not make him relent, till Haterius went with entreaties to Augusta, and was saved by her very earnest intercessions.

14. Great too was the Senate's sycophancy to Augusta. Some would have her styled "parent;" others "mother of the country," and a majority proposed that to the name of Cæsar should be added "son of Julia." The emperor repeatedly asserted that there must be a limit to the honours paid to women, and that he would observe similar moderation in those bestowed on himself, but annoyed at the invidious proposal, and indeed regarding a woman's elevation as a slight to himself, he would not allow so much as a lictor to be assigned her, and forbade the erection of an altar in memory of her adoption, and any like distinction. But for Germanicus Cæsar he asked pro-consular powers, and envoys were despatched to confer them on him, and also to express sympathy with his grief at the death of Augustus. The same request was not made for Drusus, because he was consul elect and present at Rome. Twelve candidates were named for the prætorship, the number which Augustus had handed

down, and when the Senate urged Tiberius to increase it, he bound himself by an oath not to exceed it.

15. It was then for the first time that the elections were transferred from the Campus Martius to the Senate. For up to that day, though the most important rested with the emperor's choice, some were settled by the partialities of the tribes. Nor did the people complain of having the right taken from them, except in mere idle talk, and the Senate, being now released from the necessity of bribery and of degrading solicitations, gladly upheld the change, Tiberius confining himself to the recommendation of only four candidates who were to be nominated without rejection or canvass. Meanwhile the tribunes of the people asked leave to exhibit at their own expense games to be named after Augustus and added to the Calendar as the Augustales. Money was, however, voted from the exchequer, and though the use of the triumphal robe in the circus was prescribed, it was not allowed them to ride in a chariot. Soon the annual celebration was transferred to the prætor, to whose lot fell the administration of justice between citizens and foreigners.

16. This was the state of affairs at Rome when a mutiny broke out in the legions of Pannonia, which could be traced to no fresh cause except the change of emperors and the prospect it held out of license in tumult and of profit from a civil war. In the summer camp three legions were quartered, under the command of Junius Blæsus, who on hearing of the death of Augustus and the accession of Tiberius, had allowed his men a rest from military duties, either for mourning or rejoicing. This was the beginning of demoralization among the troops, of quarreling, of listening to the talk of every pestilent fellow, in short, of craving for luxury and idleness and loathing discipline and toil. In the camp was one Percennius, who had once been a leader of one of the theatrical factions, then became a common soldier, had a saucy tongue, and had learnt from his applause of actors how to stir up a crowd. By working on ignorant minds, which doubted as to what would be the terms of military service after Augustus, this man gradually influenced them in conversations at night or at nightfall, and when the better

men had dispersed, he gathered round him all the worst spirits.

17. At last, when there were others ready to be abettors of a mutiny, he asked, in the tone of a demagogue, why, like slaves, they submitted to a few centurions and still fewer tribunes. "When," he said, "will you dare to demand relief, if you do not go with your prayers or arms to a new and yet tottering throne? We have blundered enough by our tameness for so many years, in having to endure thirty or forty campaigns till we grow old, most of us with bodies maimed by wounds. Even dismissal is not the end of our service, but, quartered under a legion's standard we toil through the same hardships under another title. If a soldier survives so many risks, he is still dragged into remote regions where, under the name of lands, he receives soaking swamps or mountainous wastes. Assuredly, military service itself is burdensome and unprofitable; ten ases a day is the value set on life and limb; out of this, clothing, arms, tents, as well as the mercy of centurions and exemptions from duty have to be purchased. But indeed of floggings and wounds, of hard winters, wearisome summers, of terrible war, or barren peace, there is no end. Our only relief can come from military life being entered on under fixed conditions, from receiving each the pay of a denarius, and from the sixteenth year terminating our service. We must be retained no longer under a standard, but in the same camp a compensation in money must be paid us. Do the prætorian cohorts, which have just got their two denarii per man, and which after sixteen years are restored to their homes, encounter more perils? We do not disparage the guards of the capital; still, here amid barbarous tribes we have to face the enemy from our tents."

18. The throng applauded from various motives, some pointing with indignation to the marks of the lash, others to their grey locks, and most of them to their threadbare garments and naked limbs. At last, in their fury they went so far as to propose to combine the three legions into one. Driven from their purpose by the jealousy with which every one sought the chief honour for his own legion, they turned to other thoughts, and set up in one spot the three eagles,

with the ensigns of the cohorts. At the same time they piled up turf and raised a mound, that they might have a more conspicuous meeting-place. Amid the bustle Blæsus came up. He upbraided them and held back man after man with the exclamation, "Better imbrue your hands in my blood: it will be less guilt to slay your commander than it is to be in revolt from the emperor. Either living I will uphold the loyalty of the legions, or pierced to the heart I will hasten on your repentance."

19. None the less however was the mound piled up, and it was quite breast high when, at last overcome by his persistency, they gave up their purpose. Blæsus, with the consummate tact of an orator, said, "It is not through mutiny and tumult that the desires of the army ought to be communicated to Cæsar, nor did our soldiers of old ever ask so novel a boon of ancient commanders, nor have you yourselves asked it of the Divine Augustus. It is far from opportune that the emperor's cares, now in their first beginning, should be aggravated. If, however, you are bent upon attempting in peace what even after your victory in the civil wars you did not demand, why, contrary to the habit of obedience, contrary to the law of discipline, do you meditate violence? Decide on sending envoys, and give them instructions in your presence."

It was carried by acclamation that the son of Blæsus, one of the tribunes, should undertake the mission, and demand for the soldiers release from service after sixteen years. He was to have the rest of their message when the first part had been successful. After the young man's departure there was comparative quiet, but there was an arrogant tone among the soldiers, to whom the fact that their commander's son was pleading their common cause clearly showed that they had wrested by compulsion what they had failed to obtain by good behaviour.

20. Meanwhile the companies which previous to the mutiny had been sent to Nauportus to make roads and bridges and for other purposes, when they heard of the tumult in the camp, tore up the standards, and having plundered the neighbouring villages and Nauportus itself, which was like a town, assailed the centurions who restrained them with

jeers and insults, last of all, with blows. Their chief rage
was against Aufidienus Rufus, the camp-prefect, whom they
dragged from a waggon, loaded with baggage, and drove on
at the head of the column, asking him in ridicule whether he
liked to bear such huge burdens and such long marches.
Rufus, who had long been a common soldier, then a centurion, and subsequently camp-prefect, tried to revive the
old severe discipline, inured as he was to work and toil, and
all the sterner because he had endured.

21. On the arrival of these troops the mutiny broke out
afresh, and straggling from the camp they plundered the
neighbourhood. Blæsus ordered a few who had conspicuously
loaded themselves with spoil to be scourged and imprisoned
as a terror to the rest; for, even as it then was, the commander was still obeyed by the centurions and by all the best
men among the soldiers. As the men were dragged off, they
struggled violently, clasped the knees of the bystanders,
called to their comrades by name, or to the company, cohort,
or legion to which they respectively belonged, exclaiming
that all were threatened with the same fate. At the same
time they heaped abuse on the commander; they appealed
to heaven and to the gods, and left nothing undone by which
they might excite resentment and pity, alarm and rage. They
all rushed to the spot, broke open the guard-house, unbound
the prisoners, and were in a moment fraternising with deserters and men convicted on capital charges.

22. Thence arose a more furious outbreak, with more
leaders of the mutiny. Vibulenus, a common soldier, was
hoisted in front of the general's tribunal on the shoulders
of the bystanders and addressed the excited throng, who
eagerly awaited his intentions. "You have indeed," he said,
"restored light and air to these innocent and most unhappy
men, but who restores to my brother his life, or my brother
to myself? Sent to you by the German army in our common
cause, he was last night butchered by the gladiators whom
the general keeps and arms for the destruction of his soldiers.
Answer, Blæsus, where you have flung aside the corpse?
Even an enemy grudges not burial. When, with embraces
and tears, I have sated my grief, order me also to be slain,
provided only that when we have been destroyed for no

crime, but only because we consulted the good of the legions, we may be buried by these men around me."

23. He inflamed their excitement by weeping and smiting his breast and face with his hands. Then, hurling aside those who bore him on their shoulders. and impetuously flinging himself at the feet of one man after another, he roused such dismay and indignation that some of the soldiers put fetters on the gladiators who were among the number of Blæsus's slaves, others did the like to the rest of his household, while a third party hurried out to look for the corpse. And had it not quickly been known that no corpse was found, that the slaves, when tortures were applied, denied the murder, and that the man never had a brother, they would have been on the point of destroying the general. As it was, they thrust out the tribunes and the camp-prefect; they plundered the baggage of the fugitives, and they killed a centurion, Lucilius, to whom, with soldiers' humour, they had given the name "Bring another," because when he had broken one vine-stick on a man's back, he would call in a loud voice for another and another. The rest sheltered themselves in concealment, and one only was detained, Clemens Julius, whom the soldiers considered a fit person to carry messages, from his ready wit. Two legions, the eighth and the fifteenth, were actually drawing swords against each other, the former demanding the death of a centurion, whom they nicknamed Sirpicus, while the men of the fifteenth defended him, but the soldiers of the ninth interposed their entreaties, and when these were disregarded, their menaces.

24. This intelligence had such an effect on Tiberius, close as he was, and most careful to hush up every very serious disaster, that he despatched his son Drusus with the leading men of the State and with two prætorian cohorts, without any definite instructions, to take suitable measures. The cohorts were strengthened beyond their usual force with some picked troops. There was in addition a considerable part of the prætorian cavalry, and the flower of the German soldiery, which was then the emperor's guard. With them too was the commander of the prætorians, Ælius Sejanus, who had been associated with his own father, Strabo, had great influence with Tiberius, and was to advise and direct

the young prince, and to hold out punishment or reward to the soldiers. When Drusus approached, the legions, as a mark of respect, met him, not as usual, with glad looks or the glitter of military decorations, but in unsightly squalor, and faces which, though they simulated grief, rather expressed defiance.

25. As soon as he entered the entrenchments, they secured the gates with sentries, and ordered bodies of armed men to be in readiness at certain points of the camp. The rest crowded round the general's tribunal in a dense mass. Drusus stood there, and with a gesture of his hand demanded silence. As often as they turned their eyes back on the throng, they broke into savage exclamations, then looking up to Drusus they trembled. There was a confused hum, a fierce shouting, and a sudden lull. Urged by conflicting emotions, they felt panic and they caused the like. At last, in an interval of the uproar, Drusus read his father's letter, in which it was fully stated that he had a special care for the brave legions with which he had endured a number of campaigns; that, as soon as his mind had recovered from its grief, he would lay their demands before the Senators; that meanwhile he had sent his son to concede unhesitatingly what could be immediately granted, and that the rest must be reserved for the Senate, which ought to have a voice in showing either favour or severity.

26. The crowd replied that they had delivered their instructions to Clemens, one of the centurions, which he was to convey to Rome. He began to speak of the soldiers' discharge after sixteen years, of the rewards of completed service, of the daily pay being a denarius, and of the veterans not being detained under a standard. When Drusus pleaded in answer reference to the Senate and to his father, he was interrupted by a tumultuous shout. "Why had he come, neither to increase the soldiers' pay, nor to alleviate their hardships, in a word, with no power to better their lot? Yet heaven knew that all were allowed to scourge and to execute. Tiberius used formerly in the name of Augustus to frustrate the wishes of the legions, and the same tricks were now revived by Drusus. Was it only sons who were to visit them? Certainly, it was a new thing for the emperor to refer to

the Senate merely what concerned the soldier's interests.
Was then the same Senate to be consulted whenever notice
was given of an execution or of a battle? Were their rewards
to be at the discretion of absolute rulers, their punishments
to be without appeal?"

27. At last they deserted the general's tribunal, and to
any prætorian soldier or friend of Cæsar's who met them,
they used those threatening gestures which are the cause of
strife and the beginning of a conflict, with special rage
against Cneius Lentulus, because they thought that he above
all others, by his age and warlike renown, encouraged Drusus, and was the first to scorn such blots on military discipline. Soon after, as he was leaving with Drusus to betake
himself in foresight of his danger to the winter camp, they
surrounded him, and asked him again and again whither he
was going; was it to the emperor or to the Senate, there
also to oppose the interests of the legions. At the same moment they menaced him savagely and flung stones. And
now, bleeding from a blow, and feeling destruction certain,
he was rescued by the hurried arrival of the throng which
had accompanied Drusus.

28. That terrible night which threatened an explosion of
crime was tranquillised by a mere accident. Suddenly in a
clear sky the moon's radiance seemed to die away. This the
soldiers in their ignorance of the cause regarded as an omen
of their condition, comparing the failure of her light to their
own efforts, and imagining that their attempts would end
prosperously should her brightness and splendour be restored
to the goddess. And so they raised a din with brazen instruments and the combined notes of trumpets and horns, with
joy or sorrow, as she brightened or grew dark. When clouds
arose and obstructed their sight, and it was thought she was
buried in the gloom, with that proneness to superstition
which steals over minds once thoroughly cowed, they lamented that this was a portent of neverending hardship,
and that heaven frowned on their deeds.

Drusus, thinking that he ought to avail himself of this
change in their temper and turn what chance had offered
to a wise account, ordered the tents to be visited. Clemens,
the centurion was summoned with all others who for their

good qualities were liked by the common soldiers. These men made their way among the patrols, sentries and guards of the camp-gates, suggesting hope or holding out threats. "How long will you besiege the emperor's son? What is to be the end of our strifes? Will Percennius and Vibulenus give pay to the soldiers and land to those who have earned their discharge? In a word, are they, instead of the Neros and the Drusi, to control the empire of the Roman people? Why are we not rather first in our repentance as we were last in the offence? Demands made in common are granted slowly; a separate favour you may deserve and receive at the same moment."

With minds affected by these words and growing mutually suspicious, they divided off the new troops from the old, and one legion from another. Then by degrees the instinct of obedience returned. They quitted the gates and restored to their places the standards which at the beginning of the mutiny they had grouped into one spot.

29. At daybreak Drusus called them to an assembly, and, though not a practised speaker, yet with natural dignity upbraided them for their past and commended their present behaviour. He was not, he said, to be conquered by terror or by threats. Were he to see them inclining to submission and hear the language of entreaty, he would write to his father, that he might be merciful and receive the legions' petition. At their prayer, Blæsus and Lucius Apronius, a Roman knight on Drusus's staff, with Justus Catonius, a first-rank centurion, were again sent to Tiberius. Then ensued a conflict of opinion among them, some maintaining that it was best to wait the envoys' return and meanwhile humour the soldiers, others, that stronger measures ought to be used, inasmuch as the rabble knows no mean, and inspires fear, unless they are afraid, though when they have once been overawed, they can be safely despised. "While superstition still swayed them, the general should apply terror by removing the leaders of the mutiny."

Drusus's temper was inclined to harsh measures. He summoned Vibulenus and Percennius and ordered them to be put to death. The common account is that they were buried in the general's tent, though according to some their bodies were flung outside the entrenchments for all to see.

30. Search was then made for all the chief mutineers. Some as they roamed outside the camp were cut down by the centurions or by soldiers of the prætorian cohorts. Some even the companies gave up in proof of their loyalty. The men's troubles were increased by an early winter with continuous storms so violent that they could not go beyond their tents or meet together or keep the standards in their places, from which they were perpetually torn by hurricane and rain. And there still lingered the dread of the divine wrath; nor was it without meaning, they thought, that, hostile to an impious host, the stars grew dim and storms burst over them. Their only relief from misery was to quit an ill-omened and polluted camp, and, having purged themselves of their guilt, to betake themselves again every one to his winter-quarters. First the eighth, then the fifteenth legion returned; the ninth cried again and again that they ought to wait for the letter from Tiberius, but soon finding themselves isolated by the departure of the rest, they voluntarily forestalled their inevitable fate. Drusus, without awaiting the envoys' return, as for the present all was quiet, went back to Rome.

31. About the same time, from the same causes, the legions of Germany rose in mutiny, with a fury proportioned to their greater numbers, in the confident hope that Germanicus Cæsar would not be able to endure another's supremacy and would offer himself to the legions, whose strength would carry everything before it. There were two armies on the bank of the Rhine; that named the upper army had Caius Silius for general; the lower was under the charge of Aulus Cæcina. The supreme direction rested with Germanicus, then busily employed in conducting the assessment of Gaul. The troops under the control of Silius, with minds yet in suspense, watched the issue of mutiny elsewhere; but the soldiers of the lower army fell into a frenzy, which had its beginning in the men of the twenty first and fifth legions, and into which the first and twentieth were also drawn. For they were all quartered in the same summer-camp, in the territory of the Ubii, enjoying ease or having

only light duties. Accordingly on hearing of the death of Augustus, a rabble of city slaves, who had been enlisted under a recent levy at Rome, habituated to laxity and impatient of hardship, filled the ignorant minds of the other soldiers with notions that the time had come when the veteran might demand a timely discharge, the young, more liberal pay, all, an end of their miseries, and vengeance on the cruelty of centurions.

It was not one alone who spoke thus, as did Percennius among the legions of Pannonia, nor was it in the ears of trembling soldiers, who looked with apprehension to other and mightier armies, but there was sedition in many a face and voice. "The Roman world," they said, "was in their hand; their victories aggrandised the State; it was from them that emperors received their titles."

32. Nor did their commander check them. Indeed, the blind rage of so many had robbed him of his resolution. In a sudden frenzy they rushed with drawn swords on the centurions, the immemorial object of the soldiers' resentment and the first cause of savage fury. They threw them to the earth and beat them sorely, sixty to one, so as to correspond with the number of centurions. Then tearing them from the ground, mangled, and some lifeless, they flung them outside the entrenchments or into the river Rhine. One Septimius, who fled to the tribunal and was grovelling at Cæcina's feet, was persistently demanded till he was given up to destruction. Cassius Chærea, who won for himself a memory with posterity by the murder of Caius Cæsar, being then a youth of high spirit, cleared a passage with his sword through the armed and opposing throng. Neither tribune nor camp-prefect maintained authority any longer. Patrols, sentries, and whatever else the needs of the time required, were distributed by the men themselves. To those who could guess the temper of soldiers with some penetration, the strongest symptom of a wide-spread and intractable commotion, was the fact that, instead of being divided or instigated by a few persons, they were unanimous in their fury and equally unanimous in their composure, with so uniform a consistency that one would have thought them to be under command.

33. Meantime Germanicus, while, as I have related, he was collecting the taxes of Gaul, received news of the death of Augustus. He was married to the granddaughter of Augustus, Agrippina, by whom he had several children, and though he was himself the son of Drusus, brother of Tiberius, and grandson of Augusta, he was troubled by the secret hatred of his uncle and grandmother, the motives for which were the more venomous because unjust. For the memory of Drusus was held in honour by the Roman people, and they believed that had he obtained empire, he would have restored freedom. Hence they regarded Germanicus with favour and with the same hope. He was indeed a young man of unaspiring temper, and of wonderful kindliness, contrasting strongly with the proud and mysterious reserve that marked the conversation and the features of Tiberius. Then, there were feminine jealousies, Livia feeling a stepmother's bitterness toward: Agrippina, and Agrippina herself too being rather excitable, only her purity and love of her husband gave a right direction to her otherwise imperious disposition.

34. But the nearer Germanicus was to the highest hope, the more laboriously did he exert himself for Tiberius, and he made the neighbouring Sequani and all the Belgic states swear obedience to him. On hearing of the mutiny in the legions, he instantly went to the spot, and met them outside the camp, eyes fixed on the ground, and seemingly repentant. As soon as he entered the entrenchments, confused murmurs became audible. Some men, seizing his hand under pretence of kissing it, thrust his fingers into their mouths, that he might touch their toothless gums; others showed him their limbs bowed with age. He ordered the throng which stood near him, as it seemed a promiscuous gathering, to separate itself into its military companies. They replied that they would hear better as they were. The standards were then to be advanced, so that thus at least the cohorts might be distinguished. The soldiers obeyed reluctantly. Then beginning with a reverent mention of Augustus, he passed on to the victories and triumphs of Tiberius, dwelling with especial praise on his glorious achievements with those legions in Germany. Next, he extolled the

unity of Italy, the loyalty of Gaul, the entire absence of turbulence or strife. He was heard in silence or with but a slight murmur.

35. As soon as he touched on the mutiny and asked what had become of soldierly obedience, of the glory of ancient discipline, whither they had driven their tribunes and centurions, they all bared their bodies and taunted him with the scars of their wounds and the marks of the lash. And then with confused exclamations they spoke bitterly of the prices of exemptions, of their scanty pay, of the severity of their tasks, with special mention of the entrenchment, the fosse, the conveyance of fodder, building-timber, firewood, and whatever else had to be procured from necessity, or as a check on idleness in the camp. The fiercest clamour arose from the veteran soldiers, who, as they counted their thirty campaigns or more, implored him to relieve worn-out men, and not let them die under the same hardships, but have an end of such harassing service, and repose without beggary. Some even claimed the legacy of the Divine Augustus, with words of good omen for Germanicus, and, should he wish for empire, they showed themselves abundantly willing. Thereupon, as though he were contracting the pollution of guilt, he leapt impetuously from the tribunal. The men opposed his departure with their weapons, threatening him repeatedly if he would not go back. But Germanicus protesting that he would die rather than cast off his loyalty, plucked his sword from his side, raised it aloft and was plunging it into his breast, when those nearest him seized his hand and held it by force. The remotest and most densely crowded part of the throng, and, what almost passes belief, some, who came close up to him, urged him to strike the blow, and a soldier, by name Calusidius, offered him a drawn sword, saying that it was sharper than his own. Even in their fury, this seemed to them a savage act and one of evil precedent, and there was a pause during which Cæsar's friends hurried him into his tent.

36. There they took counsel how to heal matters. For news was also brought that the soldiers were preparing the despatch of envoys who were to draw the upper army into their cause; that the capital of the Ubii was marked out

for destruction, and that hands with the stain of plunder on them would soon be daring enough for the pillage of Gaul. The alarm was heightened by the knowledge that the enemy was aware of the Roman mutiny, and would certainly attack if the Rhine bank were undefended. Yet if the auxiliary troops and allies were to be armed against the retiring legions, civil war was in fact begun. Severity would be dangerous; profuse liberality would be scandalous. Whether all or nothing were conceded to the soldiery, the State was equally in jeopardy.

Accordingly, having weighed their plans one against each other, they decided that a letter should be written in the prince's name, to the effect that full discharge was granted to those who had served in twenty campaigns; that there was a conditional release for those who had served sixteen, and that they were to be retained under a standard with immunity from everything except actually keeping off the enemy; that the legacies which they had asked, were to be paid and doubled.

37. The soldiers perceived that all this was invented for the occasion, and instantly pressed their demands. The discharge from service was quickly arranged by the tribunes. Payment was put off till they reached their respective winter-quarters. The men of the fifth and twenty-first legions refused to go till in the summer-camp where they stood the money was made up out of the purses of Germanicus himself and his friends, and paid in full. The first and twentieth legions were led back by their officer Cæcina to the canton of the Ubii, marching in disgrace, since sums of money which had been extorted from the general were carried among the eagles and standards. Germanicus went to the Upper Army, and the second, thirteenth, and sixteenth legions, without any delay, accepted from him the oath of allegiance. The fourteenth hesitated a little, but their money and the discharge were offered even without their demanding it.

38. Meanwhile there was an outbreak among the Chauci, begun by some veterans of the mutinous legions on garrison duty. They were quelled for a time by the instant execution of two soldiers. Such was the order of Mennius,

the camp-prefect, more as a salutary warning than as a legal act. Then, when the commotion increased, he fled and having been discovered, as his hiding place was now unsafe, he borrowed a resource from audacity. "It was not," he told them, "the camp-prefect, it was Germanicus, their general, it was Tiberius, their emperor, whom they were insulting." At the same moment, overawing all resistance, he seized the standard, faced round towards the river-bank, and exclaiming that whoever left the ranks, he would hold as a deserter, he led them back into their winter-quarters, disaffected indeed, but cowed.

39. Meanwhile envoys from the Senate had an interview with Germanicus, who had now returned, at the Altar of the Ubii. Two legions, the first and twentieth, with veterans discharged and serving under a standard, were there in winter-quarters. In the bewilderment of terror and conscious guilt they were penetrated by an apprehension that persons had come at the Senate's orders to cancel the concessions they had extorted by mutiny. And as it is the way with a mob to fix any charge, however groundless, on some particular person, they reproached Munatius Plancus, an ex-consul and the chief envoy, with being the author of the Senate's decree. At midnight they began to demand the imperial standard kept in Germanicus's quarters, and having rushed together to the entrance, burst the door, dragged Cæsar from his bed, and forced him by menaces of death to give up the standard. Then roaming through the camp-streets, they met the envoys, who on hearing of the tumult were hastening to Germanicus. They loaded them with insults, and were on the point of murdering them, Plancus especially, whose high rank had deterred him from flight. In his peril he found safety only in the camp of the first legion. There clasping the standards and the eagle, he sought to protect himself under their sanctity. And had not the eagle-bearer, Calpurnius, saved him from the worst violence, the blood of an envoy of the Roman people, an occurrence rare even among our foes, would in a Roman camp have stained the altars of the gods.

At last, with the light of day, when the general and the soldiers and the whole affair were clearly recognised. Ger-

manicus entered the camp, ordered Plancus to be conducted
to him, and received him on the tribunal. He then upbraided
them with their fatal infatuation, revived not so much by
the anger of the soldiers as by that of heaven, and explained
the reasons of the envoys' arrival. On the rights of ambassadors, on the dreadful and undeserved peril of Plancus,
and also on the disgrace into which the legion had brought
itself, he dwelt with the eloquence of pity, and while the
throng was confounded rather than appeased, he dismissed
the envoys with an escort of auxiliary cavalry.

40. Amid the alarm all condemned Germanicus for not
going to the Upper Army, where he might find obedience
and help against the rebels. "Enough and more than enough
blunders," they said, "had been made by granting discharges
and money, indeed, by conciliatory measures. Even if Germanicus held his own life cheap, why should he keep a little
son and a pregnant wife among madmen who outraged every
human right? Let these, at least, be restored safely to their
grandsire and to the State."

When his wife spurned the notion, protesting that she
was a descendant of the Divine Augustus and could face
peril with no degenerate spirit, he at last embraced her and
the son of their love with many tears, and after long delay
compelled her to depart. Slowly moved along a pitiable procession of women, a general's fugitive wife with a little son
in her bosom, her friends' wives weeping round her, as with
her they were dragging themselves from the camp. Not less
sorrowful were those who remained.

41. There was no appearance of the triumphant general
about Germanicus, and he seemed to be in a conquered city
rather than in his own camp, while groans and wailings attracted the ears and looks even of the soldiers. They came
out of their tents, asking "what was that mournful sound?
What meant the sad sight? Here were ladies of rank, not
a centurion to escort them, not a soldier, no sign of a prince's
wife, none of the usual retinue. Could they be going to the
Treveri, to be subjects of the foreigner?" Then they felt
shame and pity, and remembered his father Agrippa, her
grandfather Augustus, her father-in-law Drusus, her own
glory as a mother of children, her noble purity. And there

was her little child too, born in the camp, brought up amid the tents of the legions, whom they used to call in soldiers' fashion, Caligula, because he often wore the shoe so called, to win the men's goodwill. But nothing moved them so much as jealousy towards the Treveri. They entreated, stopped the way, that Agrippina might return and remain, some running to meet her, while most of them went back to Germanicus. He, with a grief and anger that were yet fresh, thus began to address the throng around him—

42. "Neither wife nor son are dearer to me than my father and the State. But he will surely have the protection of his own majesty, the empire of Rome that of our other armies. My wife and children whom, were it a question of your glory, I would willingly expose to destruction, I now remove to a distance from your fury, so that whatever wickedness is thereby threatened, may be expiated by my blood only, and that you may not be made more guilty by the slaughter of a great-grandson of Augustus, and the murder of a daughter-in-law of Tiberius. For what have you not dared, what have you not profaned during these days? What name shall I give to this gathering? Am I to call you soldiers, you who have beset with entrenchments and arms your general's son, or citizens, when you have trampled under foot the authority of the Senate? Even the rights of public enemies, the sacred character of the ambassador, and the law of nations have been violated by you. The Divine Julius once quelled an army's mutiny with a single word by calling those who were renouncing their military obedience 'citizens.' The Divine Augustus cowed the legions who had fought at Actium with one look of his face. Though I am not yet what they were, still, descended as I am from them, it would be a strange and unworthy thing should I be spurned by the soldiery of Spain or Syria. First and twentieth legions, you who received your standards from Tiberius, you, men of the twentieth who have shared with me so many battles and have been enriched with so many rewards, is not this a fine gratitude with which you are repaying your general? Are these the tidings which I shall have to carry to my father when he hears only joyful intelligence from our other provinces, that his own recruits, his own veterans are not satis-

fied with discharge or pay; that here only centurions are
murdered, tribunes driven away, envoys imprisoned, camps
and rivers stained with blood, while I am myself dragging
on a precarious existence amid those who hate me?

43. "Why, on the first day of our meeting, why did you,
my friends, wrest from me, in your blindness, the steel which
I was preparing to plunge into my breast? Better and more
loving was the act of the man who offered me the sword.
At any rate I should have perished before I was as yet conscious of all the disgraces of my army, while you would
have chosen a general who though he might allow my death
to pass unpunished would avenge the death of Varus and
his three legions. Never indeed may heaven suffer the Belgae, though they proffer their aid, to have the glory and
honour of having rescued the name of Rome and quelled the
tribes of Germany. It is thy spirit, Divine Augustus, now
received into heaven, thine image, father Drusus, and the
remembrance of thee, which, with these same soldiers who
are now stimulated by shame and ambition, should wipe out
this blot and turn the wrath of civil strife to the destruction
of the foe. You too, in whose faces and in whose hearts I
perceive a change, if only you restore to the Senate their
envoys, to the emperor his due allegiance, to myself my
wife and son, do you stand aloof from pollution and separate the mutinous from among you. This will be a pledge
of your repentance, a guarantee of your loyalty."

44. Thereupon, as suppliants confessing that his reproaches were true, they implored him to punish the guilty,
pardon those who had erred, and lead them against the
enemy. And he was to recall his wife, to let the nursling of
the legions return and not be handed over as a hostage to
the Gauls. As to Agrippina's return, he made the excuse of
her approaching confinement and of winter. His son, he said,
would come, and the rest they might settle themselves.
Away they hurried hither and thither, altered men, and
dragged the chief mutineers in chains to Caius Cætronius,
commander of the first legion, who tried and punished them
one by one in the following fashion. In front of the throng
stood the legions with drawn swords. Each accused man
was on a raised platform and was pointed out by a tribune.

If they shouted out that he was guilty, he was thrown headlong and cut to pieces. The soldiers gloated over the bloodshed as though it gave them absolution. Nor did Cæsar
check them, seeing that without any order from himself the
same men were responsible for all the cruelty and all the
odium of the deed.

The example was followed by the veterans, who were
soon afterwards sent into Rætia, nominally to defend the
province against a threatened invasion of the Suevi, but
really that they might tear themselves from a camp stamped
with the horror of a dreadful remedy no less than with the
memory of guilt. Then the general revised the list of centurions. Each, at his summons, stated his name, his rank,
his birthplace, the number of his campaigns, what brave
deeds he had done in battle, his military rewards, if any.
If the tribunes and the legion commended his energy and
good behaviour, he retained his rank; where they unanimously charged him with rapacity or cruelty, he was dismissed the service.

45. Quiet being thus restored for the present, a no less
formidable difficulty remained through the turbulence of the
fifth and twenty-first legions, who were in winter quarters
sixty miles away at Old Camp, as the place was called.
These, in fact, had been the first to begin the mutiny, and
the most atrocious deeds had been committed by their hands.
Unawed by the punishment of their comrades, and unmoved
by their contrition, they still retained their resentment.
Cæsar accordingly proposed to send an armed fleet with
some of our allies down the Rhine, resolved to make war
on them should they reject his authority.

46. At Rome, meanwhile, when the result of affairs in
Illyrium was not yet known, and men had heard of the
commotion among the German legions, the citizens in alarm
reproached Tiberius for the hypocritical irresolution with
which he was befooling the senate and the people, feeble
and disarmed as they were, while the soldiery were all the
time in revolt, and could not be quelled by the yet imper-
fectly-matured authority of two striplings. "He ought to
have gone himself and confronted with his imperial majesty
those who would have soon yielded, when they once saw a

sovereign of long experience, who was the supreme dispenser of rigour or of bounty. Could Augustus, with the feebleness of age on him, so often visit Germany, and is Tiberius, in the vigour of life, to sit in the Senate and criticise its members' words? He had taken good care that there should be slavery at Rome; he should now apply some soothing medicine to the spirit of soldiers, that they might be willing to endure peace."

47. Notwithstanding these remonstrances, it was the inflexible purpose of Tiberius not to quit the head-quarters of empire or to imperil himself and the State. Indeed, many conflicting thoughts troubled him. The army in Germany was the stronger; that in Pannonia the nearer; the first was supported by all the strength of Gaul; the latter menaced Italy. Which was he to prefer, without the fear that those whom he slighted would be infuriated by the affront? But his sons might alike visit both, and not compromise the imperial dignity, which inspired the greatest awe at a distance. There was also an excuse for mere youths referring some matters to their father, with the possibility that he could conciliate or crush those who resisted Germanicus or Drusus. What resource remained, if they despised the emperor? However, as if on the eve of departure, he selected his attendants, provided his camp-equipage, and prepared a fleet; then winter and matters of business were the various pretexts with which he amused, first, sensible men, then the populace, last, and longest of all, the provinces.

48. Germanicus meantime, though he had concentrated his army and prepared vengeance against the mutineers, thought that he ought still to allow them an interval, in case they might, with the late warning before them, regard their safety. He sent a despatch to Cæcina, which said that he was on the way with a strong force, and that, unless they forestalled his arrival by the execution of the guilty, he would resort to an indiscriminate massacre. Cæcina read the letter confidentially to the eagle and standard-bearers, and to all in the camp who were least tainted by disloyalty, and urged them to save the whole army from disgrace, and themselves from destruction. "In peace," he said, "the

merits of a man's case are carefully weighed; when war bursts on us, innocent and guilty alike perish."

Upon this, they sounded those whom they thought best for their purpose, and when they saw that a majority of their legions remained loyal, at the commander's suggestion they fixed a time for falling with the sword on all the vilest and foremost of the mutineers. Then, at a mutually given signal, they rushed into the tents, and butchered the unsuspecting men, none but those in the secret knowing what was the beginning or what was to be the end of the slaughter.

49. The scene was a contrast to all civil wars which have ever occurred. It was not in battle, it was not from opposing camps, it was from those same dwellings where day saw them at their common meals, night resting from labour, that they divided themselves into two factions, and showered on each other their missiles. Uproar, wounds, bloodshed, were everywhere visible; the cause was a mystery. All else was at the disposal of chance. Even some loyal men were slain, for, on its being once understood who were the objects of fury, some of the worst mutineers too had seized on weapons. Neither commander nor tribune was present to control them; the men were allowed license and vengeance to their heart's content. Soon afterwards Germanicus entered the camp, and exclaiming with a flood of tears, that this was destruction rather than remedy, ordered the bodies to be burnt.

Even then their savage spirit was seized with a desire to march against the enemy, as an atonement for their frenzy, and it was felt that the shades of their fellow-soldiers could be appeased only by exposing such impious breasts to honourable scars. Cæsar followed up the enthusiasm of the men, and having bridged over the Rhine, he sent across it 12,000 from the legions, with six-and-twenty allied cohorts, and eight squadrons of cavalry, whose discipline had been without a stain during the mutiny.

50. There was exultation among the Germans, not far off, as long as we were detained by the public mourning for the loss of Augustus, and then by our dissensions. But the Roman general in a forced march, cut through the Cæsian forest and the barrier which had been begun by Tiberius, and pitched his camp on this barrier, his front and rear

being defended by intrenchments, his flanks by timber barricades. He then penetrated some forest passes but little known, and, as there were two routes, he deliberated whether he should pursue the short and ordinary route, or that which was more difficult and unexplored, and consequently unguarded by the enemy. He chose the longer way, and hurried on every remaining preparation, for his scouts had brought word that among the Germans it was a night of festivity, with games, and one of their grand banquets. Cæcina had orders to advance with some light cohorts, and to clear away any obstructions from the woods. The legions followed at a moderate interval. They were helped by a night of bright starlight, reached the villages of the Marsi, and threw their pickets round the enemy, who even then were stretched on beds or at their tables, without the least fear, or any sentries before their camp, so complete was their carelessness and disorder; and of war indeed there was no apprehension. Peace it certainly was not—merely the languid and heedless ease of half-intoxicated people.

51. Cæsar, to spread devastation more widely, divided his eager legions into four columns, and ravaged a space of fifty miles with fire and sword. Neither sex nor age moved his compassion. Everything, sacred or profane, the temple too of Tamfana, as they called it, the special resort of all those tribes, was levelled to the ground. There was not a wound among our soldiers, who cut down a half-asleep, an unarmed, or a straggling foe. The Bructeri, Tubantes, and Usipetes, were roused by this slaughter, and they beset the forest passes through which the army had to return. The general knew this, and he marched, prepared both to advance and to fight. Part of the cavalry, and some of the auxiliary cohorts led the van; then came the first legion, and, with the baggage in the centre, the men of the twenty-first closed up the left, those of the fifth, the right flank. The twentieth legion secured the rear, and, next, were the rest of the allies.

Meanwhile the enemy moved not till the army began to defile in column through the woods, then made slight skirmishing attacks on its flanks and van, and with his whole force charged the rear. The light cohorts were thrown into confusion by the dense masses of the Germans, when Cæsar rode up to the men of the twentieth legion, and in a loud voice exclaimed that this was the time for wiping out the mutiny. "Advance," he said, "and hasten to turn your guilt into glory." This fired their courage, and at a single dash they broke through the enemy, and drove him back with great slaughter into the open country. At the same moment the troops of the van emerged from the woods and intrenched a camp. After this their march was uninterrupted, and the soldiery, with the confidence of recent success, and forgetful of the past, were placed in winter-quarters.

52. The news was a source of joy and also of anxiety to Tiberius. He rejoiced that the mutiny was crushed, but the fact that Germanicus had won the soldiers' favour by lavishing money, and promptly granting the discharge, as well as his fame as a soldier, annoyed him. Still, he brought his achievements under the notice of the Senate, and spoke much of his greatness in language elaborated for effect, more so than could be believed to come from his inmost heart. He bestowed a briefer praise on Drusus, and on the termination of the disturbance in Illyricum, but he was more earnest, and his speech more hearty. And he confirmed, too, in the armies of Pannonia all the concessions of Germanicus.

53. That same year Julia ended her days. For her profligacy she had formerly been confined by her father Augustus in the island of Pandateria, and then in the town of the Regini on the shores of the straits of Sicily. She had been the wife of Tiberius while Caius and Lucius Cæsar were in their glory, and had disdained him as an unequal match. This was Tiberius's special reason for retiring to Rhodes. When he obtained the empire, he left her in banishment and disgrace, deprived of all hope after the murder of Postumus Agrippa, and let her perish by a lingering death of destitution, with the idea that an obscurity would hang over her end from the length of her exile. He had a like motive for cruel vengeance on Sempronius Gracchus, a man of noble family, of shrewd understanding, and a perverse eloquence, who had seduced this same Julia when she was the wife of Marcus Agrippa. And this was not the end of the intrigue. When she had been handed over to Tiberius, her persistent paramour inflamed her with disobedience and hatred towards

her husband; and a letter which Julia wrote to her father, Augustus, inveighing against Tiberius, was supposed to be the composition of Gracchus. He was accordingly banished to Cercina, where he endured an exile of fourteen years. Then the soldiers who were sent to slay him, found him on a promontory, expecting no good. On their arrival, he begged a brief interval in which to give by letter his last instructions to his wife Alliaria, and then offered his neck to the executioners, dying with a courage not unworthy of the Sempronian name, which his degenerate life had dishonoured. Some have related that these soldiers were not sent from Rome, but by Lucius Asprenas, proconsul of Africa, on the authority of Tiberius, who had vainly hoped that the infamy of the murder might be shifted on Asprenas.

54. The same year witnessed the establishment of religious ceremonies in a new priesthood of the brotherhood of the Augustales, just as in former days Titus Tatius, to retain the rites of the Sabines, had instituted the Titian brotherhood. Twenty-one were chosen by lot from the chief men of the State; Tiberius, Drusus, Claudius, and Germanicus, were added to the number. The Augustal games which were then inaugurated, were disturbed by quarrels arising out of rivalry between the actors. Augustus had shown indulgence to the entertainment by way of humouring Mæcenas's extravagant passion for Bathyllus, nor did he himself dislike such amusements, and he thought it citizenlike to mingle in the pleasures of the populace. Very different was the tendency of Tiberius's character. But a people so many years indulgently treated, he did not yet venture to put under harsher control.

55. In the consulship of Drusus Cæsar and Caius Norbanus, Germanicus had a triumph decreed him, though war still lasted. And though it was for the summer campaign that he was most vigorously preparing, he anticipated it by a sudden inroad on the Chatti in the beginning of spring. There had, in fact, sprung up a hope of the enemy being divided between Arminius and Segestes, famous, respectively, for treachery and loyalty towards us. Arminius was the disturber of Germany. Segestes often revealed the fact that a rebellion was being organized, more especially at that

last banquet after which they rushed to arms, and he urged Varus to arrest himself and Arminius and all the other chiefs, assuring him that the people would attempt nothing if the leading men were removed, and that he would then have an opportunity of sifting accusations and distinguishing the innocent. But Varus fell by fate and by the sword of Arminius, with whom Segestes, though dragged into war by the unanimous voice of the nation, continued to be at feud, his resentment being heightened by personal motives, as Arminius had carried off his daughter who was betrothed to another. With a son-in-law detested, and fathers-in-law also at enmity, what are bonds of love between united hearts became with bitter foes incentives to fury.

56. Germanicus accordingly gave Cæcina four legions, five thousand auxiliaries, with some hastily raised levies from the Germans dwelling on the left bank of the Rhine. He was himself at the head of an equal number of legions and twice as many allies. Having established a fort on the site of his father's entrenchments on Mount Taunus he hurried his troops in quick marching order against the Chatti, leaving Lucius Apronius to direct works connected with roads and bridges. With a dry season and comparatively shallow streams, a rare circumstance in that climate, he had accomplished, without obstruction, a rapid march, and he feared for his return heavy rains and swollen rivers. But so suddenly did he come on the Chatti that all the helpless from age or sex were at once captured or slaughtered. Their able-bodied men had swum across the river Adrana, and were trying to keep back the Romans as they were commencing a bridge. Subsequently they were driven back by missiles and arrows, and having in vain attempted negotiations for peace, some took refuge with Germanicus, while the rest, leaving their cantons and villages dispersed themselves in their forests.

After burning Mattium, the capital of the tribe, and ravaging the open country, Germanicus marched back towards the Rhine, the enemy not daring to harass the rear of the retiring army, which was his usual practice whenever he fell back by way of stratagem rather than from panic. It had been the intention of the Cherusci to help the Chatti;

but Cæcina thoroughly cowed them, carrying his arms everywhere, and the Marsi who ventured to engage him, he repulsed in a successful battle.

57. Not long after envoys came from Segestes, imploring
aid against the violence of his fellow-countrymen, by whom
he was hemmed in, and with whom Arminius had greater
influence, because he counselled war. For with barbarians,
the more eager a man's daring, the more does he inspire
confidence, and the more highly is he esteemed in times of
revolution. With the envoys Segestes had associated his son,
by name Segimundus, but the youth hung back from a consciousness of guilt. For in the year of the revolt of Germany
he had been appointed a priest at the altar of the Ubii, and
had rent the sacred garlands, and fled to the rebels. Induced,
however, to hope for mercy from Rome, he brought his
father's message; he was graciously received and sent with
an escort to the Gallic bank of the Rhine.

It was now worth while for Germanicus to march back
his army. A battle was fought against the besiegers and
Segestes was rescued with a numerous band of kinsfolk and
dependents. In the number were some women of rank;
among them, the wife of Arminius, who was also the daughter of Segestes, but who exhibited the spirit of her husband
rather than of her father, subdued neither to tears nor to
the tones of a suppliant, her hands tightly clasped within
her bosom, and eyes which dwelt on her hope of offspring.
The spoils also taken in the defeat of Varus were brought
in, having been given as plunder to many of those who were
then being surrendered.

58. Segestes too was there in person, a stately figure,
fearless in the remembrance of having been a faithful ally.
His speech was to this effect. "This is not my first day of
steadfast loyalty towards the Roman people. From the time
that the Divine Augustus gave me the citizenship, I have
chosen my friends and foes with an eye to your advantage,
not from hatred of my fatherland (for traitors are detested
even by those whom they prefer) but because I held that
Romans and Germans have the same interests, and that
peace is better than war. And therefore I denounced to
Varus, who then commanded your army, Arminius, the

ravisher of my daughter, the violater of your treaty. I was put off by that dilatory general, and, as I found but little protection in the laws, I urged him to arrest myself, Arminius, and his accomplices. That night is my witness; would that it had been my last. What followed may be deplored rather than defended. However, I threw Arminius into chains and I endured to have them put on myself by his partisans. And as soon as you give me opportunity, I show my preference for the old over the new, for peace over commotion, not to get a reward, but that I may clear myself from treachery and be at the same time a fit mediator for a German people, should they choose repentance rather than ruin. For the youth and error of my son I entreat forgiveness. As for my daughter, I admit that it is by compulsion she has been brought here. It will be for you to consider which fact weighs most with you, that she is with child by Arminius or that she owes her being to me."

Cæsar in a gracious reply promised safety to his children and kinsfolk and a home for himself in the old province. He then led back the army and received on the proposal of Tiberius the title of Imperator. The wife of Arminius gave birth to a male child; the boy, who was brought up at Ravenna, soon afterwards suffered an insult, which at the proper time I shall relate.

59. The report of the surrender and kind reception of Segestes, when generally known, was heard with hope or grief according as men shrank from war or desired it. Arminius, with his naturally furious temper, was driven to frenzy by the seizure of his wife and the foredooming to slavery of his wife's unborn child. He flew hither and thither among the Cherusci, demanding "war against Segestes, war against Cæsar." And he refrained not from taunts. "Noble the father," he would say, "mighty the general, brave the army which, with such strength, has carried off one weak woman. Before me, three legions, three commanders have fallen. Not by treachery, not against pregnant women, but openly against armed men do I wage war. There are still to be seen in the groves of Germany the Roman standards which I hung up to our country's gods. Let Segestes dwell on the conquered bank: let him restore to his son his priestly

office; one thing there is which Germans will never thoroughly excuse, their having seen between the Elbe and the Rhine the Roman rods, axes, and toga. Other nations in their ignorance of Roman rule, have no experience of punishments, know nothing of tributes, and, as we have shaken them off, as the great Augustus, ranked among deities, and his chosen heir Tiberius, departed from us, baffled, let us not quail before an inexperienced stripling, before a mutinous army. If you prefer your fatherland, your ancestors, your ancient life to tyrants and to new colonies, follow as your leader Arminius to glory and to freedom rather than Segestes to ignominious servitude."

60. This language roused not only the Cherusci but the neighbouring tribes and drew to their side Inguiomerus, the uncle of Arminius, who had long been respected by the Romans. This increased Cæsar's alarm. That the war might not burst in all its fury on one point, he sent Cæcina through the Bructeri to the river Amisia with forty Roman cohorts to distract the enemy, while the cavalry was led by its commander Pedo by the territories of the Frisii. Germanicus himself put four legions on shipboard and conveyed them through the lakes, and the infantry, cavalry, and fleet met simultaneously at the river already mentioned. The Chauci, on promising aid, were associated with us in military fellowship. Lucius Stertinius was despatched by Germanicus with a flying column and routed the Bructeri as they were burning their possessions, and amid the carnage and plunder, found the eagle of the nineteenth legion which had been lost with Varus. The troops were then marched to the furthest frontier of the Bructeri, and all the country between the rivers Amisia and Luppia was ravaged, not far from the forest of Teutoburgium, where the remains of Varus and his legions were said to lie unburied.

61. Germanicus upon this was seized with an eager longing to pay the last honour to those soldiers and their general, while the whole army present was moved to compassion by the thought of their kinsfolk and friends, and, indeed, of the calamities of wars and the lot of mankind. Having sent on Cæcina in advance to reconnoitre the obscure forest-passes, and to raise bridges and causeways over watery

swamps and treacherous plains, they visited the mournful
scenes, with their horrible sights and associations. Varus's
first camp with its wide circumference and the measure-
ments of its central space clearly indicated the handiwork
of three legions. Further on, the partially fallen rampart
and the shallow fosse suggested the inference that it was a
shattered remnant of the army which had there taken up a
position. In the centre of the field were the whitening bones
of men, as they had fled, or stood their ground, strewn everywhere or piled in heaps. Near, lay fragments of weapons and
limbs of horses, and also human heads, prominently nailed
to trunks of trees. In the adjacent groves were the barbarous
altars, on which they had immolated tribunes and first-rank
centurions. Some survivors of the disaster who had escaped
from the battle or from captivity, described how this was
the spot where the officers fell, how yonder the eagles were
captured, where Varus was pierced by his first wound, where
too by the stroke of his own ill-starred hand he found for
himself death. They pointed out too the raised ground from
which Arminius had harangued his army, the number of
gibbets for the captives, the pits for the living, and how in
his exultation he insulted the standards and eagles.

62. And so the Roman army now on the spot, six years
after the disaster, in grief and anger, began to bury the
bones of the three legions, not a soldier knowing whether
he was interring the relics of a relative or a stranger, but
looking on all as kinsfolk and of their own blood, while
their wrath rose higher than ever against the foe. In raising
the barrow Cæsar laid the first sod, rendering thus a most
welcome honour to the dead, and sharing also in the sorrow
of those present. This Tiberius did not approve, either inter-
preting unfavourably every act of Germanicus, or because
he thought that the spectacle of the slain and unburied made
the army slow to fight and more afraid of the enemy, and
that a general invested with the augurate and its very ancient ceremonies ought not to have polluted himself with
funeral rites.

63. Germanicus, however, pursued Arminius as he fell
back into trackless wilds, and as soon as he had the opportunity, ordered his cavalry to sally forth and scour the plains

occupied by the enemy. Arminius having bidden his men to concentrate themselves and keep close to the woods, suddenly wheeled round, and soon gave those whom he had concealed in the forest-passes the signal to rush to the attack. Thereupon our cavalry was thrown into disorder by this new force, and some cohorts in reserve were sent, which, broken by the shock of flying troops, increased the panic. They were being pushed into a swamp, well known to the victorious assailants, perilous to men unacquainted with it, when Cæsar led forth his legions in battle array. This struck terror into the enemy and gave confidence to our men, and they separated without advantage to either.

Soon afterwards Germanicus led back his army to the Amisia, taking his legions by the fleet, as he had brought them up. Part of the cavalry was ordered to make for the Rhine along the sea-coast. Cæcina, who commanded a division of his own, was advised, though he was returning by a route which he knew, to pass Long Bridges with all possible speed. This was a narrow road amid vast swamps, which had formerly been constructed by Lucius Domitius; on every side were quagmires of thick clinging mud, or perilous with streams. Around were woods on a gradual slope, which Arminius now completely occupied, as soon as by a short route and quick march he had outstripped troops heavily laden with baggage and arms. As Cæcina was in doubt how he could possibly replace bridges which were ruinous from age, and at the same time hold back the enemy, he resolved to encamp on the spot, that some might begin the repair and others the attack.

64. The barbarians attempted to break through the outposts and to throw themselves on the engineering parties, which they harassed, pacing round them and continually charging them. There was a confused din from the men at work and the combatants. Everything alike was unfavourable to the Romans, the place with its deep swamps, insecure to the foot and slippery as one advanced, limbs burdened with coats of mail, and the impossibility of aiming their javelins amid the water. The Cherusci, on the other hand, were familiar with fighting in fens; they had huge frames, and lances long enough to inflict wounds even at a distance.

Night at last released the legions, which were now wavering, from a disastrous engagement. The Germans whom success rendered unwearied, without even then taking any rest, turned all the streams which rose from the slopes of the surrounding hills into the lands beneath. The ground being thus flooded and the completed portion of our works submerged, the soldiers' labour was doubled.

This was Cæcina's fortieth campaign as a subordinate or a commander, and, with such experience of success and peril, he was perfectly fearless. As he thought over future possibilities, he could devise no plan but to keep the enemy within the woods, till the wounded and the more encumbered troops were in advance. For between the hills and the swamps there stretched a plain which would admit of an extended line. The legions had their assigned places, the fifth on the right wing, the twenty-first on the left, the men of the first to lead the van, the twentieth to repel pursuers.

65. It was a restless night for different reasons, the barbarians in their festivity filling the valleys under the hills and the echoing glens with merry song or savage shouts, while in the Roman camp were flickering fires, broken exclamations, and the men lay scattered along the intrenchments or wandered from tent to tent, wakeful rather than watchful. A ghastly dream appalled the general. He seemed to see Quintilius Varus, covered with blood, rising out of the swamps, and to hear him, as it were, calling to him, but he did not, as he imagined, obey the call; he even repelled his hand, as he stretched it over him. At daybreak the legions, posted on the wings, from panic or perversity, deserted their position and hastily occupied a plain beyond the morass. Yet Arminius, though free to attack, did not at the moment rush out on them. But when the baggage was clogged in the mud and in the fosses, the soldiers around it in disorder, the array of the standards in confusion, every one in selfish haste and all ears deaf to the word of command, he ordered the Germans to charge, exclaiming again and again, "Behold a Varus and legions once more entangled in Varus's fate." As he spoke, he cut through the column with some picked men, inflicting wounds chiefly on the horses. Staggering in their blood on the slippery marsh, they

shook off their riders, driving hither and thither all in their way, and trampling on the fallen. The struggle was hottest round the eagles, which could neither be carried in the face of the storm of missiles, nor planted in the miry soil. Cæcina, while he was keeping up the battle, fell from his horse, which was pierced under him, and was being hemmed in, when the first legion threw itself in the way. The greed of the foe helped him, for they left the slaughter to secure the spoil, and the legions, towards evening, struggled on to open and firm ground.

Nor did this end their miseries. Entrenchments had to be thrown up, materials sought for earthworks, while the army had lost to a great extent their implements for digging earth and cutting turf. There were no tents for the rank and file, no comforts for the wounded. As they shared their food, soiled by mire or blood, they bewailed the darkness with its awful omen, and the one day which yet remained to so many thousand men.

66. It chanced that a horse, which had broken its halter and wandered wildly in fright at the uproar, overthrew some men against whom it dashed. Thence arose such a panic, from the belief that the Germans had burst into the camp, that all rushed to the gates. Of these the decuman gate was the point chiefly sought, as it was furthest from the enemy and safer for flight. Cæcina, having ascertained that the alarm was groundless, yet being unable to stop or stay the soldiers by authority or entreaties or even by force, threw himself to the earth in the gateway, and at last by an appeal to their pity, as they would have had to pass over the body of their commander, closed the way. At the same moment the tribunes and the centurions convinced them that it was a false alarm.

67. Having then assembled them at his headquarters, and ordered them to hear his words in silence, he reminded them of the urgency of the crisis. "Their safety," he said, "lay in their arms, which they must, however, use with discretion, and they must remain within the entrenchments, till the enemy approached closer, in the hope of storming them; then, there must be a general sortie; by that sortie the Rhine might be reached. Whereas if they fled, more forests. deeper

swamps, and a savage foe awaited them; but if they were victorious, glory and renown would be theirs." He dwelt on all that was dear to them at home, all that testified to their honour in the camp, without any allusion to disaster. Next he handed over the horses, beginning with his own, of the officers and tribunes, to the bravest fighters in the army, quite impartially, that these first, and then the infantry, might charge the enemy.

68. There was as much restlessness in the German host with its hopes, its eager longings, and the conflicting opinions of its chiefs. Arminius advised that they should allow the Romans to quit their position, and, when they had quitted it, again surprise them in swampy and intricate ground. Inguiomerus, with fiercer counsels, heartily welcome to barbarians, was for beleaguering the entrenchment in armed array, as to storm them would, he said, be easy, and there would be more prisoners and the booty unspoilt. So at daybreak they trampled in the fosses, flung hurdles into them, seized the upper part of the breastwork, where the troops were thinly distributed and seemingly paralysed by fear. When they were fairly within the fortifications, the signal was given to the cohorts, and the horns and trumpets sounded. Instantly, with a shout and sudden rush, our men threw themselves on the German rear, with taunts, that here were no woods or swamps, but that they were on equal ground, with equal chances. The sound of trumpets, the gleam of arms, which were so unexpected, burst with all the greater effect on the enemy, thinking only, as they were, of the easy destruction of a few half-armed men, and they were struck down, as unprepared for a reverse as they had been elated by success. Arminius and Inguiomerus fled from the battle, the first unhurt, the other severely wounded. Their followers were slaughtered, as long as our fury and the light of day lasted. It was not till night that the legions returned, and though more wounds and the same want of provisions distressed them, yet they found strength, healing, sustenance, everything indeed, in their victory.

69. Meanwhile a rumour had spread that our army was cut off, and that a furious German host was marching on Gaul. And had not Agrippina prevented the bridge over the

Rhine from being destroyed, some in their cowardice would
have dared that base act. A woman of heroic spirit, she assumed during those days the duties of a general, and distributed clothes or medicine among the soldiers, as they were
destitute or wounded. According to Caius Plinius, the historian of the German wars, she stood at the extremity of the
bridge, and bestowed praise and thanks on the returning
legions. This made a deep impression on the mind of Tiberius. "Such zeal," he thought, "could not be guileless; it
was not against a foreign foe that she was thus courting
the soldiers. Generals had nothing left them when a woman
went among the companies, attended the standards, ventured on bribery, as though it showed but slight ambition
to parade her son in a common soldier's uniform, and wish
him to be called Cæsar Caligula. Agrippina had now more
power with the armies than officers, than generals. A woman
had quelled a mutiny which the sovereign's name could not
check." All this was inflamed and aggravated by Sejanus,
who, with his thorough comprehension of the character of
Tiberius, sowed for a distant future hatreds which the emperor might treasure up and might exhibit when fully matured.

70. Of the legions which he had conveyed by ship, Germanicus gave the second and fourteenth to Publius Vitellius,
to be marched by land, so that the fleet might sail more
easily over a sea full of shoals, or take the ground more
lightly at the ebb-tide. Vitellius at first pursued his route
without interruption, having a dry shore, or the waves
coming in gently. After a while, through the force of the
north wind and the equinoctial season, when the sea swells
to its highest, his army was driven and tossed hither and
thither. The country too was flooded; sea, shore, fields presented one aspect, nor could the treacherous quicksands be
distinguished from solid ground or shallows from deep water.
Men were swept away by the waves or sucked under by
eddies; beasts of burden, baggage, lifeless bodies floated
about and blocked their way. The companies were mingled
in confusion, now with the breast, now with the head only
above water, sometimes losing their footing and parted from
their comrades or drowned. The voice of mutual encourage-

ment availed not against the adverse force of the waves. There was nothing to distinguish the brave from the coward, the prudent from the careless, forethought from chance; the same strong power swept everything before it. At last Vitellius struggled out to higher ground and led his men up to it. There they passed the night, without necessary food, without fire, many of them with bare or bruised limbs, in a plight as pitiable as that of men besieged by an enemy. For such, at least, have the opportunity of a glorious death, while here was destruction without honour. Daylight restored land to their sight, and they pushed their way to the river Visurgis, where Cæsar had arrived with the fleet. The legions then embarked, while a rumour was flying about that they were drowned. Nor was there a belief in their safety till they saw Cæsar and the army returned.

71. By this time Stertinius, who had been despatched to receive the surrender of Segimerus, brother of Segestes, had conducted the chief, together with his son, to the canton of the Ubii. Both were pardoned, Segimerus readily, the son with some hesitation, because it was said that he had insulted the corpse of Quintilius Varus. Meanwhile Gaul, Spain, and Italy vied in repairing the losses of the army, offering whatever they had at hand, arms, horses, gold. Germanicus having praised their zeal, took only for the war their arms and horses, and relieved the soldiers out of his own purse. And that he might also soften the remembrance of the disaster by kindness, he went round to the wounded, applauded the feats of soldier after soldier, examined their wounds, raised the hopes of one, the ambition of another, and the spirits of all by his encouragement and interest, thus strengthening their ardour for himself and for battle.

72. That year triumphal honours were decreed to Aulus Cæcina, Lucius Apronius, Caius Silius for their achievements under Germanicus. The title of "father of his country," which the people had so often thrust on him, Tiberius refused, nor would he allow obedience to be sworn to his enactments, though the Senate voted it, for he said repeatedly that all human things were uncertain, and that the more he had obtained, the more precarious was his position. But he did not thereby create a belief in his patriotism, for he

had revived the law of treason, the name of which indeed was known in ancient times, though other matters came under its jurisdiction, such as the betrayal of an army, or seditious stirring up of the people, or, in short, any corrupt act by which a man had impaired "the majesty of the people of Rome." Deeds only were liable to accusation; words went unpunished. It was Augustus who first, under colour of this law, applied legal inquiry to libellous writings, provoked, as he had been, by the licentious freedom with which Cassius Severus had defamed men and women of distinction in his insulting satires. Soon afterwards, Tiberius, when consulted by Pompeius Macer, the prætor, as to whether prosecutions for treason should be revived, replied that the laws must be enforced. He too had been exasperated by the publication of verses of uncertain authorship, pointed at his cruelty, his arrogance, and his dissensions with his mother.

73. It will not be uninteresting if I relate in the cases of Falanius and Rubrius, Roman knights of moderate fortune, the first experiments at such accusations, in order to explain the origin of a most terrible scourge, how by Tiberius's cunning it crept in among us, how subsequently it was checked, finally, how it burst into flame and consumed everything. Against Falanius it was alleged by his accuser that he had admitted among the votaries of Augustus, who in every great house were associated into a kind of brotherhood, one Cassius, a buffoon of infamous life, and that he had also in selling his gardens included in the sale a statue of Augustus. Against Rubrius the charge was that he had violated by perjury the divinity of Augustus. When this was known to Tiberius, he wrote to the consuls "that his father had not had a place in heaven decreed to him, that the honour might be turned to the destruction of the citizens. Cassius, the actor, with men of the same profession, used to take part in the games which had been consecrated by his mother to the memory of Augustus. Nor was it contrary to the religion of the State for the emperor's image, like those of other deities, to be added to a sale of gardens and houses. As to the oath, the thing ought to be considered as if the man had deceived Jupiter. Wrongs done to the gods were the gods' concern."

74. Not long afterwards, Granius Marcellus, proconsul of

Bithynia, was accused of treason by his quaestor, Cæpio Crispinus, and the charge was supported by Romanus Hispo. Crispinus then entered on a line of life afterwards rendered notorious by the miseries of the age and men's shamelessness. Needy, obscure, and restless, he wormed himself by stealthy informations into the confidence of a vindictive prince, and soon imperilled all the most distinguished citizens; and having thus gained influence with one, hatred from all besides, he left an example in following which beggars became wealthy, the insignificant, formidable, and brought ruin first on others, finally on themselves. He alleged against Marcellus that he had made some disrespectful remarks about Tiberius, a charge not to be evaded, inasmuch as the accuser selected the worst features of the emperor's character and grounded his case on them. The things were true, and so were believed to have been said.

Hispo added that Marcellus had placed his own statue above those of the Cæsars, and had set the bust of Tiberius on another statue from which he had struck off the head of Augustus. At this the emperor's wrath blazed forth, and, breaking through his habitual silence, he exclaimed that in such a case he would himself too give his vote openly on oath, that the rest might be under the same obligation. There lingered even then a few signs of expiring freedom. And so Cneius Piso asked, "In what order will you vote, Cæsar? If first, I shall know what to follow; if last, I fear that I may differ from you unwillingly." Tiberius was deeply moved, and repenting of the outburst, all the more because of its thoughtlessness, he quietly allowed the accused to be acquitted of the charges of treason. As for the question of extortion, it was referred to a special commission.

75. Not satisfied with judicial proceedings in the Senate, the emperor would sit at one end of the Prætor's tribunal, but so as not to displace him from the official seat. Many decisions were given in his presence, in opposition to improper influence and the solicitations of great men. This, though it promoted justice, ruined freedom. Pius Aurelius, for example, a senator, complained that the foundations of his house had been weakened by the pressure of a public road and aqueduct, and he appealed to the Senate for assistance.

He was opposed by the prætors of the treasury, but the emperor helped him, and paid him the value of his house, for he liked to spend money on a good purpose, a virtue which he long retained, when he cast off all others. To Propertius Celer, an ex-prætor, who sought because of his indigence to be excused from his rank as a senator, he gave a million sesterces, having ascertained that he had inherited poverty. He bade others, who attempted the same, prove their case to the Senate, as from his love of strictness he was harsh even where he acted on right grounds. Consequently every one else preferred silence and poverty to confession and relief.

76. In the same year the Tiber, swollen by continuous rains, flooded the level portions of the city. Its subsidence was followed by a destruction of buildings and of life. Thereupon Asinius Gallus proposed to consult the Sibylline books. Tiberius refused, veiling in obscurity the divine as well as the human. However, the devising of means to confine the river was intrusted to Ateius Capito and Lucius Arruntius.

Achaia and Macedonia, on complaining of their burdens, were, it was decided, to be relieved for a time from proconsular government and to be transferred to the emperor. Drusus presided over a show of gladiators which he gave in his own name and in that of his brother Germanicus, for he gloated intensely over bloodshed, however cheap its victims. This was alarming to the populace, and his father had, it was said, rebuked him. Why Tiberius kept away from the spectacle was variously explained. According to some, it was his loathing of a crowd, according to others, his gloomy temper, and a fear of contrast with the gracious presence of Augustus. I cannot believe that he deliberately gave his son the opportunity of displaying his ferocity and provoking the people's disgust, though even this was said.

77. Meanwhile the unruly tone of the theatre which first showed itself in the preceding year, broke out with worse violence, and some soldiers and a centurion, besides several of the populace, were killed, and the tribune of a prætorian cohort was wounded, while they were trying to stop insults to the magistrates and the strife of the mob. This disturbance was the subject of a debate in the Senate, and opinions

were expressed in favour of the prætors having authority to scourge actors. Haterius Agrippa, tribune of the people, interposed his veto, and was sharply censured in a speech from Asinius Gallus, without a word from Tiberius, who liked to allow the Senate such shows of freedom. Still the interposition was successful, because Augustus had once pronounced that actors were exempt from the scourge, and it was not lawful for Tiberius to infringe his decisions. Many enactments were passed to fix the amount of their pay and to check the disorderly behaviour of their partisans. Of these the chief were that no Senator should enter the house of a pantomime player, that Roman knights should not crowd round them in the public streets, that they should exhibit themselves only in the theatre, and that the prætors should be empowered to punish with banishment any riotous conduct in the spectators.

78. A request from the Spaniards that they might erect a temple to Augustus in the colony of Tarraco was granted, and a precedent thus given for all the provinces. When the people of Rome asked for a remission of the one per cent. tax on all saleable commodities, Tiberius declared by edict "that the military exchequer depended on that branch of revenue, and, further, that the State was unequal to the burden, unless the twentieth year of service were to be that of the veteran's discharge." Thus the ill-advised results of the late mutiny, by which a limit of sixteen campaigns had been extorted, were cancelled for the future.

79. A question was then raised in the Senate by Arruntius and Ateius whether, in order to restrain the inundations of the Tiber, the rivers and lakes which swell its waters should be diverted from their courses. A hearing was given to embassies from the municipal towns and colonies, and the people of Florentia begged that the Clanis might not be turned out of its channel and made to flow into the Arnus, as that would bring ruin on themselves. Similar arguments were used by the inhabitants of Interamna. The most fruitful plains of Italy, they said, would be destroyed if the river Nar (for this was the plan proposed) were to be divided into several streams and overflow the country. Nor did the people of Reate remain silent. They remonstrated against the clos-

ing up of the Veline lake, where it empties itself into the
Nar, "as it would burst in a flood on the entire neighbourhood. Nature had admirably provided for human interests
in having assigned to rivers their mouths, their channels,
and their limits, as well as their sources. Regard, too, must
be paid to the different religions of the allies, who had dedicated sacred rites, groves, and altars to the rivers of their
country. Tiber himself would be altogether unwilling to be
deprived of his neighbour streams and to flow with less
glory." Either the entreaties of the colonies, or the difficulty
of the work or superstitious motives prevailed, and they
yielded to Piso's opinion, who declared himself against any
change.

80. Poppæus Sabinus was continued in his government of
the province of Moesia with the addition of Achaia and
Macedonia. It was part of Tiberius' character to prolong
indefinitely military commands and to keep many men to the
end of their life with the same armies and in the same ad-
ministrations. Various motives have been assigned for this.
Some say that, out of aversion to any fresh anxiety, he retained what he had once approved as a permanent arrangement; others, that he grudged to see many enjoying promotion. Some, again, think that though he had an acute
intellect, his judgment was irresolute, for he did not seek
out eminent merit, and yet he detested vice. From the best
men he apprehended danger to himself, from the worst, disgrace to the State. He went so far at last in this irresolution,
that he appointed to provinces men whom he did not mean
to allow to leave Rome.

81. I can hardly venture on any positive statement about
the consular elections, now held for the first time under this
emperor, or, indeed, subsequently, so conflicting are the accounts we find not only in historians but in Tiberius' own
speeches. Sometimes he kept back the names of the candidates, describing their origin, their life and military career,
so that it might be understood who they were. Occasionally
even these hints were withheld, and, after urging them not
to disturb the elections by canvassing, he would promise his
own help towards the result. Generally he declared that only
those had offered themselves to him as candidates whose

names he had given to the consuls, and that others might offer themselves if they had confidence in their influence or merit. A plausible profession this in words, but really unmeaning and delusive, and the greater the disguise of freedom which marked it, the more cruel the enslavement into which it was soon to plunge us.

BOOK II

A.D. 16—19

1. In the consulship of Sisenna Statilius Taurus and Lucius Libo there was a commotion in the kingdoms and Roman provinces of the East. It had its origin among the Parthians, who disdained as a foreigner a king whom they had sought and received from Rome, though he was of the family of the Arsacids. This was Vonones, who had been given as an hostage to Augustus by Phraates. For although he had driven before him armies and generals from Rome, Phraates had shown to Augustus every token of reverence and had sent him some of his children, to cement the friendship, not so much from dread of us as from distrust of the loyalty of his countrymen.

2. After the death of Phraates and the succeeding kings in the bloodshed of civil wars, there came to Rome envoys from the chief men of Parthia, in quest of Vonones, his eldest son. Cæsar thought this a great honour to himself, and loaded Vonones with wealth. The barbarians, too, welcomed him with rejoicing, as is usual with new rulers. Soon they felt shame at Parthians having become degenerate, at their having sought a king from another world, one too infected with the training of the enemy, at the throne of the Arsacids now being possessed and given away among the provinces of Rome. "Where," they asked, "was the glory of the men who slew Crassus, who drove out Antonius, if Cæsar's drudge, after an endurance of so many years' slavery, were to rule over Parthians."

Vonones himself too further provoked their disdain, by his contrast with their ancestral manners, by his rare indulgence in the chase, by his feeble interest in horses, by the litter in which he was carried whenever he made a progress through their cities, and by his contemptuous dislike of their

national festivities. They also ridiculed his Greek attendants
and his keeping under seal the commonest household articles.
But he was easy of approach; his courtesy was open to all,
and he had thus virtues with which the Parthians were unfamiliar, and vices new to them. And as his ways were quite
alien from theirs they hated alike what was bad and what
was good in him.

3. Accordingly they summoned Artabanus, an Arsacid by
blood, who had grown to manhood among the Dahae, and
who, though routed in the first encounter, rallied his forces
and possessed himself of the kingdom. The conquered Vonones found a refuge in Armenia, then a free country, and
exposed to the power of Parthia and Rome, without being
trusted by either, in consequence of the crime of Antonius,
who, under the guise of friendship, had inveigled Artavasdes,
king of the Armenians, then loaded him with chains, and
finally murdered him. His son, Artaxias, our bitter foe because of his father's memory, found defence for himself and
his kingdom in the might of the Arsacids. When he was slain
by the treachery of kinsmen, Cæsar gave Tigranes to the
Armenians, and he was put in possession of the kingdom
under the escort of Tiberius Nero. But neither Tigranes nor
his children reigned long, though, in foreign fashion, they
were united in marriage and in royal power.

4. Next, at the bidding of Augustus, Artavasdes was set
on the throne, nor was he deposed without disaster to ourselves. Caius Cæsar was then appointed to restore order in
Armenia. He put over the Armenians Ariobarzanes, a Mede
by birth, whom they willingly accepted, because of his singularly handsome person and noble. spirit. On the death of
Ariobarzanes through a fatal accident, they would not endure his son. Having tried the government of a woman
named Erato and having soon afterwards driven her from
them, bewildered and disorganised, rather indeed without a
ruler than enjoying freedom, they received for their king
the fugitive Vonones. When, however, Artabanus began to
threaten, and but feeble support could be given by the
Armenians, or war with Parthia would have to be undertaken, if Vonones was to be upheld by our arms, the governor of Syria, Creticus Silanus, sent for him and kept him

under surveillance, letting him retain his royal pomp and
title. How Vonones meditated an escape from this mockery,
I will relate in the proper place.

5. Meanwhile the commotion in the East was rather pleasing to Tiberius, as it was a pretext for withdrawing Germanicus from the legions which knew him well, and placing
him over new provinces where he would be exposed both to
treachery and to disasters. Germanicus, however, in proportion to the strength of the soldiers' attachment and to his
uncle's dislike, was eager to hasten his victory, and he
pondered on plans of battle, and on the reverses or successes
which during more than three years of war had fallen to his
lot. The Germans, he knew, were beaten in the field and on
fair ground; they were helped by woods, swamps, short summers, and early winters. His own troops were affected not so
much by wounds as by long marches and damage to their
arms. Gaul had been exhausted by supplying horses; a long
baggage-train presented facilities for ambuscades, and was
embarrassing to its defenders. But by embarking on the sea,
invasion would be easy for them, and a surprise to the
enemy, while a campaign too would be more quickly begun,
the legions and supplies would be brought up simultaneously,
and the cavalry with their horses would arrive, in good condition, by the river-mouths and channels, at the heart of
Germany.

6. To this accordingly he gave his mind, and sent Publius
Vitellius and Caius Antius to collect the taxes of Gaul. Silius,
Anteius, and Cæcina had the charge of building a fleet. It
seemed that a thousand vessels were required, and they were
speedily constructed, some of small draught with a narrow
stem and stern and a broad centre, that they might bear the
waves more easily; some flat-bottomed, that they might
ground without being injured; several, furnished with a rud-
der at each end, so that by a sudden shifting of the oars
they might be run into shore either way. Many were covered in with decks, on which engines for missiles might be
conveyed, and were also fit for the carrying of horses or
supplies, and being equipped with sails as well as rapidly
moved by oars, they assumed, through the enthusiasm of
our soldiers, an imposing and formidable aspect.

The island of the Batavi was the appointed rendezvous because of its easy landing-places, and its convenience for receiving the army and carrying the war across the river. For the Rhine after flowing continuously in a single channel or encircling merely insignificant islands, divides itself, so to say, where the Batavian territory begins, into two rivers, retaining its name and the rapidity of its course in the stream which washes Germany, till it mingles with the ocean. On the Gallic bank, its flow is broader and gentler; it is called by an altered name, the Vahal, by the inhabitants of its shore. Soon that name too is changed for the Mosa river, through whose vast mouth it empties itself into the same ocean.

7. Cæsar, however, while the vessels were coming up, ordered Silius, his lieutenant-general, to make an inroad on the Chatti with a flying column. He himself, on hearing that a fort on the river Luppia was being besieged, led six legions to the spot. Silius owing to sudden rains did nothing but carry off a small booty, and the wife and daughter of Arpus, the chief of the Chatti. And Cæsar had no opportunity of fighting given him by the besiegers, who dispersed on the rumour of his advance. They had, however, destroyed the barrow lately raised in memory of Varus's legions, and the old altar of Drusus. The prince restored the altar, and himself with his legions celebrated funeral games in his father's honour. To raise a new barrow was not thought necessary. All the country between the fort Aliso and the Rhine was thoroughly secured by new barriers and earthworks.

8. By this time the fleet had arrived, and Cæsar, having sent on his supplies and assigned vessels for the legions and the allied troops, entered "Drusus's fosse," as it was called. He prayed Drusus his father to lend him, now that he was venturing on the same enterprise, the willing and favourable aid of the example and memory of his counsels and achievements, and he arrived after a prosperous voyage through the lakes and the ocean as far as the river Amisia. His fleet remained there on the left bank of the stream, and it was a blunder that he did not have it brought up the river. He disembarked the troops, which were to be marched to the country on the right, and thus several days were wasted in

the construction of bridges. The cavalry and the legions fearlessly crossed the first estuaries in which the tide had not yet risen. The rear of the auxiliaries, and the Batavi among the number, plunging recklessly into the water and displaying their skill in swimming, fell into disorder, and some were drowned. While Cæsar was measuring out his camp, he was told of a revolt of the Angrivarii in his rear. He at once despatched Stertinius with some cavalry and a light armed force, who punished their perfidy with fire and sword.

9. The waters of the Visurgis flowed between the Romans and the Cherusci. On its banks stood Arminius with the other chiefs. He asked whether Cæsar had arrived, and on the reply that he was present, he begged leave to have an interview with his brother. That brother, surnamed Flavus, was with our army, a man famous for his loyalty, and for having lost an eye by a wound, a few years ago, when Tiberius was in command. The permission was then given, and he stepped forth and was saluted by Arminius, who had removed his guards to a distance and required that the bowmen ranged on our bank should retire. When they had gone away, Arminius asked his brother whence came the scar which disfigured his face, and on being told the particular place and battle, he inquired what reward he had received. Flavus spoke of increased pay, of a neck chain, a crown, and other military gifts, while Arminius jeered at such a paltry recompense for slavery.

10. Then began a controversy. The one spoke of the greatness of Rome, the resources of Cæsar, the dreadful punishment in store for the vanquished, the ready mercy for him who surrenders, and the fact that neither Arminius's wife nor his son were treated as enemies; the other, of the claims of fatherland, of ancestral freedom, of the gods of the homes of Germany, of the mother who shared his prayers, that Flavus might not choose to be the deserter and betrayer rather than the ruler of his kinsfolk and relatives, and indeed of his own people.

By degrees they fell to bitter words, and even the river between them would not have hindered them from joining combat, had not Stertinius hurried up and put his hand on

Flavus, who in the full tide of his fury was demanding his weapons and his charger. Arminius was seen facing him, full of menaces and challenging him to conflict. Much of what he said was in Roman speech, for he had served in our camp as leader of his fellow-countrymen.

11. Next day the German army took up its position on the other side of the Visurgis. Cæsar, thinking that without bridges and troops to guard them, it would not be good generalship to expose the legions to danger, sent the cavalry across the river by the fords. It was commanded by Stertinius and Aemilius, one of the first rank centurions, who attacked at widely different points so as to distract the enemy. Chariovalda, the Batavian chief, dashed to the charge where the stream is most rapid. The Cherusci, by a pretended flight, drew him into a plain surrounded by forest-passes. Then bursting on him in a sudden attack from all points they thrust aside all who resisted, pressed fiercely on their retreat, driving them before them, when they rallied in compact array, some by close fighting, others by missiles from a distance. Chariovalda, after long sustaining the enemy's fury, cheered on his men to break by a dense formation the onset of their bands, while he himself, plunging into the thickest of the battle, fell amid a shower of darts with his horse pierced under him, and round him many noble chiefs. The rest were rescued from the peril by their own strength, or by the cavalry which came up with Stertinius and Aemilius.

12. Cæsar on crossing the Visurgis learnt by the information of a deserter that Arminius had chosen a battle-field, that other tribes too had assembled in a forest sacred to Hercules, and would venture on a night attack on his camp. He put faith in this intelligence, and, besides, several watch-fires were seen. Scouts also, who had crept close up to the enemy, reported that they had heard the neighing of horses and the hum of a huge and tumultuous host. And so thinking, as the decisive crisis drew near, that he ought thoroughly to sound the temper of his soldiers, he considered with himself how this was to be accomplished with a genuine result. Tribunes and centurions, he knew, oftener reported what was welcome than what was true; freedmen had slavish

spirits, friends a love of flattery. If an assembly were called,
there too the lead of a few was followed by the shout of the
many. He must probe their inmost thoughts, when they were
uttering their hopes and fears at the military mess, among
themselves, and unwatched.

13. At nightfall, leaving his tent of augury by a secret exit,
unknown to the sentries, with one companion, his shoulders
covered with a wild beast's skin, he visited the camp streets,
stood by the tents, and enjoyed the men's talk about himself, as one extolled his noble rank, another, his handsome
person, nearly all of them, his endurance, his gracious manner and the evenness of his temper, whether he was jesting
or was serious, while they acknowledged that they ought to
repay him with their gratitude in battle, and at the same
time sacrifice to a glorious vengeance the perfidious viola-
tors of peace. Meanwhile one of the enemy, acquainted with
the Roman tongue, spurred his horse up to the entrenchments, and in a loud voice promised in the name of Arminius
to all deserters wives and lands with daily pay of a hundred
sesterces as long as war lasted. The insult fired the wrath of
the legions. "Let daylight come," they said, "let battle be
given. The soldiers will possess themselves of the lands of
the Germans and will carry off their wives. We hail the
omen; we mean the women and riches of the enemy to be
our spoil." About midday there was a skirmishing attack on
our camp, without any discharge of missiles, when they saw
the cohorts in close array before the lines and no sign of
carelessness.

14. The same night brought with it a cheering dream to
Germanicus. He saw himself engaged in sacrifice, and his
robe being sprinkled with the sacred blood, another more
beautiful was given him by the hands of his grandmother
Augusta. Encouraged by the omen and finding the auspices
favourable, he called an assembly, and explained the precautions which wisdom suggested as suitable for the impending battle. "It is not," he said, "plains only which are
good for the fighting of Roman soldiers, but woods and
forest passes, if science be used. For the huge shields and
unwieldly lances of the barbarians cannot, amid trunks of
trees and brushwood that springs from the ground, be so

well managed as our javelins and swords and close-fitting armour. Shower your blows thickly; strike at the face with your swords' points. The German has neither cuirass nor helmet; even his shield is not strengthened with leather or steel, but is of osiers woven together or of thin and painted board. If their first line is armed with spears, the rest have only weapons hardened by fire or very short. Again, though their frames are terrible to the eye and formidable in a brief onset, they have no capacity of enduring wounds; without any shame at the disgrace, without any regard to their leaders, they quit the field and flee; they quail under disaster, just as in success they forget alike divine and human laws. If in your weariness of land and sea you desire an end of service, this battle prepares the way to it. The Elbe is now nearer than the Rhine, and there is no war beyond, provided only you enable me, keeping close as I do to my father's and my uncle's footsteps, to stand a conqueror on the same spot."

15. The general's speech was followed by enthusiasm in the soldiers, and the signal for battle was given. Nor were Arminius and the other German chiefs slow to call their respective clansmen to witness that "these Romans were the most cowardly fugitives out of Varus's army, men who rather than endure war had taken to mutiny. Half of them have their backs covered with wounds; half are once again exposing limbs battered by waves and storms to a foe full of fury, and to hostile deities, with no hope of advantage. They have, in fact, had recourse to a fleet and to a trackless ocean, that their coming might be unopposed, their flight unpursued. But when once they have joined conflict with us, the help of winds or oars will be unavailing to the vanquished. Remember only their greed, their cruelty, their pride. Is anything left for us but to retain our freedom or to die before we are enslaved?"

16. When they were thus roused and were demanding battle, their chiefs led them down into a plain named Idistavisus. It winds between the Visurgis and a hill range, its breadth varying as the river banks recede or the spurs of the hills project on it. In their rear rose a forest, with the branches rising to a great height, while there were clear

spaces between the trunks. The barbarian army occupied the plain and the outskirts of the wood. The Cherusci were posted by themselves on the high ground, so as to rush down on the Romans during the battle.

Our army advanced in the following order. The auxiliary Gauls and Germans were in the van, then the foot-archers, after them, four legions and Cæsar himself with two prætorian cohorts and some picked cavalry. Next came as many other legions, and light-armed troops with horse-bowmen, and the remaining cohorts of the allies. The men were quite ready and prepared to form in line of battle according to their marching order.

17. Cæsar, as soon as he saw the Cheruscan bands which in their impetuous spirit had rushed to the attack, ordered the finest of his cavalry to charge them in flank, Stertinius with the other squadrons to make a détour and fall on their rear, promising himself to come up in good time. Meanwhile there was a most encouraging augury. Eight eagles, seen to fly towards the woods and to enter them, caught the general's eye. "Go," he exclaimed, "follow the Roman birds, the true deities of our legions." At the same moment the infantry charged, and the cavalry which had been sent on in advance dashed on the rear and the flanks. And, strange to relate, two columns of the enemy fled in opposite directions, that, which had occupied the wood, rushing into the open, those who had been drawn up on the plains, into the wood. The Cherusci, who were between them, were dislodged from the hills, while Arminius, conspicuous among them by gesture, voice, and a wound he had received, kept up the fight. He had thrown himself on our archers and was on the point of breaking through them, when the cohorts of the Raeti, Vendelici, and Gauls faced his attack. By a strong bodily effort, however, and a furious rush of his horse, he made his way through them, having smeared his face with his blood, that he might not be known. Some have said that he was recognised by Chauci serving among the Roman auxiliaries, who let him go.

Inguiomerus owed his escape to similar courage or treachery. The rest were cut down in every direction. Many in attempting to swim across the Visurgis were overwhelmed under a storm of missiles or by the force of the current, lastly, by the rush of fugitives and the falling in of the banks. Some in their ignominious flight climbed the tops of trees, and as they were hiding themselves in the boughs, archers were brought up and they were shot for sport. Others were dashed to the ground by the felling of the trees.

18. It was a great victory and without bloodshed to us. From nine in the morning to nightfall the enemy were slaughtered, and ten miles were covered with arms and dead bodies, while there were found amid the plunder the chains which the Germans had brought with them for the Romans, as though the issue were certain. The soldiers on the battle field hailed Tiberius as Imperator, and raised a mound on which arms were piled in the style of a trophy, with the names of the conquered tribes inscribed beneath them.

19. That sight caused keener grief and rage among the Germans than their wounds, their mourning, and their losses. Those who but now were preparing to quit their settlements and to retreat to the further side of the Elbe, longed for battle and flew to arms. Common people and chiefs, young and old, rushed on the Roman army, and spread disorder. At last they chose a spot closed in by a river and by forests, within which was a narrow swampy plain. The woods too were surrounded by a bottomless morass, only on one side of it the Angrivarii had raised a broad earthwork, as a boundary between themselves and the Cherusci. Here their infantry was ranged. Their cavalry they concealed in neighbouring woods, so as to be on the legions' rear, as soon as they entered the forest.

20. All this was known to Cæsar. He was acquainted with their plans, their positions, with what met the eye, and what was hidden, and he prepared to turn the enemy's stratagems to their own destruction. To Seius Tubero, his chief officer, he assigned the cavalry and the plain. His infantry he drew up so that part might advance on level ground into the forest, and part clamber up the earthwork which confronted them. He charged himself with what was the specially difficult operation, leaving the rest to his officers. Those who had the level ground easily forced a passage. Those who had to assault the earthwork encountered heavy blows from above

as if they were scaling a wall. The general saw how unequal this close fighting was, and having withdrawn his legions to a little distance, ordered the slingers and artillerymen to discharge a volley of missiles and scatter the enemy. Spears were hurled from the engines, and the more conspicuous were the defenders of the position, the more the wounds with which they were driven from it. Cæsar with some prætorian cohorts was the first, after the storming of the ramparts, to dash into the woods. There they fought at close quarters. A morass was in the enemy's rear, and the Romans were hemmed in by the river or by the hills. Both were in a desperate plight from their position; valour was their only hope, victory their only safety.

21. The Germans were equally brave, but they were beaten by the nature of the fighting and of the weapons, for their vast host in so confined a space could neither thrust out nor recover their immense lances, or avail themselves of their nimble movements and lithe frames, forced as they were to a close engagement. Our soldiers, on the other hand, with their shields pressed to their breasts, and their hands grasping their sword-hilts, struck at the huge limbs and exposed faces of the barbarians, cutting a passage through the slaughtered enemy, for Arminius was now less active, either from incessant perils, or because he was partially disabled by his recent wound. As for Inguiomerus, who flew hither and thither over the battle-field, it was fortune rather than courage which forsook him. Germanicus, too, that he might be the better known, took his helmet off his head and begged his men to follow up the slaughter, as they wanted not prisoners, and the utter destruction of the nation would be the only conclusion of the war. And now, late in the day, he withdrew one of his legions from the field, to intrench a camp, while the rest till nightfall glutted themselves with the enemy's blood. Our cavalry fought with indecisive success.

22. Having publicly praised his victorious troops, Cæsar raised a pile of arms with the proud inscription, "The army of Tiberius Cæsar, after thoroughly conquering the tribes between the Rhine and the Elbe, has dedicated this monument to Mars, Jupiter, and Augustus." He added nothing about himself, fearing jealousy, or thinking that the con-

ciousness of the achievement was enough. Next he charged Stertinius with making war on the Angrivarii, but they hastened to surrender. And, as suppliants, by refusing nothing, they obtained a full pardon.

23. When, however, summer was at its height, some of the legions were sent back overland into winter-quarters, but most of them Cæsar put on board the fleet and brought down the river Amisia to the ocean. At first the calm waters merely sounded with the oars of a thousand vessels or were ruffled by the sailing ships. Soon, a hailstorm bursting from a black mass of clouds, while the waves rolled hither and thither under tempestuous gales from every quarter, rendered clear sight impossible, and the steering difficult, while our soldiers, terrorstricken and without any experience of disasters on the sea, by embarrassing the sailors or giving them clumsy aid, neutralized the services of the skilled crews. After a while, wind and wave shifted wholly to the south, and from the hilly lands and deep rivers of Germany came, with a huge line of rolling clouds, a strong blast, all the more frightful from the frozen north which was so near to them, and instantly caught and drove the ships hither and thither into the open ocean, or on islands with steep cliffs or which hidden shoals made perilous. These they just escaped, with difficulty, and when the tide changed and bore them the same way as the wind, they could not hold to their anchors or bale out the water which rushed in upon them. Horses, beasts of burden, baggage, were thrown overboard, in order to lighten the hulls which leaked copiously through their sides, while the waves too dashed over them.

24. As the ocean is stormier than all other seas, and as Germany is conspicuous for the terrors of its climate, so in novelty and extent did this disaster transcend every other, for all around were hostile coasts, or an expanse so vast and deep that it is thought to be the remotest shoreless sea. Some of the vessels were swallowed up; many were wrecked on distant islands, and the soldiers, finding there no form of human life, perished of hunger, except some who supported existence on carcases of horses washed on the same shores. Germanicus's trireme alone reached the country of the Chauci. Day and night, on those rocks and promontories he

would incessantly exclaim that he was himself responsible for this awful ruin, and friends scarce restrained him from seeking death in the same sea.

At last, as the tide ebbed and the wind blew favourably, the shattered vessels with but few rowers, or clothing spread as sails, some towed by the more powerful, returned, and Germanicus, having speedily repaired them, sent them to search the islands. Many by that means were recovered. The Angrivarii, who had lately been admitted to our alliance, restored to us several whom they had ransomed from the inland tribes. Some had been carried to Britain and were sent back by the petty chiefs. Every one, as he returned from some far-distant region, told of wonders, of violent hurricanes, and unknown birds, of monsters of the sea, of forms half-human, half beast-like, things they had really seen or in their terror believed.

25. Meanwhile the rumoured loss of the fleet stirred the Germans to hope for war, as it did Cæsar to hold them down. He ordered Caius Silius with thirty thousand infantry and three thousand cavalry to march against the Chatti. He himself, with a larger army, invaded the Marsi, whose leader, Mallovendus, whom we had lately admitted to surrender, pointed out a neighbouring wood, where, he said, an eagle of one of Varus's legions was buried and guarded only by a small force. Immediately troops were despatched to draw the enemy from his position by appearing in his front, others, to hem in his rear and open the ground. Fortune favoured both. So Germanicus, with increased energy, advanced into the country, laying it waste, and utterly ruining a foe who dared not encounter him, or who was instantly defeated wherever he resisted, and, as we learnt from prisoners, was never more panic-stricken. The Romans, they declared, were invincible, rising superior to all calamities; for having thrown away a fleet, having lost their arms, after strewing the shores with the carcases of horses and of men, they had rushed to the attack with the same courage, with equal spirit, and, seemingly, with augmented numbers.

26. The soldiers were then led back into winter-quarters, rejoicing in their hearts at having been compensated for their disasters at sea by a successful expedition. They were helped

too by Cæsar's bounty, which made good whatever loss any one declared he had suffered. It was also regarded as a certainty that the enemy were wavering and consulting on negotiations for peace, and that, with an additional campaign next summer the war might be ended. Tiberius, however, in repeated letters advised Germanicus to return for the triumph decreed him. "He had now had enough of success, enough of disaster. He had fought victorious battles on a great scale; he should also remember those losses which the winds and waves had inflicted, and which, though due to no fault of the general, were still grievous and shocking. He, Tiberius, had himself been sent nine times by Augustus into Germany, and had done more by policy than by arms. By this means the submission of the Sugambri had been secured, and the Suevi with their king Maroboduus had been forced into peace. The Cherusci too and the other insurgent tribes, since the vengeance of Rome had been satisfied, might be left to their internal feuds."

When Germanicus requested a year for the completion of his enterprise, Tiberius put a severer pressure on his modesty by offering him a second consulship, the functions of which he was to discharge in person. He also added that if war must still be waged, he might as well leave some materials for renown to his brother Drusus, who, as there was then no other enemy, could win only in Germany the imperial title and the triumphal laurel. Germanicus hesitated no longer, though he saw that this was a pretence, and that he was hurried away through jealousy from the glory he had already acquired.

27. About the same time Libo Drusus, of the family of Scribonii, was accused of revolutionary schemes. I will explain, somewhat minutely, the beginning, progress, and end of this affair, since then first were originated those practices which for so many years have eaten into the heart of the State. Firmius Catus, a senator, an intimate friend of Libo's, prompted the young man, who was thoughtless and an easy prey to delusions, to resort to astrologers' promises, magical rites, and interpreters of dreams, dwelling ostentatiously on his great-grandfather Pompeius, his aunt Scribonia, who had formerly been wife of Augustus, his imperial cousins, his

house crowded with ancestral busts, and urging him to extravagance and debt, himself the companion of his profligacy and desperate embarrassments, thereby to entangle him in all the more proofs of guilt.

28. As soon as he found enough witnesses, with some slaves who knew the facts, he begged an audience of the emperor, after first indicating the crime and the criminal through Flaccus Vescularius, a Roman knight, who was more intimate with Tiberius than himself. Cæsar, without disregarding the information, declined an interview, for the communication, he said, might be conveyed to him through the same messenger, Flaccus. Meanwhile he conferred the prætorship on Libo and often invited him to his table, showing no unfriendliness in his looks or anger in his words (so thoroughly had he concealed his resentment); and he wished to know all his saying and doings, though it was in his power to stop them, till one Junius, who had been tampered with by Libo for the purpose of evoking by incantations spirits of the dead, gave information to Fulcinius Trio. Trio's ability was conspicuous among informers, as well as his eagerness for an evil notoriety. He at once pounced on the accused, went to the consuls, and demanded an inquiry before the Senate. The Senators were summoned, with a special notice that they must consult on a momentous and terrible matter.

29. Libo meanwhile, in mourning apparel and accompanied by ladies of the highest rank, went to house after house, entreating his relatives, and imploring some eloquent voice to ward off his perils; which all refused, on different pretexts, but from the same apprehension. On the day the Senate met, jaded with fear and mental anguish, or, as some have related, feigning illness, he was carried in a litter to the doors of the Senate House, and leaning on his brother he raised his hands and voice in supplication to Tiberius, who received him with unmoved countenance. The emperor then read out the charges and the accusers' names, with such calmness as not to seem to soften or aggravate the accusations.

30. Besides Trio and Catus, Fonteius Agrippa and Caïus Vibius were among his accusers, and claimed with eager rivalry the privilege of conducting the case for the prosecu-

tion, till Vibius, as they would not yield one to the other, and Libo had entered without counsel, offered to state the charges against him singly, and produced an extravagantly absurd accusation, according to which Libo had consulted persons whether he would have such wealth as to be able to cover the Appian road as far as Brundisium with money There were other questions of the same sort, quite senseless and idle; if leniently regarded, pitiable. But there was one paper in Libo's handwriting, so the prosecutor alleged, with the names of Cæsars and of Senators, to which marks were affixed of dreadful or mysterious significance. When the accused denied this, it was decided that his slaves who recognised the writing should be examined by torture. As an ancient statute of the Senate forbade such inquiry in a case affecting a master's life, Tiberius, with his cleverness in devising new law, ordered Libo's slaves to be sold singly to the State-agent, so that, forsooth, without an infringement of the Senate's decree, Libo might be tried on their evidence. As a consequence, the defendant asked an adjournment till next day, and having gone home he charged his kinsman, Publius Quirinus, with his last prayer to the emperor.

31. The answer was that he should address himself to the Senate. Meanwhile his house was surrounded with soldiers; they crowded noisily even about the entrance, so that they could be heard and seen, when Libo, whose anguish drove him from the very banquet he had prepared as his last gratification, called for a minister of death, grasped the hands of his slaves, and thrust a sword into them. In their confusion, as they shrank back, they overturned the lamp on the table at his side, and in the darkness, now to him the gloom of death, he aimed two blows at a vital part. At the groans of the falling man his freedmen hurried up, and the soldiers, seeing the bloody deed, stood aloof. Yet the prosecution was continued in the Senate with the same persistency, and Tiberius declared on oath that he would have interceded for his life, guilty though he was, but for his hasty suicide.

32. His property was divided among his accusers, and prætorships out of the usual order were conferred on those who were of senators' rank. Cotta Messalinus then proposed that Libo's bust should not be carried in the funeral proces-

sion of any of his descendants; and Cneius Lentulus, that no
Scribonius should assume the surname of Drusus. Days of
public thanksgiving were appointed on the suggestion of
Pomponius Flaccus. Offerings were given to Jupiter, Mars,
and Concord, and the 13th day of September, on which Libo
had killed himself, was to be observed as a festival, on the
motion of Gallus Asinius, Papius Mutilus, and Lucius Apronius. I have mentioned the proposals and sycophancy of
these men, in order to bring to light this old-standing evil in
the State.

Decrees of the Senate were also passed to expel from Italy
astrologers and magicians. One of their number, Lucius Pitu-
anius, was hurled from the Rock. Another, Publius Marcius,
was executed, according to ancient custom, by the consuls
outside the Esquiline Gate, after the trumpets had been bidden to sound.

33. On the next day of the Senate's meeting much was
said against the luxury of the country by Quintus Haterius,
an ex-consul, and by Octavius Fronto, an ex-prætor. It was
decided that vessels of solid gold should not be made for the
serving of food, and that men should not disgrace themselves
with silken clothing from the East. Fronto went further, and
insisted on restrictions being put on plate, furniture, and
household establishments. It was indeed still usual with the
Senators, when it was their turn to vote, to suggest anything
they thought for the State's advantage. Gallus Asinius argued on the other side. "With the growth of the empire private wealth too," he said, "had increased, and there was
nothing new in this, but it accorded with the fashions of the
earliest antiquity. Riches were one thing with the Fabricii,
quite another with the Scipios. The State was the standard
of everything; when it was poor, the homes of the citizens
were humble; when it reached such magnificence, private
grandeur increased. In household establishments, and plate,
and in whatever was provided for use, there was neither excess nor parsimony except in relation to the fortune of the
possessor. A distinction had been made in the assessments of
Senators and knights, not because they differed naturally,
but that the superiority of the one class in places in the
theatre, in rank and in honour, might be also maintained in

everything else which insured mental repose and bodily recreation, unless indeed men in the highest position were to undergo more anxieties and more dangers, and to be at the same time deprived of all solace under those anxieties and dangers." Gallus gained a ready assent, under these specious phrases, by a confession of failings with which his audience sympathised. And Tiberius too had added that this was not a time for censorship, and that if there were any declension in manners, a promoter of reform would not be wanting.

34. During this debate Lucius Piso, after exclaiming against the corruption of the courts, the bribery of judges, the cruel threats of accusations from hired orators, declared that he would depart and quit the capital, and that he meant to live in some obscure and distant rural retreat. At the same moment he rose to leave the Senate House. Tiberius was much excited, and though he pacified Piso with gentle words, he also strongly urged his relatives to stop his departure by their influence or their entreaties.

Soon afterwards this same Piso gave an equal proof of a fearless sense of wrong by suing Urgulania, whom Augusta's friendship had raised above the law. Neither did Urgulania obey the summons, for in defiance of Piso she went in her litter to the emperor's house; nor did Piso give way, though Augusta complained that she was insulted and her majesty slighted. Tiberius, thinking to win popularity by so far humouring his mother as to say that he would go to the prætor's court and support Urgulania, went forth from the palace, having ordered soldiers to follow him at a distance. He was seen, as the people thronged about him, to wear a calm face, while he prolonged his time on the way with various conversations, till at last when Piso's relatives tried in vain to restrain him, Augusta directed the money which was claimed to be handed to him. This ended the affair, and Piso, in consequence, was not dishonoured, and the emperor rose in reputation. Urgulania's influence, however, was so formidable to the State, that in a certain cause which was tried by the Senate she would not condescend to appear as a witness. The prætor was sent to question her at her own house, although the Vestal virgins, according to ancient custom, were heard in the courts, before judges, whenever they gave evidence.

35. I should say nothing of the adjournment of public business in this year, if it were not worth while to notice the conflicting opinions of Cneius Piso and Asinius Gallus on the subject. Piso, although the emperor had said that he would be absent, held that all the more ought the business to be transacted, that the State might have the honour of its Senate and knights being able to perform their duties in the sovereign's absence. Gallus, as Piso had forestalled him in the display of freedom, maintained that nothing was sufficiently impressive or suitable to the majesty of the Roman people, unless done before Cæsar and under his very eyes, and that therefore the gathering from all Italy and the influx from the provinces ought to be reserved for his presence. Tiberius listened to this in silence, and the matter was debated on both sides in a sharp controversy. The business, however, was adjourned.

36. A dispute then arose between Gallus and the emperor. Gallus proposed that the elections of magistrates should be held every five years, and that the commanders of the legions who before receiving a prætorship discharged this military service should at once become prætors-elect, the emperor nominating twelve candidates every year. It was quite evident that this motion had a deeper meaning and was an attempt to explore the secrets of imperial policy. Tiberius, however, argued as if his power would be thus increased. "It would," he said, "be trying to his moderation to have to elect so many and to put off so many. He scarcely avoided giving offence from year to year, even though a candidate's rejection was solaced by the near prospect of office. What hatred would be incurred from those whose election was deferred for five years! How could he foresee through so long an interval what would be a man's temper, or domestic relations, or estate? Men became arrogant even with this annual appointment. What would happen if their thoughts were fixed on promotion for five years? It was in fact a multiplying of the magistrates five-fold, and a subversion of the laws which had prescribed proper periods for the exercise of the candidate's activity and the seeking or securing office." With

this seemingly conciliatory speech he retained the substance of power.

37. He also increased the incomes of some of the Senators. Hence it was the more surprising that he listened somewhat disdainfully to the request of Marcus Hortalus, a youth of noble rank in conspicuous poverty. He was the grandson of the orator Hortensius, and had been induced by Augustus, on the strength of a gift of a million sesterces, to marry and rear children, that one of our most illustrious families might not become extinct. Accordingly, with his four sons standing at the doors of the Senate House, the Senate then sitting in the palace, when it was his turn to speak he began to address them as follows, his eyes fixed now on the statue of Hortensius which stood among those of the orators, now on that of Augustus:—"Senators, these whose numbers and boyish years you behold I have reared, not by my own choice, but because the emperor advised me. At the same time, my ancestors deserved to have descendants. For myself, not having been able in these altered times to receive or acquire wealth or popular favour, or that eloquence which has been the hereditary possession of our house, I was satisfied if my narrow means were neither a disgrace to myself nor a burden to others. At the emperor's bidding I married. Behold the offspring and progeny of a succession of consuls and dictators. Not to excite odium do I recall such facts, but to win compassion. While you prosper, Cæsar, they will attain such promotion as you shall bestow. Meanwhile save from penury the great-grandsons of Quintus Hortensius, the foster-children of Augustus."

38. The Senate's favourable bias was an incitement to Tiberius to offer prompt opposition, which he did in nearly these words:—"If all poor men begin to come here and to beg money for their children, individuals will never be satisfied, and the State will be bankrupt. Certainly our ancestors did not grant the privilege of occasionally proposing amendments or of suggesting, in our turn for speaking, something for the general advantage in order that we might in this house increase our private business and property, thereby bringing odium on the Senate and on emperors whether they concede or refuse their bounty. In fact, it is not

a request, but an importunity, as utterly unreasonable as it is unforeseen, for a senator, when the house has met on other matters, to rise from his place and, pleading the number and age of his children, put a pressure on the delicacy of the Senate, then transfer the same constraint to myself, and, as it were, break open the exchequer, which, if we exhaust it by improper favouritism, will have to be replenished by crimes. Money was given you, Hortalus, by Augustus, but without solicitation, and not on the condition of its being always given. Otherwise industry will languish and idleness be encouraged, if a man has nothing to fear, nothing to hope from himself, and every one, in utter recklessness, will expect relief from others, thus becoming useless to himself and a burden to me."

These and like remarks, though listened to with assent by those who make it a practice to eulogise everything coming from sovereigns, both good and bad, were received by the majority in silence or with suppressed murmurs. Tiberius perceived it, and having paused a while, said that he had given Hortalus his answer, but that if the senators thought it right, he would bestow two hundred thousand sesterces on each of his children of the male sex. The others thanked him; Hortalus said nothing, either from alarm or because even in his reduced fortunes he clung to his hereditary nobility. Nor did Tiberius afterwards show any pity, though the house of Hortensius sank into shameful poverty.

39. That same year the daring of a single slave, had it not been promptly checked, would have ruined the State by discord and civil war. A servant of Postumus Agrippa, Clemens by name, having ascertained that Augustus was dead, formed a design beyond a slave's conception, of going to the island of Planasia and seizing Agrippa by craft or force and bringing him to the armies of Germany. The slowness of a merchant vessel thwarted his bold venture. Meanwhile the murder of Agrippa had been perpetrated, and then turning his thoughts to a greater and more hazardous enterprise, he stole the ashes of the deceased, sailed to Cosa, a promontory of Etruria, and there hid himself in obscure places till his hair and beard were long. In age and figure he was not unlike his master. Then through suitable emis-

saries who shared his secret, it was rumoured that Agrippa was alive, first in whispered gossip, soon, as is usual with forbidden topics, in vague talk which found its way to the credulous ears of the most ignorant people or of restless and revolutionary schemers. He himself went to the towns, as the day grew dark, without letting himself be seen publicly or remaining long in the same places, but, as he knew that truth gains strength by notoriety and time, falsehood by precipitancy and vagueness, he would either withdraw himself from publicity or else forestall it.

40. It was rumoured meanwhile throughout Italy, and was believed at Rome, that Agrippa had been saved by the blessing of Heaven. Already at Ostia, where he had arrived, he was the centre of interest to a vast concourse as well as to secret gatherings in the capital, while Tiberius was distracted by the doubt whether he should crush this slave of his by military force or allow time to dissipate a silly credulity. Sometimes he thought that he must overlook nothing, sometimes that he need not be afraid of everything, his mind fluctuating between shame and terror. At last he entrusted the affair to Sallustius Crispus, who chose two of his dependants (some say they were soldiers) and urged them to go to him as pretended accomplices, offering money and promising faithful companionship in danger. They did as they were bidden; then, waiting for an unguarded hour of night, they took with them a sufficient force, and having bound and gagged him, dragged him to the palace. When Tiberius asked him how he had become Agrippa, he is said to have replied, "As you became Cæsar." He could not be forced to divulge his accomplices. Tiberius did not venture on a public execution, but ordered him to be slain in a private part of the palace and his body to be secretly removed. And although many of the emperor's household and knights and senators were said to have supported him with their wealth and helped him with their counsels, no inquiry was made.

41. At the close of the year was consecrated an arch near the temple of Saturn to commemorate the recovery of the standards lost with Varus, under the leadership of Germanicus and the auspices of Tiberius; a temple of Fors Fortuna,

by the Tiber, in the gardens which Cæsar, the dictator, bequeathed to the Roman people; a chapel to the Julian family, and statues at Bovillæ to the Divine Augustus.

In the consulship of Caius Cæcilius and Lucius Pomponius, Germanicus Cæsar, on the 26th day of May, celebrated his triumph over the Cherusci, Chatti, and Angrivarii,
and the other tribes which extend as far as the Elbe. There
were borne in procession spoils, prisoners, representations of
the mountains, the rivers and battles; and the war, seeing
that he had been forbidden to finish it, was taken as finished.
The admiration of the beholders was heightened by the
striking comeliness of the general and the chariot which
bore his five children. Still, there was a latent dread when
they remembered how unfortunate in the case of Drusus, his
father, had been the favour of the crowd; how his uncle
Marcellus, regarded by the city populace with passionate
enthusiasm, had been snatched from them while yet a youth,
and how short-lived and ill-starred were the attachments of
the Roman people.

42. Tiberius meanwhile in the name of Germanicus gave
every one of the city populace three hundred sesterces, and
nominated himself his colleague in the consulship. Still, failing to obtain credit for sincere affection, he resolved to get
the young prince out of the way, under pretence of con-
ferring distinction, and for this he invented reasons, or
eagerly fastened on such as chance presented.

King Archelaus had been in possession of Cappadocia for
fifty years, and Tiberius hated him because he had not
shown him any mark of respect while he was at Rhodes.
This neglect of Archelaus was not due to pride, but was suggested by the intimate friends of Augustus, because, when
Caius Cæsar was in his prime and had charge of the affairs
of the East, Tiberius's friendship was thought to be dangerous. When, after the extinction of the family of the Cæsars,
Tiberius acquired the empire, he enticed Archelaus by a
letter from his mother, who without concealing her son's
displeasure promised mercy if he would come to beg for it.
Archelaus, either quite unsuspicious of treachery, or dreading compulsion, should it be thought that he saw through
it, hastened to Rome. There he was received by a pitiless

emperor, and soon afterwards was arraigned before the Senate. In his anguish and in the weariness of old age, and from being unused, as a king, to equality, much less to degradation, not, certainly, from fear of the charges fabricated against him, he ended his life, by his own act or by a natural death. His kingdom was reduced into a province, and Cæsar declared that, with its revenues, the one per cent. tax could be lightened, which, for the future, he fixed at one-half per cent.

During the same time, on the deaths of Antiochus and Philopator, kings respectively of the Commageni and Cilicians, these nations became excited, a majority desiring the Roman rule, some, that of their kings. The provinces too of Syria and Judæa, exhausted by their burdens, implored a reduction of tribute.

43. Tiberius accordingly discussed these matters and the affairs of Armenia, which I have already related, before the Senate. "The commotions in the East," he said, "could be quieted only by the wisdom of Germanicus; his own life was on the decline, and Drusus had not yet reached his maturity." Thereupon, by a decree of the Senate, the provinces beyond sea were entrusted to Germanicus, with greater powers wherever he went than were given to those who obtained their provinces by lot or by the emperor's appointment.

Tiberius had however removed from Syria Creticus Silanus, who was connected by a close tie with Germanicus, his daughter being betrothed to Nero, the eldest of Germanicus's children. He appointed to it Cneius Piso, a man of violent temper, without an idea of obedience, with indeed a natural arrogance inherited from his father Piso, who in the civil war supported with the most energetic aid against Cæsar the reviving faction in Africa, then embraced the cause of Brutus and Cassius, and, when suffered to return, refrained from seeking promotion till he was actually solicited to accept a consulship offered by Augustus. But beside the father's haughty temper there was also the noble rank and wealth of his wife Plancina, to inflame his ambition. He would hardly be the inferior of Tiberius, and as for Tiberius's children, he looked down on them as far beneath him. He thought it a certainty that he had been chosen to govern Syria in order to thwart the aspirations of Germanicus. Some believed that he had even received secret instructions from Tiberius, and it was beyond a question that Augusta, with feminine jealousy, had suggested to Plancina calumnious insinuations against Agrippina. For there was division and discord in the court, with unexpressed partialities towards either Drusus or Germanicus. Tiberius favoured Drusus, as his own son and born of his own blood. As for Germanicus, his uncle's estrangement had increased the affection which all others felt for him, and there was the fact too that he had an advantage in the illustrious rank of his mother's family, among whom he could point to his grandfather Marcus Antonius and to his great-uncle Augustus. Drusus, on the other hand, had for his great-grandfather a Roman knight, Pomponius Atticus, who seemed to disgrace the ancestral images of the Claudii. Again, the consort of Germanicus, Agrippina, in number of children and in character, was superior to Livia, the wife of Drusus. Yet the brothers were singularly united, and were wholly unaffected by the rivalries of their kinsfolk.

44. Soon afterwards Drusus was sent into Illyricum to be familiarised with military service, and to win the goodwill of the army. Tiberius also thought that it was better for the young prince, who was being demoralised by the luxury of the capital, to serve in a camp, while he felt himself the safer with both his sons in command of legions. However, he made a pretext of the Suevi, who were imploring help against the Cherusci. For when the Romans had departed and they were free from the fear of an invader, these tribes, according to the custom of the race, and then specially as rivals in fame, had turned their arms against each other. The strength of the two nations, the valour of their chiefs were equal. But the title of king rendered Maroboduus hated among his countrymen, while Arminius was regarded with favour, as the champion of freedom.

45. Thus it was not only the Cherusci and their allies, the old soldiers of Arminius, who took up arms, but even the Semnones and Langobardi from the kingdom of Maroboduus revolted to that chief. With this addition he must have had an overwhelming superiority, had not Inguiomerus deserted

with a troop of his dependants to Maroboduus, simply for the reason that the aged uncle scorned to obey a brother's youthful son. The armies were drawn up, with equal confidence on both sides, and there were not those desultory attacks or irregular bands, formerly so common with the Germans. Prolonged warfare against us had accustomed them to keep close to their standards, to have the support of reserves, and to take the word of command from their generals. On this occasion Arminius, who reviewed the whole field on horseback, as he rode up to each band, boasted of regained freedom, of slaughtered legions, of spoils and weapons wrested from the Romans, and still in the hands of many of his men. As for Maroboduus, he called him a fugitive, who had no experience of battles, who had sheltered himself in the recesses of the Hercynian forest and then with presents and embassies sued for a treaty; a traitor to his country, a satellite of Cæsar, who deserved to be driven out, with rage as furious as that with which they had slain Quintilius Varus. They should simply remember their many battles, the result of which, with the final expulsion of the Romans, sufficiently showed who could claim the crowning success in war.

46. Nor did Maroboduus abstain from vaunts about himself or from revilings of the foe. Clasping the hand of Inguiomerus, he protested "that in the person before them centred all the renown of the Cherusci, that to his counsels was due whatever had ended successfully. Arminius in his infatuation and ignorance was taking to himself the glory which belonged to another, for he had treacherously surprised three unofficered legions and a general who had not an idea of perfidy, to the great hurt of Germany and to his own disgrace, since his wife and his son were still enduring slavery. As for himself, he had been attacked by twelve legions led by Tiberius, and had preserved untarnished the glory of the Germans, and then on equal terms the armies had parted. He was by no means sorry that they had the matter in their own hands, whether they preferred to war with all their might against Rome, or to accept a bloodless peace."

To these words, which roused the two armies, was added the stimulus of special motives of their own. The Cherusci and Langobardi were fighting for ancient renown or newly-won freedom; the other side for the increase of their dominion. Never at any time was the shock of battle more tremendous or the issue more doubtful, as the right wings of both armies were routed. Further fighting was expected, when Maroboduus withdrew his camp to the hills. This was a sign of discomfiture. He was gradually stripped of his strength by desertions, and, having fled to the Marcomanni, he sent envoys to Tiberius with entreaties for help. The answer was that he had no right to invoke the aid of Roman arms against the Cherusci, when he had rendered no assistance to the Romans in their conflict with the same enemy. Drusus, however, was sent as I have related, to establish peace.

47. That same year twelve famous cities of Asia fell by an earthquake in the night, so that the destruction was all the more unforeseen and fearful. Nor were there the means of escape usual in such a disaster, by rushing out into the open country, for there people were swallowed up by the yawning earth. Vast mountains, it is said, collapsed; what had been level ground seemed to be raised aloft, and fires blazed out amid the ruin. The calamity fell most fatally on the inhabitants of Sardis, and it attracted to them the largest share of sympathy. The emperor promised ten million sesterces, and remitted for five years all they paid to the exchequer or to the emperor's purse. Magnesia, under Mount Sipylus, was considered to come next in loss and in need of help. The people of Temnus, Philadelpheia, Aegae, Apollonis, the Mostenians, and Hyrcanian Macedonians, as they were called, with the towns of Hierocæsarea, Myrina, Cyme, and Tmolus, were, it was decided, to be exempted from tribute for the same time, and some one was to be sent from the Senate to examine their actual condition and to relieve them. Marcus Aletus, one of the ex-prætors, was chosen, from a fear that, as an ex-consul was governor of Asia, there might be rivalry between men of equal rank, and consequent embarrassment.

48. To his splendid public liberality the emperor added bounties no less popular. The property of Aemilia Musa, a rich woman who died intestate, on which the imperial treas-

ury had a claim, he handed over to Æmilius Lepidus, to whose family she appeared to belong; and the estate of Patuleius, a wealthy Roman knight, though he was himself left in part his heir, he gave to Marcus Servilius, whose name he discovered in an earlier and unquestioned will. In both these cases he said that noble rank ought to have the support of wealth. Nor did he accept a legacy from any one unless he had earned it by friendship. Those who were strangers to him, and who, because they were at enmity with others, made the emperor their heir, he kept at a distance. While, however, he relieved the honourable poverty of the virtuous, he expelled from the Senate or suffered voluntarily to retire spendthrifts whose vices had brought them to penury, like Vibidius Varro, Marius Nepos, Appius Appianus, Cornelius Sulla, and Quintus Vitellius.

49. About the same time he dedicated some temples of the gods, which had perished from age or from fire, and which Augustus had begun to restore. These were temples to Liber, Libera, and Ceres, near the Great Circus, which last Aulus Postumius, when Dictator, had vowed; a temple to Flora in the same place, which had been built by Lucius and Marcus Publicius, ædiles, and a temple to Janus, which had been erected in the vegetable market by Caius Duilius, who was the first to make the Roman power successful at sea and to win a naval triumph over the Carthaginians. A temple to Hope was consecrated by Germanicus; this had been vowed by Atilius in that same war.

50. Meantime the law of treason was gaining strength. Appuleia Varilia, grand-niece of Augustus, was accused of treason by an informer for having ridiculed the Divine Augustus, Tiberius, and Tiberius's mother, in some insulting remarks, and for having been convicted of adultery, allied though she was to Cæsar's house. Adultery, it was thought, was sufficiently guarded against by the Julian law. As to the charge of treason, the emperor insisted that it should be taken separately, and that she should be condemned if she had spoken irreverently of Augustus. Her insinuations against himself he did not wish to be the subject of judicial inquiry. When asked by the consul what he thought of the unfavourable speeches she was accused of having uttered against his

mother, he said nothing. Afterwards, on the next day of the Senate's meeting, he even begged in his mother's name that no words of any kind spoken against her might in any case be treated as criminal. He then acquitted Appuleia of treason. For her adultery, he deprecated the severer penalty, and advised that she should be removed by her kinsfolk, after the example of our forefathers, to more than two hundred miles from Rome. Her paramour, Manlius, was forbidden to live in Italy or Africa.

51. A contest then arose about the election of a prætor in the room of Vipstanus Gallus, whom death had removed. Germanicus and Drusus (for they were still at Rome) supported Haterius Agrippa, a relative of Germanicus. Many, on the other hand, endeavoured to make the number of children weigh most in favour of the candidates. Tiberius rejoiced to see a strife in the Senate between his sons and the law. Beyond question the law was beaten, but not at once, and only by a few votes, in the same way as laws were defeated even when they were in force.

52. In this same year a war broke out in Africa, where the enemy was led by Tacfarinas. A Numidian by birth, he had served as an auxiliary in the Roman camp, then becoming a deserter, he at first gathered round him a roving band familiar with robbery, for plunder and for rapine. After a while, he marshalled them like regular soldiers, under standards and in troops, till at last he was regarded as the leader, not of an undisciplined rabble, but of the Musulamian people. This powerful tribe, bordering on the deserts of Africa, and even then with none of the civilisation of cities, took up arms and drew their Moorish neighbours into the war. These too had a leader, Mazippa. The army was so divided that Tacfarinas kept the picked men who were armed in Roman fashion within a camp, and familiarised them with a commander's authority, while Mazippa, with light troops, spread around him fire, slaughter, and consternation. They had forced the Ciniphii, a far from contemptible tribe, into their cause, when Furius Camillus, proconsul of Africa, united in one force a legion and all the regularly enlisted allies, and, with an army insignificant indeed compared with the multitude of the Numidians and

Moors, marched against the enemy. There was nothing however which he strove so much to avoid as their eluding an
engagement out of fear. It was by the hope of victory that
they were lured on only to be defeated. The legion was in
the army's centre; the light cohorts and two cavalry squadrons on its wings. Nor did Tacfarinas refuse battle. The
Numidians were routed, and after a number of years the
name of Furius won military renown. Since the days of the
famous deliverer of our city and his son Camillus, fame as
a general had fallen to the lot of other branches of the family, and the man of whom I am now speaking was regarded
as an inexperienced soldier. All the more willingly did
Tiberius commemorate his achievements in the Senate, and
the Senators voted him the ornaments of triumph, an honour
which Camillus, because of his unambitious life, enjoyed
without harm.

53. In the following year Tiberius held his third, Germanicus his second, consulship. Germanicus, however, entered on the office at Nicopolis, a city of Achaia, whither he
had arrived by the coast of Illyricum, after having seen his
brother Drusus, who was then in Dalmatia, and endured a
stormy voyage through the Adriatic and afterwards the
Ionian Sea. He accordingly devoted a few days to the repair
of his fleet, and, at the same time, in remembrance of his
ancestors, he visited the bay which the victory of Actium had
made famous, the spoils consecrated by Augustus, and the
camp of Antonius. For, as I have said, Augustus was his
great-uncle, Antonius his grandfather, and vivid images of
disaster and success rose before him on the spot. Thence he
went to Athens, and there, as a concession to our treaty with
an allied and ancient city, he was attended only by a single
lictor. The Greeks welcomed him with the most elaborate
honours, and brought forward all the old deeds and sayings
of their countrymen, to give additional dignity to their
flattery.

54. Thence he directed his course to Euboea and crossed
to Lesbos, where Agrippina for the last time was confined
and gave birth to Julia. He then penetrated to the remoter
parts of the province of Asia, visited the Thracian cities,
Perinthus and Byzantium; next, the narrow strait of the

Propontis and the entrance of the Pontus, from an anxious
wish to become acquainted with those ancient and celebrated
localities. He gave relief, as he went, to provinces which had
been exhausted by internal feuds or by the oppressions of
governors. In his return he attempted to see the sacred mysteries of the Samothracians, but north winds which he encountered drove him aside from his course. And so after
visiting Ilium and surveying a scene venerable from the
vicissitudes of fortune and as the birth-place of our people,
he coasted back along Asia, and touched at Colophon, to
consult the oracle of the Clarian Apollo. There, it is not a
woman, as at Delphi, but a priest chosen from certain families, generally from Miletus, who ascertains simply the
number and the names of the applicants. Then descending
into a cave and drinking a draught from a secret spring, the
man, who is commonly ignorant of letters and of poetry,
utters a response in verse answering to the thoughts conceived in the mind of any inquirer. It was said that he
prophesied to Germanicus, in dark hints, as oracles usually
do, an early doom.

55. Cneius Piso meanwhile, that he might the sooner enter
on his design, terrified the citizens of Athens by his tumultuous approach, and then reviled them in a bitter speech,
with indirect reflections on Germanicus, who, he said, had
derogated from the honour of the Roman name in having
treated with excessive courtesy, not the people of Athens,
who indeed had been exterminated by repeated disasters, but
a miserable medley of tribes. As for the men before him,
they had been Mithridates's allies against Sulla, allies of
Antonius against the Divine Augustus. He taunted them too
with the past, with their ill-success against the Macedonians,
their violence to their own countrymen, for he had his own
special grudge against this city, because they would not spare
at his intercession one Theophilus whom the Areopagus had
condemned for forgery. Then, by sailing rapidly and by
the shortest route through the Cyclades, he overtook Germanicus at the island of Rhodes. The prince was not ignorant of the slanders with which he had been assailed, but
his good nature was such that when a storm arose and drove
Piso on rocks, and his enemy's destruction could have been

referred to chance, he sent some triremes, by the help of which he might be rescued from danger. But this did not soften Piso's heart. Scarcely allowing a day's interval, he left Germanicus and hastened on in advance. When he reached Syria and the legions, he began, by bribery and favouritism, to encourage the lowest of the common soldiers, removing the old centurions and the strict tribunes and assigning their places to creatures of his own or to the vilest of the men, while he allowed idleness in the camp, licentiousness in the towns, and the soldiers to roam through the country and take their pleasure. He went such lengths in demoralizing them, that he was spoken of in their vulgar talk as the father of the legions.

Plancina too, instead of keeping herself within the proper limits of a woman, would be present at the evolutions of the cavalry and the manœuvres of the cohorts, and would fling insulting remarks at Agrippina and Germanicus. Some even of the good soldiers were inclined to a corrupt compliance, as a whispered rumour gained ground that the emperor was not averse to these proceedings. Of all this Germanicus was aware, but his most pressing anxiety was to be first in reaching Armenia.

56. This had been of old an unsettled country from the character of its people and from its geographical position, bordering, as it does, to a great extent on our provinces and stretching far away to Media. It lies between two most mighty empires, and is very often at strife with them, hating Rome and jealous of Parthia. It had at this time no king, Vonones having been expelled, but the nation's likings inclined towards Zeno, son of Polemon, king of Pontus, who from his earliest infancy had imitated Armenian manners and customs, loving the chase, the banquet, and all the popular pastimes of barbarians, and who had thus bound to himself chiefs and people alike. Germanicus accordingly, in the city of Artaxata, with the approval of the nobility, in the presence of a vast multitude, placed the royal diadem on his head. All paid him homage and saluted him as King Artaxias, which name they gave him from the city.

Cappadocia meanwhile, which had been reduced to the form of a province, received as its governor Quintus Vera-

nius. Some of the royal tributes were diminished, to inspire
hope of a gentler rule under Rome. Quintus Servæus was appointed to Commagene, then first put under a prætor's jurisdiction.

57. Successful as was this settlement of all the interests of
our allies, it gave Germanicus little joy because of the arrogance of Piso. Though he had been ordered to march part of
the legions into Armenia under his own or his son's command, he had neglected to do either. At length the two met
at Cyrrhus, the winter-quarters of the tenth legion, each
controlling his looks, Piso concealing his fears, Germanicus
shunning the semblance of menace. He was indeed, as I have
said, a kind-hearted man. But friends who knew well how
to inflame a quarrel, exaggerated what was true and added
lies, alleging various charges against Piso, Plancina, and
their sons.

At last, in the presence of a few intimate associates, Germanicus addressed him in language such as suppressed resentment suggests, to which Piso replied with haughty apolo-
gies. They parted in open enmity. After this Piso was seldom
seen at Cæsar's tribunal, and if he ever sat by him, it was
with a sullen frown and a marked display of opposition. He
was even heard to say at a banquet given by the king of the
Nabatæans, when some golden crowns of great weight were
presented to Cæsar and Agrippina and light ones to Piso and
the rest, that the entertainment was given to the son of a
Roman emperor, not of a Parthian king. At the same time
he threw his crown on the ground, with a long speech against
luxury, which, though it angered Germanicus, he still bore
with patience.

58. Meantime envoys arrived from Artabanus, king of the
Parthians. He had sent them to recall the memory of friendship and alliance, with an assurance that he wished for a
renewal of the emblems of concord, and that he would in
honour of Germanicus yield the point of advancing to the
bank of the Euphrates. He begged meanwhile that Vonones
might not be kept in Syria, where, by emissaries from an
easy distance, he might draw the chiefs of the tribes into
civil strife. Germanicus' answer as to the alliance between
Rome and Parthia was dignified: as to the king's visit and

the respect shown to himself, it was graceful and modest. Vonones was removed to Pompeiopolis, a city on the coast of Cilicia. This was not merely a concession to the request of Artabanus, but was meant as an affront to Piso, who had a special liking for Vonones, because of the many attentions and presents by which he had won Plancina's favour.

59. In the consulship of Marcus Silanus and Lucius Norbanus, Germanicus set out for Egypt to study its antiquities. His ostensible motive however was solicitude for the province. He reduced the price of corn by opening the granaries, and adopted many practices pleasing to the multitude. He would go about without soldiers, with sandalled feet, and apparelled after the Greek fashion, in imitation of Publius Scipio, who, it is said, habitually did the same in Sicily, even when the war with Carthage was still raging. Tiberius having gently expressed disapproval of his dress and manners, pronounced a very sharp censure on his visit to Alexandria without the emperor's leave, contrary to the regulations of Augustus. That prince, among other secrets of imperial policy, had forbidden senators and Roman knights of the higher rank to enter Egypt except by permission, and he had specially reserved the country, from a fear that any one who held a province containing the key of the land and of the sea, with ever so small a force against the mightiest army, might distress Italy by famine.

60. Germanicus, however, who had not yet learnt how much he was blamed for his expedition, sailed up the Nile from the city of Canopus as his starting-point. Spartans founded the place because Canopus, pilot of one of their ships, had been buried there, when Menelaus on his return to Greece was driven into a distant sea and to the shores of Libya. Thence he went to the river's nearest mouth, dedicated to a Hercules who, the natives say, was born in the country and was the original hero, others, who afterwards showed like valour, having received his name. Next he visited the vast ruins of ancient Thebes. There yet remained on the towering piles Egyptian inscriptions, with a complete account of the city's past grandeur. One of the aged priests, who was desired to interpret the language of his country, related how once there had dwelt in Thebes seven hundred

thousand men of military age, and how with such an army king Rhamses conquered Libya, Ethiopia, Media, Persia, Bactria, and Scythia, and held under his sway the countries inhabited by the Syrians, Armenians, and their neighbours, the Cappadocians, from the Bithynian to the Lycian sea. There was also to be read what tributes were imposed on these nations, the weight of silver and gold, the tale of arms and horses, the gifts of ivory and of perfumes to the temples, with the amount of grain and supplies furnished by each people, a revenue as magnificent as is now exacted by the might of Parthia or the power of Rome.

61. But Germanicus also bestowed attention on other wonders. Chief of these were the stone image of Memnon, which, when struck by the sun's rays, gives out the sound of a human voice; the pyramids, rising up like mountains amid almost impassable wastes of shifting sand, raised by the emulation and vast wealth of kings; the lake hollowed out of the earth to be a receptacle for the Nile's overflow; and elsewhere the river's narrow channel and profound depth which no line of the explorer can penetrate. He then came to Elephantine and Syene, formerly the limits of the Roman empire, which now extends to the Red Sea.

62. While Germanicus was spending the summer in visits to several provinces, Drusus gained no little glory by sowing discord among the Germans and urging them to complete the destruction of the now broken power of Maroboduus. Among the Gotones was a youth of noble birth, Catualda by name, who had formerly been driven into exile by the might of Maroboduus, and who now, when the king's fortunes were declining, ventured on revenge. He entered the territory of the Marcomanni with a strong force, and, having corruptly won over the nobles to join him, burst into the palace and into an adjacent fortress. There he found the long-accumulated plunder of the Suevi and camp followers and traders from our provinces who had been attracted to an enemy's land, each from their various homes, first by the freedom of commerce, next by the desire of amassing wealth, finally by forgetfulness of their fatherland.

63. Maroboduus, now utterly deserted, had no resource but in the mercy of Cæsar. Having crossed the Danube

where it flows by the province of Noricum, he wrote to Tiberius, not like a fugitive or a suppliant, but as one who remembered his past greatness. When as a most famous king in former days he received invitations from many nations, he had still, he said, preferred the friendship of Rome. Cæsar replied that he should have a safe and honourable home in Italy, if he would remain there, or, if his interests required something different, he might leave it under the same protection under which he had come. But in the Senate he maintained that Philip had not been so formidable to the Athenians, or Pyrrhus or Antiochus to the Roman people, as was Maroboduus. The speech is extant, and in it he magnifies the man's power, the ferocity of the tribes under his sway, his proximity to Italy as a foe, finally his own measures for his overthrow. The result was that Maroboduus was kept at Ravenna, where his possible return was a menace to the Suevi, should they ever disdain obedience. But he never left Italy for eighteen years, living to old age and losing much of his renown through an excessive clinging to life.

Catualda had a like downfall and no better refuge. Driven out soon afterwards by the overwhelming strength of the Hermundusi led by Vibilius, he was received and sent to Forum Julii, a colony of Narbonensian Gaul. The barbarians who followed the two kings, lest they might disturb the peace of the provinces by mingling with the population, were settled beyond the Danube between the rivers Marus and Cusus, under a king, Vannius, of the nation of the Quadi.

64. Tidings having also arrived of Artaxias being made king of Armenia by Germanicus, the Senate decreed that both he and Drusus should enter the city with an ovation. Arches too were raised round the sides of the temple of Mars the Avenger, with statues of the two Cæsars. Tiberius was the more delighted at having established peace by wise policy than if he had finished a war by battle. And so next he planned a crafty scheme against Rhescuporis, king of Thrace. That entire country had been in the possession of Rhœmetalces, after whose death Augustus assigned half to the king's brother Rhescuporis, half to his son Cotys. In this division the cultivated lands, the towns, and what bordered on Greek territories, fell to Cotys; the wild and barbarous

portion, with enemies on its frontier, to Rhescuporis. The kings too themselves differed. Cotys having a gentle and kindly temper, the other a fierce and ambitious spirit, which could not brook a partner. Still at first they lived in a hollow friendship, but soon Rhescuporis overstepped his bounds and appropriated to himself what had been given to Cotys, using force when he was resisted, though somewhat timidly under Augustus, who having created both kingdoms would, he feared, avenge any contempt of his arrangement. When however he heard of the change of emperor, he let loose bands of freebooters and razed the fortresses, as a provocation to war.

65. Nothing made Tiberius so uneasy as an apprehension of the disturbance of any settlement. He commissioned a centurion to tell the kings not to decide their dispute by arms. Cotys at once dismissed the forces which he had prepared. Rhescuporis, with assumed modesty, asked for a place of meeting where, he said, they might settle their differences by an interview. There was little hesitation in fixing on a time, a place, finally on terms, as every point was mutually conceded and accepted, by the one out of good nature, by the other with a treacherous intent. Rhescuporis, to ratify the treaty, as he said, further proposed a banquet; and when their mirth had been prolonged far into the night, and Cotys amid the feasting and the wine was unsuspicious of danger, he loaded him with chains, though he appealed, on perceiving the perfidy, to the sacred character of a king, to the gods of their common house, and to the hospitable board. Having possessed himself of all Thrace, he wrote word to Tiberius that a plot had been formed against him, and that he had forestalled the plotter. Meanwhile, under pretext of a war against the Bastarnian and Scythian tribes, he was strengthening himself with fresh forces of infantry and cavalry.

He received a conciliatory answer. If there was no treachery in his conduct, he could rely on his innocence, but neither the emperor nor the Senate would decide on the right or wrong of his cause without hearing it. He was therefore to surrender Cotys, come in person and transfer from himself the odium of the charge.

66. This letter Latinius Pandus, proprætor of Moesia, sent to Thrace, with soldiers to whose custody Cotys was to be delivered. Rhescuporis, hesitating between fear and rage, preferred to be charged with an accomplished rather than with an attempted crime. He ordered Cotys to be murdered and falsely represented his death as self-inflicted. Still the emperor did not change the policy which he had once for all adopted. On the death of Pandus, whom Rhescuporis accused of being his personal enemy, he appointed to the government of Moesia Pomponius Flaccus, a veteran soldier, specially because of his close intimacy with the king and his consequent ability to entrap him.

67. Flaccus on arriving in Thrace induced the king by great promises, though he hesitated and thought of his guilty deeds, to enter the Roman lines. He then surrounded him with a strong force under pretence of showing him honour, and the tribunes and centurions, by counsel, by persuasion, and by a more undisguised captivity the further he went, brought him, aware at last of his desperate plight, to Rome. He was accused before the Senate by the wife of Cotys, and was condemned to be kept a prisoner far away from his kingdom. Thrace was divided between his son Rhœmetalces, who, it was proved, had opposed his father's designs, and the sons of Cotys. As these were still minors, Trebellienus Rufus, an exprætor, was appointed to govern the kingdom in the meanwhile, after the precedent of our ancestors who sent Marcus Lepidus into Egypt as guardian to Ptolemy's children. Rhescuporis was removed to Alexandria, and there attempting or falsely charged with attempting escape, was put to death.

68. About the same time, Vonones, who, as I have related, had been banished to Cilicia, endeavoured by bribing his guards to escape into Armenia, thence to Albania and Heniochia, and to his kinsman, the king of Scythia. Quitting the sea-coast on the pretence of a hunting expedition, he struck into trackless forests, and was soon borne by his swift steed to the river Pyramus, the bridges over which had been broken down by the natives as soon as they heard of the king's escape. Nor was there a ford by which it could be crossed. And so on the river's bank he was put in chains by

Vibius Fronto, an officer of cavalry; and then Remmius, an
enrolled pensioner, who had previously been entrusted with
the king's custody, in pretended rage, pierced him with his
sword. Hence there was more ground for believing that the
man, conscious of guilty complicity and fearing accusation,
had slain Vonones.

69. Germanicus meanwhile, as he was returning from
Egypt, found that all his directions to the legions and to the
various cities had been repealed or reversed. This led to
grievous insults on Piso, while he as savagely assailed the
prince. Piso then resolved to quit Syria. Soon he was detained there by the failing health of Germanicus, but when
he heard of his recovery, while people were paying the vows
they had offered for his safety, he went attended by his
lictors, drove away the victims placed by the altars with all
the preparations for sacrifice, and the festal gathering of
the populace of Antioch. Then he left for Seleucia and
awaited the result of the illness which had again attacked
Germanicus. The terrible intensity of the malady was increased by the belief that he had been poisoned by Piso.
And certainly there were found hidden in the floor and in
the walls disinterred remains of human bodies, incantations
and spells, and the name of Germanicus inscribed on leaden
tablets, half-burnt cinders smeared with blood, and other
horrors by which in popular belief souls are devoted so the
infernal deities. Piso too was accused of sending emissaries
to note curiously every unfavourable symptom of the illness.

70. Germanicus heard of all this with anger, no less than
with fear. "If my doors," he said, "are to be besieged, if I
must gasp out my last breath under my enemies' eyes, what
will then be the lot of my most unhappy wife, of my infant
children? Poisoning seems tedious; he is in eager haste to
have the sole control of the province and the legions. But
Germanicus is not yet fallen so low, nor will the murderer
long retain the reward of the fatal deed."

He then addressed a letter to Piso, renouncing his friendship, and, as many also state, ordered him to quit the province. Piso without further delay weighed anchor, slackening
his course that he might not have a long way to return
should Germanicus' death leave Syria open to him.

71. For a brief space the prince's hopes rose; then his frame became exhausted, and, as his end drew near, he spoke as follows to the friends by his side:—

"Were I succumbing to nature, I should have just ground of complaint even against the gods for thus tearing me away in my youth by an untimely death from parents, children, country. Now, cut off by the wickedness of Piso and Plancina, I leave to your hearts my last entreaties. Describe to my father and brother, torn by what persecutions, entangled by what plots, I have ended by the worst of deaths the most miserable of lives. If any were touched by my bright prospects, by ties of blood, or even by envy towards me while I lived, they will weep that the once prosperous survivor of so many wars has perished by a woman's treachery. You will have the opportunity of complaint before the Senate, of an appeal to the laws. It is not the chief duty of friends to follow the dead with unprofitable laments, but to remember his wishes, to fulfil his commands. Tears for Germanicus even strangers will shed; vengeance must come from *you*, if you loved the man more than his fortune. Show the people of Rome her who is the granddaughter of the Divine Augustus, as well as my consort; set before them my six children. Sympathy will be on the side of the accusers, and to those who screen themselves under infamous orders belief or pardon will be refused."

His friends clasped the dying man's right hand, and swore that they would sooner lose life than revenge.

72. He then turned to his wife and implored her by the memory of her husband and by their common offspring to lay aside her high spirit, to submit herself to the cruel blows of fortune, and not, when she returned to Rome, to enrage by political rivalry those who were stronger than herself. This was said openly; other words were whispered, pointing, it was supposed, to his fears from Tiberius. Soon afterwards he expired, to the intense sorrow of the province and of the neighbouring peoples. Foreign nations and kings grieved over him, so great was his courtesy to allies, his humanity to enemies. He inspired reverence alike by look and voice, and while he maintained the greatness and dignity of the highest rank, he had escaped the hatred that waits on arrogance.

73. His funeral, though it lacked the family statues and procession, was honoured by panegyrics and a commemoration of his virtues. Some there were who, as they thought of his beauty, his age, and the manner of his death, the vicinity too of the country where he died, likened his end to that of Alexander the Great. Both had a graceful person and were of noble birth; neither had much exceeded thirty years of age, and both fell by the treachery of their own people in strange lands. But Germanicus was gracious to his friends, temperate in his pleasures, the husband of one wife, with only legitimate children. He was too no less a warrior, though rashness he had none, and, though after having cowed Germany by his many victories, he was hindered from crushing it into subjection. Had he had the sole control of affairs, had he possessed the power and title of a king, he would have attained military glory as much more easily as he had excelled Alexander in clemency, in self-restraint, and in all other virtues.

As to the body which, before it was burnt, lay bare in the forum at Antioch, its destined place of burial, it is doubtful whether it exhibited the marks of poisoning. For men according as they pitied Germanicus and were prepossessed with suspicion or were biased by partiality towards Piso, gave conflicting accounts.

74. Then followed a deliberation among the generals and other senators present about the appointment of a governor to Syria. The contest was slight among all but Vibius Marsus and Cneius Sentius, between whom there was a long dispute. Finally Marsus yielded to Sentius as an older and keener competitor. Sentius at once sent to Rome a woman infamous for poisonings in the province and a special favourite of Plancina, Martina by name, on the demand of Vitellius and Veranius and others, who were preparing the charges and the indictment as if a prosecution had already been commenced.

75. Agrippina meantime, worn out though she was with sorrow and bodily weakness, yet still impatient of everything which might delay her vengeance, embarked with the ashes of Germanicus and with her children, pitied by all. Here indeed was a woman of the highest nobility, and but lately because of her splendid union wont to be seen amid an ad

miring and sympathizing throng, now bearing in her bosom
the mournful relics of death, with an uncertain hope of
revenge, with apprehensions for herself, repeatedly at fortune's mercy by reason of the ill-starred fruitfulness of her
marriage. Piso was at the island of Coos when tidings reached
him that Germanicus was dead. He received the news with
extravagant joy, slew victims, visited the temples, with no
moderation in his transports; while Plancina's insolence increased, and she then for the first time exchanged for the
gayest attire the mourning she had worn for her lost sister.

76. Centurions streamed in, and hinted to Piso that he had
the sympathy of the legions at his command. "Go back,"
they said, "to the province which has not been rightfully
taken from you, and is still vacant." While he deliberated
what he was to do, his son, Marcus Piso, advised speedy
return to Rome. "As yet," he said, "you have not contracted
any inexpiable guilt, and you need not dread feeble suspicions or vague rumours. Your strife with Germanicus deserved hatred perhaps, but not punishment, and by your
having been deprived of the province, your enemies have
been fully satisfied. But if you return, should Sentius resist
you, civil war is begun, and you will not retain on your side
the centurions and soldiers, who are powerfully swayed by
the yet recent memory of their general and by a deep-rooted
affection for the Cæsars."

77. Against this view Domitius Celer, one of Piso's intimate friends, argued that he ought to profit by the opportunity. "It was Piso, not Sentius, who had been appointed
to Syria. It was to Piso that the symbols of power and a
prætor's jurisdiction and the legions had been given. In case
of a hostile menace, who would more rightfully confront it
by arms than the man who had received the authority and
special commission of a governor? And as for rumours, it is
best to leave time in which they may die away. Often the
innocent cannot stand against the first burst of unpopularity.
But if Piso possesses himself of the army, and increases his
resources, much which cannot be foreseen will haply turn out
in his favour. Are we hastening to reach Italy along with the
ashes of Germanicus, that, unheard and undefended, you
may be hurried to ruin by the wailings of Agrippina and the

first gossip of an ignorant mob? You have on your side the complicity of Augusta and the emperor's favour, though in secret, and none mourn more ostentatiously over the death of Germanicus than those who most rejoice at it."

78. Without much difficulty Piso, who was ever ready for violent action, was led into this view. He sent a letter to Tiberius accusing Germanicus of luxury and arrogance, and asserting that, having been driven away to make room for revolution, he had resumed the command of the army in the same loyal spirit in which he had before held it. At the same time he put Domitius on board a trireme, with an order to avoid the coast and to push on to Syria through the open sea away from the islands. He formed into regular companies the deserters who flocked to him, armed the camp-followers, crossed with his ships to the mainland, intercepted a detachment of new levies on their way to Syria, and wrote word to the petty kings of Cilicia that they were to help him with auxiliaries, the young Piso actively assisting in all the business of war, though he had advised against undertaking it.

79. And so they coasted along Lycia and Pamphylia, and on meeting the fleet which conveyed Agrippina, both sides in hot anger at first armed for battle, and then in mutual fear confined themselves to revilings, Marsus Vibius telling Piso that he was to go to Rome to defend himself. Piso mockingly replied that he would be there as soon as the prætor who had to try poisoning cases had fixed a day for the accused and his prosecutors.

Meanwhile Domitius having landed at Laodicea, a city of Syria, as he was on his way to the winter-quarters of the sixth legion, which was, he believed, particularly open to revolutionary schemes, was anticipated by its commander Pacuvius. Of this Sentius informed Piso in a letter, and warned him not to disturb the armies by agents of corruption or the province by war. He gathered round him all whom he knew to cherish the memory of Germanicus, and to be opposed to his enemies, dwelling repeatedly on the greatness of the general, with hints that the State was being threatened with an armed attack, and he put himself at the head of a strong force, prepared for battle.

80. Piso, too, though his first attempts were unsuccessful, did not omit the safest precautions under present circumstances, but occupied a very strongly fortified position in Cilicia, named Celenderis. He had raised to the strength of a legion the Cilician auxiliaries which the petty kings had sent, by mixing with them some deserters, and the lately intercepted recruits with his own and Plancina's slaves. And he protested that he, though Cæsar's legate, was kept out of the province which Cæsar had given him, not by the legions (for he had come at their invitation) but by Sentius, who was veiling private animosity under lying charges. "Only," he said, "stand in battle array, and the soldiers will not fight when they see that Piso whom they themselves once called 'father,' is the stronger, if right is to decide; if arms, is far from powerless."

He then deployed his companies before the lines of the fortress on a high and precipitous hill, with the sea surrounding him on every other side. Against him were the veteran troops drawn up in ranks and with reserves, a formidable soldiery on one side, a formidable position on the other. But his men had neither heart nor hope, and only rustic weapons, extemporised for sudden use. When they came to fighting, the result was doubtful only while the Roman cohorts were struggling up to level ground; then, the Cilicians turned their backs and shut themselves up within the fortress.

81. Meanwhile Piso vainly attempted an attack on the fleet which waited at a distance; he then went back, and as he stood before the walls, now smiting his breast, now calling on individual soldiers by name, and luring them on by rewards, sought to excite a mutiny. He had so far roused them that a standard bearer of the sixth legion went over to him with his standard. Thereupon Sentius ordered the horns and trumpets to be sounded, the rampart to be assaulted, the scaling ladders to be raised, all the bravest men to mount on them, while others were to discharge from the engines spears, stones, and brands. At last Piso's obstinacy was overcome, and he begged that he might remain in the fortress on surrendering his arms, while the emperor was being consulted about the appointment of a governor to Syria. The proposed

terms were refused, and all that was granted him were some ships and a safe return to Rome.

82. There meantime, when the illness of Germanicus was universally known, and all news, coming, as it did, from a distance, exaggerated the danger, there was grief and indignation. There was too an outburst of complaint. "Of course this was the meaning," they said, "of banishing him to the ends of the earth, of giving Piso the province; this was the drift of Augusta's secret interviews with Plancina. What elderly men had said of Drusus was perfectly true, that rulers disliked a citizen-like temper in their sons, and the young princes had been put out of the way because they had the idea of comprehending in a restored era of freedom the Roman people under equal laws."

This popular talk was so stimulated by the news of Germanicus's death that even before the magistrate's proclamation or the Senate's resolution, there was a voluntary suspension of business, the public courts were deserted, and private houses closed. Everywhere there was a silence broken only by groans; nothing was arranged for mere effect. And though they refrained not from the emblems of the mourner, they sorrowed yet the more deeply in their hearts.

It chanced that some merchants who left Syria while Germanicus was still alive, brought more cheering tidings about his health. These were instantly believed, instantly published. Every one passed on to others whom he met the intelligence, ill-authenticated as it was, and they again to many more, with joyous exaggeration. They ran to and fro through the city and broke open the doors of the temples. Night assisted their credulity, and amid the darkness confident assertion was comparatively easy. Nor did Tiberius check the false reports till by lapse of time they died away.

83. And so the people grieved the more bitterly as though Germanicus was again lost to them. New honours were devised and decreed, as men were inspired by affection for him or by genius. His name was to be celebrated in the song of the Salii; chairs of state with oaken garlands over them were to be set up in the places assigned to the priesthood of the Augustales; his image in ivory was to head the procession in the games of the circus; no flamen or augur,

except from the Julian family, was to be chosen in the room of Germanicus. Triumphal arches were erected at Rome, on the banks of the Rhine, and on mount Amanus in Syria, with an inscription recording his achievements, and how he had died in the public service. A cenotaph was raised at Antioch, where the body was burnt, a lofty mound at Epidaphna, where he had ended his life. The number of his statues, or of the places in which they were honoured, could not easily be computed. When a golden shield of remarkable size was voted him as a leader among orators, Tiberius declared that he would dedicate to him one of the usual kind, similar to the rest, for in eloquence, he said, there was no distinction of rank, and it was a sufficient glory for him to be classed among ancient writers. The knights called the seats in the theatre known as "the juniors," Germanicus's benches, and arranged that their squadrons were to ride in procession behind his effigy on the fifteenth of July. Many of these honours still remain; some were at once dropped, or became obsolete with time.

84. While men's sorrow was yet fresh, Germanicus's sister Livia, who was married to Drusus, gave birth to twin sons. This, as a rare event, causing joy even in humble homes, so delighted the emperor that he did not refrain from boasting before the senators that to no Roman of the same rank had twin offspring ever before been born. In fact, he would turn to his own glory every incident, however casual. But at such a time, even this brought grief to the people, who thought that the increase of Drusus's family still further depressed the house of Germanicus.

85. That same year the profligacy of women was checked by stringent enactments, and it was provided that no woman whose grandfather, father, or husband had been a Roman knight should get money by prostitution. Vistilia, born of a prætorian family, had actually published her name with this object on the ædile's list, according to a recognised custom of our ancestors, who considered it a sufficient punishment on unchaste women to have to profess their shame. Titidius Labeo, Vistilia's husband, was judicially called on to say why with a wife whose guilt was manifest he had neglected to inflict the legal penalty. When he pleaded that the sixty

days given for deliberation had not yet expired, it was thought sufficient to decide Vistilia's case, and she was ban- ished out of sight to the island of Seriphos.

There was a debate too about expelling the Egyptian and Jewish worship, and a resolution of the Senate was passed that four thousand of the freedmen class who were infected with those superstitions and were of military age should be transported to the island of Sardinia, to quell the brigandage of the place, a cheap sacrifice should they die from the pesti- lential climate. The rest were to quit Italy, unless before a certain day they repudiated their impious rites.

86. Next the emperor brought forward a motion for the election of a Vestal virgin in the room of Occia, who for fifty-seven years had presided with the most immaculate virtue over the Vestal worship. He formally thanked Fon- teius Agrippa and Domitius Pollio for offering their daugh- ters and so vying with one another in zeal for the common- wealth. Pollio's daughter was preferred, only because her mother had lived with one and the same husband, while Agrippa had impaired the honour of his house by a divorce. The emperor consoled his daughter, passed over though she was, with a dowry of a million sesterces.

87. As the city populace complained of the cruel dearness of corn, he fixed a price for grain to be paid by the pur- chaser, promising himself to add two sesterces on every peck for the traders. But he would not therefore accept the title of "father of the country" which once before too had been offered him, and he sharply rebuked those who called his work "divine" and himself "lord." Consequently, speech was restricted and perilous under an emperor who feared free- dom while he hated sycophancy.

88. I find it stated by some writers and senators of the period that a letter from Adgandestrius, chief of the Chatti, was read in the Senate, promising the death of Arminius, if poison were sent for the perpetration of the murder, and that the reply was that it was not by secret treachery but openly and by arms that the people of Rome avenged them- selves on their enemies. A noble answer, by which Tiberius sought to liken himself to those generals of old who had for- bidden and even denounced the poisoning of king Pyrrhus.

Arminius, meanwhile, when the Romans retired and Maroboduus was expelled, found himself opposed in aiming at the throne by his countrymen's independent spirit. He was assailed by armed force, and while fighting with various success, fell by the treachery of his kinsmen. Assuredly he was the deliverer of Germany, one too who had defied Rome, not in her early rise, as other kings and generals, but in the height of her empire's glory, had fought, indeed, indecisive battles, yet in war remained unconquered. He completed thirty-seven years of life, twelve years of power, and he is still a theme of song among barbarous nations, though to Greek historians, who admire only their own achievements, he is unknown, and to Romans not as famous as he should be, while we extol the past and are indifferent to our own times.

BOOK III

A.D. 20, 21, 22

1. WITHOUT pausing in her winter voyage Agrippina arrived at the island of Corcyra, facing the shores of Calabria. There she spent a few days to compose her mind, for she was wild with grief and knew not how to endure. Meanwhile on hearing of her arrival, all her intimate friends and several officers, every one indeed who had served under Germanicus, many strangers too from the neighbouring towns, some thinking it respectful to the emperor, and still more following their example, thronged eagerly to Brundisium, the nearest and safest landing place for a voyager.

As soon as the fleet was seen on the horizon, not only the harbour and the adjacent shores, but the city walls too and the roofs and every place which commanded the most distant prospect were filled with crowds of mourners, who incessantly asked one another, whether, when she landed, they were to receive her in silence or with some utterance of emotion. They were not agreed on what befitted the occasion when the fleet slowly approached, its crew, not joyous as is usual, but wearing all a studied expression of grief. When Agrippina descended from the vessel with her two children, clasping the funeral urn, with eyes rivetted to the earth, there was one universal groan. You could not distinguish kinsfolk from strangers, or the laments of men from those of women; only the attendants of Agrippina, worn out as they were by long sorrow, were surpassed by the mourners who now met them, fresh in their grief.

2. The emperor had despatched two prætorian cohorts with instructions that the magistrates of Calabria, Apulia, and Campania were to pay the last honours to his son's memory. Accordingly tribunes and centurions bore Germanicus's ashes on their shoulders. They were preceded by the

standards unadorned and the fasces reversed. As they passed colony after colony, the populace in black, the knights in their state robes, burnt vestments and perfumes with other usual funeral adjuncts, in proportion to the wealth of the place. Even those whose towns were out of the route, met the mourners, offered victims and built altars to the dead, testifying their grief by tears and wailings. Drusus went as far as Tarracina with Claudius, brother of Germanicus, and the children who had been at Rome. Marcus Valerius and Caius Aurelius, the consuls, who had already entered on office, and a great number of the people thronged the road in scattered groups, every one weeping as he felt inclined. Flattery there was none, for all knew that Tiberius could scarcely dissemble his joy at the death of Germanicus.

3. Tiberius and Augusta refrained from showing themselves, thinking it below their dignity to shed tears in public, or else fearing that, if all eyes scrutinised their faces, their hypocrisy would be revealed. I do not find in any historian or in the daily register that Antonia, Germanicus's mother, rendered any conspicuous honour to the deceased, though besides Agrippina, Drusus, and Claudius, all his other kinsfolk are mentioned by name. She may either have been hindered by illness, or with a spirit overpowered by grief she may not have had the heart to endure the sight of so great an affliction. But I can more easily believe that Tiberius and Augusta, who did not leave the palace, kept her within, that their sorrow might seem equal to hers, and that the grandmother and uncle might be thought to follow the mother's example in staying at home.

4. The day on which the remains were consigned to the tomb of Augustus, was now desolate in its silence, now distracted by lamentations. The streets of the city were crowded; torches were blazing throughout the Campus Martius. There the soldiers under arms, the magistrates without their symbols of office, the people in the tribes, were all incessantly exclaiming that the commonwealth was ruined, that not a hope remained, too boldly and openly to let one think that they remembered their rulers. But nothing impressed Tiberius more deeply than the enthusiasm kindled in favour of Agrippina, whom men spoke of as the glory of

the country, the sole surviving offspring of Augustus, the solitary example of the old times, while looking up to heaven and the gods they prayed for the safety of her children and that they might outlive their oppressors.

5. Some there were who missed the grandeur of a state-funeral, and contrasted the splendid honours conferred by Augustus on Drusus, the father of Germanicus. "Then the emperor himself," they said, "went in the extreme rigour of winter as far as Ticinum, and never leaving the corpse entered Rome with it. Round the funeral bier were ranged the images of the Claudii and the Julii; there was weeping in the forum, and a panegyric before the rostra; every honour devised by our ancestors or invented by their descendants was heaped on him. But as for Germanicus, even the customary distinctions due to any noble had not fallen to his lot. Granting that his body, because of the distance of the journey, was burnt in any fashion in foreign lands, still all the more honours ought to have been afterwards paid him, because at first chance had denied them. His brother had gone but one day's journey to meet him; his uncle, not even to the city gates. Where were all those usages of the past, the image at the head of the bier, the lays composed in commemoration of worth, the eulogies and laments, or at least the semblance of grief?"

6. All this was known to Tiberius, and, to silence popular talk, he reminded the people in a proclamation that many eminent Romans had died for their country and that none had been honoured with such passionate regret. This regret was a glory both to himself and to all, provided only a due mean were observed; for what was becoming in humble homes and communities, did not befit princely personages and an imperial people. Tears and the solace found in mourning were suitable enough for the first burst of grief; but now they must brace their hearts to endurance, as in former days the Divine Julius after the loss of his only daughter, and the Divine Augustus when he was bereft of his grandchildren, had thrust away their sorrow. There was no need of examples from the past, showing how often the Roman people had patiently endured the defeats of armies, the destruction of generals, the total extinction of noble

families. Princes were mortal; the State was everlasting. Let them then return to their usual pursuits, and, as the shows of the festival of the Great Goddess were at hand, even resume their amusements.

7. The suspension of business then ceased, and men went back to their occupations. Drusus was sent to the armies of Illyricum, amidst an universal eagerness to exact vengeance on Piso, and ceaseless complaints that he was meantime roaming through the delightful regions of Asia and Achaia, and was weakening the proofs of his guilt by an insolent and artful procrastination. It was indeed widely rumoured that the notorious poisoner Martina, who, as I have related, had been despatched to Rome by Cneius Sentius, had died suddenly at Brundisium; that poison was concealed in a knot of her hair, and that no symptoms of suicide were discovered on her person.

8. Piso meanwhile sent his son on to Rome with a message intended to pacify the emperor, and then made his way to Drusus, who would, he hoped, be not so much infuriated at his brother's death as kindly disposed towards himself in consequence of a rival's removal. Tiberius, to show his impartiality, received the youth courteously, and enriched him with the liberality he usually bestowed on the sons of noble families. Drusus replied to Piso that if certain insinuations were true, he must be foremost in his resentment, but he preferred to believe that they were false and groundless, and that Germanicus's death need be the ruin of no one. This he said openly, avoiding anything like secrecy. Men did not doubt that his answer was prescribed him by Tiberius, inasmuch as one who had generally all the simplicity and candour of youth, now had recourse to the artifices of old age.

9. Piso, after crossing the Dalmatian sea and leaving his ships at Ancona, went through Picenum and along the Flaminian road, where he overtook a legion which was marching from Pannonia to Rome and was then to garrison Africa. It was a matter of common talk how he had repeatedly displayed himself to the soldiers on the road during the march. From Narnia, to avoid suspicion or because the plans of fear are uncertain, he sailed down the Nar, then down the Tiber, and increased the fury of the populace by bringing his vessel

to shore at the tomb of the Cæsars. In broad daylight, when
the river-bank was thronged, he himself with a numerous
following of dependents, and Plancina with a retinue of
women, moved onward with joy in their countenances.
Among other things which provoked men's anger was his
house towering above the forum, gay with festal decorations,
his banquets and his feasts, about which there was no secrecy, because the place was so public.

10. Next day, Fulcinius Trio asked the consul's leave to
prosecute Piso. It was contended against him by Vitellius
and Veranius and the others who had been the companions
of Germanicus, that this was not Trio's proper part, and
that they themselves meant to report their instructions from
Germanicus, not as accusers, but as deponents and witnesses
to facts. Trio, abandoning the prosecution on this count,
obtained leave to accuse Piso's previous career, and the emperor was requested to undertake the inquiry. This even the
accused did not refuse, fearing, as he did, the bias of the
people and of the Senate; while Tiberius, he knew, was resolute enough to despise report, and was also entangled in his
mother's complicity. Truth too would be more easily distinguished from perverse misrepresentation by a single judge,
where a number would be swayed by hatred and ill-will.

Tiberius was not unaware of the formidable difficulty of
the inquiry and of the rumours by which he was himself assailed. Having therefore summoned a few intimate friends,
he listened to the threatening speeches of the prosecutors and
to the pleadings of the accused, and finally referred the
whole case to the Senate.

11. Drusus meanwhile, on his return from Illyricum,
though the Senate had voted him an ovation for the submission of Maroboduus and the successes of the previous summer, postponed the honour and entered Rome. Then the defendant sought the advocacy of Lucius Arruntius, Marcus
Vinicius, Asinius Gallus, Aeserninus Marcellus and Sextus
Pompeius, and on their declining for different reasons,
Marcus Lepidus, Lucius Piso, and Livineius Regulus became
his counsel, amid the excitement of the whole country, which
wondered how much fidelity would be shown by the friends
of Germanicus, on what the accused rested his hopes, and

how far Tiberius would repress and hide his feelings. Never were the people more keenly interested; never did they indulge themselves more freely in secret whispers against the emperor or in the silence of suspicion.

12. On the day the Senate met, Tiberius delivered a speech of studied moderation. "Piso," he said, "was my father's representative and friend, and was appointed by myself, on the advice of the Senate, to assist Germanicus in the administration of the East. Whether he there had provoked the young prince by wilful opposition and rivalry, and had rejoiced at his death or wickedly destroyed him, is for you to determine with minds unbiassed. Certainly if a subordinate oversteps the bounds of duty and of obedience to his commander, and has exulted in his death and in my affliction, I shall hate him and exclude him from my house, and I shall avenge a personal quarrel without resorting to my power as emperor. If however a crime is discovered which ought to be punished, whoever the murdered man may be, it is for you to give just reparation both to the children of Germanicus and to us, his parents.

"Consider this too, whether Piso dealt with the armies in a revolutionary and seditious spirit; whether he sought by intrigue popularity with the soldiers; whether he attempted to repossess himself of the province by arms, or whether these are falsehoods which his accusers have published with exaggeration. As for them, I am justly angry with their intemperate zeal. For to what purpose did they strip the corpse and expose it to the pollution of the vulgar gaze, and circulate a story among foreigners that he was destroyed by poison, if all this is still doubtful and requires investigation? For my part, I sorrow for my son and shall always sorrow for him; still I would not hinder the accused from producing all the evidence which can relieve his innocence or convict Germanicus of any unfairness, if such there was. And I implore you not to take as proven charges alleged, merely because the case is intimately bound up with my affliction. Do you, whom ties of blood or your own true-heartedness have made his advocates, help him in his peril, every one of you, as far as each man's eloquence and diligence can do so. To like exertions and like persistency I would urge the prosecutors. In this, and in this only, will we place Germanicus above the laws, by conducting the inquiry into his death in this house instead of in the forum, and before the Senate instead of before a bench of judges. In all else let the case be tried as simply as others. Let no one heed the tears of Drusus or my own sorrow, or any stories invented to our discredit."

13. Two days were then assigned for the bringing forward of the charges, and after six days' interval, the prisoner's defence was to occupy three days. Thereupon Fulcinius Trio began with some old and irrelevant accusations about intrigues and extortion during Piso's government of Spain. This, if proved, would not have been fatal to the defendant, if he cleared himself as to his late conduct, and, if refuted, would not have secured his acquittal, if he were convicted of the greater crimes. Next, Servæus, Veranius, and Vitellius, all with equal earnestness, Vitellius with striking eloquence, alleged against Piso that out of hatred of Germanicus and a desire of revolution he had so corrupted the common soldiers by licence and oppression of the allies that he was called by the vilest of them "father of the legions," while on the other hand to all the best men, especially to the companions and friends of Germanicus, he had been savagely cruel. Lastly, he had, they said, destroyed Germanicus himself by sorceries and poison, and hence came those ceremonies and horrible sacrifices made by himself and Plancina; then he had threatened the State with war, and had been defeated in battle, before he could be tried as a prisoner.

14. On all points but one the defence broke down. That he had tampered with the soldiers, that his province had been at the mercy of the vilest of them, that he had even insulted his chief, he could not deny. It was only the charge of poisoning from which he seemed to have cleared himself. This indeed the prosecutors did not adequately sustain by merely alleging that at a banquet given by Germanicus, his food had been tainted with poison by the hands of Piso who sat next above him. It seemed absurd to suppose that he would have dared such an attempt among strange servants, in the sight of so many bystanders, and under Germanicus's own eyes. And, besides, the defendant offered his slaves to

the torture, and insisted on its application to the attendants on that occasion. But the judges for different reasons were merciless, the emperor, because war had been made on a province, the Senate because they could not be sufficiently convinced that there had been no treachery about the death of Germanicus.

At the same time shouts were heard from the people in front of the Senate House, threatening violence if he escaped the verdict of the Senators. They had actually dragged Piso's statues to the Gemonian stairs, and were breaking them in pieces, when by the emperor's order they were rescued and replaced. Piso was then put in a litter and attended by a tribune of one of the prætorian cohorts, who followed him, so it was variously rumoured, to guard his person or to be his executioner.

15. Plancina was equally detested, but had stronger interest. Consequently it was considered a question how far the emperor would be allowed to go against her. While Piso's hopes were in suspense, she offered to share his lot, whatever it might be, and in the worst event, to be his companion in death. But as soon as she had secured her pardon through the secret intercessions of Augusta, she gradually withdrew from her husband and separated her defence from his. When the prisoner saw that this was fatal to him, he hesitated whether he should still persist, but at the urgent request of his sons braced his courage and once more entered the Senate. There he bore patiently the renewal of the accusation, the furious voices of the Senators, savage opposition indeed from every quarter, but nothing daunted him so much as to see Tiberius, without pity and without anger, resolutely closing himself against any inroad of emotion. He was conveyed back to his house, where, seemingly by way of preparing his defence for the next day, he wrote a few words, sealed the paper and handed it to a freedman. Then he bestowed the usual attention on his person; after a while, late at night, his wife having left his chamber, he ordered the doors to be closed, and at daybreak was found with his throat cut and a sword lying on the ground.

16. I remember to have heard old men say that a document was often seen in Piso's hands, the substance of which

he never himself divulged, but which his friends repeatedly declared contained a letter from Tiberius with instructions referring to Germanicus, and that it was his intention to produce it before the Senate and upbraid the emperor, had he not been deluded by vain promises from Sejanus. Nor did he perish, they said, by his own hand, but by that of one sent to be his executioner. Neither of these statements would I positively affirm; still it would not have been right for me to conceal what was related by those who lived up to the time of my youth.

The emperor, assuming an air of sadness, complained in the Senate that the purpose of such a death was to bring odium on himself, and he asked with repeated questionings how Piso had spent his last day and night. Receiving answers which were mostly judicious, though in part somewhat incautious, he read out a note written by Piso, nearly to the following effect:—

"Crushed by a conspiracy of my foes and the odium excited by a lying charge, since my truth and innocence find no place here, I call the immortal gods to witness that towards you Cæsar, I have lived loyally, and with like dutiful respect towards your mother. And I implore you to think of my children, one of whom, Cneius Piso, is in no way implicated in my career, whatever it may have been, seeing that all this time he has been at Rome, while the other, Marcus Piso, dissuaded me from returning to Syria. Would that I had yielded to my young son rather than he to his aged father! And therefore I pray the more earnestly that the innocent may not pay the penalty of my wickedness. By forty-five years of obedience, by my association with you in the consulate, as one who formerly won the esteem of the Divine Augustus, your father, as one who is your friend and will never hereafter ask a favour, I implore you to save my unhappy son." About Plancina he added not a word.

17. Tiberius after this acquitted the young Piso of the charge of civil war on the ground that a son could not have refused a father's orders, compassionating at the same time the high rank of the family and the terrible downfall even of Piso himself, however he might have deserved it. For Plancina he spoke with shame and conscious disgrace, alleg-

ing in excuse the intercession of his mother, secret complaints against whom from all good men were growing more
and more vehement. "So it was the duty of a grandmother,"
people said, "to look a grandson's murderess in the face, to
converse with her and rescue her from the Senate. What the
laws secure on behalf of every citizen, had to Germanicus
alone been denied. The voices of a Vitellius and Veranius
had bewailed a Cæsar, while the emperor and Augusta had
defended Plancina. She might as well now turn her poisonings, and her devices which had proved so successful, against
Agrippina and her children, and thus sate this exemplary
grandmother and uncle with the blood of a most unhappy
house."

Two days were frittered away over this mockery of a trial,
Tiberius urging Piso's children to defend their mother. While
the accusers and their witnesses pressed the prosecution with
rival zeal, and there was no reply, pity rather than anger
was on the increase. Aurelius Cotta, the consul, who was
first called on for his vote (for when the emperor put the
question, even those in office went through the duty of voting), held that Piso's name ought to be erased from the
public register, half of his property confiscated, half given
up to his son, Cneius Piso, who was to change his first name;
that Marcus Piso, stript of his rank, with an allowance of
five million sesterces, should be banished for ten years, Plancina's life being spared in consideration of Augusta's intercession.

18. Much of the sentence was mitigated by the emperor.
The name of Piso was not to be struck out of the public
register, since that of Marcus Antonius who had made war
on his country, and that of Julius Antonius who had dishonoured the house of Augustus, still remained. Marcus Piso
too he saved from degradation, and gave him his father's
property, for he was firm enough, as I have often related,
against the temptation of money, and now for very shame
at Plancina's acquittal, he was more than usually merciful.
Again, when Valerius Messalinus and Cæcina Severus proposed respectively the erection of a golden statue in the
temple of Mars the Avenger and of an altar to Vengeance,
he interposed, protesting that victories over the foreigner

were commemorated with such monuments, but that domestic woes ought to be shrouded in silent grief.

There was a further proposal of Messalinus, that Tiberius,
Augusta, Antonia, Agrippina and Drusus ought to be publicly thanked for having avenged Germanicus. He omitted
all mention of Claudius. Thereupon he was pointedly asked
by Lucius Asprenas before the Senate, whether the omission
had been intentional, and it was only then that the name of
Claudius was added. For my part, the wider the scope of my
reflection on the present and the past, the more am I impressed by their mockery of human plans in every transaction. Clearly, the very last man marked out for empire
by public opinion, expectation and general respect was he
whom fortune was holding in reserve as the emperor of the
future.

19. A few days afterwards the emperor proposed to the
Senate to confer the priesthood on Vitellius, Veranius and
Servæus. To Fulcinius he promised his support in seeking
promotion, but warned him not to ruin his eloquence by
rancour. This was the end of avenging the death of Germanicus, a subject of conflicting rumours not only among
the people then living but also in after times. So obscure
are the greatest events, as some take for granted any hearsay, whatever its source, others turn truth into falsehood,
and both errors find encouragement with posterity.

Drusus meanwhile quitted Rome to resume his command
and soon afterwards re-entered the city with an ovation. In
the course of a few days his mother Vipsania died, the only
one of all Agrippa's children whose death was without violence. As for the rest, they perished, some it is certain by the
sword, others it was believed by poison or starvation.

20. That same year Tacfarinas who had been defeated,
as I have related, by Camillus in the previous summer, renewed hostilities in Africa, first by mere desultory raids, so
swift as to be unpunished; next, by destroying villages and
carrying off plunder wholesale. Finally, he hemmed in a Roman cohort near the river Pagyda. The position was commanded by Decrius, a soldier energetic in action and experienced in war, who regarded the siege as a disgrace.
Cheering on his men to offer battle in the open plain, he

drew up his line in front of his intrenchments. At the first shock, the cohort was driven back, upon which he threw himself fearlessly amid the missiles in the path of the fugitives and cried shame on the standard-bearers for letting Roman soldiers show their backs to a rabble of deserters. At the same moment he was covered with wounds, and though pierced through the eye, he resolutely faced the enemy and ceased not to fight till he fell deserted by his men.

21. On receiving this information, Lucius Apronius, successor to Camillus, alarmed more by the dishonour of his own men than by the glory of the enemy, ventured on a deed quite exceptional at that time and derived from old tradition. He flogged to death every tenth man drawn by lot from the disgraced cohort. So beneficial was this rigour that a detachment of veterans, numbering not more than five hundred, routed those same troops of Tacfarinas on their attacking a fortress named Thala. In this engagement Rufus Helvius, a common soldier, won the honour of saving a citizen's life, and was rewarded by Apronius with a neck-chain and a spear. To these the emperor added the civic crown, complaining, but without anger, that Apronius had not used his right as pro-consul to bestow this further distinction.

Tacfarinas, however, finding that the Numidians were cowed and had a horror of siege-operations, pursued a desultory warfare, retreating when he was pressed, and then again hanging on his enemy's rear. While the barbarian continued these tactics, he could safely insult the baffled and exhausted Romans. But when he marched away towards the coast and, hampered with booty, fixed himself in a regular camp, Cæsianus was despatched by his father Apronius with some cavalry and auxiliary infantry, reinforced by the most active of the legionaries, and, after a successful battle with the Numidians, drove them into the desert.

22. At Rome meanwhile Lepida, who beside the glory of being one of the Æmilii was the great-granddaughter of Lucius Sulla and Cneius Pompeius, was accused of pretending to be a mother by Publius Quirinus, a rich and childless man. Then, too, there were charges of adulteries, of poisonings, and of inquiries made through astrologers concerning

the imperial house. The accused was defended by her brother
Manius Lepidus. Quirinus by his relentless enmity even after
his divorce, had procured for her some sympathy, infamous
and guilty as she was. One could not easily perceive the
emperor's feelings at her trial; so effectually did he interchange and blend the outward signs of resentment and compassion. He first begged the Senate not to deal with the
charges of treason, and subsequently induced Marcus Servilius, an ex-consul, to divulge what he had seemingly wished
to suppress. He also handed over to the consuls Lepida's
slaves, who were in military custody, but would not allow
them to be examined by torture on matters referring to his
own family. Drusus too, the consul-elect, he released from
the necessity of having to speak first to the question. Some
thought this a gracious act, done to save the rest of the
Senators from a compulsory assent, while others ascribed it
to malignity, on the ground that he would have yielded only
where there was a necessity of condemning.

23. On the days of the games which interrupted the trial,
Lepida went into the theatre with some ladies of rank, and
as she appealed with piteous wailings to her ancestors and
to that very Pompey, the public buildings and statues of
whom stood there before their eyes, she roused such sympathy that people burst into tears and shouted, without
ceasing, savage curses on Quirinus, "to whose childless old-
age and miserably obscure family, one once destined to be
the wife of Lucius Cæsar and the daughter-in-law of the
Divine Augustus was being sacrificed." Then, by the torture
of the slaves, her infamies were brought to light, and a motion of Rubellius Blandus was carried which outlawed her.
Drusus supported him, though others had proposed a milder
sentence. Subsequently, Scaurus, who had had a daughter by
her, obtained as a concession that her property should not be
confiscated. Then at last Tiberius declared that he had himself too ascertained from the slaves of Publius Quirinus that
Lepida had attempted their master's life by poison.

24. It was some compensation for the misfortunes of great
houses (for within a short interval the Calpurnii had lost
Piso and the Æmilii Lepida) that Decimus Silanus was now

restored to the Junian family. I will briefly relate his down-fall.

Though the Divine Augustus in his public life enjoyed unshaken prosperity, he was unfortunate at home from the profligacy of his daughter and granddaughter, both of whom he banished from Rome, and punished their paramours with death or exile. Calling, as he did, a vice so habitual among men and women by the awful name of sacrilege and treason, he went far beyond the indulgent spirit of our ancestors, beyond indeed his own legislation. But I will relate the deaths of others with the remaining events of that time, if after finishing the work I have now proposed to myself, I prolong my life for further labours.

Decimus Silanus, the paramour of the granddaughter of Augustus, though the only severity he experienced was exclusion from the emperor's friendship, saw clearly that it meant exile; and it was not till Tiberius's reign that he ventured to appeal to the Senate and to the prince, in reliance on the influence of his brother Marcus Silanus, who was conspicuous both for his distinguished rank and eloquence. But Tiberius, when Silanus thanked him, replied in the Senate's presence, "that he too rejoiced at the brother's return from his long foreign tour, and that this was justly allowable, inasmuch as he had been banished not by a decree of the Senate or under any law. Still, personally," he said, "he felt towards him his father's resentment in all its force, and the return of Silanus had not cancelled the intentions of Augustus." Silanus after this lived at Rome without attaining office.

25. It was next proposed to relax the Papia Poppæa law, which Augustus in his old age had passed subsequently to the Julian statutes, for yet further enforcing the penalties on celibacy and for enriching the exchequer. And yet, marriages and the rearing of children did not become more frequent, so powerful were the attractions of a childless state. Meanwhile there was an increase in the number of persons imperilled, for every household was undermined by the insinuations of informers; and now the country suffered from its laws, as it had hitherto suffered from its vices. This suggests to me a fuller discussion of the origin of law and of

the methods by which we have arrived at the present endless multiplicity and variety of our statutes.

26. Mankind in the earliest age lived for a time without a single vicious impulse, without shame or guilt, and, consequently, without punishment and restraints. Rewards were not needed when everything right was pursued on its own merits; and as men desired nothing against morality, they were debarred from nothing by fear. When however they began to throw off equality, and ambition and violence usurped the place of self-control and modesty, despotisms grew up and became perpetual among many nations. Some from the beginning, or when tired of kings, preferred codes of laws. These were at first simple, while men's minds were unsophisticated. The most famous of them were those of the Cretans, framed by Minos; those of the Spartans, by Lycurgus, and, subsequently, those which Solan drew up for the Athenians on a more elaborate and extensive scale. Romulus governed us as he pleased; then Numa united our people by religious ties and a constitution of divine origin, to which some additions were made by Tullus and Ancus. But Servius Tullius was our chief legislator, to whose laws even kings were to be subject.

27. After Tarquin's expulsion, the people, to check cabals among the Senators, devised many safeguards for freedom and for the establishment of unity. Decemvirs were appointed; everything specially admirable elsewhere was adopted, and the Twelve Tables drawn up, the last specimen of equitable legislation. For subsequent enactments, though occasionally directed against evildoers for some crime, were oftener carried by violence amid class dissensions, with a view to obtain honours not as yet conceded, or to banish distinguished citizens, or for other base ends. Hence the Gracchi and Saturnini, those popular agitators, and Drusus too, as flagrant a corrupter in the Senate's name; hence, the bribing of our allies by alluring promises and the cheating them by tribunes vetoes. Even the Italian and then the Civil war did not pass without the enactment of many conflicting laws, till Lucius Sulla, the Dictator, by the repeal or alteration of past legislation and by many additions, gave us a brief lull in this process, to be instantly

followed by the seditious proposals of Lepidus, and soon afterwards by the tribunes recovering their license to excite the people just as they chose. And now bills were passed, not only for national objects but for individual cases, and laws were most numerous when the commonwealth was most corrupt.

28. Cneius Pompeius was then for the third time elected consul to reform public morals, but in applying remedies more terrible than the evils and repealing the legislation of which he had himself been the author, he lost by arms what by arms he had been maintaining. Then followed twenty years of continuous strife; custom or law there was none; the vilest deeds went unpunished, while many noble acts brought ruin. At last, in his sixth consulship, Cæsar Augustus, feeling his power secure, annulled the decrees of his triumvirate, and gave us a constitution which might serve us in peace under a monarchy. Henceforth our chains became more galling, and spies were set over us, stimulated by rewards under the Papia Poppæa law, so that if men shrank from the privileges of fatherhood, the State, as universal parent, might possess their ownerless properties. But this espionage became too searching, and Rome and Italy and Roman citizens everywhere fell into its clutches. Many men's fortunes were ruined, and over all there hung a terror, till Tiberius, to provide a remedy, selected by lot five ex-consuls, five ex-prætors, and five senators, by whom most of the legal knots were disentangled and some slight temporary relief afforded.

29. About this same time he commended to the Senate's favour, Nero, Germanicus's son, who was just entering or manhood, and asked them, not without smiles of ridicule from his audience, to exempt him from serving as one of the Twenty Commissioners, and let him be a candidate for the quæstorship five years earlier than the law allowed. His excuse was that a similar decree had been made for himself and his brother at the request of Augustus. But I cannot doubt that even then there were some who secretly laughed at such a petition, though the Cæsars were but in the beginning of their grandeur, and ancient usage was more constantly before men's eyes, while also the tie be-

tween stepfather and stepson was weaker than that between
grandfather and grandchild. The pontificate was likewise
conferred on Nero, and on the day on which he first entered
the forum, a gratuity was given to the city-populace, who
greatly rejoiced at seeing a son of Germanicus now grown
to manhood. Their joy was further increased by Nero's marriage to Julia, Drusus's daughter. This news was met with
favourable comments, but it was heard with disgust that
Sejanus was to be the father-in-law of the son of Claudius.
The emperor was thought to have polluted the nobility of
his house and to have yet further elevated Sejanus, whom
they already suspected of overweening ambition.

30. Two remarkable men died at the end of the year,
Lucius Volusius and Sallustius Crispus. Volusius was of an
old family, which had however never risen beyond the prætorship. He brought into it the consulship; he also held the
office of censor for arranging the classes of the knights, and
was the first to pile up the wealth which that house enjoyed
to a boundless extent.

Crispus was of equestrian descent and grandson of a sister
of Caius Sallustius, that most admirable Roman historian,
by whom he was adopted and whose name he took. Though
his road to preferment was easy, he chose to emulate Mæcenas, and without rising to a senator's rank, he surpassed
in power many who had won triumphs and consulships. He
was a contrast to the manners of antiquity in his elegance
and refinement, and in the sumptuousness of his wealth he
was almost a voluptuary. But beneath all this was a vigorous mind, equal to the greatest labours, the more active in
proportion as he made a show of sloth and apathy. And so
while Mæcenas lived, he stood next in favour to him, and
was afterwards the chief depository of imperial secrets, and
accessory to the murder of Postumus Agrippa, till in advanced age he retained the shadow rather than the substance
of the emperor's friendship. The same too had happened to
Mæcenas, so rarely is it the destiny of power to be lasting,
or perhaps a sense of weariness steals over princes when they
have bestowed everything, or over favourites, when there is
nothing left them to desire.

31. Next followed Tiberius's fourth, Drusus's second con-

sulship, memorable from the fact that father and son were colleagues. Two years previously the association of Germanicus and Tiberius in the same honour had not been agreeable to the uncle, nor had it the link of so close a natural tie.

At the beginning of this year Tiberius, avowedly to recruit his health, retired to Campania, either as a gradual preparation for long and uninterrupted seclusion, or in order that Drusus alone in his father's absence might discharge the duties of the consulship. It happened that a mere trifle which grew into a sharp contest gave the young prince the means of acquiring popularity. Domitius Corbulo, an ex-prætor, complained to the Senate that Lucius Sulla, a young noble, had not given place to him at a gladiatorial show. Corbulo had age, national usage and the feelings of the older senators in his favour. Against him Mamercus Scaurus, Lucius Arruntius and other kinsmen of Sulla strenuously exerted themselves. There was a keen debate, and appeal was made to the precedents of our ancestors, as having censured in severe decrees disrespect on the part of the young, till Drusus argued in a strain calculated to calm their feelings. Corbulo too received an apology from Mamercus, who was Sulla's uncle and stepfather, and the most fluent speaker of that day.

It was this same Corbulo, who, after raising a cry that most of the roads in Italy were obstructed or impassable through the dishonesty of contractors and the negligence of officials, himself willingly undertook the complete management of the business. This proved not so beneficial to the State as ruinous to many persons, whose property and credit he mercilessly attacked by convictions and confiscations.

32. Soon afterwards Tiberius informed the Senate by letter that Africa was again disturbed by an incursion of Tacfarinas, and that they must use their judgment in choosing as pro-consul an experienced soldier of vigorous constitution, who would be equal to the war. Sextus Pompeius caught at this opportunity of venting his hatred against Lepidus, whom he condemned as a poor-spirited and needy man, who was a disgrace to his ancestors, and therefore deserved to lose even his chance of the province of Asia. But the Senate were against him, for they thought Lepidus gentle

rather than cowardly, and that his inherited poverty, with the high rank in which he had lived without a blot, ought to be considered a credit to him instead of a reproach. And so he was sent to Asia, and with respect to Africa it was decided that the emperor should choose to whom it was to be assigned.

33. During this debate Severus Cæcina proposed that no magistrate who had obtained a province should be accompanied by his wife. He began by recounting at length how harmoniously he had lived with his wife, who had borne him six children, and how in his own home he had observed what he was proposing for the public, by having kept her in Italy, though he had himself served forty campaigns in various provinces. "With good reason," he said, "had it been formerly decided that women were not to be taken among our allies or into foreign countries. A train of women involves delays through luxury in peace and through panic in war, and converts a Roman army on the march into the likeness of a barbarian progress. Not only is the sex feeble and unequal to hardship, but, when it has liberty, it is spiteful, intriguing and greedy of power. They show themselves off among the soldiers and have the centurions at their beck. Lately a woman had presided at the drill of the cohorts and the evolutions of the legions. You should yourselves bear in mind that, whenever men are accused of extortion, most of the charges are directed against the wives. It is to these that the vilest of the provincials instantly attach themselves; it is they who undertake and settle business; two persons receive homage when they appear; there are two centres of government, and the women's orders are the more despotic and intemperate. Formerly they were restrained by the Oppian and other laws; now, loosed from every bond, they rule our houses, our tribunals, even our armies."

34. A few heard this speech with approval, but the majority clamorously objected that there was no proper motion on the subject, and that Cæcina was no fit censor on so grave an issue. Presently Valerius Messalinus, Messala's son, in whom the father's eloquence was reproduced, replied that much of the sternness of antiquity had been changed into a better and more genial system. "Rome," he said, "is not

now, as formerly, beset with wars, nor are the provinces hostile. A few concessions are made to the wants of women, but such as are not even a burden to their husbands' homes, much less to the allies. In all other respects man and wife share alike, and this arrangement involves no trouble in peace. War of course requires that men should be unincumbered, but when they return what worthier solace can they have after their hardships than a wife's society? But some wives have abandoned themselves to scheming and rapacity. Well; even among our magistrates, are not many subject to various passions? Still, that is not a reason for sending no one into a province. Husbands have often been corrupted by the vices of their wives. Are then all unmarried men blameless? The Oppian laws were formerly adopted to meet the political necessities of the time, and subsequently there was some remission and mitigation of them on grounds of expediency. It is idle to shelter our own weakness under other names; for it is the husband's fault if the wife transgresses propriety. Besides, it is wrong that because of the imbecility of one or two men, all husbands should be cut off from their partners in prosperity and adversity. And further, a sex naturally weak will be thus left to itself and be at the mercy of its own voluptuousness and the passions of others. Even with the husband's personal vigilance the marriage tie is scarcely preserved inviolate. What would happen were it for a number of years to be forgotten, just as in a divorce? You must not check vices abroad without remembering the scandals of the capital."

Drusus added a few words on his own experience as a husband. "Princes," he said, "must often visit the extremities of their empire. How often had the Divine Augustus travelled to the West and to the East accompanied by Livia? He had himself gone to Illyricum and, should it be expedient, he would go to other countries, not always however with a contented mind, if he had to tear himself from a much loved wife, the mother of his many children."

35. Cæcina's motion was thus defeated. At the Senate's next meeting came a letter from Tiberius, which indirectly censured them for throwing on the emperor every political care, and named Marcus Lepidus and Junius Blæsus, one

of whom was to be chosen pro-consul of Africa. Both spoke on the subject, and Lepidus begged earnestly to be excused. He alleged ill-health, his children's tender age, his having a daughter to marry, and something more of which he said nothing, was well understood, the fact that Blæsus was uncle of Sejanus and so had very powerful interest. Blæsus replied with an affectation of refusal, but not with the same persistency, nor was he backed up by the acquiescence of flatterers.

36. Next was exposed an abuse, hitherto the subject of many a whispered complaint. The vilest wretches used a growing freedom in exciting insult and obloquy against respectable citizens, and escaped punishment by clasping some statue of the emperor. The very freedman or slave was often an actual terror to his patron or master whom he would menace by word and gesture. Accordingly Caius Cestius, a senator, argued that "though princes were like deities, yet even the gods listened only to righteous prayers from their suppliants, and that no one fled to the Capitol or any other temple in Rome to use it as an auxiliary in crime. There was an end and utter subversion of all law when, in the forum and on the threshold of the Senate-House, Annia Rufilla, whom he had convicted of fraud before a judge, assailed him with insults and threats, while he did not himself dare to try legal proceedings, because he was confronted by her with the emperor's image." There rose other clamorous voices, with even more flagrant complaints, and all implored Drusus to inflict exemplary vengeance, till he ordered Rufilla to be summoned, and on her conviction to be confined in the common prison.

37. Considius Aequus too and Cœlius Cursor, Roman knights, were punished on the emperor's proposal, by a decree of the Senate, for having attacked the prætor, Magius Cæcilianus, with false charges of treason. Both these results were represented as an honour to Drusus. By moving in society at Rome, amid popular talk, his father's dark policy it was thought, was mitigated. Even voluptuousness in one so young gave little offence. Better that he should incline that way, spend his days in architecture, his nights in banquets. than that he should live in solitude, cut off from every

pleasure, and absorbed in a gloomy vigilance and mischievous schemes.

38. Tiberius indeed and the informers were never weary. Ancharius Priscus had prosecuted Cæsius Cordus, proconsul of Crete, for extortion, adding a charge of treason, which then crowned all indictments. Antistius Vetus, one of the chief men of Macedonia, who had been acquitted of adultery, was recalled by the emperor himself, with a censure on the judges, to be tried for treason, as a seditious man who had been implicated in the designs of Rhescuporis, when that king after the murder of his brother Cotys had meditated war against us. The accused was accordingly outlawed, with the further sentence that he was to be confined in an island from which neither Macedonia nor Thrace were conveniently accessible.

As for Thrace, since the division of the kingdom between Rhœmetalces and the children of Cotys, who because of their tender age were under the guardianship of Trebellienus Rufus, it was divided against itself, from not being used to our rule, and blamed Rhœmetalces no less than Trebellienus for allowing the wrongs of his countrymen to go unpunished. The Cœlaletae, Odrusae and Dii, powerful tribes, took up arms, under different leaders, all on a level from their obscurity. This hindered them from combining in a formidable war. Some roused their immediate neighbourhood; others crossed Mount Hæmus, to stir up remote tribes; most of them, and the best disciplined, besieged the king in the city of Philippopolis, founded by the Macedonian Philip.

39. When this was known to Publius Vellæus who commanded the nearest army, he sent some allied cavalry and light infantry to attack those who were roaming in quest of plunder or of reinforcements, while he marched in person with the main strength of the foot to raise the siege. Every operation was at the same moment successful; the pillagers were cut to pieces; dissensions broke out among the besiegers, and the king made a well-timed sally just as the legion arrived. A battle or even a skirmish it did not deserve to be called, in which merely half-armed stragglers were slaughtered without bloodshed on our side.

40. That same year, some states of Gaul, under the pressure of heavy debts, attempted a revolt. Its most active in-
stigators were Julius Florus among the Treveri and Julius
Sacrovir among the Ædui. Both could show noble birth and
signal services rendered by ancestors, for which Roman
citizenship had formerly been granted them, when the gift
was rare and a recompense only of merit. In secret conferences to which the fiercest spirits were admitted, or any to
whom poverty or the fear of guilt was an irresistible stimulus to crime, they arranged that Florus was to rouse the
Belgae, Sacrovir the Gauls nearer home. These men accordingly talked sedition before small gatherings and popular
assemblies about the perpetual tributes, the oppressive
usury, the cruelty and arrogance of their governors, hinting
too that there was disaffection among our soldiers, since
they had heard of the murder of Germanicus. "It was,"
they said, "a grand opportunity for the recovery of freedom,
if only they would contrast their own vigour with the ex-
haustion of Italy, the unwarlike character of the city populace, and the utter weakness of Rome's armies in all but
their foreign element."

41. Scarcely a single community was untouched by the
germs of this commotion. First however in actual revolt
were the Andecavi and Turoni. Of these the former were
put down by an officer, Acilius Aviola, who had summoned
a cohort which was on garrison duty at Lugdunum. The
Turoni were quelled by some legionary troops sent by
Visellius Varro who commanded in Lower Germany, and
led by the same Aviola and some Gallic chieftains who
brought aid, in order that they might disguise their disaffection and exhibit it at a better opportunity. Sacrovir too
was conspicuous, with head uncovered, cheering on his men
to fight for Rome, to display, as he said, his valour. But
the prisoners asserted that he sought recognition that he
might not be a mark for missiles. Tiberius when consulted
on the matter disdained the information, and fostered the
war by his irresolution.

42. Florus meanwhile followed up his designs and tried
to induce a squadron of cavalry levied among the Treveri,
trained in our service and discipline, to begin hostilities by

a massacre of the Roman traders. He corrupted a few of the men, but the majority were steadfast in their allegiance. A host however of debtors and dependents took up arms, and they were on their way to the forest passes known as the Arduenna, when they were stopped by legions which Visellius and Silius had sent from their respective armies, by opposite routes, to meet them. Julius Indus from the same state, who was at feud with Florus and therefore particularly eager to render us a service, was sent on in advance with a picked force, and dispersed the undisciplined rabble. Florus after eluding the conquerors by hiding himself in one place after another, at last when he saw some soldiers who had barred every possible escape, fell by his own hand. Such was the end of the rebellion of the Treveri.

43. A more formidable movement broke out among the Ædui, proportioned to the greater wealth of the state and the distance of the force which should repress it. Sacrovir with some armed cohorts had made himself master of Augustodunum, the capital of the tribe, with the noblest youth of Gaul, there devoting themselves to a liberal education, and with such hostages he proposed to unite in his cause their parents and kinsfolk. He also distributed among the youth arms which he had had secretly manufactured. There were forty thousand, one fifth armed like our legionaries; the rest had spears and knives and other weapons used in the chase. In addition were some slaves who were being trained for gladiators, clad after the national fashion in a complete covering of steel. They were called crupellarii, and though they were ill-adapted for inflicting wounds, they were impenetrable to them. This army was continually increased, not yet by any open combination of the neighbouring states, but by zealous individual enthusiasm, as well as by strife between the Roman generals, each of whom claimed the war for himself. Varro after a while, as he was infirm and aged, yielded to Silius who was in his prime.

44. At Rome meanwhile people said that it was not only the Treveri and Ædui who had revolted, but sixty-four states of Gaul with the Germans in alliance, while Spain too was disaffected; anything in fact was believed, with rumour's usual exaggeration. All good men were saddened by anxiety

for the country, but many in their loathing of the present system and eagerness for change, rejoiced at their very perils and exclaimed against Tiberius for giving attention amid such political convulsions to the calumnies of informers. "Was Sacrovir too," they asked, "to be charged with treason before the Senate? We have at last found men to check those murderous missiles by the sword. Even war is a good exchange for a miserable peace." Tiberius all the more studiously assumed an air of unconcern. He changed neither his residence nor his look, but kept up his usual demeanour during the whole time, either from the profoundness of his reserve; or was it that he had convinced himself that the events were unimportant and much more insignificant than the rumours represented?

45. Silius meantime was advancing with two legions, and having sent forward some auxiliary troops was ravaging those villages of the Sequani, which, situated on the border, adjoin the Ædui, and were associated with them in arms. He then pushed on by forced marches to Augustodunum, his standard-bearers vying in zeal, and even the privates loudly protesting against any halt for their usual rest or during the hours of night. "Only," they said, "let us have the foe face to face; that will be enough for victory." Twelve miles from Augustodunum they saw before them Sacrovir and his army in an open plain. His men in armour he had posted in the van, his light infantry on the wings, and the half-armed in the rear. He himself rode amid the foremost ranks on a splendid charger, reminding them of the ancient glories of the Gauls, of the disasters they had inflicted on the Romans, how grand would be the freedom of the victorious, how more intolerable than ever the slavery of a second conquest.

46. His words were brief and heard without exultation. For now the legions in battle array were advancing, and the rabble of townsfolk who knew nothing of war had their faculties of sight and hearing quite paralysed. Silius, on the one hand, though confident hope took away any need for encouragement, exclaimed again and again that it was a shame to the conquerors of Germany to have to be led against Gauls, as against an enemy. "Only the other day

the rebel Turoni had been discomfited by a single cohort, the Treveri by one cavalry squadron, the Sequani by a few companies of this very army. Prove to these Ædui once for all that the more they abound in wealth and luxury, the more unwarlike are they, but spare them when they flee."

Then there was a deafening cheer; the cavalry threw itself on the flanks, and the infantry charged the van. On the wings there was but a brief resistance. The men in mail were somewhat of an obstacle, as the iron plates did not yield to javelins or swords; but our men, snatching up hatchets and pickaxes, hacked at their bodies and their armour as if they were battering a wall. Some beat down the unwieldy mass with pikes and forked poles, and they were left lying on the ground, without an effort to rise, like dead men. Sacrovir with his most trustworthy followers hurried first to Augustodunum and then, from fear of being surrendered, to an adjacent country house. There by his own hand he fell, and his comrades by mutually inflicted wounds. The house was fired over their heads, and with it they were all consumed.

47. Then at last Tiberius informed the Senate by letter of the beginning and completion of the war, without either taking away from or adding to the truth, but ascribing the success to the loyalty and courage of his generals, and to his own policy. He also gave the reasons why neither he himself nor Drusus had gone to the war; he magnified the greatness of the empire, and said it would be undignified for emperors, whenever there was a commotion in one or two states, to quit the capital, the centre of all government. Now, as he was not influenced by fear, he would go to examine and settle matters.

The Senate decreed vows for his safe return, with thanksgivings and other appropriate ceremonies. Cornelius Dolabella alone, in endeavouring to outdo the other Senators, went the length of a preposterous flattery by proposing that he should enter Rome from Campania with an ovation. Thereupon came a letter from the emperor, declaring that he was not so destitute of renown as after having subdued the most savage nations and received or refused so many triumphs in his youth, to covet now that he was old an unmeaning honour for a tour in the neighbourhood of Rome.

48. About the same time he requested the Senate to let the death of Sulpicius Quirinus be celebrated with a public funeral. With the old patrician family of the Sulpicii this Quirinus, who was born in the town of Lanuvium, was quite unconnected. An indefatigable soldier, he had by his zealous services won the consulship under the Divine Augustus, and subsequently the honours of a triumph for having stormed some fortresses of the Homonadenses in Cilicia. He was also appointed adviser to Caius Cæsar in the government of Armenia, and had likewise paid court to Tiberius, who was then at Rhodes. The emperor now made all this known to the Senate, and extolled the good offices of Quirinus to himself, while he censured Marcus Lollius, whom he charged with encouraging Caius Cæsar in his perverse and quarrelsome behaviour. But people generally had no pleasure in the memory of Quirinus, because of the perils he had brought, as I have related, on Lepida, and the meanness and dangerous power of his last years.

49. At the close of the year, Caius Lutorius Priscus, a Roman knight, who, after writing a popular poem bewailing the death of Germanicus, had received a reward in money from the emperor, was fastened on by an informer, and charged with having composed another during the illness of Drusus, which, in the event of the prince's death, might be published with even greater profit to himself. He had in his vanity read it in the house of Publius Petronius before Vitellia, Petronius's mother-in-law, and several ladies of rank. As soon as the accuser appeared, all but Vitellia were frightened into giving evidence. She alone swore that she had heard not a word. But those who criminated him fatally were rather believed, and on the motion of Haterius Agrippa, the consul-elect, the last penalty was invoked on the accused.

50. Marcus Lepidus spoke against the sentence as follows:—"Senators, if we look to the single fact of the infamous utterance with which Lutorius has polluted his own mind and the ears of the public, neither dungeon nor halter nor tortures fit for a slave would be punishment enough for him. But though vice and wicked deeds have no limit, penalties and correctives are moderated by the clemency of the

sovereign and by the precedents of your ancestors and yourselves. Folly differs from wickedness; evil words from evil
deeds, and thus there is room for a sentence by which this
offence may not go unpunished, while we shall have no cause
to regret either leniency or severity. Often have I heard our
emperor complain when any one has anticipated his mercy
by a self-inflicted death. Lutorius's life is still safe; if spared,
he will be no danger to the State; if put to death, he will
be no warning to others. His productions are as empty and
ephemeral as they are replete with folly. Nothing serious
or alarming is to be apprehended from the man who is the
betrayer of his own shame and works on the imaginations
not of men but of silly women. However, let him leave
Rome, lose his property, and be outlawed. That is my proposal, just as though he were convicted under the law of
treason."

51. Only one of the ex-consuls, Rubellius Blandus, supported Lepidus. The rest voted with Agrippa. Priscus was
dragged off to prison and instantly put to death. Of this
Tiberius complained to the Senate with his usual ambiguity,
extolling their loyalty in so sharply avenging the very slight-
est insults to the sovereign, though he deprecated such hasty
punishment of mere words, praising Lepidus and not censuring Agrippa. So the Senate passed a resolution that their decrees should not be registered in the treasury till nine days
had expired, and so much respite was to be given to condemned persons. Still the Senate had not liberty to alter
their purpose, and lapse of time never softened Tiberius.

52. Caius Sulpicius and Didius Haterius were the next
consuls. It was a year free from commotions abroad, while
at home stringent legislation was apprehended against the
luxury which had reached boundless excess in everything on
which wealth is lavished. Some expenses, though very serious, were generally kept secret by a concealment of the
real prices; but the costly preparations for gluttony and dissipation were the theme of incessant talk, and had suggested
a fear that a prince who clung to old-fashioned frugality
would be too stern in his reforms. In fact, when the ædile
Caius Bibulus broached the topic, all his colleagues had
pointed out that the sumptuary laws were disregarded, that

prohibited prices for household articles were every day on the increase, and that moderate measures could not stop the evil.

The Senate on being consulted had, without handling the matter, referred it to the emperor. Tiberius, after long considering whether such reckless tastes could be repressed, whether the repression of them would not be still more hurtful to the State, also, how undignified it would be to meddle with what he could not succeed in, or what, if effected, would necessitate the disgrace and infamy of men of distinction, at last addressed a letter to the Senate to the following purport:—

53. Perhaps in any other matter, Senators, it would be more convenient that I should be consulted in your presence, and then state what I think to be for the public good. In this debate it was better that my eyes should not be on you, for while you were noting the anxious faces of individual senators charged with shameful luxury, I too myself might observe them and, as it were, detect them. Had those energetic men, our ædiles, first taken counsel with me, I do not know whether I should not have advised them to let alone vices so strong and so matured, rather than merely attain the result of publishing what are the corruptions with which we cannot cope. They however have certainly done their duty, as I would wish all other officials likewise to fulfil their parts. For myself, it is neither seemly to keep silence nor is it easy to speak my mind, as I do not hold the office of ædile, prætor, or consul. Something greater and loftier is expected of a prince, and while everybody takes to himself the credit of right policy, one alone has to bear the odium of every person's failures. For what am I first to begin with restraining and cutting down to the old standard? The vast dimensions of country houses? The number of slaves of every nationality? The masses of silver and gold? The marvels in bronze and painting? The apparel worn indiscriminately by both sexes, or that peculiar luxury of women which, for the sake of jewels, diverts our wealth to strange or hostile nations?

54. I am not unaware that people at entertainments and social gatherings condemn all this and demand some restric-

tion. But if a law were to be passed and a penalty imposed, those very same persons will cry out that the State is revolutionised, that ruin is plotted against all our most brilliant fashion, that not a citizen is safe from incrimination. Yet as even bodily disorders of long standing and growth can be checked only by sharp and painful treatment, so the fever of a diseased mind, itself polluted and a pollution to others, can be quenched only by remedies as strong as the passions which inflame it. Of the many laws devised by our ancestors, of the many passed by the Divine Augustus, the first have been forgotten, while his (all the more to our disgrace) have become obsolete through contempt, and this has made luxury bolder than ever. The truth is, that when one craves something not yet forbidden, there is a fear that it may be forbidden; but when people once transgress prohibitions with impunity, there is no longer any fear or any shame.

Why then in old times was economy in the ascendant? Because every one practised self-control; because we were all members of one city. Nor even afterwards had we the same temptations, while our dominion was confined to Italy. Victories over the foreigner taught us how to waste the substance of others; victories over ourselves, how to squander our own. What a paltry matter is this of which the ædiles are reminding us! What a mere trifle if you look at everything else! No one represents to the Senate that Italy requires supplies from abroad, and that the very existence of the people of Rome is daily at the mercy of uncertain waves and storms. And unless masters, slaves, and estates have the resources of the provinces as their mainstay, our shrubberies, forsooth, and our country houses will have to support us.

Such, Senators, are the anxieties which the prince has to sustain, and the neglect of them will be utter ruin to the State. The cure for other evils must be sought in our own hearts. Let us be led to amendment, the poor by constraint, the rich by satiety. Or if any of our officials give promise of such energy and strictness as can stem the corruption, I praise the man, and I confess that I am relieved of a portion of my burdens. But if they wish to denounce vice, and when they have gained credit for so doing they arouse resentments and leave them to me, be assured, Senators, that I too am by no means eager to incur enmities, and though for the public good I encounter formidable and often unjust enmities, yet I have a right to decline such as are unmeaning and purposeless and will be of use neither to myself nor to you.

55. When they had heard the emperor's letter, the ædiles were excused from so anxious a task, and that luxury of the table which from the close of the war ended at Actium to the armed revolution in which Servius Galba rose to empire, had been practised with profuse expenditure, gradually went out of fashion. It is as well that I should trace the causes of this change.

Formerly rich or highly distinguished noble families often sank into ruin from a passion for splendour. Even then men were still at liberty to court and be courted by the city populace, by our allies and by foreign princes, and every one who from his wealth, his mansion and his establishment was conspicuously grand, gained too proportionate lustre by his name and his numerous *clientèle*. After the savage massacres in which greatness of renown was fatal, the survivors turned to wiser ways. The new men who were often admitted into the Senate from the towns, colonies and even the provinces, introduced their household thrift, and though many of them by good luck or energy attained an old age of wealth, still their former tastes remained. But the chief encourager of strict manners was Vespasian, himself old-fashioned both in his dress and diet. Henceforth a respectful feeling towards the prince and a love of emulation proved more efficacious than legal penalties or terrors. Or possibly there is in all things a kind of cycle, and there may be moral revolutions just as there are changes of seasons. Nor was everything better in the past, but our own age too has produced many specimens of excellence and culture for posterity to imitate. May we still keep up with our ancestors a rivalry in all that is honourable!

56. Tiberius having gained credit for forbearance by the check he had given to the growing terror of the informers, wrote a letter to the Senate, requesting the tribunitian power for Drusus. This was a phrase which Augustus devised as a designation of supremacy, so that without assuming the

name of king or dictator he might have some title to mark
his elevation above all other authority. He then chose Marcus Agrippa to be his associate in this power, and on Agrippa's death, Tiberius Nero, that there might be no uncertainty as to the succession. In this manner he thought to
check the perverse ambition of others, while he had confidence in Nero's moderation and in his own greatness.

Following this precedent, Tiberius now placed Drusus next
to the throne, though while Germanicus was alive he had
maintained an impartial attitude towards the two princes.
However in the beginning of his letter he implored heaven to
prosper his plans on behalf of the State, and then added a
few remarks, without falsehood or exaggeration, on the character of the young prince. He had, he reminded them, a wife
and three children, and his age was the same as that at
which he had himself been formerly summoned by the Divine Augustus to undertake this duty. Nor was it a precipitate step; it was only after an experience of eight years,
after having quelled mutinies and settled wars, after a triumph and two consulships, that he was adopted as a partner
in trials already familiar to him.

57. The senators had anticipated this message and hence
their flattery was the more elaborate. But they could devise
nothing but voting statues of the two princes, shrines to
certain deities, temples, arches and the usual routine, except
that Marcus Silanus sought to honour the princes by a slur
on the consulate, and proposed that on all monuments, public or private, should be inscribed, to mark the date, the
names, not of the consuls, but of those who were holding the
tribunitian power. Quintus Haterius, when he brought forward a motion that the decrees passed that day should be
set up in the Senate House in letters of gold, was laughed at
as an old dotard, who would get nothing but infamy out of
such utterly loathsome sycophancy.

58. Meantime Junius Blæsus received an extension of his
government of Africa, and Servius Maluginensis, the priest
of Jupiter, demanded to have Asia allotted to him. "It was,"
he asserted, "a popular error that it was not lawful for the
priests of Jupiter to leave Italy; in fact, his own legal position differed not from that of the priests of Mars and of

Quirinus. If these latter had provinces allotted to them, why
was it forbidden to the priests of Jupiter? There were no
resolutions of the people or anything to be found in the
books of ceremonies on the subject. Pontiffs had often performed the rites to Jupiter when his priest was hindered by
illness or by public duty. For seventy-five years after the
suicide of Cornelius Merula no successor to his office had
been appointed; yet religious rites had not ceased. If during so many years it was possible for there to be no appointment without any prejudice to religion, with what comparative ease might he be absent for one year's proconsulate?
That these priests in former days were prohibited by the
pontiffs from going into the provinces, was the result of
private feuds. Now, thank heaven, the supreme pontiff was
also the supreme man, and was influenced by no rivalry,
hatred or personal feeling."

59. As the augur Lentulus and others argued on various
grounds against this view, the result was that they awaited
the decision of the supreme pontiff. Tiberius deferred any
investigation into the priest's legal position, but he modified
the ceremonies which had been decreed in honour of Drusus's tribunitian power with special censure on the extravagance of the proposed inscription in gold, so contrary to
national usage. Letters also from Drusus were read, which,
though studiously modest in expression, were taken to be
extremely supercilious. "We have fallen so low," people said,
"that even a mere youth who has received so high an honour
does not go as a worshipper to the city's gods, does not enter
the Senate, does not so much as take the auspices on his
country's soil. There is a war, forsooth, or he is kept from
us in some remote part of the world. Why, at this very moment, he is on a tour amid the shores and lakes of Campania. Such is the training of the future ruler of mankind;
such the lesson he first learns from his father's counsels. An
aged emperor may indeed shrink from the citizen's gaze,
and plead the weariness of declining years and the toils of
the past. But, as for Drusus, what can be his hindrance but
pride?"

60. Tiberius meantime, while securing to himself the substance of imperial power, allowed the Senate some shadow of

its old constitution by referring to its investigation certain demands of the provinces. In the Greek cities license and impunity in establishing sanctuaries were on the increase. Temples were thronged with the vilest of the slaves; the same refuge screened the debtor against his creditor, as well as men suspected of capital offences. No authority was strong enough to check the turbulence of a people which protected the crimes of men as much as the worship of the gods.

It was accordingly decided that the different states were to send their charters and envoys to Rome. Some voluntarily relinquished privileges which they had groundlessly usurped; many trusted to old superstitions, or to their services to the Roman people. It was a grand spectacle on that day, when the Senate examined grants made by our ancestors, treaties with allies, even decrees of kings who had flourished before Rome's ascendancy, and the forms of worship of the very deities, with full liberty as in former days, to ratify or to alter.

61. First of all came the people of Ephesus. They declared that Diana and Apollo were not born at Delos, as was the vulgar belief. They had in their own country a river Cenchrius, a grove Ortygia, where Latona, as she leaned in the pangs of labour on an olive still standing, gave birth to those two deities, whereupon the grove at the divine intimation was consecrated. There Apollo himself, after the slaughter of the Cyclops, shunned the wrath of Jupiter; there too father Bacchus, when victorious in war, pardoned the suppliant Amazons who had gathered round the shrine. Subsequently by the permission of Hercules, when he was subduing Lydia, the grandeur of the temple's ceremonial was augmented, and during the Persian rule its privileges were not curtailed. They had afterwards been maintained by the Macedonians, then by ourselves.

62. Next the people of Magnesia relied on arrangements made by Lucius Scipio and Lucius Sulla. These generals, after respectively defeating Antiochus and Mithridates, honoured the fidelity and courage of the Magnesians by allowing the temple of Diana of the White Brow to be an inviolable sanctuary. Then the people of Aphrodisia produced a decree of the dictator Cæsar for their old services to his

party, and those of Stratonicea, one lately passed by the Divine Augustus, in which they were commended for having endured the Parthian invasion without wavering in their loyalty to the Roman people. Aphrodisia maintained the worship of Venus; Stratonicea, that of Jupiter and of Diana of the Cross Ways.

Hierocæsarea went back to a higher antiquity, and spoke of having a Persian Diana, whose fane was consecrated in the reign of Cyrus. They quoted too the names of Perperna, Isauricus, and many other generals who had conceded the same sacred character not only to the temple but to its precincts for two miles. Then came the Cyprians on behalf of three shrines, the oldest of which had been set up by their founder Aërias to the Paphian Venus, the second by his son Amathus to Venus of Amathus, and the last to Jupiter of Salamis, by Teucer when he fled from the wrath of his father Telamon.

63. Audience was also given to embassies from other states. The senators wearied by their multiplicity and seeing the party spirit that was being roused, intrusted the inquiry to the consuls, who were to sift each title and see if it involved any abuse, and then refer back the entire matter to the Senate. Besides the states already mentioned, the consuls reported that they had ascertained that at Pergamus there was a sanctuary of Æsculapius, but that the rest relied on an origin lost in the obscurity of antiquity. For example, the people of Smyrna quoted an oracle of Apollo, which had commanded them to dedicate a temple to Venus Stratonicis; and the islanders of Tenos, an utterance from the same deity, bidding them consecrate a statue and a fane to Neptune. Sardis preferred a more modern claim, a grant from the victorious Alexander. So again Miletus relied on king Darius. But in each case their religious worship was that of Diana or Apollo. The Cretans too demanded a like privilege for a statue of the Divine Augustus. Decrees of the Senate were passed, which though very respectful, still prescribed certain limits, and the petitioners were directed to set up bronze tablets in each temple, to be a sacred memorial and to restrain them from sinking into selfish aims under the mask of religion.

64. About this time Julia Augusta had an alarming ill-ness, which compelled the emperor to hasten his return to Rome, for hitherto there had been a genuine harmony between the mother and son, or a hatred well concealed. Not long before, for instance, Julia in dedicating a statue to the Divine Augustus near the theatre of Marcellus had inscribed the name of Tiberius below her own, and it was surmised that the emperor, regarding this as a slight on a sovereign's dignity, had brooded over it with deep and disguised resentment. However the Senate now decreed supplications to the gods and the celebration of the Great Games, which were to be exhibited by the pontiffs, augurs, the colleges of the Fifteen and of the Seven, with the Augustal Brotherhood. Lucius Apronius moved that the heralds too should preside over these Games. This the emperor opposed, distinguishing the peculiar privileges of the sacred guilds, and quoting precedents. Never, he argued, had the heralds this dignity. "The Augustal priests were included expressly because their sacred office was specially attached to the family for which vows were being performed."

65. My purpose is not to relate at length every motion, but only such as were conspicuous for excellence or notorious for infamy. This I regard as history's highest function, to let no worthy action be uncommemorated, and to hold out the reprobation of posterity as a terror to evil words and deeds. So corrupted indeed and debased was that age by sycophancy that not only the foremost citizens who were forced to save their grandeur by servility, but every ex-consul, most of the ex-prætors and a host of inferior senators would rise in eager rivalry to propose shameful and preposterous motions. Tradition says that Tiberius as often as he left the Senate-House used to exclaim in Greek, "How ready these men are to be slaves." Clearly, even he, with his dislike of public freedom, was disgusted at the abject abasement of his creatures.

66. From unseemly flatteries they passed by degrees to savage acts. Caius Silanus, pro-consul of Asia, was accused by our allies of extortion; whereupon Mamercus Scaurus, an ex-consul, Junius Otho, a prætor, Brutidius Niger, an ædile, simultaneously fastened on him and charged him with sacri-

lege to the divinity of Augustus, and contempt of the majesty of Tiberius, while Mamercus Scaurus quoted old precedents, the prosecutions of Lucius Cotta by Scipio Africanus, of Servius Galba by Cato the Censor and of Publius Rutilius by Scaurus. As if indeed Scipio's and Cato's vengeance fell on such offences, or that of the famous Scaurus, whom his great grandson, a blot on his ancestry, this Mamercus was now disgracing by his infamous occupation. Junius Otho's old employment had been the keeping of a preparatory school. Subsequently, becoming a senator by the influence of Sejanus, he shamed his origin, low as it was, by his unblushing effronteries. Brutidius who was rich in excellent accomplishments, and was sure, had he pursued a path of virtue, to reach the most brilliant distinction, was goaded on by an eager impatience, while he strove to outstrip his equals, then his superiors, and at last even his own aspirations. Many have thus perished, even good men, despising slow and safe success and hurrying on even at the cost of ruin to premature greatness.

67. Gellius Publicola and Marcus Paconius, respectively quæstor and lieutenant of Silanus, swelled the number of the accusers. No doubt was felt as to the defendant's conviction for oppression and extortion, but there was a combination against him, that must have been perilous even to an innocent man. Besides a host of adverse Senators there were the most accomplished orators of all Asia, who, as such, had been retained for the prosecution, and to these he had to reply alone, without any experience in pleading, and under that personal apprehension which is enough to paralyse even the most practised eloquence. For Tiberius did not refrain from pressing him with angry voice and look, himself putting incessant questions, without allowing him to rebut or evade them, and he had often even to make admissions, that the questions might not have been asked in vain. His slaves too were sold by auction to the state-agent, to be examined by torture. And that not a friend might help him in his danger, charges of treason were added, a binding guarantee for sealed lips. Accordingly he begged a few days' respite, and at last abandoned his defence, after venturing

on a memorial to the emperor, in which he mingled reproach and entreaty.

68. Tiberius, that his proceedings against Silanus might find some justification in precedent, ordered the Divine Augustus's indictment of Volesus Messala, also a proconsul of Asia, and the Senate's sentence on him to be read. He then asked Lucius Piso his opinion. After a long preliminary eulogy on the prince's clemency, Piso pronounced that Silanus ought to be outlawed and banished to the island of Gyarus. The rest concurred, with the exception of Cneius Lentulus, who, with the assent of Tiberius, proposed that the property of Silanus's mother, as she was very different from him, should be exempted from confiscation, and given to the son.

69. Cornelius Dolabella however, by way of carrying flattery yet further, sharply censured the morals of Silanus, and then moved that no one of disgraceful life and notorious infamy should be eligible for a province, and that of this the emperor should be judge. "Laws, indeed," he said, "punish crimes committed; but how much more merciful would it be to individuals, how much better for our allies, to provide against their commission."

The emperor opposed the motion. "Although," he said, "I am not ignorant of the reports about Silanus, still we must decide nothing by hearsay. Many a man has behaved in a province quite otherwise than was hoped or feared of him. Some are roused to higher things by great responsibility; others are paralysed by it. It is not possible for a prince's knowledge to embrace everything, and it is not expedient that he should be exposed to the ambitious schemings of others. Laws are ordained to meet facts, inasmuch as the future is uncertain. It was the rule of our ancestors that, whenever there was first an offence, some penalty should follow. Let us not revolutionise a wisely devised and ever approved system. Princes have enough burdens, and also enough power. Rights are invariably abridged, as despotism increases; nor ought we to fall back on imperial authority, when we can have recourse to the laws."

Such constitutional sentiments were so rare with Tiberius, that they were welcomed with all the heartier joy. Knowing, as he did, how to be forbearing, when he was not under the stimulus of personal resentment, he further said that Gyarus was a dreary and uninhabited island, and that, as a concession to the Junian family and to a man of the same order as themselves, they might let him retire by preference to Cythnus. This, he added, was also the request of Torquata, Silanus's sister, a vestal of primitive purity. The motion was carried after a division.

70. Audience was next given to the people of Cyrene, and on the prosecution of Ancharius Priscus, Cæsius Cordus was convicted of extortion. Lucius Ennius, a Roman knight, was accused of treason, for having converted a statue of the emperor to the common use of silver plate; but the emperor forbade his being put upon his trial, though Ateius Capito openly remonstrated, with a show of independence. "The Senate," he said, "ought not to have wrested from it the power of deciding a question, and such a crime must not go unpunished. Granted that the emperor might be indifferent to a personal grievance, still he should not be generous in the case of wrongs to the commonwealth." Tiberius interpreted the remark according to its drift rather than its mere expression, and persisted in his veto. Capito's disgrace was the more conspicuous, for, versed as he was in the science of law, human and divine, he had now dishonoured a brilliant public career as well as a virtuous private life.

71. Next came a religious question, as to the temple in which ought to be deposited the offering which the Roman knights had vowed to Fortune of the Knights for the recovery of Augusta. Although that Goddess had several shrines in Rome, there was none with this special designation. It was ascertained that there was a temple so called at Antium, and that all sacred rites in the towns of Italy as well as temples and images of deities were under the jurisdiction and authority of Rome. Accordingly the offering was placed at Antium.

As religious questions were under discussion, the emperor now produced his answer to Servius Maluginensis, Jupiter's priest, which he had recently deferred, and read the pontifical decree, prescribing that whenever illness attacked a priest of Jupiter, he might, with the supreme pontiff's permission, be absent more than two nights, provided it was not during the days of public sacrifice or more than twice in the same year. This regulation of the emperor Augustus sufficiently proved that a year's absence and a provincial government were not permitted to the priests of Jupiter. There was also cited the precedent of Lucius Metellus, supreme pontiff, who had detained at Rome the priest Aulus Postumius. And so Asia was allotted to the ex-consul next in seniority to Maluginensis.

72. About the same time Lepidus asked the Senate's leave to restore and embellish, at his own expense, the basilica of Paulus, that monument of the Æmilian family. Public-spirited munificence was still in fashion, and Augustus had not hindered Taurus, Philippus, or Balbus from applying the spoils of war or their superfluous wealth to adorn the capital and to win the admiration of posterity. Following these examples, Lepidus, though possessed of a moderate fortune, now revived the glory of his ancestors.

Pompeius's theatre, which had been destroyed by an accidental fire, the emperor promised to rebuild, simply because no member of the family was equal to restoring it, but Pompeius's name was to be retained. At the same time he highly extolled Sejanus on the ground that it was through his exertions and vigilance that such fury of the flames had been confined to the destruction of a single building. The Senate voted Sejanus a statue, which was to be placed in Pompeius's theatre. And soon afterwards the emperor in honouring Junius Blæsus, proconsul of Africa, with triumphal distinctions, said that he granted them as a compliment to Sejanus, whose uncle Blæsus was.

73. Still the career of Blæsus merited such a reward. For Tacfarinas, through often driven back, had recruited his resources in the interior of Africa, and had become so insolent as to send envoys to Tiberius, actually demanding a settlement for himself and his army, or else threatening us with an interminable war. Never, it is said, was the emperor so exasperated by an insult to himself and the Roman people as by a deserter and brigand assuming the character of a belligerent. "Even Spartacus when he had destroyed so many consular armies and was burning Italy with impunity,

though the State was staggering under the tremendous wars
of Sertorius and Mithridates, had not the offer of an honourable surrender on stipulated conditions; far less, in Rome's
most glorious height of power, should a robber like Tacfarinas be bought off by peace and concessions of territory."
He intrusted the affair to Blæsus, who was to hold out to
the other rebels the prospect of laying down their arms without hurt to themselves, while he was by any means to secure
the person of the chief. Many surrendered themselves on the
strength of this amnesty. Before long the tactics of Tacfarinas were encountered in a similar fashion.

74. Unequal to us in solid military strength, but better in
a war of surprises, he would attack, would elude pursuit, and
still arrange ambuscades with a multitude of detachments.
And so we prepared three expeditions and as many columns.
One of the three under the command of Cornelius Scipio,
Blæsus's lieutenant, was to stop the enemy's forays on the
Leptitani and his retreat to the Garamantes. In another
quarter, Blæsus's son led a separate force of his own, to save
the villages of Cirta from being ravaged with impunity. Between the two was the general himself with some picked
troops. By establishing redoubts and fortified lines in commanding positions, he had rendered the whole country embarrassing and perilous to the foe, for, whichever way he
turned, a body of Roman soldiers was in his face, or on his
flank, or frequently in the rear. Many were thus slain or
surprised.

Blæsus then further divided his triple army into several
detachments under the command of centurions of tried
valour. At the end of the summer he did not, as was usual,
withdraw his troops and let them rest in winter-quarters in
the old province; but, forming a chain of forts, as though he
were on the threshold of a campaign, he drove Tacfarinas by
flying columns well acquainted with the desert, from one set
of huts to another, till he captured the chief's brother, and
then returned, too soon however for the welfare of our allies,
as there yet remained those who might renew hostilities.

Tiberius however considered the war as finished, and
awarded Blæsus the further distinction of being hailed "Imperator" by the legions, an ancient honour conferred on gen-

erals who for good service to the State were saluted with cheers of joyful enthusiasm by a victorious army. Several men bore the title at the same time, without pre-eminence above their fellows. Augustus too granted the name to certain persons; and now, for the last time, Tiberius gave it to Blæsus.

75. Two illustrious men died that year. One was Asinius Saloninus, distinguished as the grandson of Marcus Agrippa, and Asinius Pollio, as the brother of Drusus and the intended husband of the emperor's granddaughter. The other was Capito Ateius, already mentioned, who had won a foremost position in the State by his legal attainments, though his grandfather was but a centurion in Sulla's army, his father having been a prætor. He was prematurely advanced to the consulship by Augustus, so that he might be raised by the honour of this promotion above Labeo Antistius, a conspicuous member of the same profession. That age indeed produced at one time two brilliant ornaments of peace. But while Labeo was a man of sturdy independence and consequently of wider fame, Capito's obsequiousness was more acceptable to those in power. Labeo, because his promotion was confined to the prætorship, gained in public favour through the wrong; Capito, in obtaining the consulship, incurred the hatred which grows out of envy.

76. Junia too, the niece of Cato, wife of Caius Cassius and sister of Marcus Brutus, died this year, the sixty-fourth after the battle of Philippi. Her will was the theme of much popular criticism, for, with her vast wealth, after having honourably mentioned almost every nobleman by name, she passed over the emperor. Tiberius took the omission graciously, and did not forbid a panegyric before the Rostra with the other customary funeral honours. The busts of twenty most illustrious families were borne in the procession, with the names of Manlius, Quinctius, and others of equal rank. But Cassius and Brutus outshone them all, from the very fact that their likenesses were not to be seen.

BOOK IV

A.D. 23—28

1. THE year when Caius Asinius and Caius Antistius were consuls was the ninth of Tiberius's reign, a period of tranquillity for the State and prosperity for his own house, for he counted Germanicus's death a happy incident. Suddenly fortune deranged everything; the emperor became a cruel tyrant, as well as an abettor of cruelty in others. Of this the cause and origin was Ælius Sejanus, commander of the prætorian cohorts, of whose influence I have already spoken. I will now fully describe his extraction, his character, and the daring wickedness by which he grasped at power.

Born at Vulsinii, the son of Seius Strabo, a Roman knight, he attached himself in his early youth to Caius Cæsar, grandson of the Divine Augustus, and the story went that he had sold his person to Apicius, a rich debauchee. Soon afterwards he won the heart of Tiberius so effectually by various artifices that the emperor, ever dark and mysterious towards others, was with Sejanus alone careless and freespoken. It was not through his craft, for it was by this very weapon that he was overthrown; it was rather from heaven's wrath against Rome, to whose welfare his elevation and his fall were alike disastrous. He had a body which could endure hardships, and a daring spirit. He was one who screened himself, while he was attacking others; he was as cringing as he was imperious; before the world he affected humility; in his heart he lusted after supremacy, for the sake of which he was sometimes lavish and luxurious, but oftener energetic and watchful, qualities quite as mischievous when hypocritically assumed for the attainment of sovereignty.

2. He strengthened the hitherto moderate powers of his office by concentrating the cohorts scattered throughout the capital into one camp, so that they might all receive orders

at the same moment, and that the sight of their numbers and strength might give confidence to themselves, while it would strike terror into the citizens. His pretexts were the demoralisation incident to a dispersed soldiery, the greater effectiveness of simultaneous action in the event of a sudden peril, and the stricter discipline which would be insured by the establishment of an encampment at a distance from the temptations of the city. As soon as the camp was completed, he crept gradually into the affections of the soldiers by mixing with them and addressing them by name, himself selecting the centurions and tribunes. With the Senate too he sought to ingratiate himself, distinguishing his partisans with offices and provinces, Tiberius readily yielding, and being so biassed that not only in private conversation but before the senators and the people he spoke highly of him as the partner of his toils, and allowed his statues to be honoured in theatres, in forums, and at the head-quarters of our legions.

3. There were however obstacles to his ambition in the imperial house with its many princes, a son in youthful manhood and grown-up grandsons. As it would be unsafe to sweep off such a number at once by violence, while craft would necessitate successive intervals in crime, he chose, on the whole, the stealthier way, and to begin with Drusus, against whom he had the stimulus of a recent resentment. Drusus, who could not brook a rival and was somewhat irascible, had, in a casual dispute, raised his fist at Sejanus, and, when he defended himself, had struck him in the face. On considering every plan, Sejanus thought his easiest revenge was to turn his attention to Livia, Drusus's wife. She was a sister of Germanicus, and though she was not handsome as a girl, she became a woman of surpassing beauty. Pretending an ardent passion for her, he seduced her, and having won his first infamous triumph, and assured that a woman after having parted with her virtue will hesitate at nothing, he lured her on to thoughts of marriage, of a share in sovereignty, and of her husband's destruction. And she, the niece of Augustus, the daughter-in-law of Tiberius, the mother of children by Drusus, for a provincial paramour, foully disgraced herself, her ancestors, and her descendants,

giving up honour and a sure position for prospects as base as they were uncertain. They took into their confidence Eudemus, Livia's friend and physician, whose profession was a pretext for frequent secret interviews. Sejanus, to avert his mistress's jealousy, divorced his wife Apicata, by whom he had had three children. Still the magnitude of the crime caused fear and delay, and sometimes a conflict of plans.

4. Meanwhile, at the beginning of this year, Drusus, one of the children of Germanicus, assumed the dress of manhood, with a repetition of the honours decreed by the Senate to his brother Nero. The emperor added a speech, with warm praise of his son for sharing a father's affection to his brother's children. Drusus indeed, difficult as it is for power and mutual harmony to exist side by side, had the character of being kindly disposed or at least not unfriendly towards the lads. And now the old plan, so often insincerely broached, of a progress through the provinces, was again discussed. The emperor's pretext was the number of veterans on the eve of discharge and the necessity of fresh levies for the army. Volunteers were not forthcoming, and even if they were sufficiently numerous, they had not the same bravery and discipline, as it is chiefly the needy and the homeless who adopt by their own choice a soldier's life. Tiberius also rapidly enumerated the legions and the provinces which they had to garrison. I too ought, I think, to go through these details, and thus show what forces Rome then had under arms, what kings were our allies, and how much narrower then were the limits of our empire.

5. Italy on both seas was guarded by fleets, at Misenum and at Ravenna, and the contiguous coast of Gaul by ships of war captured in the victory of Actium, and sent by Augustus powerfully manned to the town of Forojulium. But our chief strength was on the Rhine, as a defence alike against Germans and Gauls, and numbered eight legions. Spain, lately subjugated, was held by three. Mauretania was king Juba's, who had received it as a gift from the Roman people. The rest of Africa was garrisoned by two legions, and Egypt by the same number. Next, beginning with Syria, all within the entire tract of country stretching as far as the Euphrates, was kept in restraint by four legions, and on this

frontier were Iberian, Albanian, and other kings, to whom
our greatness was a protection against any foreign power.
Thrace was held by Rhœmetalces and the children of Cotys;
the bank of the Danube by two legions in Pannonia, two in
Mœsia, and two also were stationed in Dalmatia, which,
from the situation of the country, were in the rear of the
other four, and, should Italy suddenly require aid, not too
distant to be summoned. But the capital was garrisoned by
its own special soldiery, three city, nine prætorian cohorts,
levied for the most part in Etruria and Umbria, or ancient
Latium and the old Roman colonies. There were besides, in
commanding positions in the provinces, allied fleets, cavalry
and light infantry, of but little inferior strength. But any
detailed account of them would be misleading, since they
moved from place to place as circumstances required, and
had their numbers increased and sometimes diminished.

6. It is however, I think, a convenient opportunity for me
to review the hitherto prevailing methods of administration
in the other departments of the State, inasmuch as that year
brought with it the beginning of a change for the worse in
Tiberius's policy. In the first place, public business and the
most important private matters were managed by the Senate: the leading men were allowed freedom of discussion,
and when they stooped to flattery, the emperor himself
checked them. He bestowed honours with regard to noble
ancestry, military renown, or brilliant accomplishments as a
civilian, letting it be clearly seen that there were no better
men to choose. The consul and the prætor retained their
prestige; inferior magistrates exercised their authority; the
laws too, with the single exception of cases of treason, were
properly enforced.

As to the duties on corn, the indirect taxes and other
branches of the public revenue, they were in the hands of
companies of Roman knights. The emperor intrusted his own
property to men of the most tried integrity or to persons
known only by their general reputation, and once appointed
they were retained without any limitation, so that most of
them grew old in the same employments. The city populace
indeed suffered much from high prices, but this was no fault
of the emperor, who actually endeavoured to counteract bar-

ren soils and stormy seas with every resource of wealth and foresight. And he was also careful not to distress the provinces by new burdens, and to see that in bearing the old they were safe from any rapacity or oppression on the part of governors. Corporal punishments and confiscations of property were unknown.

7. The emperor had only a few estates in Italy, slaves on a moderate scale, and his household was confined to a few freedmen. If ever he had a dispute with a private person, it was decided in the law courts. All this, not indeed with any graciousness, but in a blunt fashion which often alarmed, he still kept up, until the death of Drusus changed everything. While he lived, the system continued, because Sejanus, as yet only in the beginning of his power, wished to be known as an upright counsellor, and there was one whose vengeance he dreaded, who did not conceal his hatred and incessantly complained "that a stranger was invited to assist in the government while the emperor's son was alive. How near was the step of declaring the stranger a colleague! Ambition at first had a steep path before it; when once the way had been entered, zealous adherents were forthcoming. Already, at the pleasure of the commander of the guards, a camp had been established; the soldiers were given into his hands; his statues were to be seen among the monuments of Cneius Pompeius; his grandsons would be of the same blood as the family of the Drusi. Henceforth they must pray that he might have self-control, and so be contented." So would Drusus talk, not unfrequently, or only in the hearing of a few persons. Even his confidences, now that his wife had been corrupted, were betrayed.

8. Sejanus accordingly thought that he must be prompt, and chose a poison the gradual working of which might be mistaken for a natural disorder. It was given to Drusus by Lygdus, a eunuch, as was ascertained eight years later. As for Tiberius, he went to the Senate house during the whole time of the prince's illness, either because he was not afraid, or to show his strength of mind, and even in the interval between his death and funeral. Seeing the consuls, in token of their grief, sitting on the ordinary benches, he reminded them of their high office and of their proper place; and when

the Senate burst into tears, suppressing a groan, he revived their spirits with a fluent speech. "He knew indeed that he might be reproached for thus encountering the gaze of the Senate after so recent an affliction. Most mourners could hardly bear even the soothing words of kinsfolk or to look on the light of day. And such were not to be condemned as weak. But he had sought a more manly consolation in the bosom of the commonwealth."

Then deploring the extreme age of Augusta, the childhood of his grandsons, and his own declining years, he begged the Senate to summon Germanicus's children, the only comfort under their present misery. The consuls went out, and having encouraged the young princes with kind words, brought them in and presented them to the emperor. Taking them by the hand he said: "Senators, when these boys lost their father, I committed them to their uncle, and begged him, though he had children of his own, to cherish and rear them as his own offspring, and train them for himself and for posterity. Drusus is now lost to us, and I turn my prayers to you, and before heaven and your country I adjure you to receive into your care and guidance the great-grandsons of Augustus, descendants of a most noble ancestry. So fulfil your duty and mine. To you, Nero and Drusus, these senators are as fathers. Such is your birth that your prosperity and adversity must alike affect the State."

9. There was great weeping at these words, and then many a benediction. Had the emperor set bounds to his speech, he must have filled the hearts of his hearers with sympathy and admiration. But he now fell back on those idle and often ridiculed professions about restoring the republic, and the wish that the consuls or some one else might undertake the government, and thus destroyed belief even in what was genuine and noble.

The same honours were decreed to the memory of Drusus as to that of Germanicus, and many more were added. Such is the way with flattery, when repeated. The funeral with its procession of statues was singularly grand. Aeneas, the father of the Julian house, all the Alban kings, Romulus, Rome's founder, then the Sabine nobility, Attus Clausus, and the busts of all the other Claudii were displayed in a long train.

10. In relating the death of Drusus I have followed the narrative of most of the best historians. But I would not pass over a rumour of the time, the strength of which is not even yet exhausted. Sejanus, it is said, having seduced Livia into crime, next secured, by the foulest means, the consent of Lygdus, the eunuch, as from his youth and beauty he was his master's favourite, and one of his principal attendants. When those who were in the secret had decided on the time and place of the poisoning, Sejanus, with the most consummate daring, reversed his plan, and, whispering an accusation against Drusus of intending to poison his father, warned Tiberius to avoid the first draught offered him as he was dining at his son's house. Thus deceived, the old emperor, on sitting down to the banquet, took the cup and handed it to Drusus. His suspicions were increased when Drusus, in perfect unconsciousness, drank it off with youthful eagerness, apparently, out of fear and shame, bringing on himself the death which he had plotted against his father.

11. These popular rumours, over and above the fact that they are not vouched for by any good writer, may be instantly refuted. For who, with moderate prudence, far less Tiberius with his great experience, would have thrust destruction on a son, without even hearing him, with his own hand too, and with an impossibility of returning to better thoughts. Surely he would rather have had the slave who handed the poison, tortured, have sought to discover the traitor, in short, would have been as hesitating and tardy in the case of an only son hitherto unconvicted of any crime, as he was naturally even with strangers. But as Sejanus had the credit of contriving every sort of wickedness, the fact that he was the emperor's special favourite, and that both were hated by the rest of the world, procured belief for any monstrous fiction, and rumour too always has a dreadful side in regard to the deaths of men in power. Besides, the whole process of the crime was betrayed by Apicata, Sejanus's wife, and fully divulged, under torture, by Eudemus and Lygdus. No writer has been found sufficiently malignant to fix the guilt on Tiberius, though every circumstance was

scrutinized and exaggerated. My object in mentioning and refuting this story is, by a conspicuous example, to put down hearsay, and to request all into whose hands my work shall come, not to catch eagerly at wild and improbable rumours in preference to genuine history which has not been perverted into romance.

12. Tiberius pronounced a panegyric on his son before the Rostra, during which the Senate and people, in appearance rather than in heart, put on the expression and accents of sorrow, while they inwardly rejoiced at the brightening future of the family of Germanicus. This beginning of popularity and the ill-concealed ambition of their mother Agrippina, hastened its downfall. Sejanus when he saw that the death of Drusus was not avenged on the murderers and was no grief to the people, grew bold in wickedness, and, now that his first attempt had succeeded, speculated on the possibility of destroying the children of Germanicus, whose succession to the throne was a certainty. There were three, and poison could not be distributed among them, because of the singular fidelity of their guardians and the unassailable virtue of Agrippina. So Sejanus inveighed against Agrippina's arrogance, and worked powerfully on Augusta's old hatred of her and on Livia's consciousness of recent guilt, and urged both these women to represent to the emperor that her pride as a mother and her reliance on popular enthusiasm were leading her to dream of empire. Livia availed herself of the cunning of accusers, among whom she had selected Julius Postumus, a man well suited to her purpose, as he had an intrigue with Mutilia Prisca, and was consequently in the confidence of Augusta, over whose mind Prisca had great influence. She thus made her aged grandmother, whose nature it was to tremble for her power, irreconcilably hostile to her grandson's widow. Agrippina's friends too were induced to be always inciting her proud spirit by mischievous talk.

13. Tiberius meanwhile, who did not relax his attention to business, and found solace in his work, occupied himself with the causes of citizens at Rome and with petitions from allies. Decrees of the Senate were passed at his proposal for relieving the cities of Cibyra and Ægium in Asia and Achaia,

which had suffered from earthquakes, by a remission of three years' tribute. Vibius Serenus too, proconsul of Further Spain, was condemned for violence in his official capacity, and was banished to the island of Amorgus for his savage temper. Carsidius Sacerdos, accused of having helped our enemy Tacfarinas with supplies of grain, was acquitted, as was also Caius Gracchus on the same charge. Gracchus's father, Sempronius, had taken him when a mere child to the island of Cercina to be his companion in exile. There he grew up among outcasts who knew nothing of a liberal education, and after a while supported himself in Africa and Sicily by petty trade. But he did not escape the dangers of high rank. Had not his innocence been protected by Ælius Lamia and Lucius Apronius, successive governors of Africa, the splendid fame of that ill-starred family and the downfall of his father would have dragged him to ruin.

14. This year too brought embassies from the Greek communities. The people of Samos and Cos petitioned for the confirmation of the ancient right of sanctuary for the respective temples of Juno and Æsculapius. The Samians relied on a decree of the Amphictyonic Council, which had the supreme decision of all questions when the Greeks, through the cities they had founded in Asia, had possession of the sea-coast. Cos could boast equal antiquity, and it had an additional claim connected with the place. Roman citizens had been admitted to the temple of Æsculapius, when king Mithridates ordered a general massacre of them throughout all the islands and cities of Asia.

Next, after various and usually fruitless complaints from the prætors, the emperor finally brought forward a motion about the licentious behaviour of the players. "They had often," he said, "sought to disturb the public peace, and to bring disgrace on private families, and the old Oscan farce, once a wretched amusement for the vulgar, had become at once so indecent and so popular, that it must be checked by the Senate's authority." The players, upon this, were banished from Italy.

15. That same year also brought fresh sorrow to the emperor by being fatal to one of the twin sons of Drusus equally too by the death of an intimate friend. This was

Lucilius Longus, the partner of all his griefs and joys, the
only senator who had been the companion of his retirement
in Rhodes. And so, though he was a man of humble origin,
the Senate decreed him a censor's funeral and a statue in
the forum of Augustus at the public expense. Everything indeed was as yet in the hands of the Senate, and consequently
Lucilius Capito, procurator of Asia, who was impeached by
his province, was tried by them, the emperor vehemently asserting "that he had merely given the man authority over
the slaves and property of the imperial establishments; that
if he had taken upon himself the powers of a prætor and
used military force, he had disregarded his instructions;
therefore they must hear the provincials." So the case was
heard and the accused condemned. The cities of Asia, gratified by this retribution and the punishment inflicted in the
previous year on Caius Silanus, voted a temple to Tiberius,
his mother, and the Senate, and were permitted to build it.
Nero thanked the Senators and his grandfather on their behalf, and carried with him the joyful sympathies of his audience, who, with the memory of Germanicus fresh in their
minds, imagined that it was his face they saw, his voice they
heard. The youth too had a modesty and a grace of person
worthy of a prince, the more charming because of his peril
from the notorious enmity of Sejanus.

16. About the same time the emperor spoke on the sub·
ject of electing a priest of Jupiter in the room of Servius
Maluginensis, deceased, and of the enactment of a new law.
"It was," he said, "the old custom to nominate together
three patricians, sons of parents wedded according to the
primitive ceremony, and of these one was to be chosen. Now
however there was not the same choice as formerly, the primitive form of marriage having been given up or being observed only by a few persons." For this he assigned several
reasons, the chief being men's and women's indifference;
then, again, the ceremony itself had its difficulties, which
were purposely avoided; and there was the objection that
the man who obtained this priesthood was emancipated from
the father's authority, as also was his wife, as passing into
the husband's control. So the Senate, Tiberius argued, ought
to apply some remedy by a decree or a law, as Augustus had

accommodated certain relics of a rude antiquity to the modern spirit.

It was then decided, after a discussion of religious questions, that the institution of the priests of Jupiter should remain unchanged. A law however was passed that the priestess, in regard to her sacred functions, was to be under the husband's control, but in other respects to retain the ordinary legal position of women. Maluginensis, the son, was chosen successor to his father. To raise the dignity of the priesthood and to inspire the priests with more zeal in attending to the ceremonial, a gift of two million sesterces was decreed to the Vestal Cornelia, chosen in the room of Scantia; and, whenever Augusta entered the theatre, she was to have a place in the seats of the Vestals.

17. In the consulship of Cornelius Cethegus and Visellius Varro, the pontiffs, whose example was followed by the other priests in offering prayers for the emperor's health, commended also Nero and Drusus to the same deities, not so much out of love for the young princes as out of sycophancy, the absence and excess of which in a corrupt age are alike dangerous. Tiberius indeed, who was never friendly to the house of Germanicus, was then vexed beyond endurance at their youth being honoured equally with his declining years. He summoned the pontiffs, and asked them whether it was to the entreaties or the threats of Agrippina that they had made this concession. And though they gave a flat denial, he rebuked them but gently, for many of them were her own relatives or were leading men in the State. However he addressed a warning to the Senate against encouraging pride in their young and excitable minds by premature honours. For Sejanus spoke vehemently, and charged them with rending the State almost by civil war. "There were those," he said, "who called themselves the party of Agrippina, and, unless they were checked, there would be more; the only remedy for the increasing discord was the overthrow of one or two of the most enterprising leaders."

18. Accordingly he attacked Caius Silius and Titius Sabinus. The friendship of Germanicus was fatal to both. As for Silius, his having commanded a great army for seven years, and won in Germany the distinctions of a triumph for his

success in the war with Sacrovir, would make his downfall all the more tremendous and so spread greater terror among others. Many thought that he had provoked further displeasure by his own presumption and his extravagant boasts that his troops had been steadfastly loyal, while other armies were falling into mutiny, and that Tiberius's throne could not have lasted had his legions too been bent on revolution. All this the emperor regarded as undermining his own power, which seemed to be unequal to the burden of such an obligation. For benefits received are a delight to us as long as we think we can requite them; when that possibility is far exceeded, they are repaid with hatred instead of gratitude.

19. Silius had a wife, Sosia Galla, whose love of Agrippina made her hateful to the emperor. The two, it was decided, were to be attacked, but Sabinus was to be put off for a time. Varro, the consul, was let loose on them, who, under colour of a hereditary feud, humoured the malignity of Sejanus to his own disgrace. The accused begged a brief respite, until the prosecutor's consulship expired, but the emperor opposed the request. "It was usual," he argued, "for magistrates to bring a private citizen to trial, and a consul's authority ought not to be impaired, seeing that it rested with his vigilance to guard the commonwealth from loss." It was characteristic of Tiberius to veil new devices in wickedness under ancient names. And so, with a solemn appeal, he summoned the Senate, as if there were any laws by which Silius was being tried, as if Varro were a real consul, or Rome a commonwealth. The accused either said nothing, or, if he attempted to defend himself, hinted, not obscurely, at the person whose resentment was crushing him. A long concealed complicity in Sacrovir's rebellion, a rapacity which sullied his victory, and his wife Sosia's conduct, were alleged against him. Unquestionably, they could not extricate themselves from the charge of extortion. The whole affair however was conducted as a trial for treason, and Silius forestalled impending doom by a self-inflicted death.

20. Yet there was a merciless confiscation of his property, though not to refund their money to the provincials, none of whom pressed any demand. But Augustus's bounty was wrested from him, and the claims of the imperial exchequer

were computed in detail. This was the first instance on
Tiberius's part of sharp dealing with the wealth of others.
Sosia was banished on the motion of Asinius Gallus, who had
proposed that half her estate should be confiscated, half left
to the children. Marcus Lepidus, on the contrary, was for
giving a fourth to the prosecutors, as the law required, and
the remainder to the children.

This Lepidus, I am satisfied, was for that age a wise and
high-principled man. Many a cruel suggestion made by the
flattery of others he changed for the better, and yet he did
not want tact, seeing that he always enjoyed an uniform
prestige, and also the favour of Tiberius. This compels me
to doubt whether the liking of princes for some men and
their antipathy to others depend, like other contingencies,
on a fate and destiny to which we are born, or, to some degree, on our own plans; so that it is possible to pursue a
course between a defiant independence and a debasing servility, free from ambition and its perils. Messalinus Cotta, of
equally illustrious ancestry as Lepidus, but wholly different
in disposition, proposed that the Senate should pass a decree
providing that even innocent governors who knew nothing
of the delinquencies of others should be punished for their
wives' offences in the provinces as much as for their own.

21. Proceedings were then taken against Calpurnius Piso,
a high-spirited nobleman. He it was, as I have related, who
had exclaimed more than once in the Senate that he would
quit Rome because of the combinations of the informers, and
had dared, in defiance of Augusta's power, to sue Urgulania
and summon her from the emperor's palace. Tiberius submitted to this at the time not ungraciously, but the remembrance of it was vividly impressed on a mind which brooded
over its resentments, even though the first impulse of his displeasure had subsided.

Quintus Granius accused Piso of secret treasonable conversation, and added that he kept poison in his house and
wore a dagger whenever he came into the Senate. This was
passed over as too atrocious to be true. He was to be tried
on the other charges, a multitude of which were heaped on
him, but his timely death cut short the trial.

Next was taken the case of Cassius Severus, an exile. A

man of mean origin and a life of crime, but a powerful pleader, he had brought on himself, by his persistent quarrelsomeness, a decision of the Senate, under oath, which banished him to Crete. There by the same practices he drew on himself, fresh odium and revived the old; stripped of his property and outlawed, he wore out his old age on the rock of Seriphos.

22. About the same time Plautius Silvanus, the prætor, for unknown reasons, threw his wife Apronia out of a window. When summoned before the emperor by Lucius Apronius, his father-in-law, he replied incoherently, representing that he was in a sound sleep and consequently knew nothing, and that his wife had chosen to destroy herself. Without a moment's delay Tiberius went to the house and inspected the chamber, where were seen the marks of her struggling and of her forcible ejection. He reported this to the Senate, and as soon as judges had been appointed, Urgulania, the grandmother of Silvanus, sent her grandson a dagger. This was thought equivalent to a hint from the emperor, because of the known intimacy between Augusta and Urgulania. The accused tried the steel in vain, and then allowed his veins to be opened. Shortly afterwards Numantina, his former wife, was charged with having caused her husband's insanity by magical incantations and potions, but she was acquitted.

23. This year at last released Rome from her long contest with the Numidian Tacfarinas. Former generals, when they thought that their successes were enough to insure them triumphal distinctions, left the enemy to himself. There were now in Rome three laurelled statues, and yet Tacfarinas was still ravaging Africa, strengthened by reinforcements from the Moors, who, under the boyish and careless rule of Ptolemæus, Juba's son, had chosen war in preference to the despotism of freedmen and slaves. He had the king of the Garamantes to receive his plunder and to be the partner of his raids, not indeed with a regular army, but with detachments of light troops whose strength, as they came from a distance, rumour exaggerated. From the province itself every needy and restless adventurer hurried to join him, for the emperor, as if not an enemy remained in Africa after the achievements of Blæsus, had ordered the ninth legion home,

and Publius Dolabella, proconsul that year, had not dared to retain it, because he feared the sovereign's orders more than the risks of war.

24. Tacfarinas accordingly spread rumours that elsewhere also nations were rending the empire of Rome and that therefore her soldiers were gradually retiring from Africa, and that the rest might be cut off by a strong effort on the part of all who loved freedom more than slavery. He thus augmented his force, and having formed a camp, he besieged the town of Thubuscum. Dolabella meanwhile collecting all the troops on the spot, raised the siege at his first approach, by the terror of the Roman name and because the Numidians cannot stand against the charge of infantry. He then fortified suitable positions, and at the same time beheaded some chiefs of the Musulamii, who were on the verge of rebellion. Next, as several expeditions against Tacfarinas had proved the uselessness of following up the enemy's desultory movements with the attack of heavy troops from a single point, he summoned to his aid king Ptolemæus and his people, and equipped four columns, under the command of his lieutenants and tribunes. Marauding parties were also led by picked Moors, Dolabella in person directing every operation.

25. Soon afterwards news came that the Numidians had fixed their tents and encamped near a half-demolished fortress, by name Auzea, to which they had themselves formerly set fire, and on the position of which they relied, as it was inclosed by vast forests. Immediately the light infantry and cavalry, without knowing whither they were being led, were hurried along at quick march. Day dawned, and with the sound of trumpets and fierce shouts, they were on the half-asleep barbarians, whose horses were tethered or roaming over distant pastures. On the Roman side, the infantry was in close array, the cavalry in its squadrons, everything prepared for an engagement, while the enemy, utterly surprised, without arms, order, or plan, were seized slaughtered, or captured like cattle. The infuriated soldiers, remembering their hardships and how often the longed-for conflict had been eluded, sated themselves to a man with vengeance and bloodshed. The word went through the com-

panies that all were to aim at securing Tacfarinas, whom, after so many battles, they knew well, as there would be no rest from war except by the destruction of the enemy's leader. Tacfarinas, his guards slain round him, his son a prisoner, and the Romans bursting on him from every side, rushed on the darts, and by a death which was not unavenged, escaped captivity.

26. This ended the war. Dolabella asked for triumphal distinctions, but was refused by Tiberius, out of compliment to Sejanus, the glory of whose uncle Blæsus he did not wish to be forgotten. But this did not make Blæsus more famous, while the refusal of the honour heightened Dolabella's renown. He had, in fact, with a smaller army, brought back with him illustrious prisoners and the fame of having slain the enemy's leader and terminated the war. In his train were envoys from the Garamantes, a rare spectacle in Rome. The nation, in its terror at the destruction of Tacfarinas, and innocent of any guilty intention, had sent them to crave pardon of the Roman people. And now that this war had proved the zealous loyalty of Ptolemæus, a custom of antiquity was revived, and one of the Senators was sent to present him with an ivory sceptre and an embroidered robe, gifts anciently bestowed by the Senate, and to confer on him the titles of king, ally, and friend.

27. The same summer, the germs of a slave war in Italy were crushed by a fortunate accident. The originator of the movement was Titus Curtisius, once a soldier of the prætorian guard. First, by secret meetings at Brundisium and the neighbouring towns, then by placards publicly exhibited, he incited the rural and savage slave-population of the remote forests to assert their freedom. By divine providence, three vessels came to land for the use of those who traversed that sea. In the same part of the country too was Curtius Lupus, the quæstor, who, according to ancient precedent, had had the charge of the "woodland pastures" assigned to him. Putting in motion a force of marines, he broke up the seditious combination in its very first beginnings. The emperor at once sent Staius, a tribune, with a strong detachment, by whom the ringleader himself, with his most daring followers, were brought prisoners to Rome,

where men already trembled at the vast scale of the slave-establishments, in which there was an immense growth, while the freeborn populace daily decreased.

28. That same consulship witnessed a horrible instance of misery and brutality. A father as defendant, a son as prosecutor, (Vibius Serenus was the name of both) were brought before the Senate; the father, dragged from exile in filth and squalor now stood in irons, while the son pleaded for his guilt. With studious elegance of dress and cheerful looks, the youth, at once accuser and witness, alleged a plot against the emperor and that men had been sent to Gaul to excite rebellion, further adding that Cæcilius Cornutus, an ex-prætor, had furnished money. Cornutus, weary of anxiety and feeling that peril was equivalent to ruin, hastened to destroy himself. But the accused with fearless spirit, looked his son in the face, shook his chains, and appealed to the vengeance of the gods, with a prayer that they would restore him to his exile, where he might live far away from such practices, and that, as for his son, punishment might sooner or later overtake him. He protested too that Cornutus was innocent and that his terror was groundless, as would easily be perceived, if other names were given up; for he never would have plotted the emperor's murder and a revolution with only one confederate.

29. Upon this the prosecutor named Cneius Lentulus and Seius Tubero, to the great confusion of the emperor, at finding a hostile rebellion and disturbance of the public peace charged on two leading men in the state, his own intimate friends, the first of whom was in extreme old age and the second in very feeble health. They were, however, at once acquitted. As for the father, his slaves were examined by torture, and the result was unfavourable to the accuser. The man, maddened by remorse, and terror-stricken by the popular voice, which menaced him with the dungeon, the rock, or a parricide's doom, fled from Rome. He was dragged back from Ravenna, and forced to go through the prosecution, during which Tiberius did not disguise the old grudge he bore the exile Serenus. For after Libo's conviction, Serenus had sent the emperor a letter, upbraiding him for not having rewarded his special zeal in that trial, with

further hints more insolent than could be safely trusted to the easily offended ears of a despot. All this Tiberius revived eight years later, charging on him various misconduct during that interval, even though the examination by torture, owing to the obstinacy of the slaves, had contradicted his guilt.

30. The Senate then gave their votes that Serenus should be punished according to ancient precedent, when the emperor, to soften the odium of the affair, interposed with his veto. Next, Gallus Asinius proposed that he should be confined in Gyaros or Donusa, but this he rejected, on the ground that both these islands were deficient in water, and that he whose life was spared, ought to be allowed the necessaries of life. And so Serenus was conveyed back to Amorgus.

In consequence of the suicide of Cornutus, it was proposed to deprive informers of their rewards whenever a person accused of treason put an end to his life by his own act before the completion of the trial. The motion was on the point of being carried when the emperor, with a harshness contrary to his manner, spoke openly for the informers, complaining that the laws would be ineffective, and the State brought to the verge of ruin. "Better," he said, "to subvert the constitution than to remove its guardians." Thus the informers. a class invented to destroy the commonwealth, and never enough controlled even by legal penalties, were stimulated by rewards.

31. Some little joy broke this long succession of horrors. Caius Cominius, a Roman knight, was spared by the emperor, against whom he was convicted of having written libellous verses, at the intercession of his brother, who was a Senator. Hence it seemed the more amazing that one who knew better things and the glory which waits on mercy, should prefer harsher courses. He did not indeed err from dulness, and it is easy to see when the acts of a sovereign meet with genuine, and when with fictitious popularity. And even he himself, though usually artificial in manner, and though his words escaped him with a seeming struggle, spoke out freely and fluently whenever he came to a man's rescue.

In another case, that of Publius Suillius, formerly quæstor to Germanicus, who was to be expelled from Italy on a con-

viction of having received money for a judicial decision, he
held that the man ought to be banished to an island, and so
intensely strong was his feeling that he bound the Senate by
an oath that this was a State necessity. The act was thought
cruel at the moment, but subsequently it redounded to his
honour when Suillius returned from exile. The next age saw
him in tremendous power and a venal creature of the emperor Claudius, whose friendship he long used, with success,
never for good.

The same punishment was adjudged to Catus Firmius, a
Senator, for having (it was alleged) assailed his sister with
a false charge of treason. Catus, as I have related, had drawn
Libo into a snare and then destroyed him by an information. Tiberius remembering this service, while he alleged
other reasons, deprecated a sentence of exile, but did not
oppose his expulsion from the Senate.

32. Much of what I have related and shall have to relate,
may perhaps, I am aware, seem petty trifles to record. But
no one must compare my annals with the writings of those
who have described Rome in old days. They told of great
wars, of the storming of cities, of the defeat and capture of
kings, or whenever they turned by preference to home affairs,
they related, with a free scope for digression, the strifes of
consuls with tribunes, land and corn-laws, and the struggles between the commons and the aristocracy. My labours
are circumscribed and inglorious; peace wholly unbroken or
but slightly disturbed, dismal misery in the capital, an emperor careless about the enlargement of the empire, such is
my theme. Still it will not be useless to study those at first
sight trifling events out of which the movements of vast
changes often take their rise.

33. All nations and cities are ruled by the people, the
nobility, or by one man. A constitution, formed by selection
out of these elements, it is easy to commend but not to
produce; or, if it is produced, it cannot be lasting. Formerly,
when the people had power or when the patricians were in
the ascendant, the popular temper and the methods of controlling it, had to be studied, and those who knew most
accurately the spirit of the Senate and aristocracy, had the
credit of understanding the age and of being wise men. So

now, after a revolution, when Rome is nothing but the realm of a single despot, there must be good in carefully noting and recording this period, for it is but few who have the foresight to distinguish right from wrong or what is sound from what is hurtful, while most men learn wisdom from the fortunes of others. Still, though this is instructive, it gives very little pleasure. Descriptions of countries, the various incidents of battles, glorious deaths of great generals, enchain and refresh a reader's mind. I have to present in succession the merciless biddings of a tyrant, incessant prosecutions, faithless friendships, the ruin of innocence, the same causes issuing in the same results, and I am everywhere confronted by a wearisome monotony in my subject matter. Then, again, an ancient historian has but few disparagers, and no one cares whether you praise more heartily the armies of Carthage or Rome. But of many who endured punishment or disgrace under Tiberius, the descendants yet survive; or even though the families themselves may be now extinct, you will find those who, from a resemblance of character, imagine that the evil deeds of others are a reproach to themselves. Again, even honour and virtue make enemies, condemning, as they do, their opposites by too close a contrast. But I return to my work.

34. In the year of the consulship of Cornelius Cossus and Asinius Agrippa, Cremutius Cordus was arraigned on a new charge, now for the first time heard. He had published a history in which he had praised Marcus Brutus and called Caius Cassius the last of the Romans. His accusers were Satrius Secundus and Pinarius Natta, creatures of Sejanus. This was enough to ruin the accused; and then too the emperor listened with an angry frown to his defence, which Cremutius, resolved to give up his life, began thus:—

"It is my words, Senators, which are condemned, so innocent am I of any guilty act; yet these do not touch the emperor or the emperor's mother, who are alone comprehended under the law of treason. I am said to have praised Brutus and Cassius, whose careers many have described and no one mentioned without eulogy. Titus Livius, pre-eminently famous for eloquence and truthfulness, extolled Cneius Pompeius in such a panegyric that Augustus called him Pompeianus, and yet this was no obstacle to their friendship. Scipio, Afranius, this very Cassius, this same Brutus, he nowhere describes as brigands and traitors, terms now applied to them, but repeatedly as illustrious men. Asinius Pollio's writings too hand down a glorious memory of them, and Messala Corvinus used to speak with pride of Cassius as his general. Yet both these men prospered to the end with wealth and preferment. Again, that book of Marcus Cicero, in which he lauded Cato to the skies, how else was it answered by Cæsar the dictator, than by a written oration in reply, as if he was pleading in court? The letters of Antonius, the harangues of Brutus contain reproaches against Augustus, false indeed, but urged with powerful sarcasm; the poems which we read of Bibaculus and Catullus are crammed with invectives on the Cæsars. Yet the Divine Julius, the Divine Augustus themselves bore all this and let it pass, whether in forbearance or in wisdom I cannot easily say. Assuredly what is despised is soon forgotten; when you resent a thing, you seem to recognise it."

35. "Of the Greeks I say nothing; with them not only liberty, but even license went unpunished, or if a person aimed at chastising, he retaliated on satire by satire. It has, however, always been perfectly open to us without any one to censure, to speak freely of those whom death has withdrawn alike from the partialities of hatred or esteem. Are Cassius and Brutus now in arms on the fields of Philippi, and am I with them rousing the people by harangues to stir up civil war? Did they not fall more than seventy years ago, and as they are known to us by statues which even the conqueror did not destroy, so too is not some portion of their memory preserved for us by historians? To every man posterity gives his due honour, and, if a fatal sentence hangs over me, there will be those who will remember me as well as Cassius and Brutus."

He then left the Senate and ended his life by starvation. His books, so the Senators decreed, were to be burnt by the aediles; but some copies were left which were concealed and afterwards published. And so one is all the more inclined to laugh at the stupidity of men who suppose that the despotism of the present can actually efface the remembrances of the next generation. On the contrary, the persecution of genius fosters its influence; foreign tyrants, and all who have imitated their oppression, have merely procured infamy for themselves and glory for their victims.

36. That year was such a continuous succession of prosecutions that on the days of the Latin festival when Drusus, as city-prefect, had ascended his tribunal for the inauguration of his office, Calpurnius Salvianus appeared before him against Sextus Marius. This the emperor openly censured, and it caused the banishment of Salvianus. Next, the people of Cyzicus were accused of publicly neglecting the established worship of the Divine Augustus, and also of acts of violence to Roman citizens. They were deprived of the franchise which they had earned during the war with Mithridates, when their city was besieged, and when they repulsed the king as much by their own bravery as by the aid of Lucullus. Then followed the acquittal of Fonteius Capito, the late proconsul of Asia, on proof that charges brought against him by Vibius Serenus were fictitious. Still this did not injure Serenus, to whom public hatred was actually a protection. Indeed any conspicuously restless informer was, so to say, inviolable; only the insignificant and undistinguished were punished.

37. About the same time Further Spain sent a deputation to the Senate, with a request to be allowed, after the example of Asia, to erect a temple to Tiberius and his mother. On this occasion, the emperor, who had generally a strong contempt for honours, and now thought it right to reply to the rumour which reproached him with having yielded to vanity, delivered the following speech:—

"I am aware, Senators, that many deplore my want of firmness in not having opposed a similar recent petition from the cities of Asia. I will therefore both explain the grounds of my previous silence and my intentions for the future. Inasmuch as the Divine Augustus did not forbid the founding of a temple at Pergamos to himself and to the city of Rome, I who respect as law all his actions and sayings, have the more readily followed a precedent once approved, seeing that with the worship of myself was linked an expression of reverence towards the Senate. But though it may be pardonable to have allowed this once, it would be a vain and arrogant thing to receive the sacred honour of images representing the divine throughout all the provinces, and the homage paid to Augustus will disappear if it is vulgarised by indiscriminate flattery.

38. "For myself, Senators, I am mortal and limited to the functions of humanity, content if I can adequately fill the highest place; of this I solemnly assure you, and would have posterity remember it. They will more than sufficiently honour my memory by believing me to have been worthy of my ancestry, watchful over your interests, courageous in danger, fearless of enmity, when the State required it. These sentiments of your hearts are my temples, these my most glorious and abiding monuments. Those built of stone are despised as mere tombs, if the judgment of posterity passes into hatred. And therefore this is my prayer to our allies, our citizens, and to heaven itself; to the last, that, to my life's close, it grant me a tranquil mind, which can discern alike human and divine claims; to the first, that, when I die, they honour my career and the reputation of my name with praise and kindly remembrance."

Henceforth Tiberius even in private conversations persisted in showing contempt for such homage to himself. Some attributed this to modesty; many to self-distrust; a few to a mean spirit. "The noblest men," it was said, "have the loftiest aspirations, and so Hercules and Bacchus among the Greeks and Quirinus among us were enrolled in the number of the gods. Augustus did better, seeing that he had aspired. All other things princes have as a matter of course; one thing they ought insatiably to pursue, that their memory may be glorious. For to despise fame is to despise merit."

39. Sejanus meanwhile, dazed by his extravagant prosperity and urged on too by a woman's passion, Livia now insisting on his promise of marriage, addressed a memorial to the emperor. For it was then the custom to apply to him by writing, even though he was at Rome. This petition was to the following effect:—The kindness of Augustus, the father, and then the many favourable testimonies of Tiberius, the son, had engendered the habit of confiding his hopes and wishes to the ears of emperors as readily as to those of

the gods. The splendour of high distinctions he had never craved; he had rather chosen watchings and hardships, like one of the common soldiers, for the emperor's safety. But there was one most glorious honour he had won, the reputation of being worthy of an alliance with a Cæsar. This was the first motive of his ambition. As he had heard that Augustus, in marrying his daughter, had even entertained some thoughts of Roman knights, so if a husband were sought for Livia, he hoped Tiberius would bear in mind a friend who would find his reward simply in the glory of the alliance. He did not wish to rid himself of the duties imposed on him; he thought it enough for his family to be secured against the unjust displeasure of Agrippina, and this for the sake of his children. For, as for himself, enough and more than enough for him would be a life completed while such a sovereign still reigned.

40. Tiberius, in reply, after praising the loyal sentiments of Sejanus and briefly enumerating the favours he had bestowed on him, asked time for impartial consideration, adding that while other men's plans depended on their ideas of their own interest, princes, who had to regulate their chief actions by public opinion, were in a different position. "Hence," he said, "I do not take refuge in an answer which it would be easy to return, that Livia can herself decide whether she considers that, after Drusus, she ought again to marry or rather to endure life in the same home, and that she has in her mother and grandmother counsellors nearer and dearer to her. I will deal more frankly. First, as to the enmity of Agrippina, I maintain that it will blaze out more fiercely if Livia's marriage rends, so to say, the house of the Cæsars into two factions. Even as it is, feminine jealousies break out, and my grandsons are torn asunder by the strife. What will happen if the rivalry is rendered more intense by such a marriage? For you are mistaken, Sejanus, if you think that you will then remain in the same position, and that Livia, who has been the wife of Caius Cæsar and afterwards of Drusus, will have the inclination to pass her old age with a mere Roman knight. Though I might allow it, do you imagine it would be tolerated by those who have seen her brother, her father, and our an-

cestors in the highest offices of state? You indeed desire to
keep within your station; but those magistrates and nobles
who intrude on you against your wishes and consult you on
all matters, openly give out that you have long overstepped
the rank of a knight and gone far beyond my father's friendships, and from their dislike of you they also condemn me.
But, you say, Augustus had thoughts of giving his daughter
to a Roman knight. Is it surprising that, with so many dis-
tracting cares, foreseeing too the immense elevation to which
a man would be raised above others by such an alliance, he
talked of Caius Proculeius and certain persons of singularly
quiet life, wholly free from political entanglements? Still, if
the hesitation of Augustus is to influence us, how much
stronger is the fact that he bestowed his daughter on Marcus
Agrippa, then on myself. All this, as a friend, I have stated
without reserve, but I will not oppose your plans or those of
Livia. My own earnest thoughts and the ties with which I
am still purposing to unite you to myself, I shall for the
present forbear to explain. This only I will declare, that
nothing is too grand to be deserved by your merits and your
goodwill towards me. When an opportunity presents itself,
either in the Senate, or in a popular assembly, I shall not
be silent."

41. Sejanus, no longer thinking of his marriage but filled
with a deeper alarm, rejoined by deprecating the whispers of
suspicion, popular rumour and the gathering storm of odium.
That he might not impair his influence by closing his doors
on the throngs of his many visitors or strengthen the hands
of accusers by admitting them, he made it his aim to induce
Tiberius to live in some charming spot at a distance from
Rome. In this he foresaw several advantages. Access to the
emperor would be under his own control, and letters, for the
most part being conveyed by soldiers, would pass through his
hands. Cæsar too, who was already in the decline of life,
would soon, when enervated by retirement, more readily
transfer to him the functions of empire; envy towards himself would be lessened when there was an end to his crowded
levées and the reality of power would be increased by the
removal of its empty show. So he began to declaim against
the laborious life of the capital, the bustling crowds and

streaming multitudes, while he praised repose and solitude, with their freedom from vexations and misunderstandings, and their special opportunities for the study of the highest questions.

42. It happened that the trial at this time of Votienus Montanus, a popular wit, convinced the hesitating Tiberius that he ought to shun all assemblies of the Senate, where speeches, often true and offensive, were flung in his very face. Votienus was charged with insulting expressions towards the emperor, and while the witness, Æmilius, a military man, in his eagerness to prove the case, repeated the whole story and amid angry clamour struggled on with loud assertion, Tiberius heard the reproaches by which he was assailed in secret, and was so deeply impressed that he exclaimed that he would clear himself either at once or on a legal inquiry, and the entreaties of friends, with the flattery of the whole assembly, hardly restored his composure. As for Votienus, he suffered the penalty of treason; but the emperor, clinging all the more obstinately to the harshness with which he had been reproached in regard to accused persons, punished Aquilia with exile for the crime of adultery with Varius Ligur, although Lentulus Gætulicus, the consul-elect, had proposed that she should be sentenced under the Julian law. He next struck off Apidius Merula from the register of the Senate for not having sworn obedience to the legislation of the Divine Augustus.

43. Then a hearing was given to embassies from the Lacedæmonians and Messenians on the question of the temple of Diana in the Marshes. The Lacedæmonians asserted that it had been dedicated by their ancestors and in their territory, and appealed to the records of their history and the hymns of poets, but it had been wrested from them, they said, by the arms of the Macedonian Philip, with whom they had fought, and subsequently restored by the decision of Caius Cæsar and Marcus Antonius. The Messenians, on the contrary, alleged the ancient division of the Peloponnesus among the descendants of Hercules, in which the territory of Denthelia (where the temple stood) had fallen to their king. Records of this event still existed, engraven on stone and ancient bronze. But if they were asked for the testimony

of poetry and of history, they had it, they said, in greater
abundance and authenticity. Philip had not decided arbitrarily, but according to fact, and king Antigonus, as also
the general Mummius, had pronounced the same judgment.
Such too had been the award of the Milesians to whom the
arbitration had been publicly entrusted, and, finally, of
Atidius Geminus, the prætor of Achaia. And so the question
was decided in favour of the Messenians.

Next the people of Segesta petitioned for the restoration
of the temple of Venus at Mount Eryx, which had fallen to
ruin from its antiquity. They repeated the well-known story
of its origin, which delighted Tiberius. He undertook the
work willingly, as being a kinsman of the goddess. After this
was discussed a petition from the city of Massilia, and sanction given to the precedent of Publius Rutilius, who having
been legally banished from Rome, had been adopted as a
citizen by the people of Smyrna. Volcatius Moschus, also an
exile, had been received with a similar privilege by the inhabitants of Massilia, and had left his property to their
community, as being now his own country.

44. Two men of noble rank died in that year, Cneius Lentulus and Lucius Domitius. It had been the glory of Lentulus, to say nothing of his consulship and his triumphal distinctions over the Gætuli, to have borne poverty with a good
grace, then to have attained great wealth, which had been
blamelessly acquired and was modestly enjoyed. Domitius
derived lustre from a father who during the civil war had
been master of the sea, till he united himself to the party of
Antonius and afterwards to that of Cæsar. His grandfather
had fallen in the battle of Pharsalia, fighting for the aristocracy. He had himself been chosen to be the husband of the
younger Antonia, daughter of Octavia, and subsequently led
an army across the Elbe, penetrating further into Germany
than any Roman before him. For this achievement he gained
triumphal honours.

Lucius Antonius too then died, of a most illustrious but
unfortunate family. His father, Julius Antonius, was capitally
punished for adultery with Julia, and the son, when a mere
youth, was banished by Augustus, whose sister's grandson
he was, to the city of Massilia, where the name of exile

might be masked under that of student. Yet honour was paid
him in death, and his bones, by the Senate's decree, were
consigned to the sepulchre of the Octavii.

45. While the same consuls were in office, an atrocious
crime was committed in Nearer Spain by a peasant of the
Termestine tribe. Suddenly attacking the prætor of the province, Lucius Piso, as he was travelling in all the carelessness
of peace, he killed him with a single wound. He then fled
on a swift horse, and reached a wooded country, where he
parted with his steed and eluded pursuit amid rocky and
pathless wilds. But he was soon discovered. The horse was
caught and led through the neighbouring villages, and its
owner ascertained. Being found and put to the torture that
he might be forced to reveal his accomplices, he exclaimed
in a loud voice, in the language of his country, that it was in
vain to question him; his comrades might stand by and look
on, but that the most intense agony would not wring the
truth from him. Next day, when he was dragged back to torture, he broke loose from his guards and dashed his head
against a stone with such violence that he instantly fell dead.
It was however believed that Piso was treacherously murdered by the Termestini. Some public money had been embezzled, and he was pressing for its payment too rigorously
for the patience of barbarians.

46. In the consulship of Lentulus Gætulicus and Caius
Calvisius, triumphal distinctions were decreed to Poppæus
Sabinus, for a crushing defeat of some Thracian tribes,
whose wild life in the highlands of a mountainous country
made them unusually fierce. Besides their natural ferocity,
the rebellion had its origin in their scornful refusal to endure
levies and to supply our armies with their bravest men. Even
native princes they would obey only according to their
caprice, and if they sent aid, they used to appoint their own
leaders and fight only against their neighbours. A rumour
had then spread itself among them that, dispersed and
mingled with other tribes, they were to be dragged away
to distant countries. Before however they took up arms, they
sent envoys with assurances of their friendship and loyalty,
which, they said, would continue, if they were not tried by
any fresh burden. But if they were doomed to slavery as a

conquered people, they had swords and young warriors and
a spirit bent on freedom or resigned to death. As they spoke,
they pointed to fortresses amid rocks whither they had
conveyed their parents and their wives, and threatened us
with a difficult, dangerous and sanguinary war.

47. Sabinus meantime, while he was concentrating his
troops, returned gentle answers; but on the arrival of Pomponius Labeo with a legion from Mœsia and of king Rhœmetalces with some reinforcements from his subjects, who
had not thrown off their allegiance, with these and the force
he had on the spot, he advanced on the enemy, who were
drawn up in some wooded defiles. Some ventured to show
themselves on the open hills; these the Roman general approached in fighting order and easily dislodged them, with
only a small slaughter of the barbarians, who had not far
to flee. In this position he soon established a camp, and held
with a strong detachment a narrow and unbroken mountain
ridge, stretching as far as the next fortress, which was
garrisoned by a large force of armed soldiers along with
some irregulars. Against the boldest of these, who after the
manner of their country were disporting themselves with
songs and dances in front of the rampart, he sent some
picked archers, who, discharging distant volleys, inflicted
many wounds without loss to themselves. As they advanced,
a sudden sortie put them to the rout, and they fell back on
the support of a Sugambrian cohort, drawn up at no great
distance by the Roman general, ready for any emergency
and as terrible as the foe, with the noise of their war songs
and the clashing of their arms.

48. He then moved his camp near to the enemy, leaving
in his former entrenchments the Thracians who, as I have
mentioned, were with us. These had permission to ravage,
burn, and plunder, provided they confined their forays to
daylight, and passed the night securely and vigilantly in
their camp. This at first they strictly observed. Soon they
resigned themselves to enjoyment, and, enriched by plunder, they neglected their guards, and amid feasts and mirth
sank down in the carelessness of the banquet, of sleep and
of wine. So the enemy, apprised of their heedlessness, prepared two detachments, one of which was to attack the

plunderers, the other, to fall on the Roman camp, not with the hope of taking it, but to hinder the din of the other battle from being heard by our soldiers, who, with shouts and missiles around them, would be all intent on their own peril. Night too was chosen for the movement to increase the panic. Those however who tried to storm the entrenchment of the legions were easily repulsed; the Thracian auxiliaries were dismayed by the suddenness of the onset, for though some were lying close to their lines, far more were straggling beyond them, and the massacre was all the more savage, inasmuch as they were taunted with being fugitives and traitors and bearing arms for their own and their country's enslavement.

49. Next day Sabinus displayed his forces in the plain, on the chance of the barbarians being encouraged by the night's success to risk an engagement. Finding that they did not quit the fortress and the adjoining hills, he began a siege by means of the works which he had opportunely began to construct; then he drew a fosse and stockade enclosing an extent of four miles, and by degrees contracted and narrowed his lines, with the view of cutting off their water and forage. He also threw up a rampart, from which to discharge stones, darts, and brands on the enemy, who was now within range. It was thirst however which chiefly distressed them, for there was only one spring for the use of a vast multitude of soldiers and non-combatants. Their cattle too, penned up close to them, after the fashion of barbarians, were dying of want of fodder; near them lay human bodies which had perished from wounds or thirst, and the whole place was befouled with rotting carcases and stench and infection. To their confusion was added the growing misery of discord, some thinking of surrender, others of destruction by mutual blows. Some there were who suggested a sortie instead of an unavenged death, and these were all men of spirit, though they differed in their plans.

50. One of their chiefs, Dinis, an old man who well knew by long experience both the strength and clemency of Rome, maintained that they must lay down their arms, this being the only remedy for their wretched plight, and he was the first to give himself up with his wife and children to the

conqueror. He was followed by all whom age or sex unfitted for war, by all too who had a stronger love of life than of renown. The young were divided between Tarsa and Turesis, both of whom had resolved to fall together with their freedom. Tarsa however kept urging them to speedy death and to the instant breaking off of all hope and fear, and, by way of example, plunged his sword into his heart. And there were some who chose the same death. Turesis and his band waited for night, not without the knowledge of our general. Consequently, the sentries were strengthened with denser masses of troops. Night was coming on with a fierce storm, and the foe, one moment with a tumultuous uproar, another in awful silence, had perplexed the besiegers, when Sabinus went round the camp, entreating the men not to give a chance to their stealthy assailants by heeding embarrassing noises or being deceived by quiet, but to keep, every one, to his post without moving or discharging their darts on false alarms.

51. The barbarians meanwhile rushed down with their bands, now hurling at the entrenchments stones such as the hand could grasp, stakes with points hardened by fire, and boughs lopped from oaks; now filling up the fosses with bushes and hurdles and dead bodies, while others advanced up to the breastwork with bridges and ladders which they had constructed for the occasion, seized it, tore it down, and came to close quarters with the defenders. Our soldiers on the other side drove them back with missiles, repelled them with their shields, and covered them with a storm of long siege-javelins and heaps of stones. Success already gained and the more marked disgrace which would follow repulse, were a stimulus to the Romans, while the courage of the foe was heightened by this last chance of deliverance and the presence of many mothers and wives with mournful cries. Darkness, which increased the daring of some and the terror of others, random blows, wounds not foreseen, failure to recognise friend or enemy, echoes, seemingly in their rear, from the winding mountain valleys, spread such confusion that the Romans abandoned some of their lines in the belief that they had been stormed. Only however a very few of the enemy had broken through them; the rest, after

their bravest men had been beaten back or wounded, were towards daybreak pushed back to the upper part of the fortress and there at last compelled to surrender. Then the immediate neighbourhood, by the voluntary action of the inhabitants, submitted. The early and severe winter of Mount Hæmus saved the rest of the population from being reduced by assault or blockade.

52. At Rome meanwhile, besides the shocks already sustained by the imperial house, came the first step towards the destruction of Agrippina, Claudia Pulchra, her cousin, being prosecuted by Domitius Afer. Lately a prætor, a man of but moderate position and eager to become notorious by any sort of deed, Afer charged her with unchastity, with having Furnius for her paramour, and with attempts on the emperor by poison and sorcery. Agrippina, always impetuous, and now kindled into fury by the peril of her kinswoman, went straight to Tiberius and found him, as it happened, offering a sacrifice to his father. This provoked an indignant outburst. "It is not," she exclaimed, "for the same man to slay victims to the Divine Augustus and to persecute his posterity. The celestial spirit has not transferred itself to the mute statue; here is the true image, sprung of heavenly blood, and she perceives her danger, and assumes its mournful emblems. Pulchra's name is a mere blind; the only reason for her destruction is that she has, in utter folly, selected Agrippina for her admiration, forgetting that Sosia was thereby ruined." These words wrung from the emperor one of the rare utterances of that inscrutable breast; he rebuked Agrippina with a Greek verse, and reminded her that "she was not wronged because she was not a queen." Pulchra and Furnius were condemned. Afer was ranked with the foremost orators, for the ability which he displayed, and which won strong praise from Tiberius, who pronounced him a speaker of natural genius. Henceforward as a counsel for the defence or the prosecution he enjoyed the fame of eloquence rather than of virtue, but old age robbed him of much of his speaking power, while, with a failing intellect, he was still impatient of silence.

53. Agrippina in stubborn rage, with the grasp of disease yet on her, when the emperor came to see her, wept long

and silently, and then began to mingle reproach and supplication. She begged him "to relieve her loneliness and provide her with a husband; her youth still fitted her for marriage, which was a virtuous woman's only solace, and there
were citizens in Rome who would not disdain to receive the
wife of Germanicus and his children." But the emperor,
who perceived the political aims of her request, but did not
wish to show displeasure or apprehension, left her, notwithstanding her urgency, without an answer. This incident, not
mentioned by any historian, I have found in the memoirs of
the younger Agrippina, the mother of the emperor Nero,
who handed down to posterity the story of her life and of
the misfortunes of her family.

54. Sejanus meanwhile yet more deeply alarmed the sor-
rowing and unsuspecting woman by sending his agents,
under the guise of friendship, with warnings that poison was
prepared for her, and that she ought to avoid her father-in-
law's table. Knowing not how to dissemble, she relaxed
neither her features nor tone of voice as she sat by him at
dinner, nor did she touch a single dish, till at last Tiberius
noticed her conduct, either casually or because he was told
of it. To test her more closely, he praised some fruit as it
was set on the table and passed it with his own hand to his
daughter-in-law. This increased the suspicions of Agrippina,
and without putting the fruit to her lips she gave it to the
slaves. Still no remark fell from Tiberius before the company, but he turned to his mother and whispered that it was
not surprising if he had decided on harsh treatment against
one who implied that he was a poisoner. Then there was a
rumour that a plan was laid for her destruction, that the
emperor did not dare to attempt it openly, and was seeking
to veil the deed in secrecy.

55. Tiberius, to divert people's talk, continually attended
the Senate, and gave an audience of several days to embassies from Asia on a disputed question as to the city in
which the temple before mentioned should be erected. Eleven
cities were rivals for the honour, of which they were all
equally ambitious, though they differed widely in resources.
With little variation they dwelt on antiquity of race and
loyalty to Rome throughout her wars with Perseus, Aristoni-

cus, and other kings. But the people of Hypæpa, Tralles, Laodicæa, and Magnesia were passed over as too insignificant; even Ilium, though it boasted that Troy was the cradle of Rome, was strong only in the glory of its antiquity. There was a little hesitation about Halicarnassus, as its inhabitants affirmed that for twelve hundred years their homes had not been shaken by an earthquake and that the foundations of their temple were on the living rock. Pergamos, it was thought, had been sufficiently honoured by having a temple of Augustus in the city, on which very fact they relied. The Ephesians and Milesians had, it seemed, wholly devoted their respective towns to the worships of Apollo and Diana. And so the question lay between Sardis and Smyrna. The envoys from Sardis read a decree of the Etrurians, with whom they claimed kindred. "Tyrrhenus and Lydus," it was said, "the sons of King Atys, divided the nation between them because of its multitude; Lydus remained in the country of his fathers; Tyrrhenus had the work assigned him of establishing new settlements, and names, taken from the two leaders, were given to the one people in Asia and to the other in Italy. The resources of the Lydians were yet further augmented by the immigration of nations into that part of Greece which afterwards took its name from Pelops. They spoke too of letters from Roman generals, of treaties concluded with us during the Macedonian war, and of their copious rivers, of their climate, and the rich countries round them.

56. The envoys from Smyrna, after tracing their city's antiquity back to such founders as either Tantalus, the son of Jupiter, or Theseus, also of divine origin, or one of the Amazons, passed on to that on which they chiefly relied, their services to the Roman people, whom they had helped with naval armaments, not only in wars abroad, but in those under which we struggled in Italy. They had also been the first, they said, to build a temple in honour of Rome, during the consulship of Marcus Porcius Cato, when Rome's power indeed was great, but not yet raised to the highest point, inasmuch as the Punic capital was still standing and there were mighty kings in Asia. They appealed too to the testimony of Lucius Sulla, whose army was once in terrible

jeopardy from a severe winter and want of clothing, and this
having been announced at Smyrna in a public assembly, all
who were present stript their clothes off their backs and sent
them to our legions. And so the Senate, when the question
was put, gave the preference to Smyrna. Vibius Marsus
moved that Marcus Lepidus, to whom the province of Asia
had been assigned, should have under him a special com-
missioner to undertake the charge of this temple. As Lepidus
himself, out of modesty, declined to appoint, Valerius Naso,
one of the ex-prætors, was chosen by lot and sent out.

57. Meanwhile, after long reflection on his purpose and
frequent deferment of it, the emperor retired into Campania
to dedicate, as he pretended, a temple to Jupiter at Capua
and another to Augustus at Nola, but really resolved to live
at a distance from Rome. Although I have followed most
historians in attributing the cause of his retirement to the
arts of Sejanus, still, as he passed six consecutive years in
the same solitude after that minister's destruction, I am
often in doubt whether it is not to be more truly ascribed
to himself, and his wish to hide by the place of his retreat
the cruelty and licentiousness which he betrayed by his actions. Some thought that in his old age he was ashamed of
his personal appearance. He had indeed a tall, singularly
slender and stooping figure, a bald head, a face full of erup-
tions, and covered here and there with plasters. In the seclusion of Rhodes he had habituated himself to shun society
and to hide his voluptuous life. According to one account his
mother's domineering temper drove him away; he was weary
of having her as his partner in power, and he could not
thrust her aside, because he had received this very power
as her gift. For Augustus had had thoughts of putting the
Roman state under Germanicus, his sister's grandson, whom
all men esteemed, but yielding to his wife's entreaties he left
Germanicus to be adopted by Tiberius and adopted Tiberius
himself. With this Augusta would taunt her son, and claim
back what she had given.

58. His departure was attended by a small retinue, one
senator, who was an ex-consul, Cocceius Nerva, learned in
the laws, one Roman knight, besides Sejanus, of the highest
order, Curtius Atticus, the rest being men of liberal culture.

for the most part Greeks, in whose conversation he might find amusement. It was said by men who knew the stars that the motions of the heavenly bodies when Tiberius left Rome were such as to forbid the possibility of his return. This caused ruin to many who conjectured that his end was near and spread the rumour; for they never foresaw the very improbable contingency of his voluntary exile from his home for eleven years. Soon afterwards it was clearly seen what a narrow margin there is between such science and delusion and in what obscurity truth is veiled. That he would not return to Rome was not a mere random assertion; as to the rest, they were wholly in the dark, seeing that he lived to extreme old age in the country or on the coast near Rome and often close to the very walls of the city.

59. It happened at this time that a perilous accident which occurred to the emperor strengthened vague rumours and gave him grounds for trusting more fully in the friendship and fidelity of Sejanus. They were dining in a country house called "The Cave," between the gulf of Amuclæ and the hills of Fundi, in a natural grotto. The rocks at its entrance suddenly fell in and crushed some of the attendants; thereupon panic seized the whole company and there was a general flight of the guests. Sejanus hung over the emperor, and with knee, face, and hand encountered the falling stones; and was found in this attitude by the soldiers who came to their rescue. After this he was greater than ever, and though his counsels were ruinous, he was listened to with confidence, as a man who had no care for himself. He pretended to act as a judge towards the children of Germanicus, after having suborned persons to assume the part of prosecutors and to inveigh specially against Nero, next in succession to the throne, who, though he had proper youthful modesty, often forgot present expediency, while freedmen and clients, eager to get power, incited him to display vigour and self-confidence. "This," they said, "was what the Roman people wished, what the armies desired, and Sejanus would not dare to oppose it, though now he insulted alike the tame spirit of the old emperor and the timidity of the young prince."

60. Nero, while he listened to this and like talk, was not

indeed inspired with any guilty ambition, but still occasionally there would break from him wilful and thoughtless expressions which spies about his person caught up and reported with exaggeration, and this he had no opportunity of
rebutting. Then again alarms under various forms were continually arising. One man would avoid meeting him; another
after returning his salutation would instantly turn away;
many after beginning a conversation would instantly break
it off, while Sejanus's friends would stand their ground and
laugh at him. Tiberius indeed wore an angry frown or a
treacherous smile. Whether the young prince spoke or held
his tongue, silence and speech were alike criminal. Every
night had its anxieties, for his sleepless hours, his dreams
and sighs were all made known by his wife to her mother
Livia and by Livia to Sejanus. Nero's brother Drusus Sejanus actually drew into his scheme by holding out to him
the prospect of becoming emperor through the removal of an
elder brother, already all but fallen. The savage temper of
Drusus, to say nothing of lust of power and the usual feuds
between brothers, was inflamed with envy by the partiality
of the mother Agrippina towards Nero. And yet Sejanus,
while he favoured Drusus, was not without thoughts of sowing the seeds of his future ruin, well knowing how very impetuous he was and therefore the more exposed to treachery.

61. Towards the close of the year died two distinguished
men, Asinius Agrippa and Quintus Haterius. Agrippa was of
illustrious rather than ancient ancestry, which his career did
not disgrace; Haterius was of a senatorian family and famous for his eloquence while he lived, though the monuments
which remain of his genius are not admired as of old. The
truth is he succeeded more by vehemence than by finish of
style. While the research and labours of other authors are
valued by an after age, the harmonious fluency of Haterius
died with him.

62. In the year of the consulship of Marcus Licinius and
Lucius Calpurnius, the losses of a great war were matched
by an unexpected disaster, no sooner begun than ended. One
Atilius, of the freedman class, having undertaken to build
an amphitheatre at Fidena for the exhibition of a show of
gladiators, failed to lay a solid foundation and to frame the

wooden superstructure with beams of sufficient strength; for he had neither an abundance of wealth, nor zeal for public popularity, but he had simply sought the work for sordid gain. Thither flocked all who loved such sights and who during the reign of Tiberius had been wholly debarred from such amusements; men and women of every age crowding to the place because it was near Rome. And so the calamity was all the more fatal. The building was densely crowded; then came a violent shock, as it fell inwards or spread outwards, precipitating and burying an immense multitude which was intently gazing on the show or standing round. Those who were crushed to death in the first moment of the accident had at least under such dreadful circumstances the advantage of escaping torture. More to be pitied were they who with limbs torn from them still retained life, while they recognised their wives and children by seeing them during the day and by hearing in the night their screams and groans. Soon all the neighbours in their excitement at the report were bewailing brothers, kinsmen or parents. Even those whose friends or relatives were away from home for quite a different reason, still trembled for them, and as it was not yet known who had been destroyed by the crash, suspense made the alarm more widespread.

63. As soon as they began to remove the débris, there was a rush to see the lifeless forms and much embracing and kissing. Often a dispute would arise, when some distorted face, bearing however a general resemblance of form and age, had baffled their efforts at recognition. Fifty thousand persons were maimed or destroyed in this disaster. For the future it was provided by a decree of the Senate that no one was to exhibit a show of gladiators, whose fortune fell short of four hundred thousand sesterces, and that no amphitheatre was to be erected except on a foundation, the solidity of which had been examined. Atilius was banished. At the moment of the calamity the nobles threw open their houses and supplied indiscriminately medicines and physicians, so that Rome then, notwithstanding her sorrowful aspect, wore a likeness to the manners of our forefathers who after a great battle always relieved the wounded with their bounty and attentions.

64. This disaster was not forgotten when a furious conflagration damaged the capital to an unusual extent, reducing Mount Cælius to ashes. "It was an ill-starred year," people began to say, "and the emperor's purpose of leaving
Rome must have been formed under evil omens." They began in vulgar fashion to trace ill-luck to guilt, when Tiberius
checked them by distributing money in proportion to losses
sustained. He received a vote of thanks in the Senate from
its distinguished members, and was applauded by the populace for having assisted with his liberality, without partiality
or the solicitations of friends, strangers whom he had himself
sought out. And proposals were also made that Mount
Cælius should for the future be called Mount Augustus, inasmuch as when all around was in flames only a single statue
of Tiberius in the house of one Junius, a senator, had remained uninjured. This, it was said, had formerly happened
to Claudia Quinta; her statue, which had twice escaped the
violence of fire, had been dedicated by our ancestors in the
temple of the Mother of Gods; hence the Claudii had been
accounted sacred and numbered among deities, and so additional sanctity ought to be given to a spot where heaven
showed such honour to the emperor.

65. It will not be uninteresting to mention that Mount
Cælius was anciently known by the name of Querquetulanus,
because it grew oak timber in abundance and was afterwards called Cælius by Cæles Vibenna, who led the Etruscan
people to the aid of Rome and had the place given him as a
possession by Tarquinius Priscus or by some other of the
kings. As to that point historians differ; as to the rest, it is
beyond a question that Vibenna's numerous forces established themselves in the plain beneath and in the neighbourhood of the forum, and that the Tuscan street was named
after these strangers.

66. But though the zeal of the nobles and the bounty of
the prince brought relief to suffering, yet every day a
stronger and fiercer host of informers pursued its victims,
without one alleviating circumstance. Quintilius Varus, a
rich man and related to the emperor, was suddenly attacked
by Domitius Afer, the successful prosecutor of Claudia
Pulchra, his mother, and no one wondered that the needy

adventurer of many years who had squandered his lately gotten recompense was now preparing himself for fresh iniquities. That Publius Dolabella should have associated himself in the prosecution was a marvel, for he was of illustrious ancestry, was allied to Varus, and was now himself seeking to destroy his own noble race, his own kindred. The Senate however stopped the proceeding, and decided to wait for the emperor, this being the only means of escaping for a time impending horrors.

67. Cæsar, meanwhile, after dedicating the temples in Campania, warned the public by an edict not to disturb his retirement and posted soldiers here and there to keep off the throngs of townsfolk. But he so loathed the towns and colonies and, in short, every place on the mainland, that he buried himself in the island of Capreæ which is separated by three miles of strait from the extreme point of the promontory of Sorrentum. The solitude of the place was, I believe, its chief attraction, for a harbourless sea surrounds it and even for a small vessel it has but few safe retreats, nor can any one land unknown to the sentries. Its air in winter is soft, as it is screened by a mountain which is a protection against cutting winds. In summer it catches the western breezes, and the open sea round it renders it most delightful. It commanded too a prospect of the most lovely bay, till Vesuvius, bursting into flames, changed the face of the country. Greeks, so tradition says, occupied those parts and Capreæ was inhabited by the Teleboi. Tiberius had by this time filled the island with twelve country houses, each with a grand name and a vast structure of its own. Intent as he had once been on the cares of state, he was now for thoroughly unbending himself in secret profligacy and a leisure of malignant schemes. For he still retained that rash proneness to suspect and to believe, which even at Rome Sejanus used to foster, and which he here excited more keenly, no longer concealing his machinations against Agrippina and Nero. Soldiers hung about them, and every message, every visit, their public and their private life were I may say regularly chronicled. And persons were actually suborned to advise them to flee to the armies of Germany, or when the Forum was most crowded, to clasp the statue of the

Divine Augustus and appeal to the protection of the people and Senate. These counsels they disdained, but they were charged with having had thoughts of acting on them.

68. The year of the consulship of Silanus and Silius Nerva opened with a foul beginning. A Roman knight of the highest rank, Titius Sabinus, was dragged to prison because he had been a friend of Germanicus. He had indeed persisted in showing marked respect towards his wife and children, as their visitor at home, their companion in public, the solitary survivor of so many clients, and he was consequently esteemed by the good, as he was a terror to the evil-minded. Latinius Latiaris, Porcius Cato, Petitius Rufus, and Marcus Opsius, ex-prætors, conspired to attack him, with an eye to the consulship, to which there was access only through Sejanus, and the good will of Sejanus was to be gained only by a crime. They arranged amongst themselves that Latiaris, who had some slight acquaintance with Sabinus, should devise the plot, that the rest should be present as witnesses, and that then they should begin the prosecution. Accordingly Latiaris, after first dropping some casual remarks, went on to praise the fidelity of Sabinus in not having, like others, forsaken after its fall the house of which he had been the friend in its prosperity. He also spoke highly of Germanicus and compassionately of Agrippina. Sabinus, with the natural softness of the human heart under calamity, burst into tears, which he followed up with complaints, and soon with yet more daring invective against Sejanus, against his cruelty, pride and ambition. He did not spare even Tiberius in his reproaches. That conversation, having united them, as it were, in an unlawful secret, led to a semblance of close intimacy. Henceforward Sabinus himself sought Latiaris, went continually to his house, and imparted to him his griefs, as to a most faithful friend.

69. The men whom I have named now consulted how these conversations might fall within the hearing of more persons. It was necessary that the place of meeting should preserve the appearance of secrecy, and, if witnesses were to stand behind the doors, there was a fear of their being seen or heard, or of suspicion casually arising. Three senators thrust themselves into the space between the roof and

ceiling, a hiding-place as shameful as the treachery was execrable. They applied their ears to apertures and crevices. Latiaris meanwhile having met Sabinus in the streets, drew him to his house and to the room, as if he was going to communicate some fresh discoveries. There he talked much about past and impending troubles, a copious topic indeed, and about fresh horrors. Sabinus spoke as before and at greater length, as sorrow, when once it has broken into utterance, is the harder to restrain. Instantly they hastened to accuse him, and having despatched a letter to the emperor, they informed him of the order of the plot and of their own infamy. Never was Rome more distracted and terror-stricken. Meetings, conversations, the ear of friend and stranger were alike shunned; even things mute and lifeless, the very roofs and walls, were eyed with suspicion.

70. The emperor in his letter on the first of January, after offering the usual prayers for the new year, referred to Sabinus, whom he reproached with having corrupted some of his freedmen and having attempted his life, and he claimed vengeance in no obscure language. It was decreed without hesitation, and the condemned man was dragged off, exclaiming as loudly as he could, with head covered and throat tightly bound, "that this was inaugurating the year; these were the victims slain to Sejanus." Wherever he turned his eyes, wherever his words fell, there was flight and solitude; the streets and public places were forsaken. A few retraced their steps and again showed themselves, shudder-ing at the mere fact that they had betrayed alarm. "What day," they asked, "will be without some execution, when amid sacrifices and prayers, a time when it is usual to refrain even from a profane word, the chain and halter are intro-duced? Tiberius has not incurred such odium blindly; this is a studied device to make us believe that there is no reason why the new magistrates should not open the dungeons as well as the temple and the altars." Thereupon there came a letter of thanks to them for having punished a bitter foe to the State, and the emperor further added that he had an anxious life, that he apprehended treachery from enemies, but he mentioned no one by name. Still there was no ques-tion that this was aimed at Nero and Agrippina.

71. But for my plan of referring each event to its own year, I should feel a strong impulse to anticipate matters and at once relate the deaths by which Latinius and Opsius and the other authors of this atrocious deed perished, some after Caius became emperor, some even while Tiberius yet ruled. For although he would not have the instruments of his wickedness destroyed by others, he frequently, when he was tired of them, and fresh ones offered themselves for the same services, flung off the old, now become a mere incubus. But these and other punishments of guilty men I shall describe in due course.

Asinius Gallus, to whose children Agrippina was aunt, then moved that the emperor should be requested to disclose his apprehensions to the Senate and allow their removal. Of all his virtues, as he counted them, there was none on which Tiberius so prided himself as his ability to dissemble, and he was therefore the more irritated at an attempt to expose what he was hiding. Sejanus however pacified him, not out of love for Gallus, but rather to wait the result of the emperor's wavering mood, knowing, as he did, that, though slow in forming his purpose, yet having once broken through his reserve, he would follow up harsh words with terrible deeds.

About the same time Julia died, the granddaughter of Augustus. He had condemned her on a conviction of adultery and had banished her to the island of Trimerus, not far from the shores of Apulia. There she endured a twenty years' exile, in which she was supported by relief from Augusta, who having overthrown the prosperity of her step-children by secret machinations, made open display of her compassion to the fallen family.

72. That same year the Frisii, a nation beyond the Rhine, cast off peace, more because of our rapacity than from their impatience of subjection. Drusus had imposed on them a moderate tribute, suitable to their limited resources, the furnishing of ox hides for military purposes. No one ever severely scrutinized the size or thickness till Olennius, a first-rank centurion, appointed to govern the Frisii, selected hides of wild bulls as the standard according to which they were to be supplied. This would have been hard for any

nation, and it was the less tolerable to the Germans, whose forests abound in huge beasts, while their home cattle are undersized. First it was their herds, next their lands, last, the persons of their wives and children, which they gave up to bondage. Then came angry remonstrances, and when they received no relief, they sought a remedy in war. The soldiers appointed to collect the tribute were seized and gibbeted. Olennius anticipated their fury by flight, and found refuge in a fortress, named Flevum, where a by no means contemptible force of Romans and allies kept guard over the shores of the ocean.

73. As soon as this was known to Lucius Apronius, propraetor of Lower Germany, he summoned from the Upper province the legionary veterans, as well as some picked auxiliary infantry and cavalry. Instantly conveying both armies down the Rhine, he threw them on the Frisii, raising at once the siege of the fortress and dispersing the rebels in defence of their own possessions. Next, he began constructing solid roads and bridges over the neighbouring estuaries for the passage of his heavy troops, and meanwhile having found a ford, he ordered the cavalry of the Canninefates, with all the Germany infantry which served with us, to take the enemy in the rear. Already in battle array, they were beating back our auxiliary horse as well as that of the legions sent to support them, when three light cohorts, then two more, and after a while the entire cavalry were sent to the attack. They were strong enough, had they charged altogether, but coming up, as they did, at intervals, they did not give fresh courage to the repulsed troops and were themselves carried away in the panic of the fugitives. Apronius entrusted the rest of the auxiliaries to Cethegus Labeo, the commander of the fifth legion, but he too, finding his men's position critical and being in extreme peril, sent messages imploring the whole strength of the legions. The soldiers of the fifth sprang forward, drove back the enemy in a fierce encounter, and saved our cohorts and cavalry, who were exhausted by their wounds. But the Roman general did not attempt vengeance or even bury the dead, although many tribunes, prefects, and first-rank centurions had fallen. Soon afterwards it was ascertained from deserters that nine

hundred Romans had been cut to pieces in a wood called
Braduhenna's, after prolonging the fight to the next day,
and that another body of four hundred, which had taken
possession of the house of one Cruptorix, once a soldier in
our pay, fearing betrayal, had perished by mutual slaughter.

74. The Frisian name thus became famous in Germany,
and Tiberius kept our losses a secret, not wishing to entrust
any one with the war. Nor did the Senate care whether dishonour fell on the extreme frontiers of the empire. Fear at
home had filled their hearts, and for this they sought relief
in sycophancy. And so, although their advice was asked on
totally different subjects, they decreed an altar to Clemency,
an altar to Friendship, and statues round them to Cæsar
and Sejanus, both of whom they earnestly begged with repeated entreaties to allow themselves to be seen in public.
Still, neither of them would visit Rome or even the neighbourhood of Rome; they thought it enough to quit the
island and show themselves on the opposite shores of Campania. Senators, knights, a number of the city populace
flocked thither, anxiously looking to Sejanus, approach to
whom was particularly difficult and was consequently sought
by intrigue and by complicity in his counsels. It was sufficiently clear that his arrogance was increased by gazing on
this foul and openly displayed servility. At Rome indeed
hurrying crowds are a familiar sight, and from the extent
of the city no one knows on what business each citizen is
bent; but there, as they lounged in promiscuous crowds in
the fields or on the shore, they had to bear day and night
alike the patronising smiles and the supercilious insolence
of hall-porters, till even this was forbidden them, and those
whom Sejanus had not deigned to accost or to look on, returned to the capital in alarm, while some felt an evil joy,
though there hung over them the dreadful doom of that
ill-starred friendship.

75. Tiberius meanwhile having himself in person bestowed
the hand of his granddaughter Agrippina, Germanicus's
daughter, on Cneius Domitius, directed the marriage to be
celebrated at Rome. In selecting Domitius he looked not
only to his ancient lineage, but also to his alliance with the
blood of the Cæsars, for he could point to Octavia as his
grandmother and through her to Augustus as his great·
uncle.

BOOK V

A. D. 29—31

1. In the consulship of Rubellius and Fufius, both of whom had the surname Geminus, died in an advanced old age Julia Augusta. A Claudia by birth and by adoption a Livia and a Julia, she united the noblest blood of Rome. Her first marriage, by which she had children, was with Tiberius Nero, who, an exile during the Perusian war, returned to Rome when peace had been concluded between Sextus Pompeius and the triumvirs. After this Cæsar, enamoured of her beauty, took her away from her husband, whether against her wish is uncertain. So impatient was he that he brought her to his house actually pregnant, not allowing time for her confinement. She had no subsequent issue, but allied as she was through the marriage of Agrippina and Germanicus to the blood of Augustus, her great-grandchildren were also his. In the purity of her home life she was of the ancient type, but was more gracious than was thought fitting in ladies of former days. An imperious mother and an amiable wife, she was a match for the diplomacy of her husband and the dissimulation of her son. Her funeral was simple, and her will long remained unexecuted. Her panegyric was pronounced from the Rostra by her great-grandson, Caius Cæsar, who afterwards succeeded to power.

2. Tiberius however, making no change in his voluptuous life, excused himself by letter for his absence from his last duty to his mother on the ground of the pressure of business. He even abridged, out of moderation, as it seemed, the honours which the Senate had voted on a lavish scale to her memory, allowing only a very few, and adding that no religious worship was to be decreed, this having been her own wish. In a part of the same letter he sneered at female friendships, with an indirect censure on the consul Fufius,

who had risen to distinction through Augusta's partiality.
Fufius was indeed a man well fitted to win the affection of
a woman; he was witty too, and accustomed to ridicule Tiberius with those bitter jests which the powerful remember
so long.

3. This at all events was the beginning of an unmitigated
and grinding despotism. As long indeed as Augusta lived,
there yet remained a refuge, for with Tiberius obedience to
his mother was the habit of a life, and Sejanus did not dare
to set himself above a parent's authority. Now, so to say,
they threw off the reins and let loose their fury. A letter
was sent, directed against Agrippina and Nero, which was
popularly believed to have been long before forwarded and
to have been kept back by Augusta, as it was publicly read
soon after her death. It contained expressions of studied
harshness, yet it was not armed rebellion or a longing for
revolution, but unnatural passions and profligacy which the
emperor imputed to his grandson. Against his daughter-in-
law he did not dare to invent this much; he merely censured her insolent tongue and defiant spirit, amid the panic-
stricken silence of the Senate, till a few who had no hope
from merit (and public calamities are ever used by individuals for interested purposes) demanded that the question should be debated. The most eager was Cotta Messalinus, who made a savage speech. Still, the other principal
senators, and especially the magistrates, were perplexed, for
Tiberius, notwithstanding his furious invective, had left
everything else in doubt.

4. There was in the Senate one Junius Rusticus, who
having been appointed by the emperor to register its debates
was therefore supposed to have an insight into his secret
purposes. This man, whether through some fatal impulse
(he had indeed never before given any evidence of courage)
or a misdirected acuteness which made him tremble at the
uncertain future, while he forgot impending perils, attached
himself to the waverers, and warned the consuls not to enter
on the debate. He argued that the highest issues turned on
trivial causes, and that the fall of the house of Germanicus
might one day move the old man's remorse. At the same
moment the people, bearing the images of Agrippina and

Nero, thronged round the Senate-house, and, with words of blessing on the emperor, kept shouting that the letter was a forgery and that it was not by the prince's will that ruin was being plotted against his house. And so that day passed without any dreadful result.

Fictitious speeches too against Sejanus were published under the names of ex-consuls, for several persons indulged, all the more recklessly because anonymously, the caprice of their imaginations. Consequently the wrath of Sejanus was the more furious, and he had ground for alleging that the Senate disregarded the emperor's trouble; that the people were in revolt; that speeches in a new style and new resolutions were being heard and read. What remained but to take the sword and chose for their generals and emperors those whose images they had followed as standards.

5. Upon this the emperor, after repeating his invectives against his grandson and his daughter-in-law and reprimanding the populace in an edict, complained to the Senate that by the trick of one senator the imperial dignity had been publicly flouted, and he insisted that, after all, the whole matter should be left to his exclusive decision. Without further deliberation, they proceeded, not indeed to pronounce the final sentence (for this was forbidden), but to declare that they were prepared for vengeance, and were restrained only by the strong hand of the sovereign.

[The remainder of the fifth book and the beginning of the sixth, recounting Sejanus' marriage and fall and covering a space of nearly three years, are lost. Newer editions of Tacitus mark the division between the fifth and sixth books at this point rather than at the end of section 11; but references are regularly made to the older numbering, and so it has been retained here. The beginning of section 6 is obviously fragmentary.]

6. . . . forty-four speeches were delivered on this subject, a few of which were prompted by fear, most by the habit of flattery. . . .

* * * * * *

"There is now a change of fortune, and even he who chose Sejanus to be his colleague and his son-in-law excuses his error. As for the rest, the man whom they encouraged by shameful baseness, they now wickedly revile. Which is the most pitiable, to be accused for friendship's sake or to have to accuse a friend, I cannot decide. I will not put any man's cruelty or compassion to the test, but, while I am free and have a clear conscience, I will anticipate peril. I implore you to cherish my memory with joy rather than with sorrow, numbering me too with those who by a noble death have fled from the miseries of our country."

7. Then detaining those of his friends who were minded to stay with him and converse, or, if otherwise, dismissing them, he thus spent part of the day, and with a numerous circle yet round him, all gazing on his fearless face, and imagining that there was still time to elapse before the last scene, he fell on a sword which he had concealed in his robe. The emperor did not pursue him after his death with either accusation or reproach, although he had heaped a number of foul charges on Blæsus.

8. Next were discussed the cases of Publius Vitellius and Pomponius Secundus. The first was charged by his accusers with having offered the keys of the treasury, of which he was prefect, and the military chest in aid of a revolution. Against the latter, Considius, an ex-prætor, alleged intimacy with Ælius Gallus, who, after the punishment of Sejanus, had fled to the gardens of Pomponius, as his safest refuge. They had no resource in their peril but in the courageous firmness of their brothers who became their sureties. Soon, after several adjournments, Vitellius, weary alike of hope and fear, asked for a penknife, avowedly, for his literary pursuits, and inflicted a slight wound in his veins, and died at last of a broken heart. Pomponius, a man of refined manners and brilliant genius, bore his adverse fortune with resignation, and outlived Tiberius.

9. It was next decided to punish the remaining children of Sejanus, though the fury of the populace was subsiding, and people generally had been appeased by the previous executions. Accordingly they were carried off to prison, the boy, aware of his impending doom, and the little girl, who was so unconscious that she continually asked what was her offence, and whither she was being dragged, saying that she

would do so no more, and a childish chastisement was enough for her correction. Historians of the time tell us that, as there was no precedent for the capital punishment of a virgin, she was violated by the executioner, with the rope on her neck. Then they were strangled and their bodies, mere children as they were, were flung down the Gemoniæ.

10. About the same time Asia and Achaia were alarmed by a prevalent but short-lived rumour that Drusus, the son of Germanicus, had been seen in the Cyclades and subsequently on the mainland. There was indeed a young man of much the same age, whom some of the emperor's freedmen pretended to recognise, and to whom they attached themselves with a treacherous intent. The renown of the name attracted the ignorant, and the Greek mind eagerly fastens on what is new and marvellous. The story indeed, which they no sooner invented than believed, was that Drusus had escaped from custody, and was on his way to the armies of his father, with the design of invading Egypt or Syria. And he was now drawing to himself a multitude of young men and much popular enthusiasm, enjoying the present and cherishing idle hopes of the future, when Poppæus Sabinus heard of the affair. At the time he was chiefly occupied with Macedonia, but he also had the charge of Achaia. So, to forestall the danger, let the story be true or false, he hurried by the bays of Torone and Thermæ, then passed on to Eubœa, an island of the Ægæan, to Piræus, on the coast of Attica, thence to the shores of Corinth and the narrow Isthmus, and having arrived by the other sea at Nicopolis, a Roman colony, he there at last ascertained that the man, when skilfully questioned, had said that he was the son of Marcus Silanus, and that, after the dispersion of a number of his followers, he had embarked on a vessel, intending, it seemed, to go to Italy. Sabinus sent this account to Tiberius, and of the origin and issue of the affair nothing more is known to me.

11. At the close of the year a long growing feud between the consuls broke out. Trio, a reckless man in incurring enmities and a practised lawyer, had indirectly censured Regulus as having been half-hearted in crushing the satellites of Sejanus. Regulus, who, unless he was provoked, loved

quietness, not only repulsed his colleague's attack, but was for dragging him to trial as a guilty accomplice in the conspiracy. And though many of the senators implored them to compose a quarrel likely to end fatally, they continued their enmity and their mutual menaces till they retired from office.

BOOK VI

A.D. 32—37

1. CNEIUS Domitius and Camillus Scribonianus had entered on the consulship when the emperor, after crossing the channel which divides Capreæ from Surrentum, sailed along Campania, in doubt whether he should enter Rome, or, possibly, simulating the intention of going thither, because he had resolved otherwise. He often landed at points in the neighbourhood, visited the gardens by the Tiber, but went back again to the cliffs and to the solitude of the sea shores, in shame at the vices and profligacies into which he had plunged so unrestrainedly that in the fashion of a despot he debauched the children of free-born citizens. It was not merely beauty and a handsome person which he felt as an incentive to his lust, but the modesty of childhood in some, and noble ancestry in others. Hitherto unknown terms were then for the first time invented, derived from the abominations of the place and the endless phases of sensuality. Slaves too were set over the work of seeking out and procuring, with rewards for the willing and threats to the reluctant, and if there was resistance from a relative or a parent, they used violence and force, and actually indulged their own passions as if dealing with captives.

2. At Rome meanwhile, in the beginning of the year, as if Livia's crimes had just been discovered and not also long ago punished, terrible decrees were proposed against her very statues and memory, and the property of Sejanus was to be taken from the exchequer and transferred to the imperial treasury, as if there was any difference. The motion was being urged with extreme persistency, in almost the same or with but slightly changed language, by such men as Scipio, Silanus, and Cassius, when suddenly Togonius Gallus intruding his own obscurity among illustrious names, was

195

heard with ridicule. He begged the emperor to select a number of senators, twenty out of whom should be chosen by lot to wear swords and to defend his person, whenever he entered the Senate House. The man had actually believed a letter from him in which he asked the protection of one of the consuls, so that he might go in safety from Capreæ to Rome. Tiberius however, who usually combined jesting and seriousness, thanked the senators for their goodwill, but asked who could be rejected, who could be chosen? "Were they always to be the same, or was there to be a succession? Were they to be men who had held office or youths, private citizens or officials? Then, again, what a scene would be presented by persons grasping their swords on the threshold of the Senate House? His life was not of so much worth if it had to be defended by arms." This was his answer to Togonius, guarded in its expression, and he urged nothing beyond the rejection of the motion.

3. Junius Gallio however, who had proposed that the prætorian soldiers, after having served their campaigns, should acquire the privilege of sitting in the fourteen rows of the theatre, received a savage censure. Tiberius, just as if he were face to face with him, asked what *he* had to do with the soldiers, who ought not to receive the emperor's orders or his rewards except from the emperor himself? He had really discovered something which the Divine Augustus had not foreseen. Or was not one of Sejanus's satellites rather seeking to sow discord and sedition, as a means of prompting ignorant minds, under the pretence of compliment, to ruin military discipline? This was Gallio's recompense for his carefully prepared flattery, with immediate expulsion from the Senate, and then from Italy. And as men complained that he would endure his exile with equanimity, since he had chosen the famous and lovely island of Lesbos, he was dragged back to Rome, and confined in the houses of different officials.

The emperor in the same letter crushed Sextius Paconianus, an ex-prætor, to the great joy of the senators, as he was a daring, mischievous man, who pried into every person's secrets, and had been the chosen instrument of Sejanus in his treacherous designs against Caius Cæsar. When this fact was divulged, there came an outburst of long-concealed hatreds, and there must have been a sentence of capital punishment, had he not himself volunteered a disclosure.

4. As soon as he named Latinius Latiaris, accuser and accused, both alike objects of execration, presented a most welcome spectacle. Latiaris, as I have related, had been foremost in contriving the ruin of Titius Sabinus, and was now the first to pay the penalty. By way of episode, Haterius Agrippa inveighed against the consuls of the previous year for now sitting silent after their threats of impeaching one another. "It must be fear," he said, "and a guilty conscience which are acting as a bond of union. But the senators must not keep back what they have heard." Regulus replied that he was awaiting the opportunity for vengeance, and meant to press it in the emperor's presence. Trio's answer was that it was best to efface the memory of rivalries between colleagues, and of any words uttered in quarrels. When Agrippa still persisted, Sanquinius Maximus, one of the ex-consuls, implored the Senate not to increase the emperor's anxieties by seeking further occasions of bitterness, as he was himself competent to provide remedies. This secured the safety of Regulus and the postponement of Trio's ruin. Haterius was hated all the more. Wan with untimely slumbers and nights of riot, and not fearing in his indolence even the cruellest of princes, he yet plotted amid his gluttony and lust the destruction of illustrious men.

5. Several charges were next brought, as soon as the opportunity offered, against Cotta Messalinus, the author of every unusually cruel proposal, and consequently, regarded with inveterate hatred. He had spoken, it was said, of Caius Cæsar, as if it were a question whether he was a man, and of an entertainment at which he was present on Augusta's birthday with the priests, as a funeral banquet. In remonstrating too against the influence of Marcus Lepidus and Lucius Arruntius, with whom he had disputes on many matters, he had added the remark, "They will have the Senate's support; I shall have that of my darling Tiberius." But the leading men of the State failed to convict him on all the charges. When they pressed the case, he appealed to the emperor. Soon afterwards, a letter arrived, in which Tiberius

traced the origin of the friendship between himself and
Cotta, enumerated his frequent services, and then requested
that words perversely misrepresented and the freedom of
table talk might not be construed into a crime.

6. The beginning of the emperor's letter seemed very
striking. It opened thus: "May all the gods and goddesses
destroy me more miserably than I feel myself to be daily
perishing, if I know at this moment what to write to you,
Senators, how to write it, or what, in short, not to write."
So completely had his crimes and infamies recoiled, as a
penalty, on himself. With profound meaning was it often
affirmed by the greatest teacher of philosophy that, could
the minds of tyrants be laid bare, there would be seen gashes
and wounds; for, as the body is lacerated by scourging, so
is the spirit by brutality, by lust and by evil thoughts. Assuredly Tiberius was not saved by his elevation or his solitude from having to confess the anguish of his heart and
his self-inflicted punishment.

7. Authority was then given to the Senate to decide the
case of Cæcilianus, one of its members, the chief witness
against Cotta, and it was agreed that the same penalty
should be inflicted as on Aruseius and Sanquinius, the accusers of Lucius Arruntius. Nothing ever happened to Cotta
more to his distinction. Of noble birth, but beggared by extravagance and infamous for his excesses, he was now by
the dignity of his revenge, raised to a level with the stainless
virtues of Arruntius.

Quintus Servæus and Minucius Thermus were next arraigned. Servæus was an ex-prætor, and had formerly been
a companion of Germanicus; Minucius was of equestrian
rank, and both had enjoyed, though discreetly, the friendship of Sejanus. Hence they were the more pitied. Tiberius,
on the contrary, denounced them as foremost in crime, and
bade Caius Cestius, the elder, tell the Senate what he had
communicated to the emperor by letter. Cestius undertook
the prosecution. And this was the most dreadful feature of
the age, that leading members of the Senate, some openly,
some secretly employed themselves in the very lowest work
of the informer. One could not distinguish between aliens
and kinsfolk, between friends and strangers, or say what

was quite recent, or what half-forgotten from lapse of time. People were incriminated for some casual remark in the forum or at the dinner-table, for every one was impatient to be the first to mark his victim, some to screen themselves, most from being, as it were, infected with the contagion of the malady.

Minucius and Servæus, on being condemned, went over to the prosecution, and then Julius Africanus with Seius Quadratus were dragged into the same ruin. Africanus was from the Santones, one of the states of Gaul; the origin of Quadratus I have not ascertained. Many authors, I am well aware, have passed over the perils and punishments of a host of persons, sickened by the multiplicity of them, or fearing that what they had themselves found wearisome and saddening, would be equally fatiguing to their readers. For myself, I have lighted on many facts worth knowing, though other writers have not recorded them.

8. A Roman knight, Marcus Terentius, at the crisis when all others had hypocritically repudiated the friendship of Sejanus, dared, when impeached on that ground, to cling to it by the following avowal to the Senate: "In my position it is perhaps less to my advantage to acknowledge than to deny the charge. Still, whatever is to be the issue of the matter, I shall admit that I was the friend of Sejanus, that I anxiously sought to be such, and was delighted when I was successful. I had seen him his father's colleague in the command of the prætorian cohorts, and subsequently combining the duties of civil and military life. His kinsfolk and connections were loaded with honours; intimacy with Sejanus was in every case a powerful recommendation to the emperor's friendship. Those, on the contrary, whom he hated, had to struggle with danger and humiliation. I take no individual as an instance. All of us who had no part in his last design, I mean to defend at the peril of myself alone. It was really not Sejanus of Vulsinii, it was a member of the Claudian and Julian houses, in which he had taken a position by his marriage-alliance, it was your son-in-law, Cæsar, your partner in the consulship, the man who administered your political functions, whom we courted. It is not for us to criticise one whom you may raise above all others, or

your motives for so doing. Heaven has intrusted you with the supreme decision of affairs, and for us is left the glory of obedience. And, again, we see what takes place before our eyes, who it is on whom you bestow riches and honours, who are the most powerful to help or to injure. That Sejanus was such, no one will deny. To explore the prince's secret thoughts, or any of his hidden plans, is a forbidden, a dangerous thing, nor does it follow that one could reach them.

"Do not, Senators, think only of Sejanus's last day, but of his sixteen years of power. We actually adored a Satrius and a Pomponius. To be known even to his freedmen and hall-porters was thought something very grand. What then is my meaning? Is this apology meant to be offered for all without difference and discrimination? No; it is to be restricted within proper limits. Let plots against the State, murderous designs against the emperor be punished. As for friendship and its obligations, the same principle must acquit both you, Cæsar, and us."

9. The courage of this speech and the fact that there had been found a man to speak out what was in all people's thoughts, had such an effect that the accusers of Terentius were sentenced to banishment or death, their previous offences being taken into account. Then came a letter from Tiberius against Sextus Vestilius, an ex-prætor, whom, as a special favourite of his brother Drusus, the emperor had admitted into his own select circle. His reason for being displeased with Vestilius was that he had either written an attack on Caius Cæsar as a profligate, or that Tiberius believed a false charge. For this Vestilius was excluded from the prince's table. He then tried the knife with his aged hand, but again bound up his veins, opening them once more however on having begged for pardon by letter and received a pitiless answer. After him a host of persons were charged with treason, Annius Pollio, Appius Silanus Scaurus, Mamercus, Sabinus Calvisius, Vinicianus too, coupled with Pollio, his father, men all of illustrious descent, some too of the highest political distinction. The senators were panic-stricken, for how few of their number were not connected by alliance or by friendship with this multitude of men of rank! Celsus however, tribune of a city cohort, and now

one of the prosecutors, saved Appius and Calvisius from the peril. The emperor postponed the cases of Pollio, Vinicianus, and Scaurus, intending to try them himself with the Senate, not however without affixing some ominous marks to the name of Scaurus.

10. Even women were not exempt from danger. Where they could not be accused of grasping at political power, their tears were made a crime. Vitia, an aged woman, mother of Fufius Geminus, was executed for bewailing the death of her son. Such were the proceedings in the Senate. It was the same with the emperor. Vescularius Atticus and Julius Marinus were hurried off to execution, two of his oldest friends, men who had followed him to Rhodes and been his inseparable companions at Capreæ. Vescularius was his agent in the plot against Libo, and it was with the co-operation of Marinus that Sejanus had ruined Curtius Atticus. Hence there was all the more joy at the recoil of these precedents on their authors.

About the same time Lucius Piso, the pontiff, died a natural death, a rare incident in so high a rank. Never had he by choice proposed a servile motion, and, whenever necessity was too strong for him, he would suggest judicious compromises. His father, as I have related, had been a censor. He lived to the advanced age of eighty, and had won in Thrace the honour of a triumph. But his chief glory rested on the wonderful tact with which as city-prefect he handled an authority, recently made perpetual and all the more galling to men unaccustomed to obey it.

11. In former days, when the kings and subsequently the chief magistrates went from Rome, an official was temporarily chosen to administer justice and provide for emergencies, so that the capital might not be left without government. It is said that Denter Romulius was appointed by Romulus, then Numa Marcius by Tullus Hostilius, and Spurius Lucretius by Tarquinius Superbus. Afterwards, the consuls made the appointment. The shadow of the old practice still survives, whenever in consequence of the Latin festival some one is deputed to exercise the consul's functions. And Augustus too during the civil wars gave Cilnius Mæcenas, a Roman knight, charge of everything in Rome

and Italy. When he rose to supreme power, in consideration
of the magnitude of the State and the slowness of legal
remedies, he selected one of the ex-consuls to overawe the
slaves and that part of the population which, unless it fears
a strong hand, is disorderly and reckless. Messala Corvinus
was the first to obtain the office, which he lost within a few
days, as not knowing how to discharge it. After him Taurus
Statilius, though in advanced years, sustained it admirably;
and then Piso, after twenty years of similar credit, was, by
the Senate's decree, honoured with a public funeral.

12. A motion was next brought forward in the Senate by
Quintilianus, a tribune of the people, respecting an alleged
book of the Sibyl. Caninius Gallus, a member of the College
of the Fifteen, had asked that it might be received among
the other volumes of the same prophetess by a decree on the
subject. This having been carried by a division, the emperor
sent a letter in which he gently censured the tribune, as ignorant of ancient usage because of his youth. Gallus he
scolded for having introduced the matter in a thin Senate,
notwithstanding his long experience in the science of religious ceremonies, without taking the opinion of the College
or having the verses read and criticised, as was usual, by its
presidents, though their authenticity was very doubtful. He
also reminded him that, as many spurious productions were
current under a celebrated name, Augustus had prescribed a
day within which they should be deposited with the city-
prætor, and after which it should not be lawful for any private person to hold them. The same regulations too had
been made by our ancestors after the burning of the Capitol
in the social war, when there was a search throughout
Samos, Ilium, Erythræ, and even in Africa, Sicily and the
Italian colonies for the verses of the Sibyl (whether there
were but one or more) and the priests were charged with
the business of distinguishing, as far as they could by human
means, what were genuine. Accordingly the book in question was now also submitted to the scrutiny of the College
of the Fifteen.

13. During the same consulship a high price of corn almost brought on an insurrection. For several days there
were many clamorous demands made in the theatre with an

unusual freedom of language towards the emperor. This provoked him to censure the magistrates and the Senate for not having used the authority of the State to put down the people. He named too the corn-supplying provinces, and dwelt on the far larger amount of grain imported by himself than by Augustus. So the Senate drew up a decree in the severe spirit of antiquity, and the consuls issued a not less stringent proclamation. The emperor's silence was not, as he had hoped, taken as a proof of patriotism, but of pride.

14. At the year's close Geminius, Celsus and Pompeius Roman knights, fell beneath a charge of conspiracy. Of these Caius Geminius, by lavish expenditure and a luxurious life, had been a friend of Sejanus, but with no serious result. Julius Celsus, a tribune, while in confinement, loosened his chain, and having twisted it around him, broke his neck by throwing himself in an opposite direction. Rubrius Fabatus was put under surveillance, on a suspicion that, in despair of the fortunes of Rome, he meant to throw himself on the mercy of the Parthians. He was, at any rate, found near the Straits of Sicily, and, when dragged back by a centurion, he assigned no adequate reason for his long journey. Still, he lived on in safety, thanks to forgetfulness rather than to mercy.

15. In the consulship of Servius Galba and Lucius Sulla, the emperor, after having long considered whom he was to choose to be husbands for his granddaughters, now that the maidens were of marriageable age, selected Lucius Cassius and Marcus Vinicius. Vinicius was of provincial descent; he was born at Cales, his father and grandfather having been consuls, and his family, on the other side, being of the rank of knights. He was a man of amiable temper and of cultivated eloquence. Cassius was of an ancient and honourable, though plebeian house, at Rome. Though he was brought up by his father under a severe training, he won esteem more frequently by his good-nature than by his diligence. To him and to Vinicius the emperor married respectively Drusilla and Julia, Germanicus's daughters, and addressed a letter on the subject to the Senate, with a slightly complimentary mention of the young men. He next assigned

some very vague reasons for his absence, then passed to
more important matters, the ill-will against him originating
in his state policy, and requested that Macro, who commanded the prætorians, with a few tribunes and centurions,
might accompany him whenever he entered the Senate-
house. But though a decree was voted by the Senate on a
liberal scale and without any restrictions as to rank or numbers, he never so much as went near the walls of Rome,
much less the State-council, for he would often go round and
avoid his native city by circuitous routes.

16. Meanwhile a powerful host of accusers fell with sudden fury on the class which systematically increased its
wealth by usury in defiance of a law passed by Cæsar the
Dictator defining the terms of lending money and of holding
estates in Italy, a law long obsolete because the public good
is sacrificed to private interest. The curse of usury was indeed of old standing in Rome and a most frequent cause of
sedition and discord, and it was therefore repressed even in
the early days of a less corrupt morality. First, the Twelve
Tables prohibited any one from exacting more than 10 per
cent., when, previously, the rate had depended on the caprice
of the wealthy. Subsequently, by a bill brought in by the
tribunes, interest was reduced to half that amount, and
finally compound interest was wholly forbidden. A check
too was put by several enactments of the people on evasions
which, though continually put down, still, through strange
artifices, reappeared. On this occasion, however, Gracchus,
the prætor, to whose jurisdiction the inquiry had fallen, felt
himself compelled by the number of persons endangered to
refer the matter to the Senate. In their dismay the senators,
not one of whom was free from similar guilt, threw themselves on the emperor's indulgence. He yielded, and a year
and six months were granted, within which every one was
to settle his private accounts conformably to the requirements of the law.

17. Hence followed a scarcity of money, a great shock
being given to all credit, the current coin too, in consequence
of the conviction of so many persons and the sale of their
property, being locked up in the imperial treasury or the
public exchequer. To meet this, the Senate had directed that

every creditor should have two-thirds of his capital secured on estates in Italy. Creditors however were suing for payment in full, and it was not respectable for persons when sued to break faith. So, at first, there were clamorous meetings and importunate entreaties; then noisy applications to the prætor's court. And the very device intended as a remedy, the sale and purchase of estates, proved the contrary, as the usurers had hoarded up all their money for buying land. The facilities for selling were followed by a fall of prices, and the deeper a man was in debt, the more reluctantly did he part with his property, and many were utterly ruined. The destruction of private wealth precipitated the fall of rank and reputation, till at last the emperor interposed his aid by distributing throughout the banks a hundred million sesterces, and allowing freedom to borrow without interest for three years, provided the borrower gave security to the State in land to double the amount. Credit was thus restored, and gradually private lenders were found The purchase too of estates was not carried out according to the letter of the Senate's decree, rigour at the outset, as usual with such matters, becoming negligence in the end.

18. Former alarms then returned, as there was a charge of treason against Considius Proculus. While he was celebrating his birthday without a fear, he was hurried before the Senate, condemned and instantly put to death. His sister Sancia was outlawed, on the accusation of Quintus Pomponius, a restless spirit, who pretended that he employed himself in this and like practices to win favour with the sovereign, and thereby alleviate the perils hanging over his brother Pomponius Secundus.

Pompeia Macrina too was sentenced to banishment. Her husband Argolicus and her father-in-law Laco, leading men of Achaia, had been ruined by the emperor. Her father likewise, an illustrious Roman knight, and her brother, an ex-prætor, seeing their doom was near, destroyed themselves. It was imputed to them as a crime that their great-grandfather Theophanes of Mitylene had been one of the intimate friends of Pompey the Great, and that after his death Greek flattery had paid him divine honours.

19. Sextus Marius, the richest man in Spain, was next ac-

cused of incest with his daughter, and thrown headlong from the Tarpeian rock. To remove any doubt that the vastness of his wealth had proved the man's ruin, Tiberius kept his gold-mines for himself, though they were forfeited to the State. Executions were now a stimulus to his fury, and he ordered the death of all who were lying in prison under accusation of complicity with Sejanus. There lay, singly or in heaps, the unnumbered dead, of every age and sex, the illustrious with the obscure. Kinsfolk and friends were not allowed to be near them, to weep over them, or even to gaze on them too long. Spies were set round them, who noted the sorrow of each mourner and followed the rotting corpses, till they were dragged to the Tiber, where, floating or driven on the bank, no one dared to burn or to touch them. The force of terror had utterly extinguished the sense of human fellowship, and, with the growth of cruelty, pity was thrust aside.

20. About this time Caius Cæsar, who became his grandfather's companion on his retirement to Capreæ, married Claudia, daughter of Marcus Silanus. He was a man who masked a savage temper under an artful guise of self-restraint, and neither his mother's doom nor the banishment of his brothers extorted from him a single utterance. Whatever the humour of the day with Tiberius, he would assume the like, and his language differed as little. Hence the fame of a clever remark from the orator Passienus, that "there never was a better slave or a worse master."

I must not pass over a prognostication of Tiberius respecting Servius Galba, then consul. Having sent for him and sounded him on various topics, he at last addressed him in Greek to this effect: "You too, Galba, will some day have a taste of empire." He thus hinted at a brief span of power late in life, on the strength of his acquaintance with the art of astrologers, leisure for acquiring which he had had at Rhodes, with Thrasyllus for instructor. This man's skill he tested in the following manner.

21. Whenever he sought counsel on such matters, he would make use of the top of the house and of the confidence of one freedman, quite illiterate and of great physical strength. The man always walked in front of the person whose science Tiberius had determined to test, through an unfrequented

and precipitous path (for the house stood on rocks), and
then, if any suspicion had arisen of imposture or of trickery,
he hurled the astrologer, as he returned, into the sea beneath, that no one might live to betray the secret. Thrasyllus
accordingly was led up the same cliffs, and when he had
deeply impressed his questioner by cleverly revealing his imperial destiny and future career, he was asked whether he
had also thoroughly ascertained his own horoscope, and the
character of that particular year and day. After surveying
the positions and relative distances of the stars, he first
paused, then trembled, and the longer he gazed, the more
was he agitated by amazement and terror, till at last he exclaimed that a perilous and well-nigh fatal crisis impended
over him. Tiberius then embraced him and congratulated
him on foreseeing his dangers and on being quite safe. Taking what he had said as an oracle, he retained him in the
number of his intimate friends.

22. When I hear of these and like occurrences, I suspend
my judgment on the question whether it is fate and un-
changeable necessity or chance which governs the revolutions
of human affairs. Indeed, among the wisest of the ancients
and among their disciples you will find conflicting theories,
many holding the conviction that heaven does not concern
itself with the beginning or the end of our life, or, in short,
with mankind at all; and that therefore sorrows are continually the lot of the good, happiness of the wicked; while
others, on the contrary, believe that, though there is a harmony between fate and events, yet it is not dependent on
wandering stars, but on primary elements, and on a combination of natural causes. Still, they leave us the capacity
of choosing our life, maintaining that, the choice once made,
there is a fixed sequence of events. Good and evil, again, are
not what vulgar opinion accounts them; many who seem to
be struggling with adversity are happy; many, amid great
affluence, are utterly miserable, if only the first bear their
hard lot with patience, and the latter make a foolish use of
their prosperity.

Most men, however, cannot part with the belief that each
person's future is fixed from his very birth, but that some
things happen differently from what has been foretold

through the impostures of those who describe what they do
not know, and that this destroys the credit of a science, clear
testimonies to which have been given both by past ages and
by our own. In fact, how the son of this same Thrasyllus
predicted Nero's reign I shall relate when the time comes,
not to digress too far from my subject.

23. That same year the death of Asinius Gallus became
known. That he died of starvation, there was not a doubt;
whether of his own choice or by compulsion, was a question.
The emperor was asked whether he would allow him to be
buried, and he blushed not to grant the favour, and actually
blamed the accident which had proved fatal to the accused
before he could be convicted in his presence. Just as if in a
three years' interval an opportunity was wanting for the trial
of an old ex-consul and the father of a number of ex-consuls.

Next Drusus perished, after having prolonged life for
eight days on the most wretched of food, even chewing the
stuffing of his bed. According to some writers, Macro had
been instructed that, in case of Sejanus attempting an armed
revolt, he was to hurry the young prince out of the confinement in which he was detained in the Palace and put him at
the head of the people. Subsequently the emperor, as a rumour was gaining ground that he was on the point of a
reconciliation with his daughter-in-law and his grandson,
chose to be merciless rather than to relent.

24. He even bitterly reviled him after his death, taunting
him with nameless abominations and with a spirit bent on his
family's ruin and hostile to the State. And, what seemed
most horrible of all, he ordered a daily journal of all that he
said and did to be read in public. That there had been spies
by his side for so many years, to note his looks, his sighs,
and even his whispered thoughts, and that his grandfather
could have heard read, and published all, was scarce credible. But letters of Attius, a centurion, and Didymus, a
freedman, openly exhibited the names of slave after slave
who had respectively struck or scared Drusus as he was quitting his chamber. The centurion had actually added, as
something highly meritorious, his own language in all its
brutality, and some utterances of the dying man in which, at
first feigning loss of reason, he imprecated in seeming mad-

ness fearful things on Tiberius, and then, when hope of life was gone, denounced him with a studied and elaborate curse. "As he had slain a daughter-in-law, a brother's son, and son's sons, and filled his whole house with bloodshed, so might he pay the full penalty due to the name and race of his ancestors as well as to future generations."

The Senate clamorously interrupted, with an affectation of horror, but they were penetrated by alarm and amazement at seeing that a hitherto cunning prince, who had shrouded his wickedness in mystery, had waxed so bold as to remove, so to speak, the walls of his house and display his grandson under a centurion's lash, amid the buffetings of slaves, craving in vain the last sustenance of life.

25. Men's grief at all this had not died away when news was heard of Agrippina. She had lived on, sustained by hope, I suppose, after the destruction of Sejanus, and, when she found no abatement of horrors, had voluntarily perished, though possibly nourishment was refused her and a fiction concocted of a death that might seem self-chosen. Tiberius, it is certain, vented his wrath in the foulest charges. He reproached her with unchastity, with having had Asinius Gallus as a paramour and being driven by his death to loathe existence. But Agrippina, who could not endure equality and loved to domineer, was with her masculine aspirations far removed from the frailties of women. The emperor further observed that she died on the same day on which Sejanus had paid the penalty of his crime two years before, a fact, he said, to be recorded; and he made it a boast that she had not been strangled by the halter and flung down the Gemonian steps. He received a vote of thanks, and it was decreed that on the seventeenth of October, the day on which both perished, through all future years, an offering should be consecrated to Jupiter.

26. Soon afterwards Cocceius Nerva, a man always at the emperor's side, a master of law both divine and human, whose position was secure and health sound, resolved to die. Tiberius, as soon as he knew it, sat by him and asked his reasons, adding intreaties, and finally protesting that it would be a burden on his conscience and a blot on his reputation, if the most intimate of his friends were to fly from

life without any cause for death. Nerva turned away from
his expostulations and persisted in his abstinence from all
food. Those who knew his thoughts said that as he saw more
closely into the miseries of the State, he chose, in anger and
alarm, an honourable death. while he was yet safe and unassailed.

Meanwhile Agrippina's ruin, strange to say, dragged Plancina with it. Formerly the wife of Cneius Piso, and one who
had openly exulted at the death of Germanicus, she had been
saved, when Piso fell, by the intreaties of Augusta, and not
less by the enmity of Agrippina. When hatred and favour
had alike passed away, justice asserted itself. Pursued by
charges universally notorious, she suffered by her own hand
a penalty tardy rather than undeserved.

27. Amid the many sorrows which saddened Rome, one
cause of grief was the marriage of Julia, Drusus's daughter
and Nero's late wife, into the humbler family of Rubellius
Blandus, whose grandfather many remembered as a Roman
knight from Tibur. At the end of the year the death of
Ælius Lamia, who, after being at last released from the farce
of governing Syria, had become city-prefect, was celebrated
with the honours of a censor's funeral. He was a man of
illustrious descent, and in a hale old age; and the fact of
the province having been withheld gained him additional esteem. Subsequently, on the death of Flaccus Pomponius,
proprætor of Syria, a letter from the emperor was read, in
which he complained that all the best men who were fit to
command armies declined the service, and that he was thus
necessarily driven to intreaties, by which some of the ex-
consuls might be prevailed on to take provinces. He forgot
that Arruntius had been kept at home now for ten years,
that he might not go to Spain.

That same year Marcus Lepidus also died. I have dwelt
at sufficient length on his moderation and wisdom in my
earlier books, and I need not further enlarge on his noble
descent. Assuredly the family of the Æmilii has been rich in
good citizens, and even the members of that house whose
morals were corrupt, still lived with a certain splendour.

28. During the consulship of Paulus Fabius and Lucius
Vitellius, the bird called the phœnix, after a long succession

of ages, appeared in Egypt and furnished the most learned
men of that country and of Greece with abundant matter for
the discussion of the marvellous phenomenon. It is my wish
to make known all on which they agree with several things,
questionable enough indeed, but not too absurd to be noticed.

That it is a creature sacred to the sun, differing from all
other birds in its beak and in the tints of its plumage, is held
unanimously by those who have described its nature. As to
the number of years it lives, there are various accounts. The
general tradition says five hundred years. Some maintain
that it is seen at intervals of fourteen hundred and sixty-one
years, and that the former birds flew into the city called
Heliopolis successively in the reigns of Sesostris, Amasis, and
Ptolemy, the third king of the Macedonian dynasty, with a
multitude of companion birds marvelling at the novelty of
the appearance. But all antiquity is of course obscure. From
Ptolemy to Tiberius was a period of less than five hundred
years. Consequently some have supposed that this was a
spurious phœnix, not from the regions of Arabia, and with
none of the instincts which ancient tradition has attributed
to the bird. For when the number of years is completed and
death is near, the phœnix, it is said, builds a nest in the land
of its birth and infuses into it a germ of life from which an
offspring arises, whose first care, when fledged, is to bury its
father. This is not rashly done, but taking up a load of
myrrh and having tried its strength by a long flight, as soon
as it is equal to the burden and to the journey, it carries its
father's body, bears it to the altar of the Sun, and leaves it
to the flames. All this is full of doubt and legendary exaggeration. Still, there is no question that the bird is occasionally seen in Egypt.

29. Rome meanwhile being a scene of ceaseless bloodshed,
Pomponius Labeo, who was, as I have related, governor of
Mœsia, severed his veins and let his life ebb from him. His
wife, Paxæa, emulated her husband. What made such deaths
eagerly sought was dread of the executioner, and the fact too
that the condemned, besides forfeiture of their property,
were deprived of burial, while those who decided their fate
themselves, had their bodies interred, and their wills re-

mained valid, a recompense this for their despatch. The emperor, however, argued in a letter to the Senate that it had been the practice of our ancestors, whenever they broke off an intimacy, to forbid the person their house, and so put an end to friendship. "This usage he had himself revived in Labeo's case, but Labeo, being pressed by charges of maladministration in his province and other crimes, had screened his guilt by bringing odium on another, and had groundlessly alarmed his wife, who, though criminal, was still free from danger."

Mamercus Scaurus was then for the second time impeached, a man of distinguished rank and ability as an advocate, but of infamous life. He fell, not through the friendship of Sejanus, but through what was no less powerful to destroy, the enmity of Macro, who practised the same arts more secretly. Macro's information was grounded on the subject of a tragedy written by Scaurus, from which he cited some verses which might be twisted into allusions to Tiberius. But Servilius and Cornelius, his accusers, alleged adultery with Livia and the practice of magical rites. Scaurus, as befitted the old house of the Æmilii, forestalled the fatal sentence at the persuasion of his wife Sextia, who urged him to die and shared his death.

30. Still the informers were punished whenever an opportunity occurred. Servilius and Cornelius, for example, whom the destruction of Scaurus had made notorious, were outlawed and transported to some islands for having taken money from Varius Ligur for dropping a prosecution. Abudius Ruso too, who had been an ædile, in seeking to imperil Lentulus Gætulicus, under whom he had commanded a legion, by alleging that he had fixed on a son of Sejanus for his son-in-law, was himself actually condemned and banished from Rome. Gætulicus at this time was in charge of the legions of Upper Germany, and had won from them singular affection, as a man of unbounded kindliness, moderate in his strictness, and popular even with the neighbouring army through his father-in-law, Lucius Apronius. Hence rumour persistently affirmed that he had ventured to send the emperor a letter, reminding him that his alliance with Sejanus had not originated in his own choice. but in the advice

of Tiberius; that he was himself as liable to be deceived as
Tiberius, and that the same mistake ought not to be held
innocent in the prince and be a source of ruin to others. His
loyalty was still untainted and would so remain, if he was
not assailed by any plot. A successor he should accept as an
announcement of his doom. A compact, so to say, ought to
be sealed between them, by which he should retain his province, and the emperor be master of all else. Strange as this
story was, it derived credibility from the fact that Gætulicus
alone of all connected with Sejanus lived in safety and in
high favour, Tiberius bearing in mind the people's hatred,
his own extreme age and how his government rested more
on prestige than on power.

31. In the consulship of Caius Cestius and Marcus Servilius, some Parthian nobles came to Rome, without the
knowledge of their king Artabanus. Dread of Germanicus
had made that prince faithful to the Romans and just to his
people, but he subsequently changed this behaviour for insolence towards us and tyranny to his subjects. He was
elated by the wars which he had successfully waged against
the surrounding nations, while he disdained the aged and, as
he thought, unwarlike Tiberius, eagerly coveting Armenia,
over which, on the death of Artaxias, he placed Arsaces, his
eldest son. He further added insult, and sent envoys to reclaim the treasures left by Vonones in Syria and Cilicia.
Then too he insisted on the ancient boundaries of Persia and
Macedonia, and intimated, with a vainglorious threat, that
he meant to seize on the country possessed by Cyrus and
afterwards by Alexander.

The chief adviser of the Parthians in sending the secret
embassy was Sinnaces, a man of distinguished family and
corresponding wealth. Next in influence was Abdus, an
eunuch, a class which, far from being despised among barbarians, actually possesses power. These, with some other
nobles whom they admitted to their counsels, as there was
not a single Arsacid whom they could put on the throne,
most of the family having been murdered by Artabanus or
being under age, demanded that Phraates, son of king
Phraates, should be sent from Rome. "Only a name," they
said, "and an authority were wanted; only, in fact, that

with Cæsar's consent, a scion of the house of Arsaces should show himself on the banks of the Euphrates."

32. This suited the wishes of Tiberius. He provided Phraates with what he needed for assuming his father's sovereignty, while he clung to his purpose of regulating foreign affairs by a crafty policy and keeping war at a distance. Artabanus meanwhile, hearing of the treacherous arrangement, was one moment perplexed by apprehension, the next fired with a longing for revenge. With barbarians, indecision is a slave's weakness, prompt action king-like. But now expediency prevailed, and he invited Abdus, under the guise of friendship, to a banquet, and disabled him by a lingering poison; Sinnaces he put off by pretexts and presents, and also by various employments. Phraates meanwhile, on arriving in Syria, where he threw off the Roman fashions to which for so many years he had been accustomed, and adapted himself to Parthian habits, unable to endure the customs of his country, was carried off by an illness. Still, Tiberius did not relinquish his purpose. He chose Tiridates, of the same stock as Artabanus, to be his rival, and the Iberian Mithridates to be the instrument of recovering Armenia, having reconciled him to his brother Pharasmanes, who held the throne of that country. He then intrusted the whole of his eastern policy to Lucius Vitellius. The man, I am aware, had a bad name at Rome, and many a foul story was told of him. But in the government of provinces he acted with the virtue of ancient times. He returned, and then, through fear of Caius Cæsar and intimacy with Claudius, he degenerated into a servility so base that he is regarded by an after-generation as the type of the most degrading adulation. The beginning of his career was forgotten in its end, and an old age of infamy effaced the virtues of youth.

33. Of the petty chiefs Mithridates was the first to persuade Pharasmanes to aid his enterprise by stratagem and force, and agents of corruption were found who tempted the servants of Arsaces into crime by a quantity of gold. At the same instant the Iberians burst into Armenia with a huge host, and captured the city of Artaxata. Artabanus, on hearing this, made his son Orodes the instrument of vengeance. He gave him the Parthian army and despatched men to hire

auxiliaries. Pharasmanes, on the other hand, allied himself with the Albanians, and procured aid from the Sarmatæ, whose highest chiefs took bribes from both sides, after the fashion of their countrymen, and engaged themselves in conflicting interests. But the Iberians, who were masters of the various positions, suddenly poured the Sarmatæ into Armenia by the Caspian route. Meanwhile those who were coming up to the support of the Parthians were easily kept back, all other approaches having been closed by the enemy except one, between the sea and the mountains on the Albanian frontier, which summer rendered difficult, as there the shallows are flooded by the force of the Etesian gales. The south wind in winter rolls back the waves, and when the sea is driven back upon itself, the shallows along the coast are exposed.

34. Meantime, while Orodes was without an ally, Pharasmanes, now strengthened by reinforcements, challenged him to battle, taunted him on his refusal, rode up to his camp and harassed his foraging parties. He often hemmed him in with his picquets in the fashion of a blockade, till the Parthians, who were unused to such insults, gathered round the king and demanded battle. Their sole strength was in cavalry; Pharasmanes was also powerful in infantry, for the Iberians and Albanians, inhabiting as they did a densely wooded country, were more inured to hardship and endurance. They claim to have been descended from the Thessalians, at the period when Jason, after the departure of Medea and the children born of her, returned subsequently to the empty palace of Æetes, and the vacant kingdom of Colchi. They have many traditions connected with his name and with the oracle of Phrixus. No one among them would think of sacrificing a ram, the animal supposed to have conveyed Phrixus, whether it was really a ram or the figure-head of a ship.

Both sides having been drawn up in battle array, the Parthian leader expatiated on the empire of the East, and the renown of the Arsacids, in contrast to the despicable Iberian chief with his hireling soldiery. Pharasmanes reminded his people that they had been free from Parthian domination, and that the grander their aims, the more glory they would

win if victorious, the more disgrace and peril they would
incur if they turned their backs. He pointed, as he spoke, to
his own menacing array, and to the Median bands with their
golden embroidery; warriors, as he said, on one side, spoil on
the other.

35. Among the Sarmatæ the general's voice was not alone
to be heard. They encouraged one another not to begin the
battle with volleys of arrows; they must, they said, anticipate attack by a hand to hand charge. Then followed every
variety of conflict. The Parthians, accustomed to pursue or
fly with equal science, deployed their squadrons, and sought
scope for their missiles. The Sarmatæ, throwing aside their
bows, which at a shorter range are effective, rushed on with
pikes and swords. Sometimes, as in a cavalry-action, there
would be alternate advances and retreats, then, again, close
fighting, in which, breast to breast, with the clash of arms,
they repulsed the foe or were themselves repulsed. And now
the Albanians and Iberians seized, and hurled the Parthians
from their steeds, and embarrassed their enemy with a
double attack, pressed as they were by the cavalry on the
heights and by the nearer blows of the infantry. Meanwhile
Pharasmanes and Orodes, who, as they cheered on the brave
and supported the wavering, were conspicuous to all, and so
recognised each other, rushed to the combat with a shout,
with javelins, and galloping chargers, Pharasmanes with the
greater impetuosity, for he pierced his enemy's helmet at a
stroke. But he could not repeat the blow, as he was hurried
onwards by his horse, and the wounded man was protected
by the bravest of his guards. A rumour that he was slain,
which was believed by mistake, struck panic into the Parthians, and they yielded the victory.

36. Artabanus very soon marched with the whole strength
of his kingdom, intent on vengeance. The Iberians from their
knowledge of the country fought at an advantage. Still Artabanus did not retreat till Vitellius had assembled his legions
and, by starting a report that he meant to invade Mesopotamia, raised an alarm of war with Rome. Armenia was then
abandoned, and the fortunes of Artabanus were overthrown,
Vitellius persuading his subjects to forsake a king who was a
tyrant in peace, and ruinously unsuccessful in war. And so

Sinnaces, whose enmity to the prince I have already mentioned, drew into actual revolt his father Abdageses and others, who had been secretly in his counsel, and were now after their continued disasters more eager to fight. By degrees, many flocked to him who, having been kept in subjection by fear rather than by goodwill, took courage as soon as they found leaders.

Artabanus had now no resources but in some foreigners who guarded his person, men exiled from their own homes, who had no perception of honour, or any scruple about a base act, mere hireling instruments of crime. With these attendants he hastened his flight into the remote country on the borders of Scythia, in the hope of aid, as he was connected by marriage alliances with the Hyrcanians and Carmanians. Meantime the Parthians, he thought, indulgent as they are to an absent prince, though restless under his presence, might turn to a better mind.

37. Vitellius, as soon as Artabanus had fled and his people were inclined to have a new king, urged Tiridates to seize the advantage thus offered, and then led the main strength of the legions and the allies to the banks of the Euphrates. While they were sacrificing, the one, after Roman custom, offering a swine, a ram and a bull; the other, a horse which he had duly prepared as a propitiation to the river-god, they were informed by the neighbouring inhabitants that the Euphrates, without any violent rains, was of itself rising to an immense height, and that the white foam was curling into circles like a diadem, an omen of a prosperous passage. Some explained it with more subtlety, of a successful commencement to the enterprise, which, however, would not be lasting, on the ground, that though a confident trust might be placed in prognostics given in the earth or in the heavens, the fluctuating character of rivers exhibited omens which vanished the same moment.

A bridge of boats having been constructed and the army having crossed, the first to enter the camp was Ornospades, with several thousand cavalry. Formerly an exile, he had rendered conspicuous aid to Tiberius in the completion of the Dalmatic war, and had for this been rewarded with Roman citizenship. Subsequently, he had again sought the friendship of his king, by whom he had been raised to high honour, and appointed governor of the plains, which, being surrounded by the waters of those famous rivers, the Euphrates and Tigris, have received the name of Mesopotamia. Soon afterwards, Sinnaces reinforced the army, and Abdageses, the mainstay of the party, came with the royal treasure and what belonged to the crown. Vitellius thought it enough to have displayed the arms of Rome, and he then bade Tiridates remember his grandfather Phraates, and his foster-father Cæsar, and all that was glorious in both of them, while the nobles were to show obedience to their king, and respect for us, each maintaining his honour and his loyalty. This done, he returned with the legions to Syria.

38. I have related in sequence the events of two summer-campaigns, as a relief to the reader's mind from our miseries at home. Though three years had elapsed since the destruction of Sejanus, neither time, intreaties, nor sated gratification, all which have a soothing effect on others, softened Tiberius, or kept him from punishing doubtful or forgotten offences as most flagrant and recent crimes. Under this dread, Fulcinius Trio, unwilling to face an onslaught of accusers, inserted in his will several terrible imputations on Macro and on the emperor's principal freedmen, while he taunted the emperor himself with the mental decay of old age, and the virtual exile of continuous retirement. Tiberius ordered these insults, which Trio's heirs had suppressed, to be publicly read, thus showing his tolerance of free speech in others and despising his own shame, or, possibly, because he had long been ignorant of the villanies of Sejanus, and now wished any remarks, however reckless, to be published, and so to ascertain, through invective, if it must be so, the truth, which flattery obscures. About the same time Granius Marcianus, a senator, who was accused of treason by Caius Gracchus, laid hands on himself. Tarius Gratianus too, an ex-prætor, was condemned under the same law to capital punishment.

39. A similar fate befell Trebellienus Rufus and Sextius Paconianus. Trebellienus perished by his own hand; Paconianus was strangled in prison for having there written some lampoons on the emperor. Tiberius received the news, no

longer parted by the sea, as he had been once, or through messengers from a distance, but in close proximity to Rome, so that on the same day, or after the interval of a single night, he could reply to the despatches of the consuls, and almost behold the bloodshed as it streamed from house to house, and the strokes of the executioner.

At the year's close Poppæus Sabinus died, a man of somewhat humble extraction, who had risen by his friendship with two emperors to the consulship and the honours of a triumph. During twenty-four years he had the charge of the most important provinces, not for any remarkable ability, but because he was equal to business and was not too great for it.

40. Quintus Plautius and Sextus Papinius were the next consuls. The fact that that year Lucius Aruseius was put to death did not strike men as anything horrible, from their familiarity with evil deeds. But there was a panic when Vibulenus Agrippa, a Roman knight, as soon as his accusers had finished their case, took from his robe, in the very Senate-house, a dose of poison, drank it off, and, as he fell expiring, was hurried away to prison by the prompt hands of lictors, where the neck of the now lifeless man was crushed with the halter. Even Tigranes, who had once ruled Armenia and was now impeached, did not escape the punishment of an ordinary citizen on the strength of his royal title.

Caius Galba meanwhile and the Blaesi perished by a voluntary death; Galba, because a harsh letter from the emperor forbade him to have a province allotted to him; while, as for the Blaesi, the priesthoods intended for them during the prosperity of their house, Tiberius had withheld, when that prosperity was shaken, and now conferred, as vacant offices, on others. This they understood as a signal of their doom, and acted on it.

Æmilia Lepida too, whose marriage with the younger Drusus I have already related, who, though she had pursued her husband with ceaseless accusations, remained unpunished, infamous as she was, as long as her father Lepidus lived, subsequently fell a victim to the informers for adultery with a slave. There was no question about her guilt, and so without an attempt at defence she put an end to her life

41. At this same time the Clitæ, a tribe subject to the Cappadocian Archelaus, retreated to the heights of Mount Taurus, because they were compelled in Roman fashion to render an account of their revenue and submit to tribute. There they defended themselves by means of the nature of the country against the king's unwarlike troops, till Marcus Trebellius, whom Vitellius, the governor of Syria, sent as his lieutenant with four thousand legionaries and some picked auxiliaries, surrounded with his lines two hills occupied by the barbarians, the lesser of which was named Cadra, the other Davara. Those who dared to sally out, he reduced to surrender by the sword, the rest by drought.

Tiridates meanwhile, with the consent of the Parthians, received the submission of Nicephorium, Anthemusias and the other cities, which having been founded by Macedonians, claim Greek names, also of the Parthian towns Halus and Artemita. There was a rivalry of joy among the inhabitants who detested Artabanus, bred as he had been among the Scythians, for his cruelty, and hoped to find in Tiridates a kindly spirit from his Roman training.

42. Seleucia, a powerful and fortified city which had never lapsed into barbarism, but had clung loyally to its founder Seleucus, assumed the most marked tone of flattery. Three hundred citizens, chosen for wealth or wisdom, form a kind of senate, and the people have powers of their own. When both act in concert, they look with contempt on the Parthians; as soon as they are at discord, and the respective leaders invite aid for themselves against their rivals, the ally summoned to help a faction crushes them all. This had lately happened in the reign of Artabanus, who, for his own interest, put the people at the mercy of the nobles. As a fact, popular government almost amounts to freedom, while the rule of the few approaches closely to a monarch's caprice.

Seleucia now celebrated the arrival of Tiridates with all the honours paid to princes of old and all which modern times, with a more copious inventiveness, have devised. Reproaches were at the same time heaped on Artabanus, as an Arsacid indeed on his mother's side, but as in all else degenerate. Tiridates gave the government of Seleucia to the people. Soon afterwards, as he was deliberating on what day

he should inaugurate his reign, he received letters from Phraates and Hiero, who held two very powerful provinces, imploring a brief delay. It was thought best to wait for men of
such commanding influence, and meanwhile Ctesiphon, the
seat of empire, was their chosen destination. But as they
postponed their coming from day to day, the Surena, in the
presence of an approving throng, crowned Tiridates, according to the national usage, with the royal diadem.

43. And now had he instantly made his way to the hear·
of the country and to its other tribes, the reluctance of those
who wavered, would have been overpowered, and all to a
man would have yielded. By besieging a fortress into which
Artabanus had conveyed his treasure and his concubines, he
gave them time to disown their compact. Phraates and
Hiero, with others who had not united in celebrating the day
fixed for the coronation, some from fear, some out of jealousy of Abdageses, who then ruled the court and the new
king, transferred their allegiance to Artabanus. They found
him in Hyrcania, covered with filth and procuring sustenance
with his bow. He was at first alarmed under the impression
that treachery was intended, but when they pledged their
honour that they had come to restore to him his dominion,
his spirit revived, and he asked what the sudden change
meant. Hiero then spoke insultingly of the boyish years of
Tiridates, hinting that the throne was not held by an Arsacid, but that a mere empty name was enjoyed by a feeble
creature bred in foreign effeminacy, while the actual power
was in the house of Abdageses.

44. An experienced king, Artabanus knew that men do not
necessarily feign hatred because they are false in friendship.
He delayed only while he was raising auxiliaries in Scythia,
and then pushed on in haste, thus anticipating the plots of
enemies and the fickleness of friends. Wishing to attract pop·
ular sympathy, he did not even cast off his miserable garb.
He stooped to wiles and to entreaties, to anything indeed by
which he might allure the wavering and confirm the willing.

He was now approaching the neighbourhood of Seleucia
with a large force, while Tiridates, dismayed by the rumour
and then by the king's presence in person, was divided in
mind, and doubted whether he should march against him or

prolong the war by delay. Those who wished for battle with its prompt decision argued that ill-arrayed levies fatigued by a long march could not even in heart be thoroughly united in obedience, traitors and enemies, as they had lately been, to the prince whom now again they were supporting Abdageses, however, advised a retreat into Mesopotamia. there, with a river in their front, they might in the interval summon to their aid the Armenians and Elymæans and other nations in their rear, and then, reinforced by allies and troops which would be sent by the Roman general, they might try the fortune of war. This advice prevailed, for Abdageses had the chief influence and Tiridates was a coward in the face of danger. But their retreat resembled a flight. The Arabs made a beginning, and then the rest went to their homes or to the camp of Artabanus, till Tiridates returned to Syria with a few followers and thus relieved all from the disgrace of desertion.

45. That same year Rome suffered from a terrible fire, and part of the circus near the Aventine hill was burnt, as well as the Aventine quarter itself. This calamity the emperor turned to his own glory by paying the values of the houses and blocks of tenements. A hundred million of sesterces was expended in this munificence, a boon all the more acceptable to the populace, as Tiberius was rather sparing in building at his private expense. He raised only two structures even at the public cost, the temple of Augustus and the stage of Pompey's theatre, and when these were completed, he did not dedicate them, either out of contempt for popularity or from his extreme age. Four commissioners, all husbands of the emperor's granddaughters—Cneius Domitius, Cassius Longinus, Marcus Vinicius, Rubellius Blandus—were appointed to assess the damage in each case, and Publius Petronius was added to their number on the nomination of the consuls. Various honours were devised and decreed to the emperor such as each man's ingenuity suggested. It is a question which of these he rejected or accepted, as the end of his life was so near.

For soon afterwards Tiberius's last consuls, Cneius Acerronius and Caius Pontius, entered on office, Macro's power being now excessive. Every day the man cultivated more as-

siduously than ever the favour of Caius Cæsar, which, indeed, he had never neglected, and after the death of Claudia,
who had, as I have related, been married to Caius, he had
prompted his wife Ennia to inveigle the young prince by a
pretence of love, and to bind him by an engagement of marriage, and the lad, provided he could secure the throne,
shrank from no conditions. For though he was of an excitable
temper, he had thoroughly learnt the falsehoods of hypocrisy
under the loving care of his grandfather.

46. This the emperor knew, and he therefore hesitated
about bequeathing the empire, first, between his grandsons.
Of these, the son of Drusus was nearest in blood and natural affection, but he was still in his childhood. Germanicus's
son was in the vigour of youth and enjoyed the people's
favour, a reason for having his grandfather's hatred. Tiberius had even thought of Claudius, as he was of sedate age
and had a taste for liberal culture, but a weak intellect was
against him. If however he were to seek a successor outside
of his house, he feared that the memory of Augustus and the
name of the Cæsars would become a laughing-stock and a
scorn. It was, in fact, not so much popularity in the present
for which he cared as for glory in the future.

Perplexed in mind, exhausted in body, he soon left to
destiny a question to which he was unequal, though he threw
out some hints from which it might be inferred that he foresaw what was to come. He taunted Macro, in no obscure
terms, with forsaking the setting and looking to the rising
sun. Once too when Caius Cæsar in a casual conversation
ridiculed Lucius Sulla, he predicted to him that he would
have all Sulla's vices and none of his virtues. At the same
moment he embraced the younger of his two grandsons with
a flood of tears, and, noting the savage face of the other
said, "You will slay this boy, and will be yourself slain by
another." But even while his strength was fast failing he
gave up none of his debaucheries. In his sufferings he would
simulate health, and was wont to jest at the arts of the
physician and at all who, after the age of thirty, require another man's advice to distinguish between what is beneficial
or hurtful to their constitutions.

47. At Rome meanwhile were being sown the seeds of

bloodshed to come even after Tiberius's death. Acutia, formerly the wife of Publius Vitellius, had been accused of treason by Lælius Balbus. When on her condemnation a reward was being voted to her prosecutor, Junius Otho, tribune of the people, interposed his veto. Hence a feud between Vitellius and Otho, ending in Otho's banishment. Then Albucilla, notorious for the number of her lovers, who had been married to Satrius Secundus, the betrayer of the late conspiracy, was charged with irreverence towards the emperor. With her were involved as her accomplices and paramours Cneius Domitius, Vibius Marsus and Lucius Arruntius. I have already spoken of the illustrious rank of Domitius. Marsus too was distinguished by the honours of his ancestors and by his own attainments. It was, however, stated in the notes of the proceedings furnished to the Senate that Macro had superintended the examination of the witnesses and the torture of the slaves, and the fact that there was no letter from the emperor against the defendants caused a suspicion that, while he was very feeble and possibly ignorant of the matter, the charge was to a great extent invented to gratify Macro's well-known enmity against Arruntius.

48. And so Domitius and Marsus prolonged their lives, Domitius, preparing his defence, Marsus, having apparently resolved on starvation. Arruntius, when his friends advised delay and temporising, replied that "the same conduct was not becoming in all persons. He had had enough of life, and all he regretted was that he had endured amid scorn and peril an old age of anxious fears, long detested by Sejanus, now by Macro, always, indeed, by some powerful minister, not for any fault, but as a man who could not tolerate gross iniquities. Granted the possibility of passing safely through the few last days of Tiberius. How was he to be secure under the youth of the coming sovereign? Was it probable that, when Tiberius with his long experience of affairs was, under the influence of absolute power, wholly perverted and changed, Caius Cæsar, who had hardly completed his boyhood, was thoroughly ignorant and bred under the vilest training, would enter on a better course, with Macro for his guide, who having been selected for his superior wickedness, to crush Sejanus had by yet more numerous crimes been the

scourge of the State? He now foresaw a still more galling slavery, and therefore sought to flee alike from the past and from the impending future."

While he thus spoke like a prophet, he opened his veins. What followed will be a proof that Arruntius rightly chose death. Albucilla, having stabbed herself with an ineffectual wound, was by the Senate's order carried off to prison. Those who had ministered to her profligacy, Carsidius Sacerdos, an ex-prætor, and Pontius Fregellanus were sentenced, respectively, to transportation to an island and to loss of a senator's rank. A like punishment was adjudged in the case of Lælius Balbus, and, indeed, with intense satisfaction, as Balbus was noted for his savage eloquence and his eagerness to assail the innocent.

49. About the same time Sextus Papinius, who belonged to a family of consular rank, chose a sudden and shocking death, by throwing himself from a height. The cause was ascribed to his mother, who, having been repeatedly repulsed in her overtures, had at last by her arts and seductions driven him to an extremity from which he could find no escape but death. She was accordingly put on her trial before the Senate, and, although she grovelled at the knees of the senators and long urged a parent's grief, the greater weakness of a woman's mind under such an affliction and other sad and pitiful pleas of the same painful kind, she was after all banished from Rome for ten years, till her younger son would have passed the frail period of youth.

50. Tiberius's bodily powers were now leaving him, but not his skill in dissembling. There was the same stern spirit; he had his words and looks under strict control, and occasionally would try to hide his weakness, evident as it was, by a forced politeness. After frequent changes of place, he at last settled down on the promontory of Misenum in a country-house once owned by Lucius Lucullus. It was there discovered that he was drawing near his end, and thus. There was a physician, distinguished in his profession, of the name of Charicles, usually employed, not indeed to have the direction of the emperor's varying health, but to put his advice at immediate disposal. This man, as if he were leaving on business of his own, clasped his hand, with a show of homage,

and touched his pulse. Tiberius noticed it. Whether he was
displeased and strove the more to hide his anger, is a question; at any rate, he ordered the banquet to be renewed,
and sat at the table longer than usual, by way, apparently,
of showing honour to his departing friend. Charicles, however, assured Macro that his breath was failing and that he
would not last more than two days. All was at once hurry;
there were conferences among those on the spot and despatches to the generals and armies. On the 15th of March,
his breath failing, he was believed to have expired, and
Caius Cæsar was going forth with a numerous throng of
congratulating followers to take the first possession of the
empire, when suddenly news came that Tiberius was recovering his voice and sight, and calling for persons to bring him
food to revive him from his faintness. Then ensued a universal panic, and while the rest fled hither and thither, every
one feigning grief or ignorance, Caius Cæsar, in silent stupor,
passed from the highest hopes to the extremity of apprehension. Macro, nothing daunted, ordered the old emperor
to be smothered under a huge heap of clothes, and all to quit
the entrance-hall.

51. And so died Tiberius, in the seventy-eighth year of his
age. Nero was his father, and he was on both sides descended
from the Claudian house, though his mother passed by adoption, first into the Livian, then into the Julian family. From
earliest infancy, perilous vicissitudes were his lot. Himself
an exile, he was the companion of a proscribed father, and
on being admitted as a stepson into the house of Augustus,
he had to struggle with many rivals, so long as Marcellus
and Agrippa and, subsequently, Caius and Lucius Cæsar
were in their glory. Again his brother Drusus enjoyed in a
greater degree the affection of the citizens. But he was more
than ever on dangerous ground after his marriage with Julia,
whether he tolerated or escaped from his wife's profligacy.
On his return from Rhodes he ruled the emperor's now heir-
less house for twelve years, and the Roman world, with absolute sway, for about twenty-three. His character too had
its distinct periods. It was a bright time in his life and reputation, while under Augustus he was a private citizen or held
high offices; a time of reserve and crafty assumption of vir-

tue, as long as Germanicus and Drusus were alive. Again,
while his mother lived, he was a compound of good and evil;
he was infamous for his cruelty, though he veiled his debaucheries, while he loved or feared Sejanus. Finally, he
plunged into every wickedness and disgrace, when fear and
shame being cast off, he simply indulged his own inclinations.

[The four following books and the beginning of Book XI,
which are lost, contained the history of a period of nearly
ten years, from A.D. 37 to A.D. 47. These years included the
reign of Caius Cæsar (Caligula), the son of Germanicus by
the elder Agrippina, and the first six years of the reign of
Claudius. Caius Cæsar's reign was three years ten months
and eight days in duration. Claudius (Tiberius Claudius
Drusus Nero Germanicus), the brother of Germanicus, succeeded him, at the age of fifty, and reigned from A.D. 41 to
A.D. 54.

The Eleventh Book of the Annals opens with the seventh
year of Claudius's reign. The power of his wife Messalina
was then at its height. She was, it seems, jealous of a certain Poppæa Sabina, who is mentioned in Book XIII., § 45,
as "having surpassed in beauty all the ladies of her day."
This Poppæa was the daughter of the Poppæus Sabinus alluded to in Book VI., § 39, and the mother of the more famous Poppæa, afterwards the wife of the emperor Nero.
Messalina contrived to involve this lady and her lover,
Valerius Asiaticus, in a ruinous charge. Asiaticus had been
twice consul, once under Caius Cæsar, a second time under
Claudius in A.D. 46. He was rich as well as noble. The
Eleventh Book, as we have it, begins with the account of his
prosecution by means of Messalina, who with the help of
Lucius Vitellius, the father of the Vitellius, afterwards em-
peror, effected his ruin.]

BOOK XI

A.D. 47, 48

1. MESSALINA believed that Valerius Asiaticus, who had been twice consul, was one of Poppæa's old lovers. At the same time she was looking greedily at the gardens which Lucullus had begun and which Asiaticus was now adorning with singular magnificence, and so she suborned Suilius to accuse both him and Poppæa. With Suilius was associated Sosibius, tutor to Britannicus, who was to give Claudius an apparently friendly warning to beware of a power and wealth which threatened the throne. Asiaticus, he said, had been the ringleader in the murder of a Cæsar, and then had not feared to face an assembly of the Roman people, to own the deed, and challenge its glory for his own. Thus grown famous in the capital, and with a renown widely spread through the provinces, he was planning a journey to the armies of Germany. Born at Vienna, and supported by numerous and powerful connections, he would find it easy to rouse nations allied to his house. Claudius made no further inquiry, but sent Crispinus, commander of the Prætorians, with troops in hot haste, as though to put down a revolt. Crispinus found him at Baiæ, loaded him with chains, and hurried him to Rome.

2. No hearing before the Senate was granted him. It was in the emperor's chamber, in the presence of Messalina, that he was heard. There Suilius accused him of corrupting the troops, of binding them by bribes and indulgences to share in every crime, of adultery with Poppæa, and finally of unmanly vice. It was at this last that the accused broke silence, and burst out with the words, "Question thy own sons, Suilius; they will own my manhood." Then he entered on his defence. Claudius he moved profoundly, and he even drew tears from Messalina. But as she left the chamber to

wipe them away, she warned Vitellius not to let the man escape. She hastened herself to effect Poppæa's destruction, and hired agents to drive her to suicide by the terrors of a prison. Cæsar meanwhile was so unconscious that a few days afterwards he asked her husband Scipio, who was dining with him, why he sat down to table without his wife, and was told in reply that she had paid the debt of nature.

3. When Claudius began to deliberate about the acquittal of Asiaticus, Vitellius, with tears in his eyes, spoke of his old friendship with the accused, and of their joint homage to the emperor's mother, Antonia. He then briefly reviewed the services of Asiaticus to the State, his recent campaign in the invasion of Britain, and everything else which seemed likely to win compassion, and suggested that he should be free to choose his death. Claudius's reply was in the same tone of mercy. Some friends urged on Asiaticus the quiet death of self-starvation, but he declined it with thanks. He took his usual exercise, then bathed and dined cheerfully, and saying that he had better have fallen by the craft of Tiberius or the fury of Caius Cæsar than by the treachery of a woman and the shameless mouth of Vitellius, he opened his veins, but not till he had inspected his funeral pyre, and directed its removal to another spot, lest the smoke should hurt the thick foliage of the trees. So complete was his calmness even to the last.

4. The senators were then convoked, and Suilius proceeded to find new victims in two knights of the first rank who bore the surname of Petra. The real cause of their destruction was that they had lent their house for the meetings of Mnester and Poppæa. But it was a vision of the night that was the actual charge against one of them. He had, it was alleged, beheld Claudius crowned with a garland of wheat, the ears of which were turned downwards, and, from this appearance, he foretold scanty harvests. Some have said that it was a vine-wreath, of which the leaves were white, which he saw, and that he interpreted it to signify the death of the emperor after the turn of autumn. It is, however, beyond dispute that in consequence of some dream, whatever it was, both the man and his brother perished.

Fifteen hundred thousand sesterces and the decorations of

the prætorship were voted to Crispinus. Vitellius bestowed a million on Sosibius, for giving Britannicus the benefit of his teaching and Claudius that of his counsels. I may add that when Scipio was called on for his opinion, he replied, "As I think what all men think about the deeds of Poppæa, sup-pose me to say what all men say." A graceful compromise this between the affection of the husband and the necessities of the senator.

5. Suilius after this plied his accusations without cessation or pity, and his audacity had many rivals. By assuming to himself all the functions of laws and magistrates, the em-peror had left exposed everything which invited plunder, and of all articles of public merchandise nothing was more venal than the treachery of advocates. Thus it happened that one Samius, a Roman knight of the first rank, who had paid four hundred thousand sesterces to Suilius, stabbed himself in the advocate's house, on ascertaining his collusion with the adversary. Upon this, following the lead of Silius, con-sul-elect, whose elevation and fall I shall in due course re-late, the senators rose in a body, and demanded the enforce-ment of the Cincian law, an old enactment, which forbade any one to receive a fee or a gift for pleading a cause.

6. When the men, at whom this strong censure was lev-elled, loudly protested, Silius, who had a quarrel with Sui-lius, attacked them with savage energy. He cited as ex-amples the orators of old who had thought fame with posterity the fairest recompense of eloquence. And, "apart from this," he said, "the first of noble accomplishments was debased by sordid services, and even good faith could not be upheld in its integrity, when men looked at the greatness of their gains. If law suits turned to no one's profit, there would be fewer of them. As it was, quarrels, accusations, hatreds and wrongs were encouraged, in order that, as the violence of disease brings fees to the physician, so the cor-ruption of the forum might enrich the advocate. They should remember Caius Asinius and Messala, and, in later days, Arruntius and Æserninus, men raised by a blameless life and by eloquence to the highest honours."

So spoke the consul-elect, and others agreed with him. A resolution was being framed to bring the guilty under the law of extortion, when Suilius and Cossutianus and the rest, who saw themselves threatened with punishment rather than trial, for their guilt was manifest, gathered round the emperor, and prayed forgiveness for the past.

7. When he had nodded assent, they began to plead their cause. "Who," they asked, "can be so arrogant as to anticipate in hope an eternity of renown? It is for the needs and the business of life that the resource of eloquence is acquired, thanks to which no one for want of an advocate is at the mercy of the powerful. But eloquence cannot be obtained for nothing; private affairs are neglected, in order that a man may devote himself to the business of others. Some support life by the profession of arms, some by cultivating land. No work is expected from any one of which he has not before calculated the profits. It was easy for Asinius and Messala, enriched with the prizes of the conflict between Antony and Augustus, it was easy for Arruntius and Æserninus, the heirs of wealthy families, to assume grand airs. We have examples at hand. How great were the fees for which Publius Clodius and Caius Curio were wont to speak! We are ordinary senators, seeking in the tranquillity of the State for none but peaceful gains. You must consider the plebeian, how he gains distinction from the gown. Take away the rewards of a profession, and the profession must perish." The emperor thought that these arguments, though less noble, were not without force. He limited the fee which might be taken to ten thousand sesterces, and those who exceeded this limit were to be liable to the penalties of extortion.

8. About this same time Mithridates, of whom I have before spoken as having ruled Armenia, and having been imprisoned by order of Caius Cæsar, made his way back to his kingdom at the suggestion of Claudius and in reliance on the help of Pharasmanes. This Pharasmanes, who was king of the Iberians and Mithridates' brother, now told him that the Parthians were divided, and that the highest questions of empire being uncertain, lesser matters were neglected Gotarzes, among his many cruelties, had caused the death of his brother Artabanus, with his wife and son. Hence his people feared for themselves and sent for Vardanes. Ever ready for daring achievements, Vardanes traversed 375 miles

in two days, and drove before him the surprised and terrified Gotarzes. Without a moment's delay, he seized the neighbouring governments, Seleucia alone refusing his rule. Rage against the place, which indeed had also revolted from his father, rather than considerations of policy, made him embarrass himself with the siege of a strong city, which the defence of a river flowing by it, with fortifications and supplies, had thoroughly secured. Gotarzes meanwhile, aided by the resources of the Dahæ and Hyrcanians, renewed the war; and Vardanes, compelled to raise the siege of Seleucia, encamped on the plains of Bactria.

9. Then it was that while the forces of the East were divided, and hesitated which side they should take, the opportunity of occupying Armenia was presented to Mithridates, who had the vigorous soldiers of Rome to storm the fortified heights, while his Iberian cavalry scoured the plain. The Armenians made no resistance after their governor, Demonax, had ventured on a battle and had been routed. Cotys, king of Lesser Armenia, to whom some of the nobles inclined, caused some delay, but he was stopped by a despatch from Claudius, and then everything passed into the hands of Mithridates, who showed more cruelty than was wise in a new ruler. The Parthian princes however, just when they were beginning battle, came to a sudden agreement, on discovering a plot among their people, which Gotarzes revealed to his brother. At first they approached each other with hesitation; then, joining right hands, they promised before the altars of their gods to punish the treachery of their enemies and to yield one to the other. Vardanes seemed more capable of retaining rule. Gotarzes, to avoid all rivalry, retired into the depths of Hyrcania. When Vardanes returned, Seleucia capitulated to him, seven years after its revolt, little to the credit of the Parthians, whom a single city had so long defied.

10. He then visited the strongest governments, and was eager to recover Armenia, but was stopped by Vibius Marsus, governor of Syria, who threatened war. Meanwhile Gotarzes, who repented of having relinquished his throne, at the solicitation of the nobility, to whom subjection is a special hardship in peace, collected a force. Vardanes

marched against him to the river Charinda; a fierce battle was fought over the passage, Vardanes winning a complete victory, and in a series of successful engagements subduing the intermediate tribes as far as the river Sindes, which is the boundary between the Dahæ and the Arians. There his successes terminated. The Parthians, victorious though they were, rebelled against distant service. So after erecting monuments on which he recorded his greatness, and the tribute won from peoples from whom no Arsacid had won it before, he returned covered with glory, and therefore the more haughty and more intolerable to his subjects than ever. They arranged a plot, and slew him when he was off his guard and intent upon the chase. He was still in his first youth, and might have been one of the illustrious few among aged princes, had he sought to be loved by his subjects as much as to be feared by his foes.

The murder of Vardanes threw the affairs of Parthia into confusion, as the people were in doubt who should be summoned to the throne. Many inclined to Gotarzes, some to Meherdates, a descendant of Phraates, who was a hostage in our hands. Finally Gotarzes prevailed. Established in the palace, he drove the Parthians by his cruelty and profligacy to send a secret entreaty to the Roman emperor that Meherdates might be allowed to mount the throne of his ancestors.

11. It was during this consulship, in the eight hundredth year after the foundation of Rome and the sixty-fourth after their celebration by Augustus that the secular games were exhibited. I say nothing of the calculations of the two princes, which I have sufficiently discussed in my history of the emperor Domitian; for he also exhibited secular games, at which indeed, being one of the priesthood of the Fifteen and prætor at the time, I specially assisted. It is in no boastful spirit that I mention this, but because this duty has immemorially belonged to the College of the Fifteen, and the prætors have performed the chief functions in these ceremonies. While Claudius sat to witness the games of the circus, some of the young nobility acted on horseback the battle of Troy. Among them was Britannicus, the emperor's son, and Lucius Domitius, who became soon afterwards by adoption heir to the empire with the surname of Nero. The

stronger popular enthusiasm which greeted him was taken
to presage his greatness. It was commonly reported that
snakes had been seen by his cradle, which they seemed to
guard, a fabulous tale invented to match the marvels of
other lands. Nero, never a disparager of himself, was wont to
say that but one snake, at most, had been seen in his chamber.

12. Something however of popular favour was bequeathed
to him from the remembrance of Germanicus, whose only
male descendant he was, and the pity felt for his mother
Agrippina was increased by the cruelty of Messalina, who,
always her enemy, and then more furious than ever, was
only kept from planning an accusation and suborning informers by a new and almost insane passion. She had grown
so frantically enamoured of Caius Silius, the handsomest of
the young nobility of Rome, that she drove from his bed
Junia Silana, a high-born lady, and had her lover wholly to
herself. Silius was not unconscious of his wickedness and his
peril; but a refusal would have insured destruction, and he
had some hope of escaping exposure; the prize too was great,
and so he consoled himself by awaiting the future and enjoying the present. As for her, careless of concealment, she
went continually with a numerous retinue to his house, she
haunted his steps, showered on him wealth and honours,
and, at last, as though empire had passed to another, the
slaves, the freedmen, the very furniture of the emperor were
to been seen in the possession of the paramour.

13. Claudius meanwhile, who knew nothing about his wife,
and was busy with his functions as censor, published edicts
severely rebuking the lawlessness of the people in the theatre, when they insulted Caius Pomponius, an ex-consul,
who furnished verses for the stage, and certain ladies of
rank. He introduced too a law restraining the cruel greed of
the usurers, and forbidding them to lend at interest sums re-
payable on a father's death. He also conveyed by an aqueduct into Rome the waters which flow from the hills of Sim-
brua. And he likewise invented and published for use some
new letters, having discovered, as he said, that even the
Greek alphabet had not been completed at once.

14. It was the Egyptians who first symbolized ideas, and

that by the figures of animals. These records, the most ancient of all human history, are still seen engraved on stone. The Egyptians also claim to have invented the alphabet, which the Phœnicians, they say, by means of their superior seamanship, introduced into Greece, and of which they appropriated the glory, giving out that they had discovered what they had really been taught. Tradition indeed says that Cadmus, visiting Greece in a Phœnician fleet, was the teacher of this art to its yet barbarous tribes. According to one account, it was Cecrops of Athens or Linus of Thebes, or Palamedes of Argos in Trojan times who invented the shapes of sixteen letters, and others, chiefly Simonides, added the rest. In Italy the Etrurians learnt them from Demaratus of Corinth, and the Aborigines from the Arcadian Evander. And so the Latin letters have the same form as the oldest Greek characters. At first too our alphabet was scanty, and additions were afterwards made. Following this precedent Claudius added three letters, which were employed during his reign and subsequently disused. These may still be seen on the tablets of brass set up in the squares and temples, on which new statutes are published.

15. Claudius then brought before the Senate the subject of the college of "haruspices," that, as he said, "the oldest of Italian sciences might not be lost through negligence. It had often happened in evil days for the State that advisers had been summoned at whose suggestion ceremonies had been restored and observed more duly for the future. The nobles of Etruria, whether of their own accord or at the instigation of the Roman Senate, had retained this science, making it the inheritance of distinct families. It was now less zealously studied through the general indifference to all sound learning and to the growth of foreign superstitions. At present all is well, but we must show gratitude to the favour of Heaven, by taking care that the rites observed during times of peril may not be forgotten in prosperity." A resolution of the Senate was accordingly passed, charging the pontiffs to see what should be retained or reformed with respect to the "haruspices."

16. It was in this same year that the Cherusci asked Rome for a king. They had lost all their nobles in their civil wars,

and there was left but one scion of the royal house, Italicus by name, who lived at Rome. On the father's side he was descended from Flavus, the brother of Arminius; his mother was a daughter of Catumerus, chief of the Chatti. The youth himself was of distinguished beauty, a skilful horseman and swordsman both after our fashion and that of his country. So the emperor made him a present of money, furnished him with an escort, and bade him enter with a good heart on the honours of his house. "Never before," he said, "had a native of Rome, no hostage but a citizen, gone to mount a foreign throne." At first his arrival was welcome to the Germans, and they crowded to pay him court, for he was untainted by any spirit of faction, and showed the same hearty goodwill to all, practising sometimes the courtesy and temperance which can never offend, but oftener those excesses of wine and lust in which barbarians delight. He was winning fame among his neighbours and even far beyond them, when some who had found their fortune in party feuds, jealous of his power, fled to the tribes on the border, protesting that Germany was being robbed of her ancient freedom, and that the might of Rome was on the rise. "Is there really," they said, "no native of this country to fill the place of king without raising the son of the spy Flavus above all his fellows? It is idle to put forward the name of Arminius. Had even the son of Arminius come to the throne after growing to manhood on a hostile soil, he might well be dreaded, corrupted as he would be by the bread of dependence, by slavery, by luxury, by all foreign habits. But if Italicus had his father's spirit, no man, be it remembered, had ever waged war against his country and his home more savagely than that father."

17. By these and like appeals they collected a large force. No less numerous were the partisans of Italicus. "He was no intruder," they said, "on an unwilling people; he had obeyed a call. Superior as he was to all others in noble birth, should they not put his valour to the test, and see whether he showed himself worthy of his uncle Arminius and his grandfather Catumerus? He need not blush because his father had never relinquished the loyalty which, with the consent of the Germans, he had promised to Rome. The name of liberty was a lying pretext in the mouths of men who, base in pri-

vate, dangerous in public life, had nothing to hope except from civil discord."

The people enthusiastically applauded him. After a fierce conflict among the barbarians, the king was victorious. Subsequently, in his good fortune, he fell into a despot's pride, was dethroned, was restored by the help of the Langobardi, and still, in prosperity or adversity, did mischief to the interests of the Cheruscan nation.

18. It was during the same period that the Chauci, free, as it happened, from dissension at home and emboldened by the death of Sanquinius, made, while Corbulo was on his way, an inroad into Lower Germany, under the leadership of Gannascus. This man was of the tribe of the Canninefates, had served long as our auxiliary, had then deserted, and, getting some light vessels, had made piratical descents specially on the coast of Gaul, inhabited, he knew, by a wealthy and unwarlike population. Corbulo meanwhile entered the province with careful preparation and soon winning a renown of which that campaign was the beginning, he brought his triremes up the channel of the Rhine and the rest of his vessels up the estuaries and canals to which they were adapted. Having sunk the enemy's flotilla, driven out Gannascus, and brought everything into good order, he restored the discipline of former days among legions which had forgotten the labours and toils of the soldier and delighted only in plunder. No one was to fall out of the line; no one was to fight without orders. At the outposts, on guard, in the duties of day and of night, they were always to be under arms. One soldier, it was said, had suffered death for working at the trenches without his sword, another for wearing nothing as he dug, but his poniard. These extreme and possibly false stories at least had their origin in the general's real severity. We may be sure that he was strict and implacable to serious offences, when such sternness in regard to trifles could be believed of him.

19. The fear thus inspired variously affected his own troops and the enemy. Our men gained fresh valour; the barbarians felt their pride broken. The Frisians, who had been hostile or disloyal since the revolt which had been begun by the defeat of Lucius Apronius, gave hostages and

settled down on territories marked out by Corbulo, who, at the same time, gave them a senate, magistrates, and a constitution. That they might not throw off their obedience, he built a fort among them, while he sent envoys to invite the Greater Chauci to submission and to destroy Gannascus by stratagem. This stealthy attempt on the life of a deserter and a traitor was not unsuccessful, nor was it anything ignoble. Yet the Chauci were violently roused by the man's death, and Corbulo was now sowing the seeds of another revolt, thus getting a reputation which many liked, but of which many thought ill. "Why," men asked, "was he irritating the foe? His disasters will fall on the State. If he is successful, so famous a hero will be a danger to peace, and a formidable subject for a timid emperor." Claudius accordingly forbade fresh attacks on Germany, so emphatically as to order the garrisons to be withdrawn to the left bank of the Rhine.

20. Corbulo was actually preparing to encamp on hostile soil when the despatch reached him. Surprised, as he was, and many as were the thoughts which crowded on him, thoughts of peril from the emperor, of scorn from the barbarians, of ridicule from the allies, he said nothing but this, "Happy the Roman generals of old," and gave the signal for retreat. To keep his soldiers free from sloth, he dug a canal of twenty-three miles in length between the Rhine and the Meuse, as a means of avoiding the uncertain perils of the ocean. The emperor, though he had forbidden war, yet granted him triumphal distinctions.

Soon afterwards Curtius Rufus obtained the same honour. He had opened mines in the territory of the Mattiaci for working certain veins of silver. The produce was small and soon exhausted. The toil meanwhile of the legions was only to a loss, while they dug channels for water and constructed below the surface works which are difficult enough in the open air. Worn out by the labour, and knowing that similar hardships were endured in several provinces, the soldiers wrote a secret despatch in the name of the armies, begging the emperor to give in advance triumphal distinctions to any one to whom he was about to entrust his forces.

21. Of the birth of Curtius Rufus, whom some affirm to

have been the son of a gladiator, I would not publish a falsehood, while I shrink from telling the truth. On reaching manhood he attached himself to a quæstor to whom Africa had been allotted, and was walking alone at midday in some unfrequented arcade in the town of Adrumetum, when he saw a female figure of more than human stature, and heard a voice, "Thou, Rufus, art the man who will one day come into this province as proconsul." Raised high in hope by such a presage, he returned to Rome, where, through the lavish expenditure of his friends and his own vigorous ability, he obtained the quæstorship. and, subsequently, in competition with well-born candidates, the prætorship, by the vote of the emperor Tiberius, who threw a veil over the discredit of his origin, saying, "Curtius Rufus seems to me to be his own ancestor." Afterwards, throughout a long old age of surly sycophancy to those above him, of arrogance to those beneath him, and of moroseness among his equals, he gained the high office of the consulship, triumphal distinctions, and, at last, the province of Africa. There he died, and so fulfilled the presage of his destiny.

22. At Rome meanwhile, without any motive then known or subsequently ascertained, Cneius Nonius, a Roman knight, was found wearing a sword amid a crowd who were paying their respects to the emperor. The man confessed his own guilt when he was being torn in pieces by torture, but gave up no accomplices, perhaps having none to hide.

During the same consulship, Publius Dolabella proposed that a spectacle of gladiators should be annually exhibited at the cost of those who obtained the quæstorship. In our ancestors' days this honour had been a reward of virtue, and every citizen, with good qualities to support him, was allowed to compete for office. At first there were no distinctions even of age, which prevented a man in his early youth from becoming a consul or a dictator. The quæstors indeed were appointed while the kings still ruled, and this the revival by Brutus of the *lex curiata* plainly shows. The consuls retained the power of selecting them, till the people bestowed this office as well as others. The first so created were Valerius Potitus and Æmilius Mamercus sixty-three years after the expulsion of the Tarquins, and they were to be attached to

the war-department. As the public business increased, two
more were appointed to attend to affairs at Rome. This
number was again doubled, when to the contributions of
Italy was added the tribute of the provinces. Subsequently
Sulla, by one of his laws, provided that twenty should be
elected to fill up the Senate, to which he had intrusted judicial functions. These functions the knights afterwards
recovered, but the quæstorship was obtained, without expense, by merit in the candidates or by the good nature of
the electors, till at Dolabella's suggestion it was, so to speak,
put up to sale.

23. In the consulship of Aulus Vitellius and Lucius Vipstanus the question of filling up the Senate was discussed,
and the chief men of Gallia Comata, as it was called, who
had long possessed the rights of allies and of Roman citizens,
sought the privilege of obtaining public offices at Rome.
There was much talk of every kind on the subject, and it
was argued before the emperor with vehement opposition.
"Italy," it was asserted, "is not so feeble as to be unable to
furnish its own capital with a senate. Once our native-born
citizens sufficed for peoples of our own kin, and we are by no
means dissatisfied with the Rome of the past. To this day we
cite examples, which under our old customs the Roman character exhibited as to valour and renown. Is it a small thing
that Veneti and Insubres have already burst into the Senate-
house, unless a mob of foreigners, a troop of captives, so to
say, is now forced upon us? What distinctions will be left
for the remnants of our noble houses, or for any impoverished senators from Latium? Every place will be crowded
with these millionaires, whose ancestors of the second and
third generations at the head of hostile tribes destroyed our
armies with fire and sword, and actually besieged the divine
Julius at Alesia. These are recent memories. What if there
were to rise up the remembrance of those who fell in Rome's
citadel and at her altar by the hands of these same barbarians! Let them enjoy indeed the title of citizens, but let
them not vulgarise the distinctions of the Senate and the
honours of office."

24. These and like arguments failed to impress the emperor. He at once addressed himself to answer them, and

thus harangued the assembled Senate. "My ancestors, the most ancient of whom was made at once a citizen and a noble of Rome, encourage me to govern by the same policy of transferring to this city all conspicuous merit, wherever found. And indeed I know, as facts, that the Julii came from Alba, the Coruncanii from Camerium, the Porcii from Tusculum, and not to inquire too minutely into the past, that new members have been brought into the Senate from Etruria and Lucania and the whole of Italy, that Italy itself was at last extended to the Alps, to the end that not only single persons but entire countries and tribes might be united under our name. We had unshaken peace at home; we prospered in all our foreign relations, in the days when Italy beyond the Po was admitted to share our citizenship, and when, enrolling in our ranks the most vigorous of the provincials, under colour of settling our legions throughout the world, we recruited our exhausted empire. Are we sorry that the Balbi came to us from Spain, and other men not less illustrious from Narbon Gaul? Their descendants are still among us, and do not yield to us in patriotism.

"What was the ruin of Sparta and Athens, but this, that mighty as they were in war, they spurned from them as aliens those whom they had conquered? Our founder Romulus, on the other hand, was so wise that he fought as enemies and then hailed as fellow-citizens several nations on the very same day. Strangers have reigned over us. That freedmen's sons should be intrusted with public offices is not, as many wrongly think, a sudden innovation, but was a common practice in the old commonwealth. But, it will be said, we have fought with the Senones. I suppose then that the Volsci and Æqui never stood in array against us. Our city was taken by the Gauls. Well, we also gave hostages to the Etruscans, and passed under the yoke of the Samnites. On the whole, if you review all our wars, never has one been finished in a shorter time than that with the Gauls. Thenceforth they have preserved an unbroken and loyal peace. United as they now are with us by manners, education, and intermarriage, let them bring us their gold and their wealth rather than enjoy it in isolation. Everything, Senators, which we now hold to be of the highest antiquity, was once new.

Plebeian magistrates came after patrician; Latin magistrates after plebeian; magistrates of other Italian peoples after Latin. This practice too will establish itself, and what we are this day justifying by precedents, will be itself a precedent."

25. The emperor's speech was followed by a decree of the Senate, and the Ædui were the first to obtain the right of becoming senators at Rome. This compliment was paid to their ancient alliance, and to the fact that they alone of the Gauls cling to the name of brothers of the Roman people.

About the same time the emperor enrolled in the ranks of the patricians such senators as were of the oldest families, and such as had had distinguished ancestors. There were now but scanty relics of the Greater Houses of Romulus and of the Lesser Houses of Lucius Brutus, as they had been called, and those too were exhausted which the Dictator Cæsar by the Cassian and the emperor Augustus by the Sænian law had chosen into their place. These acts, as being welcome to the State, were undertaken with hearty gladness by the imperial censor. Anxiously considering how he was to rid the Senate of men of notorious infamy, he preferred a gentle method, recently devised, to one which accorded with the sternness of antiquity, and advised each to examine his own case and seek the privilege of laying aside his rank. Permission, he said, would be readily obtained. He would publish in the same list those who had been expelled and those who had been allowed to retire, that by this confounding together of the decision of the censors and the modesty of voluntary resignation the disgrace might be softened.

For this, the consul Vipstanus moved that Claudius should be called "Father of the Senate." The title of "Father of the Country" had, he argued, been indiscriminately bestowed; new services ought to be recognised by unusual titles. The emperor however himself stopped the consul's flattery, as extravagant. He closed the lustrum, the census for which gave a total of 5,984,072 citizens. Then too ended his blindness as to his domestic affairs. He was soon compelled to notice and punish his wife's infamies, till he afterwards craved passionately for an unhallowed union.

26. Messalina, now grown weary of the very facility of her adulteries, was rushing into strange excesses, when even

Silius, either through some fatal infatuation or because he imagined that, amid the dangers which hung over him, danger itself was the best safety, urged the breaking off of all concealment. "They were not," he said, "in such an extremity as to have to wait for the emperor's old age. Harmless measures were for the innocent. Crime once exposed had no refuge but in audacity. They had accomplices in all who feared the same fate. For himself, as he had neither wife nor child, he was ready to marry and to adopt Britannicus. Messalina would have the same power as before, with the additional advantage of a quiet mind, if only they took Claudius by surprise, who, though unsuspicious of treachery, was hasty in his wrath."

The suggestion was coldly received, not because the lady loved her husband, but from a fear that Silius, after attaining his highest hopes, would spurn an adulteress, and soon estimate at its true value the crime which in the midst of peril he had approved. But she craved the name of wife, for the sake of the monstrous infamy, that last source of delight to the reckless. She waited only till Claudius set out for Ostia to perform a sacrifice, and then celebrated all the solemnities of marriage.

27. I am well aware that it will seem a fable that any persons in the world could have been so obtuse in a city which knows everything and hides nothing, much more, that these persons should have been a consul-elect and the emperor's wife; that, on an appointed day, before witnesses duly summoned, they should have come together as if for the purpose of legitimate marriage; that she should have listened to the words of the bridegroom's friends, should have sacrificed to the gods, have taken her place among a company of guests, have lavished her kisses and caresses, and passed the night in the freedom which marriage permits. But this is no story to excite wonder; I do but relate what I have heard and what our fathers have recorded.

28. The emperor's court indeed shuddered, its powerful personages especially, the men who had much to fear from a revolution. From secret whisperings they passed to loud complaints. "When an actor," they said, "impudently thrust himself into the imperial chamber, it certainly brought scan

dal on the State, but we were a long way from ruin. Now, a young noble of stately beauty, of vigorous intellect, with the near prospect of the consulship, is preparing himself for a loftier ambition. There can be no secret about what is to follow such a marriage." Doubtless there was a thrill of alarm when they thought of the apathy of Claudius, of his devotion to his wife and of the many murders perpetrated at Messalina's bidding. On the other hand, the very good nature of the emperor inspired confident hope that if they could overpower him by the enormity of the charge, she might be condemned and crushed before she was accused. The critical point was this, that he should not hear her defence, and that his ears should be shut even against her confession.

29. At first Callistus, of whom I have already spoken in connection with the assassination of Caius Cæsar, Narcissus, who had contrived the death of Appius, and Pallas, who was then in the height of favour, debated whether they might not by secret threats turn Messalina from her passion for Silius, while they concealed all else. Then fearing that they would be themselves involved in ruin, they abandoned the idea, Pallas out of cowardice, and Callistus, from his experience of a former court, remembering that prudent rather than vigorous counsels insure the maintenance of power. Narcissus persevered, only so far changing his plan as not to make her aware beforehand by a single word what was the charge or who was the accuser. Then he eagerly watched his opportunity, and, as the emperor lingered long at Ostia, he sought two of the mistresses to whose society Claudius was especially partial, and, by gifts, by promises, by dwelling on power increased by the wife's fall, he induced them to undertake the work of the informer.

30. On this, Calpurnia (that was the woman's name), as soon as she was allowed a private interview, threw herself at the emperor's knees, crying out that Messalina was married to Silius. At the same time she asked Cleopatra, who was standing near and waiting for the question, whether she knew it. Cleopatra nodding assent, she begged that Narcissus might be summoned. Narcissus entreated pardon for the past, for having concealed the scandal while confined to a Vettius or a Plautius. Even now, he said, he would not

make charges of adultery, and seem to be asking back the palace, the slaves, and the other belongings of imperial rank. These Silius might enjoy; only, he must give back the wife and annul the act of marriage. "Do you know," he said, "of your divorce? The people, the army, the Senate saw the marriage of Silius. Act at once, or the new husband is master of Rome."

31. Claudius then summoned all his most powerful friends. First he questioned Turranius, superintendent of the corn market; next, Lusius Geta, who commanded the prætorians. When they confessed the truth, the whole company clamoured in concert that he must go to the camp, must assure himself of the prætorian cohorts, must think of safety before he thought of vengeance. It is quite certain that Claudius was so overwhelmed by terror that he repeatedly asked whether he was indeed in possession of the empire, whether Silius was still a subject.

Messalina meanwhile, more wildly profligate than ever, was celebrating in mid autumn a representation of the vintage in her new home. The presses were being trodden; the vats were overflowing; women girt with skins were dancing, as Bacchanals dance in their worship or their frenzy. Messalina with flowing hair shook the thyrsus, and Silius at her side, crowned with ivy and wearing the buskin, moved his head to some lascivious chorus. It is said that one Vettius Valens climbed a very lofty tree in sport, and when they asked him what he saw, replied, "A terrible storm from Ostia." Possibly some such appearance had begun; perhaps, a word dropped by chance became a prophecy.

32. Meanwhile no mere rumour but messengers from all parts brought the news that everything was known to Claudius, and that he was coming, bent on vengeance. Messalina upon this went to the gardens of Lucullus; Silius, to conceal his fear, to his business in the forum. The other guests were flying in all directions when the centurions appeared and put every one in irons where they found them, either in the public streets or in hiding. Messalina, though her peril took away all power of thought, promptly resolved to meet and face her husband, a course in which she had often found safety; while she bade Britannicus and Octavia hasten to

embrace their father. She besought Vibidia, the eldest of the
Vestal Virgins, to demand audience of the supreme pontiff
and to beg for mercy. Meanwhile, with only three companions, so lonely did she find herself in a moment, she traversed the whole length of the city, and, mounting on a cart
used to remove garden refuse, proceeded along the road to
Ostia; not pitied, so overpoweringly hideous were her crimes,
by a single person.

33. There was equal alarm on the emperor's side. They
put but little trust in Geta, who commanded the prætorians,
a man swayed with equal ease to good or evil. Narcissus in
concert with others who dreaded the same fate, declared that
the only hope of safety for the emperor lay in his transferring for that one day the command of the soldiers to one of
the freedmen, and he offered to undertake it himself. And
that Claudius might not be induced by Lucius Vitellius and
Largus Cæcina to repent, while he was riding into Rome, he
asked and took a seat in the emperor's carriage.

34. It was currently reported in after times that while the
emperor broke into contradictory exclamations, now inveighing against the infamies of his wife, and now returning in
thought to the remembrance of his love and of his infant children, Vitellius said nothing but, "What audacity! what wickedness!" Narcissus indeed kept pressing him to clear up his
ambiguities and let the truth be known, but still he could not
prevail upon him to utter anything that was not vague and
susceptible of any meaning which might be put on it, or upon
Largus Cæcina, to do anything but follow his example. And
now Messalina had presented herself, and was insisting that
the emperor should listen to the mother of Octavia and Britannicus, when the accuser roared out at her the story of
Silius and her marriage. At the same moment, to draw Cæsar's eyes away from her, he handed him some papers which
detailed her debaucheries. Soon afterwards, as he was entering Rome, his children by Messalina were to have shown
themselves, had not Narcissus ordered their removal. Vibidia
he could not repel, when, with a vehemently indignant appeal, she demanded that a wife should not be given up to
death without a hearing. So Narcissus replied that the emperor would hear her, and that she should have an oppor-

tunity of disproving the charge. Meanwhile the holy virgin was to go and discharge her sacred duties.

35. All throughout, Claudius preserved a strange silence; Vitellius seemed unconscious. Everything was under the freedman's control. By his order, the paramour's house was thrown open and the emperor conducted thither. First, on the threshold, he pointed out the statue of Silius's father, which a decree of the Senate had directed to be destroyed; next, how the heirlooms of the Neros and the Drusi had been degraded into the price of infamy. Then he led the emperor, furious and bursting out in menace, into the camp, where the soldiers were purposely assembled. Claudius spoke to them a few words at the dictation of Narcissus. Shame indeed checked the utterance even of a righteous anger. Instantly there came a shout from the cohorts, demanding the names of the culprits and their punishment. Brought before the tribunal, Silius sought neither defence nor delay, but begged that his death might be hastened. A like courage made several Roman knights of the first rank desirous of a speedy doom. Titius Proculus, who had been appointed to watch Messalina and was now offering his evidence, Vettius Valens, who confessed his guilt, together with Pompeius Urbicus and Saufellus Trogus from among her accomplices, were ordered to execution. Decius Calpurnianus too, commander of the watch, Sulpicius Rufus, who had the charge of the Games, and Juncus Virgilianus, a senator, were similarly punished.

36. Mnester alone occasioned a pause. Rending off his clothes, he insisted on Claudius looking at the scars of his stripes and remembering his words when he surrendered himself, without reserve, to Messalina's bidding. The guilt of others had been the result of presents or of large promises; his, of necessity. He must have been the first victim had Silius obtained empire.

Cæsar was touched by his appeal and inclined to mercy, but his freedmen prevailed on him not to let any indulgence be shown to a player when so many illustrious citizens had fallen. "It mattered not whether he had sinned so greatly from choice or compulsion." Even the defence of Traulus Montanus, a Roman knight, was not admitted. A young man of pure life, yet of singular beauty, he had been summoned and dismissed within the space of one night by Messalina, who was equally capricious in her passions and dislikes. In the cases of Suilius Cæsoninus and Plautius Lateranus, the extreme penalty was remitted. The latter was saved by the distinguished services of his uncle; the former by his very vices, having amid that abominable throng submitted to the worst degradation.

37. Messalina meanwhile, in the gardens of Lucullus, was struggling for life, and writing letters of entreaty, as she alternated between hope and fury. In her extremity, it was her pride alone which forsook her. Had not Narcissus hurried on her death, ruin would have recoiled on her accuser. Claudius had returned home to an early banquet; then, in softened mood, when the wine had warmed him, he bade some one go and tell the "poor creature" (this is the word which they say he used) to come on the morrow and plead her cause. Hearing this, seeing too that his wrath was subsiding and his passion returning, and fearing, in the event of delay, the effect of approaching night and conjugal recollections, Narcissus rushed out, and ordered the centurions and the tribunes, who were on guard, to accomplish the deed of blood. Such, he said, was the emperor's bidding. Evodus, one of the freedmen, was appointed to watch and complete the affair. Hurrying on before with all speed to the gardens, he found Messalina stretched upon the ground, while by her side sat Lepida, her mother, who, though estranged from her daughter in prosperity, was now melted to pity by her inevitable doom, and urged her not to wait for the executioner. "Life," she said, "was over; all that could be looked for was honour in death." But in that heart, utterly corrupted by profligacy, nothing noble remained. She still prolonged her tears and idle compaints, till the gates were forced open by the rush of the new comers, and there stood at her side the tribune, sternly silent, and the freedman, overwhelming her with the copious insults of a servile tongue.

38. Then for the first time she understood her fate and put her hand to a dagger. In her terror she was applying it ineffectually to her throat and breast, when a blow from the tribune drove it through her. Her body was given up to her

mother. Claudius was still at the banquet when they told him that Messalina was dead, without mentioning whether it was by her own or another's hand. Nor did he ask the question, but called for the cup and finished his repast as usual. During the days which followed he showed no sign of hatred or joy or anger or sadness, in a word, of any human emotion, either when he looked on her triumphant accusers or on her weeping children. The Senate assisted his forgetfulness by decreeing that her name and her statues should be removed from all places, public or private. To Narcissus were voted the decorations of the quæstorship, a mere trifle to the pride of one who rose in the height of his power above Pallas and Callistus.

BOOK XII

A.D. 48—54

1. The destruction of Messalina shook the imperial house;
for a strife arose among the freedmen, who should choose a
wife for Claudius, impatient as he was of a single life and
submissive to the rule of wives. The ladies were fired with no
less jealousy. Each insisted on her rank, beauty, and fortune,
and pointed to her claims to such a marriage. But the keenest competition was between Lollia Paulina, the daughter
of Marcus Lollius, an ex-consul, and Julia Agrippina, the
daughter of Germanicus. Callistus favoured the first, Pallas
the second. Ælia Pætina however, of the family of the Tuberones, had the support of Narcissus. The emperor, who
inclined now one way, now another, as he listened to this or
that adviser, summoned the disputants to a conference and
bade them express their opinions and give their reasons.

2. Narcissus dwelt on the marriage of years gone by, on
the tie of offspring, for Pætina was the mother of Antonia,
and on the advantage of excluding a new element from his
household, by the return of a wife to whom he was accustomed, and who would assuredly not look with a stepmother's animosity on Britannicus and Octavia, who were
next in her affections to her own children. Callistus argued
that she was compromised by her long separation, and that
were she to be taken back, she would be supercilious on the
strength of it. It would be far better to introduce Lollia, for,
as she had no children of her own, she would be free from
jealousy, and would take the place of a mother towards her
stepchildren.

Pallas again selected Agrippina for special commendation
because she would bring with her Germanicus's grandson,
who was thoroughly worthy of imperial rank, the scion of a
noble house and a link to unite the descendants of the Clau-

dian family. He hoped that a woman who was the mother of many children and still in the freshness of youth, would not carry off the grandeur of the Cæsars to some other house.

3. This advice prevailed, backed up as it was by Agrippina's charms. On the pretext of her relationship, she paid frequent visits to her uncle, and so won his heart, that she was preferred to the others, and, though not yet his wife, already possessed a wife's power. For as soon as she was sure of her marriage, she began to aim at greater things, and planned an alliance between Domitius, her son by Cneius Ænobarbus, and Octavia, the emperor's daughter. This could not be accomplished without a crime, for the emperor had betrothed Octavia to Lucius Silanus, a young man otherwise famous, whom he had brought forward as a candidate for popular favour by the honour of triumphal distinctions and by a magnificent gladiatorial show. But no difficulty seemed to be presented by the temper of a sovereign who had neither partialities nor dislikes, but such as were suggested and dictated to him.

4. Vitellius accordingly, who used the name of censor to screen a slave's trickeries, and looked forward to new despotisms, already impending, associated himself in Agrippina's plans, with a view to her favour, and began to bring charges against Silanus, whose sister, Junia Calvina, a handsome and lively girl, had shortly before become his daughter-in-law. Here was a starting point for an accuser. Vitellius put an infamous construction on the somewhat incautious though not criminal love between the brother and sister. The emperor listened, for his affection for his daughter inclined him the more to admit suspicions against his son-in-law. Silanus meanwhile, who knew nothing of the plot, and happened that year to be prætor, was suddenly expelled from the Senate by an edict of Vitellius, though the roll of Senators had been recently reviewed and the lustrum closed. Claudius at the same time broke off the connection; Silanus was forced to resign his office, and the one remaining day of his prætorship was conferred on Eprius Marcellus.

5. In the year of the consulship of Caius Pompeius and Quintus Veranius, the marriage arranged between Claudius and Agrippina was confirmed both by popular rumour and

by their own illicit love. Still, they did not yet dare to celebrate the nuptials in due form, for there was no precedent
for the introduction of a niece into an uncle's house. It was
positively incest, and if disregarded, it would, people feared,
issue in calamity to the State. These scruples ceased not till
Vitellius undertook the management of the matter in his own
way. He asked the emperor whether he would yield to the
recommendations of the people and to the authority of the
Senate. When Claudius replied that he was one among the
citizens and could not resist their unanimous voice, Vitellius
requested him to wait in the palace, while he himself went to
the Senate. Protesting that the supreme interest of the commonwealth was at stake, he begged to be allowed to speak
first, and then began to urge that the very burdensome labours of the emperor in a world-wide administration, required assistance, so that, free from domestic cares, he might
consult the public welfare. How again could there be a more
virtuous relief for the mind of an imperial censor than the
taking of a wife to share his prosperity and his troubles, to
whom he might intrust his inmost thoughts and the care of
his young children, unused as he was to luxury and pleasure,
and wont from his earliest youth to obey the laws.

6. Vitellius, having first put forward these arguments in a
conciliatory speech, and met with decided acquiescence from
the Senate, began afresh to point out, that, as they all recommended the emperor's marriage, they ought to select a
lady conspicuous for noble rank and purity, herself too the
mother of children. "It cannot," he said, "be long a question
that Agrippina stands first in nobility of birth. She has given
proof too that she is not barren, and she has suitable moral
qualities. It is, again, a singular advantage to us, due to divine providence, for a widow to be united to an emperor who
has limited himself to his own lawful wives. We have heard
from our fathers, we have ourselves seen that married women
were seized at the caprice of the Cæsars. This is quite alien
to the propriety of our day. Rather let a precedent be now
set for the taking of a wife by an emperor. But, it will be
said, marriage with a brother's daughter is with us a novelty.
True; but it is common in other countries, and there is no
law to forbid it. Marriages of cousins were long unknown,

but after a time they became frequent. Custom adapts itself to expediency, and this novelty will hereafter take its place among recognized usages."

7. There were some who rushed out of the Senate, passionately protesting that if the emperor hesitated, they would use violence. A promiscuous throng assembled, and kept exclaiming that the same too was the prayer of the Roman people. Claudius without further delay presented himself in the forum to their congratulations; then entering the Senate, he asked from them a decree which should decide that for the future marriages between uncles and brothers' daughters should be legal. There was, however, found only one person who desired such a marriage, Alledius Severus, a Roman knight, who, as many said, was swayed by the influence of Agrippina. Then came a revolution in the State, and everything was under the control of a woman, who did not, like Messalina, insult Rome by loose manners. It was a stringent, and, so to say, masculine despotism; there was sternness and generally arrogance in public, no sort of immodesty at home, unless it conduced to power. A boundless greed of wealth was veiled under the pretext that riches were being accumulated as a prop to the throne.

8. On the day of the marriage Silanus committed suicide, having up to that time prolonged his hope of life, or else choosing that day to heighten the popular indignation. His sister, Calvina, was banished from Italy. Claudius further added that sacrifices after the ordinances of King Tullius, and atonements were to be offered by the pontiffs in the grove of Diana, amid general ridicule at the idea of devising penalties and propitiations for incest at such a time. Agrippina, that she might not be conspicuous only by her evil deeds, procured for Annæus Seneca a remission of his exile, and with it the prætorship. She thought this would be universally welcome, from the celebrity of his attainments, and it was her wish too for the boyhood of Domitius to be trained under so excellent an instructor, and for them to have the benefit of his counsels in their designs on the throne. For Seneca, it was believed, was devoted to Agrippina from a remembrance of her kindness, and an enemy to Claudius from a bitter sense of wrong.

9. It was then resolved to delay no longer. Memmius Pollio, the consul-elect, was induced by great promises to deliver a speech, praying Claudius to betroth Octavia to Domitius. The match was not unsuitable to the age of either, and was likely to develop still more important results. Pollio introduced the motion in much the same language as Vitellius had lately used. So Octavia was betrothed, and Domitius, besides his previous relationship, became now the emperor's affianced son-in-law, and an equal of Britannicus, through the exertions of his mother and the cunning of those who had been the accusers of Messalina, and feared the vengeance of her son.

10. About the same time an embassy from the Parthians, which had been sent, as I have stated, to solicit the return of Meherdates, was introduced into the Senate, and delivered a message to the following effect:—"They were not," they said, "unaware of the treaty of alliance, nor did their coming imply any revolt from the family of the Arsacids; indeed, even the son of Vonones, Phraates's grandson, was with them in their resistance to the despotism of Gotarzes, which was alike intolerable to the nobility and to the people. Already brothers, relatives, and distant kin had been swept off by murder after murder; wives actually pregnant, and tender children were added to Gotarzes' victims, while, slothful at home and unsuccessful in war, he made cruelty a screen for his feebleness. Between the Parthians and ourselves there was an ancient friendship, founded on a state alliance, and we ought to support allies who were our rivals in strength, and yet yielded to us out of respect. Kings' sons were given as hostages, in order that when Parthia was tired of home rule, it might fall back on the emperor and the Senate, and receive from them a better sovereign, familiar with Roman habits."

11. In answer to these and like arguments Claudius began to speak of the grandeur of Rome and the submissive attitude of the Parthians. He compared himself to the Divine Augustus, from whom, he reminded them, they had sought a king, but omitted to mention Tiberius, though he too had sent them sovereigns. He added some advice for Meherdates, who was present, and told him not to be thinking of a despot

and his slaves, but rather of a ruler among fellow citizens, and to practise clemency and justice which barbarians would like the more for being unused to them. Then he turned to the envoys and bestowed high praise on the young foster-son of Rome, as one whose self-control had hitherto been exemplary. "Still," he said, "they must bear with the caprices of kings, and frequent revolutions were bad. Rome, sated with her glory, had reached such a height that she wished even foreign nations to enjoy repose." Upon this Caius Cassius, governor of Syria, was commissioned to escort the young prince to the bank of the Euphrates.

12. Cassius was at that time preeminent for legal learning. The profession of the soldier is forgotten in a quiet period, and peace reduces the enterprising and indolent to an equality. But Cassius, as far as it was possible without war, revived ancient discipline, kept exercising the legions, in short, used as much diligence and precaution as if an enemy were threatening him. This conduct he counted worthy of his ancestors and of the Cassian family which had won renowr even in those countries.

He then summoned those at whose suggestion a king had been sought from Rome, and having encamped at Zeugma where the river was most easily fordable and awaited the arrival of the chief men of Parthia and of Acbarus, king of the Arabs, he reminded Meherdates that the impulsive enthusiasm of barbarians soon flags from delay or even changes into treachery, and that therefore he should urge on his enterprise. The advice was disregarded through the perfidy of Acbarus, by whom the foolish young prince, who thought that the highest position merely meant self-indulgence, was detained for several days in the town of Edessa. Although a certain Carenes pressed them to come and promised easy success if they hastened their arrival, they did not make for Mesopotamia, which was close to them, but, by a long détour, for Armenia, then ill-suited to their movements, as winter was beginning.

13. As they approached the plains, wearied with the snows and mountains, they were joined by the forces of Carenes, and having crossed the river Tigris they traversed the country of the Adiabeni, whose king Izates had avowedly em-

braced the alliance of Meherdates, though secretly and in better faith he inclined to Gotarzes. In their march they captured the city of Ninos, the most ancient capital of Assyria, and a fortress, historically famous, as the spot where in the last battle between Darius and Alexander the power of Persia fell. Gotarzes meantime was offering vows to the local divinities on a mountain called Sambulos, with special worship of Hercules, who at a stated time bids the priests in a dream equip horses for the chase and place them near his temple. When the horses have been laden with quivers full of arrows, they scour the forest and at length return at night with empty quivers, panting violently. Again the god in a vision of the night reveals to them the track along which he roamed through the woods, and everywhere slaughtered beasts are found.

14. Gotarzes, his army not being yet in sufficient force, made the river Corma a line of defence, and though he was challenged to an engagement by taunting messages, he contrived delays, shifted his positions and sent emissaries to corrupt the enemy and bribe them to throw off their allegiance. Izates of the Adiabeni and then Acbarus of the Arabs deserted with their troops, with their countrymen's characteristic fickleness, confirming previous experience, that barbarians prefer to seek a king from Rome than to keep him. Meherdates, stript of his powerful auxiliaries and suspecting treachery in the rest, resolved, as his last resource, to risk everything and try the issue of a battle. Nor did Gotarzes, who was emboldened by the enemy's diminished strength, refuse the challenge. They fought with terrible courage and doubtful result, till Carenes, who having beaten down all resistance had advanced too far, was surprised by a fresh detachment in his rear. Then Meherdates in despair yielded to promises from Parrhaces, one of his father's adherents, and was by his treachery delivered in chains to the conqueror. Gotarzes taunted him with being no kinsman of his or of the Arsacids, but a foreigner and a Roman, and having cut off his ears, bade him live, a memorial of his own clemency, and a disgrace to us. After this Gotarzes fell ill and died, and Vonones, who then ruled the Medes, was summoned to the throne. He was memorable neither for his good

nor bad fortune; he completed a short and inglorious reign, and then the empire of Parthia passed to his son Vologeses.

15. Mithridates of Bosporus, meanwhile, who had lost his power and was a mere outcast, on learning that the Roman general, Didius, and the main strength of his army had retired, and that Cotys, a young prince without experience, was left in his new kingdom with a few cohorts under Julius Aquila, a Roman knight, disdaining both, roused the neighbouring tribes, and drew deserters to his standard. At last he collected an army, drove out the king of the Dandaridæ, and possessed himself of his dominions. When this was known, and the invasion of Bosporus was every moment expected, Aquila and Cotys, seeing that hostilities had been also resumed by Zorsines, king of the Siraci, distrusted their own strength, and themselves too sought the friendship of the foreigner by sending envoys to Eunones, who was then chief of the Adorsi. There was no difficulty about alliance, when they pointed to the power of Rome in contrast with the rebel Mithridates. It was accordingly stipulated that Eunones should engage the enemy with his cavalry, and the Romans undertake the siege of towns.

16. Then the army advanced in regular formation, the Adorsi in the van and the rear, while the centre was strengthened by the cohorts, and native troops of Bosporus with Roman arms. Thus the enemy was defeated, and they reached Soza, a town in Dandarica, which Mithridates had abandoned, where it was thought expedient to leave a garrison, as the temper of the people was uncertain. Next they marched on the Siraci, and after crossing the river Panda besieged the city of Uspe, which stood on high ground, and had the defence of walls and fosses; only the walls, not being of stone, but of hurdles and wicker-work with earth between, were too weak to resist an assault. Towers were raised to a greater height as a means of annoying the besieged with brands and darts. Had not night stopped the conflict, the siege would have been begun and finished within one day.

17. Next day they sent an embassy asking mercy for the freeborn, and offering ten thousand slaves. As it would have been inhuman to slay the prisoners, and very difficult to keep

them under guard, the conquerors rejected the offer, preferring that they should perish by the just doom of war. The
signal for massacre was therefore given to the soldiers, who
had mounted the walls by scaling ladders. The destruction
of Uspe struck terror into the rest of the people, who thought
safety impossible when they saw how armies and ramparts,
heights and difficult positions, rivers and cities, alike yielded
to their foe. And so Zorsines, having long considered whether
he should still have regard to the fallen fortunes of Mithridates or to the kingdom of his fathers, and having at last
preferred his country's interests, gave hostages and prostrated himself before the emperor's image, to the great glory
of the Roman army, which all men knew to have come after
a bloodless victory within three days' march of the river
Tanais. In their return however fortune was not equally
favourable; some of their vessels, as they were sailing back,
were driven on the shores of the Tauri and cut off by the
barbarians, who slew the commander of a cohort and several
centurions.

18. Meanwhile Mithridates, finding arms an unavailing
resource, considered on whose mercy he was to throw himself. He feared his brother Cotys, who had once been a
traitor, then become his open enemy. No Roman was on the
spot of authority sufficient to make his promises highly valued. So he turned to Eunones, who had no personal animosity against him, and had been lately strengthened by his
alliance with us. Adapting his dress and expression of countenance as much as possible to his present condition, he entered the palace, and throwing himself at the feet of Eunones
he exclaimed, "Mithridates, whom the Romans have sought
so many years by land and sea, stands before you by his own
choice. Deal as you please with the descendant of the great
Achæmenes, the only glory of which enemies have not robbed
me."

19. The great name of Mithridates, his reverse, his prayer,
full of dignity, deeply affected Eunones. He raised the suppliant, and commended him for having chosen the nation of
the Adorsi and his own good faith in suing for mercy. He
sent at the same time envoys to Cæsar with a letter to this
effect, that friendship between emperors of Rome and sov-

ereigns of powerful peoples was primarily based on a similarity of fortune, and that between himself and Claudius there was the tie of a common victory. Wars had glorious endings, whenever matters were settled by an amnesty. The conquered Zorsines had on this principle been deprived of nothing. For Mithridates, as he deserved heavier punishment, he asked neither power nor dominions, only that he might not be led in triumph, and pay the penalty of death.

20. Claudius, though merciful to foreign princes, was yet in doubt whether it were better to receive the captive with a promise of safety or to claim his surrender by the sword. To this last he was urged by resentment at his wrongs, and by thirst for vengeance. On the other hand it was argued that it would be undertaking a war in a country without roads, on a harbourless sea, against warlike kings and wandering tribes, on a barren soil; that a weary disgust would come of tardy movements, and perils of precipitancy; that the glory of victory would be small, while much disgrace would ensue on defeat. Why should not the emperor seize the offer and spare the exile, whose punishment would be the greater, the longer he lived in poverty?

Moved by these considerations, Claudius wrote to Eunones that Mithridates had certainly merited an extreme and exemplary penalty, which he was not wanting in power to inflict, but it had been the principle of his ancestors to show as much forbearance to a suppliant as they showed persistence against a foe. As for triumphs, they were won over nations and kings hitherto unconquered.

21. After this, Mithridates was given up and brought to Rome by Junius Cilo, the procurator of Pontus. There in the emperor's presence he was said to have spoken too proudly for his position, and words uttered by him to the following effect became the popular talk: "I have not been sent, but have come back to you; if you do not believe me, let me go and pursue me." He stood too with fearless countenance when he was exposed to the people's gaze near the Rostra, under military guard. To Cilo and Aquila were voted, respectively, the consular and prætorian decorations.

22. In the same consulship, Agrippina, who was terrible in her hatred and detested Lollia, for having competed with

her for the emperor's hand, planned an accusation, through an informer who was to tax her with having consulted astrologers and magicians and the image of the Clarian Apollo, about the imperial marriage. Upon this, Claudius, without hearing the accused, first reminded the Senate of her illustrious rank, that the sister of Lucius Volusius was her mother, Cotta Messalinus her granduncle, Memmius Regulus formerly her husband (for of her marriage to Caius Cæsar he purposely said nothing), and then added that she had mischievous designs on the State, and must have the means of crime taken from her. Consequently, her property should be confiscated, and she herself banished from Italy. Thus out of immense wealth only five million sesterces were left to the exile. Calpurnia too, a lady of high rank, was ruined, simply because the emperor had praised her beauty in a casual remark, without any passion for her. And so Agrippina's resentment stopped short of extreme vengeance. A tribune was despatched to Lollia, who was to force her to suicide. Next on the prosecution of the Bithynians, Cadius Rufus, was condemned under the law against extortion.

23. Narbon Gaul, for its special reverence of the Senate, received a privilege. Senators belonging to the province, without seeking the emperor's approval, were to be allowed to visit their estates, a right enjoyed by Sicily. Ituræa and Judæa, on the death of their kings, Sohæmus and Agrippa, were annexed to the province of Syria.

It was also decided that the augury of the public safety, which for twenty-five years had been neglected, should be revived and henceforth observed. The emperor likewise widened the sacred precincts of the capital, in conformity with the ancient usage, according to which, those who had enlarged the empire were permitted also to extend the boundaries of Rome. But Roman generals, even after the conquest of great nations, had never exercised this right, except Lucius Sulla and the Divine Augustus.

24. There are various popular accounts of the ambitious and vainglorious efforts of our kings in this matter. Still, I think, it is interesting to know accurately the original plan of the precinct, as it was fixed by Romulus. From the ox market, where we see the brazen statue of a bull, because

that animal is yoked to the plough, a furrow was drawn to mark out the town, so as to embrace the great altar of Hercules; then, at regular intervals, stones were placed along the foot of the Palatine hill to the altar of Consus, soon afterwards, to the old Courts, and then to the chapel of Larunda. The Roman forum and the Capitol were not, it was supposed, added to the city by Romulus, but by Titus Tatius. In time, the precinct was enlarged with the growth of Rome's fortunes. The boundaries now fixed by Claudius may be easily recognized, as they are specified in the public records.

25. In the consulship of Caius Antistius and Marcus Suillius, the adoption of Domitius was hastened on by the influence of Pallas. Bound to Agrippina, first as the promoter of her marriage, then as her paramour, he still urged Claudius to think of the interests of the State, and to provide some support for the tender years of Britannicus. "So," he said, "it had been with the Divine Augustus, whose stepsons, though he had grandsons to be his stay, had been promoted; Tiberius too, though he had offspring of his own, had adopted Germanicus. Claudius also would do well to strengthen himself with a young prince who could share his cares with him."

Overcome by these arguments, the emperor preferred Domitius to his own son, though he was but two years older, and made a speech in the senate, the same in substance as the representations of his freedman. It was noted by learned men, that no previous example of adoption into the patrician family of the Claudii was to be found; and that from Attus Clausus there had been one unbroken line.

26. However, the emperor received formal thanks, and still more elaborate flattery was paid to Domitius. A law was passed, adopting him into the Claudian family with the name of Nero. Agrippina too was honoured with the title of Augusta. When this had been done, there was not a person so void of pity as not to feel keen sorrow at the position of Britannicus. Gradually forsaken by the very slaves who waited on him, he turned into ridicule the ill-timed attentions of his stepmother, perceiving their insincerity. For he is said to have had by no means a dull understanding; and this is either a fact, or perhaps his perils won him sympathy,

and so he possessed the credit of it, without actual evidence.

27. Agrippina, to show her power even to the allied nations, procured the despatch of a colony of veterans to the chief town of the Ubii, where she was born. The place was named after her. Agrippa, her grandfather, had, as it happened, received this tribe, when they crossed the Rhine, under our protection.

During the same time, there was a panic in Upper Germany through an irruption of plundering bands of Chatti. Thereupon Lucius Pomponius, who was in command, directed the Vangiones and Nemetes, with the allied cavalry, to anticipate the raid, and suddenly to fall upon them from every quarter while they were dispersed. The general's plan was backed up by the energy of the troops. These were divided into two columns; and those who marched to the left cut off the plunderers, just on their return, after a riotous enjoyment of their spoil, when they were heavy with sleep. It added to the men's joy that they had rescued from slavery after forty years some survivors of the defeat of Varus.

28. The column which took the right-hand and the shorter route, inflicted greater loss on the enemy who met them, and ventured on a battle. With much spoil and glory they returned to Mount Taunus, where Pomponius was waiting with the legions, to see whether the Chatti, in their eagerness for vengeance, would give him a chance of fighting. They however fearing to be hemmed in on one side by the Romans, on the other by the Cherusci, with whom they are perpetually at feud, sent envoys and hostages to Rome. To Pomponius was decreed the honour of a triumph; a mere fraction of his renown with the next generation, with whom his poems constitute his chief glory.

29. At this same time, Vannius, whom Drusus Cæsar had made king of the Suevi, was driven from his kingdom. In the commencement of his reign he was renowned and popular with his countrymen; but subsequently, with long possession, he became a tyrant, and the enmity of neighbours, joined to intestine strife, was his ruin. Vibillius, king of the Hermunduri, and Vangio and Sido, sons of a sister of Vannius, led the movement. Claudius, though often entreated, declined to interpose by arms in the conflict of the barbar-

ians, and simply promised Vannius a safe refuge in the event
of his expulsion. He wrote instructions to Publius Atellius
Hister, governor of Pannonia, that he was to have his legions, with some picked auxiliaries from the province itself,
encamped on the river-bank, as a support to the conquered
and a terror to the conqueror, who might otherwise, in the
elation of success, disturb also the peace of our empire. For
an immense host of Ligii, with other tribes, was advancing,
attracted by the fame of the opulent realm which Vannius
had enriched during thirty years of plunder and of tribute.
Vannius's own native force was infantry, and his cavalry was
from the Iazyges of Sarmatia; an army which was no match
for his numerous enemy. Consequently, he determined to
maintain himself in fortified positions, and protract the war.

30. But the Iazyges, who could not endure a siege, dispersed themselves throughout the surrounding country and
rendered an engagement inevitable, as the Ligii and Hermunduri had there rushed to the attack. So Vannius came
down out of his fortresses, and though he was defeated in
battle, notwithstanding his reverse, he won some credit by
having fought with his own hand, and received wounds on
his breast. He then fled to the fleet which was awaiting him
on the Danube, and was soon followed by his adherents, who
received grants of land and were settled in Pannonia. Vangio
and Sido divided his kingdom between them; they were admirably loyal to us, and among their subjects, whether the
cause was in themselves or in the nature of despotism, much
loved, while seeking to acquire power, and yet more hated
when they had acquired it.

31. Meanwhile, in Britain, Publius Ostorius, the proprætor, found himself confronted by disturbance. The enemy
had burst into the territories of our allies with all the more
fury, as they imagined that a new general would not march
against them with winter beginning and with an army of
which he knew nothing. Ostorius, well aware that first events
are those which produce alarm or confidence, by a rapid
movement of his light cohorts, cut down all who opposed
him, pursued those who fled, and lest they should rally, and
so an unquiet and treacherous peace might allow no rest to
the general and his troops, he prepared to disarm all whom

he suspected, and to occupy with encampments the whole country to the Avon and Severn. The Iceni, a powerful tribe, which war had not weakened, as they had voluntarily joined our alliance, were the first to resist. At their instigation the surrounding nations chose as a battlefield a spot walled in by a rude barrier, with a narrow approach, impenetrable to cavalry. Through these defences the Roman general, though he had with him only the allied troops, without the strength of the legions, attempted to break, and having assigned their positions to his cohorts, he equipped even his cavalry for the work of infantry. Then at a given signal they forced the barrier, routing the enemy who were entangled in their own defences. The rebels, conscious of their guilt, and finding escape barred, performed many noble feats. In this battle, Marius Ostorius, the general's son, won the reward for saving a citizen's life.

32. The defeat of the Iceni quieted those who were hesitating between war and peace. Then the army was marched against the Cangi; their territory was ravaged, spoil taken everywhere without the enemy venturing on an engagement, or if they attempted to harass our march by stealthy attacks, their cunning was always punished. And now Ostorius had advanced within a little distance of the sea, facing the island Hibernia, when feuds broke out among the Brigantes and compelled the general's return, for it was his fixed purpose not to undertake any fresh enterprise till he had consolidated his previous successes. The Brigantes indeed, when a few who were beginning hostilities had been slain and the rest pardoned, settled down quietly; but on the Silures neither terror nor mercy had the least effect; they persisted in war and could be quelled only by legions encamped in their country. That this might be the more promptly effected, a colony of a strong body of veterans was established at Camulodunum on the conquered lands, as a defence against the rebels, and as a means of imbuing the allies with respect for our laws.

33. The army then marched against the Silures, a naturally fierce people and now full of confidence in the might of Caractacus, who by many an indecisive and many a successful battle had raised himself far above all the other generals

of the Britons. Inferior in military strength, but deriving an advantage from the deceptiveness of the country, he at once shifted the war by a stratagem into the territory of the Ordovices, where, joined by all who dreaded peace with us, he resolved on a final struggle. He selected a position for the engagement in which advance and retreat alike would be difficult for our men and comparatively easy for his own, and then on some lofty hills, wherever their sides could be approached by a gentle slope, he piled up stones to serve as a rampart. A river too of varying depth was in his front, and his armed bands were drawn up before his defences.

34. Then too the chieftains of the several tribes went from rank to rank, encouraging and confirming the spirit of their men by making light of their fears, kindling their hopes, and by every other warlike incitement. As for Caractacus, he flew hither and thither, protesting that that day and that battle would be the beginning of the recovery of their freedom, or of everlasting bondage. He appealed, by name, to their forefathers who had driven back the dictator Cæsar, by whose valour they were free from the Roman axe and tribute, and still preserved inviolate the persons of their wives and of their children. While he was thus speaking, the host shouted applause; every warrior bound himself by his national oath not to shrink from weapons or wounds.

35. Such enthusiasm confounded the Roman general. The river too in his face, the rampart they had added to it, the frowning hilltops, the stern resistance and masses of fighting men everywhere apparent, daunted him. But his soldiers insisted on battle, exclaiming that valour could overcome all things; and the prefects and tribunes, with similar language, stimulated the ardour of the troops. Ostorius having ascertained by a survey the inaccessible and the assailable points of the position, led on his furious men, and crossed the river without difficulty. When he reached the barrier, as long as it was a fight with missiles, the wounds and the slaughter fell chiefly on our soldiers; but when we had formed the military testudo, and the rude, ill-compacted fence of stones was torn down, and it was an equal hand-to-hand engagement, the barbarians retired to the heights. Yet even there, both light and heavy-armed soldiers rushed to the attack; the first har-

assed the foe with missiles, while the latter closed with them,
and the opposing ranks of the Britons were broken, destitute
as they were of the defence of breast-plates or helmets.
When they faced the auxiliaries, they were felled by the
swords and javelins of our legionaries; if they wheeled
round, they were again met by the sabres and spears of the
auxiliaries. It was a glorious victory; the wife and daughter
of Caractacus were captured, and his brothers too were admitted to surrender.

36. There is seldom safety for the unfortunate, and Caractacus, seeking the protection of Cartismandua, queen of the
Brigantes, was put in chains and delivered up to the conquerors, nine years after the beginning of the war in Britain.
His fame had spread thence, and travelled to the neighbouring islands and provinces, and was actually celebrated in
Italy. All were eager to see the great man, who for so many
years had defied our power. Even at Rome the name of Caractacus was no obscure one; and the emperor, while he exalted his own glory, enhanced the renown of the vanquished.
The people were summoned as to a grand spectacle; the
prætorian cohorts were drawn up under arms in the plain in
front of their camp; then came a procession of the royal vassals, and the ornaments and neck-chains and the spoils which
the king had won in wars with other tribes, were displayed.
Next were to be seen his brothers, his wife and daughter;
last of all, Caractacus himself. All the rest stooped in their
fear to abject supplication; not so the king, who neither by
humble look nor speech sought compassion.

37. When he was set before the emperor's tribunal, he
spoke as follows: "Had my moderation in prosperity been
equal to my noble birth and fortune, I should have entered
this city as your friend rather than as your captive; and you
would not have disdained to receive, under a treaty of peace,
a king descended from illustrious ancestors and ruling many
nations. My present lot is as glorious to you as it is degrading to myself. I had men and horses, arms and wealth.
What wonder if I parted with them reluctantly? If you
Romans choose to lord it over the world, does it follow that
the world is to accept slavery? Were I to have been at once
delivered up as a prisoner, neither my fall nor your triumph

would have become famous. My punishment would be followed by oblivion, whereas, if you save my life, I shall be an everlasting memorial of your clemency."

Upon this the emperor granted pardon to Caractacus, to his wife, and to his brothers. Released from their bonds, they did homage also to Agrippina who sat near, conspicuous on another throne, in the same language of praise and gratitude. It was indeed a novelty, quite alien to ancient manners, for a woman to sit in front of Roman standards. In fact, Agrippina boasted that she was herself a partner in the empire which her ancestors had won.

38. The Senate was then assembled, and speeches were delivered full of pompous eulogy on the capture of Caractacus. It was as glorious, they said, as the display of Syphax by Scipio, or of Perses by Lucius Paulus, or indeed of any captive prince by any of our generals to the people of Rome. Triumphal distinctions were voted to Ostorius, who thus far had been successful, but soon afterwards met with reverses; either because, when Caractacus was out of the way, our discipline was relaxed under an impression that the war was ended, or because the enemy, out of compassion for so great a king, was more ardent in his thirst for vengeance. Instantly they rushed from all parts on the camp-prefect, and legionary cohorts left to establish fortified positions among the Silures, and had not speedy succour arrived from towns and fortresses in the neighbourhood, our forces would then have been totally destroyed. Even as it was, the camp-prefect, with eight centurions, and the bravest of the soldiers, were slain; and shortly afterwards, a foraging party of our men, with some cavalry squadrons sent to their support, was utterly routed.

39. Ostorius then deployed his light cohorts, but even thus he did not stop the flight, till our legions sustained the brunt of the battle. Their strength equalized the conflict, which after a while was in our favour. The enemy fled with trifling loss, as the day was on the decline. Now began a series of skirmishes, for the most part like raids, in woods and morasses, with encounters due to chance or to courage, to mere heedlessness or to calculation, to fury or to lust of plunder, under directions from the officers, or sometimes even

without their knowledge. Conspicuous above all in stubborn resistance were the Silures, whose rage was fired by words rumoured to have been spoken by the Roman general, to the effect, that as the Sugambri had been formerly destroyed or transplanted into Gaul, so the name of the Silures ought to be blotted out. Accordingly they cut off two of our auxiliary cohorts, the rapacity of whose officers let them make incautious forays; and by liberal gifts of spoil and prisoners to the other tribes, they were luring them too into revolt, when Ostorius, worn out by the burden of his anxieties, died, to the joy of the enemy, who thought that a campaign at least, though not a single battle, had proved fatal to a general whom none could despise.

40. The emperor on hearing of the death of his representative appointed Aulus Didius in his place, that the province might not be left without a governor. Didius, though he quickly arrived, found matters far from prosperous, for the legion under the command of Manlius Valens had meanwhile been defeated, and the disaster had been exaggerated by the enemy to alarm the new general, while he again magnified it, that he might win the more glory by quelling the movement or have a fairer excuse if it lasted. This loss too had been inflicted on us by the Silures, and they were scouring the country far and wide, till Didius hurried up and dispersed them. After the capture of Caractacus, Venutius of the Brigantes, as I have already mentioned, was preeminent in military skill; he had long been loyal to Rome and had been defended by our arms while he was united in marriage to the queen Cartismandua. Subsequently a quarrel broke out between them, followed instantly by war, and he then assumed a hostile attitude also towards us. At first, however, they simply fought against each other, and Cartismandua by cunning stratagems captured the brothers and kinsfolk of Venutius. This enraged the enemy, who were stung with shame at the prospect of falling under the dominion of a woman. The flower of their youth, picked out for war, invaded her kingdom. This we had foreseen; some cohorts were sent to her aid and a sharp contest followed, which was at first doubtful but had a satisfactory termination.

The legion under the command of Cæsius Nasica fought with a similar result. For Didius, burdened with years and covered with honours, was content with acting through his officers and merely holding back the enemy. These transactions, though occurring under two proprætors, and occupying several years, I have closely connected, lest, if related separately, they might be less easily remembered. I now return to the chronological order.

41. In the fifth consulship of Tiberius Claudius with Sextius Cornelius Orfitus for his colleague, Nero was prematurely invested with the dress of manhood, that he might be thought qualified for political life. The emperor willingly complied with the flatteries of the Senate who wished Nero to enter on the consulship in his twentieth year, and meanwhile, as consul-elect, to have proconsular authority beyond the limits of the capital with the title of "prince of the youth of Rome." A donative was also given to the soldiery in Nero's name, and presents to the city populace. At the games too of the circus which were then being celebrated to win for him popular favour, Britannicus wore the dress of boyhood, Nero the triumphal robe, as they rode in the procession. The people would thus behold the one with the decorations of a general, the other in a boy's habit, and would accordingly anticipate their respective destinies. At the same time those of the centurions and tribunes who pitied the lot of Britannicus were removed, some on false pretexts, others by way of a seeming compliment. Even of the freedmen, all who were of incorruptible fidelity were discarded on the following provocation. Once when they met, Nero greeted Britannicus by that name and was greeted in return as Domitius. Agrippina reported this to her husband, with bitter complaint, as the beginning of a quarrel, as implying, in fact, contempt of Nero's adoption and a cancelling at home of the Senate's decree and the people's vote. She said, too, that, if the perversity of such malignant suggestions were not checked, it would issue in the ruin of the State. Claudius, enraged by what he took as a grave charge, punished with banishment or death all his son's best instructors, and set persons appointed by his stepmother to have the care of him.

42. Still Agrippina did not yet dare to attempt her greatest scheme, unless Lusius Geta and Rufius Crispinus were removed from the command of the prætorian cohorts; for she thought that they cherished Messalina's memory and were devoted to her children. Accordingly, as the emperor's wife persistently affirmed that faction was rife among these cohorts through the rivalry of the two officers, and that there would be stricter discipline under one commander, the appointment was transferred to Burrus Afranius, who had a brilliant reputation as a soldier, but knew well to whose wish he owed his promotion. Agrippina, too, continued to exalt her own dignity; she would enter the Capitol in a chariot, a practice, which being allowed of old only to the priests and sacred images, increased the popular reverence for a woman who up to this time was the only recorded instance of one who, an emperor's daughter, was sister, wife, and mother of a sovereign. Meanwhile her foremost champion, Vitellius, in the full tide of his power and in extreme age (so uncertain are the fortunes of the great) was attacked by an accusation of which Junius Lupus, a senator, was the author. He was charged with treason and designs on the throne. The emperor would have lent a ready ear, had not Agrippina, by threats rather than entreaties, induced him to sentence the accuser to outlawry. This was all that Vitellius desired.

43. Several prodigies occurred in that year. Birds of evil omen perched on the Capitol; houses were thrown down by frequent shocks of earthquake, and as the panic spread, all the weak were trodden down in the hurry and confusion of the crowd. Scanty crops too, and consequent famine were regarded as a token of calamity. Nor were there merely whispered complaints; while Claudius was administering justice, the populace crowded round him with a boisterous clamour and drove him to a corner of the forum, where they violently pressed on him till he broke through the furious mob with a body of soldiers. It was ascertained that Rome had provisions for no more than fifteen days, and it was through the signal bounty of heaven and the mildness of the winter that its desperate plight was relieved. And yet in past days Italy used to send supplies for the legions into

distant provinces, and even now it is not a barren soil which causes distress. But we prefer to cultivate Africa and Egypt, and trust the life of the Roman people to ships and all their risks.

44. In the same year war broke out between the Armenians and Iberians, and was the cause of very serious disturbances between Parthia and Rome. Vologeses was king of the Parthians; on the mother's side, he was the offspring of a Greek concubine, and he obtained the throne by the retirement of his brothers. Pharasmanes had been long in possession of Iberia, and his brother, Mithridates, ruled Armenia with our powerful support. There was a son of Pharasmanes named Rhadamistus, tall and handsome, of singular bodily strength, trained in all the accomplishments of his countrymen and highly renowned among his neighbours. He boasted so arrogantly and persistently that his father's prolonged old age kept back from him the little kingdom of Iberia as to make no concealment of his ambition. Pharasmanes accordingly seeing the young prince had power in his grasp and was strong in the attachment of his people, fearing too his own declining years, tempted him with other prospects and pointed to Armenia, which, as he reminded him, he had given to Mithridates after driving out the Parthians. But open violence, he said, must be deferred; artful measures, which might crush him unawares, were better. So Rhadamistus pretended to be at feud with his father as though his stepmother's hatred was too strong for him, and went to his uncle. While he was treated by him like a son, with excessive kindness, he lured the nobles of Armenia into revolutionary schemes, without the knowledge of Mithridates, who was actually loading him with honours.

45. He then assumed a show of reconciliation with his father, to whom he returned, telling him all that could be accomplished by treachery was now ready and that he must complete the affair by the sword. Meanwhile Pharasmanes invented pretexts for war; when he was fighting with the king of the Albanians and appealing to the Romans for aid, his brother, he said, had opposed him, and he would now avenge that wrong by his destruction. At the same time he gave a large army to his son, who by a sudden invasion

drove Mithridates in terror from the open country and forced him into the fortress of Gorneas, which was strongly situated and garrisoned by some soldiers under the command of Cælius Pollio, a camp-prefect, and Casperius, a centurion.

There is nothing of which barbarians are so ignorant as military engines and the skilful management of sieges, while that is a branch of military science which we especially understand. And so Rhadamistus having attempted the fortified walls in vain or with loss, began a blockade, and, finding that his assaults were despised, tried to bribe the rapacity of the camp-prefect. Casperius protested earnestly against the overthrow of an allied king and of Armenia, the gift of the Roman people, through iniquity and greed of gain. At last, as Pollio pleaded the overpowering numbers of the enemy and Rhadamistus the orders of his father, the centurion stipulated for a truce and retired, intending, if he could not deter Pharasmanes from further hostilities, to inform Ummidius Quadratus, the governor of Syria, of the state of Armenia.

46. By the centurion's departure the camp-prefect was released, so to say, from surveillance; and he now urged Mithridates to conclude a treaty. He reminded him of the tie of brotherhood, of the seniority in age of Pharasmanes, and of their other bonds of kindred, how he was united by marriage to his brother's daughter, and was himself the father-in-law of Rhadamistus. "The Iberians," he said, "were not against peace, though for the moment they were the stronger; the perfidy of the Armenians was notorious, and he had nothing to fall back on but a fortress without stores; so he must not hesitate to prefer a bloodless negotiation to arms." As Mithridates wavered, and suspected the intentions of the camp-prefect, because he had seduced one of the king's concubines and was reputed a man who could be bribed into any wickedness, Casperius meantime went to Pharasmanes and required of him that the Iberians should raise the blockade. Pharasmanes, to his face, replied vaguely and often in a conciliatory tone, while by secret messages he recommended Rhadamistus to hurry on the siege by all possible means. Then the price of infamy was raised, and Pollio by secret corruption induced the soldiers to demand peace and to

threaten that they would abandon the garrison. Under this compulsion, Mithridates agreed to a day and a place for negotiation and quitted the fortress.

47. Rhadamistus at first threw himself into his embraces, feigning respect and calling him father-in-law and parent. He swore an oath too that he would do him no violence either by the sword or by poison. At the same time he drew him into a neighbouring grove, where he assured him that the appointed sacrifice was prepared for the confirmation of peace in the presence of the gods. It is a custom of these princes, whenever they join alliance, to unite their right hands and bind together the thumbs in a tight knot; then, when the blood has flowed into the extremities, they let it escape by a slight puncture and suck it in turn. Such a treaty is thought to have a mysterious sanctity, as being sealed with the blood of both parties. On this occasion he who was applying the knot pretended that it had fallen off, and suddenly seizing the knees of Mithridates flung him to the ground. At the same moment a rush was made by a number of persons, and chains were thrown round him. Then he was dragged along by a fetter, an extreme degradation to a barbarian; and soon the common people, whom he had held under a harsh sway, heaped insults on him with menacing gestures, though some, on the contrary, pitied such a reverse of fortune. His wife followed him with his little children, and filled every place with her wailings. They were hidden away in different covered carriages till the orders of Pharasmanes were distinctly ascertained. The lust of rule was more to him than his brother and his daughter, and his heart was steeled to any wickedness. Still he spared his eyes the seeing them slain before his face. Rhadamistus too, seemingly mindful of his oath, neither unsheathed the sword nor used poison against his sister and uncle, but had them thrown on the ground and then smothered them under a mass of heavy clothes. Even the sons of Mithridates were butchered for having shed tears over their parent's murder.

48. Quadratus, learning that Mithridates had been betrayed and that his kingdom was in the hands of his murderers, summoned a council, and, having informed them of what had occurred, consulted them whether he should take

vengeance. Few cared for the honour of the State; most
argued in favour of a safe course, saying "that any crime in
a foreign country was to be welcomed with joy, and that
the seeds of strife ought to be actually sown, on the very
principle on which Roman emperors had often under a show
of generosity given away this same kingdom of Armenia to
excite the minds of the barbarians. Rhadamistus might retain his ill-gotten gains, as long as he was hated and infamous; for this was more to Rome's interest than for him
to have succeeded with glory." To this view they assented,
but that they might not be thought to have approved the
crime and receive contrary orders from the emperor, envoys
were sent to Pharasmanes, requiring him to withdraw from
Armenian territory and remove his son.

49. Julius Pelignus was then procurator of Cappadocia, a
man despised alike for his feebleness of mind and his gro-
tesque personal appearance. He was however very intimate
with Claudius, who, when in private life, used to beguile the
dullness of his leisure with the society of jesters. This Pelignus collected some provincial auxiliaries, apparently with
the design of recovering Armenia, but, while he plundered
allies instead of enemies, finding himself, through the desertion of his men and the raids of the barbarians, utterly
defenceless, he went to Rhadamistus, whose gifts so completely overcame him that he positively encouraged him to
assume the ensigns of royalty, and himself assisted at the
ceremony, authorizing and abetting. When the disgraceful
news had spread far and wide, lest the world might judge
of other governors by Pelignus, Helvidius Priscus was sent
in command of a legion to regulate, according to circumstances, the disordered state of affairs. He quickly crossed
Mount Taurus, and had restored order to a great extent
more by moderation than by force, when he was ordered
to return to Syria, that nothing might arise to provoke a
war with Parthia.

50. For Vologeses, thinking that an opportunity presented
itself of invading Armenia, which, though the possession of
his ancestors, was now through a monstrous crime held by a
foreign prince, raised an army and prepared to establish
Tiridates on the throne, so that not a member of his house

might be without kingly power. On the advance of the Parthians, the Iberians dispersed without a battle, and the Armenian cities, Artaxata and Tigranocerta, submitted to the
yoke. Then a frightful winter or deficient supplies, with pestilence arising from both causes, forced Vologeses to abandon his present plans. Armenia was thus again without a
king, and was invaded by Rhadamistus, who was now fiercer
than ever, looking on the people as disloyal and sure to rebel
on the first opportunity. They however, though accustomed
to be slaves, suddenly threw off their tameness and gathered
round the palace in arms.

51. Rhadamistus had no means of escape but in the swiftness of the horses which bore him and his wife away. Pregnant as she was, she endured, somehow or other, out of fear
of the enemy and love of her husband, the first part of the
flight, but after a while, when she felt herself shaken by its
continuous speed, she implored to be rescued by an honourable death from the shame of captivity. He at first embraced, cheered, and encouraged her, now admiring her
heroism, now filled with a sickening apprehension at the
idea of her being left to any man's mercy. Finally, urged
by the intensity of his love and familiarity with dreadful
deeds, he unsheathed his scymitar, and having stabbed her,
dragged her to the bank of the Araxes and committed her
to the stream, so that her very body might be swept away.
Then in headlong flight he hurried to Iberia, his ancestral
kingdom. Zenobia meanwhile (this was her name), as she
yet breathed and showed signs of life on the calm water at
the river's edge, was perceived by some shepherds, who inferring from her noble appearance that she was no base-born
woman, bound up her wound and applied to it their rustic
remedies. As soon as they knew her name and her adventure, they conveyed her to the city of Artaxata, whence
she was conducted at the public charge to Tiridates, who
received her kindly and treated her as a royal person.

52. In the consulship of Faustus Sulla and Salvius Otho,
Furius Scribonianus was banished on the ground that he was
consulting the astrologers about the emperor's death. His
mother, Junia, was included in the accusation, as one who
still resented the misfortune of exile which she had suffered

in the past. His father, Camillus, had raised an armed insurrection in Dalmatia, and the emperor in again sparing a hostile family sought the credit of clemency. But the exile did not live long after this; whether he was cut off by a natural death, or by poison, was matter of conflicting rumours, according to people's belief.

A decree of the Senate was then passed for the expulsion of the astrologers from Italy, stringent but ineffectual. Next the emperor, in a speech, commended all who, from their limited means, voluntarily retired from the Senatorian order, while those were degraded from it who, by retaining their seats, added effrontery to poverty.

53. During these proceedings he proposed to the Senate a penalty on women who united themselves in marriage to slaves, and it was decided that those who had thus demeaned themselves, without the knowledge of the slave's master, should be reduced to slavery; if with his consent, should be ranked as freedwomen. To Pallas, who, as the emperor declared, was the author of this proposal, were offered on the motion of Barea Soranus, consul-elect, the decorations of the prætorship and fifteen million sesterces. Cornelius Scipio added that he deserved public thanks for thinking less of his ancient nobility as a descendant from the kings of Arcadia, than of the welfare of the State, and allowing himself to be numbered among the emperor's ministers. Claudius assured them that Pallas was content with the honour, and that he limited himself to his former poverty. A decree of the Senate was publicly inscribed on a bronze tablet, heaping the praises of primitive frugality on a freedman, the possessor of three hundred million sesterces.

54. Not equally moderate was his brother, surnamed Felix, who had for some time been governor of Judæa, and thought that he could do any evil act with impunity, backed up as he was by such power. It is true that the Jews had shown symptoms of commotion in a seditious outbreak, and when they had heard of the assassination of Caius, there was no hearty submission, as a fear still lingered that any of the emperors might impose the same orders. Felix meanwhile, by ill-timed remedies, stimulated disloyal acts; while he had, as a rival in the worst wickedness, Ventidius Cuma-

nus, who held a part of the province, which was so divided that Galilea was governed by Cumanus, Samaria by Felix. The two peoples had long been at feud, and now less than ever restrained their enmity, from contempt of their rulers. And accordingly they plundered each other, letting loose bands of robbers, forming ambuscades, and occasionally fighting battles, and carrying the spoil and booty to the two procurators, who at first rejoiced at all this, but, as the mischief grew, they interposed with an armed force, which was cut to pieces. The flame of war would have spread through the province, but it was saved by Quadratus, governor of Syria. In dealing with the Jews, who had been daring enough to slay our soldiers, there was little hesitation about their being capitally punished. Some delay indeed was occasioned by Cumanus and Felix; for Claudius on hearing the causes of the rebellion had given authority for deciding also the case of these procurators. Quadratus, however, exhibited Felix as one of the judges, admitting him to the bench with the view of cowing the ardour of the prosecutors. And so Cumanus was condemned for the crimes which the two had committed, and tranquillity was restored to the province.

55. Not long afterwards some tribes of the wild population of Cilicia, known as the Clitae, which had often been in commotion, established a camp, under a leader Troxobor, on their rocky mountains, whence rushing down on the coast, and on the towns, they dared to do violence to the farmers and townsfolk, frequently even to the merchants and shipowners. They besieged the city Anemurium, and routed some troopers sent from Syria to its rescue under the command of Curtius Severus; for the rough country in the neighbourhood, suited as it is for the fighting of infantry, did not allow of cavalry operations. After a time, Antiochus, king of that coast, having broken the unity of the barbarian forces, by cajolery of the people and treachery to their leader, slew Troxobor and a few chiefs, and pacified the rest by gentle measures.

56. About the same time, the mountain between Lake Fucinus and the river Liris was bored through, and that this grand work might be seen by a multitude of visitors, preparations were made for a naval battle on the lake, just

as formerly Augustus exhibited such a spectacle, in a basin
he had made on this side the Tiber, though with light vessels, and on a smaller scale. Claudius equipped galleys with
three and four banks of oars, and nineteen thousand men;
he lined the circumference of the lake with rafts, that there
might be no means of escape at various points, but he still
left full space for the strength of the crews, the skill of the
pilots, the impact of the vessels, and the usual operations
of a sea-fight. On the raft stood companies of the prætorian
cohorts and cavalry, with a breastwork in front of them,
from which catapults and balistas might be worked. The
rest of the lake was occupied by marines on decked vessels.
An immense multitude from the neighbouring towns, others
from Rome itself, eager to see the sight or to show respect
to the emperor, crowded the banks, the hills, and mountain
tops, which thus resembled a theatre. The emperor, with
Agrippina seated near him, presided; he wore a splendid
military cloak, she, a mantle of cloth of gold. A battle was
fought with all the courage of brave men, though it was
between condemned criminals. After much bloodshed they
were released from the necessity of mutual slaughter.

57. When the sight was over, the outlet of the water was
opened. The careless execution of the work was apparent, the
tunnel not having been bored down so low as the bottom, or
middle of the lake. Consequently after an interval the excavations were deepened, and to attract a crowd once more,
a show of gladiators was exhibited, with floating pontoons
for an infantry engagement. A banquet too was prepared
close to the outflow of the lake, and it was the means of
greatly alarming the whole company, for the water, in the
violence of its outburst, swept away the adjoining parts,
shook the more remote, and spread terror with the tremendous crash. At the same time, Agrippina availed herself of
the emperor's fright to charge Narcissus, who had been the
agent of the work, with avarice and peculation. He too was
not silent, but inveighed against the domineering temper of
her sex, and her extravagant ambition.

58. In the consulship of Didius Junius and Quintus Haterius, Nero, now sixteen years of age, married Octavia, the
emperor's daughter. Anxious to distinguish himself by noble

pursuits, and the reputation of an orator, he advocated the cause of the people of Ilium, and having eloquently recounted how Rome was the offspring of Troy, and Æneas the founder of the Julian line, with other old traditions akin to myths, he gained for his clients exemption from all public burdens. His pleading too procured for the colony of Bononia, which had been ruined by a fire, a subvention of ten million sesterces. The Rhodians also had their freedom restored to them, which had often been taken away, or confirmed, according to their services to us in our foreign wars, or their seditious misdeeds at home. Apamea, too, which had been shaken by an earthquake, had its tribute remitted for five years.

59. Claudius, on the other hand, was being prompted to exhibit the worst cruelty by the artifices of the same Agrippina. On the accusation of Tarquitius Priscus, she ruined Statilius Taurus, who was famous for his wealth, and at whose gardens she cast a greedy eye. Priscus had served under Taurus in his proconsular government of Africa, and after their return charged him with a few acts of extortion, but particularly with magical and superstitious practices. Taurus, no longer able to endure a false accusation and an undeserved humiliation, put a violent end to his life before the Senate's decision was pronounced. Tarquitius was however expelled from the Senate, a point which the senators carried, out of hatred for the accuser, notwithstanding the intrigues of Agrippina.

60. That same year the emperor was often heard to say that the legal decisions of the commissioners of the imperial treasury ought to have the same force as if pronounced by himself. Lest it might be supposed that he had stumbled inadvertently into this opinion, its principle was also secured by a decree of the Senate on a more complete and ample scale than before. It had indeed already been arranged by the Divine Augustus that the Roman knights who governed Egypt should hear causes, and that their decisions were to be as binding as those of Roman magistrates, and after a time most of the cases formerly tried by the prætors were submitted to the knights. Claudius handed over to them the whole administration of justice for which there had been by

sedition or war so many struggles; the Sempronian laws vesting judicial power in the equestrian order, and those of Servilius restoring it to the Senate, while it was for this above everything else that Marius and Sulla fought of old. But those were days of political conflict between classes, and the results of victory were binding on the State. Caius Oppius and Cornelius Balbus were the first who were able, with Cæsar's support, to settle conditions of peace and terms of war. To mention after them the Matii, Vedii, and other too influential names of Roman knights would be superfluous, when Claudius, we know, raised freedmen whom he had set over his household to equality with himself and with the laws.

61. Next the emperor proposed to grant immunity from taxation to the people of Cos, and he dwelt much on their antiquity. "The Argives or Cœus, the father of Latona, were the earliest inhabitants of the island; soon afterwards, by the arrival of Æsculapius, the art of the physician was introduced and was practised with much fame by his descendants." Claudius named them one by one, with the periods in which they had respectively flourished. He said too that Xenophon, of whose medical skill he availed himself, was one of the same family, and that they ought to grant his request and let the people of Cos dwell free from all tribute in their sacred island, as a place devoted to the sole service of their god. It was also certain that many obligations under which they had laid Rome and joint victories with her might have been recounted. Claudius however did not seek to veil under any external considerations a concession he had made, with his usual good nature, to an individual.

62. Envoys from Byzantium having received audience, in complaining to the Senate of their heavy burdens, recapitulated their whole history. Beginning with the treaty which they concluded with us when we fought against that king of Macedonia whose supposed spurious birth acquired for him the name of the Pseudo Philip, they reminded us of the forces which they had afterwards sent against Antiochus, Perses and Aristonicus, of the aid they had given Antonius in the pirate-war, of their offers to Sulla, Lucullus, and Pompeius, and then of their late services to the Cæsars.

when they were in occupation of a district peculiarly convenient for the land or sea passage of generals and armies, as well as for the conveyance of supplies.

63. It was indeed on that very narrow strait which parts Europe from Asia, at Europe's furthest extremity, that the Greeks built Byzantium. When they consulted the Pythian Apollo as to where they should found a city, the oracle replied that they were to seek a home opposite to the blind men's country. This obscure hint pointed to the people of Chalcedon, who, though they arrived there first and saw before others the advantageous position, chose the worse. For Byzantium has a fruitful soil and productive seas, as immense shoals of fish pour out of the Pontus and are driven by the sloping surface of the rocks under water to quit the windings of the Asiatic shore and take refuge in these harbours. Consequently the inhabitants were at first money-making and wealthy traders, but afterwards, under the pressure of excessive burdens, they petitioned for immunity or at least relief, and were supported by the emperor, who argued to the Senate that, exhausted as they were by the late wars in Thrace and Bosporus, they deserved help. So their tribute was remitted for five years.

64. In the year of the consulship of Marcus Asinius and Manius Acilius it was seen to be portended by a succession of prodigies that there were to be political changes for the worse. The soldiers' standards and tents were set in a blaze by lightning. A swarm of bees settled on the summit of the Capitol; births of monsters, half man, half beast, and of a pig with a hawk's talons, were reported. It was accounted a portent that every order of magistrates had had its number reduced, a quæstor, an ædile, a tribune, a prætor and consul having died within a few months. But Agrippina's terror was the most conspicuous. Alarmed by some words dropped by Claudius when half intoxicated, that it was his destiny to have to endure his wives' infamy and at last punish it, she determined to act without a moment's delay. First she destroyed Lepida from motives of feminine jealousy. Lepida indeed as the daughter of the younger Antonia, as the grandniece of Augustus, the cousin of Agrippina, and sister of her husband Cneius, thought herself of equally high rank. In

beauty, youth, and wealth they differed but slightly. Both were shameless, infamous, and intractable, and were rivals in vice as much as in the advantages they had derived from fortune. It was indeed a desperate contest whether the aunt or the mother should have most power over Nero. Lepida tried to win the young prince's heart by flattery and lavish liberality, while Agrippina on the other hand, who could give her son empire but could not endure that he should be emperor, was fierce and full of menace.

65. It was charged on Lepida that she had made attempts on the emperor's consort by magical incantations, and was disturbing the peace of Italy by an imperfect control of her troops of slaves in Calabria. She was for this sentenced to death, notwithstanding the vehement opposition of Narcissus, who, as he more and more suspected Agrippina, was said to have plainly told his intimate friends that "his destruction was certain, whether Britannicus or Nero were to be emperor, but that he was under such obligations to Claudius that he would sacrifice life to his welfare. Messalina and Silius had been convicted, and now again there were similar grounds for accusation. If Nero were to rule, or Britannicus succeed to the throne, he would himself have no claim on the then reigning sovereign. Meanwhile, a stepmother's treacherous schemes were convulsing the whole imperial house, with far greater disgrace than would have resulted from his concealment of the profligacy of the emperor's former wife. Even as it was, there was shamelessness enough, seeing that Pallas was her paramour, so that no one could doubt that she held honour, modesty and her very person, everything, in short, cheaper than sovereignty."

This, and the like, he was always saying, and he would embrace Britannicus, expressing earnest wishes for his speedy arrival at a mature age, and would raise his hand, now to heaven, now to the young prince, with entreaty that as he grew up, he would drive out his father's enemies and also take vengeance on the murderers of his mother.

66. Under this great burden of anxiety, he had an attack of illness, and went to Sinuessa to recruit his strength with its balmy climate and salubrious waters. Thereupon, Agrippina, who had long decided on the crime and eagerly

grasped at the opportunity thus offered, and did not lack instruments, deliberated on the nature of the poison to be used. The deed would be betrayed by one that was sudden and instantaneous, while if she chose a slow and lingering poison, there was a fear that Claudius, when near his end, might, on detecting the treachery, return to his love for his son. She decided on some rare compound which might derange his mind and delay death. A person skilled in such matters was selected, Locusta by name, who had lately been condemned for poisoning, and had long been retained as one of the tools of despotism. By this woman's art the poison was prepared, and it was to be administered by an eunuch, Halotus, who was accustomed to bring in and taste the dishes.

67. All the circumstances were subsequently so well known, that writers of the time have declared that the poison was infused into some mushrooms, a favourite delicacy, and its effect not at the instant perceived, from the emperor's lethargic, or intoxicated condition. His bowels too were relieved, and this seemed to have saved him. Agrippina was thoroughly dismayed. Fearing the worst, and defying the immediate obloquy of the deed, she availed herself of the complicity of Xenophon, the physician, which she had already secured. Under pretence of helping the emperor's efforts to vomit, this man, it is supposed, introduced into his throat a feather smeared with some rapid poison; for he knew that the greatest crimes are perilous in their inception, but well rewarded after their consummation.

68. Meanwhile the Senate was summoned, and prayers rehearsed by the consuls and priests for the emperor's recovery, though the lifeless body was being wrapped in blankets with warm applications, while all was being arranged to establish Nero on the throne. At first Agrippina, seemingly overwhelmed by grief and seeking comfort, clasped Britannicus in her embraces, called him the very image of his father, and hindered him by every possible device from leaving the chamber. She also detained his sisters, Antonia and Octavia, closed every approach to the palace with a military guard, and repeatedly gave out that the emperor's health was better, so that the soldiers might be encouraged

to hope, and that the fortunate moment foretold by the astrologers might arrive.

69. At last, at noon on the 13th of October, the gates of the palace were suddenly thrown open, and Nero, accompanied by Burrus, went forth to the cohort which was on guard after military custom. There, at the suggestion of the commanding officer, he was hailed with joyful shouts, and set on a litter. Some, it is said, hesitated, and looked round and asked where Britannicus was; then, when there was no one to lead a resistance, they yielded to what was offered them. Nero was conveyed into the camp, and having first spoken suitably to the occasion and promised a donative after the example of his father's bounty, he was unanimously greeted as emperor. The decrees of the Senate followed the voice of the soldiers, and there was no hesitation in the provinces. Divine honours were decreed to Claudius, and his funeral rites were solemnized on the same scale as those of Augustus; for Agrippina strove to emulate the magnificence of her great-grandmother, Livia. But his will was not publicly read, as the preference of the stepson to the son might provoke a sense of wrong and angry feeling in the popular mind.

BOOK XIII

A.D. 54—58

1. The first death under the new emperor, that of Junius Silanus, proconsul of Asia, was, without Nero's knowledge, planned by the treachery of Agrippina. Not that Silanus had provoked destruction by any violence of temper, apathetic as he was, and so utterly despised under former despotisms, that Caius Cæsar used to call him the golden sheep. The truth was that Agrippina, having contrived the murder of his brother Lucius Silanus, dreaded his vengeance; for it was the incessant popular talk that preference ought to be given over Nero, who was scarcely out of his boyhood and had gained the empire by crime, to a man of mature age, of blameless life, of noble birth, and, as a point then much regarded, of the line of the Cæsars. Silanus in fact was the son of a great-grandson of Augustus. This was the cause of his destruction. The agents of the deed were Publius Celer, a Roman knight, and Helius, a freedman, men who had the charge of the emperor's domains in Asia. They gave the proconsul poison at a banquet, too openly to escape discovery.

With no less precipitation, Narcissus, Claudius's freedman, whose quarrels with Agrippina I have mentioned, was driven to suicide by his cruel imprisonment and hopeless plight, even against the wishes of Nero, with whose yet concealed vices he was wonderfully in sympathy from his rapacity and extravagance.

2. And now they had proceeded to further murders but for the opposition of Afranius Burrus and Annæus Seneca. These two men guided the emperor's youth with an unity of purpose seldom found where authority is shared, and though their accomplishments were wholly different, they had equal

influence. Burrus, with his soldier's discipline and severe manners, Seneca, with lessons of eloquence and a dignified courtesy, strove alike to confine the frailty of the prince's youth, should he loathe virtue, within allowable indulgences. They had both alike to struggle against the domineering spirit of Agrippina, who inflamed with all the passions of an evil ascendency had Pallas on her side, at whose suggestion Claudius had ruined himself by an incestuous marriage and a fatal adoption of a son. Nero's temper however was not one to submit to slaves, and Pallas, by a surly arrogance quite beyond a freedman, had provoked disgust. Still every honour was openly heaped on Agrippina, and to a tribune who according to military custom asked the watchword, Nero gave "the best of mothers." The Senate also decreed her two lictors, with the office of priestess to Claudius, and voted to the late emperor a censor's funeral, which was soon followed by deification.

3. On the day of the funeral the prince pronounced Claudius's panegyric, and while he dwelt on the antiquity of his family and on the consulships and triumphs of his ancestors, there was enthusiasm both in himself and his audience. The praise of his graceful accomplishments, and the remark that during his reign no disaster had befallen Rome from the foreigner, were heard with favour. When the speaker passed on to his foresight and wisdom, no one could refrain from laughter, though the speech, which was composed by Seneca, exhibited much elegance, as indeed that famous man had an attractive genius which suited the popular ear of the time. Elderly men who amuse their leisure with comparing the past and the present, observed that Nero was the first emperor who needed another man's eloquence. The dictator Cæsar rivalled the greatest orators, and Augustus had an easy and fluent way of speaking, such as became a sovereign. Tiberius too thoroughly understood the art of balancing words, and was sometimes forcible in the expression of his thoughts, or else intentionally obscure. Even Caius Cæsar's disordered intellect did not wholly mar his faculty of speech. Nor did Claudius, when he spoke with preparation, lack elegance. Nero from early boyhood turned his lively genius in other directions; he carved, painted,

sang, or practised the management of horses, occasionally composing verses which showed that he had the rudiments of learning.

4. When he had done with his mimicries of sorrow he entered the Senate, and having first referred to the authority of the senators and the concurrence of the soldiery, he then dwelt on the counsels and examples which he had to guide him in the right administration of empire. "His boyhood," he said, "had not had the taint of civil wars or domestic feuds, and he brought with him no hatreds, no sense of wrong, no desire of vengeance." He then sketched the plan of his future government, carefully avoiding anything which had kindled recent odium. "He would not," he said, "be judge in all cases, or, by confining the accuser and the accused within the same walls, let the power of a few favourites grow dangerously formidable. In his house there should be nothing venal, nothing open to intrigue; his private establishment and the State should be kept entirely distinct. The Senate should retain its ancient powers; Italy and the State-provinces should plead their causes before the tribunals of the consuls, who would give them a hearing from the senators. Of the armies he would himself take charge, as specially entrusted to him."

5. He was true to his word and several arrangements were made on the Senate's authority. No one was to receive a fee or a present for pleading a cause; the quæstors-elect were not to be under the necessity of exhibiting gladiatorial shows. This was opposed by Agrippina, as a reversal of the legislation of Claudius, but it was carried by the senators who used to be summoned to the palace, in order that she might stand close to a hidden door behind them, screened by a curtain which was enough to shut her out of sight, but not out of hearing. When envoys from Armenia were pleading their nation's cause before Nero, she actually was on the point of mounting the emperor's tribunal and of presiding with him; but Seneca, when every one else was paralysed with alarm, motioned to the prince to go and meet his mother. Thus, by an apparently dutiful act, a scandalous scene was prevented.

6. With the close of the year came disquieting rumours

that the Parthians had again broken their bounds and were ravaging Armenia, from which they had driven Rhadamistus, who, having often possessed himself of the kingdom and as often been thrust out of it, had now relinquished hostilities. Rome with its love of talking began to ask how a prince of scarce seventeen was to encounter and avert this tremendous peril, how they could fall back on one who was ruled by a woman; or whether battles and sieges and the other operations of war could be directed by tutors. "Some, on the contrary, argued that this was better than it would have been, had Claudius in his feeble and spiritless old age, when he would certainly have yielded to the bidding of slaves, been summoned to the hardships of a campaign. Burrus, at least, and Seneca were known to be men of very varied experience, and, as for the emperor himself, how far was he really short of mature age, when Cneius Pompeius and Cæsar Octavianus, in their eighteenth and nineteenth years respectively, bore the brunt of civil wars? The highest rank chiefly worked through its prestige and its counsels more than by the sword and hand. The emperor would give a plain proof whether he was advised by good or bad friends by putting aside all jealousy and selecting some eminent general, rather than by promoting out of favouritism, a rich man backed up by interest."

7. Amidst this and like popular talk, Nero ordered the young recruits levied in the adjacent provinces to be brought up for the supply of the legions of the East, and the legions themselves to take up a position on the Armenian frontier while two princes of old standing, Agrippa and Antiochus, were to prepare a force for the invasion of the Parthian territories. The Euphrates too was to be spanned by bridges; Lesser Armenia was intrusted to Aristobulus, Sophene to Sohæmus, each with the ensigns of royalty. There rose up at this crisis a rival to Vologeses in his son Vardanes, and the Parthians quitted Armenia, apparently intending to defer hostilities.

8. All this however was described with exaggeration to the Senate, in the speeches of those members who proposed a public thanksgiving, and that on the days of the thanksgiving the prince should wear the triumphal robe and enter

Rome in ovation, lastly, that he should have statues on the same scale as those of Mars the Avenger, and in the same temple. To their habitual flattery was added a real joy at his having appointed Domitius Corbulo to secure Armenia, thus opening, as it seemed, a field to merit. The armies of the East were so divided that half the auxiliaries and two legions were to remain in the province of Syria under its governor, Quadratus Ummidius; while Corbulo was to have an equal number of citizen and allied troops, together with the auxiliary infantry and cavalry which were in winter quarters in Cappadocia. The confederate kings were instructed to obey orders, just as the war might require. But they had a specially strong liking for Corbulo. That general, with a view to the prestige which in a new enterprise is supremely powerful, speedily accomplished his march, and at Ægeæ, a city of Cilicia, met Quadratus who had advanced to the place under an apprehension that, should Corbulo once enter Armenia to take command of the army, he would draw all eyes on himself, by his noble stature, his imposing eloquence, and the impression he would make, not only by his wisdom and experience, but also by the mere display of showy attributes.

9. Meantime both sent messages to king Vologeses, advising him to choose peace rather than war, and to give hostages and so continue the habitual reverence of his ancestors towards the people of Rome. Vologeses, wishing to prepare for war at an advantage, or to rid himself of suspected rivals under the name of hostages, delivered up some of the noblest of the Arsacids. A centurion, Insteius, sent perhaps by Ummidius on some previous occasion, received them after an interview with the king. Corbulo, on knowing this, ordered Arrius Varus, commander of a cohort, to go and take the hostages. Hence arose a quarrel between the commander and the centurion, and to stop such a scene before foreigners, the decision of the matter was left to the hostages and to the envoys who conducted them. They preferred Corbulo, for his recent renown, and from a liking which even enemies felt for him. Then there was a feud between the two generals; Ummidius complained that he was robbed of what his prudence had achieved, while Corbulo on the other hand

appealed to the fact that Vologeses had not brought himself to offer hostages till his own appointment to the conduct of the war turned the king's hopes into fears. Nero, to compose their differences, directed the issue of a proclamation that for the successes of Quadratus and Corbulo the laurel was to be added to the imperial "fasces." I have closely connected these events, though they extend into another consulship.

10. The emperor in the same year asked the Senate for a statue to his father Domitius, and also that the consular decorations might be conferred on Asconius Labeo, who had been his guardian. Statues to himself of solid gold and silver he forbade, in opposition to offers made, and although the Senate passed a vote that the year should begin with the month of December, in which he was born, he retained for its commencement, the old sacred associations of the first of January. Nor would he allow the prosecution of Carinas Celer, a senator, whom a slave accused, or of Julius Densus, a knight, whose partiality for Britannicus was construed into a crime.

11. In the year of his consulship with Lucius Antistius, when the magistrates were swearing obedience to imperial legislation, he forbade his colleague to extend the oath to his own enactments, for which he was warmly praised by the senators, in the hope that his youthful spirit, elated with the glory won by trifles, would follow on to nobler aspirations. Then came an act of mercy to Plautius Lateranus, who had been degraded from his rank for adultery with Messalina, and whom he now restored, assuring them of his clemency in a number of speeches which Seneca, to show the purity of his teaching or to display his genius, published to the world by the emperor's mouth.

12. Meanwhile the mother's influence was gradually weakened, as Nero fell in love with a freedwoman, Acte by name, and took into his confidence Otho and Claudius Senecio, two young men of fashion, the first of whom was descended from a family of consular rank, while Senecio's father was one of the emperor's freedmen. Without the mother's knowledge, then in spite of her opposition, they had crept into his favour by debaucheries and equivocal

secrets, and even the prince's older friends did not thwart him, for here was a girl who without harm to any one gratified his desires, when he loathed his wife Octavia, high born as she was, and of approved virtue, either from some fatality, or because vice is overpoweringly attractive. It was feared too that he might rush into outrages on noble ladies, were he debarred from this indulgence.

13. Agrippina, however, raved with a woman's fury about having a freedwoman for a rival, a slave girl for a daughter-in-law, with like expressions. Nor would she wait till her son repented or wearied of his passion. The fouler her reproaches, the more powerfully did they inflame him, till completely mastered by the strength of his desire, he threw off all respect for his mother, and put himself under the guidance of Seneca, one of whose friends, Annæus Serenus, had veiled the young prince's intrigue in its beginning by pretending to be in love with the same woman, and had lent his name as the ostensible giver of the presents secretly sent by the emperor to the girl. Then Agrippina, changing her tactics, plied the lad with various blandishments, and even offered the seclusion of her chamber for the concealment of indul-gences which youth and the highest rank might claim. She went further; she pleaded guilty to an ill-timed strictness, and handed over to him the abundance of her wealth, which nearly approached the imperial treasures, and from having been of late extreme in her restraint of her son, became now, on the other hand, lax to excess. The change did not escape Nero; his most intimate friends dreaded it, and begged him to beware of the arts of a woman, who was always daring and was now false.

It happened at this time that the emperor after inspecting the apparel in which wives and mothers of the imperial house had been seen to glitter, selected a jewelled robe and sent it as a gift to his mother, with the unsparing liberality of one who was bestowing by preference on her a choice and much coveted present. Agrippina, however, publicly declared that so far from her wardrobe being furnished by these gifts, she was really kept out of the remainder, and that her son was merely dividing with her what he derived wholly from herself.

14. Some there were who put even a worse meaning on her words. And so Nero, furious with those who abetted such arrogance in a woman, removed Pallas from the charge of the business with which he had been entrusted by Claudius, and in which he acted, so to say, as the controller of the throne. The story went that as he was departing with a great retinue of attendants, the emperor rather wittily remarked that Pallas was going to swear himself out of office. Pallas had in truth stipulated that he should not be questioned for anything he had done in the past, and that his accounts with the State were to be considered as balanced. Thereupon, with instant fury, Agrippina rushed into frightful menaces, sparing not the prince's ears her solemn protest "that Britannicus was now of full age, he who was the true and worthy heir of his father's sovereignty, which a son, by mere admission and adoption, was abusing in outrages on his mother. She shrank not from an utter exposure of the wickedness of that ill-starred house, of her own marriage, to begin with, and of her poisoner's craft. All that the gods and she herself had taken care of was that her stepson was yet alive; with him she would go to the camp, where on one side should be heard the daughter of Germanicus; on the other, the crippled Burrus and the exile Seneca, claiming, forsooth, with disfigured hand, and a pedant's tongue, the government of the world." As she spoke, she raised her hand in menace and heaped insults on him, as she appealed to the deified Claudius, to the infernal shades of the Silani, and to those many fruitless crimes.

15. Nero was confounded at this, and as the day was near on which Britannicus would complete his fourteenth year, he reflected, now on the domineering temper of his mother, and now again on the character of the young prince, which a trifling circumstance had lately tested, sufficient however to gain for him wide popularity. During the feast of Saturn, amid other pastimes of his playmates, at a game of lot drawing for king, the lot fell to Nero, upon which he gave all his other companions different orders, and such as would not put them to the blush; but when he told Britannicus to step forward and begin a song, hoping for a laugh at the expense of a boy who knew nothing of sober, much less of riotous

society, the lad with perfect coolness commenced some verses which hinted at his expulsion from his father's house and from supreme power. This procured him pity, which was the more conspicuous, as night with its merriment had stript off all disguise. Nero saw the reproach and redoubled his hate. Pressed by Agrippina's menaces, having no charge against his brother and not daring openly to order his murder, he meditated a secret device and directed poison to be prepared through the agency of Julius Pollio, tribune of one of the prætorian cohorts, who had in his custody a woman under sentence for poisoning, Locusta by name, with a vast repu- tation for crime. That every one about the person of Britan- nicus should care nothing for right or honour, had long ago been provided for. He actually received his first dose of poison from his tutors and passed it off his bowels, as it was rather weak or so qualified as not at once to prove deadly. But Nero, impatient at such slow progress in crime, threat- ened the tribune and ordered the poisoner to execution for prolonging his anxiety while they were thinking of the popu- lar talk and planning their own defence. Then they prom- ised that death should be as sudden as if it were the hurried work of the dagger, and a rapid poison of previously tested ingredients was prepared close to the emperor's chamber.

16. It was customary for the imperial princes to sit during their meals with other nobles of the same age, in the sight of their kinsfolk, at a table of their own, furnished somewhat frugally. There Britannicus was dining, and as what he ate and drank was always tested by the taste of a select at- tendant, the following device was contrived, that the usage might not be dropped or the crime betrayed by the death of both prince and attendant. A cup as yet harmless, but ex- tremely hot and already tasted, was handed to Britannicus; then, on his refusing it because of its warmth, poison was poured in with some cold water, and this so penetrated his entire frame that he lost alike voice and breath. There was a stir among the company; some, taken by surprise, ran hither and thither, while those whose discernment was keener, re- mained motionless, with their eyes fixed on Nero, who, as he still reclined in seeming unconsciousness, said that this was a common occurrence from a periodical epilepsy, with

which Britannicus had been afflicted from his earliest infancy, and that his sight and senses would gradually return. As for Agrippina, her terror and confusion, though her countenance struggled to hide it, so visibly appeared, that she was clearly just as ignorant as was Octavia, Britannicus's own sister. She saw, in fact, that she was robbed of her only remaining refuge, and that here was a precedent for parricide. Even Octavia, notwithstanding her youthful inexperience, had learnt to hide her grief, her affection, and indeed every emotion.

17. And so after a brief pause the company resumed its mirth. One and the same night witnessed Britannicus's death and funeral, preparations having been already made for his obsequies, which were on a humble scale. He was however buried in the Campus Martius, amid storms so violent, that in the popular belief they portended the wrath of heaven against a crime which many were even inclined to forgive when they remembered the immemorial feuds of brothers and the impossibility of a divided throne. It is related by several writers of the period that many days before the murder, Nero had offered the worst insult to the boyhood of Britannicus; so that his death could no longer seem a premature or dreadful event, though it happened at the sacred board, without even a moment for the embraces of his sisters, hurried on too, as it was, under the eyes of an enemy, on the sole surviving offspring of the Claudii, the victim first of dishonour, then of poison. The emperor apologised for the hasty funeral by reminding people that it was the practice of our ancestors to withdraw from view any grievously untimely death, and not to dwell on it with panegyrics or display. For himself, he said, that as he had now lost a brother's help, his remaining hopes centred in the State, and all the more tenderness ought to be shown by the Senate and people towards a prince who was the only survivor of a family born to the highest greatness.

18. He then enriched his most powerful friends with liberal presents. Some there were who reproached men of austere professions with having on such an occasion divided houses and estates among themselves, like so much spoil. It was the belief of others that a pressure had been put on them

by the emperor, who, conscious as he was of guilt, hoped for merciful consideration if he could secure the most important men by wholesale bribery. But his mother's rage no lavish bounty could allay. She would clasp Octavia to her arms, and have many a secret interview with her friends; with more than her natural rapacity, she clutched at money everywhere, seemingly for a reserve, and courteously received tribunes and centurions. She honoured the names and virtues of the nobles who still were left, seeking apparently a party and a leader. Of this Nero became aware, and he ordered the departure of the military guard now kept for the emperor's mother, as it had formerly been for the imperial consort, along with some German troops, added as a further honour. He also gave her a separate establishment, that throngs of visitors might no longer wait on her, and removed her to what had been Antonia's house; and whenever he went there himself, he was surrounded by a crowd of centurions, and used to leave her after a hurried kiss.

19. Of all things human the most precarious and transitory is a reputation for power which has no strong support of its own. In a moment Agrippina's doors were deserted; there was no one to comfort or to go near her, except a few ladies, whether out of love or malice was doubtful. One of these was Junia Silana, whom Messalina had driven from her husband, Caius Silius, as I have already related. Conspicuous for her birth, her beauty, and her wantonness, she had long been a special favourite of Agrippina, till after a while there were secret mutual dislikes, because Sextius Africanus, a noble youth, had been deterred from marrying Silana by Agrippina, who repeatedly spoke of her as an immodest woman in the decline of life, not to secure Africanus for herself, but to keep the childless and wealthy widow out of a husband's control. Silana having now a prospect of vengeance, suborned as accusers two of her creatures, Iturius and Calvisius, not with the old and often-repeated charges about Agrippina's mourning the death of Britannicus or publishing the wrongs of Octavia, but with a hint that it was her purpose to encourage in revolutionary designs Rubellius Plautus, who on his mother's side was as nearly connected as Nero with the Divine Augustus; and then, by marrying

him and making him emperor, again seize the control of the State. All this Iturius and Calvisius divulged to Atimetus, a freedman of Domitia, Nero's aunt. Exulting in the opportunity, for Agrippina and Domitia were in bitter rivalry, Atimetus urged Paris, who was himself also a freedman of Domitia, to go at once and put the charge in the most dreadful form.

20. Night was far advanced and Nero was still sitting over his cups, when Paris entered, who was generally wont at such times to heighten the emperor's enjoyments, but who now wore a gloomy expression. He went through the whole evidence in order, and so frightened his hearer as to make him resolve not only on the destruction of his mother and of Plautus, but also on the removal of Burrus from the command of the guards, as a man who had been promoted by Agrippina's interest, and was now showing his gratitude. We have it on the authority of Fabius Rusticus that a note was written to Cæcina Tuscus, intrusting to him the charge of the prætorian cohorts, but that through Seneca's influence that distinguished post was retained for Burrus. According to Plinius and Cluvius, no doubt was felt about the commander's loyalty. Fabius certainly inclines to the praise of Seneca, through whose friendship he rose to honour. Proposing as I do to follow the consentient testimony of historians, I shall give the differences in their narratives under the writers' names. Nero, in his bewilderment and impatience to destroy his mother, could not be put off till Burrus answered for her death, should she be convicted of the crime, but "any one," he said, "much more a parent, must be allowed a defence. Accusers there were none forthcoming; they had before them only the word of a single person from an enemy's house, and this the night with its darkness and prolonged festivity and everything savouring of recklessness and folly, was enough to refute."

21. Having thus allayed the prince's fears, they went at daybreak to Agrippina, that she might know the charges against her, and either rebut them or suffer the penalty. Burrus fulfilled his instructions in Seneca's presence, and some of the freedmen were present to witness the interview. Then Burrus, when he had fully explained the charges with the

authors' names, assumed an air of menace. Instantly Agrippina, calling up all her high spirit, exclaimed, "I wonder not that Silana, who has never borne offspring, knows nothing of a mother's feelings. Parents do not change their children as lightly as a shameless woman does her paramours. And if Iturius and Calvisius, after having wasted their whole fortunes, are now, as their last resource, repaying an old hag for their hire by undertaking to be informers, it does not follow that I am to incur the infamy of plotting a son's murder, or that a Cæsar is to have the consciousness of like guilt. As for Domitia's enmity, I should be thankful for it, were she to vie with me in goodwill towards my Nero. Now through her paramour, Atimetus, and the actor, Paris, she is, so to say, concocting a drama for the stage. She at her Baiae was increasing the magnificence of her fishponds, when I was planning in my counsels his adoption with a proconsul's powers and a consul-elect's rank and every other step to empire. Only let the man come forward who can charge me with having tampered with the prætorian cohorts in the capital, with having sapped the loyalty of the provinces, or, in a word, with having bribed slaves and freedmen into any wickedness. Could I have lived with Britannicus in the possession of power? And if Plautus or any other were to become master of the State so as to sit in judgment on me, accusers forsooth would not be forthcoming, to charge me not merely with a few incautious expressions prompted by the eagerness of affection, but with guilt from which a son alone could absolve me."

There was profound excitement among those present, and they even tried to soothe her agitation, but she insisted on an interview with her son. Then, instead of pleading her innocence, as though she lacked confidence, or her claims on him by way of reproach, she obtained vengeance on her accusers and rewards for her friends.

22. The superintendence of the corn supply was given to Fænius Rufus, the direction of the games which the emperor was preparing, to Arruntius Stella, and the province of Egypt to Caius Balbillus. Syria was to be assigned to Publius Anteius, but he was soon put off by various artifices and finally detained at Rome. Silana was banished; Cal-

visius and Iturius exiled for a time; Atimetus was capitally punished, while Paris was too serviceable to the emperor's profligacy to allow of his suffering any penalty. Plautus for the present was silently passed over.

23. Next Pallas and Burrus were accused of having conspired to raise Cornelius Sulla to the throne, because of his noble birth and connection with Claudius, whose son-in-law he was by his marriage with Antonia. The promoter of the prosecution was one Pætus, who had become notorious by frequent purchases of property confiscated to the exchequer and was now convicted clearly of imposture. But the proved innocence of Pallas did not please men so much, as his arrogance offended them. When his freedmen, his alleged accomplices, were called, he replied that at home he signified his wishes only by a nod or a gesture, or, if further explanation was required, he used writing, so as not to degrade his voice in such company. Burrus, though accused, gave his verdict as one of the judges. The prosecutor was sentenced to exile, and the account-books in which he was reviving forgotten claims of the exchequer, were burnt.

24. At the end of the year the cohort usually on guard during the games was withdrawn, that there might be a greater show of freedom, that the soldiery too might be less demoralised when no longer in contact with the licence of the theatre, and that it might be proved whether the populace, in the absence of a guard, would maintain their self-control. The emperor, on the advice of the augurs, purified Rome by a lustration, as the temples of Jupiter and Minerva had been struck by lightning.

25. In the consulship of Quintus Volusius and Publius Scipio, there was peace abroad, but a disgusting licentiousness at home on the part of Nero, who in a slave's disguise, so as to be unrecognized, would wander through the streets of Rome, to brothels and taverns, with comrades, who seized on goods exposed for sale and inflicted wounds on any whom they encountered, some of these last knowing him so little that he even received blows himself, and showed the marks of them in his face. When it was notorious that the emperor was the assailant, and the insults on men and women of distinction were multiplied, other persons too on the strength

of a licence once granted under Nero's name, ventured with impunity on the same practices, and had gangs of their own, till night presented the scenes of a captured city. Julius Montanus, a senator, but one who had not yet held any office, happened to encounter the prince in the darkness, and because he fiercely repulsed his attack and then on recognizing him begged for mercy, as though this was a reproach, was forced to destroy himself. Nero was for the future more timid, and surrounded himself with soldiers and a number of gladiators, who, when a fray began on a small scale and seemed a private affair, were to let it alone, but, if the injured persons resisted stoutly, they rushed in with their swords. He also turned the licence of the games and the enthusiasm for the actors into something like a battle by the impunity he allowed, and the rewards he offered, and especially by looking on himself, sometimes concealed, but often in public view, till, with the people at strife and the fear of a worse commotion, the only remedy which could be devised was the expulsion of the offending actors from Italy, and the presence once more of the soldiery in the theatre.

26. During the same time there was a discussion in the Senate on the misconduct of the freedmen class, and a strong demand was made that, as a check on the undeserving, patrons should have the right of revoking freedom. There were several who supported this. But the consuls did not venture to put the motion without the emperor's knowledge, though they recorded the Senate's general opinion, to see whether he would sanction the arrangement, considering that only a few were opposed to it, while some loudly complained that the irreverent spirit which freedom had fostered, had broken into such excess, that freedmen would ask their patrons' advice as to whether they should treat them with violence, or, as legally, their equals, and would actually threaten them with blows, at the same time recommending them not to punish. "What right," it was asked, "was conceded to an injured patron but that of temporarily banishing the freedman a hundred miles off to the shores of Campania? In everything else, legal proceedings were equal and the same for both. Some weapon ought to be given to the patrons which could not be despised. It would be no grievance for

the enfranchised to have to keep their freedom by the same respectful behaviour which had procured it for them. But, as for notorious offenders, they deserved to be dragged back into slavery, that fear might be a restraint where kindness had had no effect."

27. It was argued in reply that, though the guilt of a few ought to be the ruin of the men themselves, there should be no diminution of the rights of the entire class. "For it was," they contended, "a widely diffused body; from it, the city tribes, the various public functionaries, the establishments of the magistrates and priests were for the most part supplied, as well as the cohorts of the city-guard; very many too of the knights and several of the senators derived their origin from no other source. If freedmen were to be a separate class, the paucity of the freeborn would be conspicuously apparent. Not without good reason had our ancestors, in distinguishing the position of the different orders, thrown freedom open to all. Again, two kinds of enfranchisement had been instituted, so as to leave room for retracting the boon, or for a fresh act of grace. Those whom the patron had not emancipated with the freedom-giving rod, were still held, as it were, by the bonds of slavery. Every master should carefully consider the merits of each case, and be slow to grant what once given could not be taken away."

This view prevailed, and the emperor replied to the Senate that, whenever freedmen were accused by their patrons, they were to investigate each case separately and not to annul any right to their common injury. Soon afterwards, his aunt Domitia had her freedman Paris taken from her, avowedly by civil law, much to the emperor's disgrace, by whose direction a decision that he was freeborn was obtained.

28. Still there yet remained some shadow of a free state. A contest arose between Vibullius, the prætor, and Antistius, a tribune of the people; for the tribune had ordered the release of some disorderly applauders of certain actors, whom the prætor had imprisoned. The Senate approved the imprisonment, and censured the presumption of Antistius. Tribunes were also forbidden to usurp the authority of prætors and consuls, or to summon from any part of Italy persons liable to legal proceedings. It was further proposed by Lucius

Piso, consul-elect, that tribunes were not to try any case in their own houses, that a fine imposed by them was not to be entered on the public books by the officials of the exchequer, till four months had expired, and that in the meantime appeals were to be allowed, which the consuls were to decide.

Restrictions were also put on the powers of the aediles and a limit fixed to the amount of bail or penalty which curule and plebeian aediles could respectively exact. On this, Helvidius Priscus, a tribune of the people, followed up a personal quarrel he had with Obultronius Sabinus, one of the officials of the exchequer, by insinuating that he stretched his right of confiscation with merciless rigour against the poor. The emperor then transferred the charge of the public accounts from these officers to the commissioners.

29. The arrangement of this business had been variously and frequently altered. Augustus allowed the Senate to appoint commissioners; then, when corrupt practices were suspected in the voting, men were chosen by lot for the office out of the whole number of prætors. This did not last long, as the lot strayed away to unfit persons. Claudius then again appointed quæstors, and that they might not be too lax in their duties from fear of offending, he promised them promotion out of the usual course. But what they lacked was the firmness of mature age, entering, as they did, on this office as their first step, and so Nero appointed ex-prætors of approved competency.

30. During the same consulship, Vipsanius Lænas was condemned for rapacity in his administration of the province of Sardinia. Cestius Proculus was acquitted of extortion, his accusers dropping the charge. Clodius Quirinalis, having, when in command of the crews at Ravenna, caused grievous distress to Italy by his profligacy and cruelty, just as if it was the most contemptible of countries, forestalled his doom by poison. Caninius Rebilus, one of the first men in legal knowledge and vastness of wealth, escaped the miseries of an old age of broken health by letting the blood trickle from his veins, though men did not credit him with sufficient resolution for a self-inflicted death, because of his infamous effeminacy. Lucius Volusius on the other hand died with a glorious name. There was his long life of ninety-three

years, his conspicuous wealth, honourably acquired, and his
wise avoidance of the malignity of so many emperors.

31. During Nero's second consulship with Lucius Piso for
his colleague, little occurred deserving mention, unless one
were to take pleasure in filling volumes with the praise of
the foundations and timber work on which the emperor piled
the immense amphitheatre in the Field of Mars. But we
have learnt that it suits the dignity of the Roman people to
reserve history for great achievements, and to leave such details to the city's daily register. I may mention that the
colonies of Nuceria and Capua were strengthened by an addition of veterans; to every member of the city populace
four hundred sesterces were given, and forty million paid
into the exchequer to maintain the credit of the citizens.

A tax also of four per cent. on the sale of slaves was remitted, an apparent more than a real boon, for as the seller
was ordered to pay it, purchasers found that it was added as
part of the price. The emperor by an edict forbade any magistrate or procurator in the government of a province to exhibit a show of gladiators, or of wild beasts, or indeed any
other public entertainment; for hitherto our subjects had
been as much oppressed by such bribery as by actual extortion, while governors sought to screen by corruption the
guilty deeds of arbitrary caprice.

32. The Senate next passed a decree, providing alike for
punishment and safety. If a master were murdered by his
slaves, all those who were enfranchised by his will and lived
under the same roof, were to suffer the capital punishment
with his other slaves. Lucius Varius, an ex-consul, who had
been crushed in the past under charges of extortion, was
restored to his rank as a senator. Pomponia Græcina, a distinguished lady, wife of the Plautius who returned from
Britain with an ovation, was accused of some foreign superstition and handed over to her husband's judicial decision.
Following ancient precedent, he heard his wife's cause in the
presence of kinsfolk, involving, as it did, her legal status and
character, and he reported that she was innocent. This Pomponia lived a long life of unbroken melancholy. After the
murder of Julia, Drusus's daughter, by Messalina's treachery, for forty years she wore only the attire of a mourner,

with a heart ever sorrowful. For this, during Claudius's reign, she escaped unpunished, and it was afterwards counted a glory to her.

33. The same year saw many impeached. One of these, Publius Celer, prosecuted by the province of Asia, the emperor could not acquit, and so he put off the case till the man died of old age. Celer, as I have related, had murdered Silanus, the pro-consul, and the magnitude of this crime veiled his other enormities. Cossutianus Capito was accused by the people of Cilicia; he was a man stained with the foulest guilt, and had actually imagined that his audacious wickedness had the same rights in a province as he had claimed for it at Rome. But he had to confront a determined prosecution, and at last abandoned his defence. Eprius Marcellus, from whom Lycia demanded compensation, was so powerfully supported by corrupt influence that some of his accusers were punished with exile, as though they had imperilled an innocent man.

34. Nero entered on his third consulship with Valerius Messala, whose great-grandfather, the orator Corvinus, was still remembered by a few old men, as having been the colleague of the Divine Augustus, Nero's great-grandfather, in the same office. But the honour of a noble house was further increased by an annual grant of five hundred thousand sesterces on which Messala might support virtuous poverty. Aurelius Cotta, too, and Haterius Antonius had yearly stipends assigned them by the emperor, though they had squandered their ancestral wealth in profligacy.

Early in this year a war between Parthia and Rome about the possession of Armenia, which, feebly begun, had hitherto dragged on, was vigorously resumed. For Vologeses would not allow his brother Tiridates to be deprived of a kingdom which he had himself given him, or to hold it as a gift from a foreign power, and Corbulo too thought it due to the grandeur of Rome that he should recover what Lucullus and Pompeius had formerly won. Besides, the Armenians in the fluctuations of their allegiance sought the armed protection of both empires, though by their country's position, by resemblance of manners, and by the ties of intermarriage, they were more connected with the Parthians, to whose subjection, in their ignorance of freedom, they rather inclined.

35. Corbulo however had more to struggle against in the supineness of his soldiers than in the treachery of the enemy. His legions indeed, transferred as they had been from Syria and demoralised by a long peace, endured most impatiently the duties of a Roman camp. It was well known that that army contained veterans who had never been on piquet duty or on night guard, to whom the rampart and the fosse were new and strange sights, men without helmets or breast-plates, sleek money-making traders, who had served all their time in towns. Corbulo having discharged all who were old or in ill-health, sought to supply their places, and levies were held in Galatia and Cappadocia, and to these were added a legion from Germany with its auxiliary cavalry and light infantry. The entire army was kept under canvas, though the winter was so severe that the ground, covered as it was with ice, did not yield a place for the tents without being dug up. Many of the men had their limbs frost-bitten through the intensity of the cold, and some perished on guard. A soldier was observed whose hands mortified as he was carrying a bundle of wood, so that sticking to their burden they dropped off from his arms, now mere stumps. The general, lightly clad, with head uncovered, was continually with his men on the march, amid their labours; he had praise for the brave, comfort for the feeble, and was a good example to all. And then as many shrank from the rigour of the climate and of the service, and deserted, he sought a remedy in strictness of discipline. Not, as in other armies, was a first or second offense condoned, but the soldier, who had quitted his colours, instantly paid the penalty with his life. This was shown by experience to be a wholesome measure, better than mercy; for there were fewer desertions in that camp than in those in which leniency was habitual.

36. Meanwhile Corbulo kept his legions within the camp till spring weather was fairly established, and having stationed his auxiliary infantry at suitable points, he directed them not to begin an engagement. The charge of these defensive positions he entrusted to Paccius Orfitus, who had held the post of a first-rank centurion. Though this officer

had reported that the barbarians were heedless, and that an opportunity for success presented itself, he was instructed to keep within his entrenchments and to wait for a stronger force. But he broke the order, and on the arrival of a few cavalry squadrons from the nearest forts, who in their inexperience insisted on fighting, he engaged the enemy and was routed. Panic-stricken by his disaster, those who ought to have given him support returned in precipitate flight to their respective encampments. Corbulo heard of this with displeasure; he sharply censured Paccius, the officers and soldiers, and ordered them to have their quarters outside the lines. There they were kept in disgrace, and were released only on the intercession of the whole army.

37. Tiridates meantime who, besides his own dependencies, had the powerful aid of his brother Vologeses, ravaged Armenia, not in stealthy raids as before, but in open war, plundering all whom he thought loyal to Rome, while he eluded an action with any force which was brought against him, and thus flying hither and thither, he spread panic more widely by rumour than by arms. So Corbulo, frustrated in his prolonged efforts to bring on an engagement and compelled, like the enemy, to carry hostilities everywhere, divided his army, so that his generals and officers might attack several points simultaneously. He at the same time instructed king Antiochus to hasten to the provinces on his frontier, as Pharasmanes, after having slain his son Rhadamistus as a traitor to prove his loyalty to us, was following up more keenly than ever his old feud with the Armenians. Then, for the first time, we won the friendship of the Moschi, a nation which became pre-eminently attached to Rome, and they overran the wilds of Armenia. Thus the intended plans of Tiridates were wholly reversed, and he sent envoys to ask on behalf of himself and of the Parthians, why, when hostages had lately been given and a friendship renewed which might open up a way to further acts of goodwill, he was thus driven from Armenia, his ancient possession. "As yet," he said, "Vologeses had not bestirred himself, simply because they preferred negotiation to violence. Should however war be persisted in, the Arsacids would not want the courage and good fortune which had already been

proved more than once by disaster to Rome." Corbulo in
reply, when he was certain that Vologeses was detained by
the revolt of Hyrcania, advised Tiridates to address a petition to the emperor, assuring him that he might reign securely and without bloodshed by relinquishing a prospect in
the remote future for the sake of one more solid within his
reach.

38. As no progress was made towards a final settlement of
peace by the interchange of messages, it was at last decided
to fix a time and a place for an interview between the leaders. "A thousand troopers," Tiridates said, "would be his
escort; what force of every kind was to be with Corbulo, he
did not prescribe, provided they came in peaceful fashion,
without breast-plates and helmets." Any human being, to
say nothing of an old and wary general, would have seen
through the barbarian's cunning, which assigned a limited
number on one side and offered a larger on the other, expressly with a treacherous intent; for, were they to be exposed to a cavalry trained in the use of arrows, with the
person undefended, numbers would be unavailing. Corbulo
however, pretending not to understand this, replied that they
would do better to discuss matters requiring consideration
for their common good, in the presence of the entire armies,
and he selected a place partly consisting of gently sloping
hills, suited for ranks of infantry, partly, of a spreading
plain where troops of cavalry could manœuvre. On the appointed day, arriving first, he posted his allied infantry with
the king's auxiliaries on the wings, the sixth legion in the
centre, with which he had united three thousand men of the
third, brought up in the night from another camp, with one
eagle, so as to look like a single legion. Tiridates towards
evening showed himself at some distance, whence he could be
seen rather than heard. And so the Roman general, without
any conference, ordered his troops to retire to their respective camps.

39. The king either suspecting a stratagem from these
simultaneous movements in different directions, or intending
to cut off our supplies as they were coming up from the sea
of Pontus and the town of Trapezus, hastily withdrew. He
could not however make any attack on the supplies, as they

were brought over mountains in the occupation of our forces.
Corbulo, that war might not be uselessly protracted, and also
to compel the Armenians to defend their possessions, prepared to destroy their fortresses, himself undertaking the assault on the strongest of all in that province named Volan-
dum. The weaker he assigned to Cornelius Flaccus, his
lieutenant, and to Insteius Capito, his camp-prefect. Having
then surveyed the defences and provided everything suitable for storming them, he exhorted his soldiers to strip of
his home this vagabond foe who was preparing neither for
peace nor for war, but who confessed his treachery and
cowardice by flight, and so to secure alike glory and spoil.
Then forming his army into four divisions, he led one in
the dense array of the "testudo" close up to the rampart, to
undermine it, while others were ordered to apply scaling ladders to the walls, and many more were to discharge brands
and javelins from engines. The slingers and artillerymen had
a position assigned them from which to hurl their missiles at
a distance, so that, with equal tumult everywhere, no support might be given from any point to such as were pressed.
So impetuous were the efforts of the army that within a third
part of one day the walls were stripped of their defenders,
the barriers of the gates overthrown, the fortifications scaled
and captured, and all the adult inhabitants massacred, without the loss of a soldier and with but very few wounded. The
non-military population were sold by auction; the rest of the
booty fell to the conquerors.

Corbulo's lieutenant and camp-prefect met with similar
success; three forts were stormed by them in one day, and
the remainder, some from panic, others by the consent of
the occupants, capitulated. This inspired them with confidence to attack the capital of the country, Artaxata. The legions however were not marched by the nearest route, for
should they cross the river Avaxes which washes the city's
walls by a bridge, they would be within missile-range. They
passed over it at a distance, where it was broad and shallow.

40. Meantime Tiridates, ashamed of seeming utterly powerless by not interfering with the siege, and afraid that, in
attempting to stop it, he would entangle himself and his cavalry on difficult ground, resolved finally to display his forces

and either give battle on the first opportunity, or, by a pretended flight, prepare the way for some stratagem. Suddenly,
he threw himself on the Roman columns, without however
surprising our general, who had formed his army for fighting
as well as for marching. On the right and left flanks marched
the third and sixth legions, with some picked men of the
tenth in the centre; the baggage was secured within the
lines, and the rear was guarded by a thousand cavalry, who
were ordered to resist any close attack of the enemy, but not
to pursue his retreat. On the wings were the foot-archers and
the remainder of the cavalry, with a more extended line on
the left wing, along the base of some hills, so that should the
enemy penetrate the centre, he might be encountered both
in front and flank. Tiridates faced us in skirmishing order,
but not within missile-range, now threatening attack, now
seemingly afraid, with the view of loosening our formation
and falling on isolated divisions. Finding that there was no
breaking of our ranks from rashness, and that only one cavalry officer advanced too boldly, and that he falling pierced
with arrows, confirmed the rest in obedience by the warning,
he retired on the approach of darkness.

41. Corbulo then encamped on the spot, and considered
whether he should push on his legions without their baggage
to Artaxata and blockade the city, on which, he supposed,
Tiridates had fallen back. When his scouts reported that the
king had undertaken a long march, and that it was doubtful
whether Media or Albania was its destination, he waited for
daylight, and then sent on his light-armed troops, which
were meanwhile to hover round the walls and begin the attack from a distance. The inhabitants however opened the
gates of their own accord, and surrendered themselves and
their property to the Romans. This saved their lives; the
city was fired, demolished and levelled to the ground, as it
could not be held without a strong garrison from the extent
of the walls, and we had not sufficient force to be divided between adequately garrisoning it and carrying on the war. If
again the place were left untouched and unguarded, no advantage or glory would accrue from its capture. Then too
there was a wonderful occurrence, almost a divine interposition. While the whole space outside the town, up to its build-

ings, was bright with sunlight, the enclosure within the walls was suddenly shrouded in a black cloud, seamed with lightning-flashes, and thus the city was thought to be given up to destruction, as if heaven was wroth against it.

For all this Nero was unanimously saluted emperor, and by the Senate's decree a thanksgiving was held; statues also, arches and successive consulships were voted to him, and among the holy days were to be included the day on which the victory was won, that on which it was announced, and that on which the motion was brought forward. Other proposals too of a like kind were carried, on a scale so extravagant, that Caius Cassius, after having assented to the rest of the honours, argued that if the gods were to be thanked for the bountiful favours of fortune, even a whole year would not suffice for thanksgivings, and therefore there ought to be a classification of sacred and business-days, that so they might observe divine ordinances and yet not interfere with human affairs.

42. A man who had struggled with various calamities and earned the hate of many, was then impeached and condemned, but not without angry feelings towards Seneca. This was Publius Suilius. He had been terrible and venal, while Claudius reigned, and when times were changed, he was not so much humbled as his enemies wished, and was one who would rather seem a criminal than a suppliant. With the intent of crushing him, so men believed, a decree of the Senate was revived, along with the penalty of the Cincian law against persons who had pleaded for hire. Suilius spared not complaint or indignant remonstrance; freespoken because of his extreme age as well as from his insolent temper, he taunted Seneca with his savage enmity against the friends of Claudius, under whose reign he had endured a most righteously deserved exile. "The man," he said, "familiar as he was only with profitless studies, and with the ignorance of boyhood, envied those who employed a lively and genuine eloquence in the defence of their fellow-citizens. *He* had been Germanicus's quæstor, while Seneca had been a paramour in his house. Was it to be thought a worse offence to obtain a reward for honest service with the litigant's consent, than to pollute the chambers of the imperial ladies? By what kind

of wisdom or maxims of philosophy had Seneca within four
years of royal favour amassed three hundred million sesterces? At Rome the wills of the childless were, so to say,
caught in his snare while Italy and the provinces were
drained by a boundless usury. His own money, on the other
hand, had been acquired by industry and was not excessive.
He would suffer prosecutions, perils, anything indeed rather
than make an old and self-earned position of honour to bow
before an upstart prosperity."

43. Persons were not wanting to report all this to Seneca,
in the exact words, or with a worse sense put on it. Accusers
were also found who alleged that our allies had been plundered, when Suilius governed the province of Asia, and that
there had been embezzlement of public monies. Then, as an
entire year had been granted to them for inquiries, it seemed
a shorter plan to begin with his crimes at Rome, the witnesses of which were on the spot. These men charged Suilius
with having driven Quintus Pomponius by a relentless prosecution into the extremity of civil war, with having forced
Julia, Drusus's daughter, and Sabina Poppæa to suicide,
with having treacherously ruined Valerius Asiaticus, Lusius
Saturninus and Cornelius Lupus, in fact, with the wholesale
conviction of troops of Roman knights, and with all the
cruelty of Claudius. His defence was that of all this he had
done nothing on his own responsibility but had simply
obeyed the emperor, till Nero stopped such pleadings, by
stating that he had ascertained from his father's note-books
that he had never compelled the prosecution of a single person.

Suilius then sheltered himself under Messalina's orders,
and the defence began to collapse. "Why," it was asked,
"was no one else chosen to put his tongue at the service of
that savage harlot? We must punish the instruments of atrocious acts, when, having gained the rewards of wickedness,
they impute the wickedness to others."

And so, with the loss of half his property, his son and
granddaughter being allowed to retain the other half, and
what they had inherited under their mother's or grandmother's will being also exempted from confiscation, Suilius was
banished to the Balearic isles. Neither in the crisis of his

peril nor after his condemnation did he quail in spirit. Rumour said that he supported that lonely exile by a life of ease and plenty. When the accusers attacked his son Nerullinus on the strength of men's hatred of the father and of some charges of extortion, the emperor interposed, as if implying that vengeance was fully satisfied.

44. About the same time Octavius Sagitta, a tribune of the people, who was enamoured to frenzy of Pontia, a married woman, bribed her by most costly presents into an intrigue and then into abandoning her husband. He had offered her marriage and had won her consent. But as soon as she was free, she devised delays, pretended that her father's wishes were against it, and having secured the prospect of a richer husband, she repudiated her promises. Octavius, on the other hand, now remonstrated, now threatened; his good name, he protested, was lost, his means exhausted, and as for his life, which was all that was left to him, he surrendered it to her mercy. When she spurned him, he asked the solace of one night, with which to soothe his passion, that he might set bounds to it for the future. A night was fixed, and Pontia intrusted the charge of her chamber to a female slave acquainted with her secret. Octavius attended by one freedman entered, with a dagger concealed under his dress. Then, as usual in lovers' quarrels, there were chidings, entreaties, reproaches, excuses, and some period of the darkness was given up to passion; then, when seemingly about to go, and she was fearing nothing, he stabbed her with the steel, and having wounded and scared away the slave girl who was hurrying to her, rushed out of the chamber. Next day the murder was notorious, and there was no question as to the murderer, for it was proved that he had passed some time with her. The freedman, however, declared the deed was his, that he had, in fact, avenged his patron's wrongs. He had made some impression by the nobleness of his example, when the slave girl recovered and revealed the truth. Octavius, when he ceased to be tribune, was prosecuted before the consuls by the father of the murdered woman, and was condemned by the sentence of the Senate under "the law concerning assassins."

45. A profligacy equally notorious in that same year

proved the beginning of great evils to the State. There was
at Rome one Sabina Poppæa; her father was Titus Ollius,
but she had assumed the name of her maternal grandfather
Poppæus Sabinus, a man of illustrious memory and pre-
eminently distinguished by the honours of a consulship and
a triumph. As for Ollius, before he attained promotion, the
friendship of Sejanus was his ruin. This Poppæa had everything but a right mind. Her mother, who surpassed in personal attractions all the ladies of her day, had bequeathed
to her alike fame and beauty. Her fortune adequately cor-
responded to the nobility of her descent. Her conversation
was charming and her wit anything but dull. She professed
virtue, while she practised laxity. Seldom did she appear in
public, and it was always with her face partly veiled, either
to disappoint men's gaze or to set off her beauty. Her character she never spared, making no distinction between a husband and a paramour, while she was never a slave to her
own passion or to that of her lover. Wherever there was a
prospect of advantage, there she transferred her favours.
And so while she was living as the wife of Rufius Crispinus,
a Roman knight, by whom she had a son, she was attracted
by the youth and fashionable elegance of Otho, and by the
fact too that he was reputed to have Nero's most ardent
friendship. Without any delay the intrigue was followed by
marriage.

46. Otho now began to praise his wife's beauty and accomplishments to the emperor, either from a lover's thoughtlessness or to inflame Nero's passion, in the hope of adding
to his own influence by the further tie which would arise out
of possession of the same woman. Often, as he rose from the
emperor's table, was he heard repeatedly to say that he was
going to her, to the high birth and beauty which had fallen
to his lot, to that which all men pray for, the joy of the
fortunate. These and like incitements allowed but of brief
delay. Once having gained admission, Poppæa won her way
by artful blandishments, pretending that she could not resist her passion and that she was captivated by Nero's person. Soon, as the emperor's love grew ardent, she would
change and be supercilious, and, if she were detained more
than one or two nights, would say again and again that she

was a married woman and could not give up her husband
attached as she was to Otho by a manner of life, which no
one equalled. "His ideas and his style were grand; at his
house everything worthy of the highest fortune was ever before her eyes. Nero, on the contrary, with his slave girl mistress, tied down by his attachment to Acte, had derived
nothing from his slavish associations but what was low and
degrading."

Otho was now cut off from Nero's usual familiar intercourse, and then even from interviews and from the royal
suite, and at last was appointed governor of the province of
Lusitania, that he might not be the emperor's rival at Rome.
There he lived up to the time of the civil wars, not in the
fashion of his disgraceful past, but uprightly and virtuously,
a pleasure-loving man when idle, and self-restrained when in
power.

47. Hitherto Nero had sought a veil for his abominations
and wickedness. He was particularly suspicious of Cornelius Sulla, whose apathetic temper he interpreted as really
the reverse, inferring that he was, in fact, an artful dis-
sembler. Graptus, one of the emperor's freedmen, whose age
and experience had made him thoroughly acquainted with
the imperial household from the time of Tiberius, quickened
these apprehensions by the following falsehood. The Mulvian bridge was then a famous haunt of nightly profligacy,
and Nero used to go there that he might take his pleasures
more freely outside the city. So Graptus, taking advantage
of an idle panic into which the royal attendants had chanced
to have been thrown on their return by one of those youthful frolics which were then everywhere practised, invented a
story that a treacherous attack had been planned on the
emperor, should he go back by the Flaminian road, and that
through the favour of destiny he had escaped it, as he went
home by a different way to Sallust's gardens. Sulla, he said,
was the author of this plot. Not one, however, of Sulla's
slaves or clients was recognised, and his character, despicable
as it was and incapable of a daring act, was utterly at variance with the charge. Still, just as if he had been found
guilty, he was ordered to leave his country, and confine himself within the walls of Massilia.

48. During the same consulship a hearing was given to two conflicting deputations from Puteoli, sent to the Senate by the town council and by the populace. The first spoke bitterly of the violence of the multitude; the second, of the rapacity of the magistrates and of all the chief citizens. That the disturbance, which had gone as far as stoning and threats of fire, might not lead on to bloodshed and armed fighting, Caius Cassius was appointed to apply some remedy. As they would not endure his rigour, the charge of the affair was at his own request transferred to the brothers Scribonii, to whom was given a prætorian cohort, the terror of which, coupled with the execution of a few persons, restored peace to the townspeople.

49. I should not mention a very trivial decree of the Senate which allowed the city of Syracuse to exceed the prescribed number in their gladiatorial shows, had not Pætus Thrasea spoken against it and furnished his traducers with a ground for censuring his motion. "Why," it was asked, "if he thought that the public welfare required freedom of speech in the Senate, did he pursue such trifling abuses? Why should he not speak for or against peace and war, or on the taxes and laws and other matters involving Roman interests? The senators, as often as they received the privilege of stating an opinion, were at liberty to say out what they pleased, and to claim that it should be put to the vote. Was it the only worthy object of reform to provide that the Syracusans should not give shows on a larger scale? Were all other matters in every department of the empire as admirable as if Thrasea and not Nero had the direction of them? But if the highest affairs were passed by and ignored, how much more ought there to be no meddling with things wholly insignificant."

Thrasea in reply, when his friends asked an explanation, said "that it was not in ignorance of Rome's actual condition that he sought to correct such decrees, but that he was giving what was due to the honour of the senators, in making it evident that those who attended even to the merest trifles, would not disguise their responsibility for important affairs."

50. That same year, repeated demands on the part of the people, who denounced the excessive greed of the revenue

collectors, made Nero doubt whether he should not order the
repeal of all indirect taxes, and so confer a most splendid
boon on the human race. But this sudden impulse was
checked by the senators, who, having first heartily praised
the grandeur of his conception, pointed out "that the disso-
lution of the empire must ensue if the revenues which supported the State were to be diminished; for as soon as the
customs were swept away, there would follow a demand for
the abolition of the direct taxes. Many companies for the
collection of the indirect taxes had been formed by consuls
and tribunes, when the freedom of the Roman people was
still in its vigour, and arrangements were subsequently made
to insure an exact correspondence between the amount of
income and the necessary disbursements. Certainly some restraint, they admitted, must be put on the cupidity of the
revenue collectors, that they might not by new oppressions
bring into odium what for so many years had been endured
without a complaint."

51. Accordingly the emperor issued an edict that the regulations about every branch of the public revenue, which had
hitherto been kept secret, should be published; that claims
which had been dropped should not be revived after a year;
that the prætor at Rome, the proprætor or proconsul in the
provinces, should give judicial precedence to all cases against
the collectors; that the soldiers should retain their immuni-
ties except when they traded for profit, with other very
equitable arrangements, which for a short time were maintained and were subsequently disregarded. However, the repeal of the two per cent. and two-and-a-half per cent. taxes
remains in force, as well as that of others bearing names invented by the collectors to cover their illegal exactions. In
our transmarine provinces the conveyance of corn was rendered less costly, and it was decided that merchant ships
should not be assessed with their owner's property, and that
no tax should be paid on them.

52. Two men under prosecution from Africa, in which
province they had held proconsular authority, Sulpicius
Camerinus and Pomponius Silvanus, were acquitted by the
emperor. Camerinus had against him a few private persons
who charged him with cruelty rather than with extortion.

Silvanus was beset by a host of accusers, who demanded
time for summoning their witnesses, while the defendant insisted on being at once put on his defence. And he was successful, through his wealth, his childlessness, and his old age,
which he prolonged beyond the life of those by whose corrupt influence he had escaped.

53. Up to this time everything had been quiet in Germany, from the temper of the generals, who, now that triumphal decorations had been vulgarised, hoped for greater
glory by the maintenance of peace. Paulinus Pompeius and
Lucius Vetus were then in command of the army. Still, to
avoid keeping the soldiers in idleness, the first completed the
embankment begun sixty-three years before by Drusus to
confine the waters of the Rhine, while Vetus prepared to
connect the Moselle and the Arar by a canal, so that troops
crossing the sea and then conveyed on the Rhone and Arar
might sail by this canal into the Moselle and the Rhine, and
thence to the ocean. Thus the difficulties of the route being
removed, there would be communication for ships between
the shores of the west and of the north.

Ælius Gracilis, the governor of Belgica, discouraged the
work by seeking to deter Vetus from bringing his legions
into another man's province, and so drawing to himself the
attachment of Gaul. This result he repeatedly said would
excite the fears of the emperor, an assertion by which meritorious undertakings are often hindered.

54. Meantime, from the continued inaction of our armies,
a rumour prevailed that the commanders had been deprived
of the right of leading them against the enemy. Thereupon
the Frisii moved up their youth to the forests and swamps,
and their non-fighting population, over the lakes, to the
river-bank, and established themselves in unoccupied lands,
reserved for the use of our soldiers, under the leadership of
Verritus and Malorix, the kings of the tribe, as far as Germans are under kings. Already they had settled themselves
in houses, had sown the fields, and were cultivating the soil
as if it had been their ancestors', when Dubius Avitus, who
had succeeded Paulinus in the province, by threatening them
with a Roman attack if they did not retire into their old
country or obtain a new territory from the emperor, con-

strained Verritus and Malorix to become suppliants. They
went to Rome, and while they waited for Nero, who was intent on other engagements, among the sights shown to the
barbarians they were admitted into Pompey's theatre, where
they might behold the vastness of the Roman people. There
at their leisure (for in the entertainment, ignorant as they
were, they found no amusement) they asked questions about
the crowd on the benches, about the distinctions of classes,
who were the knights, where was the Senate, till they observed some persons in a foreign dress on the seats of the
senators. Having asked who they were, when they were told
that this honour was granted to envoys from those nations
which were distinguished for their bravery and their friendship to Rome, they exclaimed that no men on earth surpassed the Germans in arms or in loyalty. Then they went
down and took their seat among the senators. The spectators
hailed the act goodnaturedly, as due to the impulsiveness of
a primitive people and to an honourable rivalry. Nero gave
both of them the Roman franchise, and ordered the Frisii to
withdraw from the territory in question. When they disdained obedience, some auxiliary cavalry by a sudden attack
made it a necessity for them, capturing or slaughtering those
who obstinately resisted.

55. Of this same territory, the Ampsivarii now possessed
themselves, a tribe more powerful not only from their numbers, but from having the sympathy of the neighbouring
peoples, as they had been expelled by the Chauci and had to
beg, as homeless outcasts, a secure exile. Their cause was
pleaded by a man, famous among those nations and loyal to
Rome, Boiocalus by name, who reminded us that on the
Cheruscan revolt he had been imprisoned by the order of
Arminius, that afterwards he had served under the leadership of Tiberius and of Germanicus, and that to a fifty
years' obedience he was adding the merit of subjecting his
tribe to our dominion. "What an extent of plain," he would
say, "lies open into which the flocks and herds of the Roman soldiers may some day be sent! Let them by all means
keep retreats for their cattle, while men are starving; only
let them not prefer a waste and a solitude to friendly nations. Once these fields belonged to the Chamavi; then to

the Tubantes; after them to the Usipii. As heaven is for the gods, so the earth has been given to mankind, and lands uninhabited are common to all." Then looking up to the sun and invoking the other heavenly bodies, he asked them, as though standing in their presence, "whether they wished to behold an empty soil; rather let them submerge it beneath the sea against the plunderers of the land."

56. Avitus was impressed by this language and said that people must submit to the rule of their betters; that the gods to whom they appealed, had willed that the decision as to what should be given or taken from them, was to rest with the Romans, who would allow none but themselves to be judges. This was his public answer to the Ampsivarii; to Boiocalus his reply was that in remembrance of past friendship he would cede the lands in question. Boiocalus spurned the offer as the price of treason, adding, "We may lack a land to live in; we cannot lack one to die in." And so they parted with mutual exasperation. The Ampsivarii now called on the Bructeri, the Tencteri, and yet more distant tribes to be their allies in war. Avitus, having written to Curtilius Mancia, commander of the Upper army, asking him to cross the Rhine and display his troops in the enemy's rear, himself led his legions into the territory of the Tencteri, and threatened them with extermination unless they dissociated themselves from the cause. When upon this the Tencteri stood aloof, the Bructeri were cowed by a like terror. And so, as the rest too were for averting perils which did not concern them, the Ampsivarian tribe in its isolation retreated to the Usipii and Tubantes. Driven out of these countries, they sought refuge with the Chatti and then with the Cherusci, and after long wanderings, as destitute outcasts, received now as friends now as foes, their entire youth were slain in a strange land, and all who could not fight, were apportioned as booty.

57. The same summer a great battle was fought between the Hermunduri and the Chatti, both forcibly claiming a river which produced salt in plenty, and bounded their territories. They had not only a passion for settling every question by arms, but also a deep-rooted superstition that such localities are specially near to heaven, and that mortal pray-

ers are nowhere more attentively heard by the gods. It is, they think, through the bounty of divine power, that in that river and in those forests salt is produced, not, as in other countries, by the drying up of an overflow of the sea, but by the combination of two opposite elements, fire and water, when the latter had been poured over a burning pile of wood. The war was a success for the Hermunduri, and the more disastrous to the Chatti because they had devoted, in the event of victory, the enemy's army to Mars and Mercury, a vow which consigns horses, men, everything indeed on the vanquished side to destruction. And so the hostile threat recoiled on themselves. Meanwhile, a state in alliance with us, that of the Ubii, suffered grievously from an unexpected calamity. Fires suddenly bursting from the earth seized everywhere on country houses, crops, and villages, and were rushing on to the very walls of the newly founded colony. Nor could they be extinguished by the fall of rain, or by river-water, or by any other moisture, till some countrymen, in despair of a remedy and in fury at the disaster, flung stones from a distance, and then, approaching nearer, as the flames began to sink, tried to scare them away, like so many wild beasts, with the blows of clubs and other weapons. At last they stript off their clothes and threw them on the fire, which they were the more likely to quench, the more they had been soiled by common use.

58. That same year, the fact that the tree in the Comitium, which 840 years before had sheltered the infancy of Romulus and Remus, was impaired by the decay of its boughs and by the withering of its stem, was accounted a portent, till it began to renew its life with fresh shoots.

BOOK XIV

A.D. 59—62

1. In the year of the consulship of Caius Vipstanus and Caius Fonteius, Nero deferred no more a long meditated crime. Length of power had matured his daring, and his passion for Poppæa daily grew more ardent. As the woman had no hope of marriage for herself or of Octavia's divorce while Agrippina lived, she would reproach the emperor with incessant vituperation and sometimes call him in jest a mere ward who was under the rule of others, and was so far from having empire that he had not even his liberty. "Why," she asked, "was her marriage put off? Was it, forsooth, her beauty and her ancestors, with their triumphal honours, that failed to please, or her being a mother, and her sincere heart? No; the fear was that as a wife at least she would divulge the wrongs of the Senate, and the wrath of the people at the arrogance and rapacity of his mother. If the only daughter-in-law Agrippina could bear was one who wished evil to her son, let her be restored to her union with Otho. She would go anywhere in the world, where she might hear of the insults heaped on the emperor, rather than witness them, and be also involved in his perils."

These and the like complaints, rendered impressive by tears and by the cunning of an adulteress, no one checked, as all longed to see the mother's power broken, while not a person believed that the son's hatred would steel his heart to her murder.

2. Cluvius relates that Agrippina in her eagerness to retain her influence went so far that more than once at midday, when Nero, even at that hour, was flushed with wine and feasting, she presented herself attractively attired to her half intoxicated son and offered him her person, and that when kinsfolk observed wanton kisses and caresses, por-

320

tending infamy, it was Seneca who sought a female's aid against a woman's fascinations, and hurried in Acte, the freed girl, who alarmed at her own peril and at Nero's disgrace, told him that the incest was notorious, as his mother boasted of it, and that the soldiers would never endure the rule of an impious sovereign. Fabius Rusticus tells us that it was not Agrippina, but Nero, who lusted for the crime, and that it was frustrated by the adroitness of that same freed-girl. Cluvius's account, however, is also that of all other authors, and popular belief inclines to it, whether it was that Agrippina really conceived such a monstrous wickedness in her heart, or perhaps because the thought of a strange passion seemed comparatively credible in a woman, who in her girlish years had allowed herself to be seduced by Lepidus in the hope of winning power, had stooped with a like ambition to the lust of Pallas, and had trained herself for every infamy by her marriage with her uncle.

3. Nero accordingly avoided secret interviews with her, and when she withdrew to her gardens or to her estates at Tusculum and Antium, he praised her for courting repose. At last, convinced that she would be too formidable, wherever she might dwell, he resolved to destroy her, merely deliberating whether it was to be accomplished by poison, or by the sword, or by any other violent means. Poison at first seemed best, but, were it to be administered at the imperial table, the result could not be referred to chance after the recent circumstances of the death of Britannicus. Again, to tamper with the servants of a woman who, from her familiarity with crime, was on her guard against treachery, appeared to be extremely difficult, and then, too, she had fortified her constitution by the use of antidotes. How again the dagger and its work were to be kept secret, no one could suggest, and it was feared too that whoever might be chosen to execute such a crime would spurn the order.

An ingenious suggestion was offered by Anicetus, a freed-man, commander of the fleet at Misenum, who had been tutor to Nero in boyhood and had a hatred of Agrippina which she reciprocated. He explained that a vessel could be constructed, from which a part might by a contrivance be detached, when out at sea, so as to plunge her unawares into

the water. "Nothing," he said, "allowed of accidents so much
as the sea, and should she be overtaken by shipwreck, who
would be so unfair as to impute to crime an offence committed by the winds and waves? The emperor would add the
honour of a temple and of shrines to the deceased lady, with
every other display of filial affection."

4. Nero liked the device, favoured as it also was by the
particular time, for he was celebrating Minerva's five days'
festival at Baiæ. Thither he enticed his mother by repeated
assurances that children ought to bear with the irritability
of parents and to soothe their tempers, wishing thus to
spread a rumour of reconciliation and to secure Agrippina's
acceptance through the feminine credulity, which easily be-
lieves what gives joy. As she approached, he went to the
shore to meet her (she was coming from Antium), welcomed
her with outstretched hand and embrace, and conducted her
to Bauli. This was the name of a country house, washed by
a bay of the sea, between the promontory of Misenum and
the lake of Baiæ. Here was a vessel distinguished from others
by its equipment, seemingly meant, among other things, to
do honour to his mother; for she had been accustomed to
sail in a trireme, with a crew of marines. And now she was
invited to a banquet, that night might serve to conceal the
crime. It was well known that somebody had been found to
betray it, that Agrippina had heard of the plot, and in doubt
whether she was to believe it, was conveyed to Baiæ in her
litter. There some soothing words allayed her fear; she was
graciously received, and seated at table above the emperor.
Nero prolonged the banquet with various conversation, passing from a youth's playful familiarity to an air of constraint,
which seemed to indicate serious thought, and then, after
protracted festivity, escorted her on her departure, clinging
with kisses to her eyes and bosom, either to crown his hypocrisy or because the last sight of a mother on the even of
destruction caused a lingering even in that brutal heart.

5. A night of brilliant starlight with the calm of a tranquil
sea was granted by heaven, seemingly, to convict the crime.
The vessel had not gone far, Agrippina having with her two
of her intimate attendants, one of whom, Crepereius Gallus,
stood near the helm, while Acerronia, reclining at Agrippina's

feet as she reposed herself, spoke joyfully of her son's repentance and of the recovery of the mother's influence, when
at a given signal the ceiling of the place, which was loaded
with a quantity of lead, fell in, and Crepereius was crushed
and instantly killed. Agrippina and Acerronia were protected
by the projecting sides of the couch, which happened to be
too strong to yield under the weight. But this was not followed by the breaking up of the vessel; for all were bewildered, and those too, who were in the plot, were hindered by
the unconscious majority. The crew then thought it best to
throw the vessel on one side and so sink it, but they could
not themselves promptly unite to face the emergency, and
others, by counteracting the attempt, gave an opportunity of
a gentler fall into the sea. Acerronia, however, thoughtlessly
exclaiming that she was Agrippina, and imploring help for
the emperor's mother, was despatched with poles and oars,
and such naval implements as chance offered. Agrippina was
silent and was thus the less recognized; still, she received a
wound in her shoulder. She swam, then met with some small
boats which conveyed her to the Lucrine lake, and so entered
her house.

6. There she reflected how for this very purpose she had
been invited by a lying letter and treated with conspicuous
honour, how also it was near the shore, not from being driven
by winds or dashed on rocks, that the vessel had in its upper
part collapsed, like a mechanism anything but nautical. She
pondered too the death of Acerronia; she looked at her own
wound, and saw that her only safeguard against treachery
was to ignore it. Then she sent her freedman Agerinus to tell
her son how by heaven's favour and his good fortune she had
escaped a terrible disaster; that she begged him, alarmed, as
he might be, by his mother's peril, to put off the duty of a
visit, as for the present she needed repose. Meanwhile, pretending that she felt secure, she applied remedies to her
wound, and fomentations to her person. She then ordered
search to be made for the will of Acerronia, and her property
to be sealed, in this alone throwing off disguise.

7. Nero, meantime, as he waited for tidings of the consummation of the deed, received information that she had
escaped with the injury of a slight wound, after having so

far encountered the peril that there could be no question as to its author. Then, paralysed with terror and protesting that she would show herself the next moment eager for vengeance, either arming the slaves or stirring up the soldiery, or hastening to the Senate and the people, to charge him with the wreck, with her wound, and with the destruction of her friends, he asked what resource he had against all this, unless something could be at once devised by Burrus and Seneca. He had instantly summoned both of them, and possibly they were already in the secret. There was a long silence on their part; they feared they might remonstrate in vain, or believed the crisis to be such that Nero must perish, unless Agrippina were at once crushed. Thereupon Seneca was so far the more prompt as to glance back on Burrus, as if to ask him whether the bloody deed must be required of the soldiers. Burrus replied "that the prætorians were attached to the whole family of the Cæsars, and remembering Germanicus would not dare a savage deed on his offspring. It was for Anicetus to accomplish his promise."

Anicetus, without a pause, claimed for himself the consummation of the crime. At those words, Nero declared that that day gave him empire, and that a freedman was the author of this mighty boon. "Go," he said, "with all speed and take with you the men readiest to execute your orders." He himself, when he had heard of the arrival of Agrippina's messenger, Agerinus, contrived a theatrical mode of accusation, and, while the man was repeating his message, threw down a sword at his feet, then ordered him to be put in irons, as a detected criminal, so that he might invent a story how his mother had plotted the emperor's destruction and in the shame of discovered guilt had by her own choice sought death.

8. Meantime, Agrippina's peril being universally known and taken to be an accidental occurrence, everybody, the moment he heard of it, hurried down to the beach. Some climbed projecting piers; some the nearest vessels; others, as far as their stature allowed, went into the sea; some, again, stood with outstretched arms, while the whole shore rung with wailings, with prayers and cries, as different questions were asked and uncertain answers given. A vast multi-

tude streamed to the spot with torches, and as soon as all knew that she was safe, they at once prepared to wish her joy, till the sight of an armed and threatening force scared them away. Anicetus then surrounded the house with a guard, and having burst open the gates, dragged off the slaves who met him, till he came to the door of her chamber, where a few still stood, after the rest had fled in terror at the attack. A small lamp was in the room, and one slave-girl with Agrippina, who grew more and more anxious, as no messenger came from her son, not even Agerinus, while the appearance of the shore was changed, a solitude one moment, then sudden bustle and tokens of the worst catastrophe. As the girl rose to depart, she exclaimed, "Do you too forsake me?" and looking round saw Anicetus, who had with him the captain of the trireme, Herculeius, and Obaritus, a centurion of marines. "If," said she, "you have come to see me, take back word that I have recovered, but if you are here to do a crime, I believe nothing about my son; he has not ordered his mother's murder."

The assassins closed in round her couch, and the captain of the trireme first struck her head violently with a club. Then, as the centurion bared his sword for the fatal deed, presenting her person, she exclaimed, "Smite my womb," and with many wounds she was slain.

9. So far our accounts agree. That Nero gazed on his mother after her death and praised her beauty, some have related, while others deny it. Her body was burnt that same night on a dining couch, with a mean funeral; nor, as long as Nero was in power, was the earth raised into a mound, or even decently closed. Subsequently, she received from the solicitude of her domestics, a humble sepulchre on the road to Misenum, near the country house of Cæsar the Dictator, which from a great height commands a view of the bay beneath. As soon as the funeral pile was lighted, one of her freedmen, surnamed Mnester, ran himself through with a sword, either from love of his mistress or from the fear of destruction.

Many years before Agrippina had anticipated this end for herself and had spurned the thought. For when she consulted the astrologers about Nero, they replied that he would be emperor and kill his mother. "Let him kill her," she said, "provided he is emperor."

10. But the emperor, when the crime was at last accomplished, realised its portentous guilt. The rest of the night, now silent and stupified, now and still oftener starting up in terror, bereft of reason, he awaited the dawn as if it would bring with it his doom. He was first encouraged to hope by the flattery addressed to him, at the prompting of Burrus, by the centurions and tribunes, who again and again pressed his hand and congratulated him on his having escaped an unforeseen danger and his mother's daring crime. Then his friends went to the temples, and, an example having once been set, the neighbouring towns of Campania testified their joy with sacrifices and deputations. He himself, with an opposite phase of hypocrisy, seemed sad, and almost angry at his own deliverance, and shed tears over his mother's death. But as the aspects of places change not, as do the looks of men, and as he had ever before his eyes the dreadful sight of that sea with its shores (some too believed that the notes of a funereal trumpet were heard from the surrounding heights, and wailings from the mother's grave), he retired to Neapolis and sent a letter to the Senate, the drift of which was that Agerinus, one of Agrippina's confidential freedmen, had been detected with the dagger of an assassin, and that in the consciousness of having planned the crime she had paid its penalty.

11. He even revived the charges of a period long past, how she had aimed at a share of empire, and at inducing the prætorian cohorts to swear obedience to a woman, to the disgrace of the Senate and people; how, when she was disappointed, in her fury with the soldiers, the Senate, and the populace, she opposed the usual donative and largess, and organised perilous prosecutions against distinguished citizens. What efforts had it cost him to hinder her from bursting into the Senate-house and giving answers to foreign nations! He glanced too with indirect censure at the days of Claudius, and ascribed all the abominations of that reign to his mother, thus seeking to show that it was the State's good fortune which had destroyed her. For he actually told the story of the shipwreck; but who could be so stupid as to

believe that it was accidental, or that a shipwrecked woman had sent one man with a weapon to break through an emperor's guards and fleets? So now it was not Nero, whose brutality was far beyond any remonstrance, but Seneca who was in ill repute, for having written a confession in such a style.

12. Still there was a marvellous rivalry among the nobles in decreeing thanksgivings at all the shrines, and the celebration with annual games of Minerva's festival, as the day on which the plot had been discovered; also, that a golden image of Minerva with a statue of the emperor by its side should be set up in the Senate-house, and that Agrippina's birthday should be classed among the inauspicious days. Thrasea Pætus, who had been used to pass over previous flatteries in silence or with brief assent, then walked out of the Senate, thereby imperilling himself, without communicating to the other senators any impulse towards freedom.

There occurred too a thick succession of portents, which meant nothing. A woman gave birth to a snake, and another was killed by a thunderbolt in her husband's embrace. Then the sun was suddenly darkened and the fourteen districts of the city were struck by lightning. All this happened quite without any providential design; so much so, that for many subsequent years Nero prolonged his reign and his crimes. Still, to deepen the popular hatred towards his mother, and prove that since her removal, his clemency had increased, he restored to their ancestral homes two distinguished ladies, Junia and Calpurnia, with two ex-prætors, Valerius Capito and Licinius Gabolus, whom Agrippina had formerly banished. He also allowed the ashes of Lollia Paulina to be brought back and a tomb to be built over them. Iturius and Calvisius, whom he had himself temporarily exiled, he now released from their penalty. Silana indeed had died a natural death at Tarentum, whither she had returned from her distant exile, when the power of Agrippina, to whose enmity she owed her fall, began to totter, or her wrath was at last appeased.

13. While Nero was lingering in the towns of Campania, doubting how he should enter Rome, whether he would find the Senate submissive and the populace enthusiastic, all the

vilest courtiers, and of these never had a court a more abundant crop, argued against his hesitation by assuring him
that Agrippina's name was hated and that her death had
heightened his popularity. "He might go without a fear,"
they said, "and experience in his person men's veneration for
him." They insisted at the same time on preceding him.
They found greater enthusiasm than they had promised, the
tribes coming forth to meet him, the Senate in holiday attire,
troops of their children and wives arranged according to sex
and age, tiers of seats raised for the spectacle, where he was
to pass, as a triumph is witnessed. Thus elated and exulting
over his people's slavery, he proceeded to the Capitol, performed the thanksgiving, and then plunged into all the excesses, which, though ill-restrained, some sort of respect for
his mother had for a while delayed.

14. He had long had a fancy for driving a four-horse
chariot, and a no less degrading taste for singing to the harp,
in a theatrical fashion, when he was at dinner. This he would
remind people was a royal custom, and had been the practice
of ancient chiefs; it was celebrated too in the praises of poets
and was meant to show honour to the gods. Songs indeed, he
said, were sacred to Apollo, and it was in the dress of a
singer that that great and prophetic deity was seen in Roman temples as well as in Greek cities. He could no longer
be restrained, when Seneca and Burrus thought it best to
concede one point that he might not persist in both. A space
was enclosed in the Vatican valley where he might manage
his horses, without the spectacle being public. Soon he actually invited all the people of Rome, who extolled him in
their praises, like a mob which craves for amusements and
rejoices when a prince draws them the same way. However,
the public exposure of his shame acted on him as an incentive instead of sickening him, as men expected. Imagining
that he mitigated the scandal by disgracing many others, he
brought on the stage descendants of noble families, who sold
themselves because they were paupers. As they have ended
their days, I think it due to their ancestors not to hand down
their names. And indeed the infamy is his who gave them
wealth to reward their degradation rather than to deter them
from degrading themselves. He prevailed too on some well-

known Roman knights, by immense presents, to offer their services in the amphitheatre; only pay from one who is able to command, carries with it the force of compulsion.

15. Still, not yet wishing to disgrace himself on a public stage, he instituted some games under the title of "juvenile sports," for which people of every class gave in their names. Neither rank nor age nor previous high promotion hindered any one from practising the art of a Greek or Latin actor and even stooping to gestures and songs unfit for a man. Noble ladies too actually played disgusting parts, and in the grove, with which Augustus had surrounded the lake for the naval fight, there were erected places for meeting and refreshment, and every incentive to excess was offered for sale. Money too was distributed, which the respectable had to spend under sheer compulsion and which the profligate gloried in squandering. Hence a rank growth of abominations and of all infamy. Never did a more filthy rabble add a worse licentiousness to our long corrupted morals. Even, with virtuous training, purity is not easily upheld; far less amid rivalries in vice could modesty or propriety or any trace of good manners be preserved. Last of all, the emperor himself came on the stage, tuning his lute with elaborate care and trying his voice with his attendants. There were also present, to complete the show, a guard of soldiers with centurions and tribunes, and Burrus, who grieved and yet applauded. Then it was that Roman knights were first enrolled under the title of Augustani, men in their prime and remarkable for their strength, some, from a natural frivolity, others from the hope of promotion. Day and night they kept up a thunder of applause, and applied to the emperor's person and voice the epithets of deities. Thus they lived in fame and honour, as if on the strength of their merits.

16. Nero however, that he might not be known only for his accomplishments as an actor, also affected a taste for poetry, and drew round him persons who had some skill in such compositions, but not yet generally recognised. They used to sit with him, stringing together verses prepared at home, or extemporised on the spot, and fill up his own expressions, such as they were, just as he threw them off. This

is plainly shown by the very character of the poems, which have no vigour or inspiration, or unity in their flow.

He would also bestow some leisure after his banquets on the teachers of philosophy, for he enjoyed the wrangles of opposing dogmatists. And some there were who liked to exhibit their gloomy faces and looks, as one of the amusements of the court.

17. About the same time a trifling beginning led to frightful bloodshed between the inhabitants of Nuceria and Pompeii, at a gladiatorial show exhibited by Livineius Regulus, who had been, as I have related, expelled from the Senate. With the unruly spirit of townsfolk, they began with abusive language of each other; then they took up stones and at last weapons, the advantage resting with the populace of Pompeii, where the show was being exhibited. And so there were brought to Rome a number of the people of Nuceria, with their bodies mutilated by wounds, and many lamented the deaths of children or of parents. The emperor entrusted the trial of the case to the Senate, and the Senate to the consuls, and then again the matter being referred back to the Senators, the inhabitants of Pompeii were forbidden to have any such public gathering for ten years, and all associations they had formed in defiance of the laws were dissolved. Livineius and the others who had excited the disturbance, were punished with exile.

18. Pedius Blæsus was also expelled from the Senate on the accusation of the people of Cyrene, that he had violated the treasury of Æsculapius and had tampered with a military levy by bribery and corruption. This same people prosecuted Acilius Strabo who had held the office of prætor, and had been sent by Claudius to adjudicate on some lands which were bequeathed by king Apion, their former possessor, together with his kingdom to the Roman people, and which had since been seized by the neighbouring proprietors, who trusted to a long continued licence in wrong, as if it constituted right and justice. Consequently, when the adjudication was against them, there arose a bitter feeling towards the judge, but the Senate replied that they knew nothing of the instructions given by Claudius, and that the emperor must be consulted. Nero, though he approved Strabo's decision,

wrote word that nevertheless he was for relieving the allies, and that he waived all claim to what had been taken into possession.

19. Then followed the deaths of two illustrious men, Domitius Afer and Marcus Servilius, who had flourished through a career of the highest honours and great eloquence. The first was a pleader; Servilius, after long practice in the courts, distinguished himself by his history of Rome and by the refinement of his life, which the contrast of his character to that of Afer, whom he equalled in genius, rendered the more conspicuous.

20. In Nero's fourth consulship with Cornelius Cossus for his colleague, a theatrical entertainment to be repeated every five years was established at Rome in imitation of the Greek festival. Like all novelties, it was variously canvassed. There were some who declared that even Cnius Pompeius was censured by the older men of the day for having set up a fixed and permanent theatre. "Formerly," they said, "the games were usually exhibited with hastily erected tiers of benches and a temporary stage, and the people stood to witness them, that they might not, by having the chance of sitting down, spend a succession of entire days in idleness. Let the ancient character of these shows be retained, whenever the prætors exhibited them, and let no citizen be under the necessity of competing. As it was, the morality of their fathers, which had by degrees been forgotten, was utterly subverted by the introduction of a lax tone, so that all which could suffer or produce corruption was to be seen at Rome, and a degeneracy bred by foreign tastes was infecting the youth who devoted themselves to athletic sports, to idle loungings and low intrigues, with the encouragement of the emperor and Senate, who not only granted licence to vice, but even applied a compulsion to drive Roman nobles into disgracing themselves on the stage, under the pretence of being orators and poets. What remained for them but to strip themselves naked, put on the boxing-glove, and practise such battles instead of the arms of legitimate warfare? Would justice be promoted, or would they serve on the knights' commissions for the honourable office of a judge, because they had listened with critical sagacity to effeminate strains of music

and sweet voices? Night too was given up to infamy, so that
virtue had not a moment left to her, but all the vilest of that
promiscuous throng dared to do in the darkness anything
they had lusted for in the day."

21. Many people liked this very licence, but they screened
it under respectable names. "Our ancestors," they said,
"were not averse to the attractions of shows on a scale suited
to the wealth of their day, and so they introduced actors
from the Etruscans and horse-races from Thurii. When we
had possessed ourselves of Achaia and Asia, games were exhibited with greater elaboration, and yet no one at Rome of
good family had stooped to the theatrical profession during
the 200 years following the triumph of Lucius Mummius,
who first displayed this kind of show in the capital. Besides,
even economy had been consulted, when a permanent edifice
was erected for a theatre, in preference to a structure raised
and fitted up yearly at vast expense. Nor would the magistrates, as hitherto, exhaust their substance, or would the
populace have the same motive for demanding of them the
Greek contests, when once the State undertakes the expenditure. The victories won by orators and poets would furnish a
stimulus to genius, and it could not be a burden for any
judge to bestow his attention on graceful pursuits or on legitimate recreations. It was to mirth rather than to profligacy
that a few nights every five years were devoted, and in these
amid such a blaze of illumination no lawless conduct could
be concealed."

This entertainment, it is true, passed off without any notorious scandal. The enthusiasm too of the populace was not
even slightly kindled, for the pantomimic actors, though permitted to return to the stage, were excluded from the sacred
contests. No one gained the first prize for eloquence, but it
was publicly announced that the emperor was victorious.
Greek dresses, in which most people showed themselves during this festival, had then gone out of fashion.

22. A comet meantime blazed in the sky, which in popular
opinion always portends revolution to kingdoms. So people
began to ask, as if Nero was already dethroned, who was to
be elected. In every one's mouth was the name of Rubellius
Blandus, who inherited through his mother the high nobility

of the Julian family. He was himself attached to the ideas of our ancestors; his manners were austere, his home was one of purity and seclusion, and the more he lived in retirement from fear, the more fame did he acquire. Popular talk was confirmed by an interpretation put with similar credulity on a flash of lightning. While Nero was reclining at dinner in his house named Sublaqueum on the Simbruine lake, the table with the banquet was struck and shattered, and as this happened close to Tibur, from which town Plautus derived his origin on his father's side, people believed him to be the man marked out by divine providence; and he was encouraged by that numerous class, whose eager and often mistaken ambition it is to attach themselves prematurely to some new and hazardous cause. This alarmed Nero, and he wrote a letter to Plautus, bidding "him consider the tranquillity of Rome and withdraw himself from mischievous gossip. He had ancestral possessions in Asia, where he might enjoy his youth safely and quietly." And so thither Plautus retired with his wife Antistia and a few intimate friends.

About the same time an excessive love of luxurious gratification involved Nero in disgrace and danger. He had plunged for a swim into the source of the stream which Quintus Marcius conveyed to Rome, and it was thought that, by thus immersing his person in it, he had polluted the sacred waters and the sanctity of the spot. A fit of illness which followed, convinced people of the divine displeasure.

23. Corbulo meanwhile having demolished Artaxata thought that he ought to avail himself of the recent panic by possessing himself of Tigranocerta, and either, by destroying it, increase the enemy's terror, or, by sparing it, win a name for mercy. Thither he marched his army, with no hostile demonstrations, lest he might cut off all hope of quarter, but still without relaxing his vigilance, knowing, as he did, the fickle temper of the people, who are as treacherous, when they have an opportunity, as they are slow to meet danger. The barbarians, following their individual inclinations, either came to him with entreaties, or quitted their villages and dispersed into their deserts. Some there were who hid themselves in caverns with all that they held dearest. The Roman general accordingly dealt variously with them;

he was merciful to suppliants, swift in pursuit of fugitives, pitiless towards those who had crept into hiding-places, burning them out after filling up the entrances and exits with brushwood and bushes. As he was on his march along the frontier of the Mardi, he was incessantly attacked by that tribe which is trained to guerilla warfare, and defended by mountains against an invader. Corbulo threw the Iberians on them, ravaged their country and punished the enemy's daring at the cost of the blood of the foreigner.

24. Both Corbulo and his army, though suffering no losses in battle, were becoming exhausted by short supplies and hardships, compelled as they were to stave off hunger solely by the flesh of cattle. Added to this was scarcity of water, a burning summer and long marches, all of which were alleviated only by the general's patient endurance. He bore indeed the same or even more burdens than the common soldier. Subsequently, they reached lands under cultivation, and reaped the crops, and of two fortresses in which the Armenians had fled for refuge, one was taken by storm; the other, which repulsed the first attack, was reduced by blockade. Thence the general crossed into the country of the Tauraunites, where he escaped an unforeseen peril. Near his tent, a barbarian of no mean rank was discovered with a dagger, who divulged under torture the whole method of the plot, its contrivance by himself, and his associates. The men who under a show of friendship planned the treachery, were convicted and punished.

Soon afterwards, Corbulo's envoys whom he had sent to Tigranocerta, reported that the city walls were open, and the inhabitants awaiting orders. They also handed him a gift denoting friendship, a golden crown, which he acknowledged in complimentary language. Nothing was done to humiliate the city, that remaining uninjured it might continue to yield a more cheerful obedience.

25. The citadel, however, which had been closed by an intrepid band of youths, was not stormed without a struggle They even ventured on an engagement under the walls, but were driven back within their fortifications and succumbed at last only to our siege-works and to the swords of furious assailants. The success was the easier, as the Parthians were

distracted by a war with the Hyrcanians, who had sent to the Roman emperor, imploring alliance, and pointing to the fact that they were detaining Vologeses as a pledge of amity. When these envoys were on their way home, Corbulo, to save them from being intercepted by the enemy's picquets after their passage of the Euphrates, gave them an escort, and conducted them to the shores of the Red Sea, whence, avoiding Parthian territory, they returned to their native possessions.

26. Corbulo too, as Tiridates was entering the Armenian frontier through Media, sent on Verulanus, his lieutenant-general with the auxiliaries, while he himself followed with the legions by forced marches, and compelled him to retreat to a distance and abandon the idea of war. Having harried with fire and sword all whom he had ascertained to be against us, he began to take possession of Armenia, when Tigranes arrived, whom Nero had selected to assume the sovereignty. Though a Cappadocian noble and grandson of king Archelaus, yet, from having long been a hostage at Rome, he had sunk into servile submissiveness. Nor was he unanimously welcomed, as some still cherished a liking for the Arsacids. Most, however, in their hatred of Parthian arrogance preferred a king given them by Rome. He was supported too with a force of a thousand legionaries, three allied cohorts and two squadrons of cavalry, that he might the more easily secure his new kingdom. Parts of Armenia, according to their respective proximities, were put under the subjection of Pharasmanes, Polemo, Aristobulus, and Antiochus. Corbulo retired into Syria, which province, as being vacant by the death of its governor Ummidius, was intrusted to him.

27. One of the famous cities of Asia, Laodicea, was that same year overthrown by an earthquake, and, without any relief from us, recovered itself by its own resources. In Italy meanwhile the old town of Puteoli obtained from Nero the privileges of a colony with an additional name. A further enrolment of veterans in Tarentum and Antium did but little for those thinly peopled places; for most scattered themselves in the provinces where they had completed their military service. Not being accustomed to tie themselves by mar-

riage and rear children, they left behind them homes without families. For whole legions were no longer transplanted, as in former days, with tribunes and centurions and soldiers of every grade, so as to form a state by their unity and mutual attachment, but strangers to one another from different companies, without a head or any community of sentiment, were suddenly gathered together, as it might be out of any other class of human beings, and became a mere crowd rather than a colony.

28. As at the elections for prætors, now generally under the Senate's control, there was the excitement of a particularly keen competition, the emperor quieted matters by promoting the three supernumerary candidates to legionary commands. He also raised the dignity of the Senate, by deciding that all who appealed from private judges to its house, were to incur the same pecuniary risk as those who referred their cause to the emperor. Hitherto such an appeal had been perfectly open, and free from penalty.

At the close of the year Vibius Secundus, a Roman knight, on the accusation of the Moors, was convicted of extortion, and banished from Italy, contriving through the influence of his brother Vibius Crispus to escape heavier punishment.

29. In the consulship of Cæsonius Pætus and Petronius Turpilianus, a serious disaster was sustained in Britain, where Aulius Didius, the emperor's legate, had merely retained our existing possessions, and his successor Veranius, after having ravaged the Silures in some trifling raids, was prevented by death from extending the war. While he lived, he had a great name for manly independence, though, in his will's final words, he betrayed a flatterer's weakness; for, after heaping adulation on Nero, he added that he should have conquered the province for him, had he lived for the next two years. Now, however, Britain was in the hands of Suetonius Paulinus, who in military knowledge and in popular favour, which allows no one to be without a rival, vied with Corbulo, and aspired to equal the glory of the recovery of Armenia by the subjugation of Rome's enemies. He therefore prepared to attack the island of Mona which had a powerful population and was a refuge for fugitives. He built flat-bottomed vessels to cope with the shallows, and uncer-

tain depths of the sea. Thus the infantry crossed, while the cavalry followed by fording, or, where the water was deep, swam by the side of their horses.

30. On the shore stood the opposing army with its dense array of armed warriors, while between the ranks dashed women, in black attire like the Furies, with hair dishevelled, waving brands. All around, the Druids, lifting up their hands to heaven, and pouring forth dreadful imprecations, scared our soldiers by the unfamiliar sight, so that, as if their limbs were paralysed, they stood motionless, and exposed to wounds. Then urged by their general's appeals and mutual encouragements not to quail before a troop of frenzied women, they bore the standards onwards, smote down all resistance, and wrapped the foe in the flames of his own brands. A force was next set over the conquered, and their groves, devoted to inhuman superstitions, were destroyed. They deemed it indeed a duty to cover their altars with the blood of captives and to consult their deities through human entrails.

31. Suetonius while thus occupied received tidings of the sudden revolt of the province. Prasutagus, king of the Iceni, famed for his long prosperity, had made the emperor his heir along with his two daughters, under the impression that this token of submission would put his kingdom and his house out of the reach of wrong. But the reverse was the result, so much so that his kingdom was plundered by centurions, his house by slaves, as if they were the spoils of war. First, his wife Boudicea was scourged, and his daughters outraged. All the chief men of the Iceni, as if Rome had received the whole country as a gift, were stript of their ancestral possessions, and the king's relatives were made slaves. Roused by these insults and the dread of worse, reduced as they now were into the condition of a province, they flew to arms and stirred to revolt the Trinobantes and others who, not yet cowed by slavery, had agreed in secret conspiracy to reclaim their freedom. It was against the veterans that their hatred was most intense. For these new settlers in the colony of Camulodunum drove people out of their houses, ejected them from their farms, called them captives and slaves, and the lawlessness of the veterans was encouraged by the soldiers,

who lived a similar life and hoped for similar licence. A temple also erected to the Divine Claudius was ever before their eyes, a citadel, as it seemed, of perpetual tyranny. Men chosen as priests had to squander their whole fortunes under the pretence of a religious ceremonial. It appeared too no difficult matter to destroy the colony, undefended as it was by fortifications, a precaution neglected by our generals, while they thought more of what was agreeable than of what was expedient.

32. Meanwhile, without any evident cause, the statue of Victory at Camulodunum fell prostrate and turned its back to the enemy, as though it fled before them. Women excited to frenzy prophesied impending destruction; ravings in a strange tongue, it was said, were heard in their Senate-house; their theatre resounded with wailings, and in the estuary of the Tamesa had been seen the appearance of an overthrown town; even the ocean had worn the aspect of blood, and, when the tide ebbed, there had been left the likenesses of human forms, marvels interpreted by the Britons, as hopeful, by the veterans, as alarming. But as Suetonius was far away, they implored aid from the procurator, Catus Decianus. All he did was to send two hundred men, and no more, without regular arms, and there was in the place but a small military force. Trusting to the protection of the temple, hindered too by secret accomplices in the revolt, who embarrassed their plans, they had constructed neither fosse nor rampart; nor had they removed their old men and women, leaving their youth alone to face the foe. Surprised, as it were, in the midst of peace, they were surrounded by an immense host of the barbarians. All else was plundered or fired in the onslaught; the temple where the soldiers had assembled, was stormed after a two days' siege. The victorious enemy met Petilius Cerialis, commander of the ninth legion, as he was coming to the rescue, routed his troops, and destroyed all his infantry. Cerialis escaped with some cavalry into the camp, and was saved by its fortifications. Alarmed by this disaster and by the fury of the province which he had goaded into war by his rapacity, the procurator Catus crossed over into Gaul.

33. Suetonius, however, with wonderful resolution,

marched amidst a hostile population to Londinium, which, though undistinguished by the name of a colony, was much frequented by a number of merchants and trading vessels. Uncertain whether he should choose it as a seat of war, as he looked round on his scanty force of soldiers, and remembered with what a serious warning the rashness of Petilius had been punished, he resolved to save the province at the cost of a single town. Nor did the tears and weeping of the people, as they implored his aid, deter him from giving the signal of departure and receiving into his army all who would go with him. Those who were chained to the spot by the weakness of their sex, or the infirmity of age, or the attractions of the place, were cut off by the enemy. Like ruin fell on the town of Verulamium, for the barbarians, who delighted in plunder and were indifferent to all else, passed by the fortresses with military garrisons, and attacked whatever offered most wealth to the spoiler, and was unsafe for defence. About seventy thousand citizens and allies, it appeared, fell in the places which I have mentioned. For it was not on making prisoners and selling them, or on any of the barter of war, that the enemy was bent, but on slaughter, on the gibbet, the fire and the cross, like men soon about to pay the penalty, and meanwhile snatching at instant vengeance.

34. Suetonius had the fourteenth legion with the veterans of the twentieth, and auxiliaries from the neighbourhood, to the number of about ten thousand armed men, when he prepared to break off delay and fight a battle. He chose a position approached by a narrow defile, closed in at the rear by a forest, having first ascertained that there was not a soldier of the enemy except in his front, where an open plain extended without any danger from ambuscades. His legions were in close array; round them, the light-armed troops, and the cavalry in dense array on the wings. On the other side, the army of the Britons, with its masses of infantry and cavalry, was confidently exulting, a vaster host than ever had assembled, and so fierce in spirit that they actually brought with them, to witness the victory, their wives riding in waggons, which they had placed on the extreme border of the plain.

35. Boudicea, with her daughters before her in a chariot, went up to tribe after tribe, protesting that it was indeed usual for Britons to fight under the leadership of women. "But now," she said, "it is not as a woman descended from noble ancestry, but as one of the people that I am avenging lost freedom, my scourged body, the outraged chastity of my daughters. Roman lust has gone so far that not our very persons, nor even age or virginity, are left unpolluted. But heaven is on the side of a righteous vengeance; a legion which dared to fight has perished; the rest are hiding themselves in their camp, or are thinking anxiously of flight. They will not sustain even the din and the shout of so many thousands, much less our charge and our blows. If you weigh well the strength of the armies, and the causes of the war, you will see that in this battle you must conquer or die. This is a woman's resolve; as for men, they may live and be slaves."

36. Nor was Suetonius silent at such a crisis. Though he confided in the valour of his men, he yet mingled encouragements and entreaties to disdain the clamours and empty threats of the barbarians. "There," he said, "you see more women than warriors. Unwarlike, unarmed, they will give way the moment they have recognised that sword and that courage of their conquerors, which have so often routed them. Even among many legions, it is a few who really decide the battle, and it will enhance their glory that a small force should earn the renown of an entire army. Only close up the ranks, and having discharged your javelins, then with shields and swords continue the work of bloodshed and destruction, without a thought of plunder. When once the victory has been won, everything will be in your power."

Such was the enthusiasm which followed the general's address, and so promptly did the veteran soldiery, with their long experience of battles, prepare for the hurling of the javelins, that it was with confidence in the result that Suetonius gave the signal of battle.

37. At first, the legion kept its position, clinging to the narrow defile as a defence; when they had exhausted their missiles, which they discharged with unerring aim on the closely approaching foe, they rushed out in a wedge-like col-

umn. Similar was the onset of the auxiliaries, while the cavalry with extended lances broke through all who offered a
strong resistance. The rest turned their back in flight, and
flight proved difficult, because the surrounding waggons had
blocked retreat. Our soldiers spared not to slay even the
women, while the very beasts of burden, transfixed by the
missiles, swelled the piles of bodies. Great glory, equal to
that of our old victories, was won on that day. Some indeed
say that there fell little less than eighty thousand of the
Britons, with a loss to our soldiers of about four hundred,
and only as many wounded. Boudicea put an end to her life
by poison. Pœnius Postumus too, camp-prefect of the second
legion, when he knew of the success of the men of the fourteenth and twentieth, feeling that he had cheated his legion
out of like glory, and had contrary to all military usage disregarded the general's orders, threw himself on his sword.

38. The whole army was then brought together and kept
under canvas to finish the remainder of the war. The emperor strengthened the forces by sending from Germany two
thousand legionaries, eight cohorts of auxiliaries, and a thousand cavalry. On their arrival the men of the ninth had their
number made up with legionary soldiers. The allied infantry
and cavalry were placed in new winter quarters, and whatever tribes still wavered or were hostile were ravaged with
fire and sword. Nothing however distressed the enemy so
much as famine, for they had been careless about sowing
corn, people of every age having gone to the war, while they
reckoned on our supplies as their own. Nations, too, so high-
spirited inclined the more slowly to peace, because Julius
Classicanus, who had been sent as successor to Catus and
was at variance with Suetonius, let private animosities interfere with the public interest, and had spread an idea that
they ought to wait for a new governor who, having neither
the anger of an enemy nor the pride of a conqueror, would
deal mercifully with those who had surrendered. At the same
time he stated in a despatch to Rome that no cessation of
fighting must be expected, unless Suetonius were superseded,
attributing that general's disasters to perverseness and his
successes to good luck.

39. Accordingly one of the imperial freedmen, Polyclitus,

was sent to survey the state of Britain, Nero having great hopes that his influence would be able not only to establish a good understanding between the governor and the procurator, but also to pacify the rebellious spirit of the barbarians. And Polyclitus, who with his enormous suite had been a burden to Italy and Gaul, failed not, as soon as he had crossed the ocean, to make his progresses a terror even to our soldiers. But to the enemy he was a laughing-stock, for they still retained some of the fire of liberty, knowing nothing yet of the power of freedmen, and so they marvelled to see a general and an army who had finished such a war cringing to slaves. Everything, however, was softened down for the emperor's ears, and Suetonius was retained in the government; but as he subsequently lost a few vessels on the shore with the crews, he was ordered, as though the war continued, to hand over his army to Petronius Turpilianus, who had just resigned his consulship. Petronius neither challenged the enemy nor was himself molested, and veiled this tame inaction under the honourable name of peace.

40. That same year two remarkable crimes were committed at Rome, one by a senator, the other by the daring of a slave. Domitius Balbus, an ex-prætor, from his prolonged old age, his childlessness and his wealth, was exposed to many a plot. His kinsman, Valerius Fabianus, who was marked out for a career of promotion, forged a will in his name with Vinicius Rufinus and Terentius Lentinus, Roman knights, for his accomplices. These men had associated with them Antonius Primus and Asinius Marcellus. Antonius was a man of ready audacity; Marcellus had the glory of being the great-grandson of Asinius Pollio, and bore a character far from contemptible, except that he thought poverty the greatest of all evils. So Fabianus, with the persons whom I have named and some others less distinguished, executed the will. The crime was proved against them before the Senate, and Fabianus and Antonius with Rufinus and Terentius were condemned under the Cornelian law. Marcellus was saved from punishment rather than from disgrace by the memory of his ancestors and the intercessions of the emperor.

41. That same day was fatal also to Pompeius Ælianus, a

young ex-quæstor, suspected of complicity in the villanies of Fabianus. He was outlawed from Italy, and from Spain, where he was born. Valerius Pontius suffered the same degradation for having indicted the defendants before the prætor to save them from being prosecuted in the court of the city-prefect, purposing meanwhile to defeat justice on some legal pretext and subsequently by collusion. A clause was added to the Senate's decree, that whoever bought or sold such a service was to be just as liable to punishment as if he had been publicly convicted of false accusation.

42. Soon afterwards one of his own slaves murdered the city-prefect, Pedanius Secundus, either because he had been refused his freedom, for which he had made a bargain, or in the jealousy of a love in which he could not brook his master's rivalry. Ancient custom required that the whole slave-establishment which had dwelt under the same roof should be dragged to execution, when a sudden gathering of the populace, which was for saving so many innocent lives, brought matters to actual insurrection. Even in the Senate there was a strong feeling on the part of those who shrank from extreme rigour, though the majority were opposed to any innovation. Of these, Caius Cassius, in giving his vote, argued to the following effect:—

43. "Often have I been present, Senators, in this assembly when new decrees were demanded from us contrary to the customs and laws of our ancestors, and I have refrained from opposition, not because I doubted but that in all matters the arrangements of the past were better and fairer and that all changes were for the worse, but that I might not seem to be exalting my own profession out of an excessive partiality for ancient precedent. At the same time I thought that any influence I possess ought not to be destroyed by incessant protests, wishing that it might remain unimpaired, should the State ever need my counsels. To-day this has come to pass, since an ex-consul has been murdered in his house by the treachery of slaves, which not one hindered or divulged, though the Senate's decree, which threatens the entire slave-establishment with execution, has been till now unshaken. Vote impunity, in heaven's name, and then who will be protected by his rank, when the prefecture of the capital has

been of no avail to its holder? Who will be kept safe by the number of his slaves when four hundred have not protected Pedanius Secundus? Which of us will be rescued by his domestics, who, even with the dread of punishment before them, regard not our dangers? Was the murderer, as some do not blush to pretend, avenging his wrongs because he had bargained about money from his father or because a family-slave was taken from him? Let us actually decide that the master was justly slain.

44. "Is it your pleasure to search for arguments in a matter already weighed in the deliberations of wiser men than ourselves? Even if we had now for the first time to come to a decision, do you believe that a slave took courage to murder his master without letting fall a threatening word or uttering a rash syllable? Granted that he concealed his purpose, that he procured his weapon without his fellows' knowledge. Could he pass the night-guard, could he open the doors of the chamber, carry in a light, and accomplish the murder, while all were in ignorance? There are many preliminaries to guilt; if these are divulged by slaves, we may live singly amid numbers, safe among a trembling throng; lastly, if we must perish, it will be with vengeance on the guilty. Our ancestors always suspected the temper of their slaves, even when they were born on the same estates, or in the same houses with themselves and thus inherited from their birth an affection for their masters. But now that we have in our households nations with different customs to our own, with a foreign worship or none at all, it is only by terror you can hold in such a motley rabble. But, it will be said, the innocent will perish. Well, even in a beaten army when every tenth man is felled by the club, the lot falls also on the brave. There is some injustice in every great precedent, which, though injurious to individuals, has its compensation in the public advantage."

45. No one indeed dared singly to oppose the opinion of Cassius, but clamorous voices rose in reply from all who pitied the number, age, or sex, as well as the undoubted innocence of the great majority. Still, the party which voted for their execution prevailed. But the sentence could not be obeyed in the face of a dense and threatening mob, with

stones and firebrands. Then the emperor reprimanded the people by edict, and lined with a force of soldiers the entire route by which the condemned had to be dragged to execution. Cingonius Varro had proposed that even all the freedmen under the same roof should be transported from Italy. This the emperor forbade, as he did not wish an ancient custom, which mercy had not relaxed, to be strained with cruel rigour.

46. During the same consulship, Tarquitius Priscus was convicted of extortion on the prosecution of the Bithynians, to the great joy of the senators, who remembered that he had impeached Statilius, his own proconsul. An assessment was made of Gaul by Quintus Volusius, Sextius Africanus, and Trebellius Maximus. There was a rivalry, on the score of rank, between Volusius and Africanus. While they both disdained Trebellius, they raised him above themselves.

47. In that year died Memmius Regulus, who from his solid worth and consistency was as distinguished as it is possible to be under the shadow of an emperor's grandeur, so much so, in fact, that Nero when he was ill, with flatterers round him, who said that if aught befell him in the course of destiny, there must be an end of the empire, replied that the State had a resource, and on their asking where it was specially to be found, he added, "in Memmius Regulus." Yet Regulus lived after this, protected by his retiring habits, and by the fact that he was a man of newly-risen family and of wealth which did not provoke envy. Nero, the same year, established a gymnasium, where oil was furnished to knights and senators after the lax fashion of the Greeks.

48. In the consulship of Publius Marius and Lucius Asinius, Antistius, the prætor, whose lawless behaviour as tribune of the people I have mentioned, composed some libellous verses on the emperor, which he openly recited at a large gathering, when he was dining at the house of Ostorius Scapula. He was upon this impeached of high treason by Cossutianus Capito, who had lately been restored to a senator's rank on the intercession of his father-in-law, Tigellinus. This was the first occasion on which the law of treason was revived, and men thought that it was not so much the ruin of Antistius which was aimed at, as the glory of the emperor,

whose veto as tribune might save from death one whom the Senate had condemned. Though Ostorius had stated that he had heard nothing as evidence, the adverse witnesses were believed, and Junius Marullus, consul-elect, proposed that the accused should be deprived of his prætorship, and be put to death in the ancient manner. The rest assented, and then Pætus Thrasea, after much eulogy of Cæsar, and most bitter censure of Antistius, argued that it was not what a guilty prisoner might deserve to suffer, which ought to be decreed against him, under so excellent a prince, and by a Senate bound by no compulsion. "The executioner and the halter," he said, "we have long ago abolished; still, there are punishments ordained by the laws, which prescribe penalties, without judicial cruelty and disgrace to our age. Rather send him to some island, after confiscating his property; there, the longer he drags on his guilty life, the more wretched will he be personally, and the more conspicuous as an example of public clemency."

49. Thrasea's freespokenness broke through the servility of the other senators. As soon as the consul allowed a division, they voted with him, with but few execeptions. Among these, the most enthusiastic in his flattery was Aulus Vitellius, who attacked all the best men with abuse, and was silent when they replied, the usual way of a cowardly temper. The consuls, however, did not dare to ratify the Senate's vote, and simply communicated their unanimous resolution to the emperor. Hesitating for a while between shame and rage, he at last wrote to them in reply "that Antistius, without having been provoked by any wrong, had uttered outrageous insults against the sovereign; that a demand for punishment had been submitted to the Senate, and that it was right that a penalty should be decreed proportioned to the offence; that for himself, inasmuch as he would have opposed severity in the sentence, he would not be an obstacle to leniency. They might determine as they pleased, and they had free liberty to acquit."

This and more to the same effect having been read out, clearly showing his displeasure, the consuls did not for that reason alter the terms of the motion, nor did Thrasea withdraw his proposal, or the Senate reject what it had once approved. Some were afraid of seeming to expose the emperor to odium; the majority felt safe in numbers, while Thrasea was supported by his usual firmness of spirit, and a determination not to let his fame perish.

50. A similar accusation caused the downfall of Fabricius Veiento. He had composed many libels on senators and pontiffs in a work to which he gave the title of "Codicils." Talius Geminus, the prosecutor, further stated that he had habitually trafficked in the emperor's favours and in the right of promotion. This was Nero's reason for himself undertaking the trial, and having convicted Veiento, he banished him from Italy, and ordered the burning of his books, which, while it was dangerous to procure them, were anxiously sought and much read. Soon full freedom for their possession caused their oblivion.

51. But while the miseries of the State were daily growing worse, its supports were becoming weaker. Burrus died, whether from illness or from poison was a question. It was supposed to be illness from the fact that from the gradual swelling of his throat inwardly and the closing up of the passage he ceased to breathe. Many positively asserted that by Nero's order his throat was smeared with some poisonous drug under the pretence of the application of a remedy, and that Burrus, who saw through the crime, when the emperor paid him a visit, recoiled with horror from his gaze, and merely replied to his question, "I indeed am well." Rome felt for him a deep and lasting regret, because of the remembrance of his worth, because too of the merely passive virtue of one of his successors and the very flagrant iniquities of the other. For the emperor had appointed two men to the command of the prætorian cohorts, Fænius Rufus, for a vulgar popularity, which he owed to his administration of the corn-supplies without profit to himself; and Sofonius Tigellinus, whose inveterate shamelessness and infamy were an attraction to him. As might have been expected from their known characters, Tigellinus had the greater influence with the prince, and was the associate of his most secret profligacy, while Rufus enjoyed the favour of the people and of the soldiers, and this, he found, prejudiced him with Nero.

52. The death of Burrus was a blow to Seneca's power, for

virtue had not the same strength when one of its companions, so to say, was removed, and Nero too began to lean on worse advisers. They assailed Seneca with various charges, representing that he continued to increase a wealth which was already so vast as to be beyond the scale of a subject, and was drawing to himself the attachment of the citizens, while in the picturesqueness of his gardens and the magnificence of his country houses he almost surpassed the emperor. They further alleged against him that he claimed for himself alone the honours of eloquence, and composed poetry more assiduously, as soon as a passion for it had seized on Nero. "Openly inimical to the prince's amusements, he disparaged his ability in driving horses, and ridiculed his voice whenever he sang. When was there to be an end of nothing being publicly admired but what Seneca was thought to have originated? Surely Nero's boyhood was over, and he was all but in the prime of youthful manhood. He ought to shake off a tutor, furnished as he was with sufficiently noble instructors in his own ancestors."

53. Seneca, meanwhile, aware of these slanders, which were revealed to him by those who had some respect for merit, coupled with the fact that the emperor more and more shunned his intimacy, besought the opportunity of an interview. This was granted, and he spoke as follows:—

"It is fourteen years ago, Cæsar, that I was first associated with your prospects, and eight years since you have been emperor. In the interval, you have heaped on me such honours and riches that nothing is wanting to my happiness but a right use of it. I will refer to great examples taken not from my own but from your position. Your great-grandfather Augustus granted to Marcus Agrippa the calm repose of Mitylene, to Caius Mæcenas what was nearly equivalent to a foreign retreat in the capital itself. One of these men shared his wars; the other struggled with many laborious duties at Rome; both received awards which were indeed splendid, but only proportioned to their great merits. For myself, what other recompense had I for your munificence, than a culture nursed, so to speak, in the shade of retirement, and to which a glory attaches itself, because I thus seem to have helped on the early training of your youth, an ample reward for the service.

"You on the other hand have surrounded me with vast influence and boundless wealth, so that I often think within myself, Am I, who am but of an equestrian and provincial family, numbered among the chief men of Rome? Among nobles who can show a long succession of glories, has my new name become famous? Where is the mind once content with a humble lot? Is this the man who is building up his garden terraces, who paces grandly through these suburban parks, and revels in the affluence of such broad lands and such widely-spread investments? Only one apology occurs to me, that it would not have been right in me to have thwarted your bounty.

54. "And yet we have both filled up our respective measures, you in giving as much as a prince can bestow on a friend, and I in receiving as much as a friend can receive from a prince. All else only fosters envy, which, like all things human, sinks powerless beneath your greatness, though on me it weighs heavily. To me relief is a necessity. Just as I should implore support if exhausted by warfare or travel, so in this journey of life, old as I am and unequal even to the lightest cares, since I cannot any longer bear the burden of my wealth, I crave assistance. Order my property to be managed by your agents and to be included in your estate. Still I shall not sink myself into poverty, but having surrendered the splendours which dazzle me, I will henceforth again devote to my mind all the leisure and attention now reserved for my gardens and country houses. You have yet before you a vigorous prime, and that on which for so many years your eyes were fixed, supreme power. We, your older friends, can answer for our quiet behaviour. It will likewise redound to your honour that you have raised to the highest places men who could also bear moderate fortune."

55. Nero's reply was substantially this:—"My being able to meet your elaborate speech with an instant rejoinder is, I consider, primarily your gift, for you taught me how to express myself not only after reflection but at a moment's notice. My great-grandfather Augustus allowed Agrippa and Mæcenas to enjoy rest after their labours, but he did it at an

age carrying with it an authority sufficient to justify any
boon, of any sort, he might have bestowed. But neither of
them did he strip of the rewards he had given. It was by
war and its perils they had earned them; for in these the
youth of Augustus was spent. And if I had passed my years
in arms, your sword and right hand would not have failed
me. But, as my actual condition required, you watched over
my boyhood, then over my youth, with wisdom, counsel, and
advice. And indeed your gifts to me will, as long as life holds
out, be lasting possessions; those which you owe to me, your
parks, investments, your country houses, are liable to accidents. Though they seem much, many far inferior to you in
merit have obtained more. I am ashamed to quote the names
of freedmen who parade a greater wealth. Hence I actually
blush to think that, standing as you do first in my affections,
you do not as yet surpass all in fortune.

56. "Yours too is a still vigorous manhood, quite equal to
the labours of business and to the fruit of those labours;
and, as for myself, I am but treading the threshold of empire. But perhaps you count yourself inferior to Vitellius,
thrice a consul, and me to Claudius. Such wealth as long
thrift has procured for Volusius, my bounty, you think, cannot fully make up to you. Why not rather, if the frailty of
my youth goes in any respect astray, call me back and guide
yet more zealously with your help the manhood which you
have instructed? It will not be your moderation, if you restore me your wealth, not your love of quiet, if you forsake
your emperor, but my avarice, the fear of my cruelty, which
will be in all men's mouths. Even if your self-control were
praised to the utmost, still it would not be seemly in a wise
man to get glory for himself in the very act of bringing
disgrace on his friend."

To these words the emperor added embraces and kisses;
for he was formed by nature and trained by habit to veil his
hatred under delusive flattery. Seneca thanked him, the usual
end of an interview with a despot. But he entirely altered
the practices of his former greatness; he kept the crowds
of his visitors at a distance, avoided trains of followers,
seldom appeared in Rome, as though weak health or philosophical studies detained him at home.

57. When Seneca had fallen, it was easy to shake the position of Fænius Rufus by making Agrippina's friendship a charge against him. Tigellinus, who was daily becoming more powerful and who thought that the wicked schemings which alone gave him strength, would be better liked if he could secure the emperor's complicity in guilt, dived into Nero's most secret apprehensions, and, as soon as he had ascertained that Plautus and Sulla were the men he most dreaded, Plautus having been lately sent away to Asia, Sulla to Gallia Narbonensis, he spoke much of their noble rank and of their respective proximity to the armies of the East and of Germany. "I have no eye," he said, "like Burrus, to two conflicting aims, but only to Nero's safety, which is at least secured against treachery in Rome by my presence. As for distant commotions, how can they be checked? Gaul is roused at the name of the great dictator, and I distrust no less the nations of Asia, because of the renown of such a grandfather as Drusus. Sulla is poor, and hence comes his surpassing audacity; he shams apathy, while he is seeking an opening for his reckless ambition. Plautus again, with his great wealth, does not so much as affect a love of repose, but he flaunts before us his imitations of the old Romans, and assumes the self-consciousness of the Stoics along with a philosophy, which makes men restless, and eager for a busy life."

There was not a moment's delay. Sulla, six days afterwards, was murdered by assassins brought over to Massilia, while he was reclining at the dinner-table, before he feared or heard of his danger. The head was taken to Rome, and Nero scoffed at its premature grey hairs as if they were a disfigurement.

58. It was less of a secret that there was a design to murder Plautus, as his life was dear to many. The distance too by land and sea, and the interval of time, had given rise to rumours, and the popular story was that he had tampered with Corbulo, who was then at the head of great armies, and would be a special mark for danger, if illustrious and innocent men were to be destroyed. Again Asia, it was said, from its partiality for the young man, had taken up arms, and the soldiers sent to do the crime, not being suf-

ficient in number or decided in purpose, and, finding themselves unable to execute their orders, had gone over to the
new cause. These absurdities, like all popular gossip, gathered strength from the idle leisure of a credulous society.

As it was, one of Plautus's freedmen, thanks to swift winds,
arrived before the centurion and brought him a message
from his father-in-law, Lucius Antistius. "He was to avoid
the obvious refuge of a coward's death, and in the pity felt
for a noble name he would soon find good men to help him,
and daring spirits would rally round him. Meantime no resource was to be rejected. If he did but repel sixty soldiers
(this was the number on the way), while tidings were being
carried back to Nero, while another force was on its march,
many events would follow which would ripen into war. Finally, by this plan he either secured safety, or he would suffer nothing worse by daring than by cowardice."

59. But all this had no effect on Plautus. Either he saw
no resource before him, an unarmed exile as he was, or he
was weary of an uncertain hope, or was swayed by his love
of his wife and of his children, to whom he thought the emperor, if harassed by no anxiety, would be more merciful.
Some say that another message came to him from his father-
in-law, representing that no dreadful peril hung over him,
and that two teachers of philosophy, Cœranus from Greece
and Musonius from Etruria, advised him to await death with
firmness rather than lead a precarious and anxious life. At
all events, he was surprised at midday, when stripped for
exercise. In that state the centurion slew him in the presence
of Pelago, an eunuch, whom Nero had set over the centurion
and his company, like a despot's minister over his satellites.

The head of the murdered man was brought to Rome. At
its sight the emperor exclaimed (I give his very words),
"Why would you have been a Nero?" Then casting off all
fear he prepared to hurry on his marriage with Poppæa,
hitherto deferred because of such alarms as I have described,
and to divorce his wife Octavia, notwithstanding her virtuous life, because her father's name and the people's affection for her made her an offence to him. He wrote, however, a letter to the Senate, confessing nothing about the
murders of Sulla and Plautus, but merely hinting that both

had a restless temper, and that he gave the most anxious thought to the safety of the State. On this pretext a thanksgiving was decreed, and also the expulsion from the Senate of Sulla and Plautus, more grievous, however, as a farce than as an actual calamity.

60. Nero, on receiving this decree of the Senate and seeing that every piece of his wickedness was regarded as a conspicuous merit, drove Octavia from him, alleging that she was barren, and then married Poppæa. The woman who had long been Nero's mistress and ruled him first as a paramour, then as her husband, instigated one of Octavia's servants to accuse her of an intrigue with a slave. The man fixed on as the guilty lover was one by name Eucærus, an Alexandrine by birth, skilled in singing to the flute. As a consequence, her slave-girls were examined under torture, and though some were forced by the intensity of agony into admitting falsehoods, most of them persisted in upholding the virtue of their mistress. One of them said, in answer to the furious menaces of Tigellinus, that Octavia's person was purer than his mouth. Octavia, however, was dismissed under the form of an ordinary divorce, and received possession of the house of Burrus and of the estates of Plautus, an ill-starred gift. She was soon afterwards banished to Campania under military surveillance. This led to incessant and outspoken remonstrances among the common people, whc have less discretion and are exposed to fewer dangers than others from the insignificance of their position. Upon this Nero, though he did not repent of his outrage, restored to Octavia her position as wife.

61. Then people in their joy went up to the Capitol and, at last, gave thanks to the gods. They threw down the statues of Poppæa; they bore on their shoulders the images of Octavia, covering them with flowers, and setting them up in the forum and in the temples. There was even a burst of applause for the emperor, men hailing the recalled Octavia. And now they were pouring into the Palace in crowds, with loud shoutings, when some companies of soldiers rushed out and dispersed the tumultuous throng with blows, and at the point of the sword. Whatever changes had been made in the riot, were reversed, and Poppæa's honours restored.

Ever relentless in her hatred, she was now enraged by the
fear that either the violence of the mob would burst on her
with yet fiercer fury, or that Nero would be swayed by the
popular bias, and so, flinging herself at his knees, she exclaimed that she was not in the position of a rival fighting
for marriage, though that was dearer to her than life, but
that her very life was brought into jeopardy by the dependants and slaves of Octavia, who had assumed the name of
the people, and dared in peace what could hardly happen in
war. "Those arms," she said, "have been taken up against
the emperor; a leader only is wanting, and he will easily be
found in a commotion. Only let her whose mere beck, though
she is far away, stirs up tumult, quit Campania, and make
her way in person to Rome. And, again, what is my sin?
What offence have I caused any one? Is it that I am about
to give to the house of the Cæsars a lawful heir? Do the
people of Rome prefer that the offspring of an Egyptian
flute-player should be raised to the imperial throne? In a
word, if it be expedient, Nero should of his own choice
rather than on compulsion send for her who ruled him, or
else secure his safety by a righteous vengeance. The beginning of a commotion has often been quieted by slight precautions; but if people once despair of Octavia being Nero's
wife, they will soon find her a husband."

62. Her various arguments, tending both to frighten and
to enrage, at once alarmed and incensed her listener. But
the suspicion about the slave was of little weight, and the
torture of the slave-girls exposed its absurdity. Consequently
it was decided to procure a confession from some one on
whom could also be fastened a charge of revolutionary designs. Fittest for this seemed the perpetrator of the mother's
murder, Anicetus, commander, as I have already mentioned,
of the fleet at Misenum, who got but scant gratitude after
that atrocious deed, and subsequently all the more vehement
hatred, inasmuch as men look on their instruments in crime
as a sort of standing reproach to them.

The emperor accordingly sent for Anicetus, and reminded
him of his former service. "He alone," he said, "had come
to the rescue of the prince's life against a plotting mother.
Close at hand was a chance of winning no less gratitude by

ridding him of a malignant wife. No violence or weapons were needed; only let him confess to an intrigue with Octavia." Nero then promised him a secret but ample immediate recompense, and some delightful retreat, while he threatened him with death in case of refusal. Anicetus, with the moral insensibility of his nature and a promptness inspired by previous atrocities, invented even more than was required of him, and confessed before friends whom the prince had called in, as a sort of judicial council. He was then banished to Sardinia, where he endured exile without poverty, and died a natural death.

63. Nero meanwhile declared by edict that the prefect had been corrupted into a design of gaining over the fleet, and added, in forgetfulness of his late charge of barrenness against Octavia, that, conscious of her profligacies, she had procured abortion, a fact he had himself ascertained. Then he confined her in the island of Pandataria. No exile ever filled the eyes of beholders with tears of greater compassion. Some still remembered Agrippina, banished by Tiberius, and the yet fresher memory of Julia, whom Claudius exiled, was present to men's thoughts. But they had life's prime for their stay; they had seen some happiness, and the horror of the moment was alleviated by recollections of a better lot in the past. For Octavia, from the first, her marriage-day was a kind of funeral, brought, as she was, into a house where she had nothing but scenes of mourning, her father and, an instant afterwards, her brother, having been snatched from her by poison; then, a slave-girl raised above the mistress; Poppæa married only to insure a wife's ruin, and, to end all, an accusation more horrible than any death.

64. And now the girl, in her twentieth year, with centurions and soldiers around her, already removed from among the living by the forecast of doom, still could not reconcile herself to death. After an interval of a few days, she received an order that she was to die, although she protested that she was now a widow and only a sister, and appealed to their common ancestors, the Germanici, and finally to the name of Agrippina, during whose life she had endured a marriage, which was miserable enough indeed, but not fatal. She was then tightly bound with cords, and the veins

of every limb were opened; but as her blood was congealed by terror and flowed too slowly, she was killed outright by the steam of an intensely hot bath. To this was added the yet more appalling horror of Poppæa beholding the severed head which was conveyed to Rome.

And for all this offerings were voted to the temples. I record the fact with a special object. Whoever would study the calamities of that period in my pages or those of other authors, is to take it for granted that as often as the emperor directed banishments or executions, so often was there a thanksgiving to the gods, and what formerly commemorated some prosperous event, was then a token of public disaster. Still, if any decree of the Senate was marked by some new flattery, or by the lowest servility, I shall not pass it over in silence.

65. That same year Nero was believed to have destroyed by poison two of his most powerful freedmen, Doryphorus, on the pretext of his having opposed the marriage with Poppæa, Pallas for still keeping his boundless wealth by a prolonged old age. Romanus had accused Seneca in stealthy calumnies, of having been an accomplice of Caius Piso, but he was himself crushed more effectually by Seneca on the same charge. This alarmed Piso, and gave rise to a huge fabric of unsuccessful conspiracies against Nero.

BOOK XV

1. Meanwhile, the Parthian king, Vologeses, when he heard of Corbulo's achievements and of a foreign prince, Tigranes, having been set over Armenia, though he longed at the same time to avenge the majesty of the Arsacids, which had been insulted by the expulsion of his brother Tiridates, was, on the other hand, drawn to different thoughts as he reflected on the greatness of Rome, and felt reverence for a hitherto unbroken treaty. Naturally irresolute, he was now hampered by a revolt of the Hyrcanians, a powerful tribe, and by several wars arising out of it. Suddenly, as he was wavering, fresh and further tidings of disgrace goaded him to action. Tigranes, quitting Armenia, had ravaged the Adiabeni, a people on its border, too extensively and continuously for mere plundering raids. The chief men of the tribes were indignant at having fallen into such contempt that they were victims to the inroads, not indeed of a Roman general, but of a daring hostage, who for so many years had been numbered among slaves. Their anger was inflamed by Monobazus, who ruled the Adiabeni, and repeatedly asked what protection he was to seek and from what quarter—"Already," he said, "Armenia has been given up, and its borders are being wrested from us, and unless the Parthians help us, we shall find that subjection to Rome is lighter for those who surrender than for the conquered." Tiridates too, exile as he was from his kingdom, by his silence or very moderate complaints made the deeper impression. "It is not," he urged, "by weak inaction that great empires are held together; there must be the struggle of brave men in arms; might is right with those who are at the summit of power. And though it is the glory of a private house to keep its

own, it is the glory of a king to fight for the possessions of others."

2. Moved by these considerations Vologeses called a council, placed Tiridates by his side, and began to speak as follows:—

"This man before you, born from the same father as myself, having waived in my favour, on the ground of age, the highest title of all, was established by me in the possession of Armenia, which is accounted the third grade of power. As for Media, Pacorus was already in possession of it. And I thought to myself that I had duly arranged our family and home so as to guard against the old feuds and rivalries of brothers. The Romans thwart me, and though they have never with success to themselves disturbed the peace between us, they are now again breaking it to their own destruction. I will not attempt to deny one thing. It was by just dealing rather than by bloodshed, by having a good cause rather than by arms, that I had wished to retain what my ancestors had won. If I have sinned through irresolution, my valour shall make amends for it. Assuredly your strength and renown are at their height, and you have in addition the repute of obedience, which the greatest of mortals must not despise, and which the gods highly esteem."

As he spoke, he encircled Tiridates' brow with a diadem, and to Moneses, a noble, he entrusted a highly efficient body of cavalry, which was the king's customary escort, giving him also some auxiliaries from the Adiabeni, and orders that Tigranes was to be driven out of Armenia. He would himself abandon his feud with the Hyrcanians, and raise his own national force in all its warlike strength by way of menace to the Roman provinces.

3. When Corbulo had heard all this from messengers he could trust, he sent two legions under Verulanus Severus and Vettius Bolanus to the support of Tigranes, with secret instructions that they were to conduct all their operations with deliberation rather than despatch, as he would prefer to sustain rather than to make war. And indeed he had written to the emperor that a general was wanted specially for the defence of Armenia, and that Syria, threatened as it was by Vologeses, was in yet more imminent peril. Mean-

while he posted his remaining legions on the bank of the Euphrates, armed a hastily collected force of provincials, and occupied with troops the enemy's approaches. And as the country was deficient in water, he established forts to guard the wells, and concealed some of the streams with heaps of sand.

4. While Corbulo was thus preparing for the defence of Syria, Moneses rapidly pushed on his forces to anticipate the rumour of his advance, but he did not any the more find Tigranes unaware of or unprepared for his movement. He had, in fact, occupied Tigranocerta, a city strong from the multitude of its defenders and the vastness of its fortifications. In addition, the river Nicephorius, the breadth of which is far from contemptible, circled a portion of its walls, and a wide fosse was drawn where they distrusted the protection of the stream. There were some soldiers too, and supplies previously provided. In the conveyance of these a few men had hurried on too eagerly, and, having been surprised by a sudden attack from the enemy, had inspired their comrades with rage rather than fear. But the Parthian has not the daring in close combat needed for a successful siege. His thin showers of arrows do not alarm men within walls, and only disappoint himself. The Adiabeni, when they began to advance their scaling ladders and engines, were easily driven back, and then cut down by a sally of our men.

5. Corbulo, however, notwithstanding his successes, thought he must use his good fortune with moderation, and sent Vologeses a message of remonstrance against the violence done to a Roman province, and the blockade of an allied and friendly king and of Roman cohorts. "He had better give up the siege, or he, Corbulo too would encamp in his territory, as on hostile ground." Casperius, a centurion selected for this mission, had an interview with the king at the town Nisibis, thirty-seven miles distant from Tigranocerta, and with fearless spirit announced his message. With Vologeses it was an old and deep conviction that he should shun the arms of Rome. Nor was the present going smoothly with him. The siege was a failure; Tigranes was safe with his troops and supplies; those who had under-

taken the storming of the place had been routed; legions
had been sent into Armenia, and other legions were ready
to rush to the attack on behalf of Syria, while his own
cavalry was crippled by want of food. A host of locusts,
suddenly appearing, had devoured every blade of grass and
every leaf. And so, hiding his fear and presenting a more
conciliatory attitude, he replied that he would send envoys
to the Roman emperor for the possession of Armenia and
the conclusion of a lasting peace. He ordered Moneses to
leave Tigranocerta, while he himself retired.

6. Many spoke highly of these results, as due to the king's
alarm and the threats of Corbulo, and as splendid successes.
Others explained them as a secret understanding that with
the cessation of war on both sides and the departure of
Vologeses, Tigranes also was to quit Armenia. "Why," it
was asked, "had the Roman army been withdrawn from
Tigranocerta? Why had they abandoned in peace what they
had defended in war? Was it better for them to have win-
tered on the confines of Cappadocia in hastily constructed
huts, than in the capital of a kingdom lately recovered?"
There had been, in short, a suspension of arms, in order
that Vologeses might fight some other foe than Corbulo, and
that Corbulo might not further risk the glory he had earned
in so many years. For, as I have related, he had asked for
a general exclusively for the defence of Armenia, and it was
heard that Cæsennius Pætus was on his way. And indeed
he had now arrived, and the army was thus divided; the
fourth and twelfth legions, with the fifth which had lately
been raised in Mœsia and the auxiliaries from Pontus, Galatia and Cappadocia, were under the command of Pætus,
while the third, sixth, and tenth legions and the old soldiery
of Syria remained with Corbulo. All else they were to share
or divide between them according to circumstances. But as
Corbulo could not endure a rival, so Pætus, who would have
been sufficiently honoured by ranking second to him, disparaged the results of the war, and said repeatedly that
there had been no bloodshed or spoil, that the sieges of cities
were sieges only in name, and that he would soon impose
on the conquered tribute and laws and Roman administration, instead of the empty shadow of a king.

7. About the same time the envoys of Vologeses, who had been sent, as I have related, to the emperor, returned without success, and the Parthians made open war. Nor did Pætus decline the challenge, but with two legions, the 4th and 12th, the first of which was then commanded by Funisulanus Vettonianus and the second by Calavius Sabinus, entered Armenia, with unlucky omen. In the passage of the Euphrates, which they crossed by a bridge, a horse which carried the consul's official emblems, took fright without any apparent cause and fled to the rear. A victim, too, standing by some of the winter-tents, which were being fortified, broke its way through them, when the work was but half finished, and got clear out of the entrenchments. Then again the soldiers' javelins gleamed with light, a prodigy the more significant because the Parthian foe fights with missiles.

8. Pætus, however, despising omens, before he had yet thoroughly fortified his winter-camp or provided for his corn supply, hurried his army across Mount Taurus, for the recovery, as he gave out, of Tigranocerta and the ravaging of the country which Corbulo had left untouched. Some forts too were taken, and some glory as well as plunder had been secured, if only he had enjoyed his glory modestly, and his plunder with vigilance. While he was overrunning in tedious expeditions districts which could not be held, the supplies which had been captured, were spoilt, and as winter was now at hand, he led back his army and wrote a letter to the emperor, as if the war was finished, in pompous language, but barren of facts.

9. Meanwhile Corbulo occupied the bank of the Euphrates, which he had never neglected, with troops at closer intervals. That he might have no hindrance in throwing a bridge over it from the enemy's cavalry, which was already scouring the adjoining plains with a formidable display, he launched on the river some vessels of remarkable size, linked together by beams, with towers rising from their decks, and with catapults and balistas he drove off the barbarians. The stones and spears penetrated their host at a range beyond the reach of the opposing volleys of arrows. The bridge was then completed, and the hills facing us were occupied by our auxiliary infantry, then, by the entrenchments of the

legions, with such rapidity and such a display of force that
the Parthians, giving up their preparations for the invasion
of Syria, concentrated all their hopes on Armenia.

10. Pætus, ignorant of the impending danger, was keeping the 5th legion at a distance in Pontus; the rest he had
weakened by indiscriminate furloughs, till it was heard that
Vologeses was approaching with a powerful force bent on
war. He summoned the 12th legion, and then was discovered
the numerical feebleness of the source from which he had
hoped for the repute of an augmented army. Yet even thus
the camp might have been held, and the Parthian foe baffled, by protracting the war, had Pætus stood firm either by
his own counsels or by those of others. But though military
men had put him on his guard against imminent disasters,
still, not wishing to seem to need the advice of others, he
would fall back on some quite different and inferior plan.
So now, leaving his winter quarters, and exclaiming that not
the fosse or the rampart, but the men's bodies and weapons
were given him for facing the foe, he led out his legions, as
if he meant to fight a battle. Then, after losing a centurion
and a few soldiers whom he had sent on in advance to reconnoitre the enemy's forces, he returned in alarm. And, as
Vologeses had not pressed his advantage with much vigour,
Pætus once again, with vain confidence, posted 3000 chosen
infantry on the adjacent ridge of the Taurus, in order to
bar the king's passage. He also stationed some Pannonian
troopers, the flower of his cavalry, in a part of the plain.
His wife and son he removed to a fortress named Arsamo-
sata, with a cohort for their defence, thus dispersing the
troops which, if kept together, could easily have checked
the desultory skirmishing of the enemy. He could, it is said,
scarcely be driven to confess to Corbulo how the enemy
was pressing him. Corbulo made no haste, that, when the
dangers thickened, the glory of the rescue might be enhanced.
Yet he ordered 1000 men from each of his three legions with
800 cavalry, and an equal number of infantry to be in instant readiness.

11. Vologeses meanwhile, though he had heard that the
roads were blocked by Pætus, here with infantry, there with
cavalry, did not alter his plan, but drove off the latter by

the menace of an attack, and crushed the legionaires, only one centurion of whom, Tarquitius Crescens, dared to defend a tower in which he was keeping guard. He had often sallied out, and cut to pieces such of the barbarians as came close up to the walls, till he was overwhelmed with volleys of firebrands. Every foot soldier still unwounded fled to remote wilds, and those who were disabled, returned to the camp, exaggerating in their terror the king's valour, and the warlike strength of his tribes, everything in short, to the simple credulity of those who trembled with like fear. Even the general did not struggle against his reverses. He had indeed wholly abandoned all the duties of a soldier, and had again sent an entreaty to Corbulo, that he would come with speed to save the standards and eagles, and the name yet left to the unfortunate army; they meantime, he said, would hold to their fidelity while life lasted.

12. Corbulo, perfectly fearless, left half his army in Syria to retain the forts built on the Euphrates, and taking the nearest route, which also was not deficient in supplies, marched through the country of Commagene, then through Cappadocia, and thence into Armenia. Beside the other usual accompaniments of war, his army was followed by a great number of camels laden with corn, to keep off famine as well as the enemy. The first he met of the defeated army was Paccius, a first-rank centurion, then many of the soldiers, whom, when they pleaded various excuses for flight, he advised to return to their standards and throw themselves on the mercy of Pætus. "For himself," he said, "he had no forgiveness but for the victorious."

As he spoke, he went up to his legions, cheering them and reminding them of their past career, and pointing the way to new glory. "It was not to villages or towns of Armenia, but to a Roman camp with two legions, a worthy recompense for their efforts, that they were bound. If each common soldier were to have bestowed on him by the emperor's hand the special honour of a crown for a rescued citizen, how wonderfully great the glory, when the numbers would be equal of those who had brought and of those who had received deliverance." Roused by these and like words into a common enthusiasm, and some too were filled with an ardour peculiarly their own by the perils of brothers and kinsfolk, they hurried on by day and night their uninterrupted march.

13. All the more vigorously did Vologeses press the besieged, now attacking the legions' entrenchments, and now again the fortress, which guarded those whose years unfitted them for war. He advanced closer than is the Parthian practice, seeking to lure the enemy to an engagement by such rashness. They, however, could hardly be dragged out of their tents, and would merely defend their lives, some held back by the general's order, others by their own cowardice; they seemed to be awaiting Corbulo, and should they be overpowered by force, they had before them the examples of Candium and Numantia. "Neither the Samnites, Italian people as they were, nor the Carthaginians, the rivals of the Roman empire, were, it seemed, equally formidable, and even the men of old, with all their strength and glory, whenever fortune was adverse, had taken thought for safety."

The general, although he was overcome by the despair of his army, first wrote a letter to Vologeses, not a suppliant petition, but in a tone of remonstrance against the doing of hostile acts on behalf of the Armenians, who always had been under Roman dominion, or subject to a king chosen by the emperor. Peace, he reminded him, was equally for the interest of both, and it would be well for him not to look only at the present. He indeed had advanced with the whole strength of his kingdom against two legions, while the Romans had all the rest of the world with which to sustain the war.

14. To this Vologeses replied nothing to the purpose, but merely that he must wait for his brothers Pacorus and Tiridates, that the place and time of their meeting had been fixed on as the occasion when they would decide about Armenia, and that heaven had granted them a further honour, well worthy of the Arsacids, the having to determine the fate of Roman legions. Messengers were then despatched by Pætus, and an interview requested with the king, who ordered Vasaces, the commander of the cavalry, to go. Thereupon Pætus dwelt on the memories of the Luculli and Pompeii, and of all that the Cæsars had done in the way of holding or giving away Armenia, while Vasaces declared that we

had the mere shadow of possession and of bestowing, but the Parthians, the reality of power. After much arguing on both sides, Monobazus of the Adiabeni was called the next day to be a witness to the stipulations into which they had entered. It was agreed that the legions should be released from the blockade, that all the troops should quit Armenian territory, and that the forts and supplies should be surrendered to the Parthians, and when all this had been completed, Vologeses was to have full permission to send envoys to Nero.

15. Meanwhile Pætus threw a bridge over the river Arsanias, which flowed by the camp, apparently with the view of facilitating his march. It was the Parthians, however, who had required this, as an evidence of their victory; for the bridge was of use to them, while our men went a different way. Rumour added that the legions had been passed under the yoke, with other miserable disgraces, of which the Armenians had borrowed imitations. For they not only entered our lines before the Roman army began to retire, but also stood about the camp streets, recognizing and dragging off slaves or beasts of burden which we had previously captured. They even seized clothes and detained weapons, for the soldiers were utterly cowed and gave up everything, so that no cause for fighting might arise. Vologeses having piled up the arms and bodies of the slain in order to attest our defeat, refrained from gazing on the fugitive legions. He sought a character for moderation after he had glutted his pride. Seated himself on an elephant, he crossed the river Arsanias, while those next to his person rushed through it at the utmost speed of their horses; for a rumour had gained ground that the bridge would give way, through the trickery of its builders. But those who ventured to go on it found it to be firm and trustworthy.

16. As for the besieged, it appeared that they had such an abundance of corn that they fired the granaries, and Corbulo declared that the Parthians on the other hand were in want of supplies, and would have abandoned the siege from their fodder being all but exhausted, and that he was himself only three days' march distant. He further stated that Pætus had guaranteed by an oath, before the standards,

in the presence of those whom the king had sent to be witnesses, that no Roman was to enter Armenia until Nero's
reply arrived as to whether he assented to the peace. Though
this may have been invented to enhance our disgrace, yet
about the rest of the story there is no obscurity, that, in a
single day Pætus traversed forty miles, leaving his wounded
behind him everywhere, and that the consternation of the
fugitives was as frightful as if they had turned their backs
in battle. Corbulo, as he met them with his forces on the
bank of the Euphrates, did not make such a display of his
standards and arms as to shame them by the contrast. His
men, in their grief and pity for the lot of their comrades,
could not even even refrain from tears. There was scarce any
mutual salutation for weeping. The spirit of a noble rivalry
and the desire of glory, emotions which stir men in success,
had died away; pity alone survived, the more strongly in the
inferior ranks.

17. Then followed a short conversation between the
generals. While Corbulo complained that his efforts had been
fruitless and that the war might have been ended with the
flight of the Parthians, Pætus replied that for neither of
them was anything lost, and urged that they should reverse
the eagles, and with their united forces invade Armenia,
much weakened, as it was, by the departure of Vologeses.
Corbulo said that he had no such instructions from the emperor; it was the peril of the legions which had stirred him
to leave his province, and, as there was uncertainty about
the designs of the Parthians, he should return to Syria, and,
even as it was, he must pray for fortune under her most
favourable aspect in order that the infantry, wearied out
with long marches, might keep pace with the enemy's un-
tiring cavalry, certain to outstrip him on the plains, which
facilitated their movements. Pætus then went into winter
quarters in Cappadocia. Vologeses, however, sent a message
to Corbulo, requiring him to remove the fortresses on the
further bank of the Euphrates, and to leave the river to be,
as formerly, the boundary between them. Corbulo also demanded the evacuation of Armenia by the garrisons posted
throughout it. At last the king yielded, all the positions

fortified by Corbulo beyond the Euphrates were destroyed, and the Armenians too left without a master.

18. At Rome meanwhile trophies for the Parthian war, and arches were erected in the centre of the Capitoline hill; these had been decreed by the Senate, while the war was yet undecided, and even now they were not given up, appearances being consulted, in disregard of known facts. And to hide his anxious fears about foreign affairs, Nero threw the people's corn, which was so old as to be spoilt, into the Tiber, with the view of keeping up a sense of security about the supplies. There was no addition to the price, although about two hundred ships were destroyed in the very harbour by a violent storm, and one hundred more, which had sailed up the Tiber, by an accidental fire. Nero next appointed three ex-consuls, Lucius Piso, Ducennius Geminus, and Pompeius Paulinus, to the management of the public revenues, and inveighed at the same time against former emperors whose heavy expenditure had exceeded their legitimate income. He himself, he said, made the state an annual present of sixty million sesterces.

19. A very demoralizing custom had at this time become rife, of fictitious adoptions of children, on the eve of the elections or of the assignment of the provinces, by a number of childless persons, who, after obtaining along with real fathers prætorships and provinces, forthwith dismissed from paternal control the sons whom they had adopted. An appeal was made to the Senate under a keen sense of wrong. Parents pleaded natural rights and the anxieties of nurture against fraudulent evasions and the brief ceremony of adoption. "It was," they argued, "sufficient reward for the childless to have influence and distinction, everything, in short, easy and open to them, without a care and without a burden. For themselves, they found that the promises held out by the laws, for which they had long waited, were turned into mockery, when one who knew nothing of a parent's solicitude or of the sorrows of bereavement could rise in a moment to the level of a father's long deferred hopes."

On this, a decree of the Senate was passed that a fictitious adoption should be of no avail in any department of the public service, or even hold good for acquiring an inheritance.

20. Next came the prosecution of Claudius Timarchus of Crete, on such charges as often fall on very influential provincials, whom immense wealth has emboldened to the oppression of the weak. But one speech of his had gone to the extremity of a gross insult to the Senate; for he had repeatedly declared that it was in his power to decide whether the proconsuls who had governed Crete should receive the thanks of the province. Pætus Thrasea, turning the occasion to public advantage, after having stated his opinion that the accused ought to be expelled from Crete, further spoke as follows:—

"It is found by experience, Senators, that admirable laws and right precedents among the good have their origin in the misdeeds of others. Thus the license of advocates resulted in the Cincian bill; the corrupt practices of candidates, in the Julian laws; the rapacity of magistrates, in the Calpurnian enactments. For, in point of time, guilt comes before punishment, and correction follows after delinquency. And therefore, to meet the new insolence of provincials, let us adopt a measure worthy of Roman good faith and resolution, whereby our allies may lose nothing of our protection, while public opinion may cease to say of us, that the estimate of a man's character is to be found anywhere rather than in the judgment of our citizens.

21. "Formerly, it was not only a prætor or a consul, but private persons also, who were sent to inspect the provinces, and to report what they thought about each man's loyalty. And nations were timidly sensitive to the opinion of individuals. But now we court foreigners and flatter them, and just as there is a vote of thanks at any one's pleasure, so even more eagerly is a prosecution decided on. Well; let it be decided on, and let the provincials retain the right of showing their power in this fashion, but as for false praise which has been extorted by entreaties, let it be as much checked as fraud or tyranny. More faults are often committed, while we are trying to oblige than while we are giving offence. Nay, some virtues are actually hated; inflexible strictness, for example, and a temper proof against par-

tiality. Consequently, our magistrates' early career is generally better than its close, which deteriorates, when we are
anxiously seeking votes, like candidates. If such practices
are stopped, our provinces will be ruled more equitably and
more steadily. For as the dread of a charge of extortion has
been a check to rapacity, so, by prohibiting the vote of
thanks, will the pursuit of popularity be restrained."

22. This opinion was hailed with great unanimity, but the
Senate's resolution could not be finally passed, as the consuls decided that there had been no formal motion on the
subject. Then, at the emperor's suggestion, they decreed
that no one was to propose to any council of our allies that
a vote of thanks ought to be given in the Senate to proprætors or pro-consuls, and that no one was to discharge
such a mission.

During the same consulship a gymnasium was wholly consumed by a stroke of lightning, and a statue of Nero within
it was melted down to a shapeless mass of bronze. An earthquake too demolished a large part of Pompeii, a populous
town in Campania. And one of the vestal virgins, Lælia, died,
and in her place was chosen Cornelia, of the family of the
Cossi.

23. During the consulship of Memmius Regulus and Verginius Rufus, Nero welcomed with something more than
mortal joy the birth of a daughter by Poppæa, whom he
called Augusta, the same title having also been given to
Poppæa. The place of her confinement was the colony of
Antium, where the emperor himself was born. Already had
the Senate commended Poppæa's safety to the gods, and had
made vows in the State's name, which were repeated again
and again and duly discharged. To these was added a public
thanksgiving, and a temple was decreed to the goddess of
fecundity, as well as games and contests after the type of
the ceremonies commemorative of Actium, and golden
images of the two Fortunes were to be set up on the throne
of Jupiter of the Capitol. Shows too of the circus were to
be exhibited in honour of the Claudian and Domitian families at Antium, like those at Bovillæ in commemoration of
the Julii. Transient distinctions all of them, as within four
months the infant died. Again there was an outburst of

flattery, men voting the honours of deification, of a shrine, a temple, and a priest.

The emperor, too, was as excessive in his grief as he had been in his joy. It was observed that when all the Senate rushed out to Antium to honour the recent birth, Thrasea was forbidden to go, and received with fearless spirit an affront which foreboded his doom. Then followed, as rumour says, an expression from the emperor, in which he boasted to Seneca of his reconciliation with Thrasea, on which Seneca congratulated him. And now henceforth the glory and the peril of these illustrious men grew greater.

24. Meanwhile, in the beginning of spring, Parthian envoys brought a message from king Vologeses, with a letter to the same effect. "He did not," it was said, "repeat his former and frequent claims to the holding of Armenia, since the gods who ruled the destinies of the most powerful nations, had handed over its possession to the Parthians, not without disgrace to Rome. Only lately, he had besieged Tigranes; afterwards, he let Pætus and his legions depart in safety when he could have destroyed them. He had tried force with a satisfactory result; he had also given clemency a trial. Nor would Tiridates refuse a journey to Rome to receive the crown, were he not detained at home by the duties of a sacred office. He was ready to go to the emperor's image in the Roman headquarters, and there in the presence of the legions inaugurate his reign."

25. As Pætus's despatch contradicted this letter from Vologeses and implied that matters were unchanged, the centurion who had arrived with the envoys was questioned as to the state of Armenia. He replied that all the Romans had quitted it. Then was perceived the mockery of the barbarians in petitioning for what they had wrested from us, and Nero consulted with the chief men of the State whether they should accept a dangerous war or a disgraceful peace. There was no hesitation about war. Corbulo, who had known our soldiers and the enemy for so many years, was appointed to conduct it, that there might be no more blunders through any other officer's incapacity; for people were utterly disgusted with Pætus.

So the envoys were sent back without an answer, but with

some presents, in order to inspire a hope that Tiridates would not make the same request in vain, if only he presented his petition in person. The administration of Syria was intrusted to Caius Itius, and the military forces to Corbulo, to which was added the fifteenth legion, under the leadership of Marius Celsus, from Pannonia. Written orders were sent to the tetrarchs, the tributaries, kings, prefects and procurators, and all the prætors who governed the neighbouring provinces, to obey Corbulo's commands, as his powers were enlarged on much the same scale as that which the Roman people had granted to Cneius Pompeius on the eve of his war against the Pirates. When Pætus returned and dreaded something worse, the emperor thought it enough to reproach him with a jest, to the effect that he pardoned him at once, lest one so ready to take fright might sink under prolonged suspense.

26. Corbulo meantime transferred to Syria the fourth and twelfth legions, which, from the loss of their bravest men and the panic of the remainder, seemed quite unfit for battle, and led thence into Armenia the third and sixth legions, troops in thorough efficiency, and trained by frequent and successful service. And he added to his army the fifth legion, which, having been quartered in Pontus, had known nothing of disaster, with men of the fifteenth, lately brought up, and picked veterans from Illyricum and Egypt, and all the allied cavalry and infantry, and the auxiliaries of the tributary princes, which had been concentrated at Melitene, where he was preparing to cross the Euphrates. Then, after the due lustration of his army, he called them together for an harangue, and began with grand allusions to the imperial auspices, and to his own achievements, while he attributed their disasters to the incapacity of Pætus. He spoke with much impressiveness, which in him, as a military man, was as good as eloquence.

27. He then pursued the route opened up in former days by Lucius Lucullus, clearing away the obstructions of long years. Envoys who came to him from Tiridates and Vologeses about peace, he did not repulse, but sent back with them some centurions with a message anything but harsh. "Matters," he said, "have not yet gone so far as to require

the extremity of war. Many successes have fallen to the lot
of Rome, some to that of Parthia, as a warning against pride.
Therefore, it is to the advantage of Tiridates to accept as a
gift a kingdom yet unhurt by the ravages of war, and Vologeses will better consult the welfare of the Parthian people
by an alliance with Rome than by mutual injuries. I know
how much there is of internal discord, and over what un-
tamably fierce tribes he reigns. My emperor, on the other
hand, has undisturbed peace all around him, and this is his
only war."

In an instant Corbulo backed up his advice by a menacing attitude. He drove from their possessions the nobles of
Armenia, who had been the first to revolt from us, destroyed
their fortresses, and spread equal panic throughout the plain
and the hill country, among the strong and among the weak.

28. Against the name of Corbulo no rage, nothing of the
hatred of an enemy, was felt by the barbarians, and they
therefore thought his advice trustworthy. Consequently
Vologeses was not implacable to the uttermost, and he even
asked a truce for some divisions of his kingdom. Tiridates
demanded a place and a day for an interview. The time was
to be soon, the place, that in which Pætus and his legions
had been lately besieged, for this was chosen by the barbarians in remembrance for their more prosperous fortune.
Corbulo did not refuse, resolved that a widely different issue
should enhance his renown. Nor did the disgrace of Pætus
trouble him, as was clearly proved by the fact that he commanded Pætus' son, who was a tribune, to take some companies with him and cover up the relics of that ill-starred
battle-field. On the day appointed, Tiberius Alexander, a
distinguished Roman knight, sent to assist in the campaign,
and Vinianus Annius, Corbulo's son-in-law, who, though not
yet of a senator's age, had the command of the fifth legion
as "legatus," entered the camp of Tiridates, by way of compliment to him, and to reassure him against treachery by so
valuable a pledge. Each then took with him twenty horsemen. The king, seeing Corbulo, was the first to dismount, and
Corbulo hesitated not a moment, but both on foot joined
their right hands.

29. Then the Roman commended the young prince for

abandoning rash courses, and adopting a safe and expedient policy. Tiridates first dwelt much on the nobility of his race, but went on to speak in a tone of moderation. He would go to Rome, and bring the emperor a new glory, a suppliant Arsacid, while Parthia was prosperous. It was then agreed that Tiridates should lay down his royal crown before Cæsar's image, and resume it only from the hand of Nero. The interview then ended with a kiss. After an interval of a few days there was a grand display on both sides; on the one, cavalry ranged in squadrons with their national ensigns; on the other, stood the columns of our legions with glittering eagles and standards and images of deities, after the appearance of a temple. In the midst, on a tribunal, was a chair of state, and on the chair a statue of Nero. To this Tiridates advanced, and having slain the customary victims, he removed the crown from his head, and set it at the foot of the statue; whereupon all felt a deep thrill of emotion, rendered the more intense by the sight which yet lingered before their eyes, of the slaughter or siege of Roman armies. "But now," they thought, "the calamity is reversed; Tiridates is about to go, a spectacle to the world, little better than a prisoner."

30. To military glory Corbulo added courtesy and hospitality. When the king continually asked the reason of whatever he noticed which was new to him, the announcements. for example, by a centurion of the beginnings of each watch, the dismissal of the guests by the sound of a trumpet, and the lighting by a torch from beneath of an altar in front of the headquarters, Corbulo, by exaggerating everything, filled him with admiration of our ancient system. Next day Tiridates begged for time which, as he was about to enter on so long a journey, might suffice for a previous visit to his brothers and his mother. Meanwhile he gave up his daughter as a hostage, and prepared a suppliant letter to Nero.

31. He then departed, and found Pacorus in Media, and Vologeses at Ecbatana, who was by no means unconcerned for his brother. In fact, Vologeses had entreated Corbulo by special messengers, that Tiridates might not have to endure any badge of slavery, or have to deliver up his sword, or be debarred the honour of embracing the governors of the prov-

inces, or have to present himself at their doors, and that he might be treated at Rome with as much respect as the consuls. Accustomed, forsooth, to foreign arrogance, he had no knowledge of us, who value the reality of empire and disregard its empty show.

32. That same year the emperor put into possession of the Latin franchise the tribes of the maritime Alps. To the Roman knights he assigned places in the circus in front of the seats of the people, for up to that time they used to enter in a promiscuous throng, as the Roscian law extended only to fourteen rows in the theatre. The same year witnessed shows of gladiators as magnificent as those of the past. Many ladies of distinction, however, and senators, disgraced themselves by appearing in the amphitheatre.

33. In the year of the consulship of Caius Læcanius and Marcus Licinius a yet keener impulse urged Nero to show himself frequently on the public stage. Hitherto he had sung in private houses or gardens, during the Juvenile games, but these he now despised, as being but little frequented, and on too small a scale for so fine a voice. As, however, he did not venture to make a beginning at Rome, he chose Neapolis, because it was a Greek city. From this as his starting-point he might cross into Achaia, and there, winning the well-known and sacred garlands of antiquity, evoke, with increased fame, the enthusiasm of the citizens. Accordingly, a rabble of the townsfolk was brought together, with those whom the excitement of such an event had attracted from the neighbouring towns and colonies, and such as followed in the emperor's train to pay him honour or for various objects. All these, with some companies of soldiers, filled the theatre at Neapolis.

34. There an incident occurred, which many thought unlucky, though to the emperor it seemed due to the providence of auspicious deities. The people who had been present, had quitted the theatre, and the empty building then fell in without harm to anyone. Thereupon Nero in an elaborate ode thanked the gods, celebrating the good luck which attended the late downfall, and as he was on his way to cross the sea of Hadria, he rested awhile at Beneventum, where a crowded gladiatorial show was being exhibited by Vatinius.

The man was one of the most conspicuously infamous sights in the imperial court, bred, as he had been, in a shoemaker's shop, of a deformed person and vulgar wit, originally introduced as a butt. After a time he grew so powerful by accusing all the best men, that in influence, wealth, and ability to injure, he was pre-eminent even in that bad company.

35. While Nero was frequently visiting the show, even amid his pleasures there was no cessation to his crimes. For during the very same period Torquatus Silanus was forced to die, because over and above his illustrious rank as one of the Junian family he claimed to be the great-grandson of Augustus. Accusers were ordered to charge him with prodigality in lavishing gifts, and with having no hope but in revolution. They said further that he had nobles about him for his letters, books, and accounts, titles all and rehearsals of supreme power. Then the most intimate of his freedmen were put in chains and torn from him, till, knowing the doom which impended, Torquatus divided the arteries in his arms. A speech from Nero followed, as usual, which stated that though he was guilty and with good reason distrusted his defence, he would yet have lived, had he awaited the clemency of the judge.

36. Soon afterwards, giving up Achaia for the present (his reasons were not certainly known), he returned to Rome, there dwelling in his secret imaginations on the provinces of the east, especially Egypt. Then having declared in a public proclamation that his absence would not be long and that all things in the State would remain unchanged and prosperous, he visited the temple of the Capitol for advice about his departure. There he adored the gods; then he entered also the temple of Vesta, and there feeling a sudden trembling throughout his limbs, either from terror inspired by the deity or because, from the remembrance of his crimes, he was never free from fear, he relinquished his purpose, repeatedly saying that all his plans were of less account than his love of his country. "He had seen the sad countenances of the citizens, he heard their secret complainings at the prospect of his entering on so long a journey, when they could not bear so much as his brief excursions, accustomed as they were to cheer themselves under mischances by the

sight of the emperor. Hence, as in private relationships the closest ties were the strongest, so the people of Rome had the most powerful claims and must be obeyed in their wish to retain him."

These and the like sentiments suited the people, who craved amusement, and feared, always their chief anxiety, scarcity of corn, should he be absent. The Senate and leading citizens were in doubt whether to regard him as more terrible at a distance or among them. After a while, as is the way with great terrors, they thought what happened the worst alternative.

37. Nero, to win credit for himself of enjoying nothing so much as the capital, prepared banquets in the public places, and used the whole city, so to say, as his private house. Of these entertainments the most famous for their notorious profligacy were those furnished by Tigellinus, which I will describe as an illustration, that I may not have again and again to narrate similar extravagance. He had a raft constructed on Agrippa's lake, put the guests on board and set it in motion by other vessels towing it. These vessels glittered with gold and ivory; the crews were arranged according to age and experience in vice. Birds and beasts had been procured from remote countries, and sea monsters from the ocean. On the margin of the lake were set up brothels crowded with noble ladies, and on the opposite bank were seen naked prostitutes with obscene gestures and movements. As darkness approached, all the adjacent grove and surrounding buildings resounded with song, and shone brilliantly with lights. Nero, who polluted himself by every lawful or lawless indulgence, had not omitted a single abomination which could heighten his depravity, till a few days afterwards he stooped to marry himself to one of that filthy herd, by name Pythagoras, with all the forms of regular wedlock. The bridal veil was put over the emperor; people saw the witnesses of the ceremony, the wedding dower, the couch and the nuptial torches; everything in a word was plainly visible, which, even when a woman weds darkness hides.

38. A disaster followed, whether accidental or treacherously contrived by the emperor, is uncertain, as authors have

given both accounts, worse, however, and more dreadful than any which have ever happened to this city by the violence of fire. It had its beginning in that part of the circus which adjoins the Palatine and Cælian hills, where, amid the shops containing inflammable wares, the conflagration both broke out and instantly became so fierce and so rapid from the wind that it seized in its grasp the entire length of the circus. For here there were no houses fenced in by solid masonry, or temples surrounded by walls, or any other obstacle to interpose delay. The blaze in its fury ran first through the level portions of the city, then rising to the hills, while it again devastated every place below them, it outstripped all preventive measures; so rapid was the mischief and so completely at its mercy the city, with those narrow winding passages and irregular streets, which characterised old Rome. Added to this were the wailings of terror-stricken women, the feebleness of age, the helpless inexperience of childhood, the crowds who sought to save themselves or others, dragging out the infirm or waiting for them, and by their hurry in the one case, by their delay in the other, aggravating the confusion. Often, while they looked behind them, they were intercepted by flames on their side or in their face. Or if they reached a refuge close at hand, when this too was seized by the fire, they found that, even places, which they had imagined to be remote, were involved in the same calamity. At last, doubting what they should avoid or whither betake themselves, they crowded the streets or flung themselves down in the fields, while some who had lost their all, even their very daily bread, and others out of love for their kinsfolk, whom they had been unable to rescue, perished, though escape was open to them. And no one dared to stop the mischief, because of incessant menaces from a number of persons who forbade the extinguishing of the flames, because again others openly hurled brands, and kept shouting that there was one who gave them authority, either seeking to plunder more freely, or obeying orders.

39. Nero at this time was at Antium, and did not return to Rome until the fire approached his house, which he had built to connect the palace with the gardens of Mæcenas. It could not. however, be stopped from devouring the palace,

the house, and everything around it. However, to relieve the people, driven out homeless as they were, he threw open to them the Campus Martius and the public buildings of Agrippa, and even his own gardens, and raised temporary structures to receive the destitute multitude. Supplies of food were brought up from Ostia and the neighbouring towns, and the price of corn was reduced to three sesterces a peck. These acts, though popular, produced no effect, since a rumour had gone forth everywhere that, at the very time when the city was in flames, the emperor appeared on a private stage and sang of the destruction of Troy, comparing present misfortunes with the calamities of antiquity.

40. At last, after five days, an end was put to the conflagration at the foot of the Esquiline hill, by the destruction of all buildings on a vast space, so that the violence of the fire was met by clear ground and an open sky. But before people had laid aside their fears, the flames returned, with no less fury this second time, and especially in the spacious districts of the city. Consequently, though there was less loss of life, the temples of the gods, and the porticoes which were devoted to enjoyment, fell in a yet more widespread ruin. And to this conflagration there attached the greater infamy because it broke out on the Æmilian property of Tigellinus, and it seemed that Nero was aiming at the glory of founding a new city and calling it by his name. Rome, indeed, is divided into fourteen districts, four of which remained uninjured, three were levelled to the ground, while in the other seven were left only a few shattered, half-burnt relics of houses.

41. It would not be easy to enter into a computation of the private mansions, the blocks of tenements, and of the temples, which were lost. Those with the oldest ceremonial, as that dedicated by Servius Tullius to Luna, the great altar and shrine raised by the Arcadian Evander to the visibly appearing Hercules, the temple of Jupiter the Stayer, which was vowed by Romulus, Numa's royal palace, and the sanctuary of Vesta, with the tutelary deities of the Roman people, were burnt. So too were the riches acquired by our many victories, various beauties of Greek art, then again the ancient and genuine historical monuments of men of genius,

and, notwithstanding the striking splendour of the restored city, old men will remember many things which could not be replaced. Some persons observed that the beginning of this conflagration was on the 19th of July, the day on which the Senones captured and fired Rome. Others have pushed a curious inquiry so far as to reduce the interval between these two conflagrations into equal numbers of years, months, and days.

42. Nero meanwhile availed himself of his country's desolation, and erected a mansion in which the jewels and gold, long familiar objects, quite vulgarised by our extravagance, were not so marvellous as the fields and lakes, with woods on one side to resemble a wilderness, and, on the other, open spaces and extensive views. The directors and contrivers of the work were Severus and Celer, who had the genius and the audacity to attempt by art even what nature had refused, and to fool away an emperor's resources. They had actually undertaken to sink a navigable canal from the lake Avernus to the mouths of the Tiber along a barren shore or through the face of hills, where one meets with no moisture which could supply water, except the Pomptine marshes. The rest of the country is broken rock and perfectly dry. Even if it could be cut through, the labour would be intolerable, and there would be no adequate result. Nero, however, with his love of the impossible, endeavoured to dig through the nearest hills to Avernus, and there still remain the traces of his disappointed hope.

43. Of Rome meanwhile, so much as was left unoccupied by his mansion, was not built up, as it had been after its burning by the Gauls, without any regularity or in any fashion, but with rows of streets according to measurement, with broad thoroughfares, with a restriction on the height of houses, with open spaces, and the further addition of colonnades, as a protection to the frontage of the blocks of tenements. These colonnades Nero promised to erect at his own expense, and to hand over the open spaces, when cleared of the débris, to the ground landlords. He also offered rewards proportioned to each person's position and property, and prescribed a period within which they were to obtain them on the completion of so many houses or blocks of building

He fixed on the marshes of Ostia for the reception of the rubbish, and arranged that the ships which had brought up corn by the Tiber, should sail down the river with cargoes of this rubbish. The buildings themselves, to a certain height, were to be solidly constructed, without wooden beams, of stone from Gabii or Alba, that material being impervious to fire. And to provide that the water which individual license had illegally appropriated, might flow in greater abundance in several places for the public use, officers were appointed, and everyone was to have in the open court the means of stopping a fire. Every building, too, was to be enclosed by its own proper wall, not by one common to others. These changes which were liked for their utility, also added beauty to the new city. Some, however, thought that its old arrangement had been more conducive to health, inasmuch as the narrow streets with the elevation of the roofs were not equally penetrated by the sun's heat, while now the open space, unsheltered by any shade, was scorched by a fiercer glow.

44. Such indeed were the precautions of human wisdom. The next thing was to seek means of propitiating the gods, and recourse was had to the Sibylline books, by the direction of which prayers were offered to Vulcanus, Ceres, and Proserpina. Juno, too, was entreated by the matrons, first, in the Capitol, then on the nearest part of the coast, whence water was procured to sprinkle the fane and image of the goddess. And there were sacred banquets and nightly vigils celebrated by married women. But all human efforts, all the lavish gifts of the emperor, and the propitiations of the gods, did not banish the sinister belief that the conflagration was the result of an order. Consequently, to get rid of the report, Nero fastened the guilt and inflicted the most exquisite tortures on a class hated for their abominations, called Christians by the populace. Christus, from whom the name had its origin, suffered the extreme penalty during the reign of Tiberius at the hands of one of our procurators, Pontius Pilatus, and a most mischievous superstition, thus checked for the moment, again broke out not only in Judæa, the first source of the evil, but even in Rome, where all things hideous and shameful from every part of the world find their

centre and become popular. Accordingly, an arrest was first
made of all who pleaded guilty; then, upon their information, an immense multitude was convicted, not so much of
the crime of firing the city, as of hatred against mankind.
Mockery of every sort was added to their deaths. Covered
with the skins of beasts, they were torn by dogs and perished, or were nailed to crosses, or were doomed to the flames
and burnt, to serve as a nightly illumination, when daylight
had expired.

Nero offered his gardens for the spectacle, and was exhibiting a show in the circus, while he mingled with the
people in the dress of a charioteer or stood aloft on a car.
Hence, even for criminals who deserved extreme and exemplary punishment, there arose a feeling of compassion;
for it was not, as it seemed, for the public good, but to glut
one man's cruelty, that they were being destroyed.

45. Meanwhile Italy was thoroughly exhausted by contributions of money, the provinces were ruined, as also the
allied nations and the free states, as they were called. Even
the gods fell victims to the plunder; for the temples in Rome
were despoiled and the gold carried off, which, for a triumph
or a vow, the Roman people in every age had consecrated in
their prosperity or their alarm. Throughout Asia and Achaia
not only votive gifts, but the images of deities were seized,
Acratus and Secundus Carinas having been sent into those
provinces. The first was a freedman ready for any wickedness; the latter, as far as speech went, was thoroughly
trained in Greek learning, but he had not imbued his heart
with sound principles. Seneca, it was said, to avert from himself the obloquy of sacrilege, begged for the seclusion of a
remote rural retreat, and, when it was refused, feigning ill
health, as though he had a nervous ailment, would not quit
his chamber. According to some writers, poison was prepared
for him at Nero's command by his own freedman, whose
name was Cleonicus. This Seneca avoided through the freedman's disclosure, or his own apprehension, while he used to
support life on the very simple diet of wild fruits, with water
from a running stream when thirst prompted.

46. During the same time some gladiators in the town of
Præneste, who attempted to break loose, were put down by

a military guard stationed on the spot to watch them, and the people, ever desirous and yet fearful of change, began at once to talk of Spartacus, and of bygone calamities. Soon afterwards, tidings of a naval disaster was received, but not from war, for never had there been so profound a peace. Nero, however, had ordered the fleet to return to Campania on a fixed day, without making any allowance for the dangers of the sea. Consequently the pilots, in spite of the fury of the waves, started from Formiæ, and while they were struggling to double the promontory of Misenum, they were dashed by a violent south-west wind on the shores of Cumæ, and lost, in all directions, a number of their triremes with some smaller vessels.

47. At the close of the year people talked much about prodigies, presaging impending evils. Never were lightning flashes more frequent, and a comet too appeared, for which Nero always made propitiation with noble blood. Human and other births with two heads were exposed to public view, or were discovered in those sacrifices in which it is usual to immolate victims in a pregnant condition. And in the district of Placentia, close to the road, a calf was born with its head attached to its leg. Then followed an explanation of the diviners, that another head was preparing for the world, which however would be neither mighty nor hidden, as its growth had been checked in the womb, and it had been born by the wayside.

48. Silius Nerva and Atticus Vestinus then entered on the consulship, and now a conspiracy was planned, and at once became formidable, for which senators, knights, soldiers, even women, had given their names with eager rivalry, out of hatred of Nero as well as a liking for Caius Piso. A descendant of the Calpurnian house, and embracing in his connections through his father's noble rank many illustrious families, Piso had a splendid reputation with the people from his virtue or semblance of virtue. His eloquence he exercised in the defence of fellow-citizens, his generosity towards friends, while even for strangers he had a courteous address and demeanour. He had, too, the fortuitous advantages of tall stature and a handsome face. But solidity of character and moderation in pleasure were wholly alien to him. He

indulged in laxity, in display, and occasionally in excess. This suited the taste of that numerous class who, when the attractions of vice are so powerful, do not wish for strictness or special severity on the throne.

49. The origin of the conspiracy was not in Piso's personal ambition. But I could not easily narrate who first planned it, or whose prompting inspired a scheme into which so many entered. That the leading spirits were Subrius Flavus, tribune of a prætorian cohort, and Sulpicius Asper, a centurion, was proved by the fearlessness of their death. Lucanus Annæus, too, and Plautius Lateranus, imported into it an intensely keen resentment. Lucanus had the stimulus of personal motives, for Nero tried to disparage the fame of his poems and, with the foolish vanity of a rival, had forbidden him to publish them. As for Lateranus, a consul-elect, it was no wrong, but love of the State which linked him with the others. Flavius Scævinus and Afranius Quintianus, on the other hand, both of senatorian rank, contrary to what was expected of them, undertook the beginning of this daring crime. Scævinus, indeed, had enfeebled his mind by excess, and his life, accordingly, was one of sleepy languor. Quintianus, infamous for his effeminate vice, had been satirised by Nero in a lampoon, and was bent on avenging the insult.

50. So, while they dropped hints among themselves or among their friends about the emperor's crimes, the approaching end of empire, and the importance of choosing some one to rescue the State in its distress, they associated with them Tullius Senecio, Cervarius Proculus, Vulcatius Araricus, Julius Augurinus, Munatius Gratus, Antonius Natalis, and Marcius Festus, all Roman knights. Of these Senecio, one of those who was specially intimate with Nero, still kept up a show of friendship, and had consequently to struggle with all the more dangers. Natalis shared with Piso all his secret plans. The rest built their hopes on revolution. Besides Subrius and Sulpicius, whom I have already mentioned, they invited the aid of military strength, of Gavius Silvanus and Statius Proximus, tribunes of prætorian cohorts, and of two centurions, Maximus Scaurus and Venetus Paulus. But their mainstay, it was thought, was Fænius Rufus, the commander of the guard, a man of esteemed life

and character, to whom Tigellinus with his brutality and shamelessness was superior in the emperor's regard. He harassed him with calumnies, and had often put him in terror by hinting that he had been Agrippina's paramour, and from sorrow at her loss was intent on vengeance. And so, when the conspirators were assured by his own repeated language that the commander of the prætorian guard had come over to their side, they once more eagerly discussed the time and place of the fatal deed. It was said that Subrius Flavus had formed a sudden resolution to attack Nero when singing on the stage, or when his house was in flames and he was running hither and thither, unattended, in the darkness. In the one case was the opportunity of solitude; in the other, the very crowd which would witness so glorious a deed, had roused a singularly noble soul; it was only the desire of escape, that foe to all great enterprises, which held him back.

51. Meanwhile, as they hesitated in prolonged suspense between hope and fear, a certain Epicharis (how she informed herself is uncertain, as she had never before had a thought of anything noble) began to stir and upbraid the conspirators. Wearied at last of their long delay, she endeavoured, when staying in Campania, to shake the loyalty of the officers of the fleet at Misenum, and to entangle them in a guilty complicity. She began thus. There was a captain in the fleet, Volusius Proculus, who had been one of Nero's instruments in his mother's murder, and had not, as he thought, been promoted in proportion to the greatness of his crime. Either, as an old acquaintance of the woman, or on the strength of a recent intimacy, he divulged to her his services to Nero and their barren result to himself, adding complaints, and his determination to have vengeance, should the chance arise. He thus inspired the hope that he could be persuaded, and could secure many others. No small help was to be found in the fleet, and there would be numerous opportunities, as Nero delighted in frequent enjoyment of the sea off Puteoli and Misenum.

Epicharis accordingly said more, and began the history of all the emperor's crimes. "The Senate," she affirmed, "had no power left it; yet means had been provided whereby he might pay the penalty of having destroyed the State. Only let Proculus gird himself to do his part and bring over to their side his bravest soldiers, and then look for an adequate recompense." The conspirators' names, however, she withheld. Consequently the information of Proculus was useless, even though he reported what he had heard to Nero. For Epicharis being summoned and confronted with the informer easily silenced him, unsupported as he was by a single witness. But she was herself detained in custody, for Nero suspected that even what was not proved to be true, was not wholly false.

52. The conspirators, however, alarmed by the fear of disclosure, resolved to hurry on the assassination at Baiæ, in Piso's villa, whither the emperor, charmed by its loveliness, often went, and where, unguarded and without the cumbrous grandeur of his rank, he would enjoy the bath and the banquet. But Piso refused, alleging the odium of an act which would stain with an emperor's blood, however bad he might be, the sanctity of the hospitable board and the deities who preside over it. "Better," he said, "in the capital, in that hateful mansion which was piled up with the plunder of the citizens, or in public, to accomplish what on the State's behalf they had undertaken."

So he said openly, with however a secret apprehension that Lucius Silanus might, on the strength of his distinguished rank and the teachings of Caius Cassius, under whom he had been trained, aspire to any greatness and seize on empire, which would be promptly offered him by all who had no part in the conspiracy, and who would pity Nero as the victim of a crime. Many thought that Piso shunned also the enterprising spirit of Vestinus, the consul, who might, he feared, rise up in the cause of freedom, or, by choosing another emperor, make the State his own gift. Vestinus, indeed, had no share in the conspiracy, though Nero on that charge gratified an old resentment against an innocent man.

53. At last they decided to carry out their design on that day of the circus games, which is celebrated in honour of Ceres, as the emperor, who seldom went out, and shut himself up in his house or gardens, used to go to the entertainments of the circus, and access to him was the easier from his keen enjoyment of the spectacle. They had so arranged

the order of the plot, that Lateranus was to throw himself
at the prince's knees in earnest entreaty, apparently craving
relief for his private necessities, and, being a man of strong
nerve and huge frame, hurl him to the ground and hold him
down. When he was prostrate and powerless, the tribunes
and centurions and all the others who had sufficient daring
were to rush up and do the murder, the first blow being
claimed by Scævinus, who had taken a dagger from the
Temple of Safety, or, according to another account, from
that of Fortune, in the town of Ferentum, and used to wear
the weapon as though dedicated to some noble deed. Piso,
meanwhile, was to wait in the sanctuary of Ceres, whence
he was to be summoned by Fænius, the commander of the
guard, and by the others, and then conveyed into the camp,
accompanied by Antonia, the daughter of Claudius Cæsar,
with a view to evoke the people's enthusiasm. So it is related
by Caius Pliny. Handed down from whatever source, I had
no intention of suppressing it, however absurd it may seem,
either that Antonia should have lent her name at her life's
peril to a hopeless project, or that Piso, with his well-known
affection for his wife, should have pledged himself to another
marriage, but for the fact that the lust of dominion inflames
the heart more than any other passion.

54. It was however wonderful how among people of different class, rank, age, sex, among rich and poor, everything
was kept in secrecy till betrayal began from the house of
Scævinus. The day before the treacherous attempt, after a
long conversation with Antonius Natalis, Scævinus returned
home, sealed his will, and, drawing from its sheath the dagger of which I have already spoken, and complaining that it
was blunted from long disuse, he ordered it to be sharpened
on a stone to a keen and bright point. This task he assigned
to his freedman Milichus. At the same time he sat down to
a more than usually sumptuous banquet, and gave his favourite slaves their freedom, and money to others. He was
himself depressed, and evidently in profound thought,
though he affected gaiety in desultory conversation. Last of
all, he directed ligatures for wounds and the means of
stanching blood to be prepared by the same Milichus, who
either knew of the conspiracy and was faithful up to this

point, or was in complete ignorance and then first caught suspicions, as most authors have inferred from what followed. For when his servile imagination dwelt on the rewards of perfidy, and he saw before him at the same moment boundless wealth and power, conscience and care for his patron's life, together with the remembrance of the freedom he had received, fled from him. From his wife, too, he had adopted a womanly and yet baser suggestion; for she even held over him a dreadful thought, that many had been present, both freedmen and slaves, who had seen what he had; that one man's silence would be useless, whereas the rewards would be for him alone who was first with the information.

55. Accordingly at daybreak Milichus went to the Servilian gardens, and, finding the doors shut against him, said again and again that he was the bearer of important and alarming news. Upon this he was conducted by the gatekeepers to one of Nero's freedmen, Epaphroditus, and by him to Nero, whom he informed of the urgent danger, of the formidable conspiracy, and of all else which he had heard or inferred. He showed him too the weapon prepared for his destruction, and bade him summon the accused.

Scævinus on being arrested by the soldiers began his defence with the reply that the dagger about which he was accused, had of old been regarded with a religious sentiment by his ancestors, that it had been kept in his chamber, and been stolen by a trick of his freedman. He had often, he said, signed his will without heeding the observance of particular days, and had previously given presents of money as well as freedom to some of his slaves, only on this occasion he gave more freely, because, as his means were now impoverished and his creditors were pressing him, he distrusted the validity of his will. Certainly his table had always been profusely furnished, and his life luxurious, such as rigid censors would hardly approve. As to the bandages for wounds, none had been prepared at his order, but as all the man's other charges were absurd, he added an accusation in which he might make himself alike informer and witness.

He backed up his words by an air of resolution. Turning on his accuser, he denounced him as an infamous and depraved wretch, with so fearless a voice and look that the in-

formation was beginning to collapse, when Milichus was reminded by his wife that Antonious Natalis had had a long
secret conversation with Scævinus, and that both were Piso's
intimate friends.

56. Natalis was therefore summoned, and they were separately asked what the conversation was, and what was its
subject. Then a suspicion arose because their answers did not
agree, and they were both put in irons. They could not endure the sight and the threat of torture. Natalis however,
taking the initiative, knowing as he did more of the whole
conspiracy, and being also more practised in accusing, first
confessed about Piso, next added the name of Annæus
Seneca, either as having been a messenger between him and
Piso, or to win the favour of Nero, who hated Seneca and
sought every means for his ruin. Then Scævinus too, when
he knew the disclosure of Natalis, with like pusillanimity, or
under the impression that everything was now divulged, and
that there could be no advantage in silence, revealed the
other conspirators. Of these, Lucanus, Quintianus, and Senecio long persisted in denial; after a time, when bribed by
the promise of impunity, anxious to excuse their reluctance,
Lucanus named his mother Atilla, Quintianus and Senecio,
their chief friends, respectively, Glitius Gallus and Annius
Pollio.

57. Nero, meanwhile, remembering that Epicharis was in
custody on the information of Volusius Proculus, and assuming that a woman's frame must be unequal to the agony,
ordered her to be torn on the rack. But neither the scourge
nor fire, nor the fury of the men as they increased the torture that they might not be a woman's scorn, overcame her
positive denial of the charge. Thus the first day's inquiry was
futile. On the morrow, as she was being dragged back on a
chair to the same torments (for with her limbs all dislocated
she could not stand), she tied a band, which she had stript
off her bosom, in a sort of noose to the arched back of the
chair, put her neck in it, and then straining with the whole
weight of her body, wrung out of her frame its little remaining breath. All the nobler was the example set by a freedwoman at such a crisis in screening strangers and those
whom she hardly knew, when freeborn men, Roman knights,

and senators, yet unscathed by torture, betrayed, every one,
his dearest kinsfolk. For even Lucanus and Senecio and
Quintianus failed not to reveal their accomplices indiscriminately, and Nero was more and more alarmed, though he
had fenced his person with a largely augmented guard.

58. Even Rome itself he put, so to say, under custody,
garrisoning its walls with companies of soldiers and occupying with troops the coast and the river-banks. Incessantly
were there flying through the public places, through private
houses, country fields, and the neighbouring villages, horse
and foot soldiers, mixed with Germans, whom the emperor
trusted as being foreigners. In long succession, troops of
prisoners in chains were dragged along and stood at the gates
of his gardens. When they entered to plead their cause, a
smile of joy on any of the conspirators, a casual conversation, a sudden meeting, or the fact of having entered a banquet or a public show in company, was construed into a
crime, while to the savage questionings of Nero and Tigellinus were added the violent menaces of Fænius Rufus, who
had not yet been named by the informers, but who, to get
the credit of complete ignorance, frowned fiercely on his accomplices. When Subius Flavus at his side asked him by a
sign whether he should draw his sword in the middle of the
trial and perpetrate the fatal deed, Rufus refused, and
checked the man's impulse as he was putting his hand to his
sword-hilt.

59. Some there were who, as soon as the conspiracy was
betrayed, urged Piso, while Milichus' story was being heard,
and Scævinus was hesitating, to go to the camp or mount the
Rostra and test the feelings of the soldiers and of the people.
"If," said they, "your accomplices join your enterprise, those
also who are yet undecided, will follow, and great will be the
fame of the movement once started, and this in any new
scheme is all-powerful. Against it Nero has taken no precaution. Even brave men are dismayed by sudden perils; far
less will that stage-player, with Tigellinus forsooth and his
concubines in his train, raise arms against you. Many things
are accomplished on trial which cowards think arduous. It is
vain to expect secrecy and fidelity from the varying tempers
and bodily constitutions of such a host of accomplices. Tor-

ture or reward can overcome everything. Men will soon come
to put you also in chains and inflict on you an ignominious
death. How much more gloriously will you die while you
cling to the State and invoke aid for liberty. Rather let the
soldiers fail, the people be traitors, provided that you, if
prematurely robbed of life, justify your death to your ancestors and descendants."

Unmoved by these considerations, Piso showed himself a
few moments in public, then sought the retirement of his
house, and there fortified his spirit against the worst, till a
troop of soldiers arrived, raw recruits, or men recently enlisted, whom Nero had selected, because he was afraid of the
veterans, imbued, though they were, with a liking for him.
Piso expired by having the veins in his arms severed. His
will, full of loathsome flatteries of Nero, was a concession to
his love of his wife, a base woman, with only a beautiful
person to recommend her, whom he had taken away from
her husband, one of his friends. Her name was Atria Galla;
that of her former husband, Domitius Silus. The tame spirit
of the man, the profligacy of the woman, blazoned Piso's
infamy.

60. In quick succession Nero added the murder of Plautius
Lateranus, consul-elect, so promptly that he did not allow
him to embrace his children or to have the brief choice of
his own death. He was dragged off to a place set apart for
the execution of slaves, and butchered by the hand of the
tribune Statius, maintaining a resolute silence, and not reproaching the tribune with complicity in the plot.

Then followed the destruction of Annæus Seneca, a special
joy to the emperor, not because he had convicted him of the
conspiracy, but anxious to accomplish with the sword what
poison had failed to do. It was, in fact, Natalis alone who
divulged Seneca's name, to this extent, that he had been
sent to Seneca when ailing, to see him and remonstrate with
him for excluding Piso from his presence, when it would
have been better to have kept up their friendship by familiar
intercourse; that Seneca's reply was that mutual conversations and frequent interviews were to the advantage of
neither, but still that his own life depended on Piso's safety.
Gavius Silvanus, tribune of a prætorian cohort, was ordered

to report this to Seneca and to ask him whether he acknowledged what Natalis said and his own answer. Either by chance or purposely Seneca had returned on that day from Campania, and had stopped at a country-house four miles from Rome. Thither the tribune came next evening, surrounded the house with troops of soldiers, and then made known the emperor's message to Seneca as he was at dinner with his wife, Pompeia Paulina, and two friends.

61. Seneca replied that Natalis had been sent to him and had complained to him in Piso's name because of his refusal to see Piso, upon which he excused himself on the ground of failing health and the desire of rest. "He had no reason," he said, for "preferring the interest of any private citizen to his own safety, and he had no natural aptitude for flattery. No one knew this better than Nero, who had oftener experienced Seneca's freespokenness than his servility." When the tribune reported this answer in the presence of Poppæa and Tigellinus, the emperor's most confidential advisers in his moments of rage, he asked whether Seneca was meditating suicide. Upon this the tribune asserted that he saw no signs of fear, and perceived no sadness in his words or in his looks. He was accordingly ordered to go back and to announce sentence of death. Fabius Rusticus tells us that he did not return the way he came, but went out of his course to Fænius, the commander of the guard, and having explained to him the emperor's orders, and asked whether he was to obey them, was by him admonished to carry them out, for a fatal spell of cowardice was on them all. For this very Silvanus was one of the conspirators, and he was now abetting the crimes which he had united with them to avenge. But he spared himself the anguish of a word or of a look, and merely sent in to Seneca one of his centurions, who was to announce to him his last doom.

62. Seneca, quite unmoved, asked for tablets on which to inscribe his will, and, on the centurion's refusal, turned to his friends, protesting that as he was forbidden to requite them, he bequeathed to them the only, but still the noblest possession yet remaining to him, the pattern of his life, which, if they remembered, they would win a name for moral worth and steadfast friendship. At the same time he called

them back from their tears to manly resolution, now with friendly talk, and now with the sterner language of rebuke. "Where," he asked again and again, "are your maxims of philosophy, or the preparation of so many years' study against evils to come? Who knew not Nero's cruelty? After a mother's and a brother's murder, nothing remains but to add the destruction of a guardian and a tutor."

63. Having spoken these and like words, meant, so to say, for all, he embraced his wife; then softening awhile from the stern resolution of the hour, he begged and implored her to spare herself the burden of perpetual sorrow, and, in the contemplation of a life virtuously spent, to endure a husband's loss with honourable consolations. She declared, in answer, that she too had decided to die, and claimed for herself the blow of the executioner. Thereupon Seneca, not to thwart her noble ambition, from an affection too which would not leave behind him for insult one whom he dearly loved, replied: "I have shown you ways of smoothing life; you prefer the glory of dying. I will not grudge you such a noble example. Let the fortitude of so courageous an end be alike in both of us, but let there be more in your decease to win fame."

Then by one and the same stroke they sundered with a dagger the arteries of their arms. Seneca, as his aged frame, attenuated by frugal diet, allowed the blood to escape but slowly, severed also the veins of his legs and knees. Worn out by cruel anguish, afraid too that his sufferings might break his wife's spirit, and that, as he looked on her tortures, he might himself sink into irresolution, he persuaded her to retire into another chamber. Even at the last moment his eloquence failed him not; he summoned his secretaries, and dictated much to them which, as it has been published for all readers in his own words, I forbear to paraphrase.

64. Nero meanwhile, having no personal hatred against Paulina and not wishing to heighten the odium of his cruelty, forbade her death. At the soldiers' prompting, her slaves and freedmen bound up her arms, and stanched the bleeding, whether with her knowledge is doubtful. For as the vulgar are ever ready to think the worst, there were persons who believed that, as long as she dreaded Nero's relentlessness,

she sought the glory of sharing her husband's death, but that after a time, when a more soothing prospect presented itself, she yielded to the charms of life. To this she added a few subsequent years, with a most praiseworthy remembrance of her husband, and with a countenance and frame white to a degree of pallor which denoted a loss of much vital energy.

Seneca meantime, as the tedious process of death still lingered on, begged Statius Annæus, whom he had long esteemed for his faithful friendship and medical skill, to produce a poison with which he had some time before provided himself, the same drug which extinguished the life of those who were condemned by a public sentence of the people of Athens. It was brought to him and he drank it in vain, chilled as he was throughout his limbs, and his frame closed against the efficacy of the poison. At last he entered a pool of heated water, from which he sprinkled the nearest of his slaves, adding the exclamation, "I offer this liquid as a libation to Jupiter the Deliverer." He was then carried into a bath, with the steam of which he was suffocated, and he was burnt without any of the usual funeral rites. So he had directed in a codicil of his will, when even in the height of his wealth and power he was thinking of his life's close.

65. There was a rumour that Sabrius Flavus had held a secret consultation with the centurions, and had planned, not without Seneca's knowledge, that when Nero had been slain by Piso's instrumentality, Piso also was to be murdered, and the empire handed over to Seneca, as a man singled out for his splendid virtues by all persons of integrity. Even a saying of Flavus was popularly current, "that it mattered not as to the disgrace if a harp-player were removed and a tragic actor succeeded him." For as Nero used to sing to the harp, so did Piso in the dress of a tragedian.

66. The soldiers' part too in the conspiracy no longer escaped discovery, some in their rage becoming informers to betray Fænius Rufus, whom they could not endure to be both an accomplice and a judge. Accordingly Scævinus, in answer to his browbeating and menaces, said with a smile that no one knew more than he did, and actually urged him to show gratitude to so good a prince. Fænius could not meet

this with either speech or silence. Halting in his words and visibly terror-stricken, while the rest, especially Cervarius Proculus, a Roman knight, did their utmost to convict him, he was, at the emperor's bidding, seized and bound by Cassius, a soldier, who because of his well-known strength of limb was in attendance.

67. Shortly afterwards, the information of the same men proved fatal to Subrius Flavus. At first he grounded his defence on his moral contrast to the others, implying that an armed soldier, like himself, would never have shared such an attempt with unarmed and effeminate associates. Then, when he was pressed, he embraced the glory of a full confession. Questioned by Nero as to the motives which had led him on to forget his oath of allegiance, "I hated you," he replied; "yet not a soldier was more loyal to you while you deserved to be loved. I began to hate you when you became the murderer of your mother and your wife, a charioteer, an actor, and an incendiary." I have given the man's very words, because they were not, like those of Seneca, generally published, though the rough and vigorous sentiments of a soldier ought to be no less known.

Throughout the conspiracy nothing, it was certain, fell with more terror on the ears of Nero, who was as unused to be told of the crimes he perpetrated as he was eager in their perpetration. The punishment of Flavus was intrusted to Veianius Niger, a tribune. At his direction, a pit was dug in a neighbouring field. Flavus, on seeing it, censured it as too shallow and confined, saying to the soldiers around him, "Even this is not according to military rule." When bidden to offer his neck resolutely, "I wish," said he, "that your stroke may be as resolute." The tribune trembled greatly, and having only just severed his head at two blows, vaunted his brutality to Nero, saying that he had slain him with a blow and a half.

68. Sulpicius Asper, a centurion, exhibited the next example of fortitude. To Nero's question why he had conspired to murder him, he briefly replied that he could not have rendered a better service to his infamous career. He then underwent the prescribed penalty. Nor did the remaining centurions forget their courage in suffering their punish-

ment. But Fænius Rufus had not equal spirit; he even put his laments into his will.

Nero waited in the hope that Vestinus also, the consul, whom he thought an impetuous and deeply disaffected man, would be involved in the charge. None however of the conspirators had shared their counsels with him, some from old feuds against him, most because they considered him a reckless and dangerous associate. Nero's hatred of him had had its origin in intimate companionship, Vestinus seeing through and despising the emperor's cowardice, while Nero feared the high spirit of his friend, who often bantered him with that rough humour which, when it draws largely on facts, leaves a bitter memory behind it. There was too a recent aggravation in the circumstance of Vestinus having married Statilia Messalina, without being ignorant that the emperor was one of her paramours.

69. As neither crime nor accuser appeared, Nero, being thus unable to assume the semblance of a judge, had recourse to the sheer might of despotism, and despatched Gerellanus, a tribune, with a cohort of soldiers, and with orders to forestall the designs of the consul, to seize what he might call his fortress, and crush his train of chosen youths. For Vestinus had a house towering over the Forum, and a host of handsome slaves of the same age. On that day he had performed all his duties as consul, and was entertaining some guests, fearless of danger, or perhaps by way of hiding his fears, when the soldiers entered and announced to him the tribune's summons. He rose without a moment's delay, and every preparation was at once made. He shut himself into his chamber; a physician was at his side; his veins were opened; with life still strong in him, he was carried into a bath, and plunged into warm water, without uttering a word of pity for himself. Meanwhile the guards surrounded those who had sat at his table, and it was only at a late hour of the night that they were dismissed, when Nero, having pictured to himself and laughed over their terror at the expectation of a fatal end to their banquet, said that they had suffered enough punishment for the consul's entertainment.

70. Next he ordered the destruction of Marcus Annæus Lucanus. As the blood flowed freely from him, and he felt a

chill creeping through his feet and hands, and the life gradually ebbing from his extremities, though the heart was still
warm and he retained his mental power, Lucanus recalled
some poetry he had composed in which he had told the story
of a wounded soldier dying a similar kind of death, and he
recited the very lines. These were his last words. After him,
Senecio, Quintianus, and Scævinus perished, not in the manner expected from the past effeminacy of their life, and then
the remaining conspirators, without deed or word deserving
record.

71. Rome all this time was thronged with funerals, the
Capitol with sacrificial victims. One after another, on the
destruction of a brother, a kinsman, or a friend, would return thanks to the gods, deck his house with laurels, prostrate himself at the knees of the emperor, and weary his
hand with kisses. He, in the belief that this was rejoicing,
rewarded with impunity the prompt informations of Antonius Natalis and Cervarius Proculus. Milichus was enriched with gifts and assumed in its Greek equivalent the
name of Saviour. Of the tribunes, Gavius Silvanus, though
acquitted, perished by his own hand; Statius Proximus threw
away the benefit of the pardon he had accepted from the
emperor by the folly of his end. Cornelius Martialis, Flavius
Nepos, Statius Domitius were then deprived of the tribune-
ship, on the ground, not of actually hating the emperor, but
of having the credit of it. Novius Priscus, as Seneca's friend,
Glitius Gallus, and Annius Pollio, as men disgraced rather
than convicted, escaped with sentences of banishment. Priscus and Gallus were accompanied respectively by their
wives, Artoria Flaccilla and Egnatia Maximilla. The latter
possessed at first a great fortune, still unimpaired, and was
subsequently deprived of it, both which circumstances enhanced her fame.

Rufius Crispinus too was banished, on the opportune pretext of the conspiracy, but he was in fact hated by Nero, because he had once been Poppæa's husband. It was the splendour of their name which drove Verginius Flavus and Musonius Rufus into exile. Verginius encouraged the studies of
our youth by his eloquence; Rufus by the teachings of philosophy. Cluvidienus Quietus, Julius Agrippa, Blitius Catu-

linus, Petronius Priscus, Julius Altinus, mere rank and file, so to say, had islands in the Ægean Sea assigned to them. Cædicia, the wife of Scævinus, and Cæsonius Maximus were forbidden to live in Italy, their penalty being the only proof they had of having been accused. Atilla, the mother of Annæus Lucanus, without either acquittal or punishment, was simply ignored.

72. All this having been completed, Nero assembled the troops and distributed two thousand sesterces to every common soldier, with an addition of as much corn without payment, as they had previously the use of at the market price. Then, as if he was going to describe successes in war, he summoned the Senate, and awarded triumphal honours to Petronius Turpilianus, an ex-consul, to Cocceius Nerva, prætor-elect, and to Tigellinus, commander of the prætorians. Tigellinus and Nerva he so distinguished as to place busts of them in the palace in addition to triumphal statues in the Forum. He granted a consul's decorations to Nymphidius, on whose origin, as he now appears for the first time, I will briefly touch. For he too will be a part of Rome's calamities.

The son of a freedwoman, who had prostituted a handsome person among the slaves and freedmen of the emperors, he gave out that he was the offspring of Caius Cæsar, for he happened to be of tall stature and to have a fierce look, or possibly Caius Cæsar, who liked even harlots, had also amused himself with the man's mother.

73. Nero meanwhile summoned the Senate, addressed them in a speech, and further added a proclamation to the people, with the evidence which had been entered on records, and the confessions of the condemned. He was indeed perpetually under the lash of popular talk, which said that he had destroyed men perfectly innocent out of jealousy or fear. However, that a conspiracy was begun, matured, and conclusively proved was not doubted at the time by those who took pains to ascertain the truth, and is admitted by those who after Nero's death returned to the capital. When every one in the Senate, those especially who had most cause to mourn, abased himself in flattery, Salienus Clemens denounced Junius Gallio, who was terror-stricken at his

brother Seneca's death and was pleading for his life. He called him an enemy and traitor to the State, till the unanimous voice of the senators deterred him from perverting public miseries into an occasion for a personal resentment, and thus importing fresh bitterness into what by the prince's clemency had been hushed up or forgotten.

74. Then offerings and thanksgivings to the gods were decreed, with special honours to the Sun, who has an ancient temple in the circus where the crime was planned, as having revealed by his power the secrets of the conspiracy. The games too of Ceres in the circus were to be celebrated with more horse-races, and the month of April was to be called after the name of Nero. A temple also was to be erected to Safety, on the spot whence Scævinus had taken his dagger. The emperor himself dedicated the weapon in the temple of the capital, and inscribed on it, "To Jupiter the Avenger." This passed without notice at the moment, but after the war of Julius Vindex it was construed as an omen and presage of impending vengeance. I find in the registers of the Senate that Cerialis Anicius, consul-elect, proposed a motion that a temple should as soon as possible be built at the public expense to the Divine Nero. He implied indeed by this proposal that the prince had transcended all mortal grandeur and deserved the adoration of mankind. Some however interpreted it as an omen of his death, seeing that divine honours are not paid to an emperor till he has ceased to live among men.

BOOK XVI

A.D. 65, 66

1. FORTUNE soon afterwards made a dupe of Nero through his own credulity and the promises of Cæsellius Bassus, a Carthaginian by birth and a man of a crazed imagination, who wrested a vision seen in the slumber of night into a confident expectation. He sailed to Rome, and having purchased admission to the emperor, he explained how he had discovered on his land a cave of immense depth, which contained a vast quantity of gold, not in the form of coin, but in the shapeless and ponderous masses of ancient days. In fact, he said, ingots of great weight lay there, with bars standing near them in another part of the cave, a treasure hidden for so many ages to increase the wealth of the present. Phœnician Dido, as he sought to show by inference, after fleeing from Tyre and founding Carthage, had concealed these riches in the fear that a new people might be demoralised by a superabundance of money, or that the Numidian kings, already for other reasons hostile, might by lust of gold be provoked to war.

2. Nero upon this, without sufficiently examining the credibility of the author of the story, or of the matter itself, or sending persons through whom he might ascertain whether the intelligence was true, himself actually encouraged the report and despatched men to bring the spoil, as if it were already acquired. They had triremes assigned them and crews specially selected to promote speed. Nothing else at the time was the subject of the credulous gossip of the people, and of the very different conversation of thinking persons. It happened, too, that the quinquennial games were being celebrated for the second time, and the orators took from this same incident their chief materials for eulogies on the emperor. "Not only," they said, "were there the usual

399

harvests, and the gold of the mine with its alloy, but the earth now teemed with a new abundance, and wealth was thrust on them by the bounty of the gods." These and other servile flatteries they invented, with consummate eloquence and equal sycophancy, confidently counting on the facility of his belief.

3. Extravagance meanwhile increased, on the strength of a chimerical hope, and ancient wealth was wasted, as apparently the emperor had lighted on treasures he might squander for many a year. He even gave away profusely from this source, and the expectation of riches was one of the causes of the poverty of the State. Bassus indeed dug up his land and extensive plains in the neighbourhood, while he persisted that this or that was the place of the promised cave, and was followed not only by our soldiers but by the rustic population who were engaged to execute the work, till at last he threw off his infatuation, and expressing wonder that his dreams had never before been false, and that now for the first time he had been deluded, he escaped disgrace and danger by a voluntary death. Some have said that he was imprisoned and soon released, his property having been taken from him as a substitute for the royal treasure.

4. Meanwhile the Senate, as they were now on the eve of the quinquennial contest, wishing to avert scandal, offered the emperor the "victory in song," and added the "crown of eloquence," that thus a veil might be thrown over a shameful exposure on the stage. Nero, however, repeatedly declared that he wanted neither favour nor the Senate's influence, as he was a match for his rivals, and was certain, in the conscientious opinion of the judges, to win the honour by merit. First, he recited a poem on the stage; then, at the importunate request of the rabble that he would make public property of all his accomplishments (these were their words), he entered the theatre, and conformed to all the laws of harp-playing, not sitting down when tired, nor wiping off the perspiration with anything but the garment he wore, or letting himself be seen to spit or clear his nostrils. Last of all, on bended knee he saluted the assembly with a motion of the hand, and awaited the verdict of the judges with pretended anxiety. And then the city-populace, who

were wont to encourage every gesture even of actors, made the place ring with measured strains of elaborate applause. One would have thought they were rejoicing, and perhaps they did rejoice, in their indifference to the public disgrace.

5. All, however, who were present from remote towns, and still retained the Italy of strict morals and primitive ways; all too who had come on embassies or on private business from distant provinces, where they had been unused to such wantonness, were unable to endure the spectacle or sustain the degrading fatigue, which wearied their unpractised hands, while they disturbed those who knew their part, and were often struck by soldiers, stationed in the seats, to see that not a moment of time passed with less vigorous applause or in the silence of indifference. It was a known fact that several knights, in struggling through the narrow approaches and the pressure of the crowd, were trampled to death, and that others while keeping their seats day and night were seized with some fatal malady. For it was a still worse danger to be absent from the show, as many openly and many more secretly made it their business to scrutinize names and faces, and to note the delight or the disgust of the company. Hence came cruel severities, immediately exercised on the humble, and resentments, concealed for the moment, but subsequently paid off, towards men of distinction. There was a story that Vespasian was insulted by Phœbus, a freedman, for closing his eyes in a doze, and that having with difficulty been screened by the intercessions of the well disposed, he escaped imminent destruction through his grander destiny.

6. After the conclusion of the games Poppæa died from a casual outburst of rage in her husband, who felled her with a kick when she was pregnant. That there was poison I cannot believe, though some writers so relate, from hatred rather than from belief, for the emperor was desirous of children, and wholly swayed by love of his wife. Her body was not consumed by fire according to Roman usage, but after the custom of foreign princes was filled with fragrant spices and embalmed, and then consigned to the sepulchre of the Julii. She had, however, a public funeral, and Nero himself from the rostra eulogized her beauty, her lot in hav

ing been the mother of a deified child, and fortune's other gifts, as though they were virtues.

7. To the death of Poppæa, which, though a public grief, was a delight to those who recalling the past thought of her shamelessness and cruelty, Nero added fresh and greater odium by forbidding Caius Cassius to attend the funeral. This was the first token of mischief. Nor was it long delayed. Silanus was coupled with Cassius, no crime being alleged, but that Cassius was eminent for his ancestral wealth and dignity of character, Silanus for the nobility of his birth and the quiet demeanour of his youth. The emperor accordingly sent the Senate a speech in which he argued that both ought to be removed from the State, and made it a reproach against Cassius that among his ancestors' busts he had specially revered that of Caius Cassius, which bore the inscription "to the Party-Leader." In fact, he had thereby sought to sow the seeds of civil war and revolt from the House of the Cæsars. And that he might not merely avail himself of the memory of a hated name to stir up strife, he had associated with him Lucius Silanus, a youth of noble birth and reckless spirit, to whom he might point as an instrument of revolution.

8. Nero next denounced Silanus himself in the same terms as he had his uncle Torquatus, implying that he was already arranging the details of imperial business, and setting freedmen to manage his accounts, papers, and correspondence, imputations utterly groundless and false. Silanus, in truth, was intensely apprehensive, and had been frightened into caution by his uncle's destruction. Nero then procured persons, under the name of informers, to invent against Lepida, the wife of Cassius and aunt of Silanus, a charge of incest with her brother's son, and of some ghastly religious ceremonial. Volcatius Tullinus, and Marcellus Cornelius, senators, and Fabatus, a Roman knight, were drawn in as accomplices. By an appeal to the emperor these men eluded an impending doom and subsequently, as being too insignificant, escaped from Nero, who was busy with crimes on a far greater scale.

9. The Senate was then consulted and sentences of exile were passed on Cassius and Silanus. As to Lepida, the em-

peror was to decide. Cassius was transported to the island of Sardinia, and he was quietly left to old age. Silanus was removed to Ostia, whence, it was pretended, he was to be conveyed to Naxos. He was afterwards confined in a town of Apulia named Barium. There, as he was wisely enduring a most undeserved calamity, he was suddenly seized by a centurion sent to slay him. When the man advised him to sever his veins, he replied that, though he had resolved in his heart to die, he would not let a cutthroat have the glory of the service. The centurion seeing that, unarmed as he was, he was very powerful, and more like an enraged than a frightened man, ordered his soldiers to overpower him. And Silanus failed not to resist and to strike blows, as well as he could with his bare hands, till he was cut down by the centurion, as though in battle, with wounds in his breast.

10. With equal courage Lucius Vetus, his mother-in-law Sextia, and his daughter Pollutia submitted to death. They were hated by the emperor because they seemed a living reproach to him for the murder of Rubellius Plautus, son-in-law of Lucius Vetus. But the first opportunity of unmasking his savage wrath was furnished by Fortunatus, a freedman, who having embezzled his patron's property, deserted him to become his accuser. He had as his accomplice Claudius Demianus, whom Vetus, when proconsul of Asia, had imprisoned for his gross misdeeds, and whom Nero now released as a recompense for the accusation.

When the accused knew this and saw that he and his freedman were pitted against each other on an equal footing, he retired to his estate at Formiæ. There he was put under the secret surveillance of soldiers. With him was his daughter, who, to say nothing of the now imminent peril, had all the fury of a long grief ever since she had seen the murderers of her husband Plautus. She had clasped his bleeding neck, and still kept by her the blood-stained apparel, clinging in her widowhood to perpetual sorrow, and using only such nourishment as might suffice to avert starvation. Then at her father's bidding she went to Neapolis. And as she was forbidden to approach Nero, she would haunt his doors and implore him to hear an innocent man, and not surrender to a freedman one who had once been his colleague in the consulship, now pleading with the cries of a woman, now again forgetting her sex and lifting up her voice in a tone of menace, till the emperor showed himself unmoved alike by entreaty and reproach.

11. She therefore told her father by message that she cast hope aside and yielded to necessity. He was at the same time informed that judicial proceedings in the Senate and a dreadful sentence were hanging over him. Some there were who advised him to name the emperor as his chief heir, and so secure the remainder for his grandchildren. But he spurned the notion, and unwilling to disgrace a life which had clung to freedom by a final act of servility, he bestowed on his slaves all his ready money, and ordered each to convey away for himself whatever he could carry, leaving only three couches for the last scene. Then in the same chamber, with the same weapon, they sundered their veins, and speedily hurried into a bath, covered each, as delicacy required, with a single garment, the father gazing intently on his daughter, the grandmother on her grandchild, she again on both, while with rival earnestness they prayed that the ebbing life might have a quick departure, each wishing to leave a relative still surviving, but just on the verge of death. Fortune preserved the due order; the oldest died first, then the others according to priority of age. They were prosecuted after their burial, and the sentence was that "they should be punished in ancient fashion." Nero interposed his veto, allowing them to die without his interference. Such were the mockeries added to murders already perpetrated.

12. Publius Gallus, a Roman knight, was outlawed for having been intimate with Fænius Rufus and somewhat acquainted with Vetus. To the freedman who was the accuser, was given, as a reward for his service, a seat in the theatre among the tribune's officers. The month too following April, or Neroneus, was changed from Maius into the name of Claudius, and Junius into that of Germanicus, Cornelius Orfitus, the proposer of the motion, publicly declaring that the month Junius had been passed over because the execution of the two Torquati for their crimes had now rendered its name inauspicious.

13. A year of shame and of so many evil deeds heaven

also marked by storms and pestilence. Campania was devastated by a hurricane, which destroyed everywhere country-houses, plantations and crops, and carried its fury to the neighbourhood of Rome, where a terrible plague was sweeping away all classes of human beings without any such derangement of the atmosphere as to be visibly apparent. Yet the houses were filled with lifeless forms and the streets with funerals. Neither age nor sex was exempt from peril. Slaves and the free-born populace alike were suddenly cut off, amid the wailings of wives and children, who were often consumed on the very funeral pile of their friends by whom they had been sitting and shedding tears. Knights and senators perished indiscriminately, and yet their deaths were less deplored because they seemed to forestal the emperor's cruelty by an ordinary death. That same year levies of troops were held in Narbon Gaul, Africa and Asia, to fill up the legions of Illyricum, all soldiers in which, worn out by age or ill-health, were receiving their discharge. Lugdunum was consoled by the prince for a ruinous disaster by a gift of four million sesterces, so that what was lost to the city might be replaced. Its people had previously offered this same amount for the distresses of Rome.

14. In the consulship of Caius Suetonius and Lucius Telesinus, Antistius Sosianus, who, as I have stated, had been punished with exile for repeated satires on Nero, having heard that there was such honour for informers and that the emperor was so partial to bloodshed, being himself too of a restless temper and quick to seize opportunities, made a friend of a man in like condition with himself, one Pammenes, an exile in the same place, noted for his skill as an astrologer, and consequently bound to many in close intimacy. He thought there must be a meaning in the frequent messages and the consultations, and he learnt at the same time that an annual payment was furnished him by Publius Anteius. He knew too that Anteius was hated by Nero for his love of Agrippina, and that his wealth was sufficiently conspicuous to provoke cupidity, and that this was the cause of the destruction of many. Accordingly he intercepted a letter from Anteius, and having also stolen some notes about the day of his nativity and his future career, which were

hidden away among Pammenes' secret papers, and having further discovered some remarks on the birth and life of Ostorius Scapula, he wrote to the emperor that he would communicate important news which would contribute to his safety, if he could but obtain a brief reprieve of his exile. Anteius and Ostorius were, he hinted, grasping at empire and prying into the destinies of themselves and of the prince. Some swift galleys were then despatched and Sosianus speedily arrived. On the disclosure of his information, Anteius and Ostorius were classed with condemned criminals rather than with men on their trial, so completely, indeed, that no one would attest the will of Anteius, till Tigellinus interposed to sanction it. Anteius had been previously advised by him not to delay this final document. Then he drank poison, but disgusted at its slowness, he hastened death by severing his veins.

15. Ostorius was living at the time on a remote estate on the Ligurian frontier. Thither a centurion was despatched to hurry on his destruction. There was a motive for promptitude arising out of the fact that Ostorius, with his great military fame and the civic crown he had won in Britain, possessed, too, as he was of huge bodily strength and skill in arms, had made Nero, who was always timid and now more frightened than ever by the lately discovered conspiracy, fearful of a sudden attack. So the centurion, having barred every exit from the house, disclosed the emperor's orders to Ostorius. That fortitude which he had often shown in fighting the enemy Ostorius now turned against himself. And as his veins, though severed, allowed but a scanty flow of blood, he used the help of a slave, simply to hold up a dagger firmly, and then pressing the man's hand towards him, he met the point with his throat.

16. Even if I had to relate foreign wars and deaths encountered in the service of the State with such a monotony of disaster, I should myself have been overcome by disgust, while I should look for weariness in my readers, sickened as they would be by the melancholy and continuous destruction of our citizens, however glorious to themselves. But now a servile submissiveness and so much wanton bloodshed at home fatigue the mind and paralyze it with grief. The only

indulgence I would ask from those who will acquaint themselves with these horrors is that I be not thought to hate men who perished so tamely. Such was the wrath of heaven against the Roman State that one may not pass over it with a single mention, as one might the defeat of armies and the capture of cities. Let us grant this privilege to the posterity of illustrious men, that just as in their funeral obsequies such men are not confounded in a common burial, so in the record of their end they may receive and retain a special memorial.

17. Within a few days, in quick succession, Annæus Mela, Cerialis Anicius, Rufius Crispinus, and Petronius fell, Mela and Crispinus being Roman knights with senatorian rank. The latter had once commanded the prætorians and had been rewarded with the decorations of the consulate. He had lately been banished to Sardinia on a charge of conspiracy, and on receiving a message that he was doomed to die had destroyed himself. Mela, son of the same parents as Gallio and Seneca, had refrained from seeking promotion out of a perverse vanity which wished to raise a Roman knight to an equality with ex-consuls. He also thought that there was a shorter road to the acquisition of wealth through offices connected with the administration of the emperor's private business. He had too in his son Annæus Lucanus a powerful aid in rising to distinction. After the death of Lucanus, he rigorously called in the debts due to his estate, and thereby provoked an accuser in the person of Fabius Romanus, one of the intimate friends of Lucanus. A story was invented that the father and son shared between them a knowledge of the conspiracy, and a letter was forged in Lucanus's name. This Nero examined, and ordered it to be conveyed to Mela, whose wealth he ravenously desired. Mela meanwhile, adopting the easiest mode of death then in fashion, opened his veins, after adding a codicil to his will bequeathing an immense amount to Tigellinus and his son-in-law, Cossutianus Capito, in order to save the remainder. In this codicil he is also said to have written, by way of remonstrance against the injustice of his death, that he died without any cause for punishment, while Rufius Crispinus and Anicius Cerialis still enjoyed life, though bitter foes to the prince. It was thought that he had invented this about Crispinus, because the man,

had been already murdered; about Cerialis, with the object
of procuring his murder. Soon afterwards Cerialis laid violent hands on himself, and received less pity than the others,
because men remembered that he had betrayed a conspiracy
to Caius Cæsar.

18. With regard to Caius Petronius, I ought to dwell a
little on his antecedents. His days he passed in sleep, his
nights in the business and pleasures of life. Indolence had
raised him to fame, as energy raises others, and he was reckoned not a debauchee and spendthrift, like most of those
who squander their substance, but a man of refined luxury.
And indeed his talk and his doings, the freer they were and
the more show of carelessness they exhibited, were the better
liked, for their look of natural simplicity. Yet as proconsul
of Bithynia and soon afterwards as consul, he showed himself a man of vigour and equal to business. Then falling back
into vice or affecting vice, he was chosen by Nero to be one
of his few intimate associates, as a critic in matters of taste,
while the emperor thought nothing charming or elegant in
luxury unless Petronius had expressed to him his approval
of it. Hence jealousy on the part of Tigellinus, who looked
on him as a rival and even his superior in the science of
pleasure. And so he worked on the prince's cruelty, which
dominated every other passion, charging Petronius with having been the friend of Scævinus, bribing a slave to become
informer, robbing him of the means of defence, and hurrying into prison the greater part of his domestics.

19. It happened at the time that the emperor was on his
way to Campania and that Petronius, after going as far as
Cumæ, was there detained. He bore no longer the suspense of
fear or of hope. Yet he did not fling away life with precipitate haste, but having made an incision in his veins and then,
according to his humour, bound them up, he again opened
them, while he conversed with his friends, not in a serious
strain or on topics that might win for him the glory of courage. And he listened to them as they repeated, not thoughts
on the immortality of the soul or on the theories of philosophers, but light poetry and playful verses. To some of his
slaves he gave liberal presents, a flogging to others. He
dined, indulged himself in sleep, that death, though forced

on him, might have a natural appearance. Even in his will he did not, as did many in their last moments, flatter Nero or Tigellinus or any other of the men in power. On the contrary, he described fully the prince's shameful excesses, with the names of his male and female companions and their novelties in debauchery, and sent the account under seal to Nero. Then he broke his signet-ring, that it might not be subsequently available for imperilling others.

20. When Nero was in doubt how the ingenious varieties of his nightly revels became notorious, Silia came into his mind, who, as a senator's wife, was a conspicuous person, and who had been his chosen associate in all his profligacy and was very intimate with Petronius. She was banished for not having, as was suspected, kept secret what she had seen and endured, a sacrifice to his personal resentment. Minucius Thermus, an ex-prætor, he surrendered to the hate of Tigellinus, because a freedman of Thermus had brought criminal charges against Tigellinus, such that the man had to atone for them himself by the torture of the rack, his patron by an undeserved death.

21. Nero after having butchered so many illustrious men, at last aspired to extirpate virtue itself by murdering Thrasea Pætus and Barea Soranus. Both men he had hated of old, Thrasea on additional grounds, because he had walked out of the Senate when Agrippina's case was under discussion, as I have already related, and had not given the Juvenile games any conspicuous encouragement. Nero's displeasure at this was the deeper, since this same Thrasea had sung in a tragedian's dress at Patavium, his birth-place, in some games instituted by the Trojan Antenor. On the day, too, on which the prætor Antistius was being sentenced to death for libels on Nero, Thrasea proposed and carried a more merciful decision. Again, when divine honours were decreed to Poppæa, he was purposely absent and did not attend her funeral. All this Capito Cossutianus would not allow to be forgotten. He had a heart eager for the worst wickedness, and he also bore ill-will to Thrasea, the weight of whose influence had crushed him, while envoys from Cilicia, supported by Thrasea's advocacy, were accusing him of extortion.

22. He alleged, too, against him the following charges:—
"Thrasea," he said, "at the beginning of the year always
avoided the usual oath of allegiance; he was not present at
the recital of the public prayers, though he had been promoted to the priesthood of the Fifteen; he had never offered
a sacrifice for the safety of the prince or for his heavenly
voice. Though formerly he had been assiduous and unwearied in showing himself a supporter or an opponent even
of the most ordinary motions of senators, he had not entered
the Senate-house for three years, and very lately, when all
were rushing thither with rival eagerness to put down Silanus and Vetus, he had attended by preference to the private business of his clients. This was political schism, and,
should many dare to do the like, it was actual war."

Capito further added, "The country in its eagerness for
discord is now talking of you, Nero, and of Thrasea, as it
talked once of Caius Cæsar and Marcus Cato. Thrasea has
his followers or rather his satellites, who copy, not indeed as
yet the audacious tone of his sentiments, but only his manners and his looks, a sour and gloomy set, bent on making
your mirthfulness a reproach to you. He is the only man
who cares not for your safety, honours not your accomplishments. The prince's prosperity he despises. Can it be that he
is not satisfied with your sorrows and griefs? It shows the
same spirit not to believe in Poppæa's divinity as to refuse
to swear obedience to the acts of the Divine Augustus and
the Divine Julius. He contemns religious rites; he annuls
laws. The daily records of the Roman people are read attentively in the provinces and the armies that they may know
what Thrasea has not done.

"Either let us go over to his system, if it is better than
ours, or let those who desire change have their leader and
adviser taken from them. That sect of his gave birth to the
Tuberones and Favonii, names hateful even to the old republic. They make a show of freedom, to overturn the empire;
should they destroy it, they will attack freedom itself. In
vain have you banished Cassius, if you are going to allow
rivals of the Bruti to multiply and flourish. Finally, write
nothing yourself about Thrasea; leave the Senate to decide
for us." Nero further stimulated the eager wrath of Cossu-

tianus, and associated with him the pungent eloquence of Marcellus Eprius.

23. As for the impeachment of Barea Soranus, Ostorius Sabinus, a Roman knight, had already claimed it for himself. It arose out of his proconsulate of Asia, where he increased the prince's animosity by his uprightness and diligence, as well as by having bestowed pains on opening the port of Ephesus and passed over without punishment the violence of the citizens of Pergamos in their efforts to hinder Acratus, one of the emperor's freedmen, from carrying off statues and pictures. But the crime imputed to him was friendship with Plautus and intrigues to lure the province into thoughts of revolt. The time chosen for the fatal sentence was that at which Tiridates was on his way to receive the sovereignty of Armenia, so that crime at home might be partially veiled amid rumours on foreign affairs, or that Nero might display his imperial grandeur by the murder of illustrious men, as though it were a kingly exploit.

24. Accordingly when all Rome rushed out to welcome the emperor and see the king, Thrasea, though forbidden to appear, did not let his spirit be cast down, but wrote a note to Nero, in which he demanded to know the charges against him, and asserted that he would clear himself, if he were informed of the crimes alleged and had an opportunity of refuting them. This note Nero received with eagerness, in the hope that Thrasea in dismay had written something to enhance the emperor's glory and to tarnish his own honour. When it turned out otherwise, and he himself, on the contrary, dreaded the glance and the defiant independence of the guiltless man, he ordered the Senate to be summoned.

25. Thrasea then consulted his most intimate friends whether he should attempt or spurn defence. Conflicting advice was offered. Those who thought it best for him to enter the Senate-house said that they counted confidently on his courage, and were sure that he would say nothing but what would heighten his renown. "It was for the feeble and timid to invest their last moments with secrecy. Let the people behold a man who could meet death. Let the Senate hear words, almost of divine inspiration, more than human. It was possible that the very miracle might impress even a Nero.

But should he persist in his cruelty, posterity would at least distinguish between the memory of an honourable death and the cowardice of those who perished in silence."

26. Those, on the other hand, who thought that he ought to wait at home, though their opinion of him was the same, hinted that mockeries and insults were in store for him. "Spare your ears," they said, "taunts and revilings. Not only are Cossutianus and Eprius eagerly bent on crime; there are numbers more, daring enough, perchance, to raise the hand of violence in their brutality. Even good men through fear do the like. Better save the Senate which you have adorned to the last the infamy of such an outrage, and leave it a matter of doubt what the senators would have decided, had they seen Thrasea on his trial. It is with a vain hope we are aiming to touch Nero with shame for his abominations, and we have far more cause to fear that he will vent his fury on your wife, your household, on all others dear to you. And therefore, while you are yet stainless and undisgraced, seek to close life with the glory of those in whose track and pursuits you have passed it."

Present at this deliberation was Rusticus Arulenus, an enthusiastic youth, who, in his ardour for renown, offered, as he was tribune of the people, to protest against the sentence of the Senate. Thrasea checked his impetuous temper, not wishing him to attempt what would be as futile, and useless to the accused, as it would be fatal to the protester. "My days," he said, "are ended, and I must not now abandon a scheme of life in which for so many years I have persevered. You are at the beginning of a career of office, and your future is yet clear. Weigh thoroughly with yourself beforehand, at such a crisis as this, the path of political life on which you enter." He then reserved for his own consideration the question whether it became him to enter the Senate.

27. Next day, however, two prætorian cohorts under arms occupied the temple of Venus Genetrix. A group of ordinary citizens with swords which they did not conceal, had blocked the approach to the Senate. Through the squares and colonnades were scattered bodies of soldiers, amid whose looks of menace the senators entered their house. A speech from the emperor was read by his quæstor. Without addressing any

one by name, he censured the senators for neglecting their public duties, and drawing by their example the Roman knights into idleness. "For what wonder is it," he asked, "that men do not come from remote provinces when many, after obtaining the consulate or some sacred office, give all their thoughts by choice to the beauty of their gardens?" Here was, so to say, a weapon for the accusers, on which they fastened.

28. Cossutianus made a beginning, and then Marcellus in more violent tones exclaimed that the whole commonwealth was at stake. "It is," he said, "the stubbornness of inferiors which lessens the clemency of our ruler. We senators have hitherto been too lenient in allowing him to be mocked with impunity by Thrasea throwing off allegiance, by his son-in-law Helvidius Priscus indulging similar frenzies, by Paconius Agrippinus, the inheritor of his father's hatred towards emperors, and by Curtius Montanus, the habitual composer of abominable verses. I miss the presence of an ex-consul in the Senate, of a priest when we offer our vows, of a citizen when we swear obedience, unless indeed, in defiance of the manners and rites of our ancestors, Thrasea has openly assumed the part of a traitor and an enemy. In a word, let the man, wont to act the senator and to screen those who disparage the prince, come among us; let him propose any reform or change he may desire. We shall more readily endure his censure of details than we can now bear the silence by which he condemns everything. Is it the peace throughout the world or victories won without loss to our armies which vex him? A man who grieves at the country's prosperity, who treats our public places, theatres and temples as if they were a desert, and who is ever threatening us with exile, let us not enable such an one to gratify his perverse vanity. To him the decrees of this house, the offices of State, the city of Rome seem as nothing. Let him sever his life from a country all love for which he has long lost and the very sight of which he has now put from him."

29. While Marcellus, with the savage and menacing look he usually wore, spoke these and like words with rising fury in his voice, countenance, and eye, that familiar grief to which a thick succession of perils had habituated the Senate

gave way to a new and profounder panic, as they saw the soldiers' hands on their weapons. At the same moment the venerable form of Thrasea rose before their imagination, and some there were who pitied Helvidius too, doomed as he was to suffer for an innocent alliance. "What again," they asked, "was the charge against Agrippinus except his father's sad fate, since he too, though guiltless as his son, fell beneath the cruelty of Tiberius? As for Montanus, a youth without a blemish, author of no libellous poem, he was positively driven out an exile because he had exhibited genius."

30. And meanwhile Ostorius Sabinus, the accuser of Soranus, entered, and began by speaking of his friendship with Rubellius Plautus and of his proconsulate in Asia which he had, he said, adapted to his own glory rather than to the public welfare, by fostering seditious movements in the various states. These were bygones, but there was a fresh charge involving the daughter in the peril of the father, to the effect that she had lavished money on astrologers. This indeed had really occurred through the filial affection of Servilia (that was the girl's name), who, out of love for her father and the thoughtlessness of youth, had consulted them, only however about the safety of her family, whether Nero could be appeased, and the trial before the Senate have no dreadful result.

She was accordingly summoned before the Senate, and there they stood facing one another before the consuls' tribunal, the aged parent, and opposite to him the daughter, in the twentieth year of her age, widowed and forlorn, her husband Annius Pollio having lately been driven into banishment, without so much as a glance at her father, whose peril she seemed to have aggravated.

31. Then on the accuser asking her whether she had sold her bridal presents or stript her neck of its ornaments to raise money for the performance of magical rites, she at first flung herself on the ground and wept long in silence. After awhile, clasping the altar steps and altar, she exclaimed, "I have invoked no impious deities, no enchantments, nor aught else in my unhappy prayers, but only that thou, Cæsar, and you, senators, might preserve unharmed this best of fathers. My jewels, my apparel, and the signs of my rank I gave up,

as I would have given up my life-blood had they demanded it. They must have seen this, those men before unknown to me, both as to the name they bear and the arts they practise. No mention was made by me of the emperor, except as one of the divinities. But my most unhappy father knows nothing, and, if it is a crime, I alone am guilty."

32. While she was yet speaking, Soranus caught up her words, and exclaimed that she had not gone with him into the province; that, from her youth, she could not have been known to Plautus, and that she was not involved in the charges against her husband. "Treat separately," he said, "the case of one who is guilty only of an exaggerated filial piety, and as for myself, let me undergo any fate." He was rushing, as he spoke, into the embraces of his daughter who hurried towards him, but the lictors interposed and stopped them both. Place was then given to the witnesses, and the appearance among them of Publius Egnatius provoked as much indignation as the cruelty of the prosecution had excited pity. A client of Soranus, and now hired to ruin his friend, he professed the dignified character of a Stoic, and had trained himself in demeanour and language to exhibit an ideal of virtue. In his heart, however, treacherous and cunning, he concealed greed and sensuality. As soon as money had brought these vices to light, he became an example, warning us to beware just as much of those who under the guise of virtuous tastes are false and deceitful in friendship, as of men wholly entangled in falsehoods and stained with every infamy.

33. That same day brought with it a noble pattern in Cassius Asclepiodotus, whose vast wealth made him a foremost man in Bithynia. He had honoured Soranus in his prosperity with a respect which he did not cast off in his fall, and he was now stript of all his property and driven into exile; so impartially indifferent is heaven to examples of virtue and vice. Thrasea, Soranus, and Servilia were allowed the choice of death. Helvidius and Paconius were banished from Italy. Montanus was spared to his father's intercessions on the understanding that he was not to be admitted to political life. The prosecutors, Eprius and Cossutianus, received

each five million sesterces, Ostorius twelve hundred thousand, with the decorations of the quæstorship.

34. Then, as evening approached, the consul's quæstor was sent to Thrasea, who was passing his time in his garden. He had had a crowded gathering of distinguished men and women, giving special attention to Demetrius, a professor of the Cynic philosophy. With him, as might be inferred from his earnest expression of face and from words heard when they raised their voices, he was speculating on the nature of the soul and on the separation of the spirit from the body, till Domitius Cæcilianus, one of his intimate friends, came to him and told him in detail what the Senate had decided. When all who were present, wept and bitterly complained, Thrasea urged them to hasten their departure and not mingle their own perils with the fate of a doomed man. Arria, too, who aspired to follow her husband's end and the example of Arria, her mother, he counselled to preserve her life, and not rob the daughter of their love of her only stay.

35. Then he went out into a colonnade, where he was found by the quæstor, joyful rather than otherwise, as he had learnt that Helvidius, his son-in-law, was merely excluded from Italy. When he heard the Senate's decision, he led Helvidius and Demetrius into a chamber, and having laid bare the arteries of each arm, he let the blood flow freely, and, as he sprinkled it on the ground, he called the quæstor to his side and said, "We pour out a libation to Jupiter the Deliverer. Behold, young man, and may the gods avert the omen, but you have been born into times in which it is well to fortify the spirit with examples of courage." Then as the slowness of his end brought with it grievous anguish, turning his eyes on Demetrius. . . .

[At this point the Annals are broken off. Much remained to be told about the last two years of Nero's reign.]

THE HISTORY

THE HISTORY

THE HISTORY

BOOK I

JANUARY-MARCH, A.D. 69

1. I BEGIN my work with the time when Servius Galba was consul for the second time with Titus Vinius for his colleague. Of the former period, the 820 years dating from the founding of the city, many authors have treated; and while they had to record the transactions of the Roman people, they wrote with equal eloquence and freedom. After the conflict at Actium, and when it became essential to peace, that all power should be centered in one man, these great intellects passed away. Then too the truthfulness of history was impaired in many ways; at first, through men's ignorance of public affairs, which were now wholly strange to them, then, through their passion for flattery, or, on the other hand, their hatred of their masters. And so between the enmity of the one and the servility of the other, neither had any regard for posterity. But while we instinctively shrink from a writer's adulation, we lend a ready ear to detraction and spite, because flattery involves the shameful imputation of servility, whereas malignity wears the false appearance of honesty. I myself knew nothing of Galba, of Otho, or of Vitellius, either from benefits or from injuries. I would not deny that my elevation was begun by Vespasian, augmented by Titus, and still further advanced by Domitian; but those who profess inviolable truthfulness must speak of all without partiality and without hatred. I have reserved as an employment for my old age, should my life be long enough, a subject at once more fruitful and less anxious in the reign of the Divine Nerva and the empire of Trajan, enjoying the rare happiness

of times, when we may think what we please, and express what we think.

2. I am entering on the history of a period rich in dis-asters, frightful in its wars, torn by civil strife, and even in peace full of horrors. Four emperors perished by the sword. There were three civil wars; there were more with foreign enemies; there were often wars that had both characters at once. There was success in the East, and disaster in the West. There were disturbances in Illyricum; Gaul wavered in its allegiance; Britain was thoroughly subdued and imme-diately abandoned; the tribes of the Suevi and the Sarmatæ rose in concert against us; the Dacians had the glory of in-flicting as well as suffering defeat; the armies of Parthia were all but set in motion by the cheat of a counterfeit Nero. Now too Italy was prostrated by disasters either entirely novel, or that recurred only after a long succession of ages; cities in Campania's richest plains were swallowed up and overwhelmed; Rome was wasted by conflagrations, its oldest temples consumed, and the Capitol itself fired by the hands of citizens. Sacred rites were profaned; there was profligacy in the highest ranks; the sea was crowded with exiles, and its rocks polluted with bloody deeds. In the capital there were yet worse horrors. Nobility, wealth, the refusal or the acceptance of office, were grounds for accusation, and virtue ensured destruction. The rewards of the informers were no less odious than their crimes; for while some seized on con-sulships and priestly offices, as their share of the spoil, others on procuratorships, and posts of more confidential authority, they robbed and ruined in every direction amid universal hatred and terror. Slaves were bribed to turn against their masters, and freedmen to betray their patrons; and those who had not an enemy were destroyed by friends.

3. Yet the age was not so barren in noble qualities, as not also to exhibit examples of virtue. Mothers accompanied the flight of their sons; wives followed their husbands into exile; there were brave kinsmen and faithful sons in law; there were slaves whose fidelity defied even torture; there were illustrious men driven to the last necessity, and enduring it with fortitude; there were closing scenes that equalled the famous deaths of antiquity. Besides the manifold vicissitudes

of human affairs, there were prodigies in heaven and earth, the warning voices of the thunder, and other intimations of the future, auspicious or gloomy, doubtful or not to be mistaken. Never surely did more terrible calamities of the Roman People, or evidence more conclusive, prove that the Gods take no thought for our happiness, but only for our punishment.

4. I think it proper, however, before I commence my purposed work, to pass under review the condition of the capital, the temper of the armies, the attitude of the provinces, and the elements of weakness and strength which existed throughout the whole empire, that so we may become acquainted, not only with the vicissitudes and the issues of events, which are often matters of chance, but also with their relations and their causes. Welcome as the death of Nero had been in the first burst of joy, yet it had not only roused various emotions in Rome, among the Senators, the people, or the soldiery of the capital, it had also excited all the legions and their generals; for now had been divulged that secret of the empire, that emperors could be made elsewhere than at Rome. The Senators enjoyed the first exercise of freedom with the less restraint, because the Emperor was new to power, and absent from the capital. The leading men of the Equestrian order sympathised most closely with the joy of the Senators. The respectable portion of the people, which was connected with the great families, as well as the dependants and freedmen of condemned and banished persons, were high in hope. The degraded populace, frequenters of the arena and the theatre, the most worthless of the slaves, and those who having wasted their property were supported by the infamous excesses of Nero, caught eagerly in their dejection at every rumour.

5. The soldiery of the capital, who were imbued with the spirit of an old allegiance to the Cæsars, and who had been led to desert Nero by intrigues and influences from without rather than by their own feelings, were inclined for change, when they found that the donative promised in Galba's name was withheld, and reflected that for great services and great rewards there was not the same room in peace as in war, and that the favour of an emperor created by the legions must be

already preoccupied. They were further excited by the trea-son of Nymphidius Sabinus, their prefect, who himself aimed at the throne. Nymphidius indeed perished in the attempt, but, though the head of the mutiny was thus removed, there yet remained in many of the soldiers the consciousness of guilt. There were even men who talked in angry terms of the feebleness and avarice of Galba. The strictness once so com-mended, and celebrated in the praises of the army, was gall-ing to troops who rebelled against the old discipline, and who had been accustomed by fourteen years' service under Nero to love the vices of their emperors, as much as they had once respected their virtues. To all this was added Galba's own expression, "I choose my soldiers, I do not buy them," noble words for the commonwealth, but fraught with peril for himself. His other acts were not after this pattern.

6. Titus Vinius and Cornelius Laco, one the most worth-less, the other the most spiritless of mankind, were ruining the weak old Emperor, who had to bear the odium of such crimes and the scorn felt for such cowardice. Galba's prog-ress had been slow and blood-stained. Cingonius Varro, con-sul elect, and Petronius Turpilianus, a man of consular rank, were put to death; the former as an accomplice of Nym-phidius, the latter as one of Nero's generals. Both had per-ished without hearing or defence, like innocent men. His entry into the capital, made after the slaughter of thousands of unarmed soldiers, was most ill-omened, and was terrible even to the executioners. As he brought into the city his Spanish legion, while that which Nero had levied from the fleet still remained, Rome was full of strange troops. There were also many detachments from Germany, Britain, and Illyria, selected by Nero, and sent on by him to the Caspian passes, for service in the expedition which he was preparing against the Albani, but afterwards recalled to crush the in-surrection of Vindex. Here there were vast materials for a revolution, without indeed a decided bias towards any one man, but ready to a daring hand.

7. In this conjuncture it happened that tidings of the deaths of Fonteius Capito and Clodius Macer reached the capital. Macer was executed in Africa, where he was un-doubtedly fomenting sedition, by Trebonius Garutianus the

procurator, who acted on Galba's authority; Capito fell in Germany, while he was making similar attempts, by the hands of Cornelius Aquinus and Fabius Valens, legates of legions, who did not wait for an order. There were however some who believed that Capito, though foully stained with avarice and profligacy, had yet abstained from all thought of revolution, that this was a treacherous accusation invented by the commanders themselves, who had urged him to take up arms, when they found themselves unable to prevail, and that Galba had approved of the deed, either from weakness of character, or to avoid investigation into the circumstances of acts which could not be altered. Both executions, however, were unfavourably regarded; indeed, when a ruler once becomes unpopular, all his acts, be they good or bad, tell against him. The freedmen in their excessive power were now putting up everything for sale; the slaves caught with greedy hands at immediate gain, and, reflecting on their master's age, hastened to be rich. The new court had the same abuses as the old, abuses as grievous as ever, but not so readily excused. Even the age of Galba caused ridicule and disgust among those whose associations were with the youth of Nero, and who were accustomed, as is the fashion of the vulgar, to value their emperors by the beauty and grace of their persons.

8. Such, as far as one can speak of so vast a multitude, was the state of feeling at Rome. Among the provinces, Spain was under the government of Cluvius Rufus, an eloquent man, who had all the accomplishments of civil life, but who was without experience in war. Gaul, besides remembering Vindex, was bound to Galba by the recently conceded privileges of citizenship, and by the diminution of its future tribute. Those Gallic states, however, which were nearest to the armies of Germany, had not been treated with the same respect, and had even in some cases been deprived of their territory; and these were reckoning the gains of others and their own losses with equal indignation. The armies of Germany were at once alarmed and angry, a most dangerous temper when allied with such strength; while elated by their recent victory, they feared because they might seem to have supported an unsuccessful party. They had been slow to re-

volt from Nero, and Verginius had not immediately declared for Galba; it was doubtful whether he had himself wished to be emperor, but all agreed that the empire had been offered to him by the soldiery. Again, the execution of Capito was a subject of indignation, even with those who could not complain of its injustice. They had no leader, for Verginius had been withdrawn on the pretext of his friendship with the Emperor. That he was not sent back, and that he was even impeached, they regarded as an accusation against themselves.

9. The army of Upper Germany despised their legate, Hordeonius Flaccus, who, disabled by age and lameness, had no strength of character and no authority; even when the soldiery were quiet, he could not control them, much more in their fits of frenzy were they irritated by the very feebleness of his restraint. The legions of Lower Germany had long been without any general of consular rank, until, by the appointment of Galba, Aulus Vitellius took the command. He was son of that Vitellius who was censor and three times consul; this was thought sufficient recommendation. In the army of Britain there was no angry feeling; indeed no troops behaved more blamelessly throughout all the troubles of these civil wars, either because they were far away and separated by the ocean from the rest of the empire, or because continual warfare had taught them to concentrate their hatred on the enemy. Illyricum too was quiet, though the legions drawn from that province by Nero had, while lingering in Italy, sent deputations to Verginius. But separated as these armies were by long distances, a thing of all others the most favourable for keeping troops to their duty, they could neither communicate their vices, nor combine their strength.

10. In the East there was as yet no movement. Syria and its four legions were under the command of Licinius Mucianus, a man whose good and bad fortune were equally famous. In his youth he had cultivated with many intrigues the friendship of the great. His resources soon failed, and his position became precarious, and as he also suspected that Claudius had taken some offence, he withdrew into a retired part of Asia, and was as like an exile, as he was aft-

erwards like an emperor. He was a compound of dissipation and energy, of arrogance and courtesy, of good and bad qualities. His self-indulgence was excessive, when he had leisure, yet whenever he had served, he had shown great qualities. In his public capacity he might be praised; his private life was in bad repute. Yet over subjects, friends, and colleagues, he exercised the influence of many fascinations. He was a man who would find it easier to transfer the imperial power to another, than to hold it for himself. Flavius Vespasian, a general of Nero's appointment, was carrying on the war in Judæa with three legions, and he had no wish or feeling adverse to Galba. He had in fact sent his son Titus to acknowledge his authority and bespeak his favour, as in its proper place I shall relate. As for the hidden decrees of fate, the omens and the oracles that marked out Vespasian and his sons for imperial power, we believed in them only after his success.

11. Ever since the time of the Divine Augustus Roman Knights have ruled Egypt as kings, and the forces by which it has to be kept in subjection. It has been thought expedient thus to keep under home control a province so difficult of access, so productive of corn, ever distracted, excitable, and restless through the superstition and licentiousness of its inhabitants, knowing nothing of laws, and unused to civil rule. Its governor was at this time Tiberius Alexander, a native of the country. Africa and its legions, now that Clodius Macer was dead, were disposed to be content with any emperor, after having experienced the rule of a smaller tyrant. The two divisions of Mauritania, Rhætia, Noricum and Thrace and the other provinces governed by procurators, as they were near this or that army, were driven by the presence of such powerful neighbours into friendship or hostility. The unarmed provinces with Italy at their head were exposed to any kind of slavery, and were ready to become the prize of victory. Such was the state of the Roman world, when Servius Galba, consul for the second time, with T. Vinius for his colleague, entered upon a year, which was to be the last of their lives, and which well nigh brought the commonwealth to an end.

12. A few days after the 1st of January, there arrived

from Belgica despatches of Pompeius Propinquus, the Procurator, to this effect; that the legions of Upper Germany had broken through the obligation of their military oath, and were demanding another emperor, but conceded the power of choice to the Senate and people of Rome, in the hope that a more lenient view might be taken of their revolt. These tidings hastened the plans of Galba, who had been long debating the subject of adoption with himself and with his intimate friends. There was indeed no more frequent subject of conversation during these months, at first because men had liberty and inclination to talk of such matters, afterwards because the feebleness of Galba was notorious. Few had any discrimination or patriotism, many had foolish hopes for themselves, and spread interested reports, in which they named this or that person to whom they might be related as friend or dependant. They were also moved by hatred of T. Vinius, who grew daily more powerful, and in the same proportion more unpopular. The very easiness of Galba's temper stimulated the greedy cupidity which great advancement had excited in his friends, because with one so weak and so credulous wrong might be done with less risk and greater gain.

13. The real power of the Empire was divided between T. Vinius, the consul, and Cornelius Laco, prefect of the Prætorian Guard. Icelus, a freedman of Galba, was in equal favour; he had been presented with the rings of knighthood, and bore the Equestrian name of Martianus. These men, being at variance, and in smaller matters pursuing their own aims, were divided in the affair of choosing a successor, into two opposing factions. T. Vinius was for Marcus Otho, Laco and Icelus agreed, not indeed in supporting any particular individual, but in striving for some one else. Galba indeed was aware of the friendship between Vinius and Otho; the gossip of those who allow nothing to pass in silence had named them as father-in-law and son-in-law, for Vinius had a widowed daughter, and Otho was unmarried. I believe that he had also at heart some care for the commonwealth, in vain, he would think, rescued from Nero, if it was to be left with Otho. For Otho's had been a neglected boyhood and a riotous youth, and he had made himself agreeable to

Nero by emulating his profligacy. For this reason the Emperor had entrusted to him, as being the confidant of his amours, Poppæa Sabina, the imperial favourite, until he could rid himself of his wife Octavia. Soon suspecting him with regard to this same Poppæa, he sent him out of the way to the province of Lusitania, ostensibly to be its governor. Otho ruled the province with mildness, and, as he was the first to join Galba's party, was not without energy, and, while the war lasted, was the most conspicuous of the Emperor's followers, he was led to cherish more and more passionately every day those hopes of adoption which he had entertained from the first. Many of the soldiers favoured him, and the court was biassed in his favour, because he resembled Nero.

14. When Galba heard of the mutiny in Germany, though nothing was as yet known about Vitellius, he felt anxious as to the direction which the violence of the legions might take, while he could not trust even the soldiery of the capital. He therefore resorted to what he supposed to be the only remedy, and held a council for the election of an emperor. To this he summoned, besides Vinius and Laco, Marius Celsus, consul elect, and Ducennius Geminus, prefect of the city. Having first said a few words about his advanced years, he ordered Piso Licinianus to be summoned. It is uncertain whether he acted on his own free choice, or, as believed by some, under the influence of Laco, who through Rubellius Plautus had cultivated the friendship of Piso. But, cunningly enough, it was as a stranger that Laco supported him, and the high character of Piso gave weight to his advice. Piso, who was the son of M. Crassus and Scribonia, and thus of noble descent on both sides, was in look and manner a man of the old type. Rightly judged, he seemed a stern man, morose to those who estimated him less favourably. This point in his character pleased his adopted father in proportion as it raised the anxious suspicions of others.

15. We are told that Galba, taking hold of Piso's hand, spoke to this effect: "If I were a private man, and were now adopting you by the Act of the Curiæ before the Pontiffs, as our custom is, it would be a high honour to me to intro-

duce into my family a descendant of Cn. Pompeius and M. Crassus; it would be a distinction to you to add to the nobility of your race the honours of the Sulpician and Lutatian houses. As it is, I, who have been called to the throne by the unanimous consent of gods and men, am moved by your splendid endowments and by my own patriotism to offer to you, a man of peace, that power, for which our ancestors fought, and which I myself obtained by war. I am following the precedent of the Divine Augustus, who placed on an eminence next to his own, first his nephew Marcellus, then his son-in-law Agrippa, afterwards his grandsons, and finally Tiberius Nero, his step-son. But Augustus looked for a successor in his own family, I look for one in the state, not because I have no relatives or companions of my campaigns, but because it was not by any private favour that I myself received the imperial power. Let the principle of my choice be shewn not only by my connections which I have set aside for you, but by your own. You have a brother, noble as yourself, and older, who would be well worthy of this dignity, were you not worthier. Your age is such as to be now free from the passions of youth, and such your life that in the past you have nothing to excuse. Hitherto, you have only borne adversity; prosperity tries the heart with keener temptations; for hardships may be endured, whereas we are spoiled by success. You indeed will cling with the same constancy to honour, freedom, friendship, the best possessions of the human spirit, but others will seek to weaken them with their servility. You will be fiercely assailed by adulation, by flattery, that worst poison of the true heart, and by the selfish interests of individuals. You and I speak together to-day with perfect frankness, but others will be more ready to address us as emperors than as men. For to urge his duty upon a prince is indeed a hard matter; to flatter him, whatever his character, is a mere routine gone through without any heart.

16. "Could the vast frame of this empire have stood and preserved its balance without a directing spirit, I was not unworthy of inaugurating a republic. As it is, we have been long reduced to a position, in which my age can confer no greater boon on the Roman people than a good successor,

your youth no greater than a good emperor. Under Tiberius, Caius, and Claudius, we were, so to speak, the inheritance of a single family. The choice which begins with us will be a substitute for freedom. Now that the family of the Julii and the Claudii has come to an end, adoption will discover the worthiest successor. To be begotten and born of a princely race is a mere accident, and is only valued as such. In adoption there is nothing that need bias the judgment, and if you wish to make a choice, an unanimous opinion points out the man. Let Nero be ever before your eyes, swollen with the pride of a long line of Cæsars; it was not Vindex with his unarmed province, it was not myself with my single legion, that shook his yoke from our necks. It was his own profligacy, his own brutality, and that, though there had been before no precedent of an emperor condemned by his own people. We, who have been called to power by the issues of war, and by the deliberate judgment of others, shall incur unpopularity, however illustrious our character. Do not however be alarmed, if, after a movement which has shaken the world, two legions are not yet quiet. I did not myself succeed to a throne without anxiety; and when men shall hear of your adoption I shall no longer be thought old, and this is the only objection which is now made against me. Nero will always be regretted by the thoroughly depraved; it is for you and me to take care, that he be not regretted also by the good. To prolong such advice, suits not this occasion, and all my purpose is fulfilled if I have made a good choice in you. The most practical and the shortest method of distinguishing between good and bad measures, is to think what you yourself would or would not like under another emperor. It is not here, as it is among nations despotically ruled, that there is a distinct governing family, while all the rest are slaves. You have to reign over men who cannot bear either absolute slavery or absolute freedom." This, with more to the same effect, was said by Galba; he spoke to Piso as if he were creating an emperor; the others addressed him as if he were an emperor already.

17. It is said of Piso that he betrayed no discomposure or excessive joy, either to the gaze to which he was immediately subjected, or afterwards when all eyes were turned

upon him. His language to the Emperor, his father, was reverential; his language about himself was modest. He shewed no change in look or manner; he seemed like one who had the power rather than the wish to rule. It was next discussed whether the adoption should be publicly pronounced in front of the Rostra, in the Senate, or in the camp. It was thought best to go to the camp. This would be a compliment to the soldiery, and their favour, base as it was to purchase it by bribery or intrigue, was not to be despised if it could be obtained by honourable means. Meanwhile the expectant people had surrounded the palace, impatient to learn the great secret, and those who sought to stifle the ill-concealed rumour did but spread it the more.

18. The 10th of January was a gloomy, stormy day, unusually disturbed by thunder, lightning, and all bad omens from heaven. Though this had from ancient time been made a reason for dissolving an assembly, it did not deter Galba from proceeding to the camp; either because he despised such things as being mere matters of chance, or because the decrees of fate, though they be foreshewn, are not escaped. Addressing a crowded assembly of the soldiers he announced, with imperial brevity, that he adopted Piso, following the precedent of the Divine Augustus, and the military custom by which a soldier chooses his comrade. Fearing that to conceal the mutiny would be to make them think it greater than it really was, he spontaneously declared that the 4th and 18th legions, led by a few factious persons, had been insubordinate, but had not gone beyond certain words and cries, and that they would soon return to their duty. To this speech he added no word of flattery, no hint of a bribe. Yet the tribunes, the centurions, and such of the soldiers as stood near, made an encouraging response. A gloomy silence prevailed among the rest, who seemed to think that they had lost by war that right to a donative which they had made good even in peace. It is certain that their feelings might have been conciliated by the very smallest liberality on the part of the parsimonious old man. He was ruined by his old-fashioned inflexibility, and by an excessive sternness which we are no longer able to endure.

19. Then followed Galba's speech in the Senate, which

was as plain and brief as his speech to the soldiery. Piso delivered a graceful oration and was supported by the feeling of the Senate. Many who wished him well, spoke with enthusiasm; those who had opposed him, in moderate terms; the majority met him with an officious homage, having aims of their own and no thought for the state. Piso neither said nor did anything else in public in the following four days which intervened between his adoption and his death. As tidings of the mutiny in Germany were arriving with daily increasing frequency, while the country was ready to receive and to credit all intelligence that had an unfavourable character, the Senate came to a resolution to send deputies to the German armies. It was privately discussed whether Piso should go with them to give them a more imposing appearance; they, it was said, would bring with them the authority of the Senate, he the majesty of the Cæsar. It was thought expedient to send with them Cornelius Laco, prefect of the Prætorian Guard, but he thwarted the design. In nominating, excusing, and changing the deputies, the Senate having entrusted the selection to Galba, the Emperor shewed a disgraceful want of firmness, yielding to individuals, who made interest to stay or to go, as their fears or their hopes prompted.

20. Next came the question of money. On a general inquiry it seemed the fairest course to demand restitution from those who had caused the public poverty. Nero had squandered in presents two thousand two hundred million sesterces. It was ordered that each recipient should be sued, but should be permitted to retain a tenth part of the bounty. They had however barely a tenth part left, having wasted the property of others in the same extravagances in which they had squandered their own, till the most rapacious and profligate among them had neither capital nor land remaining, nothing in fact but the appliances of their vices. Thirty Roman Knights were appointed to conduct the process of recovery, a novel office, and made burdensome by the number and intriguing practices of those with whom it had to deal. Everywhere were sales and brokers, and Rome was in an uproar with auctions. Yet great was the joy to think that the men whom Nero had enriched would be as poor as those

whom he had robbed. About this time were cashiered two tribunes of the Prætorian Guard, Antonius Taurus and Antonius Naso, an officer of the City cohorts, Æmilius Pacensis, and one of the watch, Julius Fronto. This led to no amendment with the rest, but only started the apprehension, that a crafty and timid policy was getting rid of individuals, while all were suspected.

21. Otho, meanwhile, who had nothing to hope while the State was tranquil, and whose whole plans depended on revolution, was being roused to action by a combination of many motives, by a luxury that would have embarrassed even an emperor, by a poverty that a subject could hardly endure, by his rage against Galba, by his envy of Piso. He even pretended to fear to make himself keener in desire. "I was," said he, "too formidable to Nero, and I must not look for another Lusitania, another honourable exile. Rulers always suspect and hate the man who has been named for the succession. This has injured me with the aged Emperor, and will injure me yet more with a young man whose temper, naturally savage, has been rendered ferocious by prolonged exile. How easy to put Otho to death! I must therefore do and dare now while Galba's authority is still unsettled, and before that of Piso is consolidated. Periods of transition suit great attempts, and delay is useless where inaction is more hurtful than temerity. Death, which nature ordains for all alike, yet admits of the distinction of being either forgotten, or remembered with honour by posterity; and, if the same lot awaits the innocent and the guilty, the man of spirit will at least deserve his fate."

22. The soul of Otho was not effeminate like his person. His confidential freedmen and slaves, who enjoyed a license unknown in private families, brought the debaucheries of Nero's court, its intrigues, its easy marriages, and the other indulgences of despotic power, before a mind passionately fond of such things, dwelt upon them as his if he dared to seize them, and reproached the inaction that would leave them to others. The astrologers also urged him to action, predicting from their observation of the heavens revolutions, and a year of glory for Otho. This is a class of men, whom the powerful cannot trust, and who deceive the aspiring, a

class which will always be proscribed in this country, and yet always retained. Many of these men were attached to the secret councils of Poppæa and were the vilest tools in the employ of the imperial household. One of them, Ptolemæus, had attended Otho in Spain, and had there foretold that his patron would survive Nero. Gaining credit by the result, and arguing from his own conjectures and from the common talk of those who compared Galba's age with Otho's youth, he had persuaded the latter that he would be called to the throne. Otho however received the prediction as the words of wisdom and the intimation of destiny, with that inclination so natural to the human mind readily to believe in the mysterious.

23. Nor did Ptolemæus fail to play his part; he now even prompted to crime, to which from such wishes it is easy to pass. Whether indeed these thoughts of crime were suddenly conceived, is doubtful. Otho had long been courting the affections of the soldiery, either in the hope of succeeding to the throne, or in preparation for some desperate act. On the march, on parade, and in their quarters, he would address all the oldest soldiers by name, and in allusion to the progresses of Nero would call them his messmates. Some he would recognise, he would inquire after others, and would help them with his money and interest. He would often intersperse his conversation with complaints and insinuations against Galba and anything else that might excite the vulgar mind. Laborious marches, a scanty commissariat, and the rigour of military discipline, were especially distasteful, when men, accustomed to sail to the lakes of Campania and the cities of Greece, had painfully to struggle under the weight of their arms over the Pyrenees, the Alps, and vast distances of road.

24. The minds of the soldiery were already on fire, when Mævius Pudens, a near relative of Tigellinus, added, so to speak, fuel to the flames. In his endeavour to win over all who were particularly weak in character, or who wanted money and were ready to plunge into revolution, he gradually went so far as to distribute, whenever Galba dined with Otho, one hundred sesterces to each soldier of the cohort on duty, under pretext of treating them. This, which

we may almost call a public bounty, Otho followed up by presents more privately bestowed on individuals; nay he bribed with such spirit, that, finding there was a dispute between Cocceius Proculus, a soldier of the bodyguard, and one of his neighbours, about some part of their boundaries, he purchased with his own money the neighbour's entire estate, and made a present of it to the soldier. He took advantage of the lazy indifference of the Prefect, who overlooked alike notorious facts and secret practices.

25. He then entrusted the conduct of his meditated treason to Onomastus, one of his freedmen, who brought over to his views Barbius Proculus, officer of the watchword to the bodyguard, and Veturius, a deputy centurion in the same force. Having assured himself by various conversations with these men that they were cunning and bold, he loaded them with presents and promises, and furnished them with money with which to tempt the cupidity of others. Thus two soldiers from the ranks undertook to transfer the Empire of Rome, and actually transferred it. Only a few were admitted to be accomplices in the plot, but they worked by various devices on the wavering minds of the remainder; on the more distinguished soldiers, by hinting that the favours of Nymphidius had subjected them to suspicion; on the vulgar herd, by the anger and despair with which the repeated postponement of the donative had inspired them. Some were fired by their recollections of Nero and their longing regrets for their old license. All felt a common alarm at the idea of having to serve elsewhere.

26. The contagion spread to the legions and the auxiliary troops, already excited by the news of the wavering loyalty of the army of Germany. So ripe were the disaffected for mutiny and so close the secresy preserved by the loyal, that they would actually have seized Otho on the 14th of January, as he was returning from dinner, had they not been deterred by the risks of darkness, the inconvenient dispersion of the troops over the whole city, and the difficulty of concerted action among a half-intoxicated crowd. It was no care for the state, which they deliberately meditated polluting with the blood of their Emperor; it was a fear lest in the darkness of night any one who presented himself to the

soldiers of the Pannonian or German army might be fixed on instead of Otho, whom few of them knew. Many symptoms of the approaching outburst were repressed by those who were in the secret. Some hints, which had reached Galba's ears, were turned into ridicule by Laco the prefect, who knew nothing of the temper of the soldiery, and who, inimical to all measures, however excellent, which he did not originate, obstinately thwarted men wiser than himself.

27. On the 15th of January, as Galba was sacrificing in front of the temple of Apollo, the Haruspex Umbricius announced to him that the entrails had a sinister aspect, that treachery threatened him, that he had an enemy at home. Otho heard, for he had taken his place close by, and interpreted it by contraries in a favourable sense, as promising success to his designs. Not long after his freedman Onomastus informed him that the architect and the contractors were waiting for him. It had been arranged thus to indicate that the soldiers were assembling, and that the preparations of the conspiracy were complete. To those who inquired the reason of his departure, Otho pretended that he was purchasing certain farm-buildings, which from their age he suspected to be unsound, and which had therefore to be first surveyed. Leaning on his freedman's arm, he proceeded thorugh the palace of Tiberius to the Velabrum, and thence to the golden milestone near the temple of Saturn. There three and twenty soldiers of the body-guard saluted him as Emperor, and, while he trembled at their scanty number, put him hastily into a chair, drew their swords, and hurried him onwards. About as many more soldiers joined them on their way, some because they were in the plot, many from mere surprise; some shouted and brandished their swords, others proceeded in silence, intending to let the issue determine their sentiments.

28. Julius Martialis was the tribune on guard in the camp. Appalled by the enormity and suddenness of the crime, or perhaps fearing that the troops were very extensively corrupted and that it would be destruction to oppose them, he made many suspect him of complicity. The rest of the tribunes and centurions preferred immediate safety to danger and duty. Such was the temper of men's minds, that,

while there were few to venture on so atrocious a treason, many wished it done, and all were ready to acquiesce.

29. Meanwhile the unconscious Galba, busy with his sacrifice, was importuning the gods of an empire that was now another's. A rumour reached him, that some senator unknown was being hurried into the camp; before long it was affirmed that this senator was Otho. At the same time came messengers from all parts of the city, where they had chanced to meet the procession, some exaggerating the danger, some, who could not even then forget to flatter, representing it as less than the reality. On deliberation it was determined to sound the feeling of the cohort on guard in the palace, but not through Galba in person, whose authority was to be kept unimpaired to meet greater emergencies. They were accordingly collected before the steps of the palace, and Piso addressed them as follows:—"Comrades, this is the sixth day since I became a Cæsar by adoption, not knowing what was to happen, whether this title was to be desired, or dreaded. It rests with you to determine what will be the result to my family and to the state. It is not that I dread on my own account the gloomier issue; for I have known adversity, and I am learning at this very moment that prosperity is fully as dangerous. It is the lot of my father, of the Senate, of the Empire itself, that I deplore, if we have either to fall this day, or to do what is equally abhorrent to the good, to put others to death. In the late troubles we had this consolation, a capital unstained by bloodshed, and power transferred without strife. It was thought that by my adoption provision was made against the possibility of war, even after Galba's death.

30. "I will lay no claim to nobleness, or moderation, for indeed, to count up virtues in comparing oneself with Otho is needless. The vices, of which alone he boasts, overthrew the Empire, even when he was but the Emperor's friend. Shall he earn that Empire now by his manner and his gait, or by those womanish adornments? They are deceived, on whom luxury imposes by its false show of liberality; he will know how to squander, he will not know how to give. Already he is thinking of debaucheries, of revels, of tribes of mistresses. These things he holds to be the prizes of princely

power, things, in which the wanton enjoyment will be for him alone, the shame and the disgrace for all. Never yet has any one exercised for good ends the power obtained by crime. The unanimous will of mankind gave to Galba the title of Cæsar, and you consented when he gave it to me. Were the Senate, the Country, the People, but empty names, yet, comrades, it is your interest that the most worthless of men should not create an Emperor. We have occasionally heard of legions mutinying against their generals, but your loyalty, your character, stand unimpeached up to this time. Even with Nero, it was he that deserted you, not you that deserted him. Shall less than thirty runaways and deserters whom no one would allow to choose a tribune or centurion for tnemselves, assign the Empire at their pleasure? Do you tolerate the precedent? Do you by your inaction make the crime your own? This lawless spirit will pass into the provinces, and though we shall suffer from this treason, you will suffer from the wars that will follow. Again, no more is offered you for murdering your Prince, than you will have if you shun such guilt. We shall give you a donative for your loyalty, as surely as others can give it for your treason."

31. The soldiers of the body-guard dispersed, but the rest of the cohort, who shewed no disrespect to the speaker, displayed their standards, acting, as often happens in a disturbance, on mere impulse and without any settled plan, rather than, as was afterwards believed, with treachery and an intention to deceive. Celsus Marius was sent to the picked troops from the army of Illyricum, then encamped in the Portico of Vipsanius. Instructions were also given to Amulius Serenus and Quintius Sabinus, centurions of the first rank, to bring up the German soldiers from the Hall of Liberty. No confidence was placed in the legion levied from the fleet, which had been enraged by the massacre of their comrades, whom Galba had slaughtered immediately on his entry into the capital. Meanwhile Cetrius Severus, Subrius Dexter, and Pompeius Longinus, all three military tribunes, proceeded to the Prætorian camp, in the hope that a sedition, which was but just commencing, and not yet fully matured, might be swayed by better counsels. Two of these tribunes, Subrius and Cetrius, the soldiers assailed with men-

aces; Longinus they seized and disarmed; it was not his
rank as an officer, but his friendship with Galba, that bound
him to that Prince, and roused a stronger suspicion in the
mutineers. The legion levied from the fleet joined the Prætorians without any hesitation. The Illyrian detachments
drove Celsus away with a shower of javelins. The German
veterans wavered long. Their frames were still enfeebled by
sickness, and their minds were favourably disposed towards
Galba, who, finding them exhausted by their long return
voyage from Alexandria, whither they had been sent on by
Nero, had supplied their wants with a most unsparing attention.

32. The whole populace and the slaves with them were
now crowding the palace, clamouring with discordant shouts
for the death of Otho and the destruction of the conspirators, just as if they were demanding some spectacle in the
circus or amphitheatre. They had not indeed any discrimination or sincerity, for on that same day they would raise
with equal zeal a wholly different cry. It was their traditional custom to flatter any ruler with reckless applause and
meaningless zeal. Meanwhile two suggestions were keeping
Galba in doubt. T. Vinius thought that he should remain
within the palace, array the slaves against the foe, secure
the approaches, and not go out to the enraged soldiers.
"You should," he said, "give the disaffected time to repent,
the loyal time to unite. Crimes gain by hasty action, better
counsels by delay. At all events, you will still have the same
facilities of going out, if need be, whereas, your retreat,
should you repent of having gone, will be in the power of
another."

33. The rest were for speedy action, "before," they said,
"the yet feeble treason of this handful of men can gather
strength. Otho himself will be alarmed, Otho, who stole
away to be introduced to a few strangers, but who now,
thanks to the hesitation and inaction in which we waste our
time, is learning how to play the Prince. We must not wait
till, having arranged matters in the camp, he bursts into the
Forum, and under Galba's very eyes makes his way to the
Capitol, while our noble Emperor with his brave friends
barricades the doors of his palace. We are to stand a siege

forsooth, and truly we shall have an admirable resource in the slaves, if the unanimous feeling of this vast multitude, and that which can do so much, the first burst of indignation, be suffered to subside. Moreover that cannot be safe which is not honourable. If we must fall, let us go to meet the danger. This will bring more odium upon Otho, and will be more becoming to ourselves." Vinius opposing this advice, Laco assailed him with threats, encouraged by Icelus, who persisted in his private animosities to the public ruin.

34. Without further delay Galba sided with these more plausible advisers. Piso was sent on into the camp, as being a young man of noble name, whose popularity was of recent date, and who was a bitter enemy to T. Vinius, that is, either he was so in reality, or these angry partisans would have it so, and belief in hatred is but too ready. Piso had hardly gone forth when there came a rumour, at first vague and wanting confirmation, that Otho had been slain in the camp; soon, as happens with these great fictions, men asserted that they had been present, and had seen the deed: and, between the delight of some and the indifference of others, the report was easily believed. Many thought the rumour had been invented and circulated by the Othonianists, who were now mingling with the crowd, and who disseminated these false tidings of success to draw Galba out of the palace.

35. Upon this not only did the people and the ignorant rabble break out into applause and vehement expressions of zeal, but many of the Knights and Senators, losing their caution as they laid aside their fear, burst open the doors of the palace, rushed in, and displayed themselves to Galba, complaining that their revenge had been snatched from them. The most arrant coward, the man, who, as the event proved, would dare nothing in the moment of danger, was the most voluble and fierce of speech. No one knew anything, yet all were confident in assertion, till at length Galba in the dearth of all true intelligence, and overborne by the universal delusion, assumed his cuirass, and as, from age and bodily weakness, he could not stand up against the crowd that was still rushing in, he was elevated on a chair. He was met in the palace by Julius Atticus, a soldier of the

body-guard, who, displaying a bloody sword, cried "I have slain Otho." "Comrade," replied Galba, "who gave the order?" So singularly resolute was his spirit in curbing the license of the soldiery; threats did not dismay him, nor flatteries seduce.

36. There was now no doubt about the feeling of all the troops in the camp. So great was their zeal, that, not content with surrounding Otho with their persons in close array, they elevated him to the pedestal, on which a short time before had stood the gilt statue of Galba, and there, amid the standards, encircled him with their colours. Neither tribunes nor centurions could approach. The common soldiers even insisted that all the officers should be watched. Everything was in an uproar with their tumultuous cries and their appeals to each other, which were not, like those of a popular assembly or a mob, the discordant expressions of an idle flattery; on the contrary, as soon as they caught sight of any of the soldiers who were flocking in, they seized him, gave him the military embrace, placed him close to Otho, dictated to him the oath of allegiance, commending sometimes the Emperor to his soldiers, sometimes the soldiers to their Emperor. Otho did not fail to play his part; he stretched out his arms, and bowed to the crowd, and kissed his hands, and altogether acted the slave, to make himself the master. It was when the whole legion from the fleet had taken the oath to him, that feeling confidence in his strength, and thinking that the men, on whose individual feeling he had been working, should be roused by a general appeal, he stood before the rampart of the camp, and spoke as follows:

37. "Comrades, I cannot say in what character I have presented myself to you; I refuse to call myself a subject, now that you have named me Prince, or Prince, while another reigns. Your title also will be equally uncertain, so long as it shall be a question, whether it is the Emperor of the Roman people, or a public enemy, whom you have in your camp. Mark you, how in one breath they cry for my punishment and for your execution. So evident it is, that we can neither perish, nor be saved, except together. Perhaps, with his usual clemency, Galba has already promised that

we should die, like the man, who, though no one demanded
it, massacred so many thousands of perfectly guiltless soldiers. A shudder comes over my soul, whenever I call to
mind that ghastly entry, Galba's solitary victory, when, before the eyes of the capital he gave orders to decimate the
prisoners, the suppliants, whom he had admitted to surrender. These were the auspices with which he entered the
city What is the glory that he has brought to the throne?
None but that he has murdered Obultronius Sabinus and
Cornelius Marcellus in Spain, Betuus Chilo in Gaul, Fonteius Capito in Germany, Clodius Macer in Africa, Cingonius on the high road, Turpilianus in the city, Nymphidius in the camp. What province, what camp in the
world, but is stained with blood and foul with crime, or, as
he expresses it himself, purified and chastened? For what
others call crimes he calls reforms, and, by similar mis-
nomers, he speaks of strictness instead of barbarity, of economy instead of avarice, while the cruelties and affronts inflicted upon you he calls discipline. Seven months only have
passed since Nero fell, and already Icelus has seized more
than the Polycleti, the Vatinii, and the Elii amassed. Vinius
would not have gone so far with his rapacity and lawlessness had he been Emperor himself; as it is, he has lorded it
over us as if we had been his own subjects, has held us as
cheap as if we had been another's. That one house would
furnish the donative, which is never given you, but with
which you are daily upbraided.

38. "Again, that we might have nothing to hope even
from his successor, Galba fetches out of exile the man in
whose ill-humour and avarice he considers that he has found
the best resemblance to himself. You witnessed, comrades,
how by a remarkable storm even the Gods discountenanced
that ill-starred adoption; and the feeling of the Senate, of
the people of Rome, is the same. It is to your valour that
they look, in you these better counsels find all their support, without you, noble as they may be, they are powerless.
It is not to war or to danger that I invite you; the swords
of all Roman soldiers are with us. At this moment Galba
has but one half-armed cohort, which is detaining, not defending him. Let it once behold you, let it receive my sig-

nal, and the only strife will be, who shall oblige me most.
There is no room for delay in a business which can only
be approved when it is done." He then ordered the armoury
to be opened. The soldiers immediately seized the arms
without regard to rule or military order, no distinction being observed between Prætorians and legionaries, both of
whom again indiscriminately assumed the shields and helmets of the auxiliary troops. No tribune or centurion encouraged them, every man acted on his own impulse and
guidance, and the vilest found their chief incitement in the
dejection of the good.

39. Meanwhile, appalled by the roar of the increasing
sedition and by the shouts which reached the city, Piso had
overtaken Galba, who in the interval had quitted the palace,
and was approaching the Forum. Already Marius Celsus
had brought back discouraging tidings. And now some advised that the Emperor should return to the palace, others
that he should make for the Capitol, many again that he
should occupy the Rostra, though most did but oppose the
opinions of others, while, as ever happens in these ill-starred
counsels, plans for which the opportunity had slipped away
seemed the best. It is said that Laco, without Galba's knowledge, meditated the death of Vinius, either hoping by this
execution to appease the fury of the soldiers, or believing
him to be an accomplice of Otho, or, it may be, out of
mere hatred. The time and the place however made him
hesitate; he knew that a massacre once begun is not easily
checked. His plan too was disconcerted by a succession of
alarming tidings, and the desertion of immediate adherents.
So languid was now the zeal of those who had at first been
eager to display their fidelity and courage.

40. Galba was hurried to and fro with every movement
of the surging crowd; the halls and temples all around
were thronged with spectators of this mournful sight. Not a
voice was heard from the people or even from the rabble.
Everywhere were terror-stricken countenances, and ears
turned to catch every sound. It was a scene neither of agitation nor of repose, but there reigned the silence of profound alarm and profound indignation. Otho however was
told that they were arming the mob. He ordered his men

to hurry on at full speed, and to anticipate the danger. Then did Roman soldiers rush forward like men who had to drive a Vologeses or Pacorus from the ancestral throne of the Arsacidæ, not as though they were hastening to murder their aged and defenceless Emperor. In all the terror of their arms, and at the full speed of their horses, they burst into the Forum, thrusting aside the crowd and trampling on the Senate. Neither the sight of the Capitol, nor the sanctity of the overhanging temples, nor the thought of rulers past or future, could deter them from committing a crime, which any one succeeding to power must avenge.

41. When this armed array was seen to approach, the standard-bearer of the cohort that escorted Galba (he is said to have been one Atilius Vergilio) tore off and dashed upon the ground Galba's effigy. At this signal the feeling of all the troops declared itself plainly for Otho. The Forum was deserted by the flying populace. Weapons were pointed against all who hesitated. Near the lake of Curtius, Galba was thrown out of his litter and fell to the ground, through the alarm of his bearers. His last words have been variously reported according as men hated or admired him. Some have said that he asked in a tone of entreaty what wrong he had done, and begged a few days for the payment of the donative. The more general account is, that he voluntarily offered his neck to the murderers, and bade them haste and strike, if it seemed to be for the good of the Common-wealth. To those who slew him it mattered not what he said. About the actual murderer nothing is clearly known. Some have recorded the name of Terentius, an enrolled pensioner, others that of Lecanius; but it is the current report that one Camurius, a soldier of the 15th legion, com-pletely severed his throat by treading his sword down upon it. The rest of the soldiers foully mutilated his arms and legs, for his breast was protected, and in their savage feroc-ity inflicted many wounds even on the headless trunk.

42. They next fell on T. Vinius; and in his case also it is not known whether the fear of instant death choked his ut-terance, or whether he cried out that Otho had not given orders to slay him. Either he invented this in his terror, or he thus confessed his share in the conspiracy. His life and

character incline us rather to believe that he was an accomplice in the crime which he certainly caused. He fell in front of the temple of the Divine Julius, and at the first blow, which struck him on the back of the knee; immediately afterwards Julius Carus, a legionary, ran him through the body.

43. A noble example of manhood was on that day witnessed by our age in Sempronius Densus. He was a centurion in a cohort of the Prætorian Guard, and had been appointed by Galba to escort Piso. Rushing, dagger in hand, to meet the armed men, and upbraiding them with their crime, he drew the attention of the murderers on himself by his exclamations and gestures, and thus gave Piso, wounded as he was, an opportunity of escape. Piso made his way to the temple of Vesta, where he was admitted by the compassion of one of the public slaves, who concealed him in his chamber. There, not indeed through the sanctity of the place or its worship, but through the obscurity of his hiding-place, he obtained a respite from instant destruction, till there came, by Otho's direction and specially eager to slay him, Sulpicius Florus, of the British auxiliary infantry, to whom Galba had lately given the citizenship, and Statius Murcus, one of the body-guard. Piso was dragged out by these men and slaughtered in the entrance of the temple.

44. There was, we are told, no death of which Otho heard with greater joy, no head which he surveyed with so insatiable a gaze. Perhaps it was, that his mind was then for the first time relieved from all anxiety, and so had leisure to rejoice; perhaps there was with Galba something to recall departed majesty, with Vinius some thought of old friendship, which troubled with mournful images even that ruthless heart; Piso's death, as that of an enemy and a rival, he felt to be a right and lawful subject of rejoicing. The heads were fixed upon poles and carried about among the standards of the cohorts, close to the eagle of the legion, while those who had struck the blow, those who had been present, those who whether truly or falsely boasted of the act, as of some great and memorable achievement, vied in displaying their bloodstained hands. Vitellius afterwards

found more than 120 memorials from persons who claimed
a reward for some notable service on that day. All these
persons he ordered to be sought out and slain, not to honour
Galba, but to comply with the traditional policy of rulers,
who thus provide protection for the present and vengeance
for the future.

45. One would have thought it a different Senate, a different people. All rushed to the camp, outran those who
were close to them, and struggled with those who were before, inveighed against Galba, praised the wisdom of the
soldiers, covered the hand of Otho with kisses; the more
insincere their demonstrations, the more they multiplied
them. Nor did Otho repulse the advances of individuals,
while he checked the greed and ferocity of the soldiers by
word and look. They demanded that Marius Celsus, consul
elect, Galba's faithful friend to the very last moment, should
be led to execution, loathing his energy and integrity as if
they were vices. It was evident that they were seeking to
begin massacre and plunder, and the proscription of all the
most virtuous citizens, and Otho had not yet sufficient authority to prevent crime, though he could command it. He
feigned anger, and ordered him to be loaded with chains,
declaring that he was to suffer more signal punishment, and
thus he rescued him from immediate destruction.

46. Every thing was then ordered according to the will
of the soldiery. The Prætorians chose their own prefects.
One was Plotius Firmus, who had once been in the ranks,
had afterwards commanded the watch, and who, while
Galba was yet alive, had embraced the cause of Otho. With
him was associated Licinius Proculus, Otho's intimate
friend, and consequently suspected of having encouraged
his schemes. Flavius Sabinus they appointed prefect of the
city, thus adopting Nero's choice, in whose reign he had
held the same office, though many in choosing him had an
eye to his brother Vespasian. A demand was then made,
that the fees for furloughs usually paid to the centurions
should be abolished. These the common soldiers paid as a
kind of annual tribute. A fourth part of every company
might be scattered on furlough, or even loiter about the
camp, provided that they paid the fees to the centurions

No one cared about the amount of the tax, or the way in which it was raised. It was by robbery, plunder, or the most servile occupations that the soldiers' holiday was purchased. The man with the fullest purse was worn out with toil and cruel usage till he bought his furlough. His means exhausted by this outlay, and his energies utterly relaxed by idleness, the once rich and vigorous soldier returned to his company a poor and spiritless man. One after another was ruined by the same poverty and license, and rushed into mutiny and dissension, and finally into civil war. Otho, however, not to alienate the affections of the centurions by an act of bounty to the ranks, promised that his own purse should pay these annual sums. It was undoubtedly a salutary reform, and was afterwards under good emperors established as a permanent rule of the service. Laco, prefect of the city, who had been ostensibly banished to an island, was assassinated by an enrolled pensioner, sent on by Otho to do the deed. Martianus Icelus, being but a freedman, was publicly executed.

47. A day spent in crime found its last horror in the rejoicings that concluded it. The Prætor of the city summoned the Senate; the rest of the Magistrates vied with each other in their flatteries. The Senators hastily assembled and conferred by decree upon Otho the tribunitial office, the name of Augustus, and every imperial honour. All strove to extinguish the remembrance of those taunts and invectives, which had been thrown out at random, and which no one supposed were rankling in his heart. Whether he had forgotten, or only postponed his resentment, the shortness of his reign left undecided. The Forum yet streamed with blood, when he was borne in a litter over heaps of dead to the Capitol, and thence to the palace. He suffered the bodies to be given up for burial, and to be burnt. For Piso, the last rites were performed by his wife Verania and his brother Scribonianus; for Vinius, by his daughter Crispina, their heads having been discovered and purchased from the murderers, who had reserved them for sale.

48. Piso, who was then completing his thirty-first year, had enjoyed more fame than good fortune. His brothers, Magnus and Crassus, had been put to death by Claudius

and Nero respectively. He was himself for many years an exile, for four days a Cæsar, and Galba's hurried adoption of him only gave him this privilege over his elder brother, that he perished first. Vinius had lived to the age of fifty-seven, with many changes of character. His father was of a prætorian family, his maternal grandfather was one of the proscribed. He had disgraced himself in his first campaign when he served under the legate Calvisius Sabinus. That officer's wife, urged by a perverse curiosity to view the camp, entered it by night in the disguise of a soldier, and after extending the insulting frolic to the watches and the general arrangements of the army, actually dared to commit the act of adultery in the head-quarters. Vinius was charged with having participated in her guilt, and by order of Caius was loaded with irons. The altered times soon restored him to liberty. He then enjoyed an uninterrupted succession of honours, first filling the prætorship, and then command-ing a legion with general satisfaction, but he subsequently incurred the degrading imputation of having pilfered a gold cup at the table of Claudius, who the next day directed that he alone should be served on earthenware. Yet as pro-consul of Gallia Narbonensis he administered the govern-ment with strict integrity. When forced by his friendship with Galba to a dangerous elevation, he shewed himself bold, crafty, and enterprising; and whether he applied his powers to vice or virtue, was always equally energetic. His will was made void by his vast wealth; that of Piso owed its validity to his poverty.

49. The body of Galba lay for a long time neglected, and subjected, through the license which the darkness permitted, to a thousand indignities, till Argius his steward, who had been one of his slaves, gave it a humble burial in his mas-ter's private gardens. His head, which the sutlers and camp-followers had fixed on a pole and mangled, was found only the next day in front of the tomb of Patrobius, a freedman of Nero's, whom Galba had executed. It was put with the body, which had by that time been reduced to ashes. Such was the end of Servius Galba, who in his seventy-three years had lived prosperously through the reigns of five Em-perors, and had been more fortunate under the rule of others

than he was in his own. His family could boast an ancient
nobility, his wealth was great. His character was of an
average kind, rather free from vices, than distinguished by
virtues. He was not regardless of fame, nor yet vainly fond
of it. Other men's money he did not covet, with his own he
was parsimonious, with that of the State avaricious. To his
freedmen and friends he shewed a forbearance, which, when
he had fallen into worthy hands, could not be blamed;
when, however, these persons were worthless, he was even
culpably blind. The nobility of his birth and the perils of
the times made what was really indolence pass for wisdom.
While in the vigour of life, he enjoyed a high military reputation in Germany; as proconsul he ruled Africa with moderation, and when advanced in years shewed the same integrity in Eastern Spain. He seemed greater than a subject
while he was yet in a subject's rank, and by common consent would have been pronounced equal to empire, had he
never been emperor.

50. The alarm of the capital, which trembled to see the
atrocity of these recent crimes, and to think of the old character of Otho, was heightened into terror by fresh news
about Vitellius, news which had been suppressed before the
murder of Galba, in order to make it appear that only the
army of Upper Germany had revolted. That two men, who
for shamelessness, indolence, and profligacy, were the most
worthless of mortals, had been selected, it would seem, by
some fatality to ruin the Empire, became the open complaint, not only of the Senate and the Knights, who had
some stake and interest in the country, but even of the
common people. It was no longer to the late horrors of a
dreadful peace, but to the recollections of the civil wars,
that men recurred, speaking of how the capital had been
taken by Roman armies, how Italy had been wasted and
the provinces spoiled, of Pharsalia, Philippi, Perusia, and
Mutina, and all the familiar names of great public disasters.
"The world," they said, "was well-nigh turned upside down
when the struggle for empire was between worthy competi-
tors, yet the Empire continued to exist after the victories
of Caius Julius and Cæsar Augustus; the Republic would
have continued to exist under Pompey and Brutus. And is

it for Otho or for Vitellius that we are now to repair to the temples? Prayers for either would be impious, vows for either a blasphemy, when from their conflict you can only learn that the conqueror must be the worse of the two." Some were speculating on Vespasian and the armies of the East. Vespasian was indeed preferable to either, yet they shuddered at the idea of another war, of other massacres. Even about Vespasian there were doubtful rumours, and he, unlike any of his predecessors, was changed for the better by power.

51. I will now describe the origin and occasion of the revolt of Vitellius. After the destruction of Julius Vindex and his whole force, the army, flushed with the delights of plunder and glory, as men might well be who had been fortunate enough to triumph without toil or danger in a most lucrative war, began to hanker after campaigns and battles, and to prefer prize money to pay. They had long endured a service which the character of the country and of the climate and the rigours of military discipline rendered at once unprofitable and severe. But that discipline, inexorable as it is in times of peace, is relaxed by civil strife, when on both sides are found the agents of corruption, and treachery goes unpunished. They had men, arms and horses, more than enough for all purposes of utility and show, but before the war they had been acquainted only with the companies and squadrons of their own force, as the various armies were separated from each other by the limits of their respective provinces. But the legions, having been concentrated to act against Vindex, and having thus learnt to measure their own strength against the strength of Gaul, were now on the look out for another war and for new conflicts. They called their neighbours, not "allies" as of old, but "the enemy" and "the vanquished." Nor did that part of Gaul which borders on the Rhine fail to espouse the same cause, and to shew the bitterest hostility in inflaming the army against the Galbianists, that being the name, which in their contempt for Vindex they had given to the party. The rage first excited against the Sequani and Ædui extended to other states in proportion to their wealth, and they revelled in imagination on the

storm of cities, the plunder of estates, the sack of dwelling-houses. But, besides the rapacity and arrogance which are the special faults of superior strength, they were exasperated by the bravadoes of the Gallic people, who in a spirit of insult to the army boasted of how they had been relieved by Galba from a fourth part of their tribute, and had received grants from the State. There was also a report, ingeniously spread and recklessly believed, to the effect that the legions were being decimated, and all the most energetic centurions dismissed. From all quarters arrived the most alarming tidings. The reports from the capital were unfavourable, while the disaffection of the colony of Lugdunum, which obstinately adhered to Nero, gave rise to a multitude of rumours. But it was in the army itself, in its hatreds, its fears, and even in the security with which a review of its own strength inspired it, that there was the most abundant material for the exercise of imagination and credulity.

52. Just before December 1 in the preceding year, Aulus Vitellius had visited Lower Germany, and had carefully inspected the winter quarters of the legions. Many had their rank restored to them, sentences of degradation were cancelled, and marks of disgrace partially removed. In most cases he did but court popularity, in some he exercised a sound discretion, making a salutary change from the meanness and rapacity which Fonteius Capito had shown in bestowing and withdrawing promotion. But he seemed a greater personage than a simple consular legate, and all his acts were invested with an unusual importance. Though sterner judges pronounced Vitellius to be a man of low tastes, those who were partial to him attributed to geniality and good nature the immoderate and indiscriminate prodigality, with which he gave away what was his own, and squandered what did not belong to him. Besides this, men themselves eager for power were ready to represent his very vices as virtues. As there were in both armies many of obedient and quiet habits, so there were many who were as unprincipled as they were energetic; but distinguished above all for boundless ambition and singular daring were the legates of the legions, Fabius Valens and Alienus Cæcina.

One of these men, Valens, had taken offence against Galba, under the notion that he had not shewn proper gratitude for his services in discovering to him the hesitation of Verginius and crushing the plans of Capito. He now began to urge Vitellius to action. He enlarged on the zeal of the soldiery. "You have," he said, "everywhere a great reputation; you will find nothing to stop you in Hordeonius Flaccus; Britain will be with you; the German auxiliaries will follow your standard. All the provinces waver in their allegiance. The Empire is held on the precarious tenure of an aged life, and must shortly pass into other hands. You have only to open your arms, and to meet the advances of fortune. It was well for Verginius to hesitate, the scion of a mere Equestrian family, and son of a father unknown to fame: he would have been unequal to empire, had he accepted it, and yet been safe though he refused it. But from the honours of a father who was thrice consul, was censor and colleague of Cæsar, Vitellius has long since derived an imperial rank, while he has lost the security that belongs to a subject."

53. These arguments roused the indolent temper of the man, yet roused him rather to wish than to hope for the throne. Meanwhile however in Upper Germany Cæcina, young and handsome, of commanding stature, and of boundless ambition, had attracted the favour of the soldiery by his skilful oratory and his dignified mien. This man had, when quæstor in Bætica, attached himself with zeal to the party of Galba, who had appointed him, young as he was, to the command of a legion, but, it being afterwards discovered that he had embezzled the public money, Galba directed that he should be prosecuted for peculation. Cæcina, grievously offended, determined to throw everything into confusion, and under the disasters of his country to conceal his private dishonour. There were not wanting in the army itself the elements of civil strife. The whole of it had taken part in the war against Vindex; it had not passed over to Galba till Nero fell; even then in this transference of its allegiance it had been anticipated by the armies of Lower Germany. Besides this, the Treveri, the Lingones, and the other states which Galba had most seriously in-

jured by his severe edicts and by the confiscation of their
territory, were particularly close to the winter-quarters of
the legions. Thence arose seditious conferences, a soldiery
demoralized by intercourse with the inhabitants of the
country, and tendencies in favour of Verginius, which could
easily be turned to the profit of any other person.

54. The Lingones, following an old custom, had sent presents to the legions, right hands clasped together, an emblem
of friendship. Their envoys, who had assumed a studied
appearance of misery and distress, passed through the head-
quarters and the men's tents, and complaining, now of their
own wrongs, now of the rewards bestowed on the neighbouring states, and, when they found the soldiers' ears open
to their words, of the perils and insults to which the army
itself was exposed, inflamed the passions of the troops. The
legions were on the verge of mutiny, when Hordeonius
Flaccus ordered the envoys to depart, and to make their
departure more secret, directed them to leave the camp by
night. Hence arose a frightful rumour, many asserting that
the envoys had been killed, and that, unless the soldiers
provided for their own safety, the next thing would be,
that the most energetic of their number, and those who had
complained of their present condition, would be slaughtered
under cover of night, when the rest of the army would
know nothing of their fate. The legions then bound themselves by a secret agreement. Into this the auxiliary troops
were admitted. At first objects of suspicion, from the idea
that their infantry and cavalry were being concentrated
in preparation for an attack on the legions, these troops
soon became especially zealous in the scheme. The bad find
it easier to agree for purposes of war than to live in harmony during peace.

55. Yet it was to Galba that the legions of Lower Germany took the oath of fidelity annually administered on
the first of January. It was done, however, after long delay, and then only by a few voices from the foremost ranks,
while the rest preserved an absolute silence, every one waiting for some bold demonstration from his neighbour, in
obedience to that innate tendency of men, which makes
them quick to follow where they are slow to lead. And

even in the various legions there was a difference of feeling. The soldiers of the 1st and of the 5th were so mutinous, that some of them threw stones at the images of Galba. The 15th and 16th legions ventured on nothing beyond uproar and threatening expressions. They were on the watch for something that might lead to an outbreak. In the Upper army, however, the 4th and 13th legions, which were stationed in the same winter-quarters, proceeded on this same first of January to break in pieces the images of Galba, the 4th legion being foremost, the 18th shewing some reluctance, but soon joining with the rest. Not however to seem to throw off all their reverence for the Empire, they sought to dignify their oath with the now obsolete names of the Senate and people of Rome. Not a single legate or tribune exerted himself for Galba; some, as is usual in a tumult, were even conspicuously active in mutiny, though no one delivered anything like a formal harangue or spoke from a tribunal. Indeed there was as yet no one to be obliged by such services.

56. Hordeonius Flaccus, the consular legate, was present and witnessed this outrage, but he dared neither check the furious mutineers, nor keep the wavering to their duty, nor encourage the well affected. Indolent and timid, he was preserved from guilt only by his sloth. Four Centurions of the 18th legion, Nonius Receptus, Donatius Valens, Romilius Marcellus, Calpurnius Repentinus, striving to protect the images of Galba, were swept away by a rush of the soldiers and put in irons. After this no one retained any sense of duty, any recollection of his late allegiance, but, as usually happens in mutinies, the side of the majority became the side of all. In the course of the night of the 1st of January, the standard-bearer of the 4th legion, coming to the Colonia Agrippinensis, announced to Vitellius, who was then at dinner, the news that the 4th and 18th legions had thrown down the images of Galba, and had sworn allegiance to the Senate and people of Rome. Such a form of oath appeared meaningless. It was determined to seize the doubtful fortune of the hour, and to offer an Emperor to their choice. Vitellius sent envoys to the legions and their legates, who were to say that the army of Upper Germany had revolted

from Galba, that it was consequently necessary for them,
either to make war on the revolters, or, if they preferred
peace and harmony, to create an Emperor, and who were to
suggest, that it would be less perilous to accept than to look
for a chief.

57. The nearest winter-quarters were those of the first
legion, and Fabius Valens was the most energetic of the
legates. This officer in the course of the following day entered the Colonia Agrippinensis with the cavalry of the legion and of the auxiliaries, and together with them saluted
Vitellius as Emperor. All the legions belonging to the same
province followed his example with prodigious zeal, and the
army of Upper Germany abandoned the specious names of
the Senate and people of Rome, and on the 3rd of January
declared for Vitellius. One could be sure that during those
previous two days it had not really been the army of the
State. The inhabitants of Colonia Agrippinensis, the Treveri,
and the Lingones, shewed as much zeal as the army, making offers of personal service, of horses, of arms and of
money, according as each felt himself able to assist the
cause by his own exertions, by his wealth, or by his talents.
Nor was this done only by the leading men in the colonies
or the camps, who had abundant means at hand, and might
indulge great expectations in the event of victory, but whole
companies down to the very ranks offered instead of money
their rations, their belts, and the bosses, which, richly deco-
rated with silver, adorned their arms; so strong were the
promptings from without, their own enthusiasm, and even
the suggestions of avarice.

58. Vitellius, after bestowing high commendation on the
zeal of the soldiers, proceeded to distribute among Roman
Knights the offices of the Imperial court usually held by
freedmen. He paid the furlough fees to the centurions out
of the Imperial treasury. While in most instances he acquiesced in the fury of the soldiers, who clamoured for
numerous executions, in some few he eluded it under the
pretence of imprisoning the accused. Pompeius Propinquus,
procurator of Belgica, was immediately put to death. Julius
Burdo, prefect of the German fleet, he contrived to withdraw from the scene of danger. The resentment of the army

had been inflamed against this officer by the belief, that it was he who had invented the charges and planned the treachery which had destroyed Capito. The memory of Capito was held in high favour, and with that enraged soldiery it was possible to slaughter in open day, but to pardon only by stealth. He was kept in prison, and only set at liberty after the victory of Vitellius, when the resentment of the soldiery had subsided. Meanwhile, by way of a victim, the centurion Crispinus was given up to them; this man had actually imbued his hands in the blood of Capito. Consequently he was to those who cried for vengeance a more notorious criminal, and to him who punished a cheaper sacrifice.

59. Julius Civilis, a man of commanding influence among the Batavi, was next rescued from like circumstances of peril, lest that high-spirited nation should be alienated by his execution. There were indeed in the territory of the Lingones eight Batavian cohorts, which formed the auxiliary force of the 14th legion, but which had, among the many dissensions of the time, withdrawn from it; a body of troops which, to whatever side they might incline, would, whether as allies or enemies, throw a vast weight into the scale. Vitellius ordered the centurions Nonnius, Donatius, Romilius, and Calpurnius, of whom I have before spoken, to be executed. They had been convicted of the crime of fidelity, among rebels the worst of crimes. New adherents soon declared themselves in Valerius Asiaticus, legate of the Province of Belgica, whom Vitellius soon after made his son-in-law, and Junius Blæsus, governor of Gallia Lugdunensis, who brought with him the Italian Legion and the Taurine Horse, which was stationed at Lugdunum. The armies of Rhætia made no delay in at once joining Vitellius, and even in Britain there was no hesitation.

60. Of that province Trebellius Maximus was governor, a man whose sordid avarice made him an object of contempt and hatred to the army. His unpopularity was heightened by the efforts of Roscius Cælius, the legate of the 20th legion, who had long been on bad terms with him, and who now seized the opportunity of a civil war to break out into greater violence. Trebellius charged him with mutinous de-

signs, and with disturbing the regularity of military discipline; Cælius retorted on Trebellius the accusation of having plundered and impoverished the legions. Meanwhile all obedience in the army was destroyed by these disgraceful quarrels between its commanders, and the feud rose to such a height that Trebellius was insulted even by the auxiliaries, and finding himself altogether isolated, as the infantry and cavalry sided with Cælius, he fled for safety to Vitellius. Yet the province still enjoyed tranquility, though its consular governor had been driven from it. It was now ruled by the legates of the legions, who were equal as to lawful authority, though the audacity of Cælius made him the more powerful.

61. After the army of Britain had joined him, Vitellius, who had now a prodigious force and vast resources, determined that there should be two generals and two lines of march for the contemplated war. Fabius Valens was ordered to win over, if possible, or, if they refused his overtures, to ravage the provinces of Gaul and to invade Italy by way of the Cottian Alps; Cæcina to take the nearer route, and to march down from the Penine range. To Valens were entrusted the picked troops of the army of Lower Germany with the eagle of the 5th legion and the auxiliary infantry and cavalry, to the number of 40,000 armed men; Cæcina commanded 30,000 from Upper Germany, the strength of his force being one legion, the 21st. Both had also some German auxiliaries, and from this source Vitellius, who was to follow with his whole military strength, completed his own forces.

62. Wonderful was the contrast between the army and the Emperor. The army was all eagerness; they cried out war, while Gaul yet wavered, and Spain hesitated. "The winter," they said, "the delays of a cowardly inaction must not stop us. We must invade Italy, we must seize the capital; in civil strife, where action is more needed than deliberation, nothing is safer than haste." Vitellius, on the contrary, was sunk in sloth, and anticipated the enjoyment of supreme power in indolent luxury and prodigal festivities. By mid-day he was half-intoxicated, and heavy with food; yet the ardour and vigour of the soldiers themselves dis-

charged all the duties of a general as well as if the Emperor
had been present to stimulate the energetic by hope and
the indolent by fear. Ready to march and eager for action,
they loudly demanded the signal for starting; the title of
Germanicus was at once bestowed on Vitellius, that of
Cæsar he refused to accept, even after his victory. It was
observed as a happy omen for Fabius Valens and the forces
which he was conducting to the campaign, that on the very
day on which they set out an eagle moved with a gentle
flight before the army as it advanced, as if to guide it on
its way. And for a long distance so loudly did the soldiers
shout in their joy, so calm and unterrified was the bird,
that it was taken as no doubtful omen of great and successful achievements.

63. The territory of the Treveri they entered with all the
security naturally felt among allies. But at Divodurum, a
town of the Mediomatrici, though they had been received
with the most courteous hospitality, a sudden panic mastered them. In a moment they took up arms to massacre
an innocent people, not for the sake of plunder, or fired by
the lust of spoil, but in a wild frenzy arising from causes so
vague that it was very difficult to apply a remedy. Soothed
at length by the entreaties of their general, they refrained
from utterly destroying the town; yet as many as four thousand human beings were slaughtered. Such an alarm was
spread through Gaul, that as the army advanced, whole
states, headed by their magistrates and with prayers on
their lips, came forth to meet it, while the women and children lay prostrate along the roads, and all else that might
appease an enemy's fury was offered, though war there was
none, to secure the boon of peace.

64. Valens received the tidings of the murder of Galba
and the accession of Otho while he was in the country of
the Leuci. The feelings of the soldiers were not seriously
affected either with joy or alarm; they were intent on war.
Gaul however ceased to hesitate; Otho and Vitellius it hated
equally, Vitellius it also feared. The next territory was that
of the Lingones, who were loyal to Vitellius. The troops
were kindly received, and they vied with each other in good
behaviour. This happy state of things, however, was of short

duration owing to the violence of the auxiliary infantry, which had detached itself, as before related, from the 14th legion, and had been incorporated by Valens with his army. First came angry words, then a brawl between the Batavi and the legionaries, which as the partialities of the soldiers espoused one or another of the parties was almost kindled into a battle, and would have been so, had not Valens by punishing a few, reminded the Batavi of the authority which they had now forgotten. Against the Ædui a pretext for war was sought in vain. That people, when ordered to furnish arms and money, voluntarily added a supply of provisions. What the Ædui did from fear, the people of Lugdunum did with delight. Yet the Italian legion and the Taurine Horse were withdrawn. It was resolved that the 18th cohort should be left there, as it was their usual winter-quarters. Manlius Valens, legate of the Italian legion, though he had served the party well, was held in no honour by Vitellius. Fabius Valens had defamed him by secret charges of which he knew nothing, publicly praising him all the while, that he might the less suspect the treachery.

65. The old feud between Lugdunum and Vienna had been kindled afresh by the late war. They had inflicted many losses on each other so continuously and so savagely that they could not have been fighting only for Nero or Galba. Galba had made his displeasure the occasion for diverting into the Imperial treasury the revenues of Lugdunum, while he had treated Vienna with marked respect. Thence came rivalry and dislike, and the two states, separated only by a river, were linked together by perpetual feud. Accordingly the people of Lugdunum began to work on the passions of individual soldiers, and to goad them into destroying Vienna, by reminding them, how that people had besieged their colony, had abetted the attempts of Vindex, and had recently raised legions for Galba. After parading these pretexts for quarrel, they pointed out how vast would be the plunder. From secret encouragement they passed to open entreaty. "Go," they said, "to avenge us and utterly destroy this home of Gallic rebellion. There all are foreigners and enemies; we are a Roman colony, a part of the Roman army, sharers in your successes and reverses.

Fortune may declare against us. Do not abandon us to an angry foe."

66. By these and many similar arguments they so wrought upon the troops, that even the legates and the leaders of the party did not think it possible to check their fury; but the people of Vienna, aware of their danger, assumed the veils and chaplets of suppliants, and, as the army approached, clasped the weapons, knees and feet of the soldiers, and so turned them from their purpose. Valens also made each soldier a present of 300 sesterces. After that the antiquity and rank of the colony prevailed, and the intercession of Valens, who charged them to respect the life and welfare of the inhabitants, received a favourable hearing. They were however publicly mulcted of their arms, and furnished the soldiers with all kinds of supplies from their private means. Report, however, has uniformly asserted, that Valens himself was bought with a vast sum. Poor for many years and suddenly growing rich, he could but ill conceal the change in his fortunes, indulging without moderation the appetites which a protracted poverty had inflamed, and, after a youth of indigence, becoming prodigal in old age. The army then proceeded by slow marches through the territory of the Allobroges and Vocontii, the very length of each day's march and the changes of encampment being made a matter of traffic by the general, who concluded disgraceful bargains to the injury of the holders of land and the magistrates of the different states, and used such menaces, that at Lucus, a municipal town of the Vocontii, he was on the point of setting fire to the place, when a present of money soothed his rage. When money was not forthcoming he was bought off by sacrifices to his lust. Thus he made his way to the Alps.

67. Cæcina revelled more freely in plunder and bloodshed. His restless spirit had been provoked by the Helvetii, a Gallic race famous once for its warlike population, afterwards for the associations of its name. Of the murder of Galba they knew nothing, and they rejected the authority of Vitellius. The war originated in the rapacity and impatience of the 21st legion, who had seized some money sent to pay the garrison of a fortress, which the Helvetii

had long held with their own troops and at their own expense. The Helvetii in their indignation intercepted some
letters written in the name of the army of Germany, which
were on their way to the legions of Pannonia, and detained
the centurion and some of his soldiers in custody. Cæcina,
eager for war, hastened to punish every delinquency, as it
occurred, before the offender could repent. Suddenly moving his camp he ravaged a place, which during a long period
of peace had grown up into something like a town, and
which was much resorted to as an agreeable watering-place.
Despatches were sent to the Rhætian auxiliaries, instruct-
ing them to attack the Helvetii in the rear while the legion
was engaging them in front.

68. Bold before the danger came and timid in the moment of peril, the Helvetii, though at the commencement
of the movement they had chosen Claudius Severus for
their leader, knew not how to use their arms, to keep their
ranks, or to act in concert. A pitched battle with veteran
troops would be destruction, a siege would be perilous with
fortifications old and ruinous. On the one side was Cæcina
at the head of a powerful army, on the other were the auxiliary infantry and cavalry of Rhætia and the youth of that
province, inured to arms and exercised in habits of warfare.
All around were slaughter and devastation. Wandering to
and fro between the two armies, the Helvetii threw aside
their arms, and with a large proportion of wounded and
stragglers fled for refuge to Mount Vocetius. They were
immediately dislodged by the attack of some Thracian infantry. Closely pursued by the Germans and Rhætians they
were cut down in their forests and even in their hiding
places. Thousands were put to the sword, thousands more
were sold into slavery. Every place having been completely
destroyed, the army was marching in regular order on Aventicum, the capital town, when a deputation was sent to surrender the city. This surrender was accepted. Julius Al-
pinus, one of the principal men, was executed by Cæcina,
as having been the promoter of the war. All the rest he left
to the mercy or severity of Vitellius.

69. It is hard to say whether the envoys from Helvetia
found the Emperor or his army less merciful. "Exterminate

the race," was the cry of the soldiers as they brandished their weapons, or shook their fists in the faces of the envoys. Even Vitellius himself did not refrain from threatening words and gestures, till at length Claudius Cossus, one of the Helvetian envoys, a man of well-known eloquence, but who then concealed the art of the orator under an assumption of alarm, and was therefore more effective, soothed the rage of the soldiers, who, like all multitudes, were liable to sudden impulses, and were now as inclined to pity as they had been extravagant in fury. Bursting into tears and praying with increasing earnestness for a milder sentence, they procured pardon and protection for the state.

70. Cæcina while halting for a few days in the Helvetian territory, till he could learn the decision of Vitellius, and at the same time making preparations for the passage of the Alps, received from Italy the good news, that Silius' Horse, which was quartered in the neighbourhood of Padus, had sworn allegiance to Vitellius. They had served under him when he was Proconsul in Africa, from which place Nero had soon afterwards brought them, intending to send them on before himself into Egypt, but had recalled them in consequence of the rebellion of Vindex. They were still in Italy, and now at the instigation of their decurions, who knew nothing of Otho, but were bound to Vitellius, and who magnified the strength of the advancing legions and the fame of the German army, they joined the Vitellianists, and by way of a present to their new Prince they secured for him the strongest towns of the country north of the Padus, Mediolanum, Novaria, Eporedia, and Vercellæ. This Cæcina had learnt from themselves. Aware that the widest part of Italy could not be held by such a force as a single squadron of cavalry, he sent on in advance the auxiliary infantry from Gaul, Lusitania, and Rhætia, with the veteran troops from Germany, and Petra's Horse, while he made a brief halt to consider whether he should pass over the Rhætian range into Noricum, to attack Petronius, the procurator, who had collected some auxiliaries, and broken down the bridges over the rivers, and was thought to be faithful to Otho. Fearing however that he might lose the infantry and cavalry which he had sent on in advance, and at the same

time reflecting that more honour was to be gained by holding possession of Italy, and that, wherever the decisive conflict might take place, Noricum would be included among
the other prizes of victory, he marched the reserves and the
heavy infantry through the Penine passes while the Alps
were still covered with the snows of winter.

71. Meanwhile Otho, to the surprise of all, was not sinking down into luxury and sloth. He deferred his pleasures,
concealed his profligacy, and moulded his whole life to suit
the dignity of empire. Men dreaded all the more virtues so
false, and vices so certain to return. Marius Celsus, consul
elect, whom he had rescued from the fury of the soldiers
by pretending to imprison him, he now ordered to be summoned to the Capitol. He sought to acquire a reputation for
clemency by sparing a distinguished man opposed to his
own party. Celsus pleaded guilty to the charge of faithful
adherence to Galba, and even made a merit of such an example of fidelity. Otho did not treat him as a man to be
pardoned, and, unwilling to blend with the grace of reconciliation the memory of past hostility, at once admitted him
to his intimate friendship, and soon afterwards appointed
him to be one of his generals. By some fatality, as it seemed,
Celsus maintained also to Otho a fidelity as irreproachable
as it was unfortunate. The escape of Celsus gratified the
leading men in the State, was generally praised by the
people, and did not displease even the soldiers, who could
not but admire the virtue which provoked their anger.

72. Then followed as great a burst of joy, though from a
less worthy cause, when the destruction of Tigellinus was
achieved. Sophonius Tigellinus, a man of obscure birth,
steeped in infamy from his boyhood, and shamelessly profligate in his old age, finding vice to be his quickest road to
such offices as the command of the watch and of the Prætorian Guard, and to other distinctions due to merit, went
on to practise cruelty, rapacity, and all the crimes of ma-
turer years. He perverted Nero to every kind of atrocity;
he even ventured on some acts without the Emperor's
knowledge, and ended by deserting and betraying him.
Hence there was no criminal, whose doom was from opposite motives more importunately demanded, as well by those

who hated Nero, as by those who regretted him. During the reign of Galba Tigellinus had been screened by the influence of Vinius, who alleged that he had saved his daughter. And doubtless he had preserved her life, not indeed out of mercy, when he had murdered so many, but to secure for himself a refuge for the future. For all the greatest villains, distrusting the present, and dreading change, look for private friendship to shelter them from public detestation, caring not to be free from guilt, but only to ensure their turn in impunity. This enraged the people more than ever, the recent unpopularity of Vinius being superadded to their old hatred against Tigellinus. They rushed from every part of the city into the palace and forum, and bursting into the circus and theatre, where the mob enjoy a special license, broke out into seditious clamours. At length Tigellinus, having received at the springs of Sinuessa a message that his last hour was come, amid the embraces and caresses of his mistresses and other unseemly delays, cut his throat with a razor, and aggravated the disgrace of an infamous life by a tardy and ignominious death.

73. About the same time a demand was made for the execution of Galvia Crispinilla. Various artifices on the part of the Emperor, who incurred much obloquy by his duplicity, rescued her from the danger. She had instructed Nero in profligacy, had passed over into Africa, that she might urge Macer into rebellion, and had openly attempted to bring a famine upon Rome. Yet she afterwards gained universal popularity on the strength of her alliance with a man of consular rank, and lived unharmed through the reigns of Galba, Otho, and Vitellius. Soon she became powerful as a rich and childless woman, circumstances which have as great weight in good as in evil times.

74. Meanwhile frequent letters, disfigured by unmanly flatteries, were addressed by Otho to Vitellius, with offers of wealth and favour and any retreat he might select for a life of prodigal indulgence. Vitellius made similar overtures. Their tone was at first pacific; and both exhibited a foolish and undignified hypocrisy. Then they seemed to quarrel, charging each other with debaucheries and the grossest crimes, and both spoke truth. Otho, having recalled the en-

voys whom Galba had sent, dispatched others, nominally
from the Senate, to both the armies of Germany, to the
Italian legion, and to the troops quartered at Lugdunum.
The envoys remained with Vitellius too readily to let it be
supposed that they were detained. Some Prætorians, whom
Otho had attached to the embassy, ostensibly as a mark of
distinction, were sent back before they could mix with the
legions. Letters were also addressed by Fabius Valens in the
name of the German army to the Prætorian and city cohorts, extolling the strength of his party, and offering terms
of peace. Valens even reproached them with having transferred the Imperial power to Otho, though it had so long
before been entrusted to Vitellius.

75. Thus they were assailed by promises as well as by
threats, were told that they were not strong enough for
war, but would lose nothing by peace. Yet all this did not
shake the loyalty of the Prætorians. Nevertheless secret
emissaries were dispatched by Otho to Germany, and by
Vitellius to Rome. Both failed in their object. Those of
Vitellius escaped without injury, unnoticed in the vast multitude, knowing none, and themselves unknown. Those of
Otho were betrayed by their strange faces in a place where
all knew each other. Vitellius wrote to Titianus, Otho's
brother, threatening him and his son with death, unless the
lives of his mother and his children were spared. Both families remained uninjured. This in Otho's reign was perhaps
due to fear; Vitellius was victorious, and gained all the
credit of mercy.

76. The first encouraging tidings came to Otho from
Illyricum. He heard that the legions of Dalmatia, Pannonia, and Mœsia had sworn allegiance to him. Similar intelligence was received from Spain, and Cluvius Rufus was
commended in an edict. Immediately afterwards it became
known that Spain had gone over to Vitellius. Even Aquitania, bound though it was by the oath of allegiance to
Otho which Julius Cordus had administered, did not long
remain firm. Nowhere was there any loyalty or affection;
men changed from one side to the other under the pressure
of fear or necessity. It was this influence of fear that drew
over to Vitellius the province of Gallia Narbonensis, which

turned readily to the side that was at once the nearer and the stronger. The distant provinces, and all the armies beyond the sea, still adhered to Otho, not from any attachment to his party, but because there was vast weight in the name of the capital and the prestige of the Senate, and also because the claims which they had first heard had prepossessed their minds. The army of Judæa under Vespasian, and the legions of Syria under Mucianus, swore allegiance to Otho. Egypt and the Eastern provinces were also governed in his name. Africa displayed the same obedience, Carthage taking the lead. In that city Crescens, one of Nero's freedmen (for in evil times even this class makes itself a power in the State), without waiting for the sanction of the proconsul, Vipstanus Apronianus, had given an entertainment to the populace by way of rejoicings for the new reign, and the people, with extravagant zeal, hastened to make the usual demonstrations of joy. The example of Carthage was followed by the other cities of Africa.

77. As the armies and provinces were thus divided, Vitellius, in order to secure the sovereign power, was compelled to fight. Otho continued to discharge his imperial duties as though it were a time of profound peace. Sometimes he consulted the dignity of the Commonwealth, but often in hasty acts, dictated by the expediency of the moment, he disregarded its honour. He was himself to be consul with his brother Titianus till the 1st of March; the two following months he assigned to Verginius as a compliment to the army of Germany. With Verginius was to be associated Pompeius Vopiscus, avowedly on the ground of their being old friends, though many regarded the appointment as meant to do honour to the people of Vienna. The other consulships still remained as Nero or Galba had arranged them. Cælius Sabinus and his brother Flavius were to be consuls till the 1st of July; Arrius Antoninus and Marius Celsus from that time to the 1st of September. Even Vitellius, after his victory, did not interfere with these appointments. On aged citizens, who had already held high office, Otho bestowed, as a crowning dignity, pontificates and augurships, while he consoled the young nobles, who had lately returned from exile, by reviving the sacerdotal offices, held by their fathers

and ancestors. Cadius Rufus, Pedius Blæsus, Sævinius Pomptinius, who in the reigns of Claudius and Nero had been convicted under indictments for extortion, were restored to their rank as Senators. Those who wished to pardon them resolved by a change of names to make, what had really been rapacity, seem to have been treason, a charge then so odious that it made even good laws a dead letter.

78. By similar bounty Otho sought to win the affections of the cities and provinces. He bestowed on the colonies of Hispalis and Emerita some additional families, on the entire people of the Lingones the privileges of Roman citizenship; to the province of Bætica he joined the states of Mauritania, and granted to Cappadocia and Africa new rights, more for display than for permanent utility. In the midst of these measures, which may find an excuse in the urgency of the crisis and the anxieties which pressed upon him, he still did not forget his old amours, and by a decree of the Senate restored the statues of Poppæa. It is even believed that he thought of celebrating the memory of Nero in the hope of winning the populace, and persons were found to exhibit statues of that Prince. There were days on which the people and the soldiers greeted him with shouts of Nero Otho, as if they were heaping on him new distinction and honour. Otho himself wavered in suspense, afraid to forbid or ashamed to acknowledge the title.

79. Men's minds were so intent on the civil war, that foreign affairs were disregarded. This emboldened the Roxolani, a Sarmatian tribe, who had destroyed two cohorts in the previous winter, to invade Mœsia with great hopes of success. They had 9000 cavalry, flushed with victory and intent on plunder rather than on fighting. They were dispersed and off their guard, when the third legion together with some auxiliaries attacked them. The Romans had everything ready for battle, the Sarmatians were scattered, and in their eagerness for plunder had encumbered themselves with heavy baggage, while the superior speed of their horses was lost on the slippery roads. Thus they were cut down as if their hands were tied. It is wonderful how entirely the courage of this people is, so to speak, external to themselves. No troops could shew so little spirit when fight-

ing on foot; when they charge in squadrons, hardly any line can stand against them. But as on this occasion the day was damp and the ice thawed, what with the continual slipping of their horses, and the weight of their coats of mail, they could make no use of their pikes or their swords, which being of an excessive length they wield with bot'' hands. These coats are worn as defensive armour by the princes and most distinguished persons of the tribe. They are formed of plates of iron or very tough hides, and though they are absolutely impenetrable to blows, yet they make it difficult for such as have been overthrown by the charge of the enemy to regain their feet. Besides, the Sarmatians were perpetually sinking in the deep and soft snow. The Roman soldier, moving easily in his cuirass, continued to harass them with javelins and lances, and whenever the occasion required, closed with them with his short sword, and stabbed the defenceless enemy; for it is not their custom to defend themselves with a shield. A few who survived the battle concealed themselves in the marshes. There they perished from the inclemency of the season and the severity of their wounds. When this success was known, Marcus Aponius, governor of Mœsia, was rewarded with a triumphal statue, while Fulvius Aurelius, Julianus Titius, and Numisius Lupus, the legates of the legions, received the ensigns of consular rank. Otho was delighted, and claimed the glory for himself, as if it were he that commanded success in war, and that had aggrandised the State by his generals and his armies.

80. Meanwhile, from a trifling cause, whence nothing wa apprehended, there arose a tumult, which had nearly provec. fatal to the capital. Otho had ordered the 17th cohort to be brought up to Rome from Ostia, and the charge of arming it was entrusted to Varius Crispinus, one of the tribunes of the Prætorian Guard. This officer, thinking that he could carry out the order more at his leisure, when the camp was quiet, opened the armoury, and ordered the waggons of the cohort to be laden at night-fall. The time provoked suspicion, the motive challenged accusation, the elaborate attempt at quiet ended in a disturbance, and the sight of arms among a drunken crowd excited the desire to use

them. The soldiers murmured, and charged the tribunes and centurions with treachery, alleging that the households of the Senators were being armed to destroy Otho; many acted in ignorance and were stupefied by wine, the worst among them were seeking an opportunity for plunder, the mass was as usual ready for any new movement, and the military obedience of the better disposed was neutralised by the darkness. The tribune, who sought to check the movement, and the strictest disciplinarians among the centurions, were cut down. The soldiers seized their arms, bared their swords, and, mounted on their horses, made for the city and the palace.

81. Otho was giving a crowded entertainment to the most distinguished men and women of Rome. In their alarm they doubted whether this was a casual outbreak of the soldiers, or an act of treachery in the Emperor, and whether to remain and be arrested was a more perilous alternative than to disperse and fly. At one time making a show of courage, at another betrayed by their terror, they still watched the countenance of Otho. And, as it happened, so ready were all to suspect, Otho felt as much alarm as he inspired. Terrified no less by the Senate's critical position than by his own, he had forthwith despatched the prefects of the Prætorian Guard to allay the fury of the soldiery, and he now ordered all to leave the banquet without delay. Then on all sides officers of state cast aside the insignia of office, and shunned the retinues of their friends and domestics; aged men and women wandered in the darkness of night about the various streets of the city; few went to their homes, most sought the houses of friends, or some obscure hiding-place in the dwelling of their humblest dependents.

82. The rush of the soldiers was not even checked by the doors of the palace. They burst in upon the banquet with loud demands that Otho should shew himself. They wounded the tribune, Julius Martialis, and the prefect, Vitellius Saturninus, who sought to stem the torrent. On every side they brandished their swords, and menaced the centurions and tribunes at one moment, the whole Senate at another. Their minds were maddened by a blind panic, and, unable to single out any one object for their fury, they

sought for indiscriminate vengeance. At last Otho, regardless of his imperial dignity, stood up on a couch, and by dint of prayers and tears contrived to restrain them. Reluctant and guilty, they returned to the camp. The next day the houses were closed as they might be in a captured city. Few of the citizens could be seen in the streets, the populace were dejected, the soldiers walked with downcast looks, and seemed gloomy rather than penitent. Licinius Proculus and Plotius Firmus, the prefects, addressed the companies in the gentler or harsher terms that suited their respective characters. The end of these harangues was that 5000 sesterces were paid to each soldier. Then did Otho venture to enter the camp; the tribunes and centurions surrounded him. They had thrown aside the insignia of their rank, and they demanded release from the toils and perils of service. The soldiers felt the reproach; returning to their duty, they even demanded the execution of the ringleaders in the riot.

83. Otho was aware how disturbed was the country, and how conflicting the feelings of the soldiery, the most respectable of whom cried out for some remedy for the existing licence, while the great mass delighted in riot and in an empire resting on popularity, and could be most easily urged to civil war by indulgence in tumult and rapine. At the same time he reflected that power acquired by crime could not be retained by a sudden assumption of the moderation and of the dignity of former times, yet he was alarmed by the critical position of the capital and by the perils of the Senate. Finally, he addressed the troops in these terms: "Comrades, I am not come that I may move your hearts to love me, or that I may rouse your courage; love and courage you have in superfluous abundance. I am come to pray you to put some restraint on your valour, some check on your affection for me. The origin of the late tumult is to be traced not to rapacity or disaffection, feelings which have driven many armies into civil strife, much less to any shrinking from, or fear of danger. It was your excessive affection for me that roused you to act with more zeal than discretion. For even honourable motives of action, unless directed by judgment, are followed by disastrous results.

We are now starting for a campaign. Does the nature of things, does the rapid flight of opportunities, admit of all intelligence being publicly announced, of every plan being discussed in the presence of all? It is as needful that the soldiers should be ignorant of some things as that they should know others. The general's authority, the stern laws of discipline, require that in many matters even the centurions and tribunes shall only receive orders. If, whenever orders are given, individuals may ask questions, obedience ceases, and all command is at an end. Will you in the field too snatch up your arms in the dead of night? Shall one or two worthless and drunken fellows, for I cannot believe that more were carried away by the frenzy of the late outbreak, imbrue their hands in the blood of centurions and tribunes, and burst into the tent of their Emperor?

84. "You indeed did this to serve me, but in the tumult, the darkness, and the general confusion, an opportunity may well occur that may be used against me. If Vitellius and his satellites were allowed to choose, what would be the temper and what the thoughts with which they would curse us? What would they wish for us but mutiny and strife, that the private should not obey the centurion, nor the centurion the tribune, that thus we should rush, horse and foot together, on our own destruction? Comrades, it is by obeying, not by questioning the orders of commanders, that military power is kept together. And that army is the most courageous in the moment of peril, which is the most orderly before the peril comes. Keep you your arms and your courage, leave it to me to plan, and to guide your valour. A few were in fault, two will be punished. Let all the rest blot out the remembrance of that night of infamy. Never let any army hear those cries against the Senate. To clamour for the destruction of what is the head of the Empire, and contains all that is distinguished in the provinces, good God! it is a thing which not even those Germans, whom Vitellius at this very moment is rousing against us, would dare to do. Shall any sons of Italy, the true youth of Rome, cry out for the massacre of an order, by whose splendid distinctions we throw into the shade the mean and obscure faction of Vitellius? Vitellius is the master of a few tribes,

and has some semblance of an army. We have the Senate. The country is with us; with them, the country's enemies. What! do you imagine that this fairest of cities is made up of dwellings and edifices and piles of stones? These dumb and inanimate things may be indifferently destroyed and rebuilt. The eternal duration of empire, the peace of nations, my safety and yours, rest on the security of the Senate. This order which was instituted under due auspices by the Father and Founder of the city, and which has lasted without interruption and without decay from the Kings down to the Emperors, we will bequeath to our descendants, as we have inherited it from our ancestors. For you give the state its Senators, and the Senate gives it its Princes."

85. This speech, which was meant to touch and to calm the feelings of the soldiers, and the moderate amount of severity exercised (for Otho had ordered two and no more to be punished), met with a grateful acceptance, and for the moment reduced to order men who could not be coerced. Yet tranquillity was not restored to the capital; there was still the din of arms and all the sights of war, and the soldiers, though they made no concerted disturbance, had dispersed themselves in disguise about private houses, and exercised a malignant surveillance over all whom exalted rank, or distinction of any kind, exposed to injurious reports. Many too believed that some of the soldiers of Vitellius had come to the capital to learn the feelings of the different parties. Hence everything was rife with suspicion, and even the privacy of the family was hardly exempt from fear. It was however in public that most alarm was felt; with every piece of intelligence that rumour brought men changed their looks and spirits, anxious not to appear discouraged by unfavourable omens, or too little delighted by success. When the Senate was summoned to the Chamber, it was hard for them to maintain in all things a safe moderation. Silence might seem contumacious, and frankness might provoke suspicion, and Otho, who had lately been a subject, and had used the same language, was familiar with flattery. Accordingly, they discussed various motions on which they had put many constructions. Vitellius they called a public enemy and a traitor to his country, the more

prudent contenting themselves with hackneyed terms of abuse, though some threw out reproaches founded in truth, yet only did so in the midst of clamour, and when many voices were heard at once, drowning their own speech in a tumult of words.

86. Prodigies which were now noised abroad from various sources increased men's terror. It was said that in the porch of the Capitol the reins of the chariot, on which stood the goddess of Victory, had dropped from her hand, that from the chapel of Juno there had rushed forth a form greater than the form of man, that the statue of the Divine Julius, which stands on the island in the Tiber, had turned from the West to the East on a calm and tranquil day, that an ox had spoken aloud in Etruria, that strange births of animals had taken place, besides many other things, such as in barbarous ages are observed even during seasons of peace, but are now heard of only in times of terror. But an alarm greater than all, because it connected immediate loss with fears for the future, arose from a sudden inundation of the Tiber. The river became vastly swollen, broke down the wooden bridge, was checked by the heap of ruins across the current, and overflowed not only the low and level districts of the capital, but also much that had been thought safe from such casualties. Many were swept away in the streets, many more were cut off in their shops and chambers. The want of employment and the scarcity of provisions caused a famine among the populace. The poorer class of houses had their foundations sapped by the stagnant waters, and fell when the river returned to its channel. When men's minds were no longer occupied by their fears, the fact, that while Otho was preparing for his campaign, the Campus Martius and the Via Flaminia, his route to the war, were obstructed by causes either fortuitous or natural, was regarded as a prodigy and an omen of impending disasters.

87. Otho, after publicly purifying the city and weighing various plans for the campaign, determined to march upon Gallia Narbonensis, as the passes of the Penine and Cottian Alps and all the other approaches to Gaul were held by the armies of Vitellius. His fleet was strong and loyal to his

cause, for he had enrolled in the ranks of the legion the survivors of the slaughter at the Milvian bridge, whom the stern policy of Galba had retained in custody, while to the rest he had held out hopes of a more honourable service for the future. To the fleet he had added some city cohorts, and many of the Prætorians, the stay and strength of his army, who might at once advise and watch the generals. The command of the expedition was entrusted to Antonius Novellus and Suedius Clemens, centurions of the first rank, and Æmilius Pacensis, to whom Otho had restored the rank of tribune, taken from him by Galba. Oscus, a freedman, retained the charge of the fleet, and went to watch the fidelity of men more honourable than himself. Suetonius Paullinus, Marius Celsus, and Annius Gallus, were appointed to command the infantry and cavalry. The Emperor, however, placed most confidence in Licinius Proculus, prefect of the Prætorian Guard; an active officer at home, without experience in war, he founded perpetual accusations on the high influence of Paullinus, on the energy of Celsus, on the mature judgment of Gallus, in fact, on each man's special excellence, a thing most easy to do; and thus the unscrupulous and the cunning were preferred before the modest and the good.

88. About this time Cornelius Dolabella was banished to the Colonia Aquinas, but he was not kept in strict or secret custody; it was not for any crime that he suffered; he was marked out for suspicion by his ancient name and by his relationship to Galba. Many of the officers of state and a large proportion of the men of consular rank Otho ordered to accompany him to the field, not indeed to share or serve in the campaign, but to form a retinue. Among them was Lucius Vitellius, whom Otho treated as he treated the rest, and not as though he were the brother either of an Emperor, or of an enemy. This roused the anxieties of the capital; no rank was free from apprehension or peril. The leading men of the Senate either suffered from the infirmities of age, or were enervated by a prolonged peace; the nobility were indolent and had forgotten how to fight; the Equestrian order knew nothing of service; and the more they endeavoured to hide and repress their alarm the more

evident was their terror. On the other hand, there were some who with senseless ostentation purchased splendid arms and magnificent horses, and some who procured by way af ¡quipments for the war the luxurious furniture of the banquet and other incentives to profligacy. The wise looked to the interests of peace and of the Commonwealth, while the giddy and those who were thoughtless of the future were inflated with idle hopes. Many whose credit had been shaken in the years of peace regained their spirits amidst the confusions of the time, and found their best safety in revolution.

89. The mob and the people generally, whose vast numbers cut them off from all interest in the state, began by degrees to feel the evils of war, now that all the currency had been diverted to the purposes of the army, and the prices of provisions were raised. These evils had not equally distressed the common people during the insurrection of Vindex; the capital was safe, and the war was in the provinces, and, fought as it was between the legions and Gaul, it seemed but a foreign campaign. Indeed from the time that the Divine Augustus consolidated the power of the Cæsars, the wars of the Roman people had been in remote places, and had caused anxiety or brought honour to but one man. Under Tiberius and Caius men dreaded for the Commonwealth only the miseries of peace. The rising of Scribonianus against Claudius was crushed as soon as heard of. Nero was driven from power by evil tidings and rumours rather than by the sword. Now the legions and the fleets were brought into action, and with them a force used but on few other occasions, the Prætorian and city soldiery. In their rear were the provinces of the East and of the West with all their forces; had they fought under other generals there was all the material for a protracted war. Many suggested to Otho, as he was setting out, a religious obstacle in the fact that the sacred shields had not been restored to their place. He spurned all delay, as having been Nero's fatal mistake; and the fact that Cæcina had now crossed the Alps urged him to action.

90. On the 14th of March, after commending the State to the care of the Senate, he presented to those who had

been recalled from exile what was left of the Neronian confiscations, or had not yet been paid into the Imperial treasury, a most equitable and apparently most splendid piece of liberality, but practically worthless, as the property had been hastily realized long before. Soon afterwards he summoned an assembly, and enlarged on the dignity of the capital and the unanimity of the Senate and people in his favour. Of the party of Vitellius he spoke with moderation, charging the legions with ignorance rather than with crime, and making no mention of Vitellius himself. This moderation was either his own, or was due to the writer of the speech, who, fearing for himself, abstained from invectives against Vitellius. For Otho was believed to avail himself of the abilities of Galerius Trachalus in civil matters, just as he employed those of Celsus and Paullinus in war. There were some who recognized the very style of speaking, which was well known from his constant pleading at the bar, and which sought to fill the popular ear with a copious and sonorous diction. The acclamations and cries which habitual flattery prompted in the people were at once extravagant and false. As if they were applauding a Dictator like Cæsar, or an Emperor like Augustus, they vied with each other in their zeal and good wishes. They acted not from fear or affection, but from the mere love of servitude; as it might be in some private household, each had his own motives, and the public honour now went for nothing. Otho set out, leaving the peace of the city and the cares of empire in the charge of his brother Salvius Titianus.

BOOK II

1. In a distant part of the world fortune was now preparing the origin and rise of a new dynasty, whose varied destinies brought happiness or misery on the State, prosperity or destruction on the Princes of its line. Titus Vespasian had been sent from Judæa by his father while Galba still lived, and alleged as a reason for his journey the homage due to the Emperor, and his age, which now qualified him to compete for office. But the vulgar, ever eager to invent, had spread the report that he was sent for to be adopted. The advanced years and childless condition of the Emperor furnished matter for such gossip, and the country never can refrain from naming many persons until one be chosen. The report gained the more credit from the genius of Titus himself, equal as it was to the most exalted fortune, from the mingled beauty and majesty of his countenance, from the prosperous fortunes of Vespasian, from the prophetic responses of oracles, and even from accidental occurrences which, in the general disposition to belief, were accepted as omens. At Corinth, the capital of Achaia, he received positive information of the death of Galba, and found men who spoke confidently of the revolt of Vitellius and of the fact of war. In the anxiety of his mind, he sent for a few of his friends, and carefully surveyed his position from both points of view. He considered that if he should proceed to Rome, he should get no thanks for a civility intended for another, while his person would be a hostage in the hands either of Vitellius or of Otho; that should he turn back, the conqueror would certainly be offended, but with the issue of the struggle still doubtful, and the father joining the party, the son would be excused; on the other hand, if Vespasian should assume the direc-

tion of the state, men who had to think of war would have to forget such causes of offence.

2. These and like thoughts made him waver between hope and fear; but hope triumphed. Some supposed that he retraced his steps for love of Queen Berenice, nor was his young heart averse to her charms, but this affection occasioned no hindrance to action. He passed, it is true, a youth enlivened by pleasure, and practised more self-restraint in his own than in his father's reign. So, after coasting Achaia and Asia, leaving the land on his left, he made for the islands of Rhodes and Cyprus, and then by a bolder course for Syria. Here he conceived a desire to visit and inspect the temple of the Paphian Venus, a place of celebrity both among natives and foreigners. It will not be a tedious digression to record briefly the origin of the worship, the ceremonial of the temple, and the form under which the goddess is adored, a form found in no other place.

3. The founder of the temple, according to old tradition, was king Aerias, though some represent this as the name of the goddess herself. Later accounts tell us that the temple was consecrated by Cinyras, and that the goddess herself after her birth from the sea was wafted to this spot, but that the wisdom and craft of the diviners was a foreign importation introduced by Tamiras of Cilicia; and that it was agreed that the descendants of both families should preside over the worship. Afterwards, that the royal family might not be without some superiority over the foreign stock, the strangers relinquished the craft which they had themselves introduced. The priest of the line of Cinyras is alone consulted. The victims are such as each worshipper has vowed, but males are selected; the surest prognostics are seen in the entrails of kids. It is forbidden to pour blood on the altar; the place of sacrifice is served only with prayers and pure flame, and though it stands in the open air, it is never wet with rain. The image of the goddess does not bear the human shape; it is a rounded mass rising like a cone from a broad base to a small circumference. The meaning of this is doubtful.

4. Titus, after surveying the treasures, the royal presents, and the other objects which the antiquarian tendencies of

the Greek arbitrarily connect with some uncertain past, first consulted the oracle about his voyage. Receiving an answer that the way was open and the sea propitious, he then, after sacrificing a number of victims, asked some questions in ambiguous phrase concerning himself. Sostratus (that was the name of the priest) seeing that the entrails presented an uniformly favourable appearance, and that the goddess signified her favour to some great enterprise, returned at the moment a brief and ordinary answer, but afterwards soliciting a private interview, disclosed the future. His spirits raised, Titus rejoined his father, and was received as a mighty pledge of success by the wavering minds of the provincials and the troops. Vespasian had all but completed the Jewish war, and only the siege of Jerusalem now remained, an operation, the difficulty and arduousness of which was due, rather to the character of its mountain citadel and the perverse obstinacy of the national superstition, than to any sufficient means of enduring extremities left to the besieged. As we have mentioned above, Vespasian himself had three legions inured to war. Mucianus had four under his command in his peaceful province. Emulation, however, and the glory won by the neighbouring army had banished all tendency to sloth, and unbroken rest and exemption from the hardships of war had given them a vigour equivalent to the hardihood which the others had gained by their perils and their toils. Each had auxiliary forces of infantry and cavalry, each had fleets and tributary kings, and each, though their renown was of a different kind, had a celebrated name.

5. Vespasian was an energetic soldier; he could march at the head of his army, choose the place for his camp, and bring by night and day his skill, or, if the occasion required, his personal courage to oppose the foe. His food was such as chance offered; his dress and appearance hardly distinguished him from the common soldier; in short, but for his avarice, he was equal to the generals of old. Mucianus, on the contrary, was eminent for his magnificence, for his wealth, and for a greatness that transcended in all respects the condition of a subject; readier of speech than the other, he thoroughly understood the arrangement and

direction of civil business. It would have been a rare combination of princely qualities, if, with their respective faults removed, their virtues only could have been united in one man. Mucianus was governor of Syria, Vespasian of Judæa. In the administration of these neighbouring provinces jealousy had produced discord between them, but on Nero's fall they had dropped their animosities and associated their counsels. At first they communicated through friends, till Titus, who was the great bond of union between them, by representing their common interests had terminated their mischievous feud. He was indeed a man formed both by nature and by education to attract even such a character as that of Mucianus. The tribunes, the centurions, and the common soldiers, were brought over to the cause by appeals to their energy or their love of license, to their virtues or to their vices, according to their different dispositions.

6. Long before the arrival of Titus, both armies had taken the oath of allegiance to Otho. The news had come, as is usual, with great speed, while there was much to delay the gigantic undertaking of a civil war, for which the East after a long period of repose was then for the first time preparing. In former times the mightiest civil conflicts had been begun in Gaul or Italy with the resources of the West. Pompey, Brutus, Cassius, and Antony, all of whom had been followed across the sea by civil war, had met with a disastrous end, and the Emperors had been oftener heard of than seen in Syria and Judæa. There had been no mutiny among the legions, nothing indeed but some demonstrations against the Parthians, attended with various success. In the last civil war, though other provinces had been disturbed, peace had been here unshaken. Then had followed a loyal adherence to Galba. But when it became notorious that Otho and Vitellius, opposed in impious strife, were ready to make a spoil of the Empire, the thought that others would engross the rewards of power, while they would have nothing left for themselves but a compulsory submission, made the soldiers murmur and take a survey of their own strength. There were close at hand seven legions; there were Syria and Judæa, with a vast number of auxiliaries. Then, without any interval of separation, there was Egypt and its

two legions, and on the other side Cappadocia, Pontus, and all the garrisons along the frontier of Armenia. There was Asia Minor; there were the other provinces, not without a military population, and well furnished with money. There were all the islands of the Mediterranean. And there was the sea itself, which during the interval of preparation for war would be both a convenience and a protection.

7. The ardour of the troops was not unknown to their generals; but it was judged advisable to wait for the issue of the struggle which others were carrying on. The conquerors and the conquered, it was said, never unite with a genuine good faith. It matters not whether fortune make Otho or Vitellius to be the victor. Even great generals grow insolent in prosperity; these men are quarrelsome, indolent, and profligate, and their own faults will make war fatal to the one, and success to the other. They therefore postponed the war until a more fitting opportunity, and though Vespasian and Mucianus had but lately resolved on concerted action, the others had done so long before. The worthiest among them were moved by patriotism; many were wrought upon by the attractions of plunder; some by their private embarrassments. And so, good and bad, from different motives, but with equal zeal, were all eager for war.

8. About this time Achaia and Asia Minor were terrified by a false report that Nero was at hand. Various rumours were current about his death; and so there were many who pretended and believed that he was still alive. The adventures and enterprises of the other pretenders I shall relate in the regular course of my work. The pretender in this case was a slave from Pontus, or, according to some accounts, a freedman from Italy, a skilful harp-player and singer, accomplishments, which, added to a resemblance in the face, gave a very deceptive plausibility to his pretensions. After attaching to himself some deserters, needy vagrants whom he bribed with great offers, he put to sea. Driven by stress of weather to the island of Cythnus, he induced certain soldiers, who were on their way from the East, to join him, and ordered others, who refused, to be executed. He also robbed the traders and armed all the most able-bodied of the slaves. The centurion Sisenna, who was the bearer of the

clasped right hands, the usual emblems of friendship, from the armies of Syria to the Prætorians, was assailed by him with various artifices, till he left the island secretly, and, fearing actual violence, made his escape with all haste. Thence the alarm spread far and wide, and many roused themselves at the well-known name, eager for change, and detesting the present state of things. The report was daily gaining credit when an accident put an end to it.

9. Galba had entrusted the government of Galatia and Pamphylia to Calpurnius Asprenas. Two triremes from the fleet of Misenum were given him to pursue the adventurer: with these he reached the island of Cythnus. Persons were found to summon the captains in the name of Nero. The pretender himself, assuming a studied appearance of sorrow, and appealing to their fidelity as old soldiers of his own, besought them to land him in Egypt or Syria. The captains, perhaps wavering, perhaps intending to deceive, declared that they must address their soldiers, and that they would return when the minds of all had been prepared. Every thing, however, was faithfully reported to Asprenas, and at his bidding the ship was boarded and taken, and the man, whoever he was, killed. The body, in which the eyes, the hair, and the savage countenance, were remarkable features, was conveyed to Asia, and thence to Rome.

10. In a state that was distracted by strife, and that from frequent changes in its rulers trembled on the verge between liberty and licence, even little matters were attended with great excitement. Vibius Crispus, whose wealth, power, and ability, made him rank among men of distinction, rather than among men of worth, demanded that Annius Faustus, of the Equestrian order, who in the days of Nero had practised the trade of the informer, should be brought to trial before the Senate. The Senators indeed had recently, during the reign of Galba, passed a resolution, that cognizance should be taken of the cases of the informers. This decree was variously carried out, and, while retained as law, was powerless or effectual, according as the person, who happened to be accused, was influential or helpless. Besides the terror of the law, Crispus had exerted his own power to the utmost to destroy the man who had informed against his

brother. He had prevailed upon a great part of the Senate to demand that he should be consigned to destruction, undefended and unheard. But, on the other hand, there were some with whom nothing helped the accused person so much as the excessive power of the accuser. They gave it as their opinion, that time ought to be allowed, that the charges ought to be specified, that, odious and guilty as the man might be, he yet ought to be heard, as precedent required. At first they carried their point, and the trial was postponed for a few days, but before long Faustus was condemned, but by no means with that unanimity on the part of the people which his detestable character had deserved. Men remembered that Crispus had followed the same profession with profit; nor was it the penalty but the prosecutor that they disliked.

11. Meanwhile the campaign had opened favourably for Otho, at whose bidding the armies of Dalmatia and Pannonia had begun to move. These comprised four legions, from each of which two thousand troops were sent on in advance. The 7th had been raised by Galba, the 11th, 13th, and 14th were veteran soldiers, the 14th having particularly distinguished itself by quelling the revolt in Britain. Nero had added to their reputation by selecting them as his most effective troops. This had made them long faithful to Nero, and kindled their zeal for Otho. But their self-confidence induced a tardiness of movement proportionate to their strength and solidity. The auxiliary infantry and cavalry moved in advance of the main body of the legions. The capital itself contributed no contemptible force, namely five Prætorian cohorts, some troops of cavalry, and the first legion, and together with these, 2000 gladiators, a disreputable kind of auxiliaries, but employed throughout the civil wars even by strict disciplinarians. Annius Gallus was put at the head of this force, and was sent on with Vestricius Spurinna to occupy the banks of the Padus, the original plan of the campaign having fallen to the ground, now that Cæcina, who they had hoped might have been kept within the limits of Gaul, had crossed the Alps. Otho himself was accompanied by some picked men of the body-guard, with whom were the rest of the Prætorian cohorts, the veteran

troops from the Prætorian camp, and a vast number of the levies raised from the fleet. No indolence or riot disgraced his march. He wore a cuirass of iron, and was to be seen in front of the standards, on foot, rough and negligent in dress, and utterly unlike what common report had pictured him.

12. Fortune seemed to smile on his efforts. Through his fleets, which commanded the sea, he held the greater part of Italy, even as far as where the chain of the Maritime Alps begins. The task of attempting the passage of this chain, and of advancing into the Provincia Narbonensis, he had entrusted to three generals, Suedius Clemens, Antonius Novellus, and Æmilius Pacensis. Pacensis, however, was put in irons by his insubordinate troops, Antonius possessed no kind of authority, and Clemens commanded only for popularity, and was as reckless in transgressing the good order of military discipline as he was eager to fight. One would not have thought that it was Italy, the fields, and the habitations of their native country, that they were passing through. They burnt, spoiled, and plundered, as if they were among the lands of the foreigner and the cities of a hostile people, and all with the more frightful effect as nowhere had there been made any provision against the danger. The fields were full of rural wealth, the houses stood with open doors; and the owners, as with their wives and children they came forth to meet the army, found themselves surrounded, in the midst of the security of peace, with all the horrors of war. Marius Maturus was then governing as procurator the province of the Maritime Alps. Raising the population, in which is no lack of able-bodied men, he resolved to drive back the Othonianists from the borders of his province; but the mountaineers were cut down and broken by the first charge, as might be expected of men who had been hastily collected, who were not familiar with camps or with regular command, who saw no glory in victory, no infamy in flight.

13. Exasperated by this conflict, the troops of Otho vented their rage on the town of Albintemilium. In the field indeed they had secured no plunder; their rustic adversaries were poor, and their arms worthless; nor could they

be taken prisoners, for they were swift of foot, and knew the country well. But the rapacity of the troops glutted itself in the ruin of an innocent population. The horror of these acts was aggravated by a noble display of fortitude in a Ligurian woman; she had concealed her son, and when the soldiers, who believed that some money had been hidden with him, questioned her with torture as to where she was hiding him, she pointed to her bosom, and replied, "It is here that he is concealed;" nor could any subsequent threats or even death itself make her falter in this courageous and noble answer.

14. Messengers now came in haste and alarm to inform Fabius Valens, how Otho's fleet was threatening the province of Gallia Narbonensis, which had sworn allegiance to Vitellius. Envoys from the colonies were already on the spot praying for aid. He despatched two cohorts of Tungrian infantry, four squadrons of horse, and all the cavalry of the Treviri under the command of Julius Classicus. Part of these troops were retained for the defence of the colony of Forum Julii, for it was feared, that if the whole army were sent by the route through the interior, the enemy's fleet might make a rapid movement on the unprotected coast. Twelve squadrons of cavalry and some picked infantry advanced against the enemy; they were reinforced by a cohort of Ligurians, an auxiliary local force of long standing, and five hundred Pannonians, not yet regularly enrolled. The conflict commenced without delay, the enemy's line of battle being so arranged, that part of the levies from the fleet, who had a number of rustics among their ranks, were posted on the slope of the hills which border on the coast, the Prætorians fully occupying the level ground between the hills and the shore, while on the sea was the fleet, moored to the land and ready for action, drawn up in line so as to present a formidable front. The Vitellianists whose infantry was inferior, but who were strong in cavalry, stationed the mountaineers on the neighbouring heights, and their infantry in close ranks behind the cavalry. The squadrons of the Treveri charged the enemy incautiously, and found themselves encountered in front by the veteran troops, while on the flanks they were also an-

noyed by showers of stones from the rustic band, who were skilful throwers, and who, mixed up as they were among the regular soldiers, whether cowardly or brave, were all equally bold in the moment of victory. The general consternation of the Vitellianists was increased by a new alarm as the fleet attacked the rear of the combatants. By this movement they were hemmed in on all sides, and the whole force would have perished, had not the shades of night checked the advance of the victorious army, and covered the retreat of the vanquished.

15. The Vitellianists, however, though beaten, did not remain inactive. They brought up reinforcements and attacked the enemy, who felt themselves secure, and whose vigilance was relaxed by success. The sentinels were cut down, the camp stormed, and the panic reached the ships, till, as the alarm gradually subsided, they again assumed the offensive under the protection of some neighbouring heights which they had occupied. A terrible slaughter ensued, and the prefects of the Tungrian cohorts, after having long maintained their line unbroken, fell beneath a shower of missiles. The Othonianists, however, did not achieve a bloodless victory, as the enemy's cavalry wheeled round, and cut off some who had imprudently prolonged the pursuit. And then, as if a sort of armistice had been concluded to provide against any sudden panic that the cavalry of the one party or the fleet of the other might cause, the Vitellianists retreated to Antipolis, a town of Gallia Narbonensis, the Othonianists to Albigaunum, in Upper Liguria.

16. Corsica, Sardinia, and the other islands of the neighbouring seas, were retained in the interests of Otho by the fame of these naval successes. Corsica, however, all but suffered fatal injury from the rash proceedings of Decumus Pacarius, the procurator, proceedings which in so gigantic a war could contribute nothing to the general result, and which only brought destruction upon their author. In his hatred of Otho he resolved to support Vitellius with the whole strength of Corsica, an insignificant assistance even had the design succeeded. He collected the chief men of the island, and explained his plans. Claudius Pyrrhicus, captain of the Liburnian ships stationed in the place, and Quintius

Certus, a Roman knight, who ventured to offer opposition,
he ordered to execution. All who were present were terrified
at their death, and, with the ignorant populace, which ever
blindly shares in the fears of others, took the oath of allegiance to Vitellius. But when Pacarius began to enlist
troops, and to weary with military duties an undisciplined
population, disgusted with the unusual toil, they began to
reflect upon their own weakness. "The country which we
inhabit," they said to themselves, "is an island: Germany
and its mighty legions are far from us, and we know that
even countries protected by infantry and cavalry have been
plundered and ravaged by the fleet." Their feelings underwent a sudden change; they did not, however, resort to
open violence, but chose an opportunity for a treacherous
attack. When the persons who usually surrounded Pacarius
had left him, and he was naked and helpless in the bath,
they slew him. His associates were slaughtered with him.
The perpetrators of the deed carried the heads of the slain
to Otho, as being the heads of public enemies; but, lost
among the crowd of greater criminals, in the vast confusion
of events, they were neither rewarded by Otho nor punished by Vitellius.

17. Silius' Horse had now, as I have already related,
opened the way into Italy, and transferred the war across
the borders. No one entertained any attachment to Otho,
yet it was not because they preferred Vitellius: long years
of peace had subdued them to any kind of servitude, had
made them ready to submit to the first comer and careless
about the better cause. The wealthiest district of Italy, the
broad plains and cities which lie between the Padus and the
Alps, was now held by the troops of Vitellius; for by this
time the infantry sent on in advance by Cæcina had also
arrived. A cohort of Pannonians had been taken prisoners
at Cremona, a hundred cavalry, and a thousand of the
levies from the fleet intercepted between Placentia and Ticinum. Elated by these successes the troops of Vitellius would
no longer be restrained by the boundaries of the river's
bank. The very sight of the Padus excited the men from
Batavia and the Transrhenane provinces. Crossing the
stream by a sudden movement, they advanced on Placentia,

and seizing some reconnoiterers so terrified the rest, that, deceived by their alarm, they announced that the whole army of Cæcina was at hand.

18. Spurinna, who now held Placentia, was sure that Cæcina had not yet arrived, and that, even were he approaching, he ought to keep his men within their fortifications, and not confront a veteran army with three Prætorian cohorts, a thousand veterans, and a handful of cavalry. But the undisciplined and inexperienced soldiery seized their standards and colours, and rushed to the attack, brandishing their weapons in the face of their general when he sought to restrain them, and spurning from them the tribunes and centurions, and even crying out that Otho was betrayed and that Cæcina had come by invitation. Spurinna associated himself with the rash movement which others had originated, at first acting under compulsion, but afterwards pretending to consent, in the hope that his counsels might have more influence should the mutinous spirit abate.

19. When the Padus was in sight and night began to fall they judged it expedient to entrench a camp. The labour, new as it was to the soldiery of the capital, broke their spirits. All the oldest among them began to inveigh against their own credulity, and to point out the difficulty and danger of their position, if on those open plains Cæcina and his army were to surround their scanty forces. By this time more temperate language was heard throughout the camp, and the tribunes and centurions, mixing with the troops, suggested commendations of the prudence of their general in selecting for the rallying point and basis of his operations a colony rich in military strength and resources. Finally, Spurinna himself, not so much reproaching them with their error as exposing it by his arguments, conducted them all back to Placentia, except some scouts whom he left, in a less turbulent temper and more amenable to command. The walls were strengthened, battlements were added, and the towers were raised in height. It was not only of the implements of war that provision and preparation were made, but of the spirit of subordination and the love of obedience. This was all that was wanting to the party, for they had no reason to be dissatisfied with their courage.

20. Cæcina, who seemed to have left his cruelty and profligacy on the other side of the Alps, advanced through Italy
with his army under excellent discipline. The towns and
colonies, however, found indications of a haughty spirit in
the general's dress, when they saw the cloak of various
colours, and the trews, a garment of foreign fashion, clothed
in which he was wont to speak to their toga-clad citizens.
And they resented, as if with a sense of personal wrong, the
conduct of his wife Salonina, though it injured no one that
she presented a conspicuous figure as she rode through their
towns on horseback in a purple habit. They were acting on
the instincts of human nature, which prompt men to scrutinize with keen eyes the recent elevation of their fellows, and
to demand a temperate use of prosperity from none more
rigorously than from those whom they have seen on a level
with themselves. Cæcina, after crossing the Padus, sought
to tamper with the loyalty of the Othonianists at a conference in which he held out hopes of reward, and he was himself assailed with the same arts. After the specious but
meaningless names of peace and concord had been thus
bandied to and fro, Cæcina turned all his thoughts and
plans on the capture of Placentia, making a formidable
show of preparation, as he knew that according to the success of his opening operations would be the subsequent
prestige of his arms.

21. The first day, however, was spent in a furious onset
rather than in the skilful approaches of a veteran army. Exposed and reckless, the troops came close under the walls,
stupefied by excess in food and wine. In this struggle the
amphitheatre, a most beautiful building, situated outside the
walls, was burnt to the ground, possibly set on fire by the
assailants, while they showered brands, fireballs, and ignited
missiles, on the besieged, possibly by the besieged themselves, while they discharged incessant volleys in return.
The populace of the town, always inclined to be suspicious,
believed that combustibles had been purposely introduced
into the building by certain persons from the neighbouring
colonies, who viewed it with envious and jealous eyes, because there was not in Italy another building so capacious.
Whatever the cause of the accident, it was thought of but

little moment as long as more terrible disasters were apprehended; but as soon as they again felt secure, they lamented it as though they could not have endured a heavier calamity. In the end Cæcina was repulsed with great slaughter among his troops, and the night was spent in the preparation of siege-works. The Vitellianists constructed mantlets, hurdles, and sheds, for undermining the walls and screening the assailants; the Othonianists busied themselves in preparing stakes and huge masses of stone and of lead and brass, with which to break and overwhelm the hostile ranks. The shame of failure, the hope of renown, wrought on both armies; both were appealed to by different arguments; on the one side they extolled the strength of the legions and of the army of Germany; on the other, the distinctions of the soldiery of the capital and the Prætorian cohorts; the one reviled their foes as slothful and indolent soldiers, demoralized by the circus and the theatres; the others retorted with the names of foreigner and barbarian. At the same time they lauded or vituperated Otho and Vitellius, but found indeed a more fruitful source of mutual provocation in invective than in praise.

22. Almost before dawn of day the walls were crowded with combatants, and the plains glittered with masses of armed men. The close array of the legions, and the skirmishing parties of auxiliaries assailed with showers of arrows and stones the loftier parts of the walls, attacking them at close quarters, where they were undefended, or old and decayed. The Othonianists, who could take a more deliberate and certain aim, poured down their javelins on the German cohorts as they recklessly advanced to the attack with fierce war-cries, brandishing their shields above their shoulders after the manner of their country, and leaving their bodies unprotected. The soldiers of the legions, working under cover of mantlets and hurdles, undermined the walls, threw up earth-works, and endeavoured to burst open the gates. The Prætorians opposed them by rolling down with a tremendous crash ponderous masses of rock, placed for the purpose. Beneath these many of the assailants were buried, and many, as the slaughter increased with the confusion, and the attack from the walls became fiercer, re-

treated wounded, fainting, and mangled, with serious damage to the prestige of the party. Cæcina, ashamed of the assault on which he had so rashly ventured, and unwilling, ridiculed and baffled as he was, to remain in the same position, again crossed the Padus, and resolved on marching to Cremona. As he was going, Turullius Cerialis with a great number of the levies from the fleet, and Julius Briganticus with a few troopers, gave themselves up to him. Julius commanded a squadron of horse; he was a Batavian. Turullius was a centurion of the first rank, not unfriendly to Cæcina, as he had commanded a company in Germany.

23. Spurinna, on discovering the enemy's route, informed Annius Gallus by letter of the successful defence of Placentia, of what had happened, and of what Cæcina intended to do. Gallus was then bringing up the first legion to the relief of Placentia; he hardly dared trust so few cohorts, fearing that they could not sustain a prolonged siege or the formidable attack of the German army. On hearing that Cæcina had been repulsed, and was making his way to Cremona, though the legion could hardly be restrained, and in its eagerness for action, even went to the length of open mutiny, he halted at Bedriacum. This is a village situated between Verona and Cremona, and has now acquired an ill-omened celebrity by two great days of disaster to Rome. About the same time Martius Macer fought a successful battle not far from Cremona. Martius, who was a man of energy, conveyed his gladiators in boats across the Padus, and suddenly threw them upon the opposite bank. The Vitellianist auxiliaries on the spot were routed; those who made a stand were cut to pieces, the rest directing their flight to Cremona. But the impetuosity of the victors was checked; for it was feared that the enemy might be strengthened by reinforcements, and change the fortune of the day. This policy excited the suspicions of the Othonianists, who put a sinister construction on all the acts of their generals. Vying with each other in an insolence of language proportioned to their cowardice of heart, they assailed with various accusations Annius Gallus, Suetonius Paullinus, and Marius Celsus. The murderers of Galba were the most ardent promoters of mutiny and discord. Frenzied

with fear and guilt, they sought to plunge everything into confusion, resorting, now to openly seditious language, now to secret letters to Otho; and he, ever ready to believe the meanest of men and suspicious of the good, irresolute in prosperity, but rising higher under reverses, was in perpetual alarm. The end of it was that he sent for his brother Titianus, and intrusted him with the direction of the campaign.

24. Meanwhile, brilliant successes were gained under the command of Celsus and Paullinus. Cæcina was greatly annoyed by the fruitlessness of all his undertakings, and by the waning reputation of his army. He had been repulsed from Placentia; his auxiliaries had been recently cut up, and even when the skirmishers had met in a series of actions, frequent indeed, but not worth relating, he had been worsted; and now that Valens was coming up, fearful that all the distinctions of the campaign would centre in that general, he made a hasty attempt to retrieve his credit, but with more impetuosity than prudence. Twelve miles from Cremona (at a place called the Castors) he posted some of the bravest of his auxiliaries, concealed in the woods that there overhang the road. The cavalry were ordered to move forward, and, after provoking a battle, voluntarily to retreat, and draw on the enemy in hasty pursuit, till the ambuscade could make a simultaneous attack. The scheme was betrayed to the Othonianist generals, and Paullinus assumed the command of the infantry, Celsus of the cavalry. The veterans of the 13th legion, four cohorts of auxiliaries, and 500 cavalry, were drawn up on the left side of the road; the raised causeway was occupied by three Prætorian cohorts, ranged in deep columns; on the right front stood the first legion with two cohorts of auxiliaries and 500 cavalry. Besides these, a thousand cavalry, belonging to the Prætorian guard and to the auxiliaries, were brought up to complete a victory or to retrieve a repulse.

25. Before the hostile lines engaged, the Vitellianists began to retreat, but Celsus, aware of the stratagem, kept his men back. The Vitellianists rashly left their position, and seeing Celsus gradually give way, followed too far in pursuit, and themselves fell into an ambuscade. The auxiliaries

assailed them on either flank, the legions were opposed to
them in front, and the cavalry, by a sudden movement, had
surrounded their rear. Suetonius Paullinus did not at once
give the infantry the signal to engage. He was a man naturally tardy in action, and one who preferred a cautious and
scientific plan of operations to any success which was the
result of accident. He ordered the trenches to be filled up,
the plain to be cleared, and the line to be extended, holding
that it would be time enough to begin his victory when he
had provided against being vanquished. This delay gave
the Vitellianists time to retreat into some vineyards, which
were obstructed by the interlacing layers of the vines, and
close to which was a small wood. From this place they again
ventured to emerge, slaughtering the foremost of the Prætorian cavalry. King Epiphanes was wounded, while he was
zealously cheering on the troops for Otho.

26. Then the Othonianist infantry charged. The enemy's
line was completely crushed, and the reinforcements who
were coming up to their aid were also put to flight. Cæcina
indeed had not brought up his cohorts in a body, but one by
one; as this was done during the battle, it increased the
general confusion, because the troops who were thus divided, not being strong at any one point, were borne away
by the panic of the fugitives. Besides this, a mutiny broke
out in the camp because the whole army was not led into
action. Julius Gratus, prefect of the camp, was put in irons,
on a suspicion of a treacherous understanding with his
brother who was serving with Otho's army, at the very
time that the Othonianists had done the same thing and on
the same grounds to that brother Julius Fronto, a tribune.
In fact such was the panic everywhere, among the fugitives
and among the troops coming up, in the lines and in front
of the entrenchments, that it was very commonly said on
both sides, that Cæcina and his whole army might have been
destroyed, had not Suetonius Paullinus given the signal of
recall. Paullinus alleged that he feared the effects of so
much additional toil and so long a march, apprehending
that the Vitellianists might issue fresh from their camp, and
attack his wearied troops, who, once thrown into confusion, would have no reserves to fall back upon. A few ap-

proved the general's policy, but it was unfavourably can-vassed by the army at large.

27. The effect of this disaster on the Vitellianists was not so much to drive them to fear as to draw them to obedience. Nor was this the case only among the troops of Cæcina, who indeed laid all the blame upon his soldiers, more ready, as he said, for mutiny than for battle. The forces also of Fabius Valens, who had now reached Ticinum, laid aside their contempt for the enemy, and anxious to retrieve their credit began to yield a more respectful and uniform obedi-ence to their general. A serious mutiny, however, had raged among them, of which, as it was not convenient to interrupt the orderly narrative of Cæcina's operations, I shall take up the history at an earlier period. I have already described how the Batavian cohorts who separated from the 14th legion during the Neronian war, hearing on their way to Britain of the rising of Vitellius, joined Fabius Valens in the country of the Lingones. They behaved themselves in-solently, boasting, as they visited the quarters of the sev-eral legions, that they had mastered the men of the 14th, that they had taken Italy from Nero, that the whole destiny of the war lay in their hands. Such language was insulting to the soldiers, and offensive to the general. The discipline of the army was relaxed by the brawls and quarrels which ensued. At last Valens began to suspect that insolence would end in actual treachery.

28. When, therefore, intelligence reached him that the cavalry of the Treveri and the Tungrian infantry had been defeated by Otho's fleet, and that Gallia Narbonensis was blockaded, anxious at once to protect a friendly population, and, like a skilful soldier, to separate cohorts so turbulent and, while they remained united, so inconveniently strong, he directed a detachment of the Batavians to proceed to the relief of the province. This having been heard and become generally known, the allies were discontented and the le-gions murmured. "We are being deprived," they said, "of the help of our bravest men. Those veteran troops victorious in so many campaigns, now that the enemy is in sight, are withdrawn, so to speak, from the very field of battle. If indeed a province be of more importance than the capital

and the safety of the Empire, let us all follow them thither, but if the reality, the support, the mainstay of success, centre in Italy, you must not tear, as it were, from a body its very strongest limbs."

29. In the midst of these fierce exclamations, Valens, sending his lictors into the crowd, attempted to quell the mutiny. On this they attacked the general himself, hurled stones at him, and, when he fled, pursued him. Crying out that he was concealing the spoil of Gaul, the gold of the men of Vienna, the hire of their own toils, they ransacked his baggage, and probed with javelins and lances the walls of the general's tent and the very ground beneath. Valens, disguised in the garb of a slave, found concealment with a subaltern officer of cavalry. After this, Alfenius Varus, prefect of the camp, seeing that the mutiny was gradually subsiding, promoted the reaction by the following device. He forbade the centurions to visit the sentinels, and discontinued the trumpet calls by which the troops are summoned to their usual military duties. Thereupon all stood paralysed, and gazed at each other in amazement, panic-stricken by the very fact that there was no one to direct them. By their silence, by their submission, finally by their tears and entreaties, they craved forgiveness. But when Valens, thus unexpectedly preserved, came forward in sad plight, shedding tears, they were moved to joy, to pity, even to affection. Their revulsion to delight was just that of a mob, always extreme in either emotion. They greeted him with praises and congratulations, and surrounding him with the eagles and standards, carried him to the tribunal. With a politic prudence he refrained from demanding capital punishment in any case; yet, fearing that he might lay himself more open to suspicion by concealment of his feelings, he censured a few persons, well aware that in civil wars the soldiers have more license than the generals.

30. While they were fortifying a camp at Ticinum, the news of Cæcina's defeat reached them, and the mutiny nearly broke out afresh from an impression that underhand dealing and delay on the part of Valens had kept them away from the battle. They refused all rest; they would not wait for their general; they advanced in front of the standards,

and hurried on the standard-bearers. After a rapid march they joined Cæcina. The character of Valens did not stand well with Cæcina's army. They complained that, though so much weaker in numbers, they had been exposed to the whole force of the enemy, thus at once excusing themselves, and extolling, in the implied flattery, the strength of the new arrivals, who might, they feared, despise them as beaten and spiritless soldiers. Though Valens had the stronger army, nearly double the number of legions and auxiliaries, yet the partialities of the soldiers inclined to Cæcina, not only from the geniality of heart, which he was thought more ready to display, but even from his vigorous age, his commanding person, and a certain superficial attractiveness which he possessed. The result was a jealousy between the two generals. Cæcina ridiculed his colleague as a man of foul and infamous character; Valens retorted with charges of emptiness and vanity. But concealing their enmity, they devoted themselves to their common interest, and in frequent letters, without any thought of pardon, heaped all manner of charges upon Otho, while the Othonianist generals, though they had the most abundant materials for invective against Vitellius, refrained from employing them.

31. In fact, before the death of these two men (and it was by his death that Otho gained high renown, as Vitellius incurred by his the foulest infamy), Vitellius with his indolent luxury was less dreaded than Otho with his ardent passions. The murder of Galba had made the one terrible and odious, while no one reckoned against the other the guilt of having begun the war. Vitellius with his sensuality and gluttony was his own enemy; Otho, with his profligacy, his cruelty, and his recklessness, was held to be more dangerous to the Commonwealth. When Cæcina and Valens had united their forces, the Vitellianists had no longer any reason to delay giving battle with their whole strength. Otho deliberated as to whether protracting the war or risking an engagement were the better course. Then Suetonius Paullinus, thinking that it befitted his reputation, which was such that no one at that period was looked upon as a more skilful soldier, to give an opinion on the whole conduct of the war, contended

that impatience would benefit the enemy, while delay would serve their own cause.

32. "The entire army of Vitellius," he said, "has already arrived. Nor have they much strength in their rear, since Gaul is ready to rise, and to abandon the banks of the Rhine, when such hostile tribes are ready to burst in, would not answer his purpose. A hostile people and an intervening sea keep from him the army of Britain: Spain is not over full of troops; Gallia Narbonensis has been cowed by the attack of our ships and by a defeat; Italy beyond the Padus is shut in by the Alps, cannot be relieved from the sea, and has been exhausted by the passage of his army. For that army there is nowhere any corn, and without supplies an army cannot be kept together. Then the Germans, the most formidable part of the enemy's forces, should the war be protracted into the summer, will sink with enfeebled frames under the change of country and climate. Many a war, formidable in its first impetuosity, has passed into nothing through the weariness of delay. We, on the other hand, have on all sides abundant resources and loyal adherents. We have Pannonia, Mœsia, Dalmatia, the East with its armies yet intact, we have Italy and Rome, the capital of the Empire, the Senate, and the people, names that never lose their splendour, though they may sometimes be eclipsed. We have the wealth of the State and of private individuals. We have a vast supply of money, which in a civil war is a mightier weapon than the sword. Our soldiers are inured to the climate of Italy or to yet greater heat. We have the river Padus on our front, and cities strongly garrisoned and fortified, none of which will surrender to the enemy, as the defence of Placentia has proved. Let Otho therefore protract the war. In a few days the 14th legion, itself highly renowned, will arrive with the troops from Mœsia. He may then again consider the question, and should a battle be resolved on, we shall fight with increased strength."

33. Marius Celsus acquiesced in the opinion of Paullinus; and Annius Gallus, who a few days before had been seriously injured by the fall of his horse, was reported to agree by those who had been sent to ascertain his opinion. Otho was inclined to risk a decisive battle. His brother Titianus,

and Proculus, the prefect of the Prætorian Guard, ignorant
and therefore impatient, declared that fortune, the Gods,
and the genius of Otho, were with their counsels, and would
be with their enterprises. That no one might dare to oppose
their views, they had taken refuge in flattery. It having
been resolved to give battle, it became a question whether
it would be better for the Emperor to be present in person,
or to withdraw. Paullinus and Celsus no longer opposed, for
they would not seem to put the Emperor in the way of peril,
and these same men who suggested the baser policy prevailed on him to retire to Brixellum, and thus secure from
the hazards of the field, to reserve himself for the administration of empire. That day first gave the death-blow to the
party of Otho. Not only did a strong detachment of the
Prætorian cohorts, of the body guard, and of the cavalry,
depart with him, but the spirit of those who remained was
broken, for the men suspected their generals, and Otho, who
alone had the confidence of the soldiers, while he himself
trusted in none but them, had left the generals' authority
on a doubtful footing.

34. Nothing of this escaped the Vitellianists, for, as is
usual in civil wars, there were many deserters, and the spies,
while busy in inquiring into the plans of the enemy, failed
to conceal their own. Meanwhile Cæcina and Valens remained quiet, and watched intently for the moment when
the enemy in his blindness should rush upon destruction,
and found the usual substitute for wisdom in waiting for
the folly of others. They began to form a bridge, making a
feint of crossing the Padus, in the face of an opposing force
of gladiators; they wished also to keep their own soldiers
from passing their unoccupied time in idleness. Boats were
ranged at equal distances from each other, connected at
both ends by strong beams, and with their heads turned
against the current, while anchors were thrown out above to
keep the bridge firm. The cables, however, instead of being
taut, hung loose in the water, in order that as the stream
rose the vessels might rise without their arrangement being
disturbed. On the end of the bridge was placed a turret; it
was built out on the last boat, and from it engines and machines might be worked to repel the enemy. The soldiers of

Otho also raised a turret on the opposite bank, and hurled from it stones and flaming missiles.

35. In the middle of the river was an island. While the gladiators were making their way to it in boats, the Germans swam and outstripped them. A considerable number, as it chanced, had effected the passage, when Macer, having manned some light gallies, attacked them with the most active of his gladiators. But the gladiator has not in battle the firmness of the regular soldier, and now, as they stood on rocking vessels, they could not direct their blows like men who had a sure footing on land. As the men in their alarm made confused movements, rowers and combatants were mingled together in disorder; upon this, the Germans themselves leapt into the shallows, laid hold of the boats, climbed over the gunwales, or sank them with their hands. All this passed in the sight of both armies, and the more it delighted the Vitellianists, the more vehemently did the Othonianists curse the cause and author of the disaster.

36. The conflict was terminated by the flight of the vanquished, who carried off what boats were left. Then they cried out for the execution of Macer. He had been wounded by a javelin thrown from a distance, and the soldiers had made a rush upon him with drawn swords, when he was saved by the interference of the tribunes and centurions. Soon after Vestricius Spurinna, having received orders to that effect from Otho, joined with his cohorts, leaving but a moderate force in garrison at Placentia. After this Otho sent Flavius Sabinus, consul elect, to take the command of the troops which had been under Macer; the soldiers were delighted by this change of generals, while the generals were led by these continual outbreaks to regard with disgust so hateful a service.

37. I find it stated by some authors that either the dread of war or the disgust felt for both Emperors, whose wickedness and infamy were coming out every day into more open notoriety, made the two armies hesitate whether they should not cease their strife, and either themselves consult together, or allow the Senate to choose an Emperor; and that, for this reason, Otho's generals recommended a certain measure of delay, Paullinus especially entertaining

hopes for himself, on the ground that he was the senior among the men of consular rank, that he was well known as a soldier, and had attained great distinction and fame by his campaigns in Britain. Though I would allow that there were some few who in their secret wishes prayed for peace in the stead of disorder, for a worthy and blameless Emperor in the room of men utterly worthless and wicked, yet I cannot suppose that Paullinus, wise as he was, could have hoped in an age thoroughly depraved to find such moderation in the common herd, as that men, who in their passion for war had trampled peace under foot, should now in their affection for peace renounce the charms of war; nor can I think that armies differing in language and in character, could have united in such an agreement; or that lieutenants and generals, who were for the most part burdened by the consciousness of profligacy, of poverty, and of crime, could have endured any Emperor who was not himself stained by vice, as well as bound by obligation to themselves.

38. That old passion for power which has been ever innate in man increased and broke out as the Empire grew in greatness. In a state of moderate dimensions equality was easily preserved; but when the world had been subdued, when all rival kings and cities had been destroyed, and men had leisure to covet wealth which they might enjoy in security, the early conflicts between the patricians and the people were kindled into flame. At one time the tribunes were factious, at another the consuls had unconstitutional power; it was in the capital and the forum that we first essayed civil wars. Then rose C. Marius, sprung from the very dregs of the populace, and L. Sulla, the most ruthless of the patricians, who perverted into absolute dominion the liberty which had yielded to their arms. After them came Cn. Pompeius, with a character more disguised but no way better. Henceforth men's sole object was supreme power. Legions formed of Roman citizens did not lay down their arms at Pharsalia and Philippi, much less were the armies of Otho and Vitellius likely of their own accord to abandon their strife. They were driven into civil war by the same wrath from heaven, the same madness among men, the same incentives to crime. That these wars were terminated by what we

may call single blows, was owing to want of energy in the chiefs. But these reflections on the character of ancient and modern times have carried me too far from my subject. I now return to the course of events.

39. Otho having started for Brixellum, the honours of supreme command devolved on his brother Titianus, while the real power and control were in the hands of the prefect Proculus. Celsus and Paullinus, as no one made any use of their skill, did but screen with their idle title of general the blunders of others. The tribunes and centurions were perplexed to see that better men were despised, and that the most worthless carried the day. The common soldiers were full of eagerness, but liked to criticise rather than to obey the orders of their officers. It was resolved to move the camp forward to the fourth milestone from Bedriacum, but it was done so unskilfully, that though it was spring, and there were so many rivers in the neighbourhood, the troops were distressed for want of water. Then the subject of giving battle was discussed, Otho in his despatches ever urging them to make haste, and the soldiers demanding that the Emperor should be present at the conflict; many begged that the troops quartered beyond the Padus should be brought up. It is not so easy to determine what was best to be done, as it is to be sure that what was done was the very worst.

40. They started for a campaign rather than for a battle, making for the confluence of the Padus and Addua, a distance of sixteen miles from their position. Celsus and Paullinus remonstrated against exposing troops wearied with a march and encumbered with baggage to any enemy, who, being himself ready for action and having marched barely four miles, would not fail to attack them, either when they were in the confusion of an advance, or when they were dispersed and busy with the work of entrenchment. Titianus and Proculus, overcome in argument, fell back on the Imperial authority. It was true that a Numidian had arrived at full gallop with an angry message from Otho, in which the Emperor, sick of delay and impatient of suspense, sharply rebuked the inactivity of the generals, and commanded that matters should be brought to an issue.

41. The same day, while Cæcina was engaged on the construction of a bridge, two tribunes of the Prætorian Guard
came to him and begged an interview. He was on the point
of hearing their proposals and sending back his own, when
the scouts arrived at headlong speed with the news that the
enemy were close at hand. The address of the tribunes was
thus abruptly terminated. Thus it remained uncertain
whether deception, or treason, or some honourable arrangement, had been in their thoughts. Cæcina dismissed the tribunes and rode back to the camp. There he found that
Fabius Valens had given the signal for battle, and that the
troops were under arms. While the legions were casting lots
for the order of march, the cavalry charged, and, strange to
say, were kept only by the courage of the Italian legion
from being driven back on the entrenchments by an inferior
force of Othonianists. These men, at the sword's point, compelled the beaten squadron to wheel round and resume the
conflict. The line of the Vitellianists was formed without
hurry, for, though the enemy was close at hand, the sight of
their arms was intercepted by the thick brushwood. In
Otho's army the generals were full of fear, and the soldiers
hated their officers; the baggage-waggons and the camp-
followers were mingled with the troops; and as there were
steep ditches on both sides the road, it would have been
found too narrow even for an undisturbed advance. Some
were gathering round their standards; others were seeking
them; everywhere was heard the confused shouting of men
who were joining the ranks, or calling to their comrades,
and each, as he was prompted by courage or by cowardice,
rushed on to the front, or slunk back to the rear.

42. From the consternation of panic their feelings passed
under the influence of a groundless joy into languid indifference, some persons spreading the lie that Vitellius' army
had revolted. Whether this rumour was circulated by the
spies of Vitellius, or originated in treachery or in accident
among the partisans of Otho, has never been clearly ascertained. Forgetting their warlike ardour, the Othonianists at
once greeted the foe; as they were answered by an angry
murmur, they caused apprehensions of treachery in many
of their own side, who did not know what the greeting

meant. Then the enemy's line charged with its ranks unbroken, in strength and in numbers superior; the Othonianists, scattered and weary as they were, met the attack
with spirit. The ground was so entangled with trees and
vineyards that the battle assumed many forms. They met
in close and in distant conflict, in line and in column. On
the raised road they stood foot to foot, they pushed with
their bodies and their shields, and ceasing to throw their
javelins, they struck through helmets and breastplates with
swords and battle-axes. Recognising each other and distinctly seen by the rest of the combatants, they were fighting to decide the whole issue of the war.

43. In an open plain between the Padus and the road, two
legions happened to meet. On the side of Vitellius was the
21st, called the Rapax, a corps of old and distinguished renown. On that of Otho was the 1st, called Adjutrix, which
had never before been brought into the field, but was high-
spirited, and eager to gain its first triumph. The men of the
1st, overthrowing the foremost ranks of the 21st, carried off
the eagle. The 21st, infuriated by this loss, not only repulsed the 1st, and slew the legate, Orfidius Benignus, but
captured many colours and standards from the enemy. In
another quarter the 13th legion was put to flight by a
charge of the 5th. The 14th was surrounded by a superior
force. Otho's generals had long since fled, and Cæcina and
Valens strengthened their army with the reserves. New reinforcements were supplied by Varus Alfenius with his Batavians. They had routed the band of gladiators, which had
been ferried across the river, and which had been cut to
pieces by the opposing cohorts while they were actually in
the water. Thus flushed with victory, they charged the flank
of the enemy.

44. The centre of their line had been penetrated, and the
Othonianists fled on all sides in the direction of Bedriacum.
The distance was very great, and the roads were blocked up
with heaps of corpses; thus the slaughter was the greater,
for captives taken in civil war can be turned to no profit.
Suetonius Paullinus and Licinius Proculus, taking different
roads, avoided the camp. Vedius Aquila, legate of the 13th
legion, in the blindness of fear, fell in the way of the furious

soldiery. Late in the day he entered the entrenchments, and found himself the centre of a mob of clamorous and mutinous fugitives. They did not refrain from abuse or actual violence; they reviled him as a deserter and traitor, not having any specific charge against him, but all, after the fashion of the mob, imputing to him their own crimes. Titianus and Celsus were favoured by the darkness. By that time the sentries had been posted, and the soldiers reduced to order. Annius Gallus had prevailed upon them by his prayers, his advice, and his personal influence, not to aggravate the disaster of their defeat by mutual slaughter. Whether the war was at an end, or whether they might choose to resume the conflict, the vanquished would find in union the sole mitigation of their lot. The spirit of the rest of the army was broken, but the Prætorians angrily complained that they had been vanquished, not by valour, but by treachery. "The Vitellianists indeed," they said, "gained no bloodless victory; their cavalry was defeated, a legion lost its eagle. We have still the troops beyond the Padus, and Otho himself. The legions of Mœsia are coming; a great part of the army remained at Bedriacum; these certainly were never vanquished; and if it must be so, it is on the battle-field that we shall fall with most honour." Amid all the exasperation or terror of these thoughts, the extremity of despair yet roused them to fury rather than to fear.

45. The army of Vitellius bivouacked at the fifth milestone from Bedriacum. The generals did not venture an assault on the enemy's camp that same day; besides, a capitulation was expected. Though they were without baggage, and had marched out only to fight, it was sufficient protection to them that they had arms, and were victorious. On the following day, as the feeling of Otho's army was evident, and those who had been most furious were inclined to repent, envoys were sent, nor did the generals of Vitellius hesitate to grant conditions of peace. The envoys indeed were detained for some little time, and this circumstance caused some doubt, as it was not known whether they had obtained their object; before long, however, they returned, and the camp was thrown open. Both victors and vanquished melted into tears, and cursed the fatality of civil

strife with a melancholy joy. There in the same tents did they dress the wounds of brothers or of kinsmen. Their hopes, their rewards, were all uncertain; death and sorrow were sure. And no one had so escaped misfortune as to have no bereavement to lament. Search was made for the body of the legate Orfidius, and it was burnt with the customary honours. A few were buried by their friends; the multitude that remained were left above ground.

46. Otho was awaiting news of the battle free from alarm and resolved in purpose. First came gloomy tidings, and then fugitives from the field, making known that all was lost. The zeal of the soldiers did not wait for the Emperor to speak. They bade him be of good cheer, telling him that he had still fresh forces, and that they would themselves endure and dare to the last. This was no flattery; they were fired by a furious impulse to seek the battle-field, and raise again the fallen fortunes of their party. Those who stood at a distance stretched out their arms, those who were near clasped the Emperor's knees, and Plotius Firmus was the most zealous of them all. This man, who was prefect of the Prætorian Guard, repeatedly besought Otho not to desert an army so loyal and soldiers so deserving; "there was more courage in bearing trouble," he said, "than in escaping from it; the brave and the energetic cling to hope, even in spite of fortune; the cowardly and the indolent are hurried into despair by their fears." While he was thus speaking, as Otho assumed a relenting or a stern expression, the soldiers cheered or groaned. Nor was it only the Prætorians, who were peculiarly Otho's troops, that thus acted; those who had been sent on from Mœsia declared that the approaching army was as firmly resolved, and that the legions had entered Aquileia. No one therefore can doubt that the war might have been renewed with its terrible disasters, and its uncertainties both for victors and vanquished.

47. Otho himself was opposed to all thoughts of war. He said, "I hold that to expose such a spirit, such a courage as yours, to any further risk is to put too high a value on my life. The more hope you hold out to me, should I choose to live, the more glorious will be my death. Fortune and I now know each other; you need not reckon for how long, for it

is peculiarly difficult to be moderate with that prosperity which you think you will not long enjoy. The civil war began with Vitellius; he was the first cause of our contending in arms for the throne; the example of not contending more than once shall belong to me. By this let posterity judge of Otho. Vitellius is welcome to his brother, his wife, his children. I need neither revenge nor consolation. Others may have held the throne for a longer time, but no one can have left it with such fortitude. Shall I suffer so large a portion of the youth of Rome and so many noble armies to be again laid low and to be lost to the State? Let this thought go with me, that you were willing to die for me. But live, and let us no longer delay, lest I interfere with your safety, you with my firmness. To say too much about one's end is a mark of cowardice. Take as the strongest proof of my determination the fact that I complain of no one. To accuse either gods or men is only for him who wishes to live."

48. After having thus spoken, he courteously entreated all in terms befitting their age and rank to go at once, and not exasperate the anger of the conqueror by staying. With the young he used his authority, with the old his prayers, and still his look was calm, his speech collected, as he checked the unseasonable tears of his friends. He gave orders that those who were departing should be furnished with boats and carriages; he destroyed all memorials and letters remarkable for their expressions of zeal for himself or their abuse of Vitellius. He distributed some gratuities, but sparingly, and not like a man who was soon to die. Then he even administered consolation to Salvius Cocceianus, his brother's son, a very young man, who was anxious and sorrowful, praising his affection while he rebuked his fear. "Do you think," he said, "that Vitellius will shew so ruthless a temper that he will not make even this return for the preservation of his whole family? By hastening my end I earn the clemency of the conqueror. It is not in the extremity of despair, but while my army yet cries for battle that I have sacrificed to the State my last chance. I have obtained enough reputation for myself, enough nobility for my family. Successor to the Julii, the Claudii, the Servii, I have been the first to bring the Imperial dignity into a new fam-

ily. Enter then on life with a brave heart, and never entirely forget, or remember too vividly, that Otho was your uncle.

49. After this he dismissed every one, and took some repose. He was now pondering in his heart the last cares of life, when his attention was distracted by a sudden tumult and he was told of the confusion and outrageous conduct of the soldiers. They were threatening with death all who attempted to depart, and were extreme in their violence against Verginius, whose house they had blockaded and were besieging. After rebuking the ringleaders of the tumult, ae returned and employed himself in granting interviews to those who were departing, till all had left in safety. Towards evening he quenched his thirst with a draught of cold water. Two daggers were brought to him; he tried the edge of each, and then put one under his head. After satisfying himself that his friends had set out, he passed a tranquil night, and it is even said that he slept. At dawn he fell with his breast upon the steel. Hearing a groan from the dying man, his freedmen and slaves, and Plotius Firmus, prefect of the Prætorian Guard, came in. They found but one wound. His funeral was hastily performed. He had made this the subject of earnest entreaties, anxious that his head might not be cut off and subjected to indignities. The Prætorian cohorts carried his body with praises and tears, covering his wound and his hands with kisses. Some of the soldiers killed themselves near the funeral pile, not moved by remorse or by fear, but by the desire to emulate his glory, and by love of their Prince. Afterwards this kind of death became a common practice among all ranks at Bedriacum, at Placentia, and in the other camps. Over Otho was built a tomb unpretending and therefore likely to stand.

50. Thus Otho ended his life in the 37th year of his age. He came from the municipal town of Ferentinum. His father was of consular, his grandfather of prætorian rank. His family on the mother's side was of less distinction, but yet respectable. What his boyhood and his youth had been, we have already shewn. By two daring acts, one most atrocious, the other singularly noble, he earned in the eyes of posterity about an equal share of infamy and of glory. I should think it unbecoming the dignity of the task which I

have undertaken, to collect fabulous marvels, and to amuse with fiction the tastes of my readers; at the same time I would not venture to impugn the credit of common report and tradition. The natives of these parts relate that on the day when the battle was being fought at Bedriacum, a bird of unfamiliar appearance settled in a much frequented grove near Regium Lepidum, and was not frightened or driven away by the concourse of people, or by the multitude of birds that flocked round it, until Otho killed himself; then it vanished. When they came to compute the time, it was found that the commencement and the end of this strange occurrence tallied with the last scenes of Otho's life.

51. At the funeral the mutinous spirit of the soldiers was kindled afresh by their sorrow and regret, and there was no one to check them. They turned to Verginius, and in threatening language, at one time besought him to accept the Imperial dignity, at another, to act as envoy to Cæcina and Valens. Verginius secretly departed by a back way from his house, and thus managed to elude them when they burst in. Rubrius Gallus was charged with the petition of the cohorts which had been quartered at Brixellum. An amnesty was immediately granted to them, while at the same time the forces which had been commanded by Flavius Sabinus signified through him their submission to the conqueror.

52. Hostilities had ceased everywhere, but a considerable number of the Senate, who had accompanied Otho from Rome, and had been afterwards left at Mutina, encountered the utmost peril. News of the defeat was brought to this place. The soldiers, however, rejected it as a false report; and judging the Senate to be hostile to Otho, watched their language, and put an unfavourable construction on their looks and manner. Proceeding at last to abuse and insults they sought a pretext for beginning a massacre, while a different anxiety also weighed upon the Senators, who, knowing that the party of Vitellius was in the ascendant, feared that they might seem to have been tardy in welcoming the conqueror. Thus they met in great alarm and distracted by a twofold apprehension; no one was ready with any advice of his own, but looked for safety in sharing any mistake with many others. The anxieties of the terrified assembly

were aggravated when the Senate of Mutina made them an offer of arms and money, and, with an ill-timed compliment, styled them "Conscript Fathers."

53. There then ensued a notable quarrel, Licinius Cæcina inveighing against Marcellus Eprius, for using ambiguous language. The rest indeed did not express their opinions, but the name of Marcellus, exposed as it was to odium from the hateful recollection of his career as an informer, had roused in Cæcina, who was an unknown man, and had lately been made a Senator, the hope of distinguishing himself by making great enemies. The moderation of wiser men put an end to the dispute. They all returned to Bononia, intending there to deliberate again, and also expecting further news in the meantime. At Bononia they posted men on the different roads to make enquiries of every new comer; one of Otho's freedmen, on being questioned as to the cause of his departure, replied that he was entrusted with his master's last commands; Otho was still alive, he said, when he left him, but his only thoughts were for posterity, and he had torn himself from all the fascinations of life. They were struck with admiration, and were ashamed to put any more questions, and then the hearts of all turned to Vitellius.

54. Lucius Vitellius, the brother of the Emperor, was present at their deliberations, and was preparing to receive their flatteries, when of a sudden Cœnus, a freedman of Nero, threw them all into consternation by an outrageous falsehood. He asserted that, by the arrival of the 14th legion, joined to the forces from Brixellum, the victorious army had been routed and the fortunes of the party changed. The object of this fabrication was that the passports of Otho, which were beginning to be disregarded, might through more favourable news recover their validity. Cœnus was conveyed with rapidity to the capital, but a few days after suffered the penalty of his crime by the order of Vitellius. The peril of the Senators was increased by the soldiers of Otho's army believing that the intelligence thus brought was authentic. Their alarm was heightened by the fact that their departure from Mutina and their desertion of the party had the appearance of a public resolution. They did not meet again for general deliberation, but every man consulted his own

safety, till letters arrived from Fabius Valens which removed their fear. Besides, the very glory of Otho's death made the news travel more quickly.

55. At Rome, however, there was no alarm; the games of Ceres were attended as usual. When trustworthy messengers brought into the theatre the news that Otho was dead, and that all the troops in the capital had taken the oath to Vitellius under the direction of Flavius Sabinus, prefect of the city, the spectators greeted the name of Vitellius with applause. The people carried round the temples images of Galba, ornamented with laurel leaves and flowers, and piled chaplets in the form of a sepulchral mound near the lake of Curtius, on the very spot which had been stained with the blood of the dying man. In the Senate all the customary honours, which had been devised during the long reigns of other Emperors, were forthwith decreed. Public acknowledgments and thanks were also given to the armies of Germany, and envoys were sent charged with congratulations. There was read a letter from Fabius Valens to the consuls, which was written in a not unbecoming style, but they liked better the modesty of Cæcina in not writing at all.

56. Italy, however, was prostrated under sufferings heavier and more terrible than the evils of war. The soldiers of Vitellius, dispersed through the municipal towns and colonies, were robbing and plundering and polluting every place with violence and lust. Everything, lawful or unlawful, they were ready to seize or to sell, sparing nothing, sacred or profane. Some persons under the soldiers' garb murdered their private enemies. The soldiers themselves, who knew the country well, marked out rich estates and wealthy owners for plunder, or for death in case of resistance; their commanders were in their power and dared not check them. Cæcina indeed was not so rapacious as he was fond of popularity; Valens was so notorious for his dishonest gains and peculations that he was disposed to conceal the crimes of others. The resources of Italy had long been impaired, and the presence of so vast a force of infantry and cavalry, with the outrages, the losses, and the wrongs they inflicted, was more than it could well endure.

57. Meanwhile Vitellius, as yet unaware of his victory

was bringing up the remaining strength of the army of Germany just as if the campaign had yet to be fought. A few
of the old soldiers were left in the winter quarters, and the
conscription throughout Gaul was hastily proceeded with,
in order that the muster-rolls of the legions which remained
behind might be filled up. The defence of the bank of the
Rhine was entrusted to Hordeonius Flaccus. Vitellius himself added to his own army 8000 men of the British conscription. He had proceeded a few days' march, when he
received intelligence of the victory at Bedriacum, and of the
termination of the war through Otho's death. He called an
assembly, and heaped praises on the valour of the soldiers.
When the army demanded that he should confer equestrian
rank on Asiaticus his freedman, he checked the disgraceful
flattery. Then, with his characteristic fickleness, in the privacy of a banquet he granted the very distinction which he
had publicly refused; and honoured with the ring of Knighthood this same Asiaticus, a slave of infamous character,
ever seeking power by unprincipled intrigues.

58. About the same time news came to Vitellius that the
procurator Albinus had fallen, and that both the provinces
of Mauritania had declared for him. Lucceius Albinus, whom
Nero had appointed to the government of Mauritania Cæsariensis, to which Galba had subsequently added the
charge of the province of Tingitana, had the disposal of no
contemptible force. He had with him 19 cohorts of infantry,
5 squadrons of cavalry, and a vast number of Moors, a force
trained to war by robbery and plunder. When Galba had
fallen, he was strongly disposed in favour of Otho. He even
looked beyond Africa and threatened Spain, which is separated from it only by a narrow strait. This alarmed Cluvius
Rufus, who ordered the 10th legion to approach the coast,
as if he intended to send them across. Some of the centurions were sent on before to gain for Vitellius the good-will
of the Moors. This was no difficult task, as the fame of the
German army was great in the provinces. Besides this, a report was circulated that Albinus, scorning the title of procurator, was assuming the insignia of royalty and the name
of Juba.

59. The tide of feeling turned, and Asinius Pollio, one of

the stanchest friends of Albinus, prefect of one of the squadrons of cavalry, with Festus and Scipio, prefects of two infantry cohorts, were killed. Albinus himself, who was sailing
from the province Tingitana to Mauritania Cæsariensis, was
murdered as he reached the shore. His wife threw herself in
the way of the murderers and was killed with him. Vitellius
made no inquiries into what was going on. He dismissed
matters of even the greatest importance with brief hearing,
and was quite unequal to any serious business. He directed
the army to proceed by land, but sailed himself down the
river Arar. His progress had nothing of imperial state about
it, but was marked by the poverty of his former condition,
till Junius Blæsus, governor of Gallia Lugdunensis, a man
of noble birth, whose munificence was equal to his wealth,
furnished him with suitable attendance, and escorted him
with a splendid retinue; a service which was of itself displeasing, though Vitellius masked his dislike under servile
compliments. At Lugdunum the generals of the two parties,
the conquerors and the conquered, were waiting for him.
Valens and Cæcina he put by his own chair of state, after
celebrating their praises before a general assembly. He then
ordered the whole army to come and greet his infant son;
he brought him out, wrapped in a military cloak, and holding him in his arms, gave him the title of Germanicus, and
surrounded him with all the insignia of the imperial rank.
It was an extravagant distinction for a day of prosperity,
but it served as a consolation in adversity.

60. Then the bravest centurions among the Othonianists
were put to death. This, more than anything else, alienated
from Vitellius the armies of Illyricum. At the same time the
other legions, influenced by the contagion of example, and
by their dislike of the German troops, were meditating war.
Vitellius detained Suetonius Paullinus and Licinus Proculus
in all the wretchedness of an odious imprisonment; when
they were heard, they resorted to a defence, necessary rather
than honourable. They actually claimed the merit of having
been traitors, attributing to their own dishonest counsels the
long march before the battle, the fatigue of Otho's troops,
the entanglement of the line with the baggage-waggons, and
many circumstances which were really accidental. Vitellius

gave them credit for perfidy, and acquitted them of the crime
of loyalty. Salvius Titianus, the brother of Otho, was never
in any peril, for his brotherly affection and his apathetic
character screened him from danger. Marius Celsus had his
consulship confirmed to him. It was commonly believed,
however, and was afterwards made a matter of accusation
in the Senate against Cæcilius Simplex, that he had sought
to purchase this honour, and with it the destruction of Celsus. Vitellius refused, and afterwards bestowed on Simplex
a consulship that had not to be bought with crime or with
money. Trachalus was protected against his accusers by
Galeria the wife of Vitellius.

61. Amid the adventures of these illustrious men, one is
ashamed to relate how a certain Mariccus, a Boian of the
lowest origin, pretending to divine inspiration, ventured to
thrust himself into fortune's game, and to challenge the
arms of Rome. Calling himself the champion of Gaul, and a
God (for he had assumed this title), he had now collected
8000 men, and was taking possession of the neighbouring
villages of the Ædui, when that most formidable state attacked him with a picked force of its native youth, to which
Vitellius attached some cohorts, and dispersed the crowd of
fanatics. Mariccus was captured in the engagement, and was
soon after exposed to wild beasts, but not having been torn
by them was believed by the senseless multitude to be invul-
nerable, till he was put to death in the presence of Vitellius.

62. No further severities were exercised on the persons of
the opposite faction, or with property in any case; the wills
of those who had fallen fighting for Otho were held to be
valid, and with those who died intestate, the law was carried out. Assuredly, could Vitellius have bridled his luxurious tastes, no one need have dreaded his rapacity. He
had a scandalous and insatiable passion for feasts; the pro-
vocatives of gluttony were conveyed to him from the capital
and from Italy, till the roads from both seas resounded with
traffic; the leading men of the various states were ruined by
having to furnish his entertainments, and the states themselves reduced to beggary; the soldiers fast degenerated
from their old activity and valour, through habitual indulgence and contempt of their leader. He sent on before him

to the capital an edict, by which he postponed his acceptance of the title of Augustus and refused that of Cæsar,
though he relinquished nothing of his actual power. The
astrologers were banished from Italy. The Roman Knights
were forbidden, under severe penalties, to degrade themselves by appearing in public entertainments, or in the arena.
Former Emperors had encouraged the practice by bribes, or
more frequently enforced it by compulsion; and many of
the towns and colonies had vied with each other in attract-
ing by large pay the most profligate of the youth.

63. Vitellius, however, when his brother joined him, and
when those who are skilled in the arts of despotism began
to creep into his confidence, grew more arrogant and cruel.
He ordered the execution of Dolabella, whose banishment
by Otho to the Colonia Aquinas I have before mentioned.
Dolabella, on hearing of the death of Otho, had entered the
capital. Plancius Varus, who had filled the office of prætor,
and had been one of Dolabella's intimate friends, founded
on this a charge, which he laid before Flavius Sabinus, prefect of the city, implying that Dolabella had escaped from
custody, and had offered to put himself at the head of the
vanquished party; and he also alleged that the cohort stationed at Ostia had been tampered with. Of these grave accusations he brought no proof whatever, and then repenting,
sought, when the crime had been consummated, a pardon
which could be of no avail. Flavius Sabinus hesitating to act
in a matter of such importance, Triaria, the wife of Lucius
Vitellius, with unfeminine ferocity, warned him not to seek a
reputation for clemency by imperilling the Emperor. Sabinus was naturally of a mild disposition, but under the
pressure of fear was easily swayed; here, the danger of another made him tremble for himself, and, lest he might seem
to have helped the accused, he precipitated his fall.

64. Upon this, Vitellius, who, besides fearing Dolabella,
hated him, because he had married Petronia, his former wife,
summoned him by letter, and at the same time gave orders
that, without passing along the much frequented thorough-
fare of the Flaminian road, he should turn aside to Interamna, and there be put to death. This seemed too tedious
to the executioner, who in a road-side tavern struck down

his prisoner, and cut his throat. The act brought great odium upon the new reign, and was noted as the first indication of its character. Triaria's recklessness was rendered more intolerable by an immediate contrast with the exemplary virtue of Galeria, the Emperor's wife, who took no part in these horrors, and with Sextilia, the mother of the two Vitellii, a woman equally blameless, and of the old type of character. She indeed is said to have exclaimed on receiving the first letter from her son, "I am the mother, not of Germanicus, but of Vitellius." And in after days no seductions of fortune, no flattery from the State, could move her to exultation; it was only the misfortunes of her family that she felt.

65. M. Cluvius Rufus, who had left his government in Spain, came up with Vitellius after his departure from Lugdunum. He wore a look of joy and congratulation, but he was anxious at heart, for he knew that he was the object of accusations. Hilarius, the Emperor's freedman, had indeed brought this charge against him, that on hearing of the contest for the throne between Vitellius and Otho, he had made an attempt to secure power for himself, and to obtain possession of Spain, and that with this view he had not headed his passports with the name of any Emperor. Some extracts from the speeches of Rufus he represented as insulting to Vitellius, and intended to win popularity for himself. So strong, however, was the influence of Cluvius, that Vitellius actually ordered the freedman to be punished. Cluvius was attached to the Emperor's retinue; Spain however was not taken from him; he still governed the province though not resident, as L. Arruntius had done before him, whom Tiberius Cæsar detained at home, because he feared him; it was not from any apprehension that Vitellius kept Cluvius with him. The same compliment was not paid to Trebellius Maximus. He had fled from Britain because of the exasperation of the soldiery. Vettius Bolanus, who was then accompanying the Emperor, was sent to succeed him.

66. Vitellius was troubled by the spirit of the vanquished legions, which was any thing but broken. Scattered through all parts of Italy, and mingled with the conquerors, they spoke the language of enemies. The soldiers of the 14th

legion were peculiarly furious. They said that they had not been vanquished; that at the battle of Bedriacum only the veterans had been beaten, and that the strength of the legion had been absent. It was resolved that these troops should be sent back to Britain, from which province Nero had summoned them, and that the Batavian cohorts should in the meantime be quartered with them, because there was an old feud between them and the 14th. In the presence of such animosities between these armed masses, harmony did not last long. At Augusta of the Taurini it happened that a Batavian soldier fiercely charged some artisan with having cheated him, and that a soldier of the legion took the part of his host. Each man's comrades gathered round him; from words they came to blows, and a fierce battle would have broken out, had not two Prætorian cohorts taken the side of the 14th, and given confidence to them, while they intimidated the Batavians. Vitellius then ordered that these latter troops should be attached to his own force, in consideration of their loyalty, and that the legion should pass over the Graian Alps, and then take that line of road, by which they would avoid passing Vienna, for the inhabitants of that place were also suspected. On the night of the departure of the legion, a part of the Colonia Taurina was destroyed by the fires which were left in every direction. This loss, like many of the evils of war, was forgotten in the greater disasters which happened to other cities. When the 14th had made the descent on the other side of the Alps, the most mutinous among them were for carrying the standards to Vienna. They were checked, however, by the united efforts of the better disposed, and the legion was transported into Britain.

67. Vitellius found his next cause of apprehension in the Prætorian cohorts. They were first divided, and then ordered, though with the gratifying compliment of an honourable discharge, to give up their arms to their tribunes. But as the arms of Vespasian gathered strength, they returned to their old service, and constituted the main stay of the Flavianist party. The first legion from the fleet was sent into Spain, that in the peaceful repose of that province their excitement might subside; the 7th and 11th were sent back to

their winter quarters; the 13th were ordered to erect amphi-
theatres, for both Cæcina at Cremona, and Valens at Bononia, were preparing to exhibit shows of gladiators. Vitellius indeed was never so intent on the cares of Empire as to
forget his pleasures.

68. Though he had thus quietly divided the conquered
party, there arose a disturbance among the conquerors. It
began in sport, but the number of those who fell aggravated
the horrors of the war. Vitellius had sat down to a banquet
at Ticinum, and had invited Verginius to be his guest. The
legates and tribunes always follow the character of the Emperor, and either imitate his strictness, or indulge in early
conviviality. And the soldiers in like manner are either diligent or lax in their duty. About Vitellius all was disorder
and drunkenness, more like a nocturnal feast and revel than
a properly disciplined camp. Thus it happened that two soldiers, one of whom belonged to the 5th legion, while the
other was one of the Gallic auxiliaries, challenged each other
in sport to a wrestling match. The legionary was thrown,
and the Gaul taunted him. The soldiers who had assembled
to witness the contest took different sides, till the legionaries
made a sudden and murderous attack on the auxiliary
troops, and destroyed two cohorts. The first disturbance
was checked only by a second. A cloud of dust and the glitter of arms were seen at a distance. A sudden cry was raised
that the 14th legion had retraced its steps, and was advancing to the attack. It was in fact the rearguard of the army,
and their recognition removed the cause of alarm. Meanwhile a slave of Verginius happened to come in their way.
He was charged with having designed the assassination of
Vitellius. The soldiers rushed to the scene of the banquet,
and loudly demanded the death of Verginius. Even Vitellius,
tremblingly alive as he was to all suspicions, had no doubt
of his innocence. Yet he could hardly check the troops when
they clamoured for the death of a man of consular rank,
formerly their own general. Indeed there was no one who
was more frequently the object of all kinds of outbreaks
than Verginius; the man still was admired, still retained his
high reputation, but they hated him with the hatred of those
who are despised.

69. The next day Vitellius, after giving audience to the envoys from the Senate whom he had ordered to wait for him there, proceeded to the camp, and actually bestowed high praise on the loyalty of the soldiers. The auxiliary troops loudly complained that such complete impunity, such privileged arrogance, was accorded to the legions. The Batavian cohorts were sent back to Germany, lest they should venture on further violence. Destiny was thus simultaneously preparing the occasions of civil and of foreign war. The Gallic auxiliaries were sent back to their respective states, a vast body of men, which in the very earliest stage of the revolt had been employed to make an idle show of strength. Besides this, in order to eke out the Imperial resources, which had been impaired by a series of bounties, directions were given that the battalions of the legions and the auxiliary forces should be reduced, all recruiting being forbidden. Discharges were offered without distinction. This measure was disastrous to the State, and distasteful to the soldier, who found that the same duty was distributed among a smaller number, and that his toils and risks came round in a more frequent succession. Their vigour too was undermined by luxury, a luxury that transgressed our ancient discipline and the customs of our ancestors, in whose days the power of Rome found a surer foundation in valour than in wealth.

70. Vitellius then directed his course to Cremona, and after witnessing the spectacle exhibited by Cæcina, he conceived a desire to visit the plains of Bedriacum and to survey the scene of the recent victory. It was a hideous and terrible sight. Not forty days had passed since the battle, and there lay mangled corpses, severed limbs, the putrefying forms of men and horses; the soil was saturated with gore, and, what with levelled trees and crops, horrible was the desolation. Not less revolting was that portion of the road which the people of Cremona had strewed with laurel leaves and roses, and on which they had raised altars, and sacrificed victims as if to greet some barbarous despot, festivities in which they delighted for the moment, but which were afterwards to work their ruin. Valens and Cæcina were present, and pointed out the various localities of the field of

battle; shewing how from one point the columns of the legions had rushed to the attack; how from another the cavalry had charged; how from a third the auxiliary troops had turned the flank of the enemy. The tribunes and prefects extolled their individual achievements, and mixed together fictions, facts, and exaggerations. The common soldiers also turned aside from the line of march with joyful shouts, and recognized the various scenes of conflict, and gazed with wonder on the piles of weapons and the heaps of slain. Some indeed there were whom all this moved to thoughts of the mutability of fortune, to pity, and to tears. Vitellius did not turn away his eyes, did not shudder to behold the unburied corpses of so many thousands of his countrymen; nay, in his exultation, in his ignorance of the doom which was so close upon himself, he actually instituted a religious ceremony in honour of the tutelary gods of the place.

71. A show of gladiators was then given by Fabius Valens at Bononia, with all the arrangements introduced from the capital. The nearer the Emperor approached to Rome, the greater was the license of his march, accompanied as it was by players and herds of eunuchs, in fact by all that had characterised the court of Nero. Indeed, Vitellius used to make a display of his admiration for Nero, and had constantly followed him when he sang, not from the compulsion to which the noblest had to yield, but because he was the slave and chattel of profligacy and gluttony. To leave some months of office open for Valens and Cæcina, the consulates of others were abridged, that of Martius Macer was ignored on the ground of his having been one of Otho's generals. Valerius Maximus, who had been nominated consul by Galba, had his dignity deferred for no offence, but because he was a man of gentle temper, and could submit tamely to an affront. Pedanius Costa was passed over. The Emperor disliked him because he had risen against Nero, and roused Verginius to revolt. Other reasons, however, were alleged. Finally, after the servile fashion of the time, thanks were voted to Vitellius.

72. A deception, which was started with considerable vigour, lasted for a few, and but a few days. There had sud

denly sprung up a man, who gave out that he was Scribonianus Camerinus; that, dreading the times of Nero, he had
concealed himself in Histria, where the old family of the
Crassi still had dependants, estates, and a popular name.
He admitted into the secret of his imposture all the most
worthless of his followers; and the credulous populace and
some of the soldiers, either from not knowing the truth, or
impatient for revolution, began eagerly to rally round him.
When he was brought before Vitellius, and asked who he
was, as his account of himself could not be trusted, and his
master recognised him as a runaway slave, by name Geta, he
was executed as slaves usually are.

73. It would almost pass belief, were I to tell to what a
degree the insolence and sloth of Vitellius grew upon him
when messengers from Syria and Judæa brought the news
that the provinces of the East had sworn allegiance to him.
Though as yet all information was but vague and uncertain,
Vespasian was the subject of much talk and rumour, and at
the mention of his name Vitellius often roused himself. But
now, both the Emperor and the army, as if they had no
rival to fear, indulging in cruelty, lust, and rapine, plunged
into all the licence of foreign manners.

74. Vespasian, on the other hand, was taking a general
survey of the chances of a campaign and of his resources
both immediate and remote. The soldiers were so entirely
devoted to him, that as he dictated the oath of allegiance
and prayed for all prosperity to Vitellius, they listened to
him in silence. Mucianus had no dislike to Vespasian, and
was strongly inclined towards Titus. Already had Alexander, the governor of Egypt, declared his adhesion. The
third legion, as it had passed over from Syria to Mœsia,
Vespasian counted upon as devoted to himself, and it was
hoped that the other legions of Illyricum would follow its
example. In fact the whole army had been kindled into indignation by the insolence of the soldiers who came among
them from Vitellius. Savage in appearance, and speaking a
rude dialect, they ridiculed every body else as their inferiors.
But in such gigantic preparations for war there is usually
delay. Vespasian was at one moment high in hope, and at
another disposed to reflect on the chances of failure. What

a day would that be when he should expose himself with
his sixty years upon him, and the two young men, his sons,
to the perils of war! In private enterprises men may advance or recede, and presume more or less upon fortune as
they may choose, whereas they who aim at empire have no
alternative between the highest success and utter downfall.

75. The strength of the army of Germany, with which as
a military man he was well acquainted, was continually before his eyes. He reflected that his own legions were wholly
without experience of a civil war, that those of Vitellius
had been victorious, and that among the conquered there
was more dissatisfaction than real strength. Civil strife had
shaken the fidelity of the Roman soldiery, and danger was
to be apprehended from individuals. What would be the
use of infantry and cavalry, should one or two men seek
the prize with which the enemy would be ready to reward
a prompt act of treason? It was thus that Scribonianus had
fallen in the days of Claudius, and his murderer, Volaginius,
had been raised from the ranks to the highest military command. It was easier to move the hearts of the multitude than
to avoid the single assassin.

76. Though staggered by these apprehensions, he was
confirmed in his purpose by others among the legates and
among his own friends, and particularly by Mucianus, who,
after many conversations with him in private, now publicly
addressed him in the following terms: "All who enter upon
schemes involving great interests, should consider whether
what they are attempting be for the advantage of the State,
for their own credit, easy of accomplishment, or at any rate
free from serious difficulty. They must also weigh the circumstances of their adviser, must see whether he will follow
up his advice by imperilling himself, and must know who,
should fortune prosper the undertaking, is to have the highest honours. I invite you, Vespasian, to a dignity which will
be as beneficial to the State, as it will be honourable to yourself. Under heaven this dignity lies within your reach. And
do not dread what may present the semblance of flattery.
To be chosen successor to Vitellius would be more of an insult than a compliment. It is not against the vigorous intellect of the Divine Augustus, it is not against the pro-

found subtlety of the aged Tiberius, it is not even against the house of Caius, Claudius, or Nero, established by a long possession of the Empire, that we are rising in revolt. You have already yielded to the prestige even of Galba's family. To persist in inaction, and to leave the State to degradation and ruin, would look like indolence and cowardice, even supposing that servitude were as safe for you as it would be infamous. The time has gone by and passed away when you might have endured the suspicion of having coveted Imperial power. That power is now your only refuge. Have you forgotten how Corbulo was murdered? His origin, I grant, was more illustrious than ours; yet in nobility of birth Nero surpassed Vitellius. The man who is afraid sees distinction enough in any one whom he fears. That an Emperor can be created by the army, Vitellius is himself a proof, who, though he had seen no service and had no military reputation, was raised to the throne by the unpopularity of Galba. Otho, who was overcome, not indeed by skilful generalship, or by a powerful enemy, but by his own premature despair, this man has made into a great and deservedly regretted Emperor, and all the while he is disbanding his legions, disarming his auxiliaries, and sowing every day fresh seeds of civil war. All the energy and high spirit which once belonged to his army is wasted in the revelry of taverns and in aping the debaucheries of their chief. You have from Judæa, Syria, and Egypt, nine fresh legions, unexhausted by battle, uncorrupted by dissension; you have a soldiery hardened by habits of warfare and victorious over foreign foes; you have strong fleets, auxiliaries both horse and foot, kings most faithful to your cause, and an experience in which you excel all other men.

77. "For myself I will claim nothing more than not to be reckoned inferior to Valens and Cæcina. But do not spurn Mucianus as an associate, because you do not find in him a rival. I count myself better than Vitellius; I count you better than myself. Your house is ennobled by the glories of a triumph; it has two youthful scions, one of whom is already equal to the cares of Empire, and in the earliest years of his military career won renown with these very armies of Germany. It would be ridiculous in me not to waive my

claims to Empire in favour of the man whose son I should
adopt, were I myself Emperor. Between us, however, there
will not be an equal distribution of the fruits of success or
failure. If we are victorious, I shall have whatever honour
you think fit to bestow on me; the danger and the peril we
shall share alike; nay, I would rather have you, as is the
better policy, direct your armies, and leave to me the conduct of the war and the hazards of battle. At this very moment a stricter discipline prevails among the conquered
than among the conquerors. The conquered are fired to
valour by anger, by hatred, by the desire of vengeance,
while the conquerors are losing their energy in pride and
insolence. War will of itself discover and lay open the hidden
and rankling wounds of the victorious party. And, indeed,
your vigilance, economy, and wisdom, do not inspire me
with greater confidence of success than do the indolence,
ignorance, and cruelty of Vitellius. Once at war, we have
a better cause than we can have in peace, for those who
deliberate on revolt have revolted already."

78. After this speech from Mucianus, the other officers
crowded round Vespasian with fresh confidence, encouraging him, and reminding him of the responses of prophets
and the movements of the heavenly bodies. Nor was Vespasian proof against this superstition, for afterwards, when
master of the world, he openly retained one Seleucus, an
astrologer, to direct his counsels, and to foretell the future.
Old omens now recurred to his thoughts. A cypress-tree of
remarkable height on his estate had suddenly fallen, and
rising again the following day on the very same spot, had
flourished with majestic beauty and even broader shade.
This, as the Haruspices agreed, was an omen of brilliant
success, and the highest distinction seemed prophesied to
Vespasian in early youth. At first, however, the honours of
a triumph, his consulate, and the glory of his victories in
Judæa, appeared to have justified the truth of the omen.
When he had won these distinctions, he began to believe
that it portended the Imperial power. Between Judæa and
Syria is Mount Carmel; this is the name both of the mountain and the Deity. They have no image of the god nor any
temple; the tradition of antiquity recognises only an altar

and its sacred association. While Vespasian was there offering sacrifice and pondering his secret hopes, Basilides the priest, after repeated inspections of the entrails, said to him, "Whatever be your purposes, Vespasian, whether you think of building a house, of enlarging your estate, or augmenting the number of your slaves, there is given you a vast habitation, boundless territory, a multitude of men." These obscure intimations popular rumour had at once caught up, and now began to interpret. Nothing was more talked about by the common people. In Vespasian's presence the topic was more frequently discussed, because to the aspirant himself men have more to say.

79. With purposes no longer doubtful they parted, Mucianus for Antioch, Vespasian for Cæsarea. These cities are the capitals of Syria and Judæa respectively. The initiative in transferring the Empire to Vespasian was taken at Alexandria under the prompt direction of Tiberius Alexander, who on the 1st of July made the legions swear allegiance to him. That day was ever after celebrated as the first of his reign, though the army of Judæa on July 3rd took the oath to Vespasian in person with such eager alacrity that they would not wait for the return of his son Titus, who was then on his way back from Syria, acting as the medium between Mucianus and his father for the communication of their plans. All this was done by the impulsive action of the soldiers without the preliminary of a formal harangue or any concentration of the legions.

80. While they were seeking a suitable time and place, and for that which in such an affair is the great difficulty, the first man to speak, while hope, fear, the chances of success or of disaster, were present to their minds, one day, on Vespasian quitting his chamber, a few soldiers who stood near, in the usual form in which they would salute their legate, suddenly saluted him as Emperor. Then all the rest hurried up, called him Cæsar and Augustus, and heaped on him all the titles of Imperial rank. Their minds had passed from apprehension to confidence of success. In Vespasian there appeared no sign of elation or arrogance, or of any change arising from his changed fortunes. As soon as he had dispelled the mist with which so astonishing a vicissi-

tude had clouded his vision, he addressed the troops in a soldier-like style, and listened to the joyful intelligence that came pouring in from all quarters. This was the very opportunity for which Mucianus had been waiting. He now at once administered to the eager soldiers the oath of allegiance to Vespasian. Then he entered the theatre at Antioch, where it is customary for the citizens to hold their public deliberations, and as they crowded together with profuse expressions of flattery, he addressed them. He could speak Greek with considerable grace, and in all that he did and said he had the art of displaying himself to advantage. Nothing excited the provincials and the army so much as the assertion of Mucianus that Vitellius had determined to remove the legions of Germany to Syria, to an easy and lucrative service, while the armies of Syria were to have given them in exchange the encampments of Germany with their inclement climate and their harassing toils. On the one hand, the provincials from long use felt a pleasure in the companionship of the soldiers, with whom many of them were connected by friendship or relationship; on the other, the soldiers from the long duration of their service loved the well-known and familiar camp as a home.

81. Before the 15th of July the whole of Syria had adopted the same allegiance. There joined him, each with his entire kingdom, Sohemus, who had no contemptible army, and Antiochus, who possessed vast ancestral wealth, and was the richest of all the subject-kings. Before long Agrippa, who had been summoned from the capital by secret despatches from his friends, while as yet Vitellius knew nothing, was crossing the sea with all speed. Queen Berenice too, who was then in the prime of youth and beauty, and who had charmed even the old Vespasian by the splendour of her presents, promoted his cause with equal zeal. All the provinces washed by the sea, as far as Asia and Achaia, and the whole expanse of country inland towards Pontus and Armenia, took the oath of allegiance. The legates, however, of these provinces were without troops, Cappadocia as yet having had no legions assigned to it. A council was held at Berytus to deliberate on the general conduct of the war. Thither came Mucianus with the legates

and tribunes and all the most distinguished centurions and
soldiers, and thither also the picked troops of the army of
Judæa. Such a vast assemblage of cavalry and infantry, and
the pomp of the kings that strove to rival each other in
magnificence, presented an appearance of Imperial splendour.

82. The first business of the campaign was to levy troops
and recall the veterans to service. The strong cities were set
apart for the manufacture of arms; at Antioch gold and
silver money was coined, every thing being vigorously carried on in its appointed place by properly qualified agents.
Vespasian himself went everywhere, urged to exertion, encouraged the industrious by praise, and with the indolent
used the stimulus of example rather than of compulsion,
and chose to be blind to the faults rather than to the merits
of his friends. Many among them he distinguished with
prefectures and governments, and several with the honours
of senatorial rank; all these were men of eminence who
soon reached the highest positions. In some cases good fortune served instead of merit. Of a donative to the troops
Mucianus in his first speech had held out only moderate
hopes, and even Vespasian offered no more in the civil war
than others had done in times of peace, thus making a noble
stand against all bribery of the soldiery, and possessing in
consequence a better army. Envoys were sent to Parthia
and Armenia, and precautions were taken that, when the
legions were engaged in the civil war, the country in their
rear might not be exposed to attack. It was arranged that
Titus should pursue the war in Judæa, while Vespasian
should secure the passes into Egypt. To cope with Vitellius,
a portion of the army, the generalship of Mucianus, the
prestige of Vespasian's name, and the destiny before which
all difficulties vanish, seemed sufficient. To all the armies
and legates letters were despatched, and instructions were
given to them that they were to attach the prætorians, who
hated Vitellius, by the inducement of renewed military service.

83. Mucianus, who acted more as a colleague than as a
servant of the Emperor, moved on with some light-armed
troops, not indeed at a tardy pace so as to give the appear-

ance of delay, yet not with extraordinary speed. Thus he allowed rumour to gather fresh strength by distance, well aware that his force was but small, and that exaggerated notions are formed about what is not seen. Behind him, however, came in a vast body the 6th legion and 13,000 veterans. He had given directions that the fleet from the Pontus should be brought up to Byzantium, not having yet made up his mind, whether, avoiding Mœsia, he should move on Dyrrachium with his infantry and cavalry, and at the same time blockade the sea on the side of Italy with his ships of war, thus leaving Asia and Achaia safe in his rear, which, being bare of troops, would be left at the mercy of Vitellius, unless they were occupied with proper garrisons. And thus too Vitellius himself, finding Brundisium, Tarentum, and the shores of Calabria and Lucania menaced by hostile fleets, would be in utter perplexity as to which part of Italy he should protect.

84. Thus the provinces echoed with the bustle of preparing fleets, armies, and the implements of war. Nothing, however, was so vexatious as the raising of money. Mucianus, with the perpetual assertion that money was the sinews of war, looked in all questions, not to right or truth, but only to the extent of a man's fortune. Informations abounded, and all the richest men were fastened on for plunder. These intolerable oppressions, which yet found some excuse in the necessities of war, were continued even in peace. Vespasian himself indeed at the beginning of his reign was not so bent on enforcing these iniquitous measures, till, spoilt by prosperity and evil counsellors, he learnt this policy and ventured to use it. Mucianus contributed to the war even from his own purse, liberal with his private means because he helped himself without scruple from the wealth of the State. The rest followed his example in contributing their money; very few enjoyed the same licence in reimbursing themselves.

85. Meanwhile the operations of Vespasian were hastened by the zeal of the army of Illyricum, which had come over to his side. The third legion set the example to the other legions of Mœsia. These were the eighth and seventh (Claudius's), who were possessed with a strong liking for

Otho, though they had not been present at the battle of Bedriacum. They had advanced to Aquileia, and by roughly repulsing the messengers who brought the tidings of Otho's defeat, by tearing the colours which displayed the name of Vitellius, by finally seizing on the military chest and dividing it among themselves, had assumed a hostile attitude. Then they began to fear; fear suggested a new thought, that acts might be made a merit of with Vespasian, which would have to be excused to Vitellius. Accordingly, the three legions of Mœsia sought by letter to win over the army of Pannonia, and prepared to use force if they refused. During this commotion, Aponius Saturnius, governor of Mœsia, ventured on a most atrocious act. He despatched a centurion to murder Tettius Julianus, the legate of the 7th legion, to gratify a private pique, which he concealed beneath the appearance of party zeal. Julianus, having discovered his danger, and procured some guides, who were acquainted with the country, fled through the pathless wastes of Mœsia beyond Mount Hæmus, nor did he afterwards take any part in the civil war. He set out to join Vespasian, but contrived to protract his journey by various pretexts, lingering or hastening on his way, according to the intelligence he received.

86. In Pannonia, however, the 13th legion and the 7th (Galba's), which still retained their vexation and rage at the defeat of Bedriacum, joined Vespasian without hesitation, mainly under the influence of Primus Antonius. This man, though an offender against the law, and convicted of fraud in the reign of Nero, had, among the other calamities of war, recovered his rank as a Senator. Having been appointed by Galba to command the 7th legion, he was commonly believed to have often written to Otho, offering the party his services as a general. Being slighted, however, by that Prince, he found no employment during the war. When the fortunes of Vitellius began to totter, he attached himself to Vespasian, and brought a vast accession of strength to his party. He was brave in battle, ready of speech, dexterous in bringing odium upon other men, powerful amidst civil strife and rebellion, rapacious, prodigal, the worst of citizens in peace, but in war no contemptible ally. United by

these means, the armies of Mœsia and Pannonia drew with
them the soldiery of Dalmatia, though the consular legates
took no part in the movement. Titus Ampius Flavianus
was the governor of Pannonia, Poppæus Silvanus of Dalmatia. They were both rich and advanced in years. The
Imperial procurator, however, was Cornelius Fuscus, a man
in the prime of life and of illustrious birth. Though in early
youth the desire of repose had led him to resign his senatorial rank, he afterwards put himself at the head of his
colony in fighting for Galba, and by this service he obtained his procuratorship. Subsequently embracing the cause
of Vespasian, he lent the movement the stimulus of a fiery
zeal. Finding his pleasure not so much in the rewards of
peril as in peril itself, to assured and long acquired possession he preferred novelty, uncertainty, and risk. Accordingly, both he and Antonius strove to agitate and disturb
wherever there was any weak point. Despatches were sent
to the 14th legion in Britain and to the 1st in Spain, for
both these legions had been on the side of Otho against
Vitellius. Letters too were scattered through every part of
Gaul, and in a moment a mighty war burst into flame, for
the armies of Illyricum were already in open revolt, and the
rest were waiting only the signal of success.

87. While Vespasian and the generals of his party were
thus occupied in the provinces, Vitellius was daily becoming more contemptible and indolent, halting to enjoy the
pleasures of every town and villa in his way, as with his
cumbrous host he advanced towards the capital. He was
followed by 60,000 armed soldiers demoralized by licence.
Still larger was the number of camp-followers; and of all
slaves, the slaves of soldiers are the most unruly. So numerous a retinue of officers and personal friends would have
been difficult to keep under restraint, even if controlled by
the strictest discipline. The crowd was made more unwieldy
by Senators and Knights who came to meet him from the
capital, some moved by fear, many by a spirit of adulation,
others, and by degrees all, that they might not be left behind while the rest were going. From the dregs of the people there thronged buffoons, players, and charioteers, known
to Vitellius from their infamous compliance with his vices;

for in such disgraceful friendships he felt a strange pleasure. And now not only were the colonies and towns exhausted by having to furnish supplies, but the very cultivator of the soil and his lands, on which the harvests were now ripe, were plundered like an enemy's territory.

88. There were many sanguinary encounters between the soldiers; for ever since the mutiny which broke out at Ticinum there had lingered a spirit of dissension between the legions and the auxiliary troops, though they could unite whenever they had to fight with the rustic population. The most terrible massacre took place at the 7th milestone from Rome. Vitellius was distributing to each soldier provisions ready dressed on the same abundant scale as the gladiators' rations, and the populace had poured forth, and spread themselves throughout the entire camp. Some with the frolicsome humour of slaves robbed the careless soldiers by slily cutting their belts, and then asked them whether they were armed. Unused to insult, the spirit of the soldiers resented the jest. Sword in hand they fell upon the unarmed people. Among the slain was the father of a soldier, who was with his son. He was afterwards recognised, and his murder becoming generally known, they spared the innocent crowd. Yet there was a panic at Rome, as the soldiers pressed on in all directions. It was to the forum that they chiefly directed their steps, anxious to behold the spot where Galba had fallen. Nor were the men themselves a less frightful spectacle, bristling as they were with the skins of wild beasts, and armed with huge lances, while in their strangeness to the place they were embarrassed by the crowds of people, or tumbling down in the slippery streets or from the shock of some casual encounter, they fell to quarrelling, and then had recourse to blows and the use of their swords. Besides, the tribunes and prefects were hurrying to and fro with formidable bodies of armed men.

89. Vitellius himself, mounted on a splendid charger, with military cloak and sword, advanced from the Mulvian bridge, driving the Senate and people before him; but deterred by the advice of his friends from marching into Rome as if it were a captured city, he assumed a civil garb, and proceeded with his army in orderly array. The eagles of

four legions were borne in front, and an equal number of
colours from other legions on either side, then came the
standards of twelve auxiliary squadrons, and the cavalry
behind the ranks of the infantry. Next came thirty-four
auxiliary cohorts, distinguished according to the names or
various equipments of the nations. Before each eagle were
the prefects of the camp, the tribunes, and the centurions of
highest rank, in white robes, and the other officers by the
side of their respective companies, glittering with arms and
decorations. The ornaments and chains of the soldiers presented a brilliant appearance. It was a glorious sight, and
the army was worthy of a better Emperor than Vitellius.
Thus he entered the capital, and he there embraced his
mother and honoured her with the title of Augusta.

90. The next day, as if he were addressing the Senate
and people of another State, he pronounced a high panegyric on himself, extolling his own energy and moderation,
though his enormities were known to the very persons who
were present and to the whole of Italy, his progress through
which had been disgraced by sloth and profligacy. Yet the
mob, who had no patriotic anxieties, and who, without distinguishing between truth and falsehood, had learnt the lesson of habitual flattery, applauded him with shouts and
acclamations, and, reluctant as he was to assume the name
of Augustus, extorted from him a compliance as idle as his
previous refusal.

91. The country, ready to find a meaning in every circumstance, regarded it as an omen of gloomy import that
Vitellius, on obtaining the office of supreme Pontiff, should
have issued a proclamation concerning the public religious
ceremonial on the 18th of July, a day which from old times
the disasters of Cremera and Allia had marked as unlucky.
Thus utterly regardless of all law human and divine, with
freedmen and friends as reckless as himself, he lived as if
he were among a set of drunkards. Still at the consular
elections he was present in company with the candidates
like an ordinary citizen, and by shewing himself as a spectator in the theatre, as a partisan in the circus, he courted
every breath of applause from the lowest rabble. Agreeable
and popular as this conduct would have been, had it been

prompted by noble qualities, it was looked upon as undignified and contemptible from the remembrance of his past
life. He habitually appeared in the Senate even when unimportant matters were under discussion; and it once happened that Priscus Helvidius, the prætor elect, had spoken
against his wishes. Though at the moment provoked, he
only called on the tribunes of the people to support his insulted authority, and then, when his friends, who feared
his resentment was deeper than it appeared, sought to appease him, he replied that it was nothing strange that two
senators in a Commonwealth should disagree: he had himself been in the habit of opposing Thrasea. Most of them
laughed at the effrontery of such a comparison, though
some were pleased at the very circumstance of his having
selected, not one of the most influential men of the time,
but Thrasea, as his model of true glory.

92. He had advanced to the command of the Prætorian
Guard Publius Sabinus, a prefect of the cohort, and Julius
Priscus, then only a centurion. It was through the influence
of Cæcina and Valens that they respectively rose to power.
Though always at variance, these two men left no authority
to Vitellius. The functions of Empire were discharged by
Cæcina and Valens. They had long before been led to suspect each other by animosities scarcely concealed amid the
cares of the campaign and the camp, and aggravated by
unprincipled friends and a state of society calculated to
produce such feuds. In their struggles for popularity, in
their long retinues, and in the vast crowds at their levees,
they vied with each other and challenged comparison, while
the favour of Vitellius inclined first to one, and then to the
other. There can never be complete confidence in a power
which is excessive. Vitellius himself, who was ever varying
between sudden irritation and unseasonable fondness, they
at once despised and feared. Still this had not made them
less keen to seize on palaces and gardens and all the wealth
of the Empire, while a sad and needy throng of nobles,
whom with their children Galba had restored to their country, received no relief from the compassion of the Emperor.
By an edict which gratified the leading men of the State,
while it approved itself even to the populace, Vitellius gave

back to the returned exiles their rights over their freedmen, although servile ingenuity sought in every way to neutralise the boon, concealing money in quarters which either obscurity or rank rendered secure. Some freedmen had made their way into the palace of the Emperor, and thus became more powerful even than their patrons.

93. Meanwhile the soldiers, as their numbers overflowed the crowded camp, dispersed throughout the porticoes, the temples, and the whole capital, did not know their own headquarters, kept no watch, and ceased to brace themselves by toil. Amidst the allurements of the city and all shameful excesses, they wasted their strength in idleness, and their energies in riot. At last, reckless even of health, a large portion of them quartered themselves in the notoriously pestilential neighbourhood of the Vatican; hence ensued a great mortality in the ranks. The Tiber was close at hand, and their extreme eagerness for the water and their impatience of the heat weakened the constitutions of the Germans and Gauls, always liable to disease. To make matters worse, the organisation of the service was deranged by unprincipled intrigue and favour. Sixteen Prætorian and four city cohorts were being raised, each to consist of a thousand men. In this levy Valens ventured to do more than his rival on the pretence of his having rescued Cæcina himself from peril. Doubtless his arrival had restored the fortunes of the party, and his victory had reversed the unfavourable rumours occasioned by his tardy advance. The entire army too of Lower Germany was attached to him; this circumstance, it is thought, first made the allegiance of Cæcina waver.

94. Much however as Vitellius indulged his generals, his soldiers enjoyed yet greater licence. Every one chose his own service. However unfit, he might, if he preferred it, be enrolled among the soldiers of the capital. Soldiers again of good character were allowed, if they so wished, to remain with the legions, or in the cavalry; and this was the choice of many who were worn out with disease, or who shrank from the unhealthiness of the climate. But the main strength of the legions and cavalry was drafted from them, while the old glory of the Prætorian camp was destroyed by these

20,000 men indiscriminately taken rather than chosen out of the whole army. While Vitellius was haranguing the troops, the men called out for the execution of Asiaticus, and of Flavius and Rufinus, the Gallic chieftains, because they had fought for Vindex. He never checked these cries; for to say nothing of the cowardice natural to that feeble soul, he was aware that the distribution of a donative was imminent, and, having no money, he lavished every thing else on the soldiers. A contribution in the form of a tax was exacted from the freedmen of former Emperors in proportion to the number of their slaves. Vitellius himself, thinking only how to squander, was building a stable for his charioteers, was filling the circus with shows of gladiators and wild beasts, and fooling away his money as if he had the most abundant supplies.

95. Moreover Cæcina and Valens celebrated the birthday of Vitellius by exhibiting in every quarter of the city shows of gladiators on a vast and hitherto unparalleled scale. He pleased the most infamous characters, but utterly disgusted all the respectable citizens, by building altars in the Campus Martius, and performing funeral rites to Nero. Victims were slaughtered and burnt in the name of the State; the pile was kindled by the Augustales, an order of the priesthood dedicated by the Emperor Tiberius to the Julian family, just as Romulus had dedicated one to king Tatius. Within four months from the victory of Bedriacum, Asiaticus, the emperor's freedman, was rivalling the Polycleti, the Patrobii, and all the old hateful names. No one sought promotion in that court by integrity or diligence; the sole road to power was to glut the insatiable appetites of Vitellius by prodigal entertainments, extravagance, and riot. The Emperor himself, thinking it enough to enjoy the present, and without a thought for the future, is believed to have squandered nine hundred million sesterces in a very few months. Rome, as miserable as she was great, afflicted in one year by an Otho and a Vitellius, what with the Vinii, the Fabii, the Iceli, and the Asiatici, passed through all vicissitudes of infamy, till there came Mucianus and Marcellus, and different men rather than a different morality.

96. The first revolt of which Vitellius received tidings

was that of the 3rd legion, despatches having been sent by
Aponius Saturninus before he too attached himself to the
party of Vespasian. Aponius, however, agitated by the unexpected occurrence, had not written all the particulars,
and flattering friends softened down its import. "It was,"
they said, "a mutiny of only a single legion; the loyalty of
the other armies was unshaken." Vitellius in addressing the
soldiers spoke to the same effect. He inveighed against the
lately disbanded Prætorians, and asserted that false rumours
were circulated by them, and that there was no fear of a
civil war. The name of Vespasian he suppressed, and soldiers
were dispersed through the city to check the popular gossip.
This more than anything else kept these rumours alive.

97. Nevertheless Vitellius summoned auxiliary troops from
Germany, Britain, and Spain, tardily, however, and with an
attempt to conceal his necessities. The legates and the provinces were equally slow. Hordeonius Flaccus, who was beginning to suspect the Batavians, feared that he should
have a war on his own hands, and Vettius Bolanus had in
Britain a province never very quiet; and both these officers
were wavering in their allegiance. Spain too, which then
was without a governor of consular rank, showed no alacrity.
The legates of the three legions, equal in authority, and
ready, while Vitellius was prosperous, to vie in obedience,
stood aloof with one consent from his falling fortunes. In
Africa, the legion, and the auxiliary infantry levied by
Clodius Macer and soon after disbanded by Galba, again
entered the service at the order of Vitellius, while all the
rest of the youth promptly gave in their names. Vitellius
had ruled that province as proconsul with integrity and
popularity; Vespasian's government had been infamous and
odious. The allies formed conjectures accordingly as to the
manner in which each would reign, but the result contradicted them.

98. At first Valerius Festus, the legate, loyally seconded
the zeal of the provincials. Soon he began to waver, supporting Vitellius in his public dispatches and edicts, Vespasian in his secret correspondence, and intending to hold
by the one or the other according as they might succeed.
Some soldiers and centurions, coming through Rhætia and

Gaul, were seized with letters and edicts from Vespasian, and on being sent to Vitellius were put to death. More, however, eluded discovery, escaping either through the faithful protection of friends or by their own tact. Thus the preparations of Vitellius became known, while the plans of Vespasian were for the most part kept secret. At first the supineness of Vitellius was in fault; afterwards the occupation of the Pannonian Alps with troops stopped all intelligence. And on the sea the prevalent Etesian winds favoured an eastward voyage, but hindered all return.

99. At length Vitellius, appalled by the irruption of the enemy and by the menacing intelligence from every quarter, ordered Cæcina and Valens to take the field. Cæcina was sent on in advance; Valens, who was just recovering from a severe illness, was delayed by weakness. Far different was the appearance of the Germany army as it marched out of the capital. All strength had departed from their bodies, all energy from their spirits. Slowly, and with thin ranks, the column moved along, their weapons feebly grasped, their horses spiritless. The soldiers, impatient of the heat, the dust, and the weather, in proportion as they were less capable of enduring toil, were more ready for mutiny. All this was aggravated by the old vanity of Cæcina, and by the indolence that had of late crept over him; presuming on the excessive favour of fortune, he had abandoned himself to luxury. Perhaps he meditated perfidy, and it was part of his policy to enervate the courage of the army. Many believe that his fidelity had been shaken by the suggestions of Flavius Sabinus, who employed Rubrius Gallus as the bearer of communications intimating that the conditions of desertion would be held binding by Vespasian. At the same time he was reminded of his hatred and jealously of Fabius Valens. Being inferior to his rival in influence with Vitellius, he should seek to secure favour and power with the new Emperor.

100. Cæcina, having embraced Vitellius and received tokens of high distinction, left him, and sent a detachment of cavalry to occupy Cremona. It was followed by the veteran troops of the 4th, 10th, and 16th legions, by the 5th and 22nd legions, and the rear was brought up by the 21st

(the Rapax) and the first Italian legion with the veteran troops of three British legions, and a chosen body of auxiliaries After the departure of Cæcina, Valens sent a despatch to the army which had been under his own command with directions that it should wait for him on the road; such, he said, was his arrangement with Cæcina. Cæcina, however, being with the army in person, and consequently having greater influence, pretended that this plan had been changed, that so the gathering forces of the enemy might be met with their whole strength. Orders were therefore given to the legions to advance with all speed upon Cremona, while a portion of the force was to proceed to Hostilia. Cæcina himself turned aside to Ravenna, on the pretext that he wished to address the fleet. Soon, however, he sought the retirement of Patavium, there to concert his treachery. Lucilius Bassus, who had been promoted by Vitellius from the command of a squadron of cavalry to be admiral of the fleets at Ravenna and Misenum, failing immediately to obtain the command of the Prætorian Guard, sought to gratify his unreasonable resentment by an atrocious act of perfidy. It cannot be certainly known whether he carried Cæcina with him, or whether (as is often the case with bad men, that they are like each other) both were actuated by the same evil motives.

101. The historians of the period, who during the ascendancy of the Flavian family composed the chronicles of this war, have in the distorted representations of flattery assigned as the motives of these men a regard for peace and a love of their country. For my own part I believe that, to say nothing of a natural fickleness and an honour which they must have held cheap after the betrayal of Galba, feelings of rivalry, and jealousy lest others should outstrip them in the favour of Vitellius, made them accomplish his ruin. Cæcina, having overtaken the legions, strove by every species of artifice to undermine the fidelity of the centurions and soldiers, who were devoted to Vitellius. Bassus, in making the same attempt, experienced less difficulty, for the fleet, remembering how recently it had served in the cause of Otho, was ready to change its allegiance.

BOOK III

SEPTEMBER–DECEMBER, A.D. 69

1. UNDER happier auspices and in a more loyal spirit the Flavianist leaders were discussing the plans of the campaign. They had assembled at Petovio, the winter-quarters of the 13th legion. There they debated, whether they should blockade the passes of the Pannonian Alps till the whole strength of their party should be gathered in their rear, or whether it would be the more vigorous policy to close with the enemy, and to contend for the possession of Italy. Those who thought it advisable to wait for reinforcements, and to protract the campaign, dwelt on the strength and reputation of the German legions. "Vitellius," they said, "has now joined them with the flower of the British army. Our numbers are not even equal to those of the legions whom they lately defeated; and the conquered, let them talk as fiercely as they will, lose something of their courage. But, if we occupy meanwhile the passes of the Alps, Mucianus will come up with the forces of the East. Vespasian has in addition the command of the sea, his fleets, and provinces loyal to his cause, in which he may collect the vast materials for what may be called another war. A salutary delay will bring us new forces, while we shall lose nothing of what we have."

2. In answer to this, Antonius Primus, who was the most energetic promoter of the war, declared that prompt action would be advantageous to themselves, and fatal to Vitellius. "Supineness," he said, "rather than confidence has grown upon the conquerors. They are not even kept under arms or within camps. In every town of Italy, sunk in sloth, formidable only to their entertainers, they have drunk of unaccustomed pleasures with an eagerness equal to the rudeness of their former life. They have been emasculated by

the circus, the theatre, and the allurements of the capital, or they are worn out with sickness. Yet even to these men, if you give them time, their old vigour will return with the preparation for war. Germany, whence their strength is drawn, is not far away; Britain is separated only by a strait; the provinces of Gaul and Spain are near; on either side they can find troops, horses, tribute; they have Italy itself, and the resources of the capital, and, should they choose themselves to take the offensive, they have two fleets, and the Illyrian sea open to them. What good then will our mountain-passes do us? What will be the use of having protracted the war into another summer? Where are we to find in the meanwhile money and supplies? Why not rather avail ourselves of the fact that the legions of Pannonia, which were cheated rather than vanquished, are hastening to rise again for vengeance, and that the armies of Mœsia have brought us their unimpaired strength? If you reckon the number of soldiers, rather than that of legions, we have greater strength, and no vices, for our very humiliation has been most helpful to our discipline. As for the cavalry, they were not vanquished even on that day; though the fortune of war was against them, they penetrated the Vitellianist lines. Two squadrons of Mœsian and Pannonian cavalry then broke through the enemy; now the united standards of sixteen squadrons will bury and overwhelm with the crash and din and storm of their onset these horses and horsemen that have forgotten how to fight. Unless any one hinders me, I who suggest will execute the plan. You, whose fortune never suffered a reverse, may keep back the legions; the light cohorts will be enough for me. Before long you will hear that Italy has been opened, and the power of Vitellius shaken. You will be delighted to follow, and to tread in the footsteps of victory."

3. With flashing eyes, and in the fierce tones that might be most widely heard (for the centurions and some of the common soldiers had intruded themselves into the deliberations), he poured out such a torrent of these and similar words, that he carried away even the cautious and prudent, while the general voice of the multitude extolled him as the one man, the one general in the army, and spurned the in-

action of the others. He had raised this reputation for himself at the very first assembly, when, after Vespasian's letters had been read, he had not, like many, used ambiguous language, on which he might put this or that construction as might serve his purpose. It was seen that he openly committed himself to the cause, and he had therefore greater weight with the soldiers, as being associated with them in what was either their crime or their glory.

4. Next to Primus in influence was Cornelius Fuscus, the procurator. He also had been accustomed to inveigh mercilessly against Vitellius, and had thus left himself no hope in the event of defeat. T. Ampius Flavianus, disposed to caution by natural temperament and advanced years, excited in the soldiers a suspicion that he still remembered his relationship to Vitellius; and as he had fled when the movement in the legions began, and had then voluntarily returned, it was believed that he had sought an opportunity for treachery. Flavianus indeed had left Pannonia, and had entered Italy, and was out of the way of danger, when his desire for revolution urged him to resume the title of Legate, and to take part in the civil strife. Cornelius Fuscus had advised him to this course, not that he needed the talents of Flavianus, but wishing that a consular name might clothe with its high prestige the very first movements of the party.

5. Still, that the passage into Italy might be safe and advantageous, directions were sent to Aponius Saturninus to hasten up with the armies of Mœsia. That the provinces might not be exposed without defence to the barbarian tribes, the princes of the Sarmatæ Iazyges, who had in their hands the government of that nation, were enrolled in the army. These chiefs also offered the service of their people, and its force of cavalry, their only effective troops; but the offer was declined, lest in the midst of civil strife they should attempt some hostile enterprise, or, influenced by higher offers from other quarters, should cast off all sense of right and duty. Sido and Italicus, kings of the Suevi, were brought over to the cause. Their loyalty to the Roman people was of long standing, and their nation was more faithful than the other to any trust reposed in them. On the flank of the army were posted some auxiliaries, for Rhætia was

hostile, Portius Septimius, the procurator, remaining incorruptibly faithful to Vitellius. Accordingly, Sextilius Felix with Aurius' Horse, eight cohorts, and the native levies of Noricum, was sent to occupy the bank of the river Ænus, which flows between Rhætia and Noricum. Neither hazarded an engagement, and the fate of the two parties was decided elsewhere.

6. Antonius, as he hurried with the veteran soldiers of the cohorts and part of the cavalry to invade Italy, was accompanied by Arrius Varus, an energetic soldier. Service under Corbulo, and successes in Armenia, had gained for him this reputation; yet it was generally said, that in secret conversations with Nero he had calumniated Corbulo's high qualities. The favour thus infamously acquired made him a centurion of the first rank, yet the ill-gotten prosperity of the moment afterwards turned to his destruction. Primus and Varus, having occupied Aquileia, were joyfully welcomed in the neighbourhood, and in the towns of Opitergium and Altinum. At Altinum a force was left to oppose the Ravenna fleet, the defection of which from Vitellius was not yet known. They next attached to their party Patavium and Ateste. There they learnt that three cohorts, belonging to Vitellius, and the Sebonian Horse had taken up a position at the Forum Alieni, where they had thrown a bridge across the river. It was determined to seize the opportunity of attacking this force, unprepared as it was; for this fact had likewise been communicated. Coming upon them at dawn, they killed many before they could arm. Orders had been given to slay but few, and to constrain the rest by fear to transfer their allegiance. Some indeed at once surrendered, but the greater part broke down the bridge, and thus cut off the advance of the pursuing enemy.

7. When this success became known, two legions, the seventh (Galba's) and the eighteenth (the Gemina), finding the campaign opening in favour of the Flavianists, repaired with alacrity to Patavium under the command of Vedius Aquila the legate. A few days were there taken for rest, and Minucius Justus, prefect of the camp in the 7th legion, who ruled with more strictness than a civil war will permit, was withdrawn from the exasperated soldiery, and sent to Ves-

pasian. An act that had been long desired was taken by a
flattering construction for more than it was worth, when
Antonius gave orders that the statues of Galba, which had
been thrown down during the troubles of the times, should
be restored in all the towns. It would, he supposed, reflect
honour on the cause, if it were thought that they had been
friendly to Galba's rule, and that his party was again rising
into strength.

8. The next question was, what place should be selected
as the seat of war. Verona seemed the most eligible, surrounded as it was with open plains, suitable for the action
of cavalry, in which they were very strong. At the same
time it was thought that in wresting from Vitellius a colony
so rich in resources there would be both profit and glory.
They secured Vicetia by simply passing through it. Though
in itself a small gain, for the town is but of moderate
strength, it was considered an important advantage when
they reflected that in this town Cæcina was born, and that
the general of the enemy had lost his native place. The people of Verona were a valuable aid; they served the cause
by the example of their zeal and by their wealth, and the
army thus occupied a position between Rhætia and the
Julian Alps. It was to cut off all passage at this point from
the armies of Germany that they had barred this route. All
this was done either without the knowledge, or against the
commands of Vespasian. He gave orders that the army
should halt at Aquileia and there await Mucianus; and
these orders he supported by the argument, that as Ægypt,
which commanded the corn supplies, and the revenues of
the wealthiest provinces were in his hands, the army of
Vitellius would be compelled to capitulate from the want of
pay and provisions. Mucianus in frequent letters advised
the same policy; a victory that should cost neither blood
nor tears, and other objects of the kind, were his pretexts;
but in truth he was greedy of glory, and anxious to keep
the whole credit of the war to himself. Owing, however, to
the vast distances, the advice came only after the matter
was decided.

9. Then Antonius by a sudden movement fell upon the
outposts of the enemy, and made trial of their courage in a

slight skirmish, the combatants separating on equal terms.
Soon afterwards, Cæcina strongly fortified a camp between
Hostilia, a village belonging to Verona, and the marshes
of the river Tartarus, where his position was secure, as his
rear was covered by the river, and his flank by intervening
marshes. Had he only been loyal, those two legions, which
had not been joined by the army of Mœsia, might have
been crushed by the united strength of the Vitellianists, or
driven back and compelled to evacuate Italy in a disgraceful
retreat. Cæcina, however, by various delays betrayed to the
enemy the early opportunities of the campaign, assailing
by letters those whom it was easy to drive out by force of
arms, until by his envoys he settled the conditions of his
treachery. In this interval Aponius Saturninus came up with
the 7th legion (Claudius's). This legion was commanded
by the tribune Vipstanus Messalla, a man of illustrious
family, himself highly distinguished, the only man who had
brought into that conflict an honest purpose. To this army,
which was far from equalling the forces of Vitellius (it in
fact consisted of three legions), Cæcina despatched a letter
reproaching them with rashness in again drawing the sword
in a vanquished cause. At the same time he extolled the
valour of the German army; of Vitellius he made but some
slight and common-place mention without any abuse of Vespasian. Certainly he said nothing which could either seduce
or terrify the enemy. The leaders of the Flavianist party,
omitting all apology for their former fortune, at once took
up a tone of high praise of Vespasian, of confidence in their
cause, of security as to their army, and of hostility to Vitellius, while hopes were held out to the tribunes and centurions of retaining the privileges which Vitellius had
granted them, and Cæcina was himself encouraged in no ambiguous terms to change sides. These letters read to the assembled army increased their confidence; for Cæcina had
written in a humble strain, as if he feared to offend Vespasian, while their own generals had used contemptuous
language, meant, it would seem, to insult Vitellius.

10. On the subsequent arrival of two legions, the third
commanded by Dillius Aponianus, the eighth by Numisius
Lupus, it was resolved to make a demonstration of their

strength, and to surround Verona with military lines. It so
happened that Galba's legion had had their work allotted to
them on that side the lines which faced the enemy, and that
some of the allied cavalry appearing in the distance were
taken for the enemy, and excited a groundless panic. They
flew to arms, and as the rage of the soldiers at the supposed
treachery fell upon T. Ampius Flavianus, not from any
proof of his guilt, but because he had been long unpopular,
they clamoured for his death in a very whirlwind of passion, vociferating that he was the kinsman of Vitellius, that
he had betrayed Otho, that he had embezzled the donative.
He could get no opportunity of defending himself, even
though he stretched out his hands in entreaty, repeatedly
prostrating himself on the ground, his garments torn, his
breast and features convulsed with sobs. This very conduct
provoked afresh these furious men, for fear so excessive
seemed to argue a consciousness of guilt. Aponius was
clamoured down by the shouts of the soldiers, when he
attempted to address them; every one else was repulsed
with noisy cries. To Antonius alone the soldiers' ears were
open; for he had eloquence, the art of soothing an angry
crowd, and personal influence. As the mutiny grew fiercer,
and the soldiers went on from abuse and taunts to use their
hands and their weapons, he ordered that Flavianus should
be put in irons. The soldiers saw what a mockery it was,
and pushing aside those who were guarding the tribunal,
were about to commit the most outrageous violence. Antonius threw himself in the way with his sword drawn, protesting that he would die either by the soldiers' hands or
by his own; whenever he saw any one who was known to
him, or who was distinguished by any military decoration,
he summoned him by name to his assistance. Then he turned
to the standards, and prayed to the gods of war, that they
would inspire the armies of the enemy, rather than his own,
with such madness and such strife. So the mutiny began to
abate, and at the close of the day the men dispersed to their
tents. The same night Flavianus set out, and being met by
letters from Vespasian, was relieved from his perilous position.

11. The legions had caught the infection of mutiny, and

next assailed Aponius Saturnius, legate of the army of
Mœsia, this time the more furiously because their rage
broke out, not as before, when they were wearied with
labour and military toils, but at mid-day. Some letters had
been published, which Saturninus was believed to have
written to Vitellius. If once they had emulated each other
in valour and obedience, so now there was a rivalry in in-
subordination and insolence, till they clamoured as violently
for the execution of Aponius as they had for that of Flavianus. The legions of Mœsia recalled how they had aided
the vengeance of the Pannonian army, while the soldiers of
Pannonia, as if they were absolved by the mutiny of others,
took a delight in repeating their fault. They hastened to
the gardens in which Saturninus was passing his time, and
it was not the efforts of Primus Antonius, Aponianus, and
Messalla, though they exerted themselves to the uttermost,
that saved him, so much as the obscurity of the hiding-
place in which he concealed himself, for he was hidden in
the furnace of some baths that happened to be out of use.
In a short time he gave up his lictors, and retired to Patavium. After the departure of the two men of consular rank,
all power and authority over the two armies centred in Antonius alone, his colleagues giving way to him, and the soldiers being strongly biassed in his favour. There were those
who believed that both these mutinies were set on foot by
the intrigues of Antonius, in order that he might engross all
the prizes of the war.

12. Nor indeed was there less restlessness among the
partisans of Vitellius, who were distracted by yet more
fatal dissensions, springing, not from the suspicions of the
common men, but from the treachery of the generals. Lucilius Bassus, prefect of the Ravenna fleet, finding that the
troops wavered in purpose, from the fact that many were
natives of Dalmatia and Pannonia, provinces held for Vespasian, had attached them to the Flavianist party. The
night-time was chosen for accomplishing the treason, because then, unknown to all the rest, the ringleaders alone
might assemble at head-quarters. Bassus, moved by shame,
or perhaps by fear, awaited the issue in his house. The captains of the triremes rushed with a great outcry on the images

or Vitellius; a few, who attempted to resist, were cut down; the great majority, with the usual love of change, were ready to join Vespasian. Then Bassus came forward and openly sanctioned the movement. The fleet appointed Cornelius Fuscus to be prefect, and he hastened to join them. Lucilius was put under honourable arrest, and conveyed as far as Adria by the Liburnian ships; there he was thrown into prison by Vivennius Rufinus, prefect of a squadron of cavalry, which was there in garrison. His chains, however, were immediately struck off on the interference of Hormus, one of the Emperor's freedmen, for he too ranked among the generals.

13. On the revolt of the fleet becoming known, Cæcina called together to head-quarters, which he purposely selected as being the most retired part of the camp, the chief centurions and some few soldiers, while the rest were dispersed on various military duties. Then he extolled the valour of Vespasian, and the strength of his party; he told them that the fleet had changed sides, that they were straitened for supplies, that Gaul and Spain were against them, that in the capital there was nothing on which to rely, thus making the worst of everything that concerned Vitellius. Then, the conspirators present setting the example, and the rest being paralysed by the strangeness of the proceeding, he made them swear allegiance to Vespasian. At the same time the images of Vitellius were torn down, and persons were despatched to convey the intelligence to Antonius. But when this treason became noised abroad throughout the camp, when the soldiers, hurrying back to head-quarters, saw the name of Vespasian written on the colours, and the images of Vitellius thrown upon the ground, first there was a gloomy silence, then all their rage burst out at once. "What," they cried, "has the glory of the army of Germany fallen so low, that without a battle, even without a wound, they should yield up hands ready bound and arms resigned to surrender? What legions indeed are these against us? Only the conquered. The first and the twelfth, the sole strength of the Othonianist army, are not there, and even them we routed and crushed on these very plains, only that so many thousands of armed men, like a herd of slaves for sale,

might be given as a present to the exile Antonius. Thus, forsooth, the adhesion of one fleet would be worth eight legions.
So it pleases Bassus and Cæcina, after robbing the Emperor
of palaces, gardens, and money, to rob the soldiers of their
Emperor. But we, who have seen nothing of toil and bloodshed, we, who must be contemptible even to the Flavianists,
what shall we answer to those who shall ask us of our victories and our defeats?"

14. Joining one and all in these cries, by which each
expressed his own vexation, they proceeded, following the
lead of the fifth legion, to replace the images of Vitellius,
and to put Cæcina in irons. They elected to the command
Fabius Fabullus, legate of the fifth legion, and Cassius
Longus, prefect of the camp; they massacred the soldiers
from three Liburnian ships, who happened to fall in their
way, but who were perfectly ignorant and innocent of these
proceedings; they then abandoned the camp, and, after
breaking down the bridge, fell back on Hostilia, and thence
on Cremona, in order to effect a junction with the two
legions, the 1st Italica and the 21st Rapax, which, with a
portion of the cavalry, Cæcina had sent on to occupy Cremona.

15. On this becoming known to Antonius, he determined
to attack the hostile armies, while they were still distracted
in feeling and divided in strength, before the generals could
recover their authority, and the soldiers their subordination
along with that confidence which would spring from the
junction of the legions. He concluded indeed that Fabius
Valens had left the capital, and would hasten his march, on
hearing of the treason of Cæcina; and Fabius was loyal to
Vitellius, and not without some military skill. At the same
time he dreaded the approach of a vast body of Germans
by way of Rhætia. Vitellius had also summoned reinforcements from Britain, Gaul, and Spain, whose arms would
have wasted like a wide-spread pestilence, had not Antonius,
fearful of this very danger, hurried on an engagement, and
thus secured his victory. He reached Bedriacum with his
whole army in two days' march from Verona. The next day,
keeping the legions to fortify the position, he sent the auxiliary infantry into the territories of Cremona, ostensibly

to collect supplies, really to imbue the soldiery with a taste for the spoils of civil war. He himself advanced with 4000 cavalry as far as the 8th milestone from Bedriacum, in order that they might plunder with greater freedom. The scouts, as usual, took a wider range.

16. It was almost eleven o'clock, when a horseman arrived at full speed with the news, that the enemy were approaching, that a small body was moving in front, but that the stir and noise could be heard far and wide. While Antonius was deliberating as to what was to be done, Arrius Varus, eager to do his best, charged with the bravest of the cavalry, and drove back the Vitellianists, inflicting upon them some slight loss; as more came up, the fortune of the day changed, and those who had been most eager in the pursuit found themselves last in the flight. This rash act did not originate with Antonius; he anticipated in fact what actually happened. He now urged his soldiers to enter on the battle with a good heart; he then drew off the squadrons of his cavalry to the two flanks, leaving in the midst an open space in which to receive Varus and his troopers; the legions were ordered to arm themselves, signals were made over the country that every man should leave plundering, and join the battle at the nearest point. Meanwhile the terror-stricken Varus plunged into the disordered ranks of his friends, and brought a panic with him. The fresh troops were driven back along with the wounded fugitives, confused by their own alarm and by the difficulties of the road.

17. In the midst of this panic Antonius omitted nothing that a self-possessed commander or a most intrepid soldier could do. He threw himself before the terrified fugitives, he held back those who were giving way, and wherever the struggle was hardest, wherever there was a gleam of hope, there he was with his ready skill, his bold hand, his encouraging voice, easily recognized by the enemy, and a conspicuous object to his own men. At last he was carried to such a pitch of excitement, that he transfixed with a lance a flying standard bearer, and then, seizing the standard, turned it towards the enemy. Touched by the reproach, a few troopers, not more than a hundred in number, made a stand. The locality favoured them, for the road was at that point

particularly narrow, while the bridge over the stream which crossed it had been broken down, and the stream itself, with its varying channel and its precipitous banks, checked their flight. It was this necessity, or a happy chance, that restored the fallen fortunes of the party. Forming themselves into strong and close ranks, they received the attack of the Vitellianists, who were now imprudently scattered. These were at once overthrown. Antonius pursued those that fled, and crushed those that encountered him. Then came the rest of his troops, who, as they were severally disposed, plundered, made prisoners, or seized on weapons and horses. Roused by the shouts of triumph, those who had lately been scattered in flight over the fields hastened to share in the victory.

18. At the fourth milestone from Cremona glittered the standards of two legions, the Italica and the Rapax, which had been advanced as far as that point during the success achieved by the first movement of their cavalry. But when fortune changed, they would not open their ranks, nor receive the fugitives, nor advance and themselves attack an enemy now exhausted by so protracted a pursuit and conflict. Vanquished by accident, these men had never in their success valued their general as much as they now in disaster felt his absence. The victorious cavalry charged the wavering line; the tribune Vipstanus Messalla followed with the auxiliary troops from Mœsia, whom, though hurriedly brought up, long service had made as good soldiers as the legionaries. The horse and foot, thus mixed together, broke through the line of the legions. The near neighbourhood of the fortifications of Cremona, while it gave more hope of escape, diminished the vigour of their resistance.

19. Antonius did not press forward, for he thought of the fatigue and the wounds with which a battle so hard fought, notwithstanding its successful termination, must have disabled his cavalry and their horses. As the shadows of evening deepened the whole strength of the Flavianist army came up. They advanced amid heaps of dead and the traces of recent slaughter, and, as if the war was over, demanded that they should advance to Cremona, and receive the capitulation of the vanquished party, or take the place by

storm. This was the motive alleged, and it sounded well, but what every one said to himself was this: "The colony, situated as it is on level ground, may be taken by assault. If we attack under cover of darkness, we shall be at least as bold, and shall enjoy more licence in plunder. If we wait for the light, we shall be met with entreaties for peace, and in return for our toil and our wounds shall receive only the empty satisfaction of clemency and praise, but the wealth of Cremona will go into the purses of the legates and the prefects. The soldiers have the plunder of a city that is stormed, the generals of one which capitulates." The centurions and tribunes were spurned away; that no man's voice might be heard, the troops clashed their weapons together, ready to break through all discipline, unless they were led as they wished.

20. Antonius then made his way into the companies. When his presence and personal authority had restored silence, he declared, "I would not snatch their glory or their reward from those who have deserved them so well. Yet there is a division of duties between the army and its generals. Eagerness for battle becomes the soldiers, but generals serve the cause by forethought, by counsel, by delay oftener than by temerity. As I promoted your victory to the utmost of my power by my sword and by my personal exertions, so now I must help you by prudence and by counsel, the qualities which belong peculiarly to a general. What you will have to encounter is indeed perfectly plain. There will be the darkness, the strange localities of the town, the enemy inside the walls, and all possible facilities for ambuscades. Even if the gates were wide open, we ought not to enter the place, except we had first reconnoitred it, and in the day-time. Shall we set about storming the town when we have no means of seeing where the ground is level, what is the height of the walls, whether the city is to be assailed by our artillery and javelins, or by siege-works and covered approaches?" He then turned to individual soldiers, asking them whether they had brought with them their axes and spades and whatever else is used when towns are to be stormed. On their admitting that they had not done so, "Can any hands," he answered, "break through and

undermine walls with swords and lances? And if it should
be found necessary to throw up an embankment and to
shelter ourselves under mantlets and hurdles, shall we stand
baffled like a thoughtless mob, marvelling at the height of
the towers and at the enemy's defences? Shall we not
rather, by delaying one night, till our artillery and engines
come up, take with us a strength that must prevail?" At
the same time he sent the sutlers and camp-followers with
the freshest of the cavalry to Bedriacum to fetch supplies
and whatever else they needed.

21. The soldiers, however, were impatient, and a mutiny
had almost broken out, when some cavalry, who had advanced to the very walls of Cremona, seized some stragglers
from the town, from whose information it was ascertained,
that the six legions of Vitellius and the entire army which
had been quartered at Hostilia had on that very day
marched a distance of thirty miles, and having heard of the
defeat of their comrades, were preparing for battle, and
would soon be coming up. This alarm opened the ears that
had before been deaf to their general's advice. The 13th
legion was ordered to take up its position on the raised
causeway of the Via Postumia, supported on the left by the
7th (Galba's) which was posted in the plain, next came the
7th (Claudius'), defended in front by a field-ditch, such
being the character of the ground. On the right was the 8th
legion, drawn up in an open space, and then the 3rd, whose
ranks were divided by some thick brushwood. Such was the
arrangement of the eagles and the standards. The soldiers
were mingled in the darkness as accident had determined.
The Prætorian colours were close to the 3rd legion; the
auxiliary infantry were stationed on the wings; the cavalry
covered the flanks and the rear. Sido and Italicus, the
Suevian chieftains, with a picked body of their countrymen,
manœuvred in the van.

22. It would have been the best policy for the army of
Vitellius to rest at Cremona, and, with strength recruited
by food and repose, to attack and crush the next day an
enemy exhausted by cold and hunger; but now, wanting a
leader, and having no settled plan, they came into collision
about nine o'clock at night with the Flavianist troops, who

stood ready, and in order of battle. Respecting the disposition of the Vitellianist army, disordered as it was by its
fury and by the darkness, I would not venture to speak
positively. Some, however, have related, that on the right
wing was the 4th legion (the Macedonian); that the 5th
and 15th, with the veterans of three British legions (the
9th, 2nd, and 20th), formed the centre, while the left wing
was made up of the 1st, the 16th, and the 22nd. Men of
the legions Rapax and Italica were mingled with all the
companies. The cavalry and the auxiliaries chose their position themselves. Throughout the night the battle raged in
many forms, indecisive and fierce, destructive, first to one
side, then to the other. Courage, strength, even the eye with
its keenest sight, were of no avail. Both armies fought with
the same weapons; the watch-word, continually asked, became known; the colours were confused together, as parties
of combatants snatched them from the enemy, and hurried
them in this or that direction. The 7th legion, recently
levied by Galba, was the hardest pressed. Six centurions of
the first rank were killed, and some of the standards taken;
but the eagle was saved by Atilius Verus, the centurion of
the first company, who, after making a great slaughter
among the enemy, at last fell.

23. The line was supported, as it began to waver, by
Antonius, who brought up the Prætorians. They took up
the conflict, repulsed the enemy, and were then themselves
repulsed. The troops of Vitellius had collected their artillery on the raised causeway, where there was a free and
open space for the discharge of the missiles, which at first
had been scattered at random, and had struck against the
trees without injury to the enemy. An engine of remarkable
size, belonging to the 15th legion, was crushing the hostile
ranks with huge stones, and would have spread destruction
far and wide, had not two soldiers ventured on a deed of
surpassing bravery. Disguising themselves with shields
snatched from the midst of the carnage, they cut the ropes
and springs of the engine. They were instantly slain, and
their names have consequently been lost; but the fact is
undoubted. Fortune favoured neither side, till at a late hour
of the night the moon rose and showed, but showed de-

ceptively, both armies. The light, however, shining from behind, favoured the Flavianists. With them a lengthened shadow fell from men and horses, and the enemy's missiles, incorrectly aimed at what seemed the substance, fell short, while the Vitellianists, who had the light shining on their faces, were unconsciously exposed to an enemy who were, so to speak, concealed while they aimed.

24. As soon as Antonius could recognize his men and be recognized by them, he sought to kindle their courage, striving to shame some with his reproaches, stirring many with praise and encouragement, and all with hopes and promises. "Why," he demanded of the legions of Pannonia, "have you again taken up arms? yonder is the field where you may wipe out the stain of past disgrace, and redeem your honour." Then turning to the troops of Mœsia, he appealed to them as the authors and originators of the war. "Idly," he said "have you challenged the Vitellianists with threatening words, if you cannot abide their attack or even their looks." So he spoke to each as he approached them. The third legion he addressed at greater length, reminding them of old and recent achievements, how under Marcus Antonius they had defeated the Parthians, under Corbulo the Armenians, and had lately discomfited the Sarmatians. Then angrily turning to the Prætorians, "Clowns," said he, "unless you are victorious, what other general, what other camp will receive you? There are your colours and your arms; defeat is death, for disgrace you have exhausted." A shout was raised on all sides, and the soldiers of the third legion saluted, as is the custom in Syria, the rising sun.

25. A vague rumour thus arose, or was intentionally suggested by the general, that Mucianus had arrived, and that the two armies had exchanged salutations. The men then charged as confidently as if they had been strengthened by fresh reinforcements, while the enemy's array was now less compact; for, as there was no one to command, it was now contracted, now extended, as the courage or fear of individual soldiers might prompt. Antonius, seeing that they gave way, charged them with a heavy column; the loose ranks were at once broken, and, entangled as they were among their waggons and artillery, could not be re-formed.

The conquerors, in the eagerness of pursuit, dispersed themselves over the entire line of road. The slaughter that followed was made particularly memorable through the murder of a father by his son. I will record the incident with the names, on the authority of Vipstanus Messalla. Julius Mansuetus, a Spaniard, enlisting in the legion Rapax, had left at home a son of tender age. The lad grew up to manhood, and was enrolled by Galba in the 7th legion. Now chancing to meet his father, he brought him to the ground with a wound, and, as he rifled his dying foe, recognized him, and was himself recognized. Clasping the expiring man in his arms, in piteous accents he implored the spirit of his father to be propitious to him, and not to turn from him with loathing as from a parricide. "This guilt," he said, "is shared by all; how small a part of a civil war is a single soldier!" With these words he raised the body, opened a grave, and discharged the last duties for his father. This was noticed by those who were on the spot, then by many others; astonishment and indignation ran through the whole army, and they cursed this most horrible war. Yet as eagerly as ever they stripped the bodies of slaughtered kinsfolk, connexions, and brothers. They talk of an impious act having been done, and they do it themselves.

26. When they reached Cremona a fresh work of vast difficulty presented itself. During the war with Otho the legions of Germany had formed their camp round the walls of the city, round this camp had drawn an entrenchment, and had again strengthened these defences. At this sight the victorious army hesitated, while the generals doubted what orders they should give. To attempt an assault with troops exhausted by the toil of a day and a night would be difficult, and with no proper reserves might be perilous. Should they return to Bedriacum, the fatigue of so long a march would be insupportable, and their victory would result in nothing. To entrench a camp with the enemy so close at hand would be dangerous, as by a sudden sortie they might cause confusion among them while dispersed and busied with the work. Above all, they were afraid of their own soldiers, who were more patient of danger than delay. Cautious measures they disliked; their rashness inspired them

with hope, and eagerness for plunder outweighed all the horrors of carnage, wounds, and bloodshed.

27. Antonius himself was this way inclined, and he ordered the entrenched camp to be invested. At first they fought from a distance with arrows and stones, the Flavianists suffering most, as the enemy's missiles were aimed at them from a superior height. Antonius then assigned to each legion the attack on some portion of the entrenchments, and on one particular gate, seeking by this division of labour to distinguish the cowardly from the brave, and to stimulate his men by an honourable rivalry. The 3rd and 7th legions took up a position close to the road from Bedriacum; more to the right of the entrenchments were stationed the 8th and the 7th (Claudius'). The 13th were carried by the impetuosity of their attack as far as the gate looking towards Brixia. There ensued a little delay, while from the neighbouring fields some were collecting spades and pickaxes, others hooks and ladders. Then raising their shields over their heads, they advanced to the rampart in a dense "testudo." Both used the arts of Roman warfare; the Vitellianists rolled down ponderous stones, and drove spears and long poles into the broken and tottering "testudo," till the dense array of shields was loosened, and the ground was strewn with a vast number of lifeless and mangled bodies.

28. Some hesitation had shewn itself, when the generals, seeing that the weary troops would not listen to what seemed to them unmeaning encouragement, pointed to Cremona. Whether this was, as Messalla relates, the device of Hormus, or whether Caius Plinius be the better authority when he charges it upon Antonius, I cannot easily determine. All I can say is this, that neither in Antonius nor in Hormus would this foulest of crimes have been a degeneracy from the character of their former lives. Wounds or bloodshed no longer kept the men back from undermining the rampart and battering the gates. Supported on the shoulders of comrades, and forming a second "testudo," they clambered up and seized the weapons and even the hands of the enemy. The unhurt and the wounded, the half-dead and the dying, were mingled together with every incident of slaughter and death in every form.

29. The fiercest struggle was maintained by the 3rd and 7th legions, and Antonius in person with some chosen auxiliaries concentrated his efforts on the same point. The Vitellianists, unable to resist the combined and resolute attack, and finding that their missiles glided off the "testudo," at last threw the engine itself on the assailants; for a moment it broke and overwhelmed those on whom it fell, but it drew after it in its fall the battlements and upper part of the rampart. At the same time an adjoining tower yielded to the volleys of stones, and, while the 7th legion in wedge-like array was endeavouring to force an entrance, the 3rd broke down the gate with axes and swords. All authors are agreed that Caius Volusius, a soldier of the 3rd legion, entered first. Beating down all who opposed him, he mounted the rampart, waved his hand, and shouted aloud that the camp was taken. The rest of the legion burst in, while the troops of Vitellius were seized with panic, and threw themselves from the rampart. The entire space between the camp and the walls of Cremona was filled with slain.

30. Difficulties of another kind presented themselves in the lofty walls of the town, its stone towers, its iron-barred gates, in the garrison who stood brandishing their weapons, in its numerous population devoted to the interests of Vitellius, and in the vast conflux from all parts of Italy which had assembled at the fair regularly held at that time. The besieged found a source of strength in these large numbers; the assailants an incentive in the prospect of booty. Antonius gave orders that fire should instantly be set to the finest buildings without the city, to see whether the inhabitants of Cremona might not be induced by the loss of their property to transfer their allegiance. Some houses near the walls, which overtopped the fortifications, he filled with the bravest of his soldiers, who, by hurling beams, tiles, and flaming missiles, dislodged the defenders from the ramparts.

31. The legions now began to form themselves into a "testudo," and the other troops to discharge volleys of stones and darts, when the courage of the Vitellianists began to flag. The higher their rank, the more readily they succumbed to fortune, fearing that when Cremona had fallen quarter could no longer be expected, and that all the

fury of the conqueror would be turned, not on the penniless crowd, but on the tribunes and centurions, by whose slaughter something was to be gained. The common soldiers, careless of the future and safer in their obscurity, still held out. Roaming through the streets or concealed in the houses, they would not sue for peace even when they had abandoned the contest. The principal officers of the camp removed the name and images of Vitellius; Cæcina, who was still in confinement, they released from his chains, imploring him to plead their cause. When he haughtily rejected their suit, they entreated him with tears; and it was indeed the last aggravation of misery, that many valiant men should invoke the aid of a traitor. Then they displayed from the walls the olive-branches and chaplets of suppliants, and when Antonius had ordered that the discharge of missiles should cease, they brought out the eagles and standards. Then followed, with eyes bent on the ground, a dismal array of unarmed men. The conquerors had gathered round; at first they heaped reproaches on them and pointed at them their weapons; then seeing how they offered their cheeks to insulting blows, how, with all their high spirit departed, they submitted, as vanquished men, to every indignity, it suddenly occurred to their recollection, that these were the very soldiers who but shortly before had used with moderation their victory at Bedriacum. Yet, when Cæcina the consul, conspicuous in his robes of state and with his train of lictors, came forward thrusting aside the crowd, the victors were fired with indignation, and reproached him with his tyranny, his cruelty, and, so hateful are such crimes, even with his treason. Antonius checked them, gave him an escort, and sent him to Vespasian.

32. Meanwhile the population of Cremona was roughly handled by the soldiers, who were just beginning a massacre, when their fury was mitigated by the entreaties of the generals. Antonius summoned them to an assembly, extolled the conquerors, spoke kindly to the conquered, but said nothing either way of Cremona. Over and above the innate love of plunder, there was an old feud which made the army bent on the destruction of the inhabitants. It was generally believed that in the war with Otho, as well as in the pres-

ent, they had supported the cause of Vitellius. Afterwards, when the 13th legion had been left to build an amphitheatre, with the characteristic insolence of a city population, they had wantonly provoked and insulted them. The ill-feeling had been aggravated by the gladiatorial show exhibited there by Cæcina, by the circumstance that their city was now for the second time the seat of war, and by the fact that they had supplied the Vitellianists with provisions in the field, and that some of their women, taken by partyzeal into the battle, had there been slain. The occurrence of the fair filled the colony, rich as it always was, with an appearance of still greater wealth. The other generals were unnoticed; Antonius from his success and high reputation was observed of all. He had hastened to the baths to wash off the blood; and when he found fault with the temperature of the water, an answer was heard, "that it would soon be warm enough." Thus the words of a slave brought on him the whole odium of having given the signal for firing the town, which was indeed already in flames.

33. Forty thousand armed men burst into Cremona, and with them a body of sutlers and camp-followers, yet more numerous and yet more abandoned to lust and cruelty. Neither age nor rank were any protection from indiscriminate slaughter and violation. Aged men and women past their prime, worthless as booty, were dragged about in wanton insult. Did a grown up maiden or youth of marked beauty fall in their way, they were torn in pieces by the violent hands of ravishers; and in the end the destroyers themselves were provoked into mutual slaughter. Men, as they carried off for themselves coin or temple-offerings of massive gold, were cut down by others of superior strength. Some, scorning what met the eye, searched for hidden wealth, and dug up buried treasures, applying the scourge and the torture to the owners. In their hands were flaming torches, which, as soon as they had carried out the spoil, they wantonly hurled into the gutted houses and plundered temples. In an army which included such varieties of language and character, an army comprising Roman citizens, allies, and foreigners, there was every kind of lust, each man had a law of his own, and nothing was forbidden. For four

days Cremona satisfied the plunderers. When all things else, sacred and profane, were settling down into the flames, the temple of Mephitis outside the walls alone remained standing, saved by its situation or by divine interposition.

34. Such was the end of Cremona, 286 years after its foundation. It was built in the consulship of Tiberius Sempronius and Cornelius Scipio, when Hannibal was threatening Italy, as a protection against the Gauls from beyond the Padus, or against any other sudden invader from the Alps. From the number of settlers, the conveniences afforded by the rivers, the fertility of the soil, and the many connexions and intermarriages formed with neighbouring nations, it grew and flourished, unharmed by foreign enemies, though most unfortunate in civil wars. Ashamed of the atrocious deed, and aware of the detestation which it was inspiring, Antonius issued a proclamation, that no one should detain in captivity a citizen of Cremona. The spoil indeed had been rendered valueless to the soldiers by a general agreement throughout Italy, which rejected with loathing the purchase of such slaves. A massacre then began; when this was known, the prisoners were secretly ransomed by their friends and relatives. The remaining inhabitants soon returned to Cremona; the temples and squares were restored by the munificence of the burghers, and Vespasian gave his exhortations.

35. The soil poisoned with blood forbade the enemy to remain long by the ruins of the buried city. They advanced to the third milestone, and gathered the dispersed and panic-stricken Vitellianists round their proper standards. The vanquished legions were then scattered throughout Illyricum; for civil war was not over, and they might play a doubtful part. Messengers carrying news of the victory were then despatched to Britain and to Spain. Julius Calenus, a tribune, was sent to Gaul, and Alpinius Montanus, prefect of a cohort, to Germany; as the one was an Æduan, the other a Trever, and both were Vitellianists, they would be a proof of the success. At the same time the passes of the Alps were occupied with troops, for it was suspected that Germany was arming itself to support Vitellius.

36. A few days after the departure of Cæcina, Vitellius

had hurried Fabius Valens to the seat of war, and was now seeking to hide his apprehensions from himself by indulgence. He made no military preparation; he did not seek to invigorate the soldiers by encouraging speeches or warlike exercises; he did not keep himself before the eyes of the people. Buried in the shades of his gardens, like those sluggish animals which, if you supply them with food, lie motionless and torpid, he had dismissed with the same forgetfulness the past, the present, and the future. While he thus lay wasting his powers in sloth among the woods of Aricia, he was startled by the treachery of Lucilius Bassus and the defection of the fleet at Ravenna. Then came the news about Cæcina, and he heard with a satisfaction mingled with distress, first, that he had revolted, and then, that he had been put in irons by the army. In that dull soul joy was more powerful than apprehension. In great exultation he returned to Rome, and before a crowded assembly of the people heaped praises on the dutiful obedience of the soldiers. He ordered Publius Sabinus, prefect of the Prætorian Guard, to be thrown into prison, because of his friendship with Cæcina, and substituted in his place Alfenius Varus.

37. He then addressed the Senate in a speech of studied grandiloquence, and was extolled by the Senators with elaborate adulation. A savage resolution against Cæcina was moved by Lucius Vitellius; the rest affected indignation at the idea that a consul had betrayed the State, a general his Emperor, a man loaded with wealth so vast and honours so numerous his benefactor, and seemed to deplore the wrongs of Vitellius, while they uttered their private griefs. Not a word from any one of them disparaged the Flavianist leaders; they censured the delusion and recklessness of the armies, and with a prudent circumlocution avoided the name of Vespasian. A man was found, who, while all regarded with great contempt both giver and receiver, wormed himself by flattery into the one day of office which remained to complete the consulate of Cæcina. On the last day of October Rosius Regulus both assumed and resigned the office. The learned remarked that never before had a new consul been elected without a formal act of deprivation and the passing of a law. Before this indeed Caninius Rebilus

had been consul for a single day during the dictatorship of Caius Cæsar, when the prizes of the civil war had to be enjoyed in haste.

38. At this time the murder of Junius Blæsus obtained an infamous notoriety. Of this act I have heard the following account. Vitellius, who was suffering from severe illness, observed from the Servilian gardens a neighbouring turret brilliantly illuminated throughout the night. Inquiring the cause, he was told that Cæcina Tuscus was entertaining a large party, of whom Junius Blæsus was the most distinguished. Other particulars were given with much exaggeration about the splendour of the banquet and the unrestrained gaiety of the guests. There were persons who charged Tuscus and his guests, and Blæsus more vindictively than any, with passing their days in merriment while the Emperor was sick. As soon as it was sufficiently clear to those who keenly watch the angry moods of princes, that Vitellius was exasperated, and that Blæsus might be destroyed, the part of the informer was intrusted to Lucius Vitellius. An unworthy jealousy made him the enemy of Blæsus, whose illustrious character raised him far above one who was stained with every infamy; he burst into the Imperial chamber, and clasping to his bosom the Emperor's son, fell at his knees. On Vitellius enquiring the cause of his emotion: "It is not," he replied, "from any private apprehension, or because I am anxious for myself; it is for a brother and for a brother's children that I have come hither with my prayers and tears. It is idle to fear Vespasian, when there are so many legions of Germany, so many provinces with their valour and their loyalty, and lastly, so vast an extent of sea and land with enormous distances, to keep him from us. In the capital, in the very bosom of the empire, there is the foe of whom we must beware, a foe who boasts of Junii and Antonii among his ancestors, and who, claiming an Imperial descent, displays to the soldiers his condescension and his magnificence. On him all thoughts are fixed, while Vitellius, regardless alike of friends and foes, is cherishing a rival, who from his banqueting table gazes at the sufferings of his sovereign. For such ill-timed mirth let him be recompensed with a night of

sorrow and of death, that he may know and feel that Vitellius still lives and reigns, and has a son, if in the course of destiny anything should happen to himself."

39. Vitellius, after wavering between his guilty purpose and his fears, dreading lest to postpone the murder of Blæsus might hasten his own ruin, while openly to order it might provoke terrible odium, determined to destroy him by poison. He gave a proof of his guilt by his marked joy when he visited Blæsus. He was even heard to utter a most brutal speech, in which (I will relate the very words) he boasted that he had feasted his eyes on the spectacle of his enemy's death. Besides his noble birth and refinement of character, Blæsus was a man of resolute loyalty. In the flourishing days of the party, when canvassed by Cæcina and the leading men, who were beginning to despise Vitellius, he persevered in rejecting their solicitations. A righteous man and a lover of peace, who coveted no sudden elevation, much less the throne, he could not escape being thought to deserve it.

40. Meanwhile Fabius Valens, who was moving along with a vast and luxurious train of concubines and eunuchs too tardily for a general about to take the field, received speedy intelligence of the betrayal of the Ravenna fleet by Lucilius Bassus. Had he hastened the march which he had then begun, he might have come up with Cæcina while still undecided, or have reached the legions previous to the decisive action. Some advised him to take a few of his most devoted soldiers, and, avoiding Ravenna, to hurry on by unfrequented paths to Hostilia or Cremona. Others thought that he should summon the Prætorian cohorts from Rome, and then force his way with a strong body of troops. But with a ruinous delay he wasted in deliberation the opportunities of action. Eventually he rejected both plans, and did what is the very worst thing in circumstances of peril, attempted a middle course, and was neither bold enough on the one hand, nor cautious enough on the other.

41. He wrote to Vitellius asking for aid. Three cohorts with some British cavalry arrived, a force too numerous to elude observation, too small to force its way. Even amidst such perils Valens could not keep himself clear of the in-

famous reputation of grasping at unlawful gratifications, and of polluting the houses of his hosts with intrigue and violation. He had power, he had money, and he indulged the lusts that are the last solace of desperate fortunes. At length on the arrival of the infantry and cavalry the folly of his plans became evident. With so small a force, even had it been thoroughly loyal, he could not have made his way through the enemy, and the loyalty they had brought with them was not beyond suspicion. Yet shame and respect for the presence of their general held them in check, no lasting restraint with men who loved danger and were careless of disgrace. Moved by this apprehension, Valens, while he retained a few attendants whom adversity had not changed, sent on the infantry to Ariminum and ordered the cavalry to cover his rear. He then himself made his way to Umbria, and thence to Etruria, where, having learnt the issue of the battle of Cremona, he conceived a plan not wanting in vigour, and which, had it succeeded, would have had terrible results. This was to seize some ships, to land on some part of Gallia Narbonensis, to rouse Gaul with its armies as well as the tribes of Germany, and so to kindle a fresh war.

42. The garrison of Ariminum were discouraged by the departure of Valens, and Cornelius Fuscus, bringing up his army and disposing his Liburnian ships at the nearest points of the shore, invested the place by sea and land. His troops occupied the plains of Umbria and that portion of the Picentine territory that is washed by the Adriatic, and now the whole of Italy was divided by the range of the Apennines between Vespasian and Vitellius. Valens, having started from the bay of Pisa, was compelled, either by a calm or a contrary wind, to put in at the port of Hercules Monœcus. Near this place was stationed Marius Maturus, procurator of the Maritime Alps, who was loyal to Vitellius, and who, though every thing around him was hostile, had not yet thrown off his allegiance. While courteously receiving Valens, he deterred him by his advice from rashly invading Gallia Narbonensis. And now the fidelity of the rest of the party was weakened by their fears. In fact the procurator Valerius Paullinus, an enterprising officer, who had

been a friend of Vespasian before his elevation to the throne, had made the neighbouring States swear allegiance to that Prince.

43. Paullinus had collected all the troops who, having been disbanded by Vitellius, were now spontaneously taking up arms, and was holding with this force the colony of Forum Julii, which commanded the sea. His influence was all the greater, because Forum Julii was his native place, and because he was respected by the Prætorians, in which force he had once been a tribune. The inhabitants themselves, favouring a fellow-townsman, and anticipating his future greatness, did their best to promote the cause. When these preparations, which were really formidable and were exaggerated by report, became known among the now distracted Vitellianists, Fabius Valens returned to his ships with four soldiers of the body-guard, three personal friends, and as many centurions, while Maturus and the rest chose to remain behind and swear allegiance to Vespasian. For Valens indeed the open sea was safer than the coast or the towns, yet, all uncertain about the future, and knowing rather what he must avoid than what he could trust, he was thrown by adverse weather on the Stœchades, islands off Massilia. There he was captured by some Liburnian ships, dispatched by Paullinus.

44. Valens once captured, every thing turned to swell the resources of the conqueror; the lead was taken in Spain by the 1st legion (the "Adjutrix"), whose recollections of Otho made them hate Vitellius; they drew with them the 6th and 10th. Gaul did not hesitate to follow. A partiality long felt in Britain for Vespasian, who had there commanded the 2nd legion by the appointment of Claudius, and had served with distinction, attached that province to his cause, though not without some commotion among the other legions, in which were many centurions and soldiers promoted by Vitellius, who felt uneasy in exchanging for another ruler one whom they knew already.

45. These dissensions, and the continual rumours of civil war, raised the courage of the Britons. They were led by one Venutius, who, besides being naturally high spirited, and hating the name of Rome, was fired by his private ani-

mosity against Queen Cartismandua. Cartismandua ruled
the Brigantes in virtue of her illustrious birth; and she
strengthened her throne, when, by the treacherous capture
of king Caractacus, she was regarded as having given its
chief distinction to the triumph of Claudius Cæsar. Then
followed wealth and the self-indulgence of prosperity. Spurning her husband Venutius, she made Vellocatus, his armour-
bearer, the partner of her bed and throne. By this enormity
the power of her house was at once shaken to its base. On
the side of the husband were the affections of the people, on
that of the adulterer, the lust and savage temper of the
Queen. Accordingly Venutius collected some auxiliaries,
and, aided at the same time by a revolt of the Brigantes,
brought Cartismandua into the utmost peril. She asked for
some Roman troops, and our auxiliary infantry and cavalry,
after fighting with various success, contrived to rescue the
Queen from her peril. Venutius retained the kingdom, and
we had the war on our hands.

46. About the same time, Germany suffered from the
supineness of our generals and the mutinous conduct of our
legions; the assaults of enemies and the perfidy of allies all
but overthrew the power of Rome. Of this war, its origin
and its issue, for it lasted long, I shall hereafter speak. The
Dacians also were in motion, a people which never can be
trusted, and which, now that our legions were withdrawn
from Mœsia, had nothing to fear. They quietly watched the
opening of the campaign, but when they heard that Italy
was in a blaze of war, and that the whole Empire was divided against itself, they stormed the winter quarters of the
auxiliary infantry and cavalry, and occupied both banks of
the Danube. They were then preparing to destroy the camp
of the legions, but Mucianus sent the 6th legion against
them, for he knew of the victory of Cremona, and he feared
this double pressure of barbarian power with Dacians and
Germans invading Italy from opposite sides. We were
helped, as often before, by the good fortune of the Roman
people, which brought to the spot Mucianus with the armies
of the East, and by the decisive settlement which in the
meantime was effected at Cremona. Fonteius Agrippa was
removed from Asia (which province he had governed as

proconsul for a year) to Mœsia, and had some troops given him from the army of Vitellius. That this army should be dispersed through the provinces and closely occupied with foreign wars, was sound policy and essential to peace.

47. All other nations were equally restless. A sudden outbreak had been excited in Pontus by a barbarian slave, who had before commanded the royal fleet. This was Anicetus, a freedman of Polemon, once a very powerful personage, who, when the kingdom was converted into a Roman province, ill brooked the change. Accordingly he raised in the name of Vitellius the tribes that border on Pontus, bribed a number of very needy adventurers by the hope of plunder, and, at the head of a force by no means contemptible, made a sudden attack on the old and famous city of Trapezus, founded by the Greeks on the furthest shore of the Pontus. There he destroyed a cohort, once a part of the royal contingent. They had afterwards received the privileges of citizenship, and while they carried their arms and banners in Roman fashion, they still retained the indolence and licence of the Greek. Anicetus also set fire to the fleet, and, as the sea was not guarded, escaped, for Mucianus had brought up to Byzantium the best of the Liburnian ships and all the troops. The barbarians even insolently scoured the sea in hastily constructed vessels of their own called "camaræ," built with narrow sides and broad bottoms, and joined together without fastenings of brass or iron. Whenever the water is rough, they raise the bulwarks with additional planks according to the increasing height of the waves, till the vessel is covered in like a house. Thus they roll about amid the billows, and, as they have a prow at both extremities alike and a convertible arrangement of oars, they may be paddled in one direction or another indifferently and without risk.

48. The matter attracted the attention of Vespasian, and induced him to dispatch some veterans from the legions under Virdius Geminus, a tried soldier. Finding the enemy in disorder and dispersed in the eager pursuit of plunder, he attacked them, and drove them to their ships. Hastily fitting out a fleet of Liburnian ships, he pursued Anicetus, and overtook him at the mouth of the river Cohibus, where he was protected by the king of the Sedochezi, whose alli-

ance he had secured by a sum of money and other presents. This prince at first endeavoured to protect the suppliant by a threat of hostilities; when, however, the choice was presented to him between war and the profit to be derived from treachery, he consented, with the characteristic perfidy of barbarians, to the destruction of Anicetus, and delivered up the refugees. So ended this servile war. Amidst the joy of this success, while everything was prosperous beyond his hopes, tidings of the victory of Cremona reached Vespasian in Egypt. This made him hasten his advance to Alexandria, for, now that the army of Vitellius was shattered, he sought to apply the pressure of famine to the capital, which is always dependent on foreign supplies. He was indeed also preparing to invade by sea and land the province of Africa, which lies on the same line of coast, intending by thus closing the supplies of corn to cause famine and dissension among the enemy.

49. While with this world-wide convulsion the Imperial power was changing hands, the conduct of Primus Antonius, after the fall of Cremona, was by no means as blameless as before. Either he believed that the necessities of the war had been satisfied, and that all else would follow easily, or, perhaps, success, working on such a temperament, developed his latent pride, rapacity, and other vices. He swept through Italy as if it were a conquered country, and caressed the legions as if they were his own; by all his words and acts he sought to pave for himself the way to power. To imbue the army with a spirit of licence, he offered to the legions the commissions of the centurions killed in the war. By their vote the most turbulent men were elected. The soldiers in fact were not under the control of the generals, but the generals were themselves constrained to follow the furious impulses of the soldiers. These mutinous proceedings, so ruinous to discipline, Antonius soon turned to his own profit, regardless of the near approach of Mucianus, a neglect more fatal than any contempt for Vespasian.

50. As winter was approaching, and the low country was flooded by the Padus, the army marched on without its heavy baggage. The standards and eagles of the victorious legions, the old and wounded soldiers, and even many effec-

tive men, were left at Verona. The auxiliary infantry and cavalry, with some picked troops from the legions, appeared sufficient for a war that was all but finished. They had been joined by the 11th legion, which at first had hesitated, but now in the hour of success felt alarm at having stood aloof A recent levy of 6000 Dalmatians was attached to the legion. They were under the command of Pompeius Silvanus, a man of consular rank; the real direction of affairs was in the hands of Annius Bassus, the legate of the legion. This officer contrived, under an appearance of submission, to govern Silvanus, a leader without vigour, and apt to waste in words the opportunities of action. Bassus, with his unobtrusive energy, was ready for every thing that had to be done. To these forces were added the *élite* of the marines of the Ravenna fleet, who demanded permission to serve in the legions. The crews were made up with Dalmatians. The army and generals halted at the Temple of Fortune, undecided as to their line of action. They had heard that the Prætorian Guard had marched out of Rome, and they supposed that the Apennines were occupied with troops. The generals, finding themselves in a country utterly impoverished by war, were terrified by the scarcity of provisions and the mutinous clamours of the soldiery, who incessantly demanded the "clavarium," as the donative was called. They had provided neither money nor corn, and they were embarrassed by the general impatience and rapacity; for what they might have obtained was plundered.

51. I have the very highest authority for asserting, that there was among the conquerors such an impious disregard of right and wrong, that a private cavalry soldier declared he had slain his brother in the late battle, and claimed a reward from the generals. The common law of humanity on the one hand forbade them to reward this act of blood, the necessities of the war on the other forbade them to punish it. They put him off, on the ground that the obligation was too great to be immediately discharged. Nothing more is recorded. In the earlier civil wars indeed a similar horror had occurred. In the battle with Cinna at the Janiculum, a soldier in Pompey's army, as Sisenna tells us, slew his own brother, and, on discovering the horrible deed he had com

mitted, destroyed himself. So much more earnest among our
ancestors was the honour paid to virtue, and the remorse
that waited on crime. These and like instances, drawn from
the recollections of the past, I shall mention not irrele-
vantly, whenever the subject and the occasion shall call for
some example of goodness or some solace in the presence
of evil.

52. Antonius and the other generals of the party judged
it expedient to send forward the cavalry and explore the
whole of Umbria for some point where the Apennines presented a more gentle ascent, and also to bring up the eagles
and standards and all the troops at Verona, while they were
to cover the Padus and the sea with convoys. Some there
were among the generals who were contriving delays, for
Antonius in fact was now becoming too great a man, and
their hopes from Mucianus were more definite. That commander, troubled at so speedy a success, and imagining that
unless he occupied Rome in person he should lose all share
in the glory of the war, continued to write in ambiguous
terms to Varus and Antonius, enlarging at one time on the
necessity of following up their operations, at another on the
advantage of delay, and with expressions so worded that he
could, according to the event, repudiate a disastrous, or
claim a successful policy. To Plotius Griphus, who had
lately been raised by Vespasian to the senatorial rank and
appointed to command a legion, as well as to all others on
whom he could fully rely, he gave plainer instructions. All
these men sent replies reflecting unfavourably on the precipitancy of Varus and Antonius, and suiting the wishes of
Mucianus. By forwarding these letters to Vespasian he had
accomplished this much, that the measures and achievements of Antonius were not valued according to his hopes.

53. Antonius was indignant, and blamed Mucianus, whose
calumnies had depreciated his own hazardous achievements.
Nor was he temperate in his expressions, for he was habitually violent in language, and was unaccustomed to obey. He
wrote a letter to Vespasian in terms more arrogant than
should be addressed to an Emperor, and not without implied
reproach against Mucianus. "It was I," he said, "who
brought into the field the legions of Pannonia; my instiga-

tions roused the generals in Mœsia; my courageous resolution forced a passage through the Alps, seized on Italy, and cut off the succours from Germany and Rhætia. The discomfiture of the disunited and scattered legions of Vitellius by a fierce charge of cavalry, and afterwards by the steady strength of the infantry in a conflict that lasted for a day and a night, was indeed a most glorious achievement, and it was my work. For the destruction of Cremona the war must be answerable; the civil strifes of former days cost the State more terrible loss and the overthrow of many cities. Not with messages and letters, but with my arm and my sword, have I served my Emperor. I would not seek to hinder the renown of those who in the meanwhile have reduced Asia to tranquillity. They had at heart the peace of Mœsia, I the safety and security of Italy. By my earnest representations Gaul and Spain, the most powerful region of the world, have been won for Vespasian. But all my efforts have been wasted, if they alone who have not shared the peril obtain its rewards." The meaning of all this did not escape Mucianus, and there arose a deadly feud, cherished by Antonius with frankness, by Mucianus with reserve, and therefore with the greater bitterness.

54. Vitellius, after his power had been shattered at Cremona, endeavoured to suppress the tidings of the disaster, and by this foolish attempt at concealment he put off, not indeed his troubles, but only the application of the remedy. Had he avowed and discussed his position, he had some chance, some strength, left; whereas, on the contrary, when he pretended that all was prosperous, he aggravated his perils by falsehood. A strange silence was observed in his presence as to the war; throughout the country all discussion was prohibited, and so, many who would have told the truth had it been allowed, finding it forbidden, spread rumours exaggerating the calamity. The generals of the enemy failed not to magnify the report of their strength, for they sent back any spies of Vitellius whom they captured, after conducting them round the camp in order that they might learn the force of the victorious army. All of these persons Vitellius questioned in secret, and then ordered that they should be put to death. Singular bravery

was displayed by a centurion, Julius Agrestis, who, after several interviews, in which he had in vain endeavoured to rouse Vitellius to courage, prevailed on the Emperor to send him in person to see what was the strength of the enemy's resources, and what had happened at Cremona. He did not seek to escape the notice of Antonius by making his observations in secret, but avowed the Emperor's instructions and his own purpose, and asked leave to see everything. Persons were sent to shew him the field of battle, the remains of Cremona, and the captured legions. He then made his way back to Vitellius, and when the Emperor denied the truth of the intelligence which he brought, and even charged him with having been bribed, "Since," he replied, "you require some decisive proof, and I can no longer serve you in any other way either by my life or death, I will give you a proof which you can believe." So he departed, and confirmed his statement by a voluntary death. Some say that he was slain by order of Vitellius, but they bear the same testimony to his loyalty and courage.

55. Vitellius, who seemed like a man roused from slumber, ordered Julius Priscus and Alfenius Varus, with fourteen of the Prætorian cohorts and the entire force of cavalry, to occupy the Apennines. A legion of troops drafted from the fleet followed. So many thousand troops, comprising the picked men and horses of the army, had they been under the direction of a different general, would have been quite equal even to aggressive operations. The rest of the Prætorian cohorts were entrusted to Lucius Vitellius, brother of the Emperor, for the defence of the capital. Vitellius, while he abated nothing of his habitual indulgence, with a precipitancy prompted by alarm, anticipated the elections, at which he appointed consuls for several years. With a profuse liberality, he granted treaties to allies, and the rights of Latin citizenship to foreigners; some he relieved by the remission of tribute, others by exemptions; in a word, utterly careless of the future, he mutilated the resources of the Empire. But the mob was attracted by the magnificence of his bounties. The most foolish bought these favours with money; the wise held that to be invalid, which could neither be given nor received without ruin to the

State. Yielding at length to the importunity of the army, which had taken up its position at Mevania, and accompanied by a numerous train of senators, into which many were brought by ambition and more by fear, he entered the camp, undecided in purpose and at the mercy of faithless counsels.

56. While he was haranguing his troops (marvellous to relate) such a multitude of ill-omened birds flew over him, as to obscure with a dark cloud the light of day. There occurred another terrible presage. A bull escaped from the altar, scattered the preparations for sacrifice, and was finally slain far from the spot where the victims are usually struck down. But the most portentous spectacle of all was Vitellius himself, ignorant of military matters and without forethought in his plans, even asking others about the order of march, about the business of reconnoitring, and the discretion to be used in pushing on or protracting the campaign, betraying in his countenance and gait his alarm at every fresh piece of intelligence, and finally drinking to intoxication. At last, weary of the camp, and having received tidings of the defection of the fleet at Misenum, he returned to Rome, trembling at every new disaster, but reckless of the final result. For though it was open to him to have crossed the Apennines with an army in unimpaired vigour, and to have attacked in the field an enemy suffering from cold and scant supplies, yet, by dividing his forces, he abandoned to destruction or captivity troops of the keenest courage and faithful to the last, against the judgment of the most experienced among the centurions, who, had they been consulted, would have told him the truth. They were all kept at a distance by the intimate friends of Vitellius; for the Emperor's ears were so formed, that all profitable counsels were offensive to him, and that he would hear nothing but what would please and ruin.

57. The fleet at Misenum, so much can be done in times of civil discord by the daring of even a single man, was drawn into revolt by Claudius Faventinus, a centurion cashiered by Galba, who forged letters in the name of Vespasian offering a reward for treachery. The fleet was under the command of Claudius Apollinaris, a man neither firm in his

loyalty, nor energetic in his treason. Apinius Tiro, who had filled the office of prætor, and who then happened to be at Minturnæ, offered to head the revolt. By these men the colonies and municipal towns were drawn into the movement, and as Puteoli was particularly zealous for Vespasian, while Capua on the other hand remained loyal to Vitellius, they introduced their municipal jealousy into the civil war. Claudius Julianus, who had lately exercised an indulgent rule over the fleet at Misenum, was selected by Vitellius to soothe the irritation of the soldiery. He was supported by a city cohort and a troop of gladiators whose chief officer he was. As soon as the two camps were pitched, Julianus, without much hesitation, went over to the side of Vespasian, and they then occupied Tarracina, which was protected by its fortifications and position rather than by any ability of theirs.

58. Vitellius, when informed of these events, left a portion of his army at Narnia under the command of the prefect of the Prætorian Guard, and deputed his brother Lucius with six cohorts of infantry and 500 cavalry to encounter the danger that now threatened him on the side of Campania. Sick at heart, he found relief in the zeal of the soldiers and in the shouts with which the people clamoured for arms, while he gave the delusive name of an army and of Roman legions to a cowardly mob, that would not venture on any thing beyond words. At the instance of his freedmen (for his friends were the less faithful the more distinguished their rank) he ordered the tribes to be convoked, and to those who gave in their names administered the oath of service. As the numbers were excessive, he divided the business of enrolment between the consuls. He required the Senators to furnish a prescribed number of slaves and a certain weight of silver. The Roman Knights offered their services and money, and even the freedmen voluntarily sought the privilege of doing the same. This pretence of loyalty, dictated at first by fear, passed into enthusiasm, and many expressed compassion, not so much for Vitellius, as for the fallen condition of the Imperial power. Vitellius himself failed not to draw out their sympathies by his pitiable looks, his voice, and his tears; he was liberal in his

promises and even extravagant, as men in their alarm naturally are. He even expressed a wish to be saluted as Cæsar,
a title which he had formerly rejected. But now he had a
superstitious feeling about the name; and it is a fact that
in the moment of terror the counsels of the wise and the
voice of the rabble are listened to with equal respect. But
as all movements that originate in thoughtless impulse,
however vigorous in their beginnings, become feeble after a
time, the throng of Senators and Knights gradually melted
away, dispersing at first tardily and during the absence of
the Emperor, but before long with a contemptuous indifference to his presence, till, ashamed of the failure of his
efforts, Vitellius waived his claims to services which were
not offered.

59. As the occupation of Mevania, and the apparent revival of the war with new vigour, had struck terror into
Italy, so now did the timorous retreat of Vitellius give an
unequivocal bias in favour of the Flavianists. The Samnites,
the Peligni, and the Marsi, roused themselves, jealous at
having been anticipated by Campania, and, as men who
serve a new master, were energetic in all the duties of war.
The army, however, was much distressed by bad weather
in its passage over the Apennines, and since they could
hardly struggle through the snow, though their march was
unmolested, they perceived what danger they would have
had to encounter, had not Vitellius been made to turn back
by that good fortune, which, not less often than the wisdom
of their counsels, helped the Flavianist generals. Here they
fell in with Petilius Cerialis, who had escaped the sentries
of Vitellius by a rustic disguise and by his knowledge of the
country. There was a near relationship between Cerialis and
Vespasian, and he was not without reputation as a soldier.
He was therefore admitted to rank among the generals. It
has been said by many that the means of escape were likewise open to Flavius Sabinus and to Domitian, and indeed
messengers, dispatched by Antonius, contrived under various disguises to make their way to them, offering them a
place of refuge and a protecting force. Sabinus pleaded his
ill health, unsuited to toil and adventure. Domitian did not
want the courage, but he feared that the guards whom

Vitellius had set over him, though they offered to accompany him in his flight, had treacherous designs. And Vitellius himself, out of a regard for his own connexions, did not meditate any cruelty against Domitian.

60. The Flavianist generals on their arrival at Carsulæ took a few days for repose, while the eagles and standards of the legions were coming up. Carsulæ appeared a good position for an encampment, for it commanded an extensive prospect, provisions could be safely brought up, and there were in its rear several very wealthy towns. They also calculated on interviews with the Vitellianists, who were only ten miles distant, and on the chances of defection. The soldiers were dissatisfied with this prospect, and wished for victory rather than for peace. They would not even await the arrival of their own legions, whom they looked upon as sharers in the spoil rather than in the dangers of the campaign. Antonius summoned them to an assembly, and explained to them that Vitellius had still forces, which would waver in their loyalty if they had time to reflect, but would be fierce foes if driven to despair. "The opening of a civil war must," he said, "be left to chance; the final triumph is perfected by wise counsels and skill. The fleet of Misenum and the fairest portion of Campania have already revolted, and out of the whole world Vitellius has nothing left but the country between Tarracina and Narnia. From our victory at Cremona sufficient glory has accrued to us, and from the destruction of that city only too much disgrace. Let us not be eager to capture rather than to preserve the capital. Greater will be our reward, far higher our reputation, if we secure without bloodshed the safety of the Senate and of the people of Rome." By this and similar language their impatience was allayed.

61. Soon after, the legions arrived. Alarmed by the report of this increase to the army, the Vitellianist cohorts began to waver; no one urged them to fight, many urged them to change sides, each more eager than the other to hand over his company or troop, a present to the conqueror, and a source of future advantage to himself. From these men it was ascertained that Interamna, situated in the adjoining plain, was occupied by a garrison of 400 cavalry. Varus was

at once dispatched with a lightly equipped force, and cut to pieces a few who attempted to resist; the greater number threw down their arms, and begged for quarter. Some fled back into the camp, and spread panic everywhere by exaggerated reports of the courage and strength of the enemy, seeking thus to mitigate the disgrace of having lost the position. Among the Vitellianists treason went unpunished; all loyalty was subverted by the rewards of desertion, and nothing was left but emulation in perfidy. There were numerous desertions among the tribunes and centurions; the common soldiers remained obstinately faithful to Vitellius, till Priscus and Alfenius, deserting the camp and returning to Vitellius, relieved all from any shame they might feel at being traitors.

62. About the same time Fabius Valens was put to death while in confinement at Urbinum. His head was displayed to the Vitellianist cohorts, that they might not cherish any further hope, for they generally believed that Valens had made his way into Germany, and was there bringing into the field veteran as well as newly levied armies. The bloody spectacle reduced them to despair, and it was amazing how the army of Vespasian welcomed in their hearts the destruc· tion of Valens as the termination of the war. Valens was a native of Anagnia, and belonged to an Equestrian family; he was a man of loose character, but of no small ability, who sought to gain by profligacy a reputation for elegance. In the theatricals performed by young men during the reign of Nero, at first apparently from compulsion, afterwards of his own free choice, he repeatedly acted in the farces, with more cleverness than propriety. While legate of a legion, he first supported, then slandered, Verginius. Fonteius Capito he murdered, either after he had corrupted him, or because he had failed to do so. Though a traitor to Galba he was loyal to Vitellius, and gained a lustre from the perfidy of others.

63. Finding all their hopes cut off, the troops of Vitellius, intending to pass over to the side of the conqueror, but to do so with honour, marched down with their standards and colours into the plains beneath Narnia. The army of Vespasian, prepared and equipped as if for action, was drawn

up in dense array on both sides of the road. The Vitellianists were received between the two columns; when they
were thus surrounded, Antonius addressed them kindly. One
division was ordered to remain at Narnia, another at Interamna; with them were left some of the victorious legions,
which would not be formidable to them if they remained
quiet, but were strong enough to crush all turbulence. At
the same time Primus and Varus did not neglect to forward
continual messages to Vitellius, offering him personal safety,
the enjoyment of wealth, and a quiet retreat in Campania,
provided he would lay down his arms and surrender himself
and his children to Vespasian. Mucianus also wrote to him
to the same effect, and Vitellius was often disposed to trust
these overtures, and even discussed the number of his household and the choice of a residence on the coast. Such a
lethargy had come over his spirit, that, had not others remembered he had been an Emperor, he would have himself
forgotten it.

64. The leading men in the State had secret conferences
with Flavius Sabinus, prefect of the city, urging him to
secure a share in the credit of the victory. "You have," they
said, "a force of your own in the city cohorts; the cohorts
of the watch will not fail you, and there are also our own
slaves, there is the prestige of the party, there is the fact
that to the victorious every thing is easy. You should not
yield the glory of the war to Antonius and Varus. Vitellius
has but a few cohorts, and they are alarmed by gloomy tidings from every quarter. The feelings of the people are
easily swayed, and, if you put yourself at their head, there
will soon be the same flatteries ready for Vespasian. Vitellius even in prosperity was unequal to his position, and he
is proportionately unnerved by disaster. The merit of having finished the war will belong to him who may have possessed himself of the capital. It would well become Sabinus
to keep the Empire for his brother, and Vespasian equally
well, to count his other adherents inferior to Sabinus."

65. Old and infirm as he was, it was with any thing but
eagerness that he listened to these suggestions. Some indeed
assailed him with dark insinuations, implying that from motives of envy and rivalry he was seeking to retard the ele-

vation of his brother. It was true, that while both were in a
private station, Flavius Sabinus, who was the elder, was the
superior of Vespasian in influence and in wealth. He was
believed indeed to have sustained the failing credit of his
brother, while taking a mortgage of his house and lands;
and hence, though the outward appearance of harmony was
preserved, some secret grudge was feared. It is more chari-
table to suppose that the mild temper of the man shrank
from bloodshed and slaughter, and that for this reason he
had held frequent conferences with Vitellius to discuss the
question of peace and the cessation of hostilities upon certain conditions. After many private interviews, they finally,
so report said, ratified an agreement in the temple of Apollo.
The words of their conversation had two witnesses in Cluvius Rufus and Silius Italicus. Their looks were noted by
the more distant spectators; the expression of Vitellius was
abject and mean, that of Sabinus not triumphant, but rather
akin to pity.

66. Could Vitellius have swayed the feelings of his partisans as easily as he had himself yielded, the army of Vespasian might have entered the capital without bloodshed.
But the more loyal his adherents, the more did they protest
against peace and negotiation. They pointed out the danger
and disgrace of a submission in which the caprice of the
conqueror would be their sole guarantee. "And Vespasian,"
they said, "is not so arrogant as to tolerate such a subject
as Vitellius. Even the vanquished would not endure it. Their
pity would be dangerous to him. You certainly are an old
man, and have had enough both of prosperity and of adversity, but think what a name, what a position, you will leave
to your son Germanicus. Now indeed they promise you
wealth, and a large establishment, and a luxurious retreat
in Campania; but when Vespasian has once seized the
throne, neither he, nor his friends, nor even his armies, will
feel themselves secure till all rivalry has been extinguished.
Fabius Valens, captive as he was, and reserved against the
chance of disaster, was yet too formidable to them; and
certainly Primus, Fuscus, and Mucianus, who exhibits the
temper of his party, will not be allowed power over Vitellius
except to put him to death. Cæsar did not leave Pompey,

Augustus did not leave Antony in safety, though, perhaps, Vespasian may show a more lofty spirit, Vespasian, who was a dependant of Vitellius, when Vitellius was the colleague of Claudius. If you would act as becomes the censorship, the thrice-repeated consulate of your father, and all the honours of your illustrious house, let despair at any rate arm you to courageous action. The troops are still firm, and among the people there is abundant zeal. Lastly, nothing can happen to us more terrible than that upon which we are voluntarily rushing. If we are conquered, we must die; we must die, if we capitulate. All that concerns us is this; shall we draw our last breath amidst scorn and insult, or in a valiant struggle?"

67. The ears of Vitellius were deaf to manly counsels. His whole soul was overwhelmed by a tender anxiety, lest by an obstinate resistance he might leave the conqueror less mercifully disposed to his wife and children. He had also a mother old and feeble, but she, expiring a few days before, escaped by her opportune death the ruin of her house, having gained from the Imperial dignity of her son nothing but sorrow and a good name. On the 18th of December, after hearing of the defection of the legion and the auxiliary infantry which had surrendered at Narnia, he left the palace, clad in mourning robes, and surrounded by his weeping household. With him went his little son, carried in a litter, as though in a funeral procession. The greetings of the people were flattering, but ill-suited to the time; the soldiers preserved an ominous silence.

68. There could hardly be a man so careless of human interests as not to be affected by this spectacle. There was the Roman Emperor, lord but a few days before of the whole human race, leaving the seat of his power, and passing through the midst of his people and his capital, to abdicate his throne. Men had never before seen or heard of such an event. Cæsar, the Dictator, had fallen by sudden violence, Caligula by secret treason. The shades of night and the obscurity of a rural hiding-place had veiled the flight of Nero. Piso and Galba had, it might be said, fallen in battle. In an assembly of his own people, and in the midst of his own soldiers, with the very women of his family looking on,

Vitellius stood and spoke a few words suitable to the sad conjuncture. "He gave way," he said, "for the sake of peace, for the sake of his country; let them only remember him, and think with compassion of his brother, of his wife, of his young and innocent children." At the same time he held out his son, commending him first to individual bystanders, then to the whole assembly. At last, unable to speak for weeping, he unfastened the dagger from his side, and offered it to the Consul, Cæcilius Simplex, who was standing by him, as if to indicate that he surrendered the power of life and death over the citizens. The Consul rejecting it, and those who were standing by in the assembly shouting remonstrance, he departed, as if with the intention of laying aside the emblems of Imperial power in the Temple of Concord, and of betaking himself to his brother's house. Louder shouts here met him from the crowd, which hindered him from entering a private house, and invited him to return to the palace. Every other route was closed, and the only one open was one which led into the Via Sacra. Then in utter perplexity he returned to the palace. The rumour that he had renounced the Imperial dignity had preceded him thither, and Flavius Sabinus had sent written orders to the tribunes of the cohorts to keep their soldiers under restraint.

69. Then, as if the whole State had passed into the hands of Vespasian, the leading men of the Senate, many of the Equestrian order, with all the city soldiery and the watch, thronged the dwelling of Sabinus. Intelligence was there brought to him of the enthusiasm of the populace and of the threatening attitude of the German cohorts. He had now gone too far to be able to retreat, and every one, fearing for himself, should the Vitellianists come upon them while they were scattered and comparatively weak, urged him, in spite of his reluctance, to hostilities. As usually happens, however, in such cases, all gave the advice, but few shared the risk. The armed retinue which was escorting Sabinus was met, as it was coming down by the Lake Fundanus, by some of the most determined of the Vitellianists. From this unforeseen collision resulted an encounter slight indeed, but terminating favourably for the Vitellianists. In the hurry of the moment Sabinus adopted the safest course open to him,

and occupied the Capitol with a miscellaneous body of soldiery, and some Senators and Knights. It is not easy to give
the names of these persons, since after the triumph of Vespasian many pretended to have rendered this service to his
party. There were even women who braved the dangers of
the siege; the most conspicuous among them being Verulana
Gratilla, who was taken thither, not by the love of children
or kindred, but by the fascination of war. The Vitellianists
kept but a careless watch over the besieged, and thus at the
dead of night Sabinus was able to bring into the Capitol his
own children and Domitian his brother's son, and to send by
an unguarded route a messenger to the generals of the Flavianist party, with information that they were besieged, and
that, unless succour arrived, they must be reduced to distress. The night passed so quietly that he might have
quitted the place without loss; for, brave as were the soldiers of Vitellius in encountering danger, they were far from
attentive to the laborious duties of watching. Besides this,
the sudden fall of a winter storm baffled both sight and
hearing.

70. At dawn of day, before either side commenced hostilities, Sabinus sent Cornelius Martialis, a centurion of the
first rank, to Vitellius, with instructions to complain of the
infraction of the stipulated terms. "There has evidently,"
he said, "been a mere show and pretence of abdicating the
Empire, with the view of deceiving a number of distinguished men. If not, why, when leaving the Rostra, had he
gone to the house of his brother, looking as it did over the
Forum, and certain to provoke the gaze of the multitude,
rather than to the Aventine, and the family house of his
wife? This would have befitted a private individual anxious
to shun all appearance of Imperial power. But on the contrary, Vitellius retraced his steps to the palace, the very
stronghold of Empire; thence issued a band of armed men.
One of the most frequented parts of the city was strewed
with the corpses of innocent persons. The Capitol itself had
not been spared. "I," said Sabinus, "was only a civilian and
a member of the Senate, while the rivalry of Vitellius and
Vespasian was being settled by conflicts between legions, by
the capture of cities, by the capitulation of cohorts; with

Spain, Germany, and Britain in revolt, the brother of Vespasian still remained firm to his allegiance, till actually invited to discuss terms of agreement. Peace and harmony bring advantage to the conquered, but only credit to the conqueror. If you repent of your compact, it is not against me, whom you treacherously deceived, that you must draw the sword, nor is it against the son of Vespasian, who is yet of tender age. What would be gained by the slaughter of one old man and one stripling? You should go and meet the legions, and fight there for Empire; everything else will follow the issue of that struggle." To these representations the embarrassed Vitellius answered a few words in his own exculpation, throwing all the blame upon the soldiers, with whose excessive zeal his moderation was, he said, unable to cope. He advised Martialis to depart unobserved through a concealed part of the palace, lest he should be killed by the soldiers, as the negotiator of this abhorred convention. Vitellius had not now the power either to command or to forbid. He was no longer Emperor, he was merely the cause of war.

71. Martialis had hardly returned to the Capitol, when the infuriated soldiery arrived, without any leader, every man acting on his own impulse. They hurried at quick march past the Forum and the temples which hang over it, and advanced their line up the opposite hill as far as the outer gates of the Capitol. There were formerly certain colonnades on the right side of the slope as one went up; the defenders, issuing forth on the roof of these buildings, showered tiles and stones on the Vitellianists. The assailants were not armed with anything but swords, and it seemed too tedious to send for machines and missiles. They threw lighted brands on a projecting colonnade, and following the track of the fire would have burst through the half-burnt gates of the Capitol, had not Sabinus, tearing down on all sides the statues, the glories of former generations, formed them into a barricade across the opening. They then assailed the opposite approaches to the Capitol, near the grove of the Asylum, and where the Tarpeian rock is mounted by a hundred steps. Both these attacks were unexpected; the closer and fiercer of the two threatened the Asylum. The

HISTORY 3.71-73

assailants could not be checked as they mounted the continuous line of buildings, which, as was natural in a time of profound peace, had grown up to such a height as to be on a level with the soil of the Capitol. A doubt arises at this point, whether it was the assailants who threw lighted brands on to the roofs, or whether, as the more general account has it, the besieged thus sought to repel the assailants, who were now making vigorous progress. From them the fire passed to the colonnades adjoining the temples; the eagles supporting the pediment, which were of old timber, caught the flames. And so the Capitol, with its gates shut, neither defended by friends, nor spoiled by a foe, was burnt to the ground.

72. This was the most deplorable and disgraceful event that had happened to the Commonwealth of Rome since the foundation of the city; for now, assailed by no foreign enemy, with Heaven ready to be propitious, had our vices only allowed, the seat of Jupiter Supremely Good and Great, founded by our ancestors with solemn auspices to be the pledge of Empire, the seat, which neither Porsenna, when the city was surrendered, nor the Gauls, when it was captured, had been able to violate, was destroyed by the madness of our Emperors. Once before indeed during civil war the Capitol had been consumed by fire, but then only through the crime of individuals; now it was openly besieged, and openly set on fire. And what were the motives of this conflict? what the compensation for so great a disaster? was it for our country we were fighting? King Tarquinius Priscus had vowed its erection in his war with the Sabines, and had laid the foundations on a scale which suited the hopes of future greatness rather than what the yet moderate resources of Rome could achieve. After him, Servius Tullius, heartily assisted by the allies, and Tarquinius Superbus, employing the spoils of war from the conquered Suessa Pometia, raised the superstructure. But the glory of its completion was reserved for the days of liberty. After the expulsion of the Kings, Horatius Pulvillus, in his second consulate, dedicated it, a building so magnificent, that the vast wealth afterwards acquired by the people of Rome served to embellish rather than increase it. It was re-

built on the same site, when, after an interval of 415 years, it was burnt to the ground in the consulate of Lucius Scipio and Caius Norbanus. Sulla, after his final triumph, undertook the charge of restoring it, but did not live to dedicate it, the one thing denied to his uniform good fortune. The name of Lutatius Catulus, the dedicator, remained among all the vast erections of the Emperors, down to the days of Vitellius. This was the building that was now on fire.

73. The catastrophe, however, caused more panic among the besieged than among the besiegers. In fact, the troops of Vitellius lacked neither skill nor courage in the midst of peril. Opposed to them were soldiers without self-possession, and a spiritless and, so to speak, infatuated commander, who had not the use of his tongue or his ears, who would not be guided by other men's counsels, and could not carry out his own, who, hurried to and fro by the shouts of the enemy, forbade what he had just ordered, and ordered what he had just forbidden. Then, as usually happens when everything is lost, all gave orders, and no one obeyed. At last, they threw away their arms, and began to look about for ways of escape and means of concealment. The Vitellianists burst in, carrying everywhere with indiscriminate ferocity the firebrand and the sword. A few of the military men, among whom the most conspicuous were Cornelius Martialis, Æmilius Pacensis, Casperius Niger, and Didius Sceva, ventured to resist, and were cut down. Flavius Sabinus, who was unarmed, and who did not attempt to fly, was surrounded, and with him the consul Quinctius Atticus, marked out by his clinging to the shadow of office, and by his folly in having scattered among the people edicts highly eulogistic of Vespasian and insulting to Vitellius. The rest escaped by various chances, some disguised as slaves, others concealed by the fidelity of dependants, and hiding among the baggage. Some caught the watchword by which the Vitellianists recognised each other, and, themselves challenging others and giving it when challenged, found in their audacity an effectual disguise.

74. When the enemy first burst in, Domitian concealed himself in the house of a servant of the temple. At the ingenious suggestion of a freedman, he assumed a linen vest-

ment, and passing unnoticed among a crowd of acolytes,
found a refuge with Cornelius Primus, one of his father's
dependants, in a house near the Velabrum. When his father
mounted the throne, he pulled down the chamber of the
temple-servant, and built a small chapel, dedicated to Jupiter the Preserver, with an altar on which his own adventures were represented in marble. Afterwards, on his own
accession to the Imperial power, he consecrated a vast
temple to Jupiter the Guardian, with an effigy of himself in
the arms of the god. Sabinus and Atticus were loaded with
chains, and conducted to Vitellius, who received them with
anything but anger in his words and looks, amidst the murmurs of those who demanded the privilege of slaying them
and their pay for the work they had done. Those who were
standing near began the clamour, and the degraded rabble
cried out for the execution of Sabinus, and mingled threats
with their flatteries. Vitellius, who was standing before the
steps of the palace, and was preparing to intercede, was
induced to desist. The body of Sabinus, pierced and mutilated and with the head severed from it, was dragged to the
Gemoniæ.

75. Such was the end of a man in no wise contemptible.
In five and thirty campaigns he had served the State, and
had gained distinction both at home and abroad. His blame-
lessness and integrity no one could question. He was somewhat boastful; this was the only fault of which rumour accused him in the seven years during which he had governed
Mœsia, and the twelve during which he was prefect of the
city. In the closing scene of his life some have seen pusillanimity, many a moderate temper, sparing of the blood of
his countrymen. One thing is allowed by all, that, before
the accession of Vespasian, the distinction of the family was
centred in Sabinus. I have heard that his death gratified
Mucianus, and many indeed asserted that the interests of
peace were promoted by the removal of the rivalry between
these two men, one of whom felt himself to be the brother
of the Emperor, while the other thought himself his colleague. Vitellius resisted the demands of the people for the
execution of the Consul; he was now pacified, and wished,
it would seem, to recompense Atticus, who, when asked who

had set fire to the Capitol, had confessed his own guilt, and by this confession, which may indeed have been an opportune falsehood, was thought to have taken upon himself the odium of the crime, and to have acquitted the Vitellianist party.

76. Meanwhile Lucius Vitellius, who was encamped near Feronia, was threatening Tarracina with destruction. There were shut up in the place a few gladiators and seamen, who dared not leave the walls and risk an engagement in the plain. I have mentioned before that Julianus was in command of the gladiators, Apollinaris of the seamen, two men whose profligacy and indolence made them resemble gladiators rather than generals. They kept no watch; they did not strengthen the weak points of the fortifications; but, making each pleasant spot ring with the noise of their daily and nightly dissipation, they dispersed their soldiers on errands which were to minister to their luxury, and never spoke of war, except at their banquets. Apinius Tiro had quitted the place a few days before, and was now, by the harsh exaction of presents and contributions from the towns, adding to the unpopularity rather than to the resources of his party.

77. Meanwhile a slave belonging to Verginius Capito deserted to L. Vitellius, and having engaged, on being furnished with a force, to put him in possession of the unoccupied citadel, proceeded at a late hour of the night to place some light-armed cohorts on the summit of a range of hills which commanded the enemy's position. From this place the troops descended to what was more a massacre than a conflict. Many whom they slew were unarmed or in the act of arming themselves, some were just awaking from sleep, amid the confusion of darkness and panic, the braying of trumpets, and the shouts of the foe. A few of the gladiators resisted, and fell not altogether unavenged. The rest made a rush for the ships, where everything was involved in a general panic, the troops being mingled with country people, whom the Vitellianists slaughtered indiscriminately. Six Liburnian ships with Apollinaris, prefect of the fleet, escaped in the first confusion. The rest were either seized upon the beach, or were swamped by the weight of the crowds that

rushed on board. Julianus was brought before L. Vitellius, and, after being ignominiously scourged, was put to death in his presence. Some persons accused Triaria, the wife of L. Vitellius, of having armed herself with a soldier's sword, and of having behaved with arrogance and cruelty amid the horrors and massacres of the storm of Tarracina. Lucius himself sent to his brother a laurelled dispatch with an account of his success, and asked whether he wished him at once to return to Rome, or to complete the subjugation of Campania. This circumstance was advantageous to the State as well as to the cause of Vespasian. Had the army fresh from victory, and with all the pride of success added to its natural obstinacy, marched upon Rome, a conflict of no slight magnitude, and involving the destruction of the capital, must have ensued. Lucius Vitellius, infamous as he was, had yet some energy, but it was not through his virtues, as is the case with the good, but through his vices, that he, like the worst of villains, was formidable.

78. While these successes were being achieved on the side of Vitellius, the army of Vespasian had left Narnia, and was passing the holiday of the Saturnalia in idleness at Ocriculum. The reason alleged for so injurious a delay was that they might wait for Mucianus. Some persons indeed there were who assailed Antonius with insinuations, that he lingered with treacherous intent, after receiving private letters from Vitellius, which conveyed to him the offer of the consulship and of the Emperor's daughter in marriage with a vast dowry, as the price of treason. Others asserted that this was all a fiction, invented to please Mucianus. Some again alleged that the policy agreed upon by all the generals was to threaten rather than actually to attack the capital, as Vitellius' strongest cohorts had revolted from him, and it seemed likely that, deprived of all support, he would abdicate the throne, but that the whole plan was ruined by the impatience and subsequent cowardice of Sabinus, who, after rashly taking up arms, had not been able to defend against three cohorts the great stronghold of the Capitol, which might have defied even the mightiest armies. One cannot, however, easily fix upon one man the blame which belongs to all. Mucianus did in fact delay the conquerors by ambig-

uously-worded dispatches; Antonius, by a perverse acquiescence, or by an attempt to throw the odium upon another,
laid himself open to blame; the other generals, by imag
ining that the war was over, contrived a distinction for its
closing scene. Even Petilius Cerialis, though he had been
sent on with a thousand cavalry by cross roads through the
Sabine district so as to enter Rome by the Via Salaria, had
not been sufficiently prompt in his movements, when the
report of the siege of the Capitol put all alike on the alert.

79. Antonius marched by the Via Flaminia, and arrived
at Saxa Rubra, when the night was far spent, too late to
give any help. There he received nothing but gloomy intelligence, that Sabinus was dead, that the Capitol had been
burnt to the ground, that Rome was in consternation, and
also that the populace and the slaves were arming themselves for Vitellius. And Petilius Cerialis had been defeated
in a cavalry skirmish. While he was hurrying on without
caution, as against a vanquished enemy, the Vitellianists,
who had disposed some infantry among their cavalry, met
him. The conflict took place not far from the city among
buildings, gardens, and winding lanes, which were well
known to the Vitellianists, but disconcerting to their opponents, to whom they were strange. Nor indeed were all
the cavalry one in heart, for there were with them some who
had lately capitulated at Narnia, and who were anxiously
watching the fortunes of the rival parties. Tullius Flavianus, commanding a squadron, was taken prisoner; the rest
fled in disgraceful confusion, but the victors did not continue the pursuit beyond Fidenæ.

80. By this success the zeal of the people was increased.
The mob of the city armed itself. Some few had military
shields, the greater part seized such arms as came to hand
and loudly demanded the signal of battle. Vitellius expressed
his thanks to them, and bade them sally forth to defend the
capital. Then the Senate was called together, and envoys
were selected to meet the armies and urge them in the name
of the Commonwealth to union and peace. The reception of
these envoys was not everywhere the same. Those who fell
in with Petilius Cerialis were exposed to extreme peril, for
the troops disdained all offers of peace. The prætor Arulenus

Rusticus was wounded. This deed seemed all the more atrocious, when, over and above the insult offered to the dignity
of the envoy and prætor, men considered the private worth
of the man. His companions were dispersed, and the lictor
that stood next to him, venturing to push aside the crowd,
was killed. Had they not been protected by an escort provided by the general, the dignity of the ambassador, respected even by foreign nations, would have been profaned
with fatal violence by the madness of Roman cizitens before the very walls of their Country. The envoys who met
Antonious were more favourably received, not because the
troops were of quieter temper, but because the general had
more authority.

81. One Musonius Rufus, a man of equestrian rank,
strongly attached to the pursuit of philosophy and to the
tenets of the Stoics, had joined the envoys. He mingled with
the troops, and, enlarging on the blessings of peace and the
perils of war, began to admonish the armed crowd. Many
thought it ridiculous; more thought it tiresome; some were
ready to throw him down and trample him under foot, had
he not yielded to the warnings of the more orderly and the
threats of others, and ceased to display his ill-timed wisdom. The Vestal virgins also presented themselves with a
letter from Vitellius to Antonius. He asked for one day of
truce before the final struggle, and said, that if they would
permit some delay to intervene, everything might be more
easily arranged. The sacred virgins were sent back with
honour, but the answer returned to Vitellius was, that all
ordinary intercourse of war had been broken off by the murder of Sabinus and the conflagration of the Capitol.

82. Antonius, however, summoned the legions to an assembly, and endeavoured to calm them, proposing that they
should encamp near the Mulvian bridge, and enter the capital on the following day. His reason for delay was the fear
that the soldiers, once exasperated by conflict, would respect
neither the people nor the Senate, nor even the shrines and
temples of the Gods. They, however, looked with dislike on
all procrastination as inimical to victory. At the same time
the colours that glittered among the hills, though followed
by an unwarlike population, presented the appearance of a

hostile array. They advanced in three divisions, one column straight from where they had halted along the Via Flaminia, another along the bank of the Tiber, a third moved on the Colline Gate by the Via Salaria. The mob was routed by a charge of the cavalry. Then the Vitellianist troops, themselves also drawn up in three columns of defence, met the foe. Numerous engagements with various issue took place before the walls, but they generally ended in favour of the Flavianists, who had the advantage of more skilful generalship. Only that division suffered which had wound its way along narrow and slippery roads to the left quarter of the city as far as the gardens of Sallust. The Vitellianists, taking their stand on the garden-walls, kept off the assailants with stones and javelins till late in the day, when they were taken in the rear by the cavalry, which had then forced an entrance by the Colline Gate. In the Campus Martius also the hostile armies met, the Flavianists with all the prestige of fortune and repeated victory, the Vitellianists rushing on in sheer despair. Though defeated, they rallied again in the city.

83. The populace stood by and watched the combatants; and, as though it had been a mimic conflict, encouraged first one party and then the other by their shouts and plaudits. Whenever either side gave way, they cried out that those who concealed themselves in the shops, or took refuge in any private house, should be dragged out and butchered, and they secured the larger share of the booty; for, while the soldiers were busy with bloodshed and massacre, the spoils fell to the crowd. It was a terrible and hideous sight that presented itself throughout the city. Here raged battle and death; there the bath and the tavern were crowded. In one spot were pools of blood and heaps of corpses, and close by prostitutes and men of character as infamous; there were all the debaucheries of luxurious peace, all the horrors of a city most cruelly sacked, till one was ready to believe the Country to be mad at once with rage and lust. It was not indeed the first time that armed troops had fought within the city; they had done so twice when Sulla, once when Cinna triumphed. The bloodshed then had not been less, but now there was an unnatural recklessness, and men's pleasures

were not interrupted even for a moment. As if it were a
new delight added to their holidays, they exulted in and enjoyed the scene, indifferent to parties, and rejoicing over the
sufferings of the Commonwealth.

84. The most arduous struggle was the storming of the
camp, which the bravest of the enemy still held as a last
hope. It was, therefore, with peculiar energy that the conquerors, among whom the veteran cohorts were especially
forward, brought to bear upon it at once all the appliances
which have been discovered in reducing the strongest cities,
the testudo, the catapult, the earth-work, and the firebrand.
They repeatedly shouted "that all the toil and danger they
had endured in so many conflicts would be crowned by this
achievement. The capital has been restored to the Senate
and people of Rome, and their temples to the Gods; but the
soldier's peculiar distinction is in the camp; this is his country, and this his home; unless this be recovered forthwith,
the night must be passed under arms." On the other hand
the Vitellianists, though unequal in numbers and doomed to
defeat, could yet disturb the victory, delay the conclusion
of peace, and pollute both hearth and altar with blood; and
they clung to these last consolations of the vanquished.
Many, desperately wounded, breathed their last on the towers and ramparts. When the gates were torn down, the survivors threw themselves in a body on the conquerors, and
fell to a man, with their wounds in front and their faces
turned towards the foe, so anxious were they even in their
last hours to die with honour. When the city had been taken,
Vitellius caused himself to be carried in a litter through the
back of the palace to the Aventine, to his wife's dwelling,
intending, if by any concealment he could escape for that
day, to make his way to his brother's cohorts at Tarracina.
Then, with characteristic weakness, and following the instincts of fear, which, dreading everything, shrinks most
from what is immediately before it, he retraced his steps to
the desolate and forsaken palace, whence even the meanest
slaves had fled, or where they avoided his presence. The
solitude and silence of the place scared him; he tried the
closed doors, he shuddered in the empty chambers, till,
wearied out with his miserable wanderings, he concealed

himself in an unseemly hiding-place, from which he was dragged out by the tribune Julius Placidus. His hands were bound behind his back, and he was led along with tattered robes, a revolting spectacle, amidst the invectives of many, the tears of none. The degradation of his end had extinguished all pity. One of the German soldiers met the party, and aimed a deadly blow at Vitellius, perhaps in anger, perhaps wishing to release him the sooner from insult. Possibly the blow was meant for the Tribune. He struck off that officer's ear, and was immediately dispatched.

85. Vitellius, compelled by threatening swords, first to raise his face and offer it to insulting blows, then to behold his own statues falling round him, and more than once to look at the Rostra and the spot where Galba was slain, was then driven along till they reached the Gemoniæ, the place where the corpse of Flavius Sabinus had lain. One speech was heard from him shewing a spirit not utterly degraded, when to the insults of a tribune he answered, "Yet I was your Emperor." Then he fell under a shower of blows, and the mob reviled the dead man with the same heartlessness with which they had flattered him when he was alive.

86. Luceria was his native place. He had nearly completed his 57th year. His consulate, his priesthood, his high reputation, his place among the first men of the State, he owed, not to any energy of his own, but to the renown of his father. The throne was offered him by men who did not know him. Seldom have the affections of the army attached themselves to any man who sought to gain them by his virtues as firmly as they did to him from the indolence of his character. Yet he had a certain frankness and generosity, qualities indeed which turn to a man's ruin, unless tempered with discretion. Believing that friendship may be retained by munificent gifts rather than by consistency of character, he deserved more of it than he secured. Doubtless it was good for the State that Vitellius should be overthrown, but they who betrayed Vitellius to Vespasian cannot make a merit of their treachery, since they had themselves revolted from Galba. The day was now fast drawing to a close, and the Senate could not be convened, owing to the panic of the magistrates and Senators, who had stolen

out of the city, or were concealing themselves in the houses of dependants. When nothing more was to be feared from the enemy, Domitian came forward to meet the leaders of the party; he was universally saluted by the title of Cæsar, and the troops, in great numbers, armed as they were, conducted him to his father's house.

BOOK IV

JANUARY-NOVEMBER, A.D. 70

1. WHEN Vitellius was dead, the war had indeed come to an end, but peace had yet to begin. Sword in hand, throughout the capital, the conquerors hunted down the conquered with merciless hatred. The streets were choked with carnage, the squares and temples reeked with blood, for men were massacred everywhere as chance threw them in the way. Soon, as their license increased, they began to search for and drag forth hidden foes. Whenever they saw a man tall and young they cut him down, making no distinction between soldiers and civilians. But the ferocity, which in the first impulse of hatred could be gratified only by blood, soon passed into the greed of gain. They let nothing be kept secret, nothing be closed; Vitellianists, they pretended, might be thus concealed. Here was the first step to breaking open private houses; here, if resistance were made, a pretext for slaughter. The most needy of the populace and the most worthless of the slaves did not fail to come forward and betray their wealthy masters; others were denounced by friends. Everywhere were lamentations, and wailings, and all the miseries of a captured city, till the license of the Vitellianist and Othonianist soldiery, once so odious, was remembered with regret. The leaders of the party, so energetic in kindling civil strife, were incapable of checking the abuse of victory. In stirring up tumult and strife the worst men can do the most, but peace and quiet cannot be established without virtue.

2. Domitian had entered into possession of the title and residence of Cæsar, but not yet applying himself to business, was playing the part of a son of the throne with debauchery and intrigue. The office of prefect of the Prætorian Guard was held by Arrius Varus, but the supreme power was in the

hands of Primus Antonius, who carried off money and slaves from the establishment of the Emperor, as if they were the spoils of Cremona. The other generals, whose moderation or insignificance had shut them out from distinction in the war, had accordingly no share in its prizes. The country, terror-stricken and ready to acquiesce in servitude, urgently demanded that Lucius Vitellius with his cohorts should be intercepted on his way from Tarracina, and that the last sparks of war should be trodden out. The cavalry were sent on to Aricia, the main body of the legions halted on this side of Bovillæ. Without hesitation Vitellius surrendered himself and his cohorts to the discretion of the conqueror, and the soldiers threw down their ill-starred arms in rage quite as much as in alarm. The long train of prisoners, closely guarded by armed men, passed through the capital. Not one of them wore the look of a suppliant; sullen and savage, they were unmoved by the shouts and jests of the insulting rabble. A few, who ventured to break away, were overpowered by the force that hemmed them in; the rest were thrown into prison. Not one of them uttered an unworthy word; even in disaster the honour of the soldier was preserved. After this Lucius Vitellius was executed. Equally vicious with his brother, he had yet shewn greater vigilance during that brother's reign, and may be said, not so much to have shared his elevation, as to have been dragged down by his fall.

3. About the same time Lucilius Bassus was sent with some light cavalry to establish order in Campania, where the towns were still disturbed, but by mutual animosities rather than by any spirit of opposition to the new Emperor. The sight of the soldiery restored quiet, and the smaller colonies escaped unpunished. At Capua, however, the third legion was stationed to pass the winter, and the noble families suffered severely. Tarracina, on the other hand, received no relief; so much more inclined are we to requite an injury than an obligation. Gratitude is a burden, while there seems to be a profit in revenge. They were consoled by seeing the slave of Verginius Capito, whom I have mentioned as the betrayer of Tarracina, gibbeted in the very rings of knighthood, the gift of Vitellius, which they had seen him wear.

At Rome the Senate, delighted and full of confident hope, decreed to Vespasian all the honours customarily bestowed on the Emperors. And indeed the civil war, which, beginning in Gaul and Spain, and afterwards drawing into the struggle first Germany and then Illyricum, had traversed Ægypt, Judæa, and Syria, every province, and every army, this war, now that the whole earth was, as it were, purged from guilt, seemed to have reached its close. Their alacrity was increased by a letter from Vespasian, written during the continuance of the war. Such indeed was its character at first sight; the writer, however, expressed himself as an Emperor, speaking modestly about himself, in admirable language about the State. There was no want of deference on the part of the Senate. On the Emperor and his son Titus the consulship was bestowed by decree; on Domitian the office of prætor with consular authority.

4. Mucianus had also forwarded to the Senate certain letters which furnished matter for talk. It was said, "Why, if he is a private citizen, does he speak like a public man? In a few days' time he might have said the very same words in his place as a Senator. And even the invective against Vitellius comes too late, and is ungenerous; while certainly it is arrogance to the State and an insult to the Emperor to boast that he had the Imperial power in his hands, and made a present of it to Vespasian." Their dislike, however, was concealed; their adulation was open enough. In most flattering language they voted a triumph to Mucianus, a triumph for a civil war, though the expedition against the Sarmatæ was the pretext. On Antonius Primus were bestowed the insignia of consular rank, on Arrius Varus and Cornelius Fuscus prætorian honours. Then they remembered the Gods. It was determined that the Capitol should be restored. All these motions Valerius Asiaticus, consul elect, proposed. Most of the Senators signified their assent by their looks, or by raising the hand; but a few, who either held a distinguished rank, or had a practised talent for flattery, declared their acquiescence in studied speeches. When it came to the turn of Helvidius Priscus, prætor elect, to vote, he delivered an opinion, full of respect indeed to a worthy Emperor, and yet wholly free from insincerity; and he was strongly sup-

ported by the sympathies of the Senate. To Priscus indeed this day was in an especial manner the beginning of a great quarrel and a great renown.

5. As I have again happened to mention a man of whom I shall often have to speak, the subject seems to demand that I should give a brief account of his life and pursuits, and of his fortunes. Helvidius Priscus was a native of the town of Carecina in Italy, and was the son of one Cluvius, who had been a centurion of the first rank. In early youth he devoted his distinguished talents to the loftiest pursuits, not wishing, as do many, to cloak under an imposing name a life of indolence, but to be able to enter upon public life with a spirit fortified against the chances of fortune. He followed those teachers of philosophy who hold nothing to be good but what is honourable, nothing evil but what is base, and who refuse to count either among things good or evil, power, rank, or indeed any thing not belonging to the mind. While still holding the quæstorship, he was selected by Pætus Thrasea to be his son-in-law, and from the example of his father-in-law imbibed with peculiar eagerness a love of liberty. As a citizen and as a Senator, as a husband, as a son-in-law, as a friend, and in all the relations of life, he was ever the same, despising wealth, steadily tenacious of right, and undaunted by danger.

6. There were some who thought him too eager for fame, and indeed the desire of glory is the last infirmity cast off even by the wise. The fall of his father-in-law drove him into exile, but he returned when Galba mounted the throne, and proceeded to impeach Marcellus Eprius, who had been the informer against Thrasea. This retribution, as great as it was just, had divided the Senate into two parties; for, if Marcellus fell, a whole army of fellow culprits was struck down. At first there was a fierce struggle, as is proved by the great speeches delivered by both men. But afterwards, as the feelings of Galba were doubtful, and many Senators interceded, Priscus dropped the charge, amidst comments varying with the tempers of men, some praising his moderation, and others deploring a lack of courage. On the day, however, that the Senate was voting about the Imperial dignities of Vespasian, it had been resolved that envoys should

be sent to the new Emperor. Hence arose a sharp altercation between Helvidius and Eprius. Priscus proposed that
they should be chosen by name by the magistrates on oath,
Marcellus demanded the ballot; and this had been the opinion expressed by the Consul elect.

7. It was the dread of personal humiliation that made
Marcellus so earnest, for he feared that, if others were
chosen, he should himself appear slighted. From an angry
conversation they passed by degrees to long and bitter
speeches. Helvidius asked, "Why should Marcellus be so
afraid of the judgment of the magistrates? He has wealth
and eloquence, which might make him superior to many,
were he not oppressed by the consciousness of guilt. The
chances of the ballot do not discriminate men's characters;
the voting and the judgment of the Senate were devised to
reach the lives and reputations of individuals. It concerns
the interests of the Commonwealth, it concerns the honour
due to Vespasian, that he should be met by those whom the
Senate counts to be peculiarly blameless, and who may fill
the Emperor's ear with honourable counsels. Vespasian was
the friend of Thrasea, Soranus, and Sextius; and the accusers of these men, though it may not be expedient to punish them, ought not to be paraded before him. By this selection on the part of the Senate the Emperor will, so to speak,
be advised whom he should mark with approval, and from
whom he should shrink. There can be no more effectual instrument of good government than good friends. Let Marcellus be satisfied with having urged Nero to destroy so
many innocent victims; let him enjoy the wages of his
crimes and his impunity, but let him leave Vespasian to
worthier advisers."

8. Marcellus declared, "It is not my opinion that is assailed; the Consul elect has made a motion in accordance
with old precedents, which directed the use of the ballot in
the appointment of envoys, in order that there might be no
room for intrigue or private animosities. Nothing has happened why customs of long standing should fall into disuse,
or why the honour due to the Emperor should be turned
into an insult to any man. All Senators are competent to
pay their homage. What we have rather to avoid is this, that

a mind unsettled by the novelty of power, and which will keenly watch the very looks and language of all, should be irritated by the obstinacy of certain persons. I do not forget the times in which I have been born, or the form of government which our fathers and grandfathers established. I may regard with admiration an earlier period, but I acquiesce in the present, and, while I pray for good Emperors, I can endure whomsoever we may have. It was not through my speech any more than it was through the judgment of the Senate that Thrasea fell. The savage temper of Nero amused itself under these forms, and I found the friendship of such a Prince as harassing as others found their exile. Finally, Helvidius may rival the Catos and the Bruti of old in constancy and courage; I am but one of the Senate which bows to the same yoke. Besides, I would advise Priscus not to climb higher than the throne, or to impose his counsels on Vespasian, an old man, who has won the honours of a triumph, and has two sons grown to manhood. For as the worst Emperors love an unlimited despotism, so the noblest like some check on liberty." These speeches, which were delivered with much vehemence on both sides, were heard with much diversity of feeling. That party prevailed which preferred that the envoys should be taken by lot, as even the neutral section in the Senate exerted themselves to retain the old practice, while the more conspicuous members inclined to the same view, dreading jealousy, should the choice fall on themselves.

9. Another struggle ensued. The prætors of the Treasury (the Treasury was at this time managed by prætors) complained of the poverty of the State, and demanded a retrenchment of expenditure. The Consul elect, considering how great was the evil and how difficult the remedy, was for reserving the matter for the Emperor. Helvidius gave it as his opinion that measures should be taken at the discretion of the Senate. When the Consuls came to take the votes, Vulcatius Tertullinus, tribune of the people, put his veto on any resolution being adopted in so important a matter in the absence of the Emperor. Helvidius had moved that the Capitol should be restored at the public expense, and that Vespasian should give his aid. All the more moderate of the

Senators let this opinion pass in silence, and in time forgot
it; but there were some who remembered it.

10. Musonius Rufus then made a violent attack on Publius Celer, accusing him of having brought about the destruction of Barea Soranus by perjury. By this impeachment all the hatreds of the days of the informers seemed to
be revived; but the accused person was so worthless and so
guilty that he could not be protected. For indeed the memory of Soranus was held in reverence; Celer had been a professor of philosophy, and had then given evidence against
Barea, thus betraying and profaning the friendship of which
he claimed to be a teacher. The next day was fixed for the
trial. But it was not of Musonius or Publius, it was of Priscus, of Marcellus, and his brother informers, that men were
thinking, now that their hearts were once roused to vengeance.

11. While things were in this state, while there was division in the Senate, resentment among the conquered, no real
authority in the conquerors, and in the country at large no
laws and no Emperor, Mucianus entered the capital, and at
once drew all power into his own hands. The influence of
Primus Antonius and Varus Arrius was destroyed; for the
irritation of Mucianus against them, though not revealed in
his looks, was but ill-concealed, and the country, keen to
discover such dislikes, had changed its tone and transferred
its homage. He alone was canvassed and courted, and he,
surrounding himself with armed men, and bargaining for
palaces and gardens, ceased not, what with his magnificence
his proud bearing, and his guards, to grasp at the power,
while he waved the titles of Empire. The murder of Calpurnius Galerianus caused the utmost consternation. He was
a son of Caius Piso, and had done nothing, but a noble name
and his own youthful beauty made him the theme of common talk; and while the country was still unquiet and delighted in novel topics, there were persons who associated
him with idle rumours of Imperial honours. By order of
Mucianus he was surrounded with a guard of soldiers. Lest
his execution in the capital should excite too much notice,
they conducted him to the fortieth milestone from Rome on
the Appian Road, and there put him to death by opening

his veins. Julius Priscus, who had been prefect of the Præ-torian Guard under Vitellius, killed himself rather out of shame than by compulsion. Alfenius Varus survived the dis-grace of his cowardice. Asiaticus, who was only a freedman, expiated by the death of a slave his evil exercise of power.

12. At this time the country was hearing with anything but sorrow rumours that daily gained strength of disasters in Germany. Men began to speak of slaughtered armies, of captured encampments, of Gaul in revolt, as if such things were not calamities. Beginning at an earlier period I will dis-cuss the causes in which this war had its origin, and the extent of the movements which it kindled among independ-ent and allied nations.

The Batavians, while they dwelt on the other side of the Rhine, formed a part of the tribe of the Chatti. Driven out by a domestic revolution, they took possession of an unin-habited district on the extremity of the coast of Gaul, and also of a neighbouring island, surrounded by the ocean in front, and by the river Rhine in the rear and on either side. Not weakened by the power of Rome or by alliance with a people stronger than themselves, they furnished to the Em-pire nothing but men and arms. They had had a long train-ing in the German wars, and they had gained further re-nown in Britain, to which country their cohorts had been transferred, commanded, according to ancient custom, by the noblest men in the nation. They had also at home a select body of cavalry, who practised with special devotion the art of swimming, so that they could stem the stream of the Rhine with their arms and horses, without breaking the order of their squadrons.

13. Julius Paullus and Claudius Civilis, scions of the royal family, ranked very high above the rest of their nation. Paullus was executed by Fonteius Capito on a false charge of rebellion. Civilis was put in chains and sent to Nero, and, though acquitted by Galba, again stood in peril of his life in the time of Vitellius, when the army clamoured for his execution. Here were causes of deep offence; hence arose hopes built on our disasters. Civilis, however, was naturally politic to a degree rarely found among barbarians. He was wont to represent himself as Sertorius or Hannibal, on the

strength of a similar disfigurement of his countenance. To avoid the opposition which he would encounter as a public enemy, were he openly to revolt from Rome, he affected a friendship for Vespasian and a zealous attachment to his party; and indeed a letter had been despatched to him by Primus Antonius, in which he was directed to divert the reinforcements which Vitellius had called up, and to keep the legions where they were by the feint of an outbreak in Germany. The same policy was suggested by Hordeonius in person; he had a bias towards Vespasian, and feared for the Empire, the utter ruin of which would be very near, were a fresh war with so many thousands of armed men to burst upon Italy.

14. Civilis, who was resolved on rebellion, and intended, while concealing his ulterior designs, to reveal his other plans as occasion presented itself, set about the work of revolution in this way. By command of Vitellius all the Batavian youth was then being summoned to the conscription, a thing naturally vexatious, and which the officials made yet more burdensome by their rapacity and profligacy, while they selected aged and infirm persons, whom they might discharge for a consideration, and mere striplings, but of distinguished beauty (and many attain even in boyhood to a noble stature), whom they dragged off for infamous purposes. This caused indignation, and the ringleaders of the concerted rebellion prevailed upon the people to refuse the conscription. Civilis collected at one of the sacred groves, ostensibly for a banquet, the chiefs of the nation and the boldest spirits of the lower class. When he saw them warmed with the festivities of the night, he began by speaking of the renown and glory of their race, and then counted the wrongs and the oppressions which they endured, and all the other evils of slavery. "There is," he said, "no alliance, as once there was; we are treated as slaves. When does even a legate come among us, though he come only with a burdensome retinue and in all the haughtiness of power? We are handed over to prefects and centurions, and when they are glutted with our spoils and our blood, then they are changed, and new receptacles for plunder, new terms for spoliation, are discovered. Now the conscription is at hand, tearing, we

may say, for ever children from parents, and brothers from brothers. Never has the power of Rome been more depressed. In the winter quarters of the legions there is nothing but property to plunder and a few old men. Only dare to look up, and cease to tremble at the empty names of legions. For we have a vast force of horse and foot; we have the Germans our kinsmen; we have Gaul bent on the same objects. Even to the Roman people this war will not be displeasing; if defeated, we shall still reckon it a service to Vespasian, and for success no account need be rendered."

15. Having been listened to with great approval, he bound the whole assembly with barbarous rites and the national forms of oath. Envoys were sent to the Canninefates to urge a common policy. This is a tribe which inhabits part of the island, and closely resembles the Batavians in their origin, their language, and their courageous character, but is inferior in numbers. After this he sent messengers to tamper with the British auxiliaries and with the Batavian cohorts, who, as I have before related, had been sent into Germany, and were then stationed at Mogontiacum. Among the Canninefates there was a certain Brinno, a man of a certain stolid bravery and of distinguished birth. His father, after venturing on many acts of hostility, had scorned with impunity the ridiculous expedition of Caligula. His very name, the name of a family of rebels, made him popular. Raised aloft on a shield after the national fashion, and balanced on the shoulders of the bearers, he was chosen general. Immediately summoning to arms the Frisii, a tribe of the further bank of the Rhine, he assailed by sea the winter quarters of two cohorts, which was the nearest point to attack. The soldiers had not anticipated the assault of the enemy; even had they done so, they had not strength to repulse it. Thus the camp was taken and plundered. Then the enemy fell upon the sutlers and Roman traders, who were wandering about in every direction, as they would in a time of peace. At the same time they were on the point of destroying the forts, but the prefects of the cohorts, seeing that they could not hold them, set them on fire. The standards, the colours, and what soldiers there were, concentrated themselves in the upper part of the island under the command of Aquilius,

a centurion of the first rank, an army in name rather than in strength. Vitellius in fact, after withdrawing the effective troops from the cohorts, had loaded with arms a crowd of idlers from the neighbouring villages of the Nervii and the Germans.

16. Civilis, thinking that he must proceed by craft, actually blamed the prefects for having deserted the forts, saying that he would himself, with the cohort under his command, quell the disturbance among the Canninefates, and that they had better return to their respective winter quarters. In was evident, however, that there was some treacherous design beneath this advice, that the cohorts would be dispersed only to be more easily crushed, and that the guiding hand in the war was not Brinno but Civilis; for indications of the truth, which the Germans, a people who delight in war, could not long conceal, were gradually coming to light. When stratagem proved ineffectual, he resorted to force, arranging in distinct columns the Canninefates, the Batavians, and the Frisii. The Roman army was drawn up to meet them not far from the river Rhine, and the ships, which, after burning the forts, they had stranded at that point, were arranged so as to front the enemy. Before the struggle had lasted long, a cohort of Tungrians carried over their standards to Civilis. The other troops, paralysed by the unexpected desertion, were cut down alike by friends and foes. In the fleet there was the same treachery. Some of the rowers were Batavians, and they hindered the operations of the sailors and combatants by an apparent want of skill; then they began to back water, and to run the sterns on to the hostile shore. At last they killed the pilots and centurions, unless these were willing to join them. The end was that the whole fleet of four and twenty vessels either deserted or was taken.

17. For the moment this was a brilliant success, and it had its use for the future. They possessed themselves of some arms and some vessels, both of which they wanted, while they became very famous throughout Germany as the champions of liberty. The tribes of Germany immediately sent envoys with offers of troops. The co-operation of Gaul Civilis endeavoured to secure by politic liberality, sending

back to their respective states the captured prefects of cohorts, and giving permission to their men to go or stay as
they preferred. He offered to those who stayed service on
honourable terms, to those who departed the spoils of the
Roman army. At the same time he reminded them in confidential conversations of the wrongs which they had endured for so many years, while they falsely gave to a
wretched slavery the name of peace. "The Batavians," he
said, "though free of tribute, have yet taken up arms against
our common masters. In the first conflict the soldiers of
Rome have been routed and vanquished. What will be the
result if Gaul throws off the yoke? What strength is there
yet left in Italy? It is by the blood of the provinces that the
provinces are conquered. Think not of how it fared with the
armies of Vindex. It was by Batavian cavalry that the Ædui
and the Arverni were trampled down, and among the auxiliaries of Verginius there were found Belgian troops. To
those who will estimate the matter aright it is evident that
Gaul fell by her own strength. But now all are on the same
side, and we have whatever remnant of military vigour still
flourished in the camps of Rome. With us too are the veteran cohorts to which the legions of Otho lately succumbed.
Let Syria, Asia Minor, and the East, habituated as it is to
despotism, submit to slavery; there are many yet alive in
Gaul who were born before the days of tribute. It was only
lately indeed that Quintilius Varus was slain, and slavery
driven out of Germany. And the Emperor who was challenged by that war was not a Vitellius, but a Cæsar Augustus. Freedom is a gift bestowed by nature even on the
dumb animals. Courage is the peculiar excellence of man, and
the Gods help the braver side. Let us then, who are free to
act and vigorous, fall on a distracted and exhausted enemy.
While some are supporting Vespasian, and others Vitellius,
opportunities are opening up for acting against both."

18. Civilis, bent on winning Gaul and Germany if his purposes should prosper, was on the point of securing supremacy over the most powerful and most wealthy of the states.
His first attempts Hordeonius Flaccus had encouraged by
affecting ignorance. But when messengers came hurrying in
with intelligence that a camp had been stormed, that cohorts

had been cut to pieces, and that the Roman power had been expelled from the island of the Batavians, the general ordered the legate, Munius Lupercus, who was in command of the winter quarters of two legions, to advance against the enemy. Lupercus in great haste threw across the Rhine such legionaries as were on the spot, some Ubian troops who were close at hand, and some cavalry of the Treveri, who were stationed at no great distance; these were accompanied by some Batavian horse, who, though they had been long disaffected, yet still simulated loyalty in order that by betraying the Romans in the moment of actual conflict they might receive a higher price for their desertion. Civilis, surrounding himself with the standards of the captured cohorts, to keep their recent honours before the eyes of his own men, and to terrify the enemy by the remembrance of defeat, now directed his own mother and sisters, and the wives and children of all his men, to stand in the rear, where they might encourage to victory, or shame defeat. The war-song of the men, and the shrill cries of the women, rose from the whole line, and an answering but far less vigorous cheer, came from the legions and auxiliaries. The Batavians had exposed the left wing by their desertion, and they immediately turned against our men. Still the legionaries, though their position was alarming, kept their arms and their ranks. The auxiliaries of the Ubii and the Treveri broke at once in shameful flight, and dispersed over the whole country. On that side the Germans threw the weight of their attack. Meanwhile the legions had an opportunity of retreating into what was called the Old Camp. Claudius Labeo, prefect of the Batavian horse, who had been the rival of Civilis in some local contest, was sent away into the country of the Frisii; to kill him might be to give offence to his countrymen, while to keep him with the army might be to sow the seeds of discord.

19. About the same time the messenger despatched by Civilis came up with the cohorts of the Batavians and the Canninefates, while by the orders of Vitellius they were advancing towards Rome. At once, inflated with pride and haughtiness, they demanded, by way of remuneration for their march, a donative, double pay, and an increase in the

number of cavalry, things indeed which Vitellius had promised, but which they now asked, not with the thought of obtaining them, but as a pretext for mutiny. Flaccus, by his
many concessions, had produced no other effect but to make
them insist with more energy on what they knew he must
refuse. Treating him with contempt, they made their way
towards Lower Germany, to join Civilis. Hordeonius, assembling the tribunes and centurions, asked their opinion as
to whether he should use coercion with those who refused
obedience. Soon, yielding to his natural timidity and to the
alarm of his officers, who were troubled by the suspicious
temper of the auxiliaries and by the fact that the ranks of
the legions had been recruited by a hurried conscription, he
resolved to confine his troops to the camp. Then, repenting
of his resolve, and finding that the very men who had advised it now disapproved it, he seemed bent on pursuing the
enemy, and wrote to Herennius Gallus, legate of the first
legion, who was then holding Bonna, that he was to prevent
the Batavians from crossing the Rhine, and that he would
himself hang on their rear with his army. They might have
been crushed, if Hordeonius, moving from one side, and
Gallus from the other, had enclosed them between their
armies. But Flaccus abandoned his purpose, and, in other
despatches to Gallus, recommended him not to threaten the
departing foe. Thence arose a suspicion that the war was
being kindled with the consent of the legates, and that everything which had happened, or was apprehended, was due,
not to the cowardice of the troops, or to the strength of the
enemy, but to the treachery of the generals.

20. When the Batavians were near the camp at Bonna,
they sent on before them delegates, commissioned to deliver
to Herennius Gallus a message from the cohorts. It was to
this effect: "We have no quarrel with the Romans, for whom
we have so often fought. Wearied with a protracted and
fruitless service, we long for our native land and for rest.
If no one oppose us, our march will be harmless, but if an
armed force encounter us, we will make a way with the
sword." The soldiers prevailed upon the hesitating legate to
risk the chances of a battle. Three thousand legionaries,
some raw Belgian cohorts, and with them a mob of rustics

and camp-followers, cowardly, but bold of speech before the moment of danger, rushed out of all the gates, thinking to surround the Batavians, who were inferior in number. But the enemy, being veteran troops, formed in columns, presenting on every side a dense array, with front, flanks, and rear secure. Thus they were able to break the thin line of our soldiers. The Belgians giving way, the legion was driven back, retreating in confusion on the entrenchments and the gates. It was there that the greatest slaughter took place. The trenches were heaped up with corpses. Nor was it only from the deadly blows of the enemy that they suffered; many perished in the crush and by their own weapons. The victorious army, who avoided the Colonia Agrippinensis, did not venture on any other hostile act during the remainder of their march, and excused the conflict at Bonna, alleging that they had asked for peace, and that when it was refused they had but looked to their own safety.

21. Civilis, who now on the arrival of these veteran cohorts was at the head of a complete army, but who was undecided in his plans, and still reflected on the power of Rome, made all who were with him swear allegiance to Vespasian, and sent envoys to the two legions which after their defeat in the previous engagement had retreated into the Old Camp, advising them to accept the same allegiance. Their reply was: "We do not follow the advice of traitors or enemies. Vitellius is our Emperor; to him we will retain our fealty and devote our swords till our last breath. Then let not a Batavian refugee affect to decide the destinies of Rome; let him rather await the merited penalty of his guilt." When this reply was delivered to Civilis, he was furious with anger, and hurried the whole Batavian nation into open war. The Bructeri and the Tencteri joined him, and messengers summoned all Germany to share in his plunder and his glory.

22. To meet the threatened dangers of the gathering war, the legates of the legions, Munius Lupercus and Numisius Rufus, strengthened their entrenchments and walls. The buildings, which during a long period of peace had grown up like a town near the camp, were destroyed, lest they might be useful to the enemy. Little care, however, was taken

about the conveyance of supplies into the camp. These the generals allowed to be plundered; and so, what might long have sufficed for their necessities, was wantonly wasted in a few days. Civilis, who occupied the centre of the army with the *élite* of the Batavian troops, wishing to add a new terror to his demonstration, covered both banks of the Rhine with columns of his German allies, while his cavalry galloped about the plains. At the same time the fleet was moved up the stream. Here were the standards of the veteran cohorts; there the images of wild beasts, brought out of the woods and sacred groves, under the various forms which each tribe is used to follow into battle, and these mingled emblems of civil and of foreign warfare utterly confounded the besieged. The extent of the entrenchment raised the hopes of the besiegers. Constructed for two legions, it was now held by not more than five thousand Roman soldiers. But there was with them a great number of camp-followers, who had assembled there on the disturbance of peace, and who could be employed in the contest.

23. Part of the camp occupied the gentle slope of a hill; to part was a level approach. By this encampment Augustus had thought the German tribes might be watched and checked; never had he contemplated such a pitch of disaster, as that these tribes should themselves advance to attack our legions. Hence no laubour was bestowed on the ground or on the defences. Our valour and our arms seemed defence enough. The Batavians and the Transrhenane tribes took up their position, each tribe by itself, to distinguish and so the better to display the valour of each; first annoying us by a distant volley; then, as they found that very many of their missiles fixed themselves harmlessly in the turrets and battlements of the walls, and they themselves suffered from the stones showered down on them, they fell on the entrenchment with a shout and furious rush, many placing their scaling-ladders against the ramparts, and others mounting on a testudo formed by their comrades. Some were in the act of climbing over when they were thrust down by the swords of the enemy, and fell overwhelmed by a storm of javelins and stakes. Always very daring at first and excessively elated by success, they now in their eagerness for

plunder bore up against reverse. They also ventured to use what to them was a novelty, engines of war; they had themselves no skill in handling them, but the prisoners and deserters taught them to pile up timber in the shape of a bridge, under which they put wheels, and so propelled it, some standing on the top, and fighting as they would from an earth-work, others concealing themselves within and undermining the walls. But the stones thrown by the catapults prostrated the ill-constructed fabric, and when they set themselves to prepare hurdles and mantlets, burning spears were thrown on them by the engines, fire being thus actually used against the assailants. At last, despairing of success by force, they changed their plans, and resolved to wait, for they were well aware that only a few days' provisions were in the camp, and that there was a great crowd of non-combatants; and they counted at the same time on the treachery that might follow on scarcity, on the wavering fidelity of the slaves, and on the chances of war.

24. Meanwhile Flaccus, who had heard of the siege of the camp, and had sent into all parts of Gaul to collect auxiliaries, put under command of Dillius Vocula, legate of the 18th legion, some troops picked from the legions with orders to hasten by forced marches along the banks of the Rhine. Flaccus himself, who was weak in health and disliked by his troops, travelled with the fleet. The troops indeed complained in unmistakeable language that their general had despatched the Batavian cohorts from Mogontiacum, had feigned ignorance of the plans of Civilis, and was inviting the German tribes to join the league. "This," they said, "has strengthened Vespasian no less than the exertions of Primus Antonius and Mucianus. Declared enmity and hostility may be openly repulsed, but treachery and fraud work in darkness, and so cannot be avoided. Civilis stands in arms against us, and arranges the order of his battle; Hordeonius from his chamber or his litter gives such orders as may best serve the enemy. The swords of thousands of brave men are directed by one old man's sick caprice. How much better by slaying the traitor, to set free our valour and our fortune from these evil auspices!" The passions already kindled by the language which they thus held among themselves were

yet more inflamed by a despatch from Vespasian, which
Flaccus, finding that it could not be concealed, read before
an assembly of the troops, sending the persons who had
brought it in chains to Vitellius.

25. With feelings somewhat appeased, they arrived at
Bonna, the winter-camp of the first legion. The troops there
were even more enraged against Hordeonius, and laid on him
the blame of the late disaster. They said that it was by his
orders that they had offered battle to the Batavians, supposing that the legions from Mogontiacum were following
them; that it was through his treachery that they had been
slaughtered, no reinforcements coming up; that all these
events were unknown to the other legions, and were not told
to their Emperor, though the sudden outburst of treason
might have been crushed by the prompt action of so many
provinces. Hordeonius read to the army copies of all the letters which he had sent about Gaul, begging for reinforcements, and established as a precedent a most disgraceful
practice, namely, the handing over the despatches to the
standard-bearers of the legions, through whose means they
were read by the soldiers sooner than by the generals. He
then ordered one of the mutineers to be put in irons, more
for the sake of asserting his authority than because any one
man was in fault. The army was then moved from Bonna to
the Colonia Agrippinensis, while auxiliaries from Gaul continued to flow in; for at first that nation zealously supported
the cause of Rome. Soon indeed as the Germans increased in
power, many of the states took up arms against us, moved
by the hope of freedom and, could they once shake off the
yoke, even by the lust of empire. The irritation of the legions still increased, nor had the imprisonment of a single
soldier struck them with terror. This fellow indeed actually
charged the general with complicity; he had, he said, acted
as a messenger between Civilis and Flaccus, and because he
might tell the truth he was now being crushed under a false
charge. With wonderful firmness Vocula ascended the tribunal, and ordered the man who had been seized by the
lictors, and was loudly remonstrating, to be led off to execution. All the best men acquiesced in the order, while the ill-
affected were struck with terror. Then, as all with common

consent demanded that Vocula should be their general, Hordeonius handed over to him the supreme command.

26. But there were many things to exasperate the already
divided feelings of the soldiery. Pay and provisions were
scanty, Gaul was rebelling against conscription and taxes,
while the Rhine, owing to a drought unexampled in that climate, would hardly admit of navigation, and thus supplies
were straitened at the same time that outposts had to be
established along the entire bank to keep the Germans from
fording the stream; the self-same cause thus bringing about
a smaller supply of grain and a greater number of con-
sumers. Among ignorant persons the very failure of the
stream was regarded as a prodigy, as if the very rivers, the
old defences of the Empire, were deserting us. What, in
peace, would have seemed chance or nature, was now spoken
of as destiny and the anger of heaven. As the army entered
Novesium the sixteenth legion joined it; Herennius Gallus,
its legate, was associated with Vocula in the responsibilities
of command. As they did not venture to advance upon the
enemy, they constructed a camp at a place called Gelduba.
Here the generals sought to give steadiness to the troops by
such exercises as forming in order of battle, constructing
fortifications, making entrenchments, and whatever else
might train them for war. In the hope that they might be
fired to courage by the delights of plunder, Vocula led the
army against the nearest villages of the Gugerni, who had
accepted the alliance of Civilis. Some of the troops remained
permanently with Herennius Gallus.

27. One day it happened that at no great distance from
the camp the Germans were endeavouring to drag off to their
own bank a vessel laden with corn, which had run aground
in the shallows. Gallus could not endure this, and sent a cohort to help. The numbers of the Germans also increased;
as fresh troops continued to join both sides, a regular battle
ensued. The Germans, besides inflicting great loss on our
men, carried off the vessel. The vanquished troops, following
what had become a regular practice, laid the blame not on
their own cowardice, but on supposed treachery in the legate. Dragged out of his tent, his garments torn, and his person severely beaten, he was commanded to declare for what

bribe and with what accomplices he had betrayed the army. Their old hatred of Hordeonius reappeared. He, they declared, was the instigator of the crime, Gallus his tool. At last, utterly terrified by their threats of instant death, the legate himself charged Hordeonius with treachery. He was then put in irons, and only released on the arrival of Vocula, who the next day inflicted capital punishment on the ringleaders of the mutiny; such wide extremes of license and of subordination were to be found in that army. The common soldiers were undoubtedly loyal to Vitellius, but all the most distinguished men were in favour of Vespasian. The result was an alternation of outbreaks and executions, and a strange mixture of obedience and frenzy, which made it impossible to restrain the men whom it was yet possible to punish.

28. Meanwhile all Germany was raising the power of Civilis by vast additions of strength, and the alliance was secured by hostages of the noblest rank. He directed that the territories of the Ubii and the Treveri should be ravaged by the several tribes on which they bordered, and that another detachment should cross the river Mosa, to threaten the Menapii and the Morini and the frontiers of Gaul. In both quarters plunder was collected; with peculiar hostility in the case of the Ubii, because this nation, being of German origin, had forsworn its native country, and assumed the Roman name of the Agrippinenses. Their cohorts were cut up at the village of Marcodurum, where they lay in careless security, presuming on their distance from the river-bank. The Ubii did not remain quiet, but made predatory excursions into Germany, escaping at first with impunity, though they were afterwards cut off. Throughout the whole of this war, they were more loyal than fortunate. Civilis, grown more formidable now that the Ubii had been crushed, and elated by the success of his operations, pressed on the siege of the legions, keeping a strict watch to prevent any secret intelligence of advancing succours from reaching them. He entrusted to the Batavians the care of the machines and the vast siege works, and when the Transrhenane tribes clamoured for battle, he bade them go and cut through the ramparts, and, if repulsed, renew the struggle; their numbers

were superfluously large, and their loss was not felt. Even darkness did not terminate the struggle.

29. Piling up logs of wood round the walls and lighting them, they sat feasting, and rushed to the conflict, as each grew heated with wine, with a useless daring. Their missiles were discharged without effect in the darkness, but to the Romans the ranks of the barbarians were plainly discernible, and they singled out with deliberate aim anyone whose boldness or whose decorations made him conspicuous. Civilis saw this, and, extinguishing the fires, threw the confusion of darkness over the attack. Then ensued a scene of discordant clamour, of accident, and uncertainty, where no one could see how to aim or to avoid a blow. Wherever a shout was heard, they wheeled round and strained hand and foot. Valour was of no avail, accident disturbed every plan, and the bravest frequently were struck down by the missiles of the coward. The Germans fought with inconsiderate fury; our men, more alive to the danger, threw, but not at random, stakes shod with iron and heavy stones. Where the noise of the assailants was heard, or where the ladders placed against the walls brought the enemy within reach of their hands, they pushed them back with their shields, and followed them with their javelins. Many, who had struggled on to the walls, they stabbed with their short swords. After a night thus spent, day revealed a new method of attack.

30. The Batavians had raised a tower two stories high, which they brought up to the Prætorian gate of the camp, where the ground was most level. But our men, pushing forward strong poles, and battering it with beams, broke it down, causing great destruction among the combatants on the top. The enemy were attacked in their confusion by a sudden and successful sally. All this time many engines were constructed by the legionaries, who were superior to the enemy in experience and skill. Peculiar consternation was caused by a machine, which, being poised in the air over the heads of the enemy, suddenly descended, and carried up one or more of them past the faces of their friends, and then, by a shifting of the weights, projected them within the limits of the camp. Civilis, giving up all hope of a successful assault, again sat down to blockade the camp at his leisure

and undermined the fidelity of the legions by the promises
of his emissaries.

31. All these events in Germany took place before the
battle of Cremona, the result of which was announced in a
despatch from Antonius, accompanied by Cæcina's proclamation. Alpinius Montanus, prefect of a cohort in the vanquished army, was on the spot, and acknowledged the fate
of his party. Various were the emotions thus excited; the
Gallic auxiliaries, who felt neither affection nor hatred towards either party, and who served without attachment, at
once, at the instance of their prefects, deserted Vitellius. The
veteran soldiers hesitated. Nevertheless, when Hordeonius
administered the oath, under a strong pressure from their
tribunes, they pronounced the words, which their looks and
their temper belied, and, while they adopted every other expression, they hesitated at the name of Vespasian, passing it
over with a slight murmur, and not unfrequently in absolute
silence.

32. After this, certain letters from Antonius to Civilis
were read in full assembly, and provoked the suspicions of
the soldiery, as they seemed to be addressed to a partisan
of the cause and to be unfriendly to the army of Germany.
Soon the news reached the camp at Gelduba, and the same
language and the same acts were repeated. Montanus was
sent with a message to Civilis, bidding him desist from hostilities, and not seek to conceal the designs of an enemy by
fighting under false colours, and telling him that, if he had
been attempting to assist Vespasian, his purpose had been
fully accomplished. Civilis at first replied in artful language,
but soon perceiving that Montanus was a man of singularly
high spirit and was himself disposed for change, he began
with lamenting the perils through which he had struggled
for five-and-twenty years in the camps of Rome. "It is,"
he said, "a noble reward that I have received for my toils;
my brother murdered, myself imprisoned, and the savage
clamour of this army, a clamour which demanded my execution, and for which by the law of nations I demand vengeance. You, Treveri, and other enslaved creatures, what reward do you expect for the blood which you have shed so
often? What but a hateful service, perpetual tribute, the

rod, the axe, and the passions of a ruling race? See how I, the prefect of a single cohort, with the Batavians and the Canninefates, a mere fraction of Gaul, have destroyed their vast but useless camps, or are pressing them with the close blockade of famine and the sword. In a word, either freedom will follow on our efforts, or, if we are vanquished, we shall but be what we were before." Having thus fired the man's ambition, Civilis dismissed him, but bade him carry back a milder answer. He returned, pretending to have failed in his mission, but not revealing the other facts; these indeed soon came to light.

33. Civilis, retaining a part of his forces, sent the veteran cohorts and the bravest of his German troops against Vocula and his army, under the command of Julius Maximus and Claudius Victor, his sister's son. On their march they plundered the winter camp of a body of horse stationed at Ascibergium, and they fell on Vocula's camp so unexpectedly that he could neither harangue his army, nor even get it into line. All that he could do in the confusion was to order the veteran troops to strengthen the centre. The auxiliaries were dispersed in every part of the field. The cavalry charged, but, received by the orderly array of the enemy, fled to their own lines. What ensued was a massacre rather than a battle. The Nervian infantry, from panic or from treachery, exposed the flank of our army. Thus the attack fell upon the legions, who had lost their standards and were being cut down within the entrenchments, when the fortune of the day was suddenly changed by a reinforcement of fresh troops. Some Vascon infantry, levied by Galba, which had by this time been sent for, heard the noise of the combatants as they approached the camp, attacked the rear of the preoccupied enemy, and spread a panic more than proportionate to their numbers, some believing that all the troops from Novesium, others that all from Mogontiacum, had come up. This delusion restored the courage of the Romans, and in relying on the strength of others they recovered their own. All the bravest of the Batavians, of the infantry at least, fell, but the cavalry escaped with the standards and with the prisoners whom they had secured in the early part of the engagement. Of the slain on that day the greater number be-

longed to our army, but to its less effective part. The Germans lost the flower of their force.

34. The two generals were equally blameworthy; they deserved defeat, they did not make the most of success. Had Civilis given battle in greater force, he could not have been outflanked by so small a number of cohorts, and he might have destroyed the camp after once forcing an entrance. As for Vocula, he did not reconnoitre the advancing enemy, and consequently he was vanquished as soon as he left the camp; and then, mistrusting his victory, he fruitlessly wasted several days before marching against the enemy, though, had he at once resolved to drive them back, and to follow up his success, he might, by one and the same movement, have raised the siege of the legions. Meanwhile Civilis had tried to work on the feelings of the besieged by representing that with the Romans all was lost, and that victory had declared for his own troops. The standards and colours were carried round the ramparts, and the prisoners also were displayed. One of them, with noble daring, declared the real truth in a loud voice, and, as he was cut down on the spot by the Germans, all the more confidence was felt in his information. At the same time it was becoming evident, from the devastation of the country and from the flames of burning houses, that the victorious army was approaching. Vocula issued orders that the standards should be planted within sight of the camp, and should be surrounded with a ditch and rampart, where his men might deposit their knapsacks, and so fight without encumbrance. On this, the General was assailed by a clamorous demand for instant battle. They had now grown used to threaten. Without even taking time to form into line, disordered and weary as they were, they commenced the action. Civilis was on the field, trusting quite as much to the faults of his adversaries as to the valour of his own troops. With the Romans the fortune of the day varied, and the most violently mutinous shewed themselves cowards. But some, remembering their recent victory, stood their ground and struck fiercely at the foe, now encouraging each other and their neighbours, and now, while they re-formed their lines, imploring the besieged not to lose the opportunity. These latter, who saw everything from the walls, sallied

out from every gate. It so happened that Civilis was thrown
to the ground by the fall of his horse. A report that he had
been either wounded or slain gained belief throughout both
armies, and spread incredible panic among his own troops,
and gave as great encouragement to their opponents. But
Vocula, leaving the flying foe, began to strengthen the rampart and the towers of the camp, as if another siege were
imminent. He had misused success so often that he was
rightly suspected of a preference for war.

35. Nothing distressed our troops so much as the scarcity
of supplies. The baggage of the legions was therefore sent
to Novesium with a crowd of non-combatants to fetch corn
from that place overland, for the enemy commanded the
river. The march of the first body was accomplished in security, as Civilis had not yet recovered. But when he heard
that officers of the commissariat had been again sent to
Novesium, and that the infantry detached as an escort were
advancing just as if it was a time of profound peace. with
but few soldiers round the standards, the arms stowed away
in the wagons, and all wandering about at their pleasure, he
attacked them in regular form, having first sent on troops to
occupy the bridges and the defiles in the road. The battle
extended over a long line of march, lasting with varying success till night parted the combatants. The infantry pushed
on to Gelduba, while the camp remained in the same state
as before, garrisoned by such troops as had been left in it.
There could be no doubt what peril a convoy, heavily laden
and panic stricken, would have to encounter in attempting
to return. Vocula added to his force a thousand picked men
from the fifth and fifteenth legions besieged in the Old
Camp, a body of troops undisciplined and ill-affected to
their officers. But more than the number specified came forward, and openly protested, as they marched, that they
would not endure any longer the hardships of famine and the
treachery of the legates. On the other hand, those who had
stayed behind complained that they were being left to their
fate by this withdrawal of a part of the legions. A twofold
mutiny was the result, some calling upon Vocula to come
back, while the others refused to return to the camp.

36. Meanwhile Civilis blockaded the Old Camp. Vocula

retired first to Gelduba, afterwards to Novesium; Civilis took possession of Gelduba, and not long after was victorious in a cavalry engagement near Novesium. But reverses and successes seemed equally to kindle in the troops the one desire of murdering their officers. The legions, increased in number by the arrival of the men from the fifth and fifteenth, demanded a donative, for they had discovered that some money had been sent by Vitellius. After a short delay Hordeonius gave the donative in the name of Vespasian. This, more than anything else, fostered the mutinous spirit. The men, abandoning themselves to debauchery and revelry and all the license of nightly gatherings, revived their old grudge against Hordeonius. Without a single legate or tribune venturing to check them, for the darkness seems to have taken from them all sense of shame, they dragged him out of his bed and killed him. The same fate was intended for Vocula, but he assumed the dress of a slave, and escaped unrecognized in the darkness. When their fury had subsided and their alarm returned, they sent centurions with despatches to the various states of Gaul, imploring help in money and troops.

37. These men, headstrong, cowardly, and spiritless, as a mob without a leader always is, on the approach of Civilis hastily took up arms, and, as hastily abandoning them, betook themselves to flight. Disaster produced disunion, the troops from the Upper army dissociating their cause from that of their comrades. Nevertheless the statues of Vitellius were again set up in the camp and in the neighbouring Belgian towns, and this at a time when Vitellius himself had fallen. Then the men of the 1st, the 4th, and the 18th legions, repenting of their conduct, followed Vocula, and again taking in his presence the oath of allegiance to Vespasian, were marched by him to the relief of Mogontiacum. The besieging army, an heterogeneous mass of Chatti, Usipii, and Mattiaci, had raised the siege, glutted with spoils, but not without suffering loss. Our troops attacked them on the way, dispersed and unprepared. Moreover the Treveri had constructed a breastwork and rampart across their territory, and they and the Germans continued to contend with great losses on both sides up to the time when they tarnished by

rebellion their distinguished services to the Roman people.

38. Meanwhile Vespasian (now consul for the second time) and Titus entered upon their office, both being absent from Rome. People were gloomy and anxious under the pressure of manifold fears, for, over and above immediate perils, they had taken groundless alarm under the impression that Africa was in rebellion through the revolutionary movements of Lucius Piso. He was governor of that province, and was far from being a man of turbulent disposition. The fact was that the wheat-ships were detained by the severity of the weather, and the lower orders, who were accustomed to buy their provisions from day to day, and to whom cheap corn was the sole subject of public interest, feared and believed that the ports had been closed and the supplies stopped, the Vitellianists, who had not yet given up their party feelings, helping to spread the report, which was not displeasing even to the conquerors. Their ambition, which even foreign campaigns could not fill to the full, was not satisfied by any triumphs that civil war could furnish.

39. On the 1st of January, at a meeting of the Senate, convoked for the purpose by Julius Frontinus, prætor of the city, votes of thanks were passed to the legates, to the armies, and to the allied kings. The office of prætor was taken away from Tettius Julianus, as having deserted his legion when it passed over to the party of Vespasian, with a view to its being transferred to Plotius Griphus. Equestrian rank was conferred on Hormus. Then, on the resignation of Frontinus, Cæsar Domitian assumed the office of prætor of the city. His name was put at the head of despatches and edicts, but the real authority was in the hands of Mucianus, with this exception, that Domitian ventured on several acts of power, at the instigation of his friends, or at his own caprice. But Mucianus found his principal cause of apprehension in Primus Antonius and Varus Arrius, who, in the freshness of their fame, while distinguished by great achievements and by the attachment of the soldiery, were also supported by the people, because in no case had they extended their severities beyond the battle-field. It was also reported that Antonius had urged Scribonianus Crassus, whom an illus-trious descent added to the honours of his brother made a

conspicuous person, to assume the supreme power; and it was understood that a number of accomplices would not have failed to support him, had not the proposal been rejected by Scribonianus, who was a man not easily to be tempted even by a certainty, and was proportionately apprehensive of risk. Mucianus, seeing that Antonius could not be openly crushed, heaped many praises upon him in the Senate, and loaded him with promises in secret, holding out as a prize the government of Eastern Spain, then vacant in consequence of the departure of Cluvius Rufus. At the same time he lavished on his friends tribuneships and prefectures; and then, when he had filled the vain heart of the man with hope and ambition, he destroyed his power by sending into winter quarters the 7th legion, whose affection for Antonius was particularly vehement. The 3rd legion, old troops of Varus Arrius, were sent back to Syria. Part of the army was on its way to Germany. Thus all elements of disturbance being removed, the usual appearance of the capital, the laws, and the jurisdiction of the magistrates, were once more restored.

40. Domitian, on the day of his taking his seat in the Senate, made a brief and measured speech in reference to the absence of his father and brother, and to his own youth. He was graceful in his bearing, and, his real character being yet unknown, the frequent blush on his countenance passed for modesty. On his proposing the restoration of the Imperial honours of Galba, Curtius Montanus moved that respect should also be paid to the memory of Piso. The Senate passed both motions, but that which referred to Piso was not carried out. Certain commissioners were then appointed by lot, who were to see to the restitution of property plundered during the war, to examine and restore to their place the brazen tables of the laws, which had fallen down through age, to free the Calendar from the additions with which the adulatory spirit of the time had disfigured it, and to put a check on the public expenditure. The office of prætor was restored to Tettius Julianus, as soon as it was known that he had fled for refuge to Vespasian. Griphus still retained his rank. It was then determined that the cause of Musonius Rufus against Publius Celer should be again brought on.

Publius was condemned, and thus expiation was made to the shade of Soranus. The day thus marked by an example of public justice was not barren of distinction to individuals. Musonius was thought to have fulfilled the righteous duty of an accuser, but men spoke very differently of Demetrius, a disciple of the Cynical school of philosophy, who pleaded the cause of a notorious criminal by appeals to corrupt influences rather than by fair argument. Publius himself, in his peril, had neither spirit nor power of speech left. The signal for vengeance on the informers having been thus given, Junius Mauricus asked Cæsar to give the Senate access to the Imperial registers, from which they might learn what impeachments the several informers had proposed. Cæsar answered, that in a matter of such importance the Emperor must be consulted.

41. The Senate, led by its principal members, then framed a form of oath, which was eagerly taken by all the magistrates and by the other Senators in the order in which they voted. They called the Gods to witness, that nothing had been done by their instrumentality to prejudice the safety of any person, and that they had gained no distinction or advantage by the ruin of Roman citizens. Great was the alarm, and various the devices for altering the words of the oath, among those who felt the consciousness of guilt. The Senate appreciated the scruple, but denounced the perjury. This public censure, as it might be called, fell with especial severity on three men, Sariolenus Vocula, Nonnius Attianus, and Cestius Severus, all of them infamous for having practised the trade of the informer in the days of Nero. Sariolenus indeed laboured under an imputation of recent date. It was said that he had attempted the same practices during the reign of Vitellius. The Senators did not desist from threatening gestures, till he quitted the chamber; then passing to Paccius Africanus, they assailed him in the same way. It was he, they said, who had singled out as victims for Nero the brothers Scribonius, renowned for their mutual affection and for their wealth. Africanus dared not confess his guilt, and could not deny it; but he himself turned on Vibius Crispus, who was pressing him with questions, and complicating a charge which he could not rebut, shifted the

blame from himself by associating another with his guilt.

42. Great was the reputation for brotherly affection, as well as for eloquence, which Vipstanus Messalla earned for himself on that day, by venturing, though not yet of Senatorial age, to plead for his brother Aquilius Regulus. The fall of the families of the Crassi and Orfitus had brought Regulus into the utmost odium. Of his own free will, as it seemed, and while still a mere youth, he had undertaken the prosecution, not to ward off any peril from himself, but in the hope of gaining power. The wife of Crassus, Sulpicia Prætextata, and her four children were ready, should the Senate take cognizance of the cause, to demand vengeance. Accordingly, Messalla, without attempting to defend the case or the person accused, had simply thrown himself in the way of the perils that threatened his brother, and had thus wrought upon the feelings of several Senators. On this Curtius Montanus met him with a fierce speech, in which he went to the length of asserting, that after the death of Galba money had been given by Regulus to the murderer of Piso, and that he had even fastened his teeth in the murdered man's head. "Certainly," he said, "Nero did not compel this act; you did not secure by this piece of barbarity either your rank or your life. We may bear with the defence put forward by men who thought it better to destroy others than to come into peril themselves. As for you, the exile of your father, and the division of his property among his creditors, had left you perfectly safe, besides that your youth incapacitated you for office; there was nothing in you which Nero could either covet or dread. It was from sheer lust of slaughter and greed of gain that you, unknown as you were, you, who had never pleaded in any man's defence, steeped your soul in noble blood, when, though you had snatched from the very grave of your Country the spoils of a man of consular rank, had been fed to the full with seven million sesterces, and shone with all sacerdotal honours, you yet overwhelmed in one common ruin innocent boys, old men of illustrious name, and noble ladies, when you actually blamed the tardy movements of Nero in wearying himself and his informers with the overthrow of single families, and declared that the whole Senate might be destroyed by one word. Keep, Conscript Fathers,

preserve a man of such ready counsels, that every age may
be furnished with its teacher, and that our young men may
imitate Regulus, just as our old men imitate Marcellus and
Crispus. Even unsuccessful villany finds some to emulate it:
what will happen, if it flourish and be strong? And the man,
whom we dare not offend when he holds only quæstor's rank,
are we to see him rise to the dignities of prætor and consul?
Do you suppose that Nero will be the last of the tyrants?
Those who survived Tiberius, those who survived Caligula,
thought the same; and yet after each there arose another
ruler yet more detestable and more cruel. We are not afraid
of Vespasian; the age and moderation of the new Emperor
reassure us. But the influence of an example outlives the
individual character. We have lost our vigour, Conscript
Fathers; we are no longer that Senate, which, when Nero
had fallen, demanded that the informers and ministers of
the tyrant should be punished according to ancient custom.
The first day after the downfall of a wicked Emperor is the
best of opportunities."

43. Montanus was heard with such approval on the part
of the Senate, that Helvidius conceived a hope that Marcellus also might be overthrown. He therefore began with a
panegyric on Cluvius Rufus, who, though not less rich nor
less renowned for eloquence, had never imperilled a single
life in the days of Nero. By this comparison, as well as by
direct accusations, he pressed Eprius hard, and stirred the
indignation of the Senators. When Marcellus perceived this,
he made as if he would leave the House, exclaiming, "We
go, Priscus, and leave you your Senate; act the king, though
Cæsar himself be present." Crispus followed. Both were enraged, but their looks were different; Marcellus cast furious
glances about him, while Crispus smiled. They were drawn
back, however, into the Senate by the hasty interference of
friends. The contest grew fiercer, while the well-disposed
majority on the one side, and a powerful minority on the
other, fought out their obstinate quarrel, and thus the day
was spent in altercation.

44. At the next meeting of the Senate Cæsar began by
recommending that the wrongs, the resentments, and the
terrible necessities of former times, should be forgotten, and

Mucianus spoke at great length in favour of the informers. At the same time he admonished in gentle terms and in a tone of entreaty those who were reviving indictments, which they had before commenced and afterwards dropped. The Senators, when they found themselves opposed, relinquished the liberty which they had begun to exercise. That it might not be thought that the opinion of the Senate was disregarded, or that impunity was accorded to all acts done in the days of Nero, Mucianus sent back to their islands two men of Senatorial rank, Octavius Sagitta and Antistius Sosianus, who had quitted their places of banishment. Octavius had seduced one Pontia Postumia, and, on her refusing to marry him, in the frenzy of passion had murdered her. Sosianus by his depravity had brought many to ruin. Both had been condemned and banished by a solemn decision of the Senate, and, though others were permitted to return, were kept under the same penalty. But this did not mitigate the hatred felt against Mucianus. Sosianus and Sagitta were utterly insignificant, even if they did return; but men dreaded the abilities of the informers, their wealth, and the power which they exercised in many sinister ways.

45. A trial, conducted in the Senate according to ancient precedents, brought into harmony for a time the feelings of its members. Manlius Patruitus, a Senator, laid a complaint, that he had been beaten by a mob in the colony of Sena, and that by order of the magistrates; that the wrong had not stopped here, but that lamentations and wailings, in fact a representation of funeral obsequies, had been enacted in his presence, accompanied with contemptuous and insulting expressions levelled against the whole Senate. The persons accused were summoned to appear, and after the case had been investigated, punishment was inflicted on those who were found guilty. A resolution of the Senate was also passed, recommending more orderly behaviour to the people of Sena. About the same time Antonius Flamma was condemned under the law against extortion, at the suit of the people of Cyrene, and was banished for cruel practices.

46. Amidst all this a mutiny in the army all but broke out. The troops who, having been disbanded by Vitellius, had flocked to support Vespasian, asked leave to serve again in

the Prætorian Guard, and the soldiers who had been selected from the legions with the same prospect now clamoured for their promised pay. Even the Vitellianists could not be got rid of without much bloodshed. But the money required for retaining in the service so vast a body of men was immensely large. Mucianus entered the camp to examine more accurately the individual claims. The victorious army, wearing their proper decorations and arms, he drew up with moderate intervals of space between the divisions; then the Vitellianists, whose capitulation at Bovillæ I have already related, and the other troops of the party, who had been collected from the capital and its neighbourhood, were brought forth almost naked. Mucianus ordered these men to be drawn up apart, making the British, the German, and any other troops that there were belonging to other armies, take up separate positions. The very first view of their situation paralyzed them. They saw opposed to them what seemed a hostile array, threatening them with javelin and sword. They saw themselves hemmed in, without arms, filthy and squalid. And when they began to be separated, some to be marched to one spot, and some to another, a thrill of terror ran through them all. Among the troops from Germany the panic was particularly great; for they believed that this separation marked them out for slaughter. They embraced their fellow-soldiers, clung to their necks, begged for parting kisses, and entreated that they might not be deserted, or doomed in a common cause to suffer a different lot. They invoked now Mucianus, now the absent Emperor, and, as a last resource, heaven and the Gods, till Mucianus came forward, and calling them "soldiers bound by the same oath and servants of the same Emperor," stopped the groundless panic. And indeed the victorious army seconded the tears of the vanquished with their approving shouts. This terminated the proceedings for that day. But when Domitian harangued them a few days afterwards, they received him with increased confidence. The land that was offered them they contemptuously rejected, and begged for regular service and pay. Theirs were prayers indeed, but such as it was impossible to reject. They were therefore received into the Prætorian camp. Then such as had reached the prescribed age, or had served the proper number of campaigns, received an honourable discharge; others were dismissed for misconduct; but this was done by degrees and in detail, always the safest mode of reducing the united strength of a multitude.

47. It is a fact that, whether suggested by real poverty or by a wish to give the appearance of it, a proposition passed the Senate to the effect that a loan of sixty million sesterces from private persons should be accepted. Pompeius Silvanus was appointed to manage the affair. Before long, either the necessity ceased or the pretence was dropped. After this, on the motion of Domitian, the consulships conferred by Vitellius were cancelled, and the honours of a censor's funeral were paid to Sabinus; great lessons both of the mutability of fortune, ever bringing together the highest honours and the lowest humiliations.

48. About the same time the proconsul Lucius Piso was murdered. I shall make the account of this murder as exact as possible by first reviewing a few earlier circumstances, which have a bearing on the origin and motives of such deeds. The legion and the auxiliaries stationed in Africa to guard the frontiers of the Empire were under the proconsul's authority during the reigns of the divine Augustus and Tiberius. But in course of time Caligula, prompted by his restless temper and by his fear of Marcus Silanus, who then held Africa, took away the legion from the proconsul, and handed it over to a legate whom he sent for that purpose. The patronage was equally divided between the two officers. A source of disagreement was thus studiously sought in the continual clashing of their authority, and it was further developed by an unprincipled rivalry. The power of the legates grew through their lengthened tenure of office, and, perhaps, because an inferior feels greater interest in such a competition. All the more distinguished of the proconsuls cared more for security than for power.

49. At this time the legion in Africa was commanded by Valerius Festus, a young man of extravagant habits and immoderate ambition, who was now made uneasy by his relationship to Vitellius. Whether this man in their frequent interviews tempted Piso to revolt, or whether he resisted

such overtures, is not known for certain, for no one was
present at their confidential meetings, and, after Piso's death,
many were disposed to ingratiate themselves with the murderer. There is no doubt that the province and the troops
entertained feelings of hostility to Vespasian, and some of
the Vitellianists, who had escaped from the capital, incessantly represented to Piso that Gaul was hesitating and
Germany ready to revolt, that his own position was perilous,
and that for one who in peace must be suspected war was
the safer course. While this was going on, Claudius Sagitta,
prefect of Petra's Horse, making a very quick passage,
reached Africa before Papirius, the centurion despatched by
Mucianus. He declared that an order to put Piso to death
had been given to the centurion, and that Galerianus, his
cousin and son-in-law, had perished; that his only hope of
safety was in bold action; that in such action two paths
were open; he might defend himself on the spot, or he might
sail for Gaul and offer his services as general to the Vitellianist armies. Piso was wholly unmoved by this statement.
The centurion despatched by Mucianus, on landing in the
port of Carthage, raised his voice, and invoked in succession
all blessings on the head of Piso, as if he were Emperor, and
bade the bystanders, who were astonished by this sudden
and strange proceeding, take up the same cry. The credulous
mob rushed into the market-place, and demanded that Piso
should shew himself. They threw everything into an uproar
with their clamorous shouts of joy, careless of the truth, and
only eager to flatter. Piso, acting on the information of
Sagitta, or, perhaps, from natural modesty, would not make
his appearance in public, or trust himself to the zeal of the
populace. On questioning the centurion, and finding that he
had sought a pretext for accusing and murdering him, he
ordered the man to be executed, moved, not so much by any
hope of saving his life, as by indignation against the assassin; for this fellow had been one of the murderers of Macer,
and was now come to slay the proconsul with hands already
stained with the blood of the legate. He then severely blamed
the people of Carthage in an edict which betrayed his anxiety, and ceased to discharge even the usual duties of his
office, shutting himself up in his palace, to guard against

any casual occurrence that might lead to a new outbreak.

50. But when the agitation of the people, the execution of the centurion, and other news, true or false, exaggerated as usual by report, came to the ears of Festus, he sent some cavalry to put Piso to death. They rode over at full speed, and broke into the dwelling of the proconsul in the dim light of early dawn, with their swords drawn in their hands. Many of them were unacquainted with the person of Piso, for the legate had selected some Moorish and Carthaginian auxiliaries to perpetrate the deed. Near the proconsul's chamber they chanced to meet a slave, and asked him who he was, and where Piso was to be found? The slave with a noble untruth replied, "I am he," and was immediately cut down. Soon after Piso was killed, for there was on the spot one who recognized him, Bæbius Massa, one of the procura- tors of Africa, a name even then fatal to the good, and des- tined often to reappear among the causes of the sufferings which he had ere long to endure. From Adrumetum, where he had stayed to watch the result, Festus went to the legion, and gave orders that Cetronius Pisanus, prefect of the camp, should be put in irons. He did this out of private pique, but he called the man an accomplice of Piso. Some few cen- turions and soldiers he punished, others he rewarded, neither the one nor the other deservedly, but he wished men to be- lieve that he had extinguished a war. He then put an end to a quarrel between the Œenses and the Leptitani, which, originating in robberies of corn and cattle by two rustic populations, had grown from this insignificant beginning till it was carried on in pitched battles. The people of Œea, who were inferior in numbers, had summoned to their aid the Garamantes, a wild race incessantly occupied in robbing their neighbours. This had brought the Leptitani to extremi- ties; their territories had been ravaged far and wide, and they were trembling within their walls, when the Garamantes were put to flight by the arrival of the auxiliary infantry and cavalry, and the whole of the booty was recaptured, with the exception of some which the plunderers, in their wanderings through inaccessible hamlets, had sold to more distant tribes.

51. Vespasian had heard of the victory of Cremona, and

had received favourable tidings from all quarters, and he was now informed of the fall of Vitellius by many persons of every rank, who, with a good fortune equal to their courage, risked the perils of the wintry sea. Envoys had come from king Vologesus to offer him 40,000 Parthian cavalry. It was a matter of pride and joy to him to be courted with such splendid offers of help from the allies, and not to want them. He thanked Vologesus, and recommended him to send ambassadors to the Senate, and to learn for himself that peace had been restored. While his thoughts were fixed on Italy and on the state of the capital, he heard an unfavourable account of Domitian, which represented him as overstepping the limits of his age and the privileges of a son. He therefore entrusted Titus with the main strength of the army to complete what had yet to be done in the Jewish war.

52. It was said that Titus before his departure had a long interview with his father, in which he implored him not to let himself be easily excited by the reports of slanderers, but to shew an impartial and forgiving temper towards his son. "Legions and fleets," he reminded him, "are not such sure bulwarks of Imperial power as a numerous family. As for friends, time, altered fortunes, perhaps their passions or their errors, may weaken, may change, may even destroy, their affection. A man's own race can never be dissociated from him, least of all with Princes, whose prosperity is shared by others, while their reverses touch but their nearest kin. Even between brothers there can be no lasting affection, except the father sets the example." Vespasian, delighted with the brotherly affection of Titus rather than reconciled to Domitian, bade his son be of good cheer, and aggrandise the State by war and deeds of arms. He would himself provide for the interests of peace, and for the welfare of his family. He then had some of the swiftest vessels laden with corn, and committed them to the perils of the still stormy sea. Rome indeed was in the very critical position of not having more than ten days' consumption in the granaries, when the supplies from Vespasian arrived.

53. The work of rebuilding the Capitol was assigned by him to Lucius Vestinius, a man of the Equestrian order.

who, however, for high character and reputation ranked
among the nobles. The soothsayers whom he assembled directed that the remains of the old shrine should be removed
to the marshes, and the new temple raised on the original
site. The Gods, they said, forbade the old form to be
changed. On the 21st of June, beneath a cloudless sky, the
entire space devoted to the sacred enclosure was encom-
passed with chaplets and garlands. Soldiers, who bore auspicious names, entered the precincts with sacred boughs.
Then the vestal virgins, with a troop of boys and girls,
whose fathers and mothers were still living, sprinkled the
whole space with water drawn from the fountains and rivers.
After this, Helvidius Priscus, the prætor, first purified the
spot with the usual sacrifice of a sow, a sheep, and a bull,
and duly placed the entrails on turf; then, in terms dictated
by Publius Ælianus, the high-priest, besought Jupiter, Juno,
Minerva, and the tutelary deities of the place, to prosper the
undertaking, and to lend their divine help to raise the abodes
which the piety of men had founded for them. He then
touched the wreaths, which were wound round the foundation stone and entwined with the ropes, while at the same
moment all the other magistrates of the State, the Priests,
the Senators, the Knights, and a number of the citizens,
with zeal and joy uniting their efforts, dragged the huge
stone along. Contributions of gold and silver and virgin
ores, never smelted in the furnace, but still in their natural
state, were showered on the foundations. The soothsayers
had previously directed that no stone or gold which had
been intended for any other purpose should profane the
work. Additional height was given to the structure; this was
the only variation which religion would permit, and the one
feature which had been thought wanting in the splendour
of the old temple.

54. Meanwhile the tidings of the death of Vitellius, spreading through Gaul and Germany, had caused a second war.
Civilis had thrown aside all disguise, and was now openly
assailing the Roman power, while the legions of Vitellius
preferred even a foreign yoke to the rule of Vespasian. Gaul
had gathered fresh courage from the belief that the fortunes
of our armies had been everywhere disastrous; for a report

was rife that our winter camps in Mœsia and Pannonia were hemmed in by the Sarmatians and Dacians. Rumours equally false were circulated respecting Britain. Above all, the conflagration of the Capitol had made them believe that the end of the Roman Empire was at hand. The Gauls, they remembered, had captured the city in former days, but, as the abode of Jupiter was uninjured, the Empire had survived; whereas now the Druids declared, with the prophetic utterances of an idle superstition, that this fatal conflagration was a sign of the anger of heaven, and portended universal empire for the Transalpine nations. A rumour had also gone forth that the chiefs of Gaul, whom Otho had sent against Vitellius, had, before their departure, bound themselves by a compact not to fail the cause of freedom, should the power of Rome be broken by a continuous succession of civil wars and internal calamities.

55. Before the murder of Flaccus Hordeonius nothing had come out by which any conspiracy could be discovered. After his death, messengers passed to and fro between Civilis and Classicus, commander of the cavalry of the Treveri. Classicus was first among his countrymen in rank and wealth; he was of a royal house, of a race distinguished both in peace and war, and he himself claimed to be by family tradition the foe rather than the ally of the Romans. Julius Tutor and Julius Sabinus joined him in his schemes. One was a Trever, the other a Lingon. Tutor had been made by Vitellius guardian of the banks of the Rhine. Sabinus, over and above his natural vanity, was inflamed with the pride of an imaginary descent, for he asserted that his great-grandmother had, by her personal charms, attracted the admiration of the divine Julius, when he was campaigning in Gaul. These two men held secret conferences to sound the views of the rest of their countrymen, and when they had secured as accomplices such as they thought suitable for their purpose, they met together in a private house in the Colonia Agrippinensis; for the State in its public policy was strongly opposed to all such attempts. Some, however, of the Ubii and Tungri were present, but the Treveri and Lingones had the greatest weight in the matter. Nor could they endure the delay of deliberation; they rivalled each other in

vehement assertions that the Romans were in a frenzy of discord, that their legions had been cut to pieces, that Italy was laid waste, that Rome itself was at that very moment undergoing capture, while all her armies were occupied by wars of their own. If they were but to secure the passes of the Alps with bodies of troops, Gaul, with her own freedom firmly established, might look about her, and fix the limits of her dominion.

56. These views were no sooner stated than approved. As to the survivors of the Vitellianist army, they doubted what to do; many voted for putting to death men so turbulent and faithless, stained too with the blood of their generals. Still the policy of mercy prevailed. To cut off all hope of quarter might provoke an obstinate resistance. It would be better to draw them into friendly union. If only the legates of the legions were put to death, the remaining multitude, moved by the consciousness of guilt and the hope of escape, would readily join their cause. Such was the outline of their original plan. Emissaries were likewise despatched through-out Gaul to stir up war, while they themselves feigned sub-mission, that they might be the better able to crush the un-suspecting Vocula. Persons, however, were found to convey information to him, but he had not sufficient strength to suppress the movement, as the legions were incomplete in numbers and disloyal. So, what with soldiers of doubtful fidelity and secret enemies, he thought it best, under the circumstances, to make his way by meeting deceit with de-ceit, and by using the same arts with which he was himself assailed. He therefore went down to the Colonia Agrippinen-sis. Thither Claudius Labeo, who, as I have related, had been taken prisoner and sent out of the province into the country of the Frisii, made his escape by bribing his gaolers. This man undertook, if a force were given him, to enter the Batavian territory and bring back to the Roman alliance the more influential part of that State; but, though he ob-tained a small force of infantry and cavalry, he did not venture to attempt anything among the Batavi, but only induced some of the Nervii and Betasii to take up arms, and made continual attacks on the Canninefates and the Marsaci more in the way of robbery than of war.

57. Lured on by the treacherous representations of the Gauls, Vocula marched against the enemy. He was near the Old Camp, when Classicus and Tutor, who had gone on in advance under the pretence of reconnoitring, concluded an agreement with the German chiefs. They then for the first time separated themselves from the legions, and formed a camp of their own, with a separate line of entrenchment, while Vocula protested that the power of Rome was not so utterly shaken by civil war as to have become contempti- ble even to Treveri and Lingones. "There are still," he said, "faithful provinces, victorious armies, the fortune of the Empire, and avenging Gods. Thus it was that Sacrovir and the Ædui in former days, Vindex and the Gauls in more recent times, were crushed in a single battle. The breakers of treaties may look for the vengeance of the same Deities, and the same doom. Julius and Augustus understood far better the character of the people. Galba's policy and the diminution of their tribute have inspired them with hostile feelings. They are now enemies, because their yoke is easy; when they have been plundered and stripped, they will be friends." After uttering this defiance, finding that Classicus and Tutor persisted in their treachery, he changed his line of march, and retired to Novesium. The Gauls encamped at a distance of two miles, and plied with bribes the cen- turions and soldiers who visited them there, striving to make a Roman army commit the unheard-of baseness of swearing allegiance to foreigners, and pledge itself to the perpetration of this atrocious crime by murdering or imprisoning its of- ficers. Vocula, though many persons advised him to escape, thought it best to be bold, and, summoning an assembly, spoke as follows.

58. "Never, when I have addressed you, have I felt more anxious for your welfare, never more indifferent about my own. Of the destruction that threatens me I can hear with cheerfulness; and amid so many evils I look forward to death as the end of my sufferings. For you I feel shame and compassion. Against you indeed no hostile ranks are gather- ing. That would be but the lawful course of war, and the right which an enemy may claim. But Classicus hopes to wage with your strength his war against Rome, and proudly

offers to your allegiance an empire of Gaul. Though our fortune and courage have for the moment failed us, have we so
utterly forgotten the old memories of those many times
when the legions of Rome resolved to perish but not to be
driven from their post? Often have our allies endured to see
their cities destroyed, and with their wives and children to
die in the flames, with only this reward in their death, the
glory of untarnished loyalty. At this very moment our legions at the Old Camp are suffering the horrors of famine
and of siege, and cannot be shaken by threats or by promises.
We, besides our arms, our numbers, and the singular
strength of our fortifications, have corn and supplies sufficient for a campaign however protracted. We had lately
money enough even to furnish a donative; and, whether you
choose to refer the bounty to Vitellius or Vespasian, it was
at any rate from a Roman Emperor that you received it.
If you, who have been victorious in so many campaigns,
who have so often routed the enemy at Gelduba and at the
Old Camp, yet shrink from battle, this indeed is an unworthy fear. Still you have an entrenched camp; you have
fortifications and the means of prolonging the war, till suc-
couring armies pour in from the neighbouring provinces. It
may be that I do not satisfy you; you may fall back on
other legates or tribunes, on some centurion, even on some
common soldier. Let not this monstrous news go forth to the
whole world, that with you in their train Civilis and Classicus are about to invade Italy. Should the Germans and the
Gauls lead you to the walls of the capital, will you lift up
arms against your Country? My soul shudders at the imagination of so horrible a crime. Will you mount guard for
Tutor, the Trever? Shall a Batavian give the signal for
battle? Will you serve as recruits in the German battalions?
What will be the issue of your wickedness when the Roman
legions are marshalled against you? Will you be a second
time deserters, a second time traitors, and brave the anger
of heaven while you waver between your old and your new
allegiance? I implore and entreat thee, O Jupiter, supremely
good and great, to whom through eight hundred and twenty
years we have paid the honours of so many triumphs, and
thou, Quirinus father of Rome, that, if it be not your pleas-

ure that this camp should be preserved pure and inviolate under my command, you will at least not suffer it to be polluted and defiled by a Tutor and a Classicus. Grant that the soldiers of Rome may either be innocent of crime, or at least experience a repentance speedy and without remorse."

59. They received his speech with feelings that varied between hope, fear, and shame. Vocula then left them, and was preparing to put an end to his life, when his freedmen and slaves prevented him from anticipating by his own act a most miserable death. Classicus despatched one Æmilius Longinus, a deserter from the first legion, and speedily accomplished the murder. With respect to the two legates, Herennius and Numisius, it was thought enough to put them in chains. Classicus then assumed the insignia of Roman Imperial power, and entered the camp. Hardened though he was to every sort of crime, he could only find words enough to go through the form of oath. All who were present swore allegiance to the empire of Gaul. He distinguished the murderer of Vocula by high promotion, and the others by rewards proportioned to their services in crime.

Tutor and Classicus then divided the management of the war between them. Tutor, investing the Colonia Agrippinensis with a strong force, compelled the inhabitants and all the troops on the Upper Rhine to take the same oath. He did this after having first put to death the tribunes at Mogontiacum, and driven away the prefect of the camp, because they refused obedience. Classicus picked out all the most unprincipled men from the troops who had capitulated, and bade them go to the besieged, and offer them quarter, if they would accept the actual state of affairs; otherwise there was no hope for them; they would have to endure famine, the sword, and the direst extremities. The messengers whom he sent supported their representations by their own example.

60. The ties of loyalty on the one hand, and the necessities of famine on the other, kept the besieged wavering between the alternatives of glory and infamy. While they thus hesitated, all usual and even unusual kinds of food failed them, for they had consumed their horses and beasts of burden and all the other animals, which, though unclean

and disgusting, necessity compelled them to use. At last they tore up shrubs and roots and the grass that grew between the stones, and thus shewed an example of patience under privations, till at last they shamefully tarnished the lustre of their fame by sending envoys to Civilis to beg for their lives. Their prayers were not heard, till they swore allegiance to the empire of Gaul. Civilis then stipulated for the plunder of the camp, and appointed guards who were to secure the treasure, the camp-followers, and the baggage, and accompany them as they departed, stripped of everything. About five miles from the spot the Germans rose upon them, and attacked them as they marched without thought of danger. The bravest were cut down where they stood; the greater part, as they were scattered in flight. The rest made their escape to the camp, while Civilis certainly complained of the proceeding, and upbraided the Germans with breaking faith by this atrocious act. Whether this was mere hypocrisy, or whether he was unable to restrain their fury, is not positively stated. They plundered and then fired the camp, and all who survived the battle the flames destroyed.

61. Then Civilis fulfilled a vow often made by barbarians; his hair, which he had let grow long and coloured with a red dye from the day of taking up arms against Rome, he now cut short, when the destruction of the legions had been accomplished. It was also said that he set up some of the prisoners as marks for his little son to shoot at with a child's arrows and javelins. He neither took the oath of allegiance to Gaul himself, nor obliged any Batavian to do so, for he relied on the resources of Germany, and felt that, should it be necessary to fight for empire with the Gauls, he should have on his side a great name and superior strength. Munius Lupercus, legate of one of the legions, was sent along with other gifts to Veleda, a maiden of the tribe of the Bructeri, who possessed extensive dominion; for by ancient usage the Germans attributed to many of their women prophetic powers and, as the superstition grew in strength, even actual divinity. The authority of Veleda was then at its height, because she had foretold the success of the Germans and the destruction of the legions. Lupercus, however, was murdered on the road. A few of the centurions and tribunes, who were

natives of Gaul, were reserved as hostages for the maintenance of the alliance. The winter encampments of the auxiliary infantry and cavalry and of the legions, with the sole
exception of those at Mogontiacum and Vindonissa, were
pulled down and burnt.

62. The 16th legion, with the auxiliary troops that capitulated at the same time, received orders to march from Novesium to the Colony of the Treveri, a day having been
fixed by which they were to quit the camp. The whole of
this interval they spent in many anxious thoughts. The
cowards trembled to think of those who had been massacred
at the Old Camp; the better men blushed with shame at the
infamy of their position. "What a march is this before us!"
they cried, "Who will lead us on our way? Our all is at
the disposal of those whom we have made our masters for
life or death." Others, without the least sense of their disgrace, stowed away about their persons their money and
what else they prized most highly, while some got their arms
in readiness, and girded on their weapons as if for battle.
While they were thus occupied, the time for their departure
arrived, and proved even more dismal than their anticipation. For in their intrenchments their woeful appearance had
not been so noticeable; the open plain and the light of day
revealed their disgrace. The images of the Emperors were
torn down; the standards were borne along without their
usual honours, while the banners of the Gauls glittered on
every side. The train moved on in silence like a long funeral
procession. Their leader was Claudius Sanctus; one of his
eyes had been destroyed; he was repulsive in countenance
and even more feeble in intellect. The guilt of the troops
seemed to be doubled, when the other legion, deserting the
camp at Bonna, joined their ranks. When the report of the
capture of the legions became generally known, all who but
a short time before trembled at the name of Rome rushed
forth from the fields and houses, and spread themselves
everywhere to enjoy with extravagant delight the strange
spectacle. The Picentine Horse could not endure the triumph
of the insulting rabble, and, disregarding the promises and
threats of Sanctus, rode off to Mogontiacum. Chancing to
fall in with Longinus the murderer of Vocula, they over-

whelmed him with a shower of darts, and thus made a beginning towards a future expiation of their guilt. The legions
did not change the direction of their march, and encamped
under the walls of the colony of the Treveri.

63. Elated with their success, Civilis and Classicus
doubted whether they should not give up the Colonia Agrippinensis to be plundered by their troops. Their natural
ferocity and lust for spoil prompted them to destroy the
city; but the necessities of war, and the advantage of a
character for clemency to men founding a new empire, forbade them to do so. Civilis was also influenced by recollections of kindness received; for his son, who at the beginning
of the war had been arrested in the Colony, had been kept
in honourable custody. But the tribes beyond the Rhine disliked the place for its wealth and increasing power, and held
that the only possible way of putting an end to war would
be, either to make it an open city for all Germans, or to
destroy it and so disperse the Ubii.

64. Upon this the Tencteri, a tribe separated by the
Rhine from the Colony, sent envoys with orders to make
known their instructions to the Senate of the Agrippinenses.
These orders the boldest spirit among the ambassadors thus
expounded: "For your return into the unity of the German
nation and name we give thanks to the Gods whom we
worship in common and to Mars, the chief of our divinities,
and we congratulate you that at length you will live as free
men among the free. Up to this day have the Romans closed
river and land and, in a way, the very air, that they may
bar our converse and prevent our meetings, or, what is a
still worse insult to men born to arms, may force us to assemble unarmed and all but stripped, watched by sentinels,
and taxed for the privilege. But that our friendship and
union may be established for ever, we require of you to
strip your city of its walls, which are the bulwarks of slavery. Even savage animals, if you keep them in confinement,
forget their natural courage. We require of you to massacre
all Romans within your territory; liberty and a dominant
race cannot well exist together. Let the property of the
slain come into a common stock, so that no one may be able
to secrete anything, or to detach his own interest from ours.

Let it be lawful for us and for you to inhabit both banks of the Rhine, as it was of old for our ancestors. As nature has given light and air to all men, so has she thrown open every land to the brave. Resume the manners and customs of your country, renouncing the pleasures, through which, rather than through their arms, the Romans secure their power against subject nations. A pure and untainted race, forgetting your past bondage, you will be the equals of all, or will even rule over others."

65. The inhabitants of the Colony took time for deliberation, and, as dread of the future would not allow them to accept the offered terms, while their actual condition forbade an open and contemptuous rejection, they replied to the following effect: "The very first chance of freedom that presented itself we seized with more eagerness than caution, that we might unite ourselves with you and the other Germans, our kinsmen by blood. With respect to our fortifications, as at this very moment the Roman armies are assembling, it is safer for us to strengthen than to destroy them. All strangers from Italy or the provinces, that may have been in our territory, have either perished in the war, or have fled to their own homes. As for those who in former days settled here, and have been united to us by marriage, and as for their offspring, this is their native land. We cannot think you so unjust as to wish that we should slay our parents, our brothers, and our children. All duties and restrictions on trade we repeal. Let there be a free passage across the river, but let it be during the day-time and for persons unarmed, till the new and recent privileges assume by usage the stability of time. As arbiters between us we will have Civilis and Veleda; under their sanction the treaty shall be ratified." The Tencteri were thus appeased, and ambassadors were sent with presents to Civilis and Veleda, who settled everything to the satisfaction of the inhabitants of the Colony. They were not, however, allowed to approach or address Veleda herself. In order to inspire them with more respect they were prevented from seeing her. She dwelt in a lofty tower, and one of her relatives, chosen for the purpose, conveyed, like the messenger of a divinity, the questions and answers.

66. Thus strengthened by his alliance with the Colonia Agrippinensis, Civilis resolved to attach to himself the neighbouring States, or to make war on them if they offered any opposition. He occupied the territory of the Sunici, and formed the youth of the country into regular cohorts. To hinder his further advance, Claudius Labeo encountered him with a hastily assembled force of Betasii, Tungri, and Nervii, relying on the strength of his position, as he had occupied a bridge over the river Mosa. They fought in a narrow defile without any decided result, till the Germans swam across and attacked Labeo's rear. At the same moment, Civilis, acting either on some bold impulse or by a preconcerted plan, rushed into the Tungrian column, exclaiming in a loud voice, "We have not taken up arms in order that the Batavi and Treveri may rule over the nations. Far from us be such arrogance! Accept our alliance. I am ready to join your ranks, whether you would prefer me to be your general or your comrade." The multitude was moved by the appeal, and were beginning to sheathe their swords, when Campanus and Juvenalis, two of the Tungrian chieftains, surrendered the whole tribe to Civilis. Labeo made his escape before he could be intercepted. The Betasii and Nervii, also capitulating, were incorporated by Civilis into his army. He now commanded vast resources, as the States were either completely cowed, or else were naturally inclined in his favour.

67. Meanwhile Julius Sabinus, after having thrown down the pillars that recorded the treaty with Rome, bade his followers salute him as Emperor, and hastened at the head of a large and undisciplined crowd of his countrymen to attack the Sequani, a neighbouring people, still faithful to Rome. The Sequani did not decline the contest. Fortune favoured the better cause, and the Lingones were defeated. Sabinus fled from the battle with a cowardice equal to the rashness with which he had precipitated it, and, in order to spread a report of his death, he set fire to a country-house where he had taken refuge. It was believed that he there perished by a death of his own seeking. The various shifts by which he contrived to conceal himself and to prolong his life for nine years, the firm fidelity of his friends, and the noble example

of his wife Epponina, I shall relate in their proper place. By
this victory of the Sequani the tide of war was stayed. The
States began by degrees to recover their senses, and to reflect
on the claims of justice and of treaties. The Remi were fore·
most in this movement, announcing throughout Gaul that
deputies were to be sent to consult in common assembly
whether they should make freedom or peace their object.

68. At Rome report exaggerated all these disasters, and
disturbed Mucianus with the fear that the generals, though
distinguished men (for he had already appointed Gallus
Annius and Petilius Cerialis to the command), would be unequal to the weight of so vast a war. Yet the capital could
not be left without a ruler, and men feared the ungoverned
passions of Domitian, while Primus Antonius and Varus
Arrius were also, as I have said, objects of suspicion. Varus,
who had been made commander of the Prætorian Guard,
had still at his disposal much military strength. Mucianus
ejected him from his office, and, not to leave him without
consolation, made him superintendent of the sale of corn. To
pacify the feelings of Domitian, which were not unfavourable to Varus, he appointed Arretinus Clemens, who was
closely connected with the house of Vespasian, and who was
also a great favourite with Domitian, to the command of the
Prætorian Guard, alleging that his father, in the reign of
Caligula, had admirably discharged the duties of that office.
The old name, he said, would please the soldiers, and Clemens himself, though on the roll of Senators, would be equal
to both duties. He selected the most eminent men in the
State to accompany him, while others were appointed
through interest. At the same time Domitian and Mucianus
prepared to set out, but in a very different mood; Domitian
in all the hope and impatience of youth, Mucianus ever contriving delays to check his ardent companion, who, he
feared, were he to intrude himself upon the army, might be
led by the recklessness of youth or by bad advisers to compromise at once the prospects of war and of peace. Two of
the victorious legions, the 6th and 8th, the 21st, which belonged to the Vitellianist army, the 2nd, which consisted of
new levies, were marched into Gaul, some over the Penine
and Cottian, some over the Graian Alps. The 14th legion

were summoned from Britain, and the 6th and 10th from Spain. Thus rumours of an advancing army, as well as their own temper, inclined the States of Gaul which assembled in the country of the Remi to more peaceful counsels. Envoys from the Treveri were awaiting them there, and among them Tullius Valentinus, the most vehement promoter of the war, who in a set speech poured forth all the charges usually made against great empires, and levelled against the Roman people many insulting and exasperating expressions. The man was a turbulent fomenter of sedition, and pleased many by his frantic eloquence.

69. On the other hand Julius Auspex, one of the leading chieftains among the Remi, dwelt on the power of Rome and the advantages of peace. Pointing out that war might be commenced indeed by cowards, but must be carried on at the peril of the braver spirits, and that the Roman legions were close at hand, he restrained the most prudent by considerations of respect and loyalty, and held back the younger by representations of danger and appeals to fear. The result was, that, while they extolled the spirit of Valentinus, they followed the counsels of Auspex. It is certain that the Treveri and Lingones were injured in the eyes of the Gallic nations by their having sided with Verginius in the movement of Vindex. Many were deterred by the mutual jealousy of the provinces. "Where," they asked, "could a head be found for the war? Where could they look for civil authority, and the sanction of religion? If all went well with them, what city could they select as the seat of empire?" The victory was yet to be gained; dissension had already begun. One State angrily boasted of its alliances, another of its wealth and military strength, or of the antiquity of its origin. Disgusted with the prospect of the future, they acquiesced in their present condition. Letters were written to the Treveri in the name of the states of Gaul, requiring them to abstain from hostilities, and reminding them that pardon might yet be obtained, and that friends were ready to intercede for them, should they repent. Valentinus still opposed, and succeeded in closing the ears of his countrymen to this advice, though he was not so diligent in preparing for war as he was assiduous in haranguing.

70. Accordingly neither the Treveri, the Lingones, nor the other revolted States, took measures at all proportioned to the magnitude of the peril they had incurred. Even their generals did not act in concert. Civilis was traversing the pathless wilds of the Belgæ in attempting to capture Claudius Labeo, or to drive him out of the country. Classicus for the most part wasted his time in indolent repose, as if he had only to enjoy an empire already won. Even Tutor made no haste to occupy with troops the upper bank of the Rhine and the passes of the Alps. Meanwhile the 21st legion, by way of Vindonissa, and Sextilius Felix with the auxiliary infantry, by way of Rhætia, penetrated into the province. They were joined by the Singularian Horse, which had been raised some time before by Vitellius, and had afterwards gone over to the side of Vespasian. Their commanding officer was Julius Briganticus. He was sister's son to Civilis, and he was hated by his uncle and hated him in return with all the extreme bitterness of a family feud. Tutor, having augmented the army of the Treveri with fresh levies from the Vangiones, the Cæracates, and the Triboci, strengthened it with a force of veteran infantry and cavalry, men from the legions whom he had either corrupted by promises or overborne by intimidation. Their first act was to cut to pieces a cohort, which had been sent on in advance by Sextilius Felix; soon afterwards, however, on the approach of the Roman generals at the head of their army, they returned to their duty by an act of honourable desertion, and the Triboci, Vangiones, and Cæracates, followed their example. Avoiding Mogontiacum, Tutor retired with the Treveri to Bingium, trusting to the strength of the position, as he had broken down the bridge over the river Nava. A sudden attack, however, was made by the infantry under the command of Sextilius; a ford was discovered, and he found himself betrayed and routed. The Treveri were panic-stricken by this disaster, and the common people threw down their arms, and dispersed themselves through the country. Some of the chiefs, anxious to seem the first to cease from hostilities, fled to those States which had not renounced the Roman alliance. The legions, which had been removed, as I have before related, from Novesium and Bonna to the ter-

ritory of the Treveri, voluntarily swore allegiance to Vespasian. These proceedings took place in the absence of
Valentinus. When he returned, full of fury and bent on again
throwing everything into confusion and ruin, the legions
withdrew to the Mediomatrici, a people in alliance with
Rome. Valentinus and Tutor again involved the Treveri in
war, and murdered the two legates, Herennius and Numisius, that by diminishing the hope of pardon they might
strengthen the bond of crime.

71. Such was the state of the war, when Petilius Cerialis
reached Mogontiacum. Great expectations were raised by his
arrival. Eager for battle, and more ready to despise than to
be on his guard against the enemy, he fired the spirit of the
troops by his bold language; for he would, he said, fight
without a moment's delay, as soon as it was possible to meet
the foe. The levies which had been raised in Gaul he ordered
back to their respective States, with instructions to proclaim
that the legions sufficed to defend the Empire, and that the
allies might return to the duties of peace, secure in the
thought that a war which Roman arms had undertaken was
finished. This proceeding strengthened the loyalty of the
Gauls. Now that their youth were restored to them they
could more easily bear the burden of the tribute; and, finding themselves despised, they were more ready to obey.
Civilis and Classicus, having heard of the defeat of Tutor
and of the rout of the Treveri, and indeed of the complete
success of the enemy, hastened in their alarm to concentrate
their own scattered forces, and meanwhile sent repeated
messages to Valentinus, warning him not to risk a decisive
battle. This made Cerialis move with more rapidity. He sent
to the Mediomatrici persons commissioned to conduct the
legions which were there by the shortest route against the
enemy; and, collecting such troops as there were at Mogontiacum and such as he had brought with himself, he arrived
in three days' march at Rigodulum. Valentinus, at the head
of a large body of Treveri, had occupied this position, which
was protected by hills, and by the river Mosella. He had also
strengthened it with ditches and breastworks of stones.
These defences, however, did not deter the Roman general
from ordering his infantry to the assault, and making his

cavalry advance up the hill; he scorned the enemy, whose forces, hastily levied, could not, he knew, derive any advantage from their position, but what would be more than counterbalanced by the courage of his own men. There was some little delay in the ascent, while the troops were passing through the range of the enemy's missiles. As soon as they came to close fighting, the barbarians were dislodged and hurled like a falling house from their position. A detachment of the cavalry rode round where the hills were less steep, and captured the principal Belgic chiefs, and among them Valentinus, their general.

72. On the following day Cerialis entered the Colony of the Treveri. The soldiers were eager to destroy the city. "This," they said, "is the birthplace of Classicus and Tutor; it was by the treason of these men that our legions were besieged and massacred. What had Cremona done like this, Cremona which was torn from the very bosom of Italy, because it had occasioned to the conquerors the delay of a single night? Here on the borders of Germany stands unharmed a city which exults in the spoils of our armies and the blood of our generals. Let the plunder be brought into the Imperial treasury; we shall be satisfied with the fire that will destroy a rebellious colony and compensate for the overthrow of so many camps." Cerialis, fearing the disgrace of being thought to have imbued his soldiers with a spirit of licence and cruelty, checked their fury. They submitted, for, now that civil war was at an end, they were tractable enough in dealing with an enemy. Their thoughts were then diverted by the pitiable aspect of the legions which had been summoned from the Mediomatrici. They stood oppressed by the consciousness of guilt, their eyes fixed on the earth. No friendly salutations passed between the armies as they met, they made no answer to those who would console or encourage them, but hid themselves in their tents, and shrank from the very light of day. Nor was it so much their peril or their alarm that confounded them, as their shame and humiliation. Even the conquerors were struck dumb, and dared not utter a word of entreaty, but pleaded for pardon by their silent tears, till Cerialis at last soothed their minds by declaring that destiny had brought about all that had hap-

pened through the discords of soldiers and generals or through the treachery of the foe. They must consider that day as the first of their military service and of their allegiance. Their past crimes would be remembered neither by the Emperor nor by himself. They were thus admitted into the same camp with the rest, and an order was read in every company, that no soldier was in any contention or altercation to reproach a comrade with mutiny or defeat.

73. Cerialis then convoked an assembly of the Treveri and Lingones, and thus addressed them: "I have never cultivated eloquence; it is by my sword that I have asserted the excellence of the Roman people. Since, however, words have very great weight with you, since you estimate good and evil, not according to their real value, but according to the representations of seditious men, I have resolved to say a few words, which, as the war is at an end, it may be useful for you to have heard rather than for me to have spoken. Roman generals and Emperors entered your territory, as they did the rest of Gaul, with no ambitious purposes, but at the solicitation of your ancestors, who were wearied to the last extremity by intestine strife, while the Germans, whom they had summoned to their help, had imposed their yoke alike on friend and foe. How many battles we have fought against the Cimbri and Teutones, at the cost of what hardships to our armies, and with what result we have waged our German wars, is perfectly well known. It was not to defend Italy that we occupied the borders of the Rhine, but to insure that no second Ariovistus should seize the empire of Gaul. Do you fancy yourselves to be dearer in the eyes of Civilis and the Batavi and the Transrhenane tribes, than your fathers and grandfathers were to their ancestors? There have ever been the same causes at work to make the Germans cross over into Gaul, lust, avarice, and the longing for a new home, prompting them to leave their own marshes and deserts, and to possess themselves of this most fertile soil and of you its inhabitants. Liberty, indeed, and the like specious names are their pretexts; but never did any man seek to enslave his fellows and secure dominion for himself without using the very same words.

74. "Gaul always had its petty kingdoms and intestine

wars, till you submitted to our authority. We, though so often provoked, have used the right of conquest to burden you only with the cost of maintaining peace. For the tranquillity of nations cannot be preserved without armies; armies cannot exist without pay; pay cannot be furnished without tribute; all else is common between us. You often command our legions. You rule these and other provinces. There is no privilege, no exclusion. From worthy Emperors you derive equal advantage, though you dwell so far away, while cruel rulers are most formidable to their neighbours. Endure the passions and rapacity of your masters, just as you bear barren seasons and excessive rains and other natural evils. There will be vices as long as there are men. But they are not perpetual, and they are compensated by the occurrence of better things. Perhaps, however, you expect a milder rule under Tutor and Classicus, and fancy that armies to repel the Germans and the Britons will be furnished by less tribute than you now pay. Should the Romans be driven out (which God forbid) what can result but wars between all these nations? By the prosperity and order of eight hundred years has this fabric of empire been consolidated, nor can it be overthrown without destroying those who overthrow it. Yours will be the worst peril, for you have gold and wealth, and these are the chief incentives to war. Give therefore your love and respect to the cause of peace, and to that capital in which we, conquerors and conquered, claim an equal right. Let the lessons of fortune in both its forms teach you not to prefer rebellion and ruin to submission and safety." With words to this effect he quieted and encouraged his audience, who feared harsher treatment.

75. The territory of the Treveri was occupied by the victorious army, when Civilis and Classicus sent letters to Cerialis, the purport of which was as follows: "Vespasian, though the news is suppressed, is dead. Rome and Italy are thoroughly wasted by intestine war. Mucianus and Domitian are mere empty and powerless names. If Cerialis wishes for the empire of Gaul, we can be content with the boundaries of our own States. If he prefers to fight, we do not refuse that alternative." Cerialis sent no answer to Civilis and Classicus, but despatched the bearer and the letter itself

to Domitian. The enemy advanced from every quarter in several bodies. Cerialis was generally censured for allowing them to unite, when he might have destroyed them in detail. The Roman army surrounded their camp with a fosse and rampart, for up to that time they had been rash enough to occupy it without any defence. Among the Germans there was a conflict of opinions.

76. Civilis said: "We must await the arrival of the Transrhenane tribes, the terror of whose name will break down the shattered strength of Rome. As for the Gauls, what are they but the prey of the conqueror? And yet the chief strength of the nation, the Belgæ, are with us, either openly, or in heart." Tutor maintained that the power of Rome would only increase with delay, as her armies were assembling from all quarters. "One legion," he said, "has already been brought over from Britain; others have been summoned from Spain, or are advancing from Italy. Nor are these troops newly raised levies, but they are veteran soldiers, experienced in war. But the Germans, whom we are expecting, do not obey orders, and cannot be controlled, but always act according to their own caprice. The money too and other presents by which alone they can be bribed are more plentiful among the Romans, and no one can be so bent on fighting as not to prefer repose to peril, when the profit is the same. But if we at once meet the foe, Cerialis has no legions but those that survive from the wreck of the German army, and these are bound by treaties to the States of Gaul. And the very fact of their having, contrary to their expectations, lately routed the undisciplined force of Valentinus will confirm in their rashness both them and their general. They will venture again, and will find themselves in the hands, not of an ignorant stripling, whose thoughts were of speeches and harangues rather than of battle and the sword, but in those of Civilis and Classicus, whom when they once behold they will be reminded of panic, of flight, of famine, and of the many times when as captives they had to beg for life. Nor are the Treveri and Lingones bound by any ties of affection; once let their fear cease, and they will resume their arms." Classicus put an end to these dif-

ferences of opinion by giving his approval to the suggestions of Tutor, which were at once acted on.

77. The centre was the post assigned to the Ubii and Lingones. On the right were the Batavian cohorts; on the left the Bructeri and the Tencteri. One division marching over the hills, another passing between the high road and the river Mosella, made the attack with such suddenness, that Cerialis, who had not slept in the camp, was in his chamber and even in his bed, when he heard at the same moment that the battle had begun, and that his men were being worsted. He rebuked the alarm of the messengers, till the whole extent of the disaster became visible, and he saw that the camp of the legions had been forced, that the cavalry were routed, that the bridge over the Mosella, which connected the further bank of the river with the Colony, was held by the Germans. Undismayed by the confusion, Cerialis held back the fugitives with his own hand, and readily exposing himself, with his person entirely unprotected, to the missiles of the enemy, he succeeded by a daring and successful effort, with the prompt aid of his bravest soldiers, in recovering the bridge and holding it with a picked force. Then returning to the camp, he saw the broken companies of the legions, which had been captured at Bonna and Novesium, with but few soldiers round the standards, and the eagles all but surrounded by the foe. Fired with indignation, he exclaimed, "It is not Flaccus or Vocula, whom you are thus abandoning. There is no treachery here; I have nothing to excuse but that I rashly believed that you, forgetting your alliance with Gaul, had again recollected your allegiance to Rome. I shall be added to the number of the Numisii and Herennii, so that all your commanders will have fallen by the hands of their soldiers or of the enemy. Go, tell Vespasian, or, since they are nearer, Civilis and Classicus, that you have deserted your general on the battlefield. Legions will come who will not leave me unavenged or you unpunished."

78. All this was true, and the tribunes and prefects heaped on their men the same reproaches. The troops formed themselves in cohorts and companies, for they could not deploy into line, as the enemy were scattered everywhere, while

from the fact that the battle was raging within the entrenchments, they were themselves hampered with their tents and
baggage. Tutor, Classicus, and Civilis, each at his post,
animated the combatants; the Gauls they urged to fight for
freedom, the Batavi for glory, the Germans for plunder.
Everything seemed in favour of the enemy, till the 21st legion, having more room than the others, formed itself into a
compact body, withstood, and soon drove back the assailants. Nor was it without an interposition of heaven, that
by a sudden change of temper the conquerors turned their
backs and fled. Their own account was, that they were
alarmed by the sight of the cohorts, which, after being
broken at the first onset, rallied on the top of the hills, and
presented the appearance of reinforcements. What checked
them in their course of victory was a mischievous struggle
among themselves to secure plunder while they forgot the
enemy. Cerialis, having thus all but ruined everything by his
carelessness, restored the day by his resolution; following
up his success, he took and destroyed the enemy's camp on
the same day.

79. No long time was allowed to the soldiers for repose.
The Agrippinenses were begging for help, and were offering
to give up the wife and sister of Civilis and the daughter of
Classicus, who had been left with them as pledges for the
maintenance of the alliance. In the meanwhile they had
massacred all the Germans who were scattered throughout
their dwellings. Hence their alarm and reasonable importunity in begging for help, before the enemy, recovering
their strength, could raise their spirits for a new effort or for
thoughts of revenge. And indeed Civilis had marched in
their direction, nor was he by any means weak, as he had
still, in unbroken force, the most warlike of his cohorts,
which consisted of Chauci and Frisii, and which was posted
at Tolbiacum, on the frontiers of the Agrippinenses. He was,
however, diverted from his purpose by the deplorable news
that this cohort had been entirely destroyed by a stratagem
of the Agrippinenses, who, having stupefied the Germans by
a profuse entertainment and abundance of wine, fastened
the doors, set fire to the houses, and burned them. At the
same time Cerialis advanced by forced marches, and re-

lieved the city. Civilis too was beset by other fears. He was afraid that the 14th legion, supported by the fleet from Britain, might do mischief to the Batavi along their line of coast. The legion was, however, marched overland under the command of Fabius Priscus into the territory of the Nervii and Tungri, and these two states were allowed to capitulate. The Canninefates, taking the offensive, attacked our fleet, and the larger part of the ships was either sunk or captured. The same tribe also routed a crowd of Nervii, who by a spontaneous movement had taken up arms on the Roman side. Classicus also gained a victory over some cavalry, who had been sent on to Novesium by Cerialis. These reverses, which, though trifling, came in rapid succession, destroyed by degrees the prestige of the recent victory.

80. About the same time Mucianus ordered the son of Vitellius to be put to death, alleging that dissension would never cease, if he did not destroy all seeds of civil war. Nor would he suffer Antonius Primus to be taken into the number of Domitian's attendants, for he felt uneasy at his popularity with the troops, and feared the proud spirit of the man, who could not endure an equal, much less a superior. Antonius then went to Vespasian, who received him, not indeed as he expected, but in a not unfriendly spirit. Two opposite influences acted on the Emperor; on the one hand were the merits of Antonius, under whose conduct the war had beyond all doubt been terminated; on the other, were the letters of Mucianus. And everyone else inveighed against him, as an ill-affected and conceited man, nor did they forget the scandals of his early life. Antonius himself failed not to provoke offence by his arrogance and his excessive propensity to dwell on his own services. He reproached other men with being cowards; Cæcina he stigmatized as a captive and a prisoner of war. Thus by degrees he came to be thought of less weight and worth, though his friendship with the Emperor to all appearance remained the same.

81. In the months during which Vespasian was waiting at Alexandria for the periodical return of the summer gales and settled weather at sea, many wonders occurred which seemed to point him out as the object of the favour of heaven and of the partiality of the Gods. One of the com-

mon people of Alexandria, well-known for his blindness,
threw himself at the Emperor's knees, and implored him
with groans to heal his infirmity. This he did by the advice
of the God Serapis, whom this nation, devoted as it is to
many superstitions, worships more than any other divinity.
He begged Vespasian that he would deign to moisten his
cheeks and eye-balls with his spittle. Another with a diseased hand, at the counsel of the same God, prayed that the
limb might feel the print of a Cæsar's foot. At first Vespasian ridiculed and repulsed them. They persisted; and he,
though on the one hand he feared the scandal of a fruitless
attempt, yet, on the other, was induced by the entreaties of
the men and by the language of his flatterers to hope for
success. At last he ordered that the opinion of physicians
should be taken, as to whether such blindness and infirmity
were within the reach of human skill. They discussed the
matter from different points of view. "In the one case," they
said, "the faculty of sight was not wholly destroyed, and
might return, if the obstacles were removed; in the other
case, the limb, which had fallen into a diseased condition,
might be restored, if a healing influence were applied; such,
perhaps, might be the pleasure of the Gods, and the Emperor might be chosen to be the minister of the divine will;
at any rate, all the glory of a successful remedy would be
Cæsar's, while the ridicule of failure would fall on the suf-
ferers." And so Vespasian, supposing that all things were
possible to his good fortune, and that nothing was any
longer past belief, with a joyful countenance, amid the intense expectation of the multitude of bystanders, accomplished what was required. The hand was instantly restored
to its use, and the light of day again shone upon the blind.
Persons actually present attest both facts, even now when
nothing is to be gained by falsehood.

82. Vespasian thus came to conceive a deeper desire to
visit the sanctuary of Serapis, that he might consult the
God about the interests of his throne. He gave orders that
all persons should be excluded from the temple. He had entered, and was absorbed in worship, when he saw behind
him one of the chief men of Egypt, named Basilides, whom
he knew at the time to be detained by sickness at a consid-

erable distance, as much as several days' journey, from Alexandria. He enquired of the priests, whether Basilides had on this day entered the temple. He enquired of others whom he met, whether he had been seen in the city. At length, sending some horsemen, he ascertained that at that very instant the man had been eighty miles distant. He then concluded that it was a divine apparition, and discovered an oracular force in the name of Basilides.

83. The origin of this God Serapis has not hitherto been made generally known by our writers. The Egyptian priests give this account. While Ptolemy, the first Macedonian king who consolidated the power of Egypt, was setting up in the newly-built city of Alexandria fortifications, temples, and rites of worship, there appeared to him in his sleep a youth of singular beauty and more than human stature, who counselled the monarch to send his most trusty friends to Pontus, and fetch his effigy from that country. This, he said, would bring prosperity to the realm, and great and illustrious would be the city which gave it a reception. At the same moment he saw the youth ascend to heaven in a blaze of fire. Roused by so significant and strange an appearance, Ptolemy disclosed the vision of the night to the Egyptian priests, whose business it is to understand such matters. As they knew but little of Pontus or of foreign countries, he enquired of Timotheus, an Athenian, one of the family of the Eumolpids, whom he had invited from Eleusis to preside over the sacred rites, what this worship was, and who was the deity. Timotheus, questioning persons who had found their way to Pontus, learnt that there was there a city Sinope, and near it a temple, which, according to an old tradition of the neighbourhood, was sacred to the infernal Jupiter, for there also stood close at hand a female figure, to which many gave the name of Proserpine. Ptolemy, however, with the true disposition of a despot, though prone to alarm, was, when the feeling of security returned, more intent on pleasures than on religious matters; and he began by degrees to neglect the affair, and to turn his thoughts to other concerns, till at length the same apparition, but now more terrible and peremptory, denounced ruin against the king and his realm, unless his bidding were performed.

Ptolemy then gave directions that an embassy should be despatched with presents to king Scydrothemis, who at that time ruled the people of Sinope, and instructed them, when they were on the point of sailing, to consult the Pythian Apollo. Their voyage was prosperous, and the response of the oracle was clear. The God bade them go and carry back with them the image of his father, but leave that of his sister behind.

84. On their arrival at Sinope, they delivered to Scydrothemis the presents from their king, with his request and message. He wavered in purpose, dreading at one moment the anger of the God, terrified at another by the threats and opposition of the people. Often he was wrought upon by the gifts and promises of the ambassadors. And so three years passed away, while Ptolemy did not cease to urge his zealous solicitations. He continued to increase the dignity of his embassies, the number of his ships, and the weight of his gold. A terrible vision then appeared to Scydrothemis, warning him to thwart no longer the purposes of the God. As he yet hesitated, various disasters, pestilence, and the unmistakeable anger of heaven, which grew heavier from day to day, continued to harass him. He summoned an assembly, and explained to them the bidding of the God, the visions of Ptolemy and himself, and the miseries that were gathering about them. The people turned away angrily from their king, were jealous of Egypt, and, fearing for themselves, thronged around the temple. The story becomes at this point more marvellous, and relates that the God of his own will conveyed himself on board the fleet, which had been brought close to shore, and, wonderful to say, vast as was the extent of sea that they traversed, they arrived at Alexandria on the third day. A temple, proportioned to the grandeur of the city, was erected in a place called Rhacotis, where there had stood a chapel consecrated in old times to Serapis and Isis. Such is the most popular account of the origin and introduction of the God Serapis. I am aware indeed that there are some who say that he was brought from Seleucia, a city of Syria, in the reign of Ptolemy III., while others assert that it was the act of the same king, but that the place from which he was brought was Memphis, once a famous city

and the strength of ancient Egypt. The God himself, because he heals the sick, many identified with Æsculapius; others with Osiris, the deity of the highest antiquity among these nations; not a few with Jupiter, as being supreme ruler of all things; but most people with Pluto, arguing from the emblems which may be seen on his statues, or from conjectures of their own.

85. Domitian and Mucianus received, before they reached the Alps, favourable news of the operations among the Treveri. The best proof of the victory was seen in the enemy's general Valentinus, who with undaunted courage shewed in his look his habitual high spirit. He was heard, but only that they might judge of his character; and he was condemned. During his execution he replied to one who taunted him with the subjection of his country, "That I take as my consolation in death." Mucianus now brought forward as a new thought a plan he had long concealed. "Since," he said, "by the blessing of the Gods the strength of the enemy has been broken, it would little become Domitian, now that the war is all but finished, to interfere with the glory of others. If the stability of the Empire or the safety of Gaul were in danger, it would have been right for Cæsar to take his place in the field; but the Canninefates and Batavi should be handed over to inferior generals. Let the Emperor display from the near neighbourhood of Lugdunum the might and prestige of imperial power, not meddling with trifling risks, though he would not be wanting on greater occasions."

86. His artifices were understood, but it was a part of their respect not to expose them. Thus they arrived at Lugdunum. It is believed that from this place Domitian despatched secret emissaries to Cerialis, and tempted his loyalty with the question whether, on his shewing himself, he would hand over to him the command of the army. Whether in this scheme Domitian was thinking of war with his father, or of collecting money and men to be used against his brother, was uncertain; for Cerialis, by a judicious temporising, eluded the request as prompted by an idle and childish ambition. Domitian, seeing that his youth was despised by the older officers, gave up even the less im-

portant functions of government which he had before exercised. Under a semblance of simple and modest tastes, he wrapped himself in a profound reserve, and affected a devotion to literature and a love of poetry, thus seeking to throw a veil over his character, and to withdraw himself from the jealousy of his brother, of whose milder temper, so unlike his own, he judged most falsely.

BOOK V

A.D. 70

1. EARLY in this year Titus Cæsar, who had been selected
by his father to complete the subjugation of Judæa, and
who had gained distinction as a soldier while both were still
subjects, began to rise in power and reputation, as armies
and provinces emulated each other in their attachment to
him. The young man himself, anxious to be thought superior
to his station, was ever displaying his gracefulness and his
energy in war. By his courtesy and affability he called forth
a willing obedience, and he often mixed with the common
soldiers, while working or marching, without impairing his
dignity as general. He found in Judæa three legions, the 5th.
the 10th, and the 15th, all old troops of Vespasian's. To
these he added the 12th from Syria, and some men belonging
to the 18th and 3rd, whom he had withdrawn from Alexandria. This force was accompanied by twenty cohorts of
allied troops and eight squadrons of cavalry, by the two
kings Agrippa and Sohemus, by the auxiliary forces of king
Antiochus, by a strong contingent of Arabs, who hated the
Jews with the usual hatred of neighbours, and, lastly, by
many persons brought from the capital and from Italy by
private hopes of securing the yet unengaged affections of the
Prince. With this force Titus entered the enemy's territory,
preserving strict order on his march, reconnoitring every
spot, and always ready to give battle. At last he encamped
near Jerusalem.

2. As I am about to relate the last days of a famous city,
it seems appropriate to throw some light on its origin.

Some say that the Jews were fugitives from the island of
Crete, who settled on the nearest coast of Africa about the
time when Saturn was driven from his throne by the power

of Jupiter. Evidence of this is sought in the name. There is a famous mountain in Crete called Ida; the neighbouring tribe, the Idæi, came to be called Judæi by a barbarous lengthening of the national name. Others assert that in the reign of Isis the overflowing population of Egypt, led by Hierosolymus and Judas, discharged itself into the neighbouring countries. Many, again, say that they were a race of Ethiopian origin, who in the time of king Cepheus were driven by fear and hatred of their neighbours to seek a new dwelling-place. Others describe them as an Assyrian horde who, not having sufficient territory, took possession of part of Egypt, and founded cities of their own in what is called the Hebrew country, lying on the borders of Syria. Others, again, assign a very distinguished origin to the Jews, alleging that they were the Solymi, a nation celebrated in the poems of Homer, who called the city which they founded Hierosolyma after their own name.

3. Most writers, however, agree in stating that once a disease, which horribly disfigured the body, broke out over Egypt; that king Bocchoris, seeking a remedy, consulted the oracle of Hammon, and was bidden to cleanse his realm, and to convey into some foreign land this race detested by the gods. The people, who had been collected after diligent search, finding themselves left in a desert, sat for the most part in a stupor of grief, till one of the exiles, Moyses by name, warned them not to look for any relief from God or man, forsaken as they were of both, but to trust to themselves, taking for their heaven-sent leader that man who should first help them to be quit of their present misery. They agreed, and in utter ignorance began to advance at random. Nothing, however, distressed them so much as the scarcity of water, and they had sunk ready to perish in all directions over the plain, when a herd of wild asses was seen to retire from their pasture to a rock shaded by trees. Moyses followed them, and, guided by the appearance of a grassy spot, discovered an abundant spring of water. This furnished relief. After a continuous journey for six days, on the seventh they possessed themselves of a country, from which they expelled the inhabitants, and in which they founded a city and a temple.

4. Moyses, wishing to secure for the future his authority over the nation, gave them a novel form of worship, opposed to all that is practised by other men. Things sacred with us, with them have no sanctity, while they allow what with us is forbidden. In their holy place they have consecrated an image of the animal by whose guidance they found deliverance from their long and thirsty wanderings. They slay the ram, seemingly in derision of Hammon, and they sacrifice the ox, because the Egyptians worship it as Apis. They abstain from swine's flesh, in consideration of what they suffered when they were infected by the leprosy to which this animal is liable. By their frequent fasts they still bear witness to the long hunger of former days, and the Jewish bread, made without leaven, is retained as a memorial of their hurried seizure of corn. We are told that the rest of the seventh day was adopted, because this day brought with it a termination of their toils; after a while the charm of indolence beguiled them into giving up the seventh year also to inaction. But others say that it is an observance in honour of Saturn, either from the primitive elements of their faith having been transmitted from the Idæi, who are said to have shared the flight of that God, and to have founded the race, or from the circumstance that of the seven stars which rule the destinies of men Saturn moves in the highest orbit and with the mightiest power, and that many of the heavenly bodies complete their revolutions and courses in multiples of seven.

5. This worship, however introduced, is upheld by its antiquity; all their other customs, which are at once perverse and disgusting, owe their strength to their very badness. The most degraded out of other races, scorning their national beliefs, brought to them their contributions and presents. This augmented the wealth of the Jews, as also did the fact, that among themselves they are inflexibly honest and ever ready to shew compassion, though they regard the rest of mankind with all the hatred of enemies. They sit apart at meals, they sleep apart, and though, as a nation, they are singularly prone to lust, they abstain from intercourse with foreign women; among themselves nothing is unlawful. Circumcision was adopted by them as a mark of difference

from other men. Those who come over to their religion adopt the practice, and have this lesson first instilled into them, to despise all gods, to disown their country, and set at nought parents, children, and brethren. Still they provide for the increase of their numbers. It is a crime among them to kill any newly-born infant. They hold that the souls of all who perish in battle or by the hands of the executioner are immortal. Hence a passion for propagating their race and a contempt for death. They are wont to bury rather than to burn their dead, following in this the Egyptian custom; they bestow the same care on the dead, and they hold the same belief about the lower world. Quite different is their faith about things divine. The Egyptians worship many animals and images of monstrous form; the Jews have purely mental conceptions of Deity, as one in essence. They call those profane who make representations of God in human shape out of perishable materials. They believe that Being to be supreme and eternal, neither capable of representation, nor of decay. They therefore do not allow any images to stand in their cities, much less in their temples. This flattery is not paid to their kings, nor this honour to our Emperors. From the fact, however, that their priests used to chant to the music of flutes and cymbals, and to wear garlands of ivy, and that a golden vine was found in the temple, some have thought that they worshipped Father Liber, the conqueror of the East, though their institutions do not by any means harmonize with the theory; for Liber established a festive and cheerful worship, while the Jewish religion is tasteless and mean.

6. Eastward the country is bounded by Arabia; to the south lies Egypt; on the west are Phœnicia and the Mediterranean. Northward it commands an extensive prospect over Syria. The inhabitants are healthy and able to bear fatigue. Rain is uncommon, but the soil is fertile. Its products resemble our own. They have, besides, the balsam-tree and the palm. The palm-groves are tall and graceful. The balsam is a shrub; each branch, as it fills with sap, may be pierced with a fragment of stone or pottery. If steel is employed, the veins shrink up. The sap is used by physicians. Libanus is the principal mountain, and has, strange to say,

amidst these burning heats, a summit shaded with trees and never deserted by its snows. The same range supplies and sends forth the stream of the Jordan. This river does not discharge itself into the sea, but flows entire through two lakes, and is lost in the third. This is a lake of vast circumference; it resembles the sea, but is more nauseous in taste; it breeds pestilence among those who live near by its noisome odour; it cannot be moved by the wind, and it affords no home either to fish or water-birds. These strange waters support what is thrown upon them, as on a solid surface, and all persons, whether they can swim or no, are equally buoyed up by the waves. At a certain season of the year the lake throws up bitumen, and the method of collecting it has been taught by that experience which teaches all other arts. It is naturally a fluid of dark colour; when vinegar is sprinkled upon it, it coagulates and floats upon the surface. Those whose business it is take it with the hand, and draw it on to the deck of the boat; it then continues of itself to flow in and lade the vessel till the stream is cut off. Nor can this be done by any instrument of brass or iron. It shrinks from blood or any cloth stained by the menstrua of women. Such is the account of old authors; but those who know the country say that the bitumen moves in heaving masses on the water, that it is drawn by hand to the shore, and that there, when dried by the evaporation of the earth and the power of the sun, it is cut into pieces with axes and wedges just as timber or stone would be.

7. Not far from this lake lies a plain, once fertile, they say, and the site of great cities, but afterwards struck by lightning and consumed. Of this event, they declare, traces still remain, for the soil, which is scorched in appearance, has lost its productive power. Everything that grows spontaneously, as well as what is planted by hand, either when the leaf or flower have been developed, or after maturing in the usual form, becomes black and rotten, and crumbles into a kind of dust. I am ready to allow, on the one hand, that cities, once famous, may have been consumed by fire from heaven, while, on the other, I imagine that the earth is infected by the exhalations of the lake, that the surrounding air is tainted, and that thus the growth of harvest and the

fruits of autumn decay under the equally noxious influences of soil and climate. The river Belus also flows into the Jewish sea. About its mouth is a kind of sand which is collected, mixed with nitre, and fused into glass. This shore is of limited extent, but furnishes an inexhaustible supply to the exporter.

8. A great part of Judæa consists of scattered villages. They have also towns. Jerusalem is the capital. There stood a temple of immense wealth. First came the city with its fortifications, then the royal palace, then, within the innermost defences, the temple itself. Only the Jew might approach the gates; all but priests were forbidden to pass the threshold. While the East was under the sway of the Assyrians, the Medes, and the Persians, Jews were the most contemptible of the subject tribes. When the Macedonians became supreme, King Antiochus strove to destroy the national superstition, and to introduce Greek civilization, but was prevented by his war with the Parthians from at all improving this vilest of nations; for at this time the revolt of Arsaces had taken place. The Macedonian power was now weak, while the Parthian had not yet reached its full strength, and, as the Romans were still far off, the Jews chose kings for themselves. Expelled by the fickle populace, and regaining their throne by force of arms, these princes, while they ventured on the wholesale banishment of their subjects, on the destruction of cities, on the murder of brothers, wives, and parents, and the other usual atrocities of despots, fostered the national superstition by appropriating the dignity of the priesthood as the support of their political power.

9. Cneius Pompeius was the first of our countrymen to subdue the Jews. Availing himself of the right of conquest, he entered the temple. Thus it became commonly known that the place stood empty with no similitude of gods within, and that the shrine had nothing to reveal. The walls of Jerusalem were destroyed, the temple was left standing. After these provinces had fallen, in the course of our civil wars, into the hands of Marcus Antonius, Pacorus, king of the Parthians, seized Judæa. He was slain by Publius Ventidius, and the Parthians were driven back over the Euphrates.

Caius Sosius reduced the Jews to subjection. The royal power, which had been bestowed by Antony on Herod, was augmented by the victorious Augustus. On Herod's death, one Simon, without waiting for the approbation of the Emperor, usurped the title of king. He was punished by Quintilius Varus then governor of Syria, and the nation, with its liberties curtailed, was divided into three provinces under the sons of Herod. Under Tiberius all was quiet. But when the Jews were ordered by Caligula to set up his statue in the temple, they preferred the alternative of war. The death of the Emperor put an end to the disturbance. The kings were either dead, or reduced to insignificance, when Claudius entrusted the province of Judæa to the Roman Knights or to his own freedmen, one of whom, Antonius Felix, indulging in every kind of barbarity and lust, exercised the power of a king in the spirit of a slave. He had married Drusilla, the granddaughter of Antony and Cleopatra, and so was the grandson-in-law, as Claudius was the grandson, of Antony.

10. Yet the endurance of the Jews lasted till Gessius Florus was procurator. In his time the war broke out. Cestius Gallus, legate of Syria, who attempted to crush it, had to fight several battles, generally with ill-success. Cestius dying, either in the course of nature, or from vexation, Vespasian was sent by Nero, and by help of his good fortune, his high reputation, and his excellent subordinates, succeeded within the space of two summers in occupying with his victorious army the whole of the level country and all the cities, except Jerusalem. The following year had been wholly taken up with civil strife, and had passed, as far as the Jews were concerned, in inaction. Peace having been established in Italy, foreign affairs were once more remembered. Our indignation was heightened by the circumstance that the Jews alone had not submitted. At the same time it was held to be more expedient, in reference to the possible results and contingencies of the new reign, that Titus should remain with the army.

Accordingly he pitched his camp, as I have related, before the walls of Jerusalem, and displayed his legions in order of battle.

11. The Jews formed their line close under their walls

whence, if successful, they might venture to advance, and where, if repulsed, they had a refuge at hand. The cavalry with some light infantry was sent to attack them, and fought without any decisive result. Shortly afterwards the enemy retreated. During the following days they fought a series of engagements in front of the gates, till they were driven within the walls by continual defeats. The Romans then began to prepare for an assault. It seemed beneath them to await the result of famine. The army demanded the more perilous alternative, some prompted by courage, many by sheer ferocity and greed of gain. Titus himself had Rome with all its wealth and pleasures before his eyes. Jerusalem must fall at once, or it would delay his enjoyment of them. But the commanding situation of the city had been strengthened by enormous works which would have been a thorough defence even for level ground. Two hills of great height were fenced in by walls which had been skilfully obliqued or bent inwards, in such a manner that the flank of an assailant was exposed to missiles. The rock terminated in a precipice; the towers were raised to a height of sixty feet, where the hill lent its aid to the fortifications, where the ground fell, to a height of one hundred and twenty. They had a marvellous appearance, and to a distant spectator seemed to be of uniform elevation. Within were other walls surrounding the palace, and, rising to a conspicuous height, the tower Antonia, so called by Herod, in honour of Marcus Antonius.

12. The temple resembled a citadel, and had its own walls, which were more laboriously constructed than the others. Even the colonnades with which it was surrounded formed an admirable outwork. It contained an inexhaustible spring; there were subterranean excavations in the hill, and tanks and cisterns for holding rain water. The founders of the state had foreseen that frequent wars would result from the singularity of its customs, and so had made every provision against the most protracted siege. After the capture of their city by Pompey, experience and apprehension taught them much. Availing themselves of the sordid policy of the Claudian era to purchase the right of fortification, they raised in time of peace such walls as were suited for war. Their num-

bers were increased by a vast rabble collected from the overthrow of the other cities. All the most obstinate rebels had escaped into the place, and perpetual seditions were the consequence. There were three generals, and as many armies. Simon held the outer and larger circuit of walls. John, also called Bargioras, occupied the middle city. Eleazar had fortified the temple. John and Simon were strong in numbers and equipment, Eleazar in position. There were continual skirmishes, surprises, and incendiary fires, and a vast quantity of corn was burnt. Before long John sent some emissaries, who, under pretence of sacrificing, slaughtered Eleazar and his partisans, and gained possession of the temple. The city was thus divided between two factions, till, as the Romans approached, war with the foreigner brought about a reconciliation.

13. Prodigies had occurred, which this nation, prone to superstition, but hating all religious rites, did not deem it lawful to expiate by offering and sacrifice. There had been seen hosts joining battle in the skies, the fiery gleam of arms, the temple illuminated by a sudden radiance from the clouds. The doors of the inner shrine were suddenly thrown open, and a voice of more than mortal tone was heard to cry that the Gods were departing. At the same instant there was a mighty stir as of departure. Some few put a fearful meaning on these events, but in most there was a firm persuasion, that in the ancient records of their priests was contained a prediction of how at this very time the East was to grow powerful, and rulers, coming from Judæa, were to acquire universal empire. These mysterious prophecies had pointed to Vespasian and Titus, but the common people, with the usual blindness of ambition, had interpreted these mighty destinies of themselves, and could not be brought even by disasters to believe the truth. I have heard that the total number of the besieged, of every age and both sexes, amounted to six hundred thousand. All who were able bore arms, and a number, more than proportionate to the population, had the courage to do so. Men and women showed equal resolution, and life seemed more terrible than death, if they were to be forced to leave their country. Such was this city and nation; and Titus Cæsar, seeing that the posi-

tion forbad an assault or any of the more rapid operations
of war, determined to proceed by earthworks and covered
approaches. The legions had their respective duties assigned
to them, and there was a cessation from fighting, till all the
inventions, used in ancient warfare, or devised by modern
ingenuity for the reduction of cities, were constructed.

14. Meanwhile Civilis, having recruited his army from
Germany after his defeat among the Treveri, took up his
position at the Old Camp, where his situation would protect
him, and where the courage of his barbarian troops would
be raised by the recollection of successes gained on the spot.
He was followed to this place by Cerialis, whose forces had
now been doubled by the arrival of the 2nd, 6th, and 14th
legions. The auxiliary infantry and cavalry, summoned long
before, had hastened to join him after his victory. Neither
of the generals loved delay. But a wide extent of plain
naturally saturated with water kept them apart. Civilis had
also thrown a dam obliquely across the Rhine, so that the
stream, diverted by the obstacle, might overflow the adjacent country. Such was the character of the district, full of
hidden perils from the varying depth of the fords, and unfavourable to our troops. The Roman soldier is heavily
armed and afraid to swim, while the German, who is accustomed to rivers, is favoured by the lightness of his equipment and the height of his stature.

15. The Batavi provoking a conflict, the struggle was at
once begun by all the boldest spirits among our troops, but
a panic arose, when they saw arms and horses swallowed up
in the vast depths of the marshes. The Germans leapt lightly
through the well-known shallows, and frequently, quitting
the front, hung on the rear and flanks of our army. It was
neither the close nor the distant fighting of a land-battle; it
was more like a naval contest. Struggling among the waters,
or exerting every limb where they found any firm footing,
the wounded and the unhurt, those who could swim and
those who could not, were involved in one common destruction. The loss however was less than might have been expected from the confusion, for the Germans, not venturing
to leave the morass, returned to their camp. The result of
this battle roused both generals, though from different mo-

tives, to hasten on the final struggle. Civilis was anxious to follow up his success; Cerialis to wipe out his disgrace. The Germans were flushed with success; the Romans were thoroughly roused by shame. The barbarians spent the night in singing and shouting; our men in rage and threats of vengeance.

16. Next morning Cerialis formed his front with the cavalry and auxiliary infantry; in the second line were posted the legions, the general reserving a picked force for unforeseen contingencies. Civilis confronted him with his troops ranged, not in line, but in columns. On the right were the Batavi and the Gugerni; the left, which was nearer the river, was occupied by the Transrhenane tribes. The exhortations of the generals were not addressed as formal harangues to the assembled armies, but to the divisions separately, as they rode along the line. Cerialis spoke of the old glory of the Roman name, of former and of recent victories; he told them that in destroying for ever their treacherous, cowardly, and beaten foe, they had to execute a punishment, rather than to fight a battle. They had lately contended with a superior force, and yet the Germans, the strength of the hostile army, had been routed; a few were left, who carried terror in their hearts and scars upon their backs. He addressed to the several legions appropriate appeals. The 14th were styled the 'Conquerors of Britain'; the powerful influence of the 6th had made Galba Emperor; the men of the 2nd were in that battle first to consecrate their new standards and new eagle. Then riding up to the army of Germany, he stretched forth his hand, and implored them to recover their river-bank and their camp by the slaughter of the foe. A joyful shout arose from the whole army, some of whom after long peace lusted for battle, while others, weary of war, desired peace; all were looking for rewards and for future repose.

17. Nor did Civilis marshal his army in silence. He called the field of battle to bear witness to their valour. He told the Germans and Batavians that they were standing on the monuments of their glory, that they were treading under foot the ashes and bones of legions. "Wherever," he said, "the Roman turns his eyes, captivity, disaster, and everything that is terrible, confront him. Do not be alarmed by the

adverse result of the battle among the Treveri. There, their own success proved hurtful to the Germans, for, throwing away their arms, they hampered their hands with plunder. Since then everything has been favourable to us, and against the foe. All precautions, which the skill of a general should take, have been taken. Here are these flooded plains which we know so well, here the marshes so fatal to the enemy. The Rhine and the Gods of Germany are in your sight. Under their auspices give battle, remembering your wives, your parents, and your father-land. This day will either be the most glorious among the deeds of the past, or will be infamous in the eyes of posterity." These words were hailed, according to their custom, with the clash of arms and with wild antics, and then the battle was commenced by a discharge of stones, leaden balls, and other missiles, our soldiers not entering the morass, while the Germans sought to provoke, and so draw them on.

18. When their store of missiles was spent, and the battle grew hotter, a fiercer onslaught was made by the enemy. Their tall stature and very long spears enabled them, without closing, to wound our men, who were wavering and unsteady. At the same time a column of the Bructeri swam across from the dam, which I have described as carried out into the river. Here there was some confusion. The line of the allied infantry was being driven back, when the legions took up the contest. The fury of the enemy was checked, and the battle again became equal. At the same time a Batavian deserter came up to Cerialis, offering an opportunity of attacking the enemy's rear, if some cavalry were sent along the edge of the morass. The ground there was firm, and the Gugerni, to whom the post had been allotted, were careless. Two squadrons were sent with the deserter, and outflanked the unsuspecting enemy. At the shout that announced this success, the legions charged in front. The Germans were routed, and fled towards the Rhine. The war would have been finished that day, if the fleet had hastened to come up. As it was, the cavalry did not pursue, for a storm of rain suddenly fell, and night was at hand.

19. The next day the 14th legion was sent into the Upper Province to join Gallus Annius. The 10th, which had arrived

from Spain, supplied its place in the army of Cerialis. Civilis was joined by some auxiliaries from the Chauci. Nevertheless he did not venture to fight for the defence of the Batavian capital, but carrying off property that could be removed, and setting fire to the remainder, he retreated into the island, aware that there were not vessels enough for constructing a bridge, and that the Roman army could not cross the river in any other way. He also demolished the dyke, constructed by Drusus Germanicus, and, by destroying this barrier, sent the river flowing down a steep channel on the side of Gaul. The river having been thus, so to speak, diverted, the narrowness of the channel between the island and Germany created an appearance of an uninterrupted surface of dry ground. Tutor, Classicus, and one hundred and thirteen senators of the Treveri, also crossed the Rhine. Among them was Alpinius Montanus, of whose mission into Gaul by Antonius I have already spoken. He was accompanied by his brother Decimus Alpinius. His other adherents were now endeavouring to collect auxiliaries among these danger-loving tribes by appeals to their pity and their greed.

20. The war was so far from being at an end, that Civilis in one day attacked on four points the positions of the auxiliary infantry and cavalry and of the legions, assailing the tenth legion at Arenacum, the second at Batavodurum, and the camp of the auxiliary infantry and cavalry at Grinnes and Vada, and so dividing his forces, that he himself, his sister's son Verax, Classicus, and Tutor, led each his own division. They were not confident of accomplishing all these objects, but they hoped that, if they made many ventures, fortune would favour them on some one point. Besides, Cerialis was not cautious, and might easily be intercepted, as the multiplicity of tidings hurried him from place to place. The force, which had to attack the tenth legion, thinking it a hard matter to storm a legionary encampment, surprised some troops, who had gone out, and were busy felling timber, killed the prefect of the camp, five centurions of the first rank, and a few soldiers; the rest found shelter behind the fortifications. At Batavodurum the German troops tried to break down the bridge partly built. Night terminated an indecisive conflict.

21. There was greater danger at Grinnes and Vada. Civilis attacked Vada, Classicus Grinnes, and they could not be checked, for our bravest men had fallen, among them Briganticus, who commanded a squadron of cavalry, and of whose loyalty to the Roman cause and enmity to his uncle Civilis I have already spoken. But when Cerialis came up with a picked body of cavalry, the fortune of the day changed, and the Germans were driven headlong into the river. Civilis, who was recognised while seeking to stop his flying troops, became the mark of many missiles, left his horse, and swam across the river. Verax escaped in the same way. Some light vessels were brought up, and carried off Tutor and Classicus. Even on this occasion the Roman fleet was not present at the engagement, though orders had been given to that effect. Fear kept them away, and their crews were dispersed about other military duties. Cerialis in fact allowed too little time for executing his commands; he was hasty in his plans, though eminently successful in their results. Fortune helped him even where skill had failed, and so both the general and his army became less careful about discipline. A few days after this he escaped the peril of actual capture, but not without great disgrace.

22. He had gone to Novesium and Bonna, to inspect the camps which were then in course of erection for the winter abode of the legions, and was making his way back with the fleet, his escort being in disorder, and his sentries negligent. This was observed by the Germans, and they planned a surprise. They chose a dark and cloudy night, and moving rapidly down the stream, entered the entrenchments without opposition. The carnage was at first helped on by a cunning device. They cut the ropes of the tents, and slaughtered the soldiers as they lay buried beneath their own dwellings. Another force put the fleet into confusion, threw their grappling irons on the vessels, and dragged them away by the sterns. They sought at first to elude notice by silence, but when the slaughter was begun, by way of increasing the panic they raised on all sides a deafening shout. The Romans, awakened by wounds, looked for their arms and rushed through the passages of the camp, some few with their proper accoutrements, but most with their garments

wrapped round their shoulders, and with drawn swords in their hands. The general, who was half asleep, and all but naked, was saved by the enemy's mistake. They carried off the prætorian vessel, which was distinguished by a flag, believing that the general was on board. Cerialis indeed had passed the night elsewhere, in the company, as many believed, of an Ubian woman, Claudia Sacrata. The sentinels sought to excuse their own scandalous neglect by the disgraceful conduct of the general, alleging that they had been ordered to be silent, that they might not disturb his rest, and that, from omitting the watchwords and the usual challenges, they had themselves fallen asleep. The enemy rowed back in broad daylight with the captured vessels. The prætorian trireme they towed up the river Lupia as a present to Veleda.

23. Civilis was seized by a desire to make a naval demonstration. He manned all the biremes that he had, and such vessels as were propelled by a single bank of oars. To these he added a vast number of boats. He put in each three or four hundred men, the usual complement of a Liburnian galley. With these were the captured vessels, in which, picturesquely enough, plaids of various colours were used for sails. The place selected was an expanse of water, not unlike the sea, where the mouth of the Mosa serves to discharge the Rhine into the ocean. The motive for equipping this fleet was, to say nothing of the natural vanity of this people, a desire to intercept, by this alarming demonstration, the supplies that were approaching from Gaul. Cerialis, more in astonishment than alarm, drew up his fleet in line, and, though inferior in numbers, it had the advantage in the experience of the crews, the skill of the pilots, and the size of the vessels. The Romans had the stream with them, the enemy's vessels were propelled by the wind. Thus passing each other, they separated after a brief discharge of light missiles. Civilis attempted nothing more, and retired to the other side of the Rhine. Cerialis mercilessly ravaged the Island of the Batavi, but, with a policy familiar to commanders, left untouched the estates and houses of Civilis. Meanwhile, however, the autumn was far advanced, and the river, swollen by the continual rains of the season, overflowed the island, marshy and low-lying as it is, till it resembled a lake. There

were no ships, no provisions at hand, and the camp, which was situated on low ground, was in process of being carried away by the force of the stream.

24. That the legions might then have been crushed, and that the Germans wished to crush them, but were turned from their purpose by his own craft, was claimed as a merit by Civilis; nor is it unlike the truth, since a capitulation followed in a few days. Cerialis, sending secret emissaries, had held out the prospect of peace to the Batavi, and of pardon to Civilis, while he advised Veleda and her relatives to change by a well-timed service to the Roman people the fortune of war, which so many disasters had shown to be adverse. He reminded them that the Treveri had been beaten, that the Ubii had submitted, that the Batavi had had their country taken from them, and that from the friendship of Civilis nothing else had been gained but wounds, defeat, and mourning; an exile and a fugitive he could only be a burden to those who entertained him, and they had already trespassed enough in crossing the Rhine so often. If they attempted anything more, on their side would be the wrong and the guilt, with the Romans the vengeance of heaven.

25. Thus promises were mingled with threats. When the fidelity of the Transrhenane tribes had been thus shaken, among the Batavi also there arose debates. "We can no longer," they said, "postpone our ruin. The servitude of the whole world cannot be averted by a single nation. What has been accomplished by destroying legions with fire and sword, but that more legions and stronger have been brought up? If it was for Vespasian that we fought this war, then Vespasian rules the world; if we meant to challenge to battle the Roman people, then what a mere fraction of the human race are the Batavi! Look at the Rhætians and Noricans, at the burdens borne by the other allies. No tribute, but valour and manhood are demanded of us. This is the next thing to liberty, and if we must choose between masters, then we may more honourably bear with the Emperors of Rome, than with the women of the Germans." Such were the murmurs of the lower class; the nobles spoke in fiercer language. "We have been driven into war," they said, "by the fury of Civilis. He sought to counterbalance his private wrongs by the

destruction of his nation. Then were the Gods angry with the Batavi when the legions were besieged, when the legates were slain, when the war, so necessary to that one man, so fatal to us, was begun. We are at the last extremity, unless we think of repenting, and avow our repentance by punishing the guilty."

26. These dispositions did not escape the notice of Civilis. He determined to anticipate them, moved not only by weariness of his sufferings, but also by that clinging to life which often breaks the noblest spirits. He asked for a conference. The bridge over the river Nabalia was cut down, and the two generals advanced to the broken extremities. Civilis thus opened the conference:—"If it were before a legate of Vitellius that I were defending myself, my acts would deserve no pardon, my words no credit. All the relations between us were those of hatred and hostility, first made so by him, and afterwards embittered by me. My respect for Vespasian is of long standing. While he was still a subject, we were called friends. This was known to Primus Antonius, whose letters urged me to take up arms, for he feared lest the legions of Germany and the youth of Gaul should cross the Alps. What Antonius advised by his letters, Hordeonius suggested by word of mouth. I fought the same battle in Germany, as did Mucianus in Syria, Aponius in Mœsia, Flavianus in Pannonia."

[At this point the *History* breaks off. We do not know what happened to Civilis. The Batavians seem to have received favorable treatment.]

THE LIFE OF
CNÆUS JULIUS AGRICOLA

THE LIFE OF
CNÆUS JULIUS AGRICOLA

1. To bequeath to posterity a record of the deeds and characters of distinguished men is an ancient practice which even the present age, careless as it is of its own sons, has not abandoned whenever some great and conspicuous excellence has conquered and risen superior to that failing, common to petty and to great states, blindness and hostility to goodness. But in days gone by, as there was a greater inclination and a more open path to the achievement of memorable actions, so the man of highest genius was led by the simple reward of a good conscience to hand on without partiality or self-seeking the remembrance of greatness. Many too thought that to write their own lives showed the confidence of integrity rather than presumption. Of Rutilius and Scaurus no one doubted the honesty or questioned the motives. So true is it that merit is best appreciated by the age in which it thrives most easily. But in these days, I, who have to record the life of one who has passed away, must crave an indulgence, which I should not have had to ask had I only to inveigh against an age so cruel, so hostile to all virtue.

2. We have read that the panegyrics pronounced by Arulenus Rusticus on Pætus Thrasea, and by Herennius Senecio on Priscus Helvidius, were made capital crimes, that not only their persons but their very books were objects of rage, and that the triumvirs were commissioned to burn in the forum those works of splendid genius. They fancied, forsooth, that in that fire the voice of the Roman people, the freedom of the Senate, and the conscience of the human race were perishing, while at the same time they banished the teachers of philosophy, and exiled every noble pursuit, that nothing good might anywhere confront them. Certainly we

showed a magnificent example of patience; as a former age
had witnessed the extreme of liberty, so we witnessed the
extreme of servitude, when the informer robbed us of the
interchange of speech and hearing. We should have lost
memory as well as voice, had it been as easy to forget as to
keep silence.

3. Now at last our spirit is returning. And yet, though at
the dawn of a most happy age Nerva Cæsar blended things
once irreconcilable, sovereignty and freedom, though Nerva
Trajan is now daily augmenting the prosperity of the time,
and though the public safety has not only our hopes and
good wishes, but has also the certain pledge of their fulfill-
ment, still, from the necessary condition of human frailty,
the remedy works less quickly than the disease. As our bodies
grow but slowly, perish in a moment, so it is easier to crush
than to revive genius and its pursuits. Besides, the charm of
indolence steals over us, and the idleness which at first we
loathed we afterwards love. What if during those fifteen
years, a large portion of human life, many were cut off by
ordinary casualties, and the ablest fell victims to the Emperor's rage, if a few of us survive, I may almost say, not
only others but our ownselves, survive, though there have
been taken from the midst of life those many years which
brought the young in dumb silence to old age, and the old
almost to the very verge and end of existence! Yet we shall
not regret that we have told, though in language unskilful
and unadorned, the story of past servitude, and borne our
testimony to present happiness. Meanwhile this book, intended to do honour to Agricola, my father-in-law, will, as
an expression of filial regard, be commended, or at least
excused.

4. Cnæus Julius Agricola was born at the ancient and
famous colony of Forum Julii. Each of his grandfathers was
an Imperial procurator, that is, of the highest equestrian
rank. His father, Julius Græcinus, a member of the Senatorian order, and distinguished for his pursuit of eloquence
and philosophy, earned for himself by these very merits the
displeasure of Caius Cæsar. He was ordered to impeach
Marcus Silanus, and because he refused was put to death.
His mother was Julia Procilla, a lady of singular virtue.

Brought up by her side with fond affection, he passed his boyhood and youth in the cultivation of every worthy attainment. He was guarded from the enticements of the profligate not only by his own good and straightforward character, but also by having, when quite a child, for the scene and guide of his studies, Massilia, a place where refinement and provincial frugality were blended and happily combined. I remember that he used to tell us how in his early youth he would have imbibed a keener love of philosophy than became a Roman and a senator, had not his mother's good sense checked his excited and ardent spirit. It was the case of a lofty and aspiring soul craving with more eagerness than caution the beauty and splendour of great and glorious renown. But it was soon mellowed by reason and experience, and he retained from his learning that most difficult of lessons—moderation.

5. He served his military apprenticeship in Britain to the satisfaction of Suetonius Paullinus, a painstaking and judicious officer, who, to test his merits, selected him to share his tent. Without the recklessness with which young men often make the profession of arms a mere pastime, and without indolence, he never availed himself of his tribune's rank or his inexperience to procure enjoyment or to escape from duty. He sought to make himself acquainted with the province and known to the army; he would learn from the skilful, and keep pace with the bravest, would attempt nothing for display, would avoid nothing from fear, and would be at once careful and vigilant.

Never indeed had Britain been more excited, or in a more critical condition. Veteran soldiers had been massacred, colonies burnt, armies cut off. The struggle was then for safety; it was soon to be for victory. And though all this was conducted under the leadership and direction of another, though the final issue and the glory of having won back the province belonged to the general, yet skill, experience, and ambition were acquired by the young officer. His soul too was penetrated with the desire of warlike renown, a sentiment unwelcome to an age which put a sinister construction on eminent merit, and made glory as perilous as infamy.

6. From Britain he went to Rome, to go through the regu-

lar course of office, and there allied himself with Domitia
Decidiana, a lady of illustrious birth. The marriage was one
which gave a man ambitious of advancement distinction and
support. They lived in singular harmony, through their mutual affection and preference of each other to self. However,
the good wife deserves the greater praise, just as the bad
incurs a heavier censure.

Appointed Quæstor, the ballot gave him Asia for his province, Salvius Titianus for his proconsul. Neither the one nor
the other corrupted him, though the province was rich and
an easy prey to the wrongdoer, while the proconsul, a man
inclined to every species of greed, was ready by all manner
of indulgence to purchase a mutual concealment of guilt.

A daughter was there added to his family to be his stay
and comfort, for shortly after he lost the son that had before
been born to him. The year between his quæstorship and
tribunate, as well as the year of the tribunate itself, he
passed in retirement and inaction, for he knew those times
of Nero when indolence stood for wisdom. His prætorship
was passed in the same consistent quietude, for the usual
judicial functions did not fall to his lot. The games and the
pageantry of his office he ordered according to the mean
between strictness and profusion, avoiding extravagance, but
not missing distinction. He was afterwards appointed by
Galba to draw up an account of the temple offerings, and
his searching scrutiny relieved the conscience of the state
from the burden of all sacrileges but those committed by
Nero.

7. The following year inflicted a terrible blow on his affections and his fortunes. Otho's fleet, while cruising idly about,
cruelly ravaged Intemelii, a district of Liguria; his mother,
who was living here on her own estate, was murdered. The
estate itself and a large part of her patrimony were plundered. This was indeed the occasion of the crime. Agricola,
who instantly set out to discharge the duties of affection,
was overtaken by the tidings that Vespasian was aiming at
the throne. He at once joined his party. Vespasian's early
policy, and the government of Rome were directed by Mucianus, for Domitian was a mere youth, and from his father's
elevation sought only the opportunities of indulgence.

Agricola, having been sent by Mucianus to conduct a levy of troops, and having done his work with integrity and energy, was appointed to command the 20th Legion, which had been slow to take the new oath of allegiance, and the retiring officer of which was reported to be acting disloyally. It was a trying and formidable charge for even officers of consular rank, and the late prætorian officer, perhaps from his own disposition, perhaps from that of the soldiers, was powerless to restrain them. Chosen thus at once to supersede and to punish, Agricola, with a singular moderation, wished it to be thought that he had found rather than made an obedient soldiery.

8. Britain was then under Vettius Bolanus, who governed more mildly than suited so turbulent a province. Agricola moderated his energy and restrained his ardour, that he might not grow too important, for he had learnt to obey, and understood well how to combine expediency with honour. Soon afterwards Britain received for its governor a man of consular rank, Petilius Cerialis. Agricola's merits had now room for display. Cerialis let him share at first indeed only the toils and dangers, but before long the glory of war, often by way of trial putting him in command of part of the army, and sometimes, on the strength of the result, of larger forces. Never to enhance his own renown did Agricola boast of his exploits; he always referred his success, as though he were but an instrument, to his general and director. Thus by his valour in obeying orders and by his modesty of speech he escaped jealousy without losing distinction.

9. As he was returning from the command of the legion, Vespasian admitted him into the patrician order, and then gave him the province of Aquitania, a preeminently splendid appointment both from the importance of its duties and the prospect of the consulate to which the Emperor destined him. Many think the genius of the soldier wants subtlety, because military law, which is summary and blunt, and apt to appeal to the sword, finds no exercise for the refinements of the forum. Yet Agricola, from his natural good sense, though called to act among civilians, did his work with ease and correctness. And, besides, the times of business and relaxation were kept distinct. When his public and judicial

duties required it, he was dignified, thoughtful, austere, and yet often merciful; when business was done with, he wore no longer the official character. He was altogether without harshness, pride, or the greed of gain. With a most rare felicity, his good nature did not weaken his authority, nor his strictness the attachment of his friends. To speak of uprightness and purity in such a man would be an insult to his virtues. Fame itself, of which even good men are often weakly fond, he did not seek by an ostentation of virtue or by artifice. He avoided rivalry with his colleagues, contention with his procurator, thinking such victories no honour and defeat disgrace. For somewhat less than three years he was kept in his governorship, and was then recalled with an immediate prospect of the consulate. A general belief went with him that the province of Britain was to be his, not because he had himself hinted it, but because he seemed worthy of it. Public opinion is not always mistaken; sometimes even it chooses the right man. He was consul, and I but a youth, when he betrothed to me his daughter, a maiden even then of noble promise. After his consulate he gave her to me in marriage, and was then at once appointed to the government of Britain, with the addition of the sacred office of the pontificate.

10. The geography and inhabitants of Britain, already described by many writers, I will speak of, not that my research and ability may be compared with theirs, but because the country was then for the first time thoroughly subdued. And so matters, which as being still not accurately known my predecessors embellished with their eloquence, shall now be related on the evidence of facts.

Britain, the largest of the islands which Roman geography includes, is so situated that it faces Germany on the east, Spain on the west; on the south it is even within sight of Gaul; its northern extremities, which have no shores opposite to them, are beaten by the waves of a vast open sea. The form of the entire country has been compared by Livy and Fabius Rusticus, the most graphic among ancient and modern historians, to an oblong shield or battle-axe. And this no doubt is its shape without Caledonia, so that it has become the popular description of the whole island. There is, however, a large and irregular tract of land which juts out from its furthest shores, tapering off in a wedge-like form. Round these coasts of remotest ocean the Roman fleet then for the first time sailed, ascertained that Britain is an island, and simultaneously discovered and conquered what are called the Orcades, islands hitherto unknown. Thule too was descried in the distance, which as yet had been hidden by the snows of winter. Those waters, they say, are sluggish, and yield with difficulty to the oar, and are not even raised by the wind as other seas. The reason, I suppose, is that lands and mountains, which are the cause and origin of storms, are here comparatively rare, and also that the vast depths of that unbroken expanse are more slowly set in motion. But to investigate the nature of the ocean and the tides is no part of the present work, and many writers have discussed the subject. I would simply add, that nowhere has the sea a wider dominion, that it has many currents running in every direction, that it does not merely flow and ebb within the limits of the shore, but penetrates and winds far inland, and finds a home among hills and mountains as though in its own domain.

11. Who were the original inhabitants of Britain, whether they were indigenous or foreign, is, as usual among barbarians, little known. Their physical characteristics are various, and from these conclusions may be drawn. The red hair and large limbs of the inhabitants of Caledonia point clearly to a German origin. The dark complexion of the Silures, their usually curly hair, and the fact that Spain is the opposite shore to them, are an evidence that Iberians of a former date crossed over and occupied these parts. Those who are nearest to the Gauls are also like them, either from the permanent influence of original descent, or, because in countries which run out so far to meet each other, climate has produced similar physical qualities. But a general survey inclines me to believe that the Gauls established themselves in an island so near to them. Their religious belief may be traced in the strongly-marked British superstition. The language differs but little; there is the same boldness in challenging danger, and, when it is near, the same timidity in shrinking from it. The Britons, however, exhibit more spirit, as being a people

whom a long peace has not yet enervated. Indeed we have understood that even the Gauls were once renowned in war; but, after a while, sloth following on ease crept over them, and they lost their courage along with their freedom. This too has happened to the long-conquered tribes of Britain; the rest are still what the Gauls once were.

12. Their strength is in infantry. Some tribes fight also with the chariot. The higher in rank is the charioteer; the dependants fight. They were once ruled by kings, but are now divided under chieftains into factions and parties. Our greatest advantage in coping with tribes so powerful is that they do not act in concert. Seldom is it that two or three states meet together to ward off a common danger. Thus, while they fight singly, all are conquered.

Their sky is obscured by continual rain and cloud. Severity of cold is unknown. The days exceed in length those of our part of the world; the nights are bright, and in the extreme north so short that between sunlight and dawn you can perceive but a slight distinction. It is said that, if there are no clouds in the way, the splendour of the sun can be seen throughout the night, and that he does not rise and set, but only crosses the heavens. The truth is, that the low shadow thrown from the flat extremities of the earth's surface does not raise the darkness to any height, and the night thus fails to reach the sky and stars.

With the exception of the olive and vine, and plants which usually grow in warmer climates, the soil will yield, and even abundantly, all ordinary produce. It ripens indeed slowly, but is of rapid growth, the cause in each case being the same, namely, the excessive moisture of the soil and of the atmosphere. Britain contains gold and silver and other metals, as the prize of conquest. The ocean, too, produces pearls, but of a dusky and bluish hue. Some think that those who collect them have not the requisite skill, as in the Red Sea the living and breathing pearl is torn from the rocks, while in Britain they are gathered just as they are thrown up. I could myself more readily believe that the natural properties of the pearls are in fault than our keenness for gain.

13. The Britons themselves bear cheerfully the conscrip-

tion, the taxes, and the other burdens imposed on them by the Empire, if there be no oppression. Of this they are impatient; they are reduced to subjection, not as yet to slavery. The deified Julius, the very first Roman who entered Britain with an army, though by a successful engagement he struck terror into the inhabitants and gained possession of the coast, must be regarded as having indicated rather than transmitted the acquisition to future generations. Then came the civil wars, and the arms of our leaders were turned against their country, and even when there was peace, there was a long neglect of Britain. This Augustus spoke of as policy, Tiberius as an inherited maxim. That Caius Cæsar meditated an invasion of Britain is perfectly clear, but his purposes, rapidly formed, were easily changed, and his vast attempts on Germany had failed. Claudius was the first to renew the attempt, and conveyed over into the island some legions and auxiliaries, choosing Vespasian to share with him the campaign, whose approaching elevation had this beginning. Several tribes were subdued and kings made prisoners, and destiny learnt to know its favourite.

14. Aulus Plautius was the first governor of consular rank, and Ostorius Scapula the next. Both were famous soldiers, and by degrees the nearest portions of Britain were brought into the condition of a province, and a colony of veterans was also introduced. Some of the states were given to king Cogidumnus, who lived down to our day a most faithful ally. So was maintained the ancient and long-recognised practice of the Roman people, which seeks to secure among the instruments of dominion even kings themselves. Soon after, Didius Gallus consolidated the conquests of his predecessors, and advanced a very few positions into parts more remote, to gain the credit of having enlarged the sphere of government. Didius was succeeded by Veranius, who died within the year. Then Suetonius Paullinus enjoyed success for two years; he subdued several tribes and strengthened our military posts. Thus encouraged, he made an attempt on the island of Mona, as a place from which the rebels drew reinforcements; but in doing this he left his rear open to attack.

15. Relieved from apprehension by the legate's absence, the Britons dwelt much among themselves on the miseries of

subjection, compared their wrongs, and exaggerated them in the discussion. "All we get by patience," they said, "is that heavier demands are exacted from us, as from men who will readily submit. A single king once ruled us; now two are set over us; a legate to tyrannise over our lives, a procurator to tyrannise over our property. Their quarrels and their harmony are alike ruinous to their subjects. The centurions of the one, the slaves of the other, combine violence with insult. Nothing is now safe from their avarice, nothing from their lust. In war it is the strong who plunders; now, it is for the most part by cowards and poltroons that our homes are rifled, our children torn from us, the conscription enforced, as though it were for our country alone that we could not die. For, after all, what a mere handful of soldiers has crossed over, if we Britons look at our own numbers. Germany did thus actually shake off the yoke, and yet its defence was a river, not the ocean. With us, fatherland, wives, parents, are the motives to war; with them, only greed and profligacy. They will surely fly, as did the now deified Julius, if once we emulate the valour of our sires. Let us not be panicstricken at the result of one or two engagements. The miserable have more fury and greater resolution. Now even the gods are beginning to pity us, for they are keeping away the Roman general, and detaining his army far from us in another island. We have already taken the hardest step; we are deliberating. And indeed, in all such designs, to dare is less perilous than to be detected."

16. Rousing each other by this and like language, under the leadership of Boudicea, a woman of kingly descent (for they admit no distinction of sex in their royal successions), they all rose in arms. They fell upon our troops, which were scattered on garrison duty, stormed the forts, and burst into the colony itself, the head-quarters, as they thought, of tyranny. In their rage and their triumph, they spared no variety of a barbarian's cruelty. Had not Paullinus on hearing of the outbreak in the province rendered prompt succour, Britain would have been lost. By one successful engagement, he brought it back to its former obedience, though many, troubled by the conscious guilt of rebellion and by particular dread of the legate, still clung to their arms. Excellent as he

was in other respects, his policy to the conquered was arrogant, and exhibited the cruelty of one who was avenging private wrongs. Accordingly Petronius Turpilianus was sent out to initiate a milder rule. A stranger to the enemy's misdeeds and so more accessible to their penitence, he put an end to old troubles, and, attempting nothing more, handed the province over to Trebellius Maximus. Trebellius, who was somewhat indolent, and never ventured on a campaign, controlled the province by a certain courtesy in his administration. Even the barbarians now learnt to excuse many attractive vices, and the occurrence of the civil war gave a good pretext for inaction. But we were sorely troubled with mutiny, as troops habituated to service grew demoralised by idleness. Trebellius, who had escaped the soldiers' fury by flying and hiding himself, governed henceforth on sufferance, a disgraced and humbled man. It was a kind of bargain; the soldiers had their licence, the general had his life; and so the mutiny cost no bloodshed. Nor did Vettius Bolanus, during the continuance of the civil wars, trouble Britain with discipline. There was the same inaction with respect to the enemy, and similar unruliness in the camp, only Bolanus, an upright man, whom no misdeeds made odious, had secured affection in default of the power of control.

17. When however Vespasian had restored to unity Britain as well as the rest of the world, in the presence of great generals and renowned armies the enemy's hopes were crushed. They were at once panic-stricken by the attack of Petilius Cerialis on the state of the Brigantes, said to be the most prosperous in the entire province. There were many battles, some by no means bloodless, and his conquests, or at least his wars, embraced a large part of the territory of the Brigantes. Indeed he would have altogether thrown into the shade the activity and renown of any other successor; but Julius Frontinus was equal to the burden, a great man as far as greatness was then possible, who subdued by his arms the powerful and warlike tribe of the Silures, surmounting the difficulties of the country as well as the valour of the enemy.

18. Such was the state of Britain, and such were the vicissitudes of the war, which Agricola found on his crossing over about midsummer. Our soldiers made it a pretext for care-

lessness, as if all fighting was over, and the enemy were bid-
ing their time. The Ordovices, shortly before Agricola's arrival, had destroyed nearly the whole of a squadron of allied
cavalry quartered in their territory. Such a beginning raised
the hopes of the country, and all who wished for war approved the precedent, and anxiously watched the temper of
the new governor. Meanwhile Agricola, though summer was
past and the detachments were scattered throughout the
province, though the soldiers' confident anticipation of inaction for that year would be a source of delay and difficulty
in beginning a campaign, and most advisers thought it best
simply to watch all weak points, resolved to face the peril.
He collected a force of veterans and a small body of auxiliaries; then as the Ordovices would not venture to descend
into the plain, he put himself in front of the ranks to inspire
all with the same courage against a common danger, and led
his troops up a hill. The tribe was all but exterminated.

Well aware that he must follow up the prestige of his
arms, and that in proportion to his first success would be the
terror of the other tribes, he formed the design of subju-
gating the island of Mona, from the occupation of which
Paullinus had been recalled, as I have already related, by
the rebellion of the entire province. But, as his plans were
not matured, he had no fleet. The skill and resolution of the
general accomplished the passage. With some picked men of
the auxiliaries, disencumbered of all baggage, who knew the
shallows and had that national experience in swimming
which enables the Britons to take care not only of themselves but of their arms and horses, he delivered so unexpected an attack that the astonished enemy who were looking for a fleet, a naval armament, and an assault by sea,
thought that to such assailants nothing could be formidable
or invincible. And so, peace having been sued for and the
island given up, Agricola became great and famous as one
who, when entering on his province, a time which others
spend in vain display and a round of ceremonies, chose
rather toil and danger. Nor did he use his success for self-
glorification, or apply the name of campaigns and victories
to the repression of a conquered people. He did not even
describe his achievements in a laurelled letter. Yet by thus

disguising his renown he really increased it, for men inferred
the grandeur of his aspirations from his silence about services so great.

19. Next, with thorough insight into the feelings of his
province, and taught also, by the experience of others, that
little is gained by conquest if followed by oppression, he
determined to root out the causes of war. Beginning first
with himself and his dependants, he kept his household
under restraint, a thing as hard to many as ruling a province. He transacted no public business through freedmen or
slaves; no private leanings, no recommendations or entreaties of friends, moved him in the selection of centurions
and soldiers, but it was ever the best man whom he thought
most trustworthy. He knew everything, but did not always
act on his knowledge. Trifling errors he treated with leniency, serious offences with severity. Nor was it always punishment, but far oftener penitence, which satisfied him. He
preferred to give office and power to men who would not
transgress, rather than have to condemn a transgressor. He
lightened the exaction of corn and tribute by an equal distribution of the burden, while he got rid of those contrivances
for gain which were more intolerable than the tribute itself.
Hitherto the people had been compelled to endure the farce
of waiting by the closed granary and of purchasing corn un-
necessarily and raising it to a fictitious price. Difficult by-
roads and distant places were fixed for them, so that states
with a winter-camp close to them had to carry corn to remote and inaccessible parts of the country, until what was
within the reach of all became a source of profit to the few.

20. Agricola, by the repression of these abuses in his very
first year of office, restored to peace its good name, when,
from either the indifference or the harshness of his predecessors, it had come to be as much dreaded as war. When,
however, summer came, assembling his forces, he continually showed himself in the ranks, praised good discipline,
and kept the stragglers in order. He would himself choose
the position of the camp, himself explore the estuaries and
forests. Meanwhile he would allow the enemy no rest, laying
waste his territory with sudden incursions, and, having sufficiently alarmed him, would then by forbearance display

the allurements of peace. In consequence, many states, which up to that time had been independent, gave hostages, and laid aside their animosities; garrisons and forts were established among them with a skill and diligence with which no newly-acquired part of Britain had before been treated.

21. The following winter passed without disturbance, and was employed in salutary measures. For, to accustom to rest and repose through the charms of luxury a population scattered and barbarous and therefore inclined to war, Agricola gave private encouragement and public aid to the building of temples, courts of justice and dwelling-houses, praising the energetic, and reproving the indolent. Thus an honourable rivalry took the place of compulsion. He likewise provided a liberal education for the sons of the chiefs, and showed such a preference for the natural powers of the Britons over the industry of the Gauls that they who lately disdained the tongue of Rome now coveted its eloquence. Hence, too, a liking sprang up for our style of dress, and the "toga" became fashionable. Step by step they were led to things which dispose to vice, the lounge, the bath, the elegant banquet. All this in their ignorance, they called civilization, when it was but a part of their servitude.

22. The third year of his campaigns opened up new tribes, our ravages on the native population being carried as far as the Taus, an estuary so called. This struck such terror into the enemy that he did not dare to attack our army, harassed though it was by violent storms; and there was even time for the erection of forts. It was noted by experienced officers that no general had ever shown more judgment in choosing suitable positions, and that not a single fort established by Agricola was either stormed by the enemy or abandoned by capitulation or flight. Sorties were continually made; for these positions were secured from protracted siege by a year's supply. So winter brought with it no alarms, and each garrison could hold its own, as the baffled and despairing enemy, who had been accustomed often to repair his summer losses by winter successes, found himself repelled alike both in summer and winter.

Never did Agricola in a greedy spirit appropriate the achievements of others; the centurion and the prefect both found in him an impartial witness of their every action. Some persons used to say that he was too harsh in his reproofs, and that he was as severe to the bad as he was gentle to the good. But his displeasure left nothing behind it; reserve and silence in him were not to be dreaded. He thought it better to show anger than to cherish hatred.

23. The fourth summer he employed in securing what he had overrun. Had the valour of our armies and the renown of the Roman name permitted it, a limit to our conquests might have been found in Britain itself. Clota and Bodotria, estuaries which the tides of two opposite seas carry far back into the country, are separated by but a narrow strip of land. This Agricola then began to defend with a line of forts, and, as all the country to the south was now occupied, the enemy were pushed into what might be called another island.

24. In the fifth year of the war Agricola, himself in the leading ship, crossed the Clota, and subdued in a series of victories tribes hitherto unknown. In that part of Britain which looks towards Ireland, he posted some troops, hoping for fresh conquests rather than fearing attack, inasmuch as Ireland, being between Britain and Spain and conveniently situated for the seas round Gaul, might have been the means of connecting with great mutual benefit the most powerful parts of the empire. Its extent is small when compared with Britain, but exceeds the islands of our seas. In soil and climate, in the disposition, temper, and habits of its population, it differs but little from Britain. We know most of its harbours and approaches, and that through the intercourse of commerce. One of the petty kings of the nation, driven out by internal faction, had been received by Agricola, who detained him under the semblance of friendship till he could make use of him. I have often heard him say that a single legion with a few auxiliaries could conquer and occupy Ireland, and that it would have a salutary effect on Britain for the Roman arms to be seen everywhere, and for freedom, so to speak, to be banished from its sight.

25. In the summer in which he entered on the sixth year of his office, his operations embraced the states beyond Bodotria, and, as he dreaded a general movement among the remoter tribes, as well as the perils which would beset an

invading army, he explored the harbours with a fleet, which, at first employed by him as an integral part of his force, continued to accompany him. The spectacle of war thus pushed on at once by sea and land was imposing; while often infantry, cavalry, and marines, mingled in the same encampment and joyously sharing the same meals, would dwell on their own achievements and adventures, comparing, with a soldier's boastfulness, at one time the deep recesses of the forest and the mountain with the dangers of waves and storms, or, at another, battles by land with victories over the ocean. The Britons too, as we learnt from the prisoners, were confounded by the sight of a fleet, as if, now that their inmost seas were penetrated, the conquered had their last refuge closed against them. The tribes inhabiting Caledonia flew to arms, and with great preparations, made greater by the rumours which always exaggerate the unknown, themselves advanced to attack our fortresses, and thus challenging a conflict, inspired us with alarm. To retreat south of the Bodotria, and to retire rather than to be driven out, was the advice of timid pretenders to prudence, when Agricola learnt that the enemy's attack would be made with more than one army. Fearing that their superior numbers and their knowledge of the country might enable them to hem him in, he too distributed his forces into three divisions, and so advanced.

26. This becoming known to the enemy, they suddenly changed their plan, and with their whole force attacked by night the ninth Legion, as being the weakest, and cutting down the sentries, who were asleep or panic-stricken, they broke into the camp. And now the battle was raging within the camp itself, when Agricola, who had learnt from his scouts the enemy's line of march and had kept close on his track, ordered the most active soldiers of his cavalry and infantry to attack the rear of the assailants, while the entire army were shortly to raise a shout. Soon his standards glittered in the light of daybreak. A double peril thus alarmed the Britons, while the courage of the Romans revived; and feeling sure of safety, they now fought for glory. In their turn they rushed to the attack, and there was a furious conflict within the narrow passages of the gates till the enemy

were routed. Both armies did their utmost, the one for the honour of having given aid, the other for that of not having needed support. Had not the flying enemy been sheltered by morasses and forests, this victory would have ended the war.

27. Knowing this, and elated by their glory, our army exclaimed that nothing could resist their valour—that they must penetrate the recesses of Caledonia, and at length after an unbroken succession of battles, discover the furthest limits of Britain. Those who but now were cautious and prudent, became after the event eager and boastful. It is the singularly unfair peculiarity of war that the credit of success is claimed by all, while a disaster is attributed to one alone. But the Britons thinking themselves baffled, not so much by our valour as by our general's skilful use of an opportunity, abated nothing of their arrogant demeanour, arming their youth, removing their wives and children to a place of safety, and assembling together to ratify, with sacred rites, a confederacy of all their states. Thus, with angry feelings on both sides, the combatants parted.

28. The same summer a Usipian cohort, which had been levied in Germany and transported into Britain, ventured on a great and memorable exploit. Having killed a centurion and some soldiers, who, to impart military discipline, had been incorporated with their ranks and were employed at once to instruct and command them, they embarked on board three swift galleys with pilots pressed into their service. Under the direction of one of them—for two of the three they suspected and consequently put to death—they sailed past the coast in the strangest way before any rumour about them was in circulation. After a while, dispersing in search of water and provisions, they encountered many of the Britons, who sought to defend their property. Often victorious, though now and then beaten, they were at last reduced to such an extremity of want as to be compelled to eat, at first, the feeblest of their number, and then victims selected by lot. Having sailed round Britain and lost their vessels from not knowing how to manage them, they were looked upon as pirates and were intercepted, first by the Suevi and then by the Frisii. Some who were sold as slaves in the way of trade, and were brought through the process of barter as far as our

side of the Rhine, gained notoriety by the disclosure of this extraordinary adventure.

29. Early in the summer Agricola sustained a domestic affliction in the loss of a son born a year before, a calamity which he endured, neither with the ostentatious fortitude displayed by many brave men, nor, on the other hand, with womanish tears and grief. In his sorrow he found one source of relief in war. Having sent on a fleet, which by its ravages at various points might cause a vague and wide-spread alarm, he advanced with a lightly equipped force, including in its ranks some Britons of remarkable bravery, whose fidelity had been tried through years of peace, as far as the Grampian mountains, which the enemy had already occupied. For the Britons, indeed, in no way cowed by the result of the late engagement, had made up their minds to be either avenged or enslaved, and convinced at length that a common danger must be averted by union, had, by embassies and treaties, summoned forth the whole strength of all their states. More than 30,000 armed men were now to be seen, and still there were pressing in all the youth of the country, with all whose old age was yet hale and vigorous, men renowned in war and bearing each decorations of his own. Meanwhile, among the many leaders, one superior to the rest in valour and in birth, Galgacus by name, is said to have thus harangued the multitude gathered around him and clamouring for battle:—

30. "Whenever I consider the origin of this war and the necessities of our position, I have a sure confidence that this day, and this union of yours, will be the beginning of freedom to the whole of Britain. To all of us slavery is a thing unknown; there are no lands beyond us, and even the sea is not safe, menaced as we are by a Roman fleet. And thus in war and battle, in which the brave find glory, even the coward will find safety. Former contests, in which, with varying fortune, the Romans were resisted, still left in us a last hope of succour, inasmuch as being the most renowned nation of Britain, dwelling in the very heart of the country, and out of sight of the shores of the conquered, we could keep even our eyes unpolluted by the contagion of slavery. To us who dwell on the uttermost confines of the earth and

of freedom, this remote sanctuary of Britain's glory has up to this time been a defence. Now, however, the furthest limits of Britain are thrown open, and the unknown always passes for the marvellous. But there are no tribes beyond us, nothing indeed but waves and rocks, and the yet more terrible Romans, from whose oppression escape is vainly sought by obedience and submission. Robbers of the world, having by their universal plunder exhausted the land, they rifle the deep. If the enemy be rich, they are rapacious; if he be poor, they lust for dominion; neither the east nor the west has been able to satisfy them. Alone among men they covet with equal eagerness poverty and riches. To robbery, slaughter, plunder, they give the lying name of empire; they make a solitude and call it peace.

31. "Nature has willed that every man's children and kindred should be his dearest objects. Yet these are torn from us by conscriptions to be slaves elsewhere. Our wives and our sisters, even though they may escape violation from the enemy, are dishonoured under the names of friendship and hospitality. Our goods and fortunes they collect for their tribute, our harvests for their granaries. Our very hands and bodies, under the lash and in the midst of insult, are worn down by the toil of clearing forests and morasses. Creatures born to slavery are sold once for all, and are, moreover, fed by their masters; but Britain is daily purchasing, is daily feeding, her own enslaved people. And as in a household the last comer among the slaves is always the butt of his companions, so we in a world long used to slavery, as the newest and the most contemptible, are marked out for destruction. We have neither fruitful plains, nor mines, nor harbours, for the working of which we may be spared. Valour, too, and high spirit in subjects, are offensive to rulers; besides, remoteness and seclusion, while they give safety, provoke suspicion. Since then you cannot hope for quarter, take courage, I beseech you, whether it be safety or renown that you hold most precious. Under a woman's leadership the Brigantes were able to burn a colony, to storm a camp, and had not success ended in supineness, might have thrown off the yoke. Let us, then, a fresh and unconquered people, never likely to abuse our freedom, show forthwith

at the very first onset what heroes Caledonia has in reserve.

32. "Do you suppose that the Romans will be as brave in war as they are licentious in peace? To our strifes and discords they owe their fame, and they turn the errors of an enemy to the renown of their own army, an army which, composed as it is of every variety of nations, is held together by success and will be broken up by disaster. These Gauls and Germans, and, I blush to say, these numerous Britons, who, though they lend their lives to support a stranger's rule, have been its enemies longer than its subjects, you cannot imagine to be bound by fidelity and affection. Fear and terror there certainly are, feeble bonds of attachment; remove them, and those who have ceased to fear will begin to hate. All the incentives to victory are on our side. The Romans have no wives to kindle their courage; no parents to taunt them with flight; many have either no country or one far away. Few in number, dismayed by their ignorance, looking around upon a sky, a sea, and forests which are all unfamiliar to them; hemmed in, as it were, and enmeshed, the Gods have delivered them into our hands. Be not frightened by idle display, by the glitter of gold and of silver, which can neither protect nor wound. In the very ranks of the enemy we shall find our own forces. Britons will acknowledge their own cause; Gauls will remember past freedom; the other Germans will abandon them, as but lately did the Usipii. Behind them there is nothing to dread. The forts are ungarrisoned; the colonies in the hands of aged men; what with disloyal subjects and oppressive rulers, the towns are ill-affected and rife with discord. On the one side you have a general and an army; on the other, tribute, the mines, and all the other penalties of an enslaved people. Whether you endure these for ever, or instantly avenge them, this field is to decide. Think, therefore, as you advance to battle, at once of your ancestors and of your posterity."

33. They received his speech with enthusiasm, and as is usual among barbarians, with songs, shouts and discordant cries. And now was seen the assembling of troops and the gleam of arms, as the boldest warriors stepped to the front. As the line was forming, Agricola, who, though his troops

were in high spirits and could scarcely be kept within the entrenchments, still thought it right to encourage them, spoke as follows—

"Comrades, this is the eighth year since, thanks to the greatness and good fortune of Rome and to your own loyalty and energy, you conquered Britain. In our many campaigns and battles, whether courage in meeting the foe, or toil and endurance in struggling, I may say, against nature herself, have been needed, I have ever been well satisfied with my soldiers, and you with your commander. And so you and I have passed beyond the limits reached by former armies or by former governors, and we now occupy the last confines of Britain, not merely in rumour and report, but with an actual encampment and armed force. Britain has been both discovered and subdued. Often on the march, when morasses, mountains, and rivers were wearing out your strength, did I hear our bravest men exclaim, 'When shall we have the enemy before us?—when shall we fight?' He is now here, driven from his lair, and your wishes and your valour have free scope, and everything favours the conqueror, everything is adverse to the vanquished. For as it is a great and glorious achievement, if we press on, to have accomplished so great a march, to have traversed forests and to have crossed estuaries, so, if we retire, our present most complete success will prove our greatest danger. We have not the same knowledge of the country or the same abundance of supplies, but we have arms in our hands, and in them we have everything. For myself I have long been convinced that neither for an army nor for a general is retreat safe. Better, too, is an honourable death than a life of shame, and safety and renown are for us to be found together. And it would be no inglorious end to perish on the extreme confines of earth and of nature.

34. "If unknown nations and an untried enemy confronted you, I should urge you on by the example of other armies. As it is, look back upon your former honours, question your own eyes. These are the men who last year under cover of darkness attacked a single legion, whom you routed by a shout. Of all the Britons these are the most confirmed runaways, and this is why they have survived so long. Just as

when the huntsman penetrates the forest and the thicket, all the most courageous animals rush out upon him, while the timid and feeble are scared away by the very sound of his approach, so the bravest of the Britons have long since fallen; and the rest are a mere crowd of spiritless cowards. You have at last found them, not because they have stood their ground, but because they have been overtaken. Their desperate plight, and the extreme terror that paralyses them, have rivetted their line to this spot, that you might achieve in it a splendid and memorable victory. Put an end to campaigns; crown your fifty years' service with a glorious day; prove to your country that her armies could never have been fairly charged with protracting a war or with causing a rebellion."

35. While Agricola was yet speaking, the ardour of the soldiers was rising to its height, and the close of his speech was followed by a great outburst of enthusiasm. In a moment they flew to arms. He arrayed his eager and impetuous troops in such a manner that the auxiliary infantry, 8,000 in number, strengthened his centre, while 3,000 cavalry were posted on his wings. The legions were drawn up in front of the intrenched camp; his victory would be vastly more glorious if won without the loss of Roman blood, and he would have a reserve in case of repulse. The enemy, to make a formidable display, had posted himself on high ground; his van was on the plain, while the rest of his army rose in an arch-like form up the slope of a hill. The plain between resounded with the noise and with the rapid movements of chariots and cavalry. Agricola, fearing that from the enemy's superiority of force he would be simultaneously attacked in front and on the flanks, widened his ranks, and though his line was likely to be too extended, and several officers advised him to bring up the legions, yet, so sanguine was he, so resolute in meeting danger, he sent away his horse and took his stand on foot before the colours.

36. The action began with distant fighting. The Britons with equal steadiness and skill used their huge swords and small shields to avoid or to parry the missiles of our soldiers, while they themselves poured on us a dense shower of darts, till Agricola encouraged three Batavian and two Tun-

grian cohorts to bring matters to the decision of close fighting with swords. Such tactics were familiar to these veteran
soldiers, but were embarrassing to an enemy armed with
small bucklers and unwieldy weapons. The swords of the
Britons are not pointed, and do not allow them to close with
the foe, or to fight in the open field. No sooner did the Batavians begin to close with the enemy, to strike them with
their shields, to disfigure their faces, and overthrowing the
force on the plain to advance their line up the hill, than the
other auxiliary cohorts joined with eager rivalry in cutting
down all the nearest of the foe. Many were left behind half
dead, some even unwounded, in the hurry of victory. Meantime the enemy's cavalry had fled, and the charioteers had
mingled in the engagement of the infantry. But although
these at first spread panic, they were soon impeded by the
close array of our ranks and by the inequalities of the
ground. The battle had anything but the appearance of a
cavalry action, for men and horses were carried along in
confusion together, while chariots, destitute of guidance, and
terrified horses without drivers, dashed as panic urged them,
sideways, or in direct collision against the ranks.

37. Those of the Britons who, having as yet taken no part
in the engagement, occupied the hill-tops, and who without
fear for themselves sat idly disdaining the smallness of our
numbers, had begun gradually to descend and to hem in the
rear of the victorious army, when Agricola, who feared this
very movement, opposed their advance with four squadrons
of cavalry held in reserve by him for any sudden emergencies of battle. Their repulse and rout was as severe as
their onset had been furious. Thus the enemy's design recoiled on himself, and the cavalry which by the general's
order had wheeled round from the van of the contending
armies, attacked his rear. Then, indeed, the open plain presented an awful and hideous spectacle. Our men pursued,
wounded, made prisoners of the fugitives only to slaughter
them when others fell in their way. And now the enemy, as
prompted by their various dispositions, fled in whole battalions with arms in their hands before a few pursuers, while
some, who were unarmed, actually rushed to the front and
gave themselves up to death. Everywhere there lay scattered

arms, corpses, and mangled limbs, and the earth reeked with
blood. Even the conquered now and then felt a touch of fury
and of courage. On approaching the woods, they rallied, and
as they knew the ground, they were able to pounce on the
foremost and least cautious of the pursuers. Had not Agricola, who was present everywhere, ordered a force of strong
and lightly-equipped cohorts, with some dismounted troopers for the denser parts of the forest, and a detachment of
cavalry where it was not so thick, to scour the woods like a
party of huntsmen, serious loss would have been sustained
through the excessive confidence of our troops. When, however, the enemy saw that we again pursued them in firm
and compact array, they fled no longer in masses as before,
each looking for his comrade; but dispersing and avoiding
one another, they sought the shelter of distant and pathless
wilds. Night and weariness of bloodshed put an end to the
pursuit. About 10,000 of the enemy were slain; on our side
there fell 360 men, and among them Aulus Atticus, the
commander of the cohort, whose youthful impetuosity and
mettlesome steed had borne him into the midst of the enemy.

38. Elated by their victory and their booty, the conquerors passed a night of merriment. Meanwhile the Britons,
wandering amidst the mingled wailings of men and women,
were dragging off their wounded, calling to the unhurt, deserting their homes, and in their rage actually firing them,
choosing places of concealment only instantly to abandon
them. One moment they would take counsel together, the
next, part company, while the sight of those who were dearest to them sometimes melted their hearts, but oftener
roused their fury. It was an undoubted fact that some of
them vented their rage on their wives and children, as if in
pity for their lot. The following day showed more fully the
extent of the calamity, for the silence of desolation reigned
everywhere: the hills were forsaken, houses were smoking in
the distance, and no one was seen by the scouts. These were
despatched in all directions; and it having been ascertained
that the track of the flying enemy was uncertain, and that
there was no attempt at rallying, it being also impossible, as
summer was now over, to extend the war, Agricola led back
his army into the territory of the Boresti. He received hos-

tages from them, and then ordered the commander of the fleet to sail round Britain. A force for this purpose was given him, which great panic everywhere preceded. Agricola himself, leading his infantry and cavalry by slow marches, so as to overawe the newly-conquered tribes by the very tardiness of his progress, brought them into winter-quarters, while the fleet with propitious breezes and great renown entered the harbour of Trutulium, to which it had returned after having coasted along the entire southern shore of the island.

39. Of this series of events, though not exaggerated in the despatches of Agricola by any boastfulness of language, Domitian heard, as was his wont, with joy in his face but anxiety in his heart. He felt conscious that all men laughed at his late mock triumph over Germany, for which there had been purchased from traders people whose dress and hair might be made to resemble those of captives, whereas now a real and splendid victory, with the destruction of thousands of the enemy, was being celebrated with just applause. It was, he thought, a very alarming thing for him that the name of a subject should be raised above that of the Emperor; it was to no purpose that he had driven into obscurity the pursuit of forensic eloquence and the graceful accomplishments of civil life, if another were to forestall the distinctions of war. To other glories he could more easily shut his eyes, but the greatness of a good general was a truly imperial quality. Harassed by these anxieties, and absorbed in an incommunicable trouble, a sure prognostic of some cruel purpose, he decided that it was best for the present to suspend his hatred until the freshness of Agricola's renown and his popularity with the army should begin to pass away.

40. For Agricola was still the governor of Britain. Accordingly the Emperor ordered that the usual triumphal decorations, the honour of a laurelled statue, and all that is commonly given in place of the triumphal procession, with the addition of many laudatory expressions, should be decreed in the senate, together with a hint to the effect that Agricola was to have the province of Syria, then vacant by the death of Atilius Rufus, a man of consular rank, and generally reserved for men of distinction. It was believed by many persons that one of the freedmen employed on confidential serv-

ices was sent to Agricola, bearing a despatch in which Syria was offered him, and with instructions to deliver it should he be in Britain; that this freedman in crossing the straits met Agricola, and without even saluting him made his way back to Domitian; though I cannot say whether the story is true, or is only a fiction invented to suit the Emperor's character.

Meanwhile Agricola had handed over his province in peace and safety to his successor. And not to make his entrance into Rome conspicuous by the concourse of welcoming throngs, he avoided the attentions of his friends by entering the city at night, and at night too, according to orders, proceded to the palace, where, having been received with a hurried embrace and without a word being spoken, he mingled in the crowd of courtiers. Anxious henceforth to temper the military renown, which annoys men of peace, with other merits, he studiously cultivated retirement and leisure, simple in dress, courteous in conversation, and never accompanied but by one or two friends, so that the many who commonly judge of great men by their external grandeur, after having seen and attentively surveyed him, asked the secret of a greatness which but few could explain.

41. During this time he was frequently accused before Domitian in his absence, and in his absence acquitted. The cause of his danger lay not in any crime, nor in any complaint of injury, but in a ruler who was the foe of virtue, in his own renown, and in that worst class of enemies—the men who praise. And then followed such days for the commonwealth as would not suffer Agricola to be forgotten; days when so many of our armies were lost in Mœsia, Dacia, Germany, and Pannonia, through the rashness or cowardice of our generals, when so many of our officers were besieged and captured with so many of our auxiliaries, when it was no longer the boundaries of empire and the banks of rivers which were imperilled, but the winter-quarters of our legions and the possession of our territories. And so when disaster followed upon disaster, and the entire year was marked by destruction and slaughter, the voice of the people called Agricola to the command; for they all contrasted his vigour, firmness, and experience in war, with the inertness and ti-

midity of other generals. This talk, it is quite certain, assailed the ears of the Emperor himself, while affection and loyalty in the best of his freedmen, malice and envy in the worst, kindled the anger of a prince ever inclined to evil. And so at once, by his own excellences and by the faults of others, Agricola was hurried headlong to a perilous elevation.

42. The year had now arrived in which the pro-consulate of Asia or Africa was to fall to him by lot, and, as Civica had been lately murdered, Agricola did not want a warning, or Domitian a precedent. Persons well acquainted with the Emperor's feelings came to ask Agricola, as if on their own account, whether he would go. First they hinted their purpose by praises of tranquillity and leisure; then offered their services in procuring acceptance for his excuses; and at last, throwing off all disguise, brought him by entreaties and threats to Domitian. The Emperor, armed beforehand with hypocrisy, and assuming a haughty demeanour, listened to his prayer that he might be excused, and having granted his request allowed himself to be formally thanked, nor blushed to grant so sinister a favour. But the salary usually granted to a pro-consul, and which he had himself given to some governors, he did not bestow on Agricola, either because he was offended at its not having been asked, or was warned by his conscience that he might be thought to have purchased the refusal which he had commanded. It is, indeed, human nature to hate the man whom you have injured; yet the Emperor, notwithstanding his irascible temper and an implacability proportioned to his reserve, was softened by the moderation and prudence of Agricola, who neither by a perverse obstinacy nor an idle parade of freedom challenged fame or provoked his fate. Let it be known to those whose habit it is to admire the disregard of authority, that there may be great men even under bad emperors, and that obedience and submission, when joined to activity and vigour, may attain a glory which most men reach only by a perilous career, utterly useless to the state, and closed by an ostentatious death.

43. The end of his life, a deplorable calamity to us and a grief to his friends, was regarded with concern even by strangers and those who knew him not. The common people

and this busy population continually inquired at his house, and talked of him in public places and in private gatherings. No man when he heard of Agricola's death could either be glad or at once forget it. Men's sympathy was increased by a prevalent rumour that he was destroyed by poison. For myself, I have nothing which I should venture to state for fact. Certainly during the whole of his illness the Emperor's chief freedmen and confidential physicians came more frequently than is usual with a court which pays its visits by means of messengers. This was, perhaps, solicitude, perhaps espionage. Certain it is, that on the last day the very agonies of his dying moments were reported by a succession of couriers, and no one believed that there would be such haste about tidings which would be heard with regret. Yet in his manner and countenance the Emperor displayed some signs of sorrow, for he could now forget his enmity, and it was easier to conceal his joy than his fear. It was well known that on reading the will, in which he was named co-heir with Agricola's excellent wife and most dutiful daughter, he expressed delight, as if it had been a complimentary choice. So blinded and perverted was his mind by incessant flattery, that he did not know that it was only a bad Emperor whom a good father would make his heir.

44. Agricola was born on the 13th of June, in the third consulate of Caius Cæsar; he died on the 23rd of August, during the consulate of Collega and Priscus, being in the fifty-sixth year of his age. Should posterity wish to know something of his appearance, it was graceful rather than commanding. There was nothing formidable in his appearance; a gracious look predominated. One would easily believe him a good man, and willingly believe him to be great. As for himself, though taken from us in the prime of a vigorous manhood, yet, as far as glory is concerned, his life was of the longest. Those true blessings, indeed, which consist in virtue, he had fully attained; and on one who had reached the honours of a consulate and a triumph, what more had fortune to bestow? Immense wealth had no attractions for him, and wealth he had, even to splendour. As his daughter and his wife survived him, it may be thought that he was even fortunate—fortunate, in that while his honours

had suffered no eclipse, while his fame was at its height, while his kindred and his friends still prospered, he escaped from the evil to come. For, though to survive until the dawn of this most happy age and to see a Trajan on the throne was what he would speculate upon in previsions and wishes confided to my ears, yet he had this mighty compensation for his premature death, that he was spared those later years during which Domitian, leaving now no interval or breathing space of time, but, as it were, with one continuous blow, drained the life-blood of the Commonwealth.

45. Agricola did not see the senate-house besieged, or the senate hemmed in by armed men, or so many of our consulars falling at one single massacre, or so many of Rome's noblest ladies exiles and fugitives. Carus Metius had as yet the distinction of but one victory, and the noisy counsels of Messalinus were not heard beyond the walls of Alba, and Massa Bæbius was then answering for his life. It was not long before our hands dragged Helvidius to prison, before we gazed on the dying looks of Manricus and Rusticus, before we were steeped in Senecio's innocent blood. Even Nero turned his eyes away, and did not gaze upon the atrocities which he ordered; with Domitian it was the chief part of our miseries to see and to be seen, to know that our sighs were being recorded, to have, ever ready to note the pallid looks of so many faces, that savage countenance reddened with the hue with which he defied shame.

Thou wast indeed fortunate, Agricola, not only in the splendour of thy life, but in the opportune moment of thy death. Thou submittedst to thy fate, so they tell us who were present to hear thy last words, with courage and cheerfulness, seeming to be doing all thou couldst to give thine Emperor full acquittal. As for me and thy daughter, besides all the bitterness of a father's loss, it increases our sorrow that it was not permitted us to watch over thy failing health, to comfort thy weakness, to satisfy ourselves with those looks, those embraces. Assuredly we should have received some precepts, some utterances to fix in our inmost hearts. This is the bitterness of our sorrow, this the smart of our wound, that from the circumstance of so long an absence thou wast lost to us four years before. Doubtless, best of

fathers, with that most loving wife at thy side, all the dues
of affection were abundantly paid thee, yet with too few
tears thou wast laid to thy rest, and in the light of thy last
day there was something for which thine eyes longed in vain.

46. If there is any dwelling-place for the spirits of the
just; if, as the wise believe, noble souls do not perish with
the body, rest thou in peace; and call us, thy family, from
weak regrets and womanish laments to the contemplation
of thy virtues, for which we must not weep nor beat the
breast. Let us honour thee not so much with transitory
praises as with our reverence, and, if our powers permit us,
with our emulation. That will be true respect, that the true
affection of thy nearest kin. This, too, is what I would en-
join on daughter and wife, to honour the memory of that
father, that husband, by pondering in their hearts all his
words and acts, by cherishing the features and lineaments
of his character rather than those of his person. It is not
that I would forbid the likenesses which are wrought in
marble or in bronze; but as the faces of men, so all simili-
tudes of the face are weak and perishable things, while the
fashion of the soul is everlasting, such as may be expressed
not in some foreign substance, or by the help of art, but in
our own lives. Whatever we loved, whatever we admired in
Agricola, survives, and will survive in the hearts of men, in
the succession of the ages, in the fame that waits on noble
deeds. Over many indeed, of those who have gone before, as
over the inglorious and ignoble, the waves of oblivion will
roll; Agricola, made known to posterity by history and tradition, will live for ever.

GERMANY AND ITS TRIBES

GERMANY AND ITS TRIBES

1. Germany is separated from the Galli, the Rhæti, and Pannonii, by the rivers Rhine and Danube; mountain ranges, or the fear which each feels for the other, divide it from the Sarmatæ and Daci. Elsewhere ocean girds it, embracing broad peninsulas and islands of unexplored extent, where certain tribes and kingdoms are newly known to us, revealed by war. The Rhine springs from a precipitous and inaccessible height of the Rhætian Alps, bends slightly westward, and mingles with the Northern Ocean. The Danube pours down from the gradual and gently rising slope of Mount Abnoba, and visits many nations, to force its way at last through six channels into the Pontus; a seventh mouth is lost in marshes.

2. The Germans themselves I should regard as aboriginal, and not mixed at all with other races through immigration or intercourse. For, in former times, it was not by land but on shipboard that those who sought to emigrate would arrive; and the boundless and, so to speak, hostile ocean beyond us, is seldom entered by a sail from our world. And, beside the perils of rough and unknown seas, who would leave Asia, or Africa, or Italy for Germany, with its wild country, its inclement skies, its sullen manners and aspect, unless indeed it were his home? In their ancient songs, their only way of remembering or recording the past, they celebrate an earth-born god, Tuisco, and his son Mannus, as the origin of their race, as their founders. To Mannus they assign three sons, from whose names, they say, the coast tribes are called Ingævones; those of the interior, Herminones; all the rest, Istævones. Some, with the freedom of conjecture permitted by antiquity, assert that the god had several descendants, and the nation several appellations, as Marsi, Gambrivii, Suevi, Vandilii, and that these are genu-

ine old names. The name Germany, on the other hand, they say, is modern and newly introduced, from the fact that the tribes which first crossed the Rhine and drove out the Gauls, and are now called Tungrians, were then called Germans. Thus what was the name of a tribe, and not of a race, gradually prevailed, till all called themselves by this self-invented name of Germans, which the conquerors had first employed to inspire terror.

3. They say that Hercules, too, once visited them; and when going into battle, they sing of him first of all heroes. They have also those songs of theirs, by the recital of which ("baritus," they call it), they rouse their courage, while from the note they augur the result of the approaching con- flict. For, as their line shouts, they inspire or feel alarm. It is not so much an articulate sound, as a general cry of valour. They aim chiefly at a harsh note and a confused roar, put- ting their shields to their mouth, so that, by reverberation, it may swell into a fuller and deeper sound. Ulysses, too, is believed by some, in his long legendary wanderings, to have found his way into this ocean, and, having visited German soil, to have founded and named the town of Asciburgium, which stands on the bank of the Rhine, and is to this day inhabited. They even say that an altar dedicated to Ulysses, with the addition of the name of his father, Laertes, was formerly discovered on this same spot, and that certain monuments and tombs, with Greek inscriptions, still exist on the borders of Germany and Rhætia. These statements I have no intention of sustaining by proofs, or of refuting; every one may believe or disbelieve them as he feels inclined.

4. For my own part, I agree with those who think that the tribes of Germany are free from all taint of inter- marriages with foreign nations, and that they appear as a distinct, unmixed race, like none but themselves. Hence, too, the same physical peculiarities throughout so vast a popu- lation. All have fierce blue eyes, red hair, huge frames, fit only for a sudden exertion. They are less able to bear la- borious work. Heat and thirst they cannot in the least en- dure; to cold and hunger their climate and their soil inure them.

5. Their country, though somewhat various in appearance,

yet generally either bristles with forests or reeks with swamps; it is more rainy on the side of Gaul, bleaker on that of Noricum and Pannonia. It is productive of grain, but unfavourable to fruit-bearing trees; it is rich in flocks and herds, but these are for the most part undersized, and even the cattle have not their usual beauty or noble head. It is number that is chiefly valued; they are in fact the most highly prized, indeed the only riches of the people. Silver and gold the gods have refused to them, whether in kindness or in anger I cannot say. I would not, however, affirm that no vein of German soil produces gold or silver, for who has ever made a search? They care but little to possess or use them. You may see among them vessels of silver, which have been presented to their envoys and chieftains, held as cheap as those of clay. The border population, however, value gold and silver for their commercial utility, and are familiar with, and show preference for, some of our coins. The tribes of the interior use the simpler and more ancient practice of the barter of commodities. They like the old and well-known money, coins milled, or showing a two-horse chariot. They likewise prefer silver to gold, not from any special liking, but because a large number of silver pieces is more convenient for use among dealers in cheap and common articles.

6. Even iron is not plentiful with them, as we infer from the character of their weapons. But few use swords or long lances. They carry a spear (*framea* is their name for it), with a narrow and short head, but so sharp and easy to wield that the same weapon serves, according to circumstances, for close or distant conflict. As for the horse-soldier, he is satisfied with a shield and spear; the foot-soldiers also scatter showers of missiles, each man having several and hurling them to an immense distance, and being naked or lightly clad with a little cloak. There is no display about their equipment: their shields alone are marked with very choice colours. A few only have corslets, and just one or two here and there a metal or leathern helmet. Their horses are remarkable neither for beauty nor for fleetness. Nor are they taught various evolutions after our fashion, but are driven straight forward, or so as to make one wheel to the

right in such a compact body that none is left behind another. On the whole, one would say that their chief strength is in their infantry, which fights along with the cavalry; admirably adapted to the action of the latter is the swiftness of certain foot-soldiers, who are picked from the entire youth of their country, and stationed in front of the line. Their number is fixed,—a hundred from each canton; and from this they take their name among their countrymen, so that what was originally a mere number has now become a title of distinction. Their line of battle is drawn up in a wedge-like formation. To give ground, provided you return to the attack, is considered prudence rather than cowardice. The bodies of their slain they carry off even in indecisive engagements. To abandon your shield is the basest of crimes; nor may a man thus disgraced be present at the sacred rites, or enter their council; many, indeed, after escaping from battle, have ended their infamy with the halter.

7. They choose their kings by birth, their generals for merit. These kings have not unlimited or arbitrary power, and the generals do more by example than by authority. If they are energetic, if they are conspicuous, if they fight in the front, they lead because they are admired. But to reprimand, to imprison, even to flog, is permitted to the priests alone, and that not as a punishment, or at the general's bidding, but, as it were, by the mandate of the god whom they believe to inspire the warrior. They also carry with them into battle certain figures and images taken from their sacred groves. And what most stimulates their courage is, that their squadrons or battalions, instead of being formed by chance or by a fortuitous gathering, are composed of families and clans. Close by them, too, are those dearest to them, so that they hear the shrieks of women, the cries of infants. *They* are to every man the most sacred witnesses of his bravery—*they* are his most generous applauders. The soldier brings his wounds to mother and wife, who shrink not from counting or even demanding them and who administer both food and encouragement to the combatants.

8. Tradition says that armies already wavering and giving way have been rallied by women who, with earnest en-

treaties and bosoms laid bare, have vividly represented the horrors of captivity, which the Germans fear with such extreme dread on behalf of their women, that the strongest tie by which a state can be bound is the being required to give, among the number of hostages, maidens of noble birth. They even believe that the sex has a certain sanctity and prescience, and they do not despise their counsels, or make light of their answers. In Vespasian's days we saw Veleda, long regarded by many as a divinity. In former times, too, they venerated Aurinia, and many other women, but not with servile flatteries, or with sham deification.

9. Mercury is the deity whom they chiefly worship, and on certain days they deem it right to sacrifice to him even with human victims. Hercules and Mars they appease with more lawful offerings. Some of the Suevi also sacrifice to Isis. Of the occasion and origin of this foreign rite I have discovered nothing, but that the image, which is fashioned like a light galley, indicates an imported worship. The Germans, however, do not consider it consistent with the grandeur of celestial beings to confine the gods within walls, or to liken them to the form of any human countenance. They consecrate woods and groves, and they apply the names of deities to the abstraction which they see only in spiritual worship.

10. Augury and divination by lot no people practise more diligently. The use of the lots is simple. A little bough is lopped off a fruit-bearing tree, and cut into small pieces; these are distinguished by certain marks, and thrown carelessly and at random over a white garment. In public questions the priest of the particular state, in private the father of the family, invokes the gods, and, with his eyes towards heaven, takes up each piece three times, and finds in them a meaning according to the mark previously impressed on them. If they prove unfavourable, there is no further consultation that day about the matter; if they sanction it, the confirmation of augury is still required. For they are also familiar with the practice of consulting the notes and the flight of birds. It is peculiar to this people to seek omens and monitions from horses. Kept at the public expense, in these same woods and groves, are white horses, pure from

the taint of earthly labour; these are yoked to a sacred car,
and accompanied by the priest and the king, or chief of the
tribe, who note their neighings and snortings. No species of
augury is more trusted, not only by the people and by the
nobility, but also by the priests, who regard themselves as
the ministers of the gods, and the horses as acquainted with
their will. They have also another method of observing auspices, by which they seek to learn the result of an important
war. Having taken, by whatever means, a prisoner from the
tribe with whom they are at war, they pit him against a
picked man of their own tribe, each combatant using the
weapons of their country. The victory of the one or the
other is accepted as an indication of the issue.

11. About minor matters the chiefs deliberate, about the
more important the whole tribe. Yet even when the final
decision rests with the people, the affair is always thoroughly
discussed by the chiefs. They assemble, except in the case
of a sudden emergency, on certain fixed days, either at new
or at full moon; for this they consider the most auspicious
season for the transaction of business. Instead of reckoning
by days as we do, they reckon by nights, and in this manner fix both their ordinary and their legal appointments.
Night they regard as bringing on day. Their freedom has
this disadvantage, that they do not meet simultaneously or
as they are bidden, but two or three days are wasted in the
delays of assembling. When the multitude think proper, they
sit down armed. Silence is proclaimed by the priests, who
have on these occasions the right of keeping order. Then the
king or the chief, according to age, birth, distinction in war,
or eloquence, is heard, more because he has influence to persuade than because he has power to command. If his sentiments displease them, they reject them with murmurs; if
they are satisfied, they brandish their spears. The most complimentary form of assent is to express approbation with
their weapons.

12. In their councils an accusation may be preferred or a
capital crime prosecuted. Penalties are distinguished according to the offence. Traitors and deserters are hanged on
trees; the coward, the unwarlike, the man stained with
abominable vices, is plunged into the mire of the morass,

with a hurdle put over him. This distinction in punishment means that crime, they think, ought, in being punished, to be exposed, while infamy ought to be buried out of sight. Lighter offences, too, have penalties proportioned to them; he who is convicted, is fined in a certain number of horses or of cattle. Half of the fine is paid to the king or to the state, half to the person whose wrongs are avenged and to his relatives. In these same councils they also elect the chief magistrates, who administer law in the cantons and the towns. Each of these has a hundred associates chosen from the people, who support him with their advice and influence.

13. They transact no public or private business without being armed. It is not, however, usual for anyone to wear arms till the state has recognised his power to use them. Then in the presence of the council one of the chiefs, or the young man's father, or some kinsman, equips him with a shield and a spear. These arms are what the "toga" is with us, the first honour with which youth is invested. Up to this time he is regarded as a member of a household, afterwards as a member of the commonwealth. Very noble birth or great services rendered by the father secure for lads the rank of a chief; such lads attach themselves to men of mature strength and of long approved valour. It is no shame to be seen among a chief's followers. Even in his escort there are gradations of rank, dependent on the choice of the man to whom they are attached. These followers vie keenly with each other as to who shall rank first with his chief, the chiefs as to who shall have the most numerous and the bravest followers. It is an honour as well as a source of strength to be thus always surrounded by a large body of picked youths; it is an ornament in peace and a defence in war. And not only in his own tribe but also in the neighbouring states it is the renown and glory of a chief to be distinguished for the number and valour of his followers, for such a man is courted by embassies, is honoured with presents, and the very prestige of his name often settles a war.

14. When they go into battle, it is a disgrace for the chief to be surpassed in valour, a disgrace for his followers not to equal the valour of the chief. And it is an infamy and a reproach for life to have survived the chief, and returned

from the field. To defend, to protect him, to ascribe one's own brave deeds to his renown, is the height of loyalty. The chief fights for victory; his vassals fight for their chief. If their native state sinks into the sloth of prolonged peace and repose, many of its noble youths voluntarily seek those tribes which are waging some war, both because inaction is odious to their race, and because they win renown more readily in the midst of peril, and cannot maintain a numerous following except by violence and war. Indeed, men look to the liberality of their chief for their war-horse and their blood-stained and victorious lance. Feasts and entertainments, which, though inelegant, are plentifully furnished, are their only pay. The means of this bounty come from war and rapine. Nor are they as easily persuaded to plough the earth and to wait for the year's produce as to challenge an enemy and earn the honour of wounds. Nay, they actually think it tame and stupid to acquire by the sweat of toil what they might win by their blood.

15. Whenever they are not fighting, they pass much of their time in the chase, and still more in idleness, giving themselves up to sleep and to feasting, the bravest and the most warlike doing nothing, and surrendering the management of the household, of the home, and of the land, to the women, the old men, and all the weakest members of the family. They themselves lie buried in sloth, a strange combination in their nature that the same men should be so fond of idleness, so averse to peace. It is the custom of the states to bestow by voluntary and individual contribution on the chiefs a present of cattle or of grain, which, while accepted as a compliment, supplies their wants. They are particularly delighted by gifts from neighbouring tribes, which are sent not only by individuals but also by the state, such as choice steeds, heavy armour, trappings, and neck-chains. We have now taught them to accept money also.

16. It is well known that the nations of Germany have no cities, and that they do not even tolerate closely contiguous dwellings. They live scattered and apart, just as a spring, a meadow, or a wood has attracted them. Their villages they do not arrange in our fashion, with the buildings connected and joined together, but every person surrounds

his dwelling with an open space, either as a precaution against the disasters of fire, or because they do not know how to build. No use is made by them of stone or tile; they employ timber for all purposes, rude masses without ornament or attractiveness. Some parts of their buildings they stain more carefully with a clay so clear and bright that it resembles painting, or a coloured design. They are wont also to dig out subterranean caves, and pile on them great heaps of dung, as a shelter from winter and as a receptacle for the year's produce, for by such places they mitigate the rigour of the cold. And should an enemy approach, he lays waste the open country, while what is hidden and buried is either not known to exist, or else escapes him from the very fact that it has to be searched for.

17. They all wrap themselves in a cloak which is fastened with a clasp, or, if this is not forthcoming, with a thorn, leaving the rest of their persons bare. They pass whole days on the hearth by the fire. The wealthiest are distinguished by a dress which is not flowing, like that of the Sarmatæ and Parthi, but is tight, and exhibits each limb. They also wear the skins of wild beasts; the tribes on the Rhine and Danube in a careless fashion, those of the interior with more elegance, as not obtaining other clothing by commerce. These select certain animals, the hides of which they strip off and vary them with the spotted skins of beasts, the produce of the outer ocean, and of seas unknown to us. The women have the same dress as the men, except that they generally wrap themselves in linen garments, which they embroider with purple, and do not lengthen out the upper part of their clothing into sleeves. The upper and lower arm is thus bare, and the nearest part of the bosom is also exposed.

18. Their marriage code, however, is strict, and indeed no part of their manners is more praiseworthy. Almost alone among barbarians they are content with one wife, except a very few among them, and these not from sensuality, but because their noble birth procures for them many offers of alliance. The wife does not bring a dower to the husband, but the husband to the wife. The parents and relatives are present, and pass judgment on the marriage-gifts, gifts not meant to suit a woman's taste, nor such as a bride would

deck herself with, but oxen, a caparisoned steed, a shield, a lance, and a sword. With these presents the wife is espoused, and she herself in her turn brings her husband a gift of arms. This they count their strongest bond of union, these their sacred mysteries, these their gods of marriage. Lest the woman should think herself to stand apart from aspirations after noble deeds and from the perils of war, she is reminded by the ceremony which inaugurates marriage that she is her husband's partner in toil and danger, destined to suffer and to dare with him alike both in peace and in war. The yoked oxen, the harnessed steed, the gift of arms, proclaim this fact. She must live and die with the feeling that she is receiving what she must hand down to her children neither tarnished nor depreciated, what future daughters-in-law may receive, and may be so passed on to her grand-children.

19. Thus with their virtue protected they live uncorrupted by the allurements of public shows or the stimulant of feastings. Clandestine correspondence is equally unknown to men and women. Very rare for so numerous a population is adultery, the punishment for which is prompt, and in the husband's power. Having cut off the hair of the adulteress and stripped her naked, he expels her from the house in the presence of her kinsfolk, and then flogs her through the whole village. The loss of chastity meets with no indulgence; neither beauty, youth, nor wealth will procure the culprit a husband. No one in Germany laughs at vice, nor do they call it the fashion to corrupt and to be corrupted. Still better is the condition of those states in which only maidens are given in marriage, and where the hopes and expectations of a bride are then finally terminated. They receive one husband, as having one body and one life, that they may have no thoughts beyond, no further-reaching desires, that they may love not so much the husband as the married state. To limit the number of their children or to destroy any of their subsequent offspring is accounted infamous, and good habits are here more effectual than good laws elsewhere.

20. In every household the children, naked and filthy, grow up with those stout frames and limbs which we so much admire. Every mother suckles her own offspring, and

never entrusts it to servants and nurses. The master is not distinguished from the slave by being brought up with greater delicacy. Both live amid the same flocks and lie on the same ground till the freeborn are distinguished by age and recognised by merit. The young men marry late, and their vigour is thus unimpaired. Nor are the maidens hurried into marriage; the same age and a similar stature is required; well-matched and vigorous they wed, and the offspring reproduce the strength of the parents. Sister's sons are held in as much esteem by their uncles as by their fathers; indeed, some regard the relation as even more sacred and binding, and prefer it in receiving hostages, thinking thus to secure a stronger hold on the affections and a wider bond for the family. But every man's own children are his heirs and successors, and there are no wills. Should there be no issue, the next in succession to the property are his brothers and his uncles on either side. The more relatives he has, the more numerous his connections, the more honoured is his old age; nor are there any advantages in childlessness.

21. It is a duty among them to adopt the feuds as well as the friendships of a father or a kinsman. These feuds are not implacable; even homicide is expiated by the payment of a certain number of cattle and of sheep, and the satisfaction is accepted by the entire family, greatly to the advantage of the state, since feuds are dangerous in proportion to a people's freedom.

No nation indulges more profusely in entertainments and hospitality. To exclude any human being from their roof is thought impious; every German, according to his means, receives his guest with a well-furnished table. When his supplies are exhausted, he who was but now the host becomes the guide and companion to further hospitality, and without invitation they go to the next house. It matters not; they are entertained with like cordiality. No one distinguishes between an acquaintance and a stranger, as regards the rights of hospitality. It is usual to give the departing guest whatever he may ask for, and a present in return is asked with as little hesitation. They are greatly charmed with gifts, but they expect no return for what they give, nor feel any obligation for what they receive.

22. On waking from sleep, which they generally prolong to a late hour of the day, they take a bath, oftenest of warm water, which suits a country where winter is the longest of the seasons. After their bath they take their meal, each having a separate seat and table of his own. Then they go armed to business, or no less often to their festal meetings. To pass an entire day and night in drinking disgraces no one. Their quarrels, as might be expected with intoxicated people, are seldom fought out with mere abuse, but commonly with wounds and bloodshed. Yet it is at their feasts that they generally consult on the reconciliation of enemies, on the forming of matrimonial alliances, on the choice of chiefs, finally even on peace and war, for they think that at no time is the mind more open to simplicity of purpose or more warmed to noble aspirations. A race without either natural or acquired cunning, they disclose their hidden thoughts in the freedom of the festivity. Thus the sentiments of all having been discovered and laid bare, the discussion is renewed on the following day, and from each occasion its own peculiar advantage is derived. They deliberate when they have no power to dissemble; they resolve when error is impossible.

23. A liquor for drinking is made out of barley or other grain, and fermented into a certain resemblance to wine. The dwellers on the river-bank also buy wine. Their food is of a simple kind, consisting of wild-fruit, fresh game, and curdled milk. They satisfy their hunger without elaborate preparation and without delicacies. In quenching their thirst they are not equally moderate. If you indulge their love of drinking by supplying them with as much as they desire, they will be overcome by their own vices as easily as by the arms of an enemy.

24. One and the same kind of spectacle is always exhibited at every gathering. Naked youths who practise the sport bound in the dance amid swords and lances that threaten their lives. Experience gives them skill, and skill again gives grace; profit or pay are out of the question; however reckless their pastime, its reward is the pleasure of the spectators. Strangely enough they make games of hazard a serious

occupation even when sober, and so venturesome are they about gaining or losing, that, when every other resource has failed, on the last and final throw they stake the freedom of their own persons. The loser goes into voluntary slavery; though the younger and stronger, he suffers himself to be bound and sold. Such is their stubborn persistency in a bad practice; they themselves call it honour. Slaves of this kind the owners part with in the way of commerce, and also to relieve themselves from the scandal of such a victory.

25. The other slaves are not employed after our manner with distinct domestic duties assigned to them, but each one has the management of a house and home of his own. The master requires from the slave a certain quantity of grain, of cattle, and of clothing, as he would from a tenant, and this is the limit of subjection. All other household functions are discharged by the wife and children. To strike a slave or to punish him with bonds or with hard labour is a rare occurrence. They often kill them, not in enforcing strict discipline, but on the impulse of passion, as they would an enemy, only it is done with impunity. The freedmen do not rank much above slaves, and are seldom of any weight in the family, never in the state, with the exception of those tribes which are ruled by kings. There indeed they rise above the freedborn and the noble; elsewhere the inferiority of the freedman marks the freedom of the state.

26. Of lending money on interest and increasing it by compound interest they know nothing,—a more effectual safeguard than if it were prohibited.

Land proportioned to the number of inhabitants is occupied by the whole community in turn, and afterwards divided among them according to rank. A wide expanse of plains makes the partition easy. They till fresh fields every year, and they have still more land than enough; with the richness and extent of their soil, they do not laboriously exert themselves in planting orchards, inclosing meadows, and watering gardens. Corn is the only produce required from the earth; hence even the year itself is not divided by them into as many seasons as with us. Winter, spring, and summer have both a meaning and a name; the name and blessings of autumn are alike unknown.

27. In their funerals there is no pomp; they simply observe the custom of burning the bodies of illustrious men with certain kinds of wood. They do not heap garments or spices on the funeral pile. The arms of the dead man and in some cases his horse are consigned to the fire. A turf mound forms the tomb. Monuments with their lofty elaborate splendour they reject as oppressive to the dead. Tears and lamentations they soon dismiss; grief and sorrow but slowly. It is thought becoming for women to bewail, for men to remember, the dead.

Such on the whole is the account which I have received of the origin and manners of the entire German people. I will now touch on the institutions and religious rites of the separate tribes, pointing out how far they differ, and also what nations have migrated from Germany into Gaul.

28. That highest authority, the great Julius, informs us that Gaul was once more powerful than Germany. Consequently we may believe that Gauls even crossed over into Germany. For what a trifling obstacle would a river be to the various tribes, as they grew in strength and wished to possess in exchange settlements which were still open to all, and not partitioned among powerful monarchies! Accordingly the country between the Hercynian forest and the rivers Rhine and Mœnus, and that which lies beyond, was occupied respectively by the Helvetii and Boii, both tribes of Gaul. The name Boiemum still survives, marking the old tradition of the place, though the population has been changed. Whether however the Aravisci migrated into Pannonia from the Osi, a German race, or whether the Osi came from the Aravisci into Germany, as both nations still retain the same language, institutions, and customs, is a doubtful matter; for as they were once equally poor and equally free, either bank had the same attractions, the same drawbacks. The Treveri and Nervii are even eager in their claims of a German origin, thinking that the glory of this descent distinguishes them from the uniform level of Gallic effeminacy. The Rhine bank itself is occupied by tribes unquestionably German,—the Vangiones, the Triboci, and the Nemetes. Nor do even the Ubii, though they have earned the distinction of being a Roman colony, and prefer to be

called Agrippinenses, from the name of their founder, blush to own their origin. Having crossed the sea in former days, and given proof of their allegiance, they were settled on the Rhine-bank itself, as those who might guard it but need not be watched.

29. Foremost among all these nations in valour, the Batavi occupy an island within the Rhine and but a small portion of the bank. Formerly a tribe of the Chatti, they were forced by internal dissension to migrate to their present settlements and there become a part of the Roman Empire. They yet retain the honourable badge of an ancient alliance; for they are not insulted by tribute, nor ground down by the tax-gatherer. Free from the usual burdens and contributions, and set apart for fighting purposes, like a magazine of arms, we reserve them for our wars. The subjection of the Mattiaci is of the same character. For the greatness of the Roman people has spread reverence for our empire beyond the Rhine and the old boundaries. Thus this nation, whose settlements and territories are on their own side of the river, are yet in sentiment and purpose one with us; in all other respects they resemble the Batavi, except that they still gain from the soil and climate of their native land a keener vigour. I should not reckon among the German tribes the cultivators of the tithe-lands, although they are settled on the further side of the Rhine and Danube. Reckless adventurers from Gaul, emboldened by want, occupied this land of questionable ownership. After a while, our frontier having been advanced, and our military positions pushed forward, it was regarded as a remote nook of our empire and a part of a Roman province.

30. Beyond them are the Chatti, whose settlements begin at the Hercynian forest, where the country is not so open and marshy as in the other cantons into which Germany stretches. They are found where there are hills, and with them grow less frequent, for the Hercynian forest keeps close till it has seen the last of its native Chatti. Hardy frames, close-knit limbs, fierce countenances, and a peculiarly vigorous courage, mark the tribe. For Germans, they have much intelligence and sagacity; they promote their picked men to power, and obey those whom they promote;

they keep their ranks, note their opportunities, check their impulses, portion out the day, intrench themselves by night, regard fortune as a doubtful, valour as an unfailing, resource; and what is most unusual, and only given to systematic discipline, they rely more on the general than on the army. Their whole strength is in their infantry, which, in addition to its arms, is laden with iron tools and provisions. Other tribes you see going to battle, the Chatti to a campaign. Seldom do they engage in mere raids and casual encounters. It is indeed the peculiarity of a cavalry force quickly to win and as quickly to yield a victory. Fleetness and timidity go together; deliberateness is more akin to steady courage.

31. A practice, rare among the other German tribes, and simply characteristic of individual prowess, has become general among the Chatti, of letting the hair and beard grow as soon as they have attained manhood, and not till they have slain a foe laying aside that peculiar aspect which devotes and pledges them to valour. Over the spoiled and bleeding enemy they show their faces once more; then, and not till then, proclaiming that they have discharged the obligations of their birth, and proved themselves worthy of their country and of their parents. The coward and the unwarlike remain unshorn. The bravest of them also wear an iron ring (which otherwise is a mark of disgrace among the people) until they have released themselves by the slaughter of a foe. Most of the Chatti delight in these fashions. Even hoary-headed men are distinguished by them, and are thus conspicuous alike to enemies and to fellow-countrymen. To begin the battle always rests with *them; they* form the first line, an unusual spectacle. Nor even in peace do they assume a more civilised aspect. They have no home or land or occupation; they are supported by whomsoever they visit, as lavish of the property of others as they are regardless of their own, till at length the feebleness of age makes them unequal to so stern a valour.

32. Next to the Chatti on the Rhine, which has now a well-defined channel, and serves as a boundary, dwell the Usipii and Tencteri. The latter, besides the more usual military distinctions, particularly excel in the organisation of

cavalry, and the Chatti are not more famous for their foot-soldiers than are the Tencteri for their horsemen. What their forefathers originated, posterity maintain. This supplies sport to their children, rivalry to their youths: even the aged keep it up. Horses are bequeathed along with the slaves, the dwelling-house, and the usual rights of inheritance; they go to the son, not to the eldest, as does the other property, but to the most warlike and courageous.

33. After the Tencteri came, in former days, the Bructeri; but the general account now is, that the Chamavi and Angrivarii entered their settlements, drove them out and utterly exterminated them with the common help of the neighbouring tribes, either from hatred of their tyranny, or from the attractions of plunder, or from heaven's favourable regard for us. It did not even grudge us the spectacle of the conflict. More than sixty thousand fell, not beneath the Roman arms and weapons, but, grander far, before our delighted eyes. May the tribes, I pray, ever retain if not love for us, at least hatred for each other; for while the destinies of empire hurry us on, fortune can give no greater boon than discord among our foes.

34. The Angrivarii and Chamavi are bounded in the rear by the Dulgubini and Chasuarii, and other tribes not equally famous. Towards the river are the Frisii, distinguished as the Greater and Lesser Frisii, according to their strength. Both these tribes, as far as the ocean, are skirted by the Rhine, and their territory also embraces vast lakes which Roman fleets have navigated. We have even ventured on the ocean itself in these parts. Pillars of Hercules, so rumour commonly says, still exist; whether Hercules really visited the country, or whether we have agreed to ascribe every work of grandeur, wherever met with, to his renown. Drusus Germanicus indeed did not lack daring; but the ocean barred the explorer's access to itself and to Hercules. Subsequently no one has made the attempt, and it has been thought more pious and reverential to believe in the actions of the gods than to inquire.

35. Thus far we have taken note of Western Germany. Northwards the country takes a vast sweep. First comes the tribe of the Chauci, which, beginning at the Frisian

settlements, and occupying a part of the coast, stretches
along the frontier of all the tribes which I have enumerated,
till it reaches with a bend as far as the Chatti. This vast
extent of country is not merely possessed, but densely peopled, by the Chauci, the noblest of the German races, a nation who would maintain their greatness by righteous dealing. Without ambition, without lawless violence, they live
peaceful and secluded, never provoking a war or injuring
others by rapine and robbery. Indeed, the crowning proof
of their valour and their strength is, that they keep up their
superiority without harm to others. Yet all have their weapons in readiness, and an army if necessary, with a multitude
of men and horses; and even while at peace they have the
same renown of valour.

36. Dwelling on one side of the Chauci and Chatti, the
Cherusci long cherished, unassailed, an excessive and ener-
vating love of peace. This was more pleasant than safe, for
to be peaceful is self-deception among lawless and powerful
neighbours. Where the strong hand decides, moderation and
justice are terms applied only to the more powerful; and so
the Cherusci, ever reputed good and just, are now called
cowards and fools, while in the case of the victorious Chatti
success has been identified with prudence. The downfall of
the Cherusci brought with it also that of the Fosi, a neighbouring tribe, which shared equally in their disasters, though
they had been inferior to them in prosperous days.

37. In the same remote corner of Germany, bordering on
the ocean dwell the Cimbri, a now insignificant tribe, but of
great renown. Of their ancient glory widespread traces yet
remain; on both sides of the Rhine are encampments of vast
extent, and by their circuit you may even now measure the
warlike strength of the tribe, and find evidence of that
mighty emigration. Rome was in her 640th year when we
first heard of the Cimbrian invader in the consulship of
Cæcilius Metellus and Papirius Carbo, from which time to
the second consulship of the Emperor Trajan we have to
reckon about 210 years. So long have we been in conquering
Germany. In the space of this long epoch many losses have
been sustained on both sides. Neither Samnite nor Carthaginian, neither Spain nor Gaul, not even the Parthians, have

given us more frequent warnings. German independence truly is fiercer than the despotism of an Arsaces. What else, indeed, can the East taunt us with but the slaughter of Crassus, when it has itself lost Pacorus, and been crushed under a Ventidius? But Germans, by routing or making prisoners of Carbo, Cassius, Scaurus Aurelius, Servilius Cæpio, and Marcus Manlius, deprived the Roman people of five consular armies, and they robbed even a Cæsar of Varus and his three legions. Not without loss to us were they discomfited by Marius in Italy, by the great Julius in Gaul, and by Drusus, Nero, and Germanicus, on their own ground. Soon after, the mighty menaces of Caius Cæsar were turned into a jest. Then came a lull, until on the occasion of our discords and the civil war, they stormed the winter camp of our legions, and even designed the conquest of Gaul. Again were they driven back; and in recent times we have celebrated triumphs rather than won conquests over them.

38. I must now speak of the Suevi, who are not one nation as are the Chatti and Tencteri, for they occupy the greater part of Germany, and have hitherto been divided into separate tribes with names of their own, though they are called by the general designation of "Suevi." A national peculiarity with them is to twist their hair back, and fasten it in a knot. This distinguishes the Suevi from the other Germans, as it also does their own freeborn from their slaves. With other tribes, either from some connection with the Suevic race, or, as often happens, from imitation, the practice is an occasional one, and restricted to youth. The Suevi, till their heads are grey, affect the fashion of drawing back their unkempt locks, and often they are knotted on the very top of the head. The chiefs have a more elaborate style; so much do they study appearance, but in perfect innocence, not with any thoughts of love-making; but arranging their hair when they go to battle, to make themselves tall and terrible, they adorn themselves, so to speak, for the eyes of the foe.

39. The Semnones give themselves out to be the most ancient and renowned branch of the Suevi. Their antiquity is strongly attested by their religion. At a stated period, all the tribes of the same race assemble by their representatives in a grove consecrated by the auguries of their forefathers, and

by immemorial associations of terror. Here, having publicly slaughtered a human victim, they celebrate the horrible beginning of their barbarous rite. Reverence also in other ways is paid to the grove. No one enters it except bound with a chain, as an inferior acknowledging the might of the local divinity. If he chance to fall, it is not lawful for him to be lifted up, or to rise to his feet; he must crawl out along the ground. All this superstition implies the belief that from this spot the nation took its origin, that here dwells the supreme and all-ruling deity, to whom all else is subject and obedient. The fortunate lot of the Semnones strengthens this belief; a hundred cantons are in their occupation, and the vastness of their community makes them regard themselves as the head of the Suevic race.

40. To the Langobardi, on the contrary, their scanty numbers are a distinction. Though surrounded by a host of most powerful tribes, they are safe, not by submitting, but by daring the perils of war. Next come the Reudigni, the Aviones, the Anglii, the Varini, the Eudoses, the Suardones, and Nuithones who are fenced in by rivers or forests. None of these tribes have any noteworthy feature, except their common worship of Ertha, or mother-Earth, and their belief that she interposes in human affairs, and visits the nations in her car. In an island of the ocean there is a sacred grove, and within it a consecrated chariot, covered over with a garment. Only one priest is permitted to touch it. *He* can perceive the presence of the goddess in this sacred recess, and walks by her side with the utmost reverence as she is drawn along by heifers. It is a season of rejoicing, and festivity reigns wherever she deigns to go and be received. They do not go to battle or wear arms; every weapon is under lock; peace and quiet are known and welcomed only at these times, till the goddess, weary of human intercourse, is at length restored by the same priest to her temple. Afterwards the car, the vestments, and, if you like to believe it, the divinity herself, are purified in a secret lake. Slaves perform the rite, who are instantly swallowed up by its waters. Hence arises a mysterious terror and a pious ignorance concerning the nature of that which is seen only by men doomed

to die. This branch indeed of the Suevi stretches into the remoter regions of Germany.

41. Nearer to us is the state of the Hermunduri (I shall follow the course of the Danube as I did before that of the Rhine), a people loyal to Rome. Consequently they, alone of the Germans, trade not merely on the banks of the river, but far inland, and in the most flourishing colony of the province of Rætia. Everywhere they are allowed to pass without a guard; and while to the other tribes we display only our arms and our camps, to them we have thrown open our houses and country-seats, which they do not covet. It is in their lands that the Elbe takes its rise, a famous river known to us in past days; now we only hear of it.

42. The Narisci border on the Hermunduri, and then follow the Marcomanni and Quadi. The Marcomanni stand first in strength and renown, and their very territory, from which the Boii were driven in a former age, was won by valour. Nor are the Narisci and Quadi inferior to them. This I may call the frontier of Germany, so far as it is completed by the Danube. The Marcomanni and Quadi have, up to our time, been ruled by kings of their own nation, descended from the noble stock of Maroboduus and Tudrus. They now submit even to foreigners; but the strength and power of the monarch depend on Roman influence. He is occasionally supported by our arms, more frequently by our money, and his authority is none the less.

43. Behind them the Marsigni, Gotini, Osi, and Buri, close in the rear of the Marcomanni and Quadi. Of these, the Marsigni and Buri, in their language and manner of life, resemble the Suevi. The Gotini and Osi are proved by their respective Gallic and Pannonian tongues, as well as by the fact of their enduring tribute, not to be Germans. Tribute is imposed on them as aliens, partly by the Sarmatæ, partly by the Quadi. The Gotini, to complete their degradation, actually work iron mines. All these nations occupy but little of the plain country, dwelling in forests and on mountain-tops. For Suevia is divided and cut in half by a continuous mountain-range, beyond which live a multitude of tribes. The name of Ligii, spread as it is among many states, is the most widely extended. It will be enough to mention the most

powerful, which are the Harii, the Helvecones, the Manimi, the Helisii and the Nahanarvali. Among these last is shown a grove of immemorial sanctity. A priest in female attire has the charge of it. But the deities are described in Roman language as Castor and Pollux. Such, indeed, are the attributes of the divinity, the name being Alcis. They have no images, or, indeed, any vestige of foreign superstition, but it is as brothers and as youths that the deities are worshipped. The Harii, besides being superior in strength to the tribes just enumerated, savage as they are, make the most of their natural ferocity by the help of art and opportunity. Their shields are black, their bodies dyed. They choose dark nights for battle, and, by the dread and gloomy aspect of their death-like host, strike terror into the foe, who can never confront their strange and almost infernal appearance. For in all battles it is the eye which is first vanquished.

44. Beyond the Ligii are the Gothones, who are ruled by kings, a little more strictly than the other German tribes, but not as yet inconsistently with freedom. Immediately adjoining them, further from the coast, are the Rugii and Lemovii, the badge of all these tribes being the round shield, the short sword, and servile submission to their kings.

And now begin the states of the Suiones, situated on the Ocean itself, and these, besides men and arms, are powerful in ships. The form of their vessels is peculiar in this respect, that a prow at either extremity acts as a forepart, always ready for running into shore. They are not worked by sails, nor have they a row of oars attached to their sides; but, as on some rivers, the apparatus of rowing is unfixed, and shifted from side to side as circumstances require. And they likewise honour wealth, and so a single ruler holds sway with no restrictions, and with no uncertain claim to obedience. Arms are not with them, as with the other Germans, at the general disposal, but are in the charge of a keeper, who is actually a slave; for the ocean forbids the sudden inroad of enemies, and, besides, an idle multitude of armed men is easily demoralized. And indeed it is by no means the policy of a monarch to place either a nobleman, a freeborn citizen, or even a freedman, at the head of an armed force.

45. Beyond the Suiones is another sea, sluggish and al-

most motionless, which, we may certainly infer, girdles and surrounds the world, from the fact that the last radiance of the setting sun lingers on till sunrise, with a brightness sufficient to dim the light of the stars. Even the very sound of his rising, as popular belief adds, may be heard, and the forms of gods and the glory round his head may be seen. Only thus far (and here rumour seems truth) does the world extend.

At this point the Suevic sea, on its eastern shore, washes the tribes of the Æstii, whose rites and fashions and style of dress are those of the Suevi, while their language is more like the British. They worship the mother of the gods, and wear as a religious symbol the device of a wild boar. This serves as armour, and as a universal defence, rendering the votary of the goddess safe even amidst enemies. They often use clubs, iron weapons but seldom. They are more patient in cultivating corn and other produce than might be expected from the general indolence of the Germans. But they also search the deep, and are the only people who gather amber (which they call "glesum"), in the shallows, and also on the shore itself. Barbarians as they are they have not investigated or discovered what natural cause or process produces it. Nay, it even lay amid the sea's other refuse, till our luxury gave it a name. To them it is utterly useless; they gather it in its raw state, bring it to us in shapeless lumps, and marvel at the price which they receive. It is however a juice from trees, as you may infer from the fact that there are often seen shining through it, reptiles, and even winged insects, which, having become entangled in the fluid, are gradually enclosed in the substance as it hardens. I am therefore inclined to think that the islands and countries of the West, like the remote recesses of the East, where frankincense and balsam exude, contain fruitful woods and groves; that these productions, acted on by the near rays of the sun, glide in a liquid state into the adjacent sea, and are thrown up by the force of storms on the opposite shores. If you test the composition of amber by applying fire, it burns like pinewood, and sends forth a rich and fragrant flame; it is soon softened into something like pitch or resin.

Closely bordering on the Suiones are the tribes of the

Sitones, which, resembling them in all else, differ only in being ruled by a woman. So low have they fallen, not merely from freedom, but even from slavery itself. Here Suevia ends.

46. As to the tribes of the Peucini, Veneti, and Fenni, I am in doubt whether I should class them with the Germans or the Sarmatæ, although indeed the Peucini called by some Bastarnæ, are like Germans in their language, mode of life, and in the permanence of their settlements. They all live in filth and sloth, and by the intermarriages of the chiefs they are becoming in some degree debased into a resemblance to the Sarmatæ. The Veneti have borrowed largely from the Sarmatian character; in their plundering expeditions they roam over the whole extent of forest and mountain between the Peucini and Fenni. They are however to be rather referred to the German race, for they have fixed habitations, carry shields, and delight in strength and fleetness of foot, thus presenting a complete contrast to the Sarmatæ, who live in waggons and on horseback. The Fenni are strangely beastlike and squalidly poor; neither arms nor homes have they; their food is herbs, their clothing skins, their bed the earth. They trust wholly to their arrows, which, for want of iron, are pointed with bone. The men and the women are alike supplied by the chase; for the latter are always present, and demand a share of the prey. The little children have no shelter from wild beasts and storms but a covering of interlaced boughs. Such are the homes of the young, such the resting place of the old. Yet they count this greater happiness than groaning over field-labour, toiling at building, and poising the fortunes of themselves and others between hope and fear. Heedless of men, heedless of gods, they have attained that hardest of results, the not needing so much as a wish. All else is fabulous, as that the Hellusii and Oxiones have the faces and expressions of men, with the bodies and limbs of wild beasts. All this is unauthenticated, and I shall leave it open.

A DIALOGUE ON ORATORY

A DIALOGUE ON ORATORY

1. YOU often ask me, Justus Fabius, how it is that while the genius and the fame of so many distinguished orators have shed a lustre on the past, our age is so forlorn and so destitute of the glory of eloquence that it scarce retains the very name of orator. That title indeed we apply only to the ancients, and the clever speakers of this day we call pleaders, advocates, counsellors, anything rather than orators. To answer this question of yours, to undertake the burden of so serious an inquiry, involving, as it must, a mean opinion either of our capacities, if we cannot reach the same standard, or of our tastes, if we have not the wish, is a task on which I should scarcely venture had I to give my own views instead of being able to reproduce a conversation among men, for our time, singularly eloquent, whom, when quite a youth, I heard discussing this very question. And so it is not ability, it is only memory and recollection which I require. I have to repeat now, with the same divisions and arguments, following closely the course of that discussion, those subtle reflections which I heard, powerfully expressed, from men of the highest eminence, each of whom assigned a different but plausible reason, thereby displaying the peculiarities of his individual temper and genius. Nor indeed did the opposite side lack an advocate, who, after much criticism and ridicule of old times, maintained the superiority of the eloquence of our own days to the great orators of the past.

2. It was the day after Curiatius Maternus had given a reading of his Cato, by which it was said that he had irritated the feelings of certain great personages, because in the subject of his tragedy he had apparently forgotten himself and thought only of Cato. While all Rome was discussing the subject, he received a visit from Marcus Aper and Julius

Secundus, then the most famous men of genius at our bar
Of both I was a studious hearer in court, and I also would
follow them to their homes and when they appeared in public, from a singular zeal for my profession, and a youthful
enthusiasm which urged me to listen diligently to their
trivial talk, their more serious debates, and their private and
esoteric descourse. Yet many ill-naturedly thought that Secundus had no readiness of speech, and that Aper had won
his reputation for eloquence by his cleverness and natural
powers, more than by training and culture. As a fact, Secundus had a pure, terse, and a sufficiently fluent style,
while Aper, who was imbued with learning of all kinds, pretended to despise the culture which he really possessed. He
would have, so he must have thought, a greater reputation
for industry and application, if it should appear that his
genius did not depend on any supports from pursuits alien
to his profession.

3. So we entered the study of Maternus, and found him
seated with the very book which he had read the day before,
in his hands. Secundus began. Has the talk of ill-natured
people no effect in deterring you, Maternus, from clinging
to your Cato with its provocations? Or have you taken up
the book to revise it more carefully, and, after striking out
whatever has given a handle for a bad interpretation, will
you publish, if not a better, at least a safer, Cato?

You shall read, was the answer, what Maternus owed it
to himself to write, and all that you heard you will recognise
again. Anything omitted in the Cato Thyestes shall supply
in my next reading. This is a tragedy, the plan of which I
have in my own mind arranged and formed. I am therefore
bent on hurrying on the publication of the present book,
that, as soon as my first work is off my hands, I may devote
my whole soul to a fresh task.

It seems, said Aper, so far from these tragedies contenting you, that you have abandoned the study of the orator
and pleader, and are giving all your time to Medea and now
to Thyestes, although your friends, with their many causes,
and your clients from the colonies, municipalities, and towns,
are calling you to the courts. You could hardly answer their
demands even if you had not imposed new work on your-

self, the work of adding to the dramas of Greece a Domitius and a Cato, histories and names from our own Rome.

4. This severity of yours, replied Maternus, would be quite a blow to us, had not our controversy from its frequency and familiarity become by this time almost a regular practice. You, in fact, never cease from abusing and inveighing against poets, and I, whom you reproach with neglect of my professional duties, every day undertake to plead against you in defence of poetry. So I am all the more delighted at the presence of a judge who will either forbid me for the future to write verses, or who will compel me by his additional authority to do what I have long desired, to give up the petty subleties of legal causes, at which I have toiled enough, and more than enough, and to cultivate a more sacred and more stately eloquence.

5. For my part, said Secundus, before Aper refuses me as a judge, I will do as is usually done by upright and sensible judges, who excuse themselves in cases in which it is evident that one side has an undue influence with them. Who knows not that no one is nearer my heart from long friendship and uninterrupted intercourse than Saleius Bassus, an excellent man, as well as a most accomplished poet? Besides, if poetry is to be put on her defence, I know not a more influential defendant.

He may rest secure, said Aper, both Saleius Bassus himself, and anyone else who is devoted to the pursuit of poetry and the glory of song, if he has not the gift of pleading causes. But assuredly, as I have found an arbiter for this dispute, I will not allow Maternus to shelter himself behind a number of associates. I single him out for accusation before you on the ground that, though naturally fittest for that manly eloquence of the orator by which he might create and retain friendships, acquire connections, and attach the provinces, he is throwing away a pursuit than which it is impossible to imagine one in our state richer in advantages, more splendid in its prospects, more attractive in fame at home, more illustrious in celebrity throughout our whole empire and all the world. If, indeed, what is useful in life should be the aim of all our plans and actions, what can be safer than to practise an art armed with which a man can always bring

aid to friends, succour to strangers, deliverance to the imperilled, while to malignant foes he is an actual fear and
terror, himself the while secure and intrenched, so to say,
within a power and a position of lasting strength? When we
have a flow of prosperity, the efficacy and use of this art are
seen in the help and protection of others; if, however, we
hear the sound of danger to ourselves, the breast-plate and
the sword are not, I am well assured, a stronger defence on
the battle-field than eloquence is to a man amid the perils of
a prosecution. It is both a shield and a weapon; you can use
it alike for defence and attack, either before a judge, before
the senate, or before the emperor. What but his eloquence
did Eprius Marcellus oppose the other day to the senators
in their fury? Armed with this, and consequently terrible, he
baffled the sagacious but untrained wisdom of Helvidius
Priscus, which knew nothing of such encounters. Of its use-
fulness I say no more. It is a point which I think my friend
Maternus will be the last to dispute.

6. I pass now to the pleasure derived from the orator's eloquence. Its delights are enjoyed not for a single moment, but
almost on every day and at every hour. To the mind of an
educated gentleman, naturally fitted for worthy enjoyments,
what can be more delightful than to see his house always
thronged and crowded by gatherings of the most eminent
men, and to know that the honour is paid not to his wealth,
his childlessness, or his possession of some office, but to himself? Nay, more; the childless, the rich, and the powerful
often go to one who is both young and poor, in order to
intrust him with difficulties affecting themselves or their
friends. Can there be any pleasure from boundless wealth
and vast power equal to that of seeing men in years, and
even in old age, men backed by the influence of the whole
world, readily confessing, amid the utmost affluence of every
kind, that they do not possess that which is the best of all?
Again, look at the respectable citizens who escort the pleader
to and from the court. Look at his appearance in public, and
the respect shown him before the judges. What a delight it
must be to rise and stand amid the hushed crowd, with every
eye on him alone, the people assembling and gathering round
him in a circle, and taking from the orator any emotion he

has himself assumed. I am now reckoning the notorious joys of an orator, those which are open to the sight even of the uneducated; the more secret, known only to the advocate himself, are yet greater. If he produces a careful and well-prepared speech, there is a solidity and stedfastness in his satisfaction, just as there is in his style; if, again, he offers his audience, not without some tremblings at heart, the result of a fresh and sudden effort, his very anxiety enhances the joy of success, and ministers to his pleasure. In fact, audacity at the moment, and rashness itself, have quite a peculiar sweetness. As with the earth, so with genius. Though time must be bestowed on the sowing and cultivation of some plants, yet those which grow spontaneously are the more pleasing.

7. To speak my own mind, I did not experience more joy on the day on which I was presented with the robe of a senator, or when, as a new man, born in a far from influential state, I was elected quæstor, or tribune, or prætor, than on those on which it was my privilege, considering the insignificance of my ability as a speaker, to defend a prisoner with success, to win a verdict in a cause before the Court of the Hundred, or to give the support of my advocacy in the emperor's presence to the great freedmen themselves, or to ministers of the crown. On such occasions I seem to rise above tribunates, prætorships, and consulships, and to possess that which, if it be not of natural growth, is not bestowed by mandate, nor comes through interest. Again, is there an accomplishment, the fame and glory of which are to be compared with the distinction of the orator, who is an illustrious man at Rome, not only with the busy class, intent on public affairs, but even with people of leisure, and with the young, those at least who have a right disposition and a worthy confidence in themselves? Whose name does the father din into his children's ears before that of the orator? Whom, as he passes by, do the ignorant mob and the men with the tunic oftener speak of by name and point out with the finger? Strangers too and foreigners, having heard of him in their towns and colonies, as soon as they have arrived at Rome, ask for him and are eager, as it were to recognise him.

8. As for Marcellus Eprius, whom I have just mentioned, and Crispus Vibius (it is pleasanter to me to cite recent and modern examples than those of a distant and forgotten past), I would venture to argue that they are quite as great men in the remotest corners of the world as at Capua or Vercellae, where they are said to have been born. Nor do they owe this to the three hundred million sesterces of the one, although it may seem that they must thank their eloquence for having attained such wealth. Eloquence itself is the cause. Its inspiration and superhuman power have throughout all times shown by many an example what a height of fortune men have reached by the might of genius. But there are, as I said but now, instances close at hand, and we may know them, not by hearsay, but may see them with our eyes. The lower and meaner their birth, the more notorious the poverty and the straitened means amid which their life began, the more famous and brilliant are they as examples to show the efficacy of an orator's eloquence. Without the recommendation of birth, without the support of riches, neither of the two distinguished for virtue, one even despised for the appearance of his person, they have now for many years been the most powerful men in the state, and, as long as it suited them, they were the leaders of the bar. At this moment, as leading men in the emperor's friendship they carry all before them, and even the leading man himself of the State esteems and almost reverences them. Vespasian indeed, venerable in his old age and most tolerant of truth, knows well that while his other friends are dependent on what he has given them, and on what it is easy for him to heap and pile on others, Marcellus and Crispus, in becoming his friends, brought with them something which they had not received and which could not be received from a prince. Amid so much that is great, busts, inscriptions, and statues hold but a very poor place. Yet even these they do not disregard, and certainly not riches and affluence, which it is easier to find men denouncing than despising. It is these honours and splendours, aye and substantial wealth, that we see filling the homes of those who from early youth have given themselves to practice at the bar and to the study of oratory.

9. As for song and verse to which Maternus wishes to devote his whole life (for this was the starting-point of his
entire argument), they bring no dignity to the author, nor
do they improve his circumstances. Although your ears, Maternus, may loathe what I am about to say, I ask what good
it is if Agamemnon or Jason speaks eloquently in your composition. Who the more goes back to his home saved from
danger and bound to you? Our friend Saleius is an admirable poet, or, if the phrase be more complimentary, a most
illustrious bard; but who walks by his side or attends his
receptions or follows in his train? Why, if his friend or relative or even he himself stumbles into some troublesome affair, he will run to Secundus here, or to you, Maternus, not
because you are a poet or that you may make verses for
him; for verses come naturally to Bassus in his own home,
and pretty and charming they are, though the result of them
is that when, with the labour of a whole year, through entire
days and the best part of the nights, he has hammered out,
with the midnight oil, a single book, he is forced actually to
beg and canvass for people who will condescend to be his
hearers, and not even this without cost to himself. He gets
the loan of a house, fits up a room, hires benches, and scat-
ters programmes. Even if his reading is followed by a complete success, all the glory is, so to say, cut short in the
bloom and the flower, and does not come to any real and
substantial fruit. He carries away with him not a single
friendship, not a single client, not an obligation that will
abide in anyone's mind, only idle applause, meaningless acclamations and a fleeting delight. We lately praised Vespasian's bounty, in giving Bassus four thousand pounds, as
something marvellous and splendid. It is no doubt a fine
thing to win an emperor's favour by talent; but how much
finer, if domestic circumstances so require, to cultivate oneself, to make one's own genius propitious, to fall back on
one's own bounty. Consider too that a poet, if he wishes to
work out and accomplish a worthy result, must leave the
society of his friends, and the attractions of the capital; he
must relinquish every other duty, and must, as poets themselves say, retire to woods and groves, in fact, into solitude

10. Nor again do even reputation and fame, the only ob-

ject of their devotion, the sole reward of their labours, by
their own confession, cling to the poet as much as to the
orator; for indifferent poets are known to none, and the
good but to a few. When does the rumour of the very
choicest readings penetrate every part of Rome, much less
is talked of throughout our numerous provinces? How few,
when they visit the capital from Spain or Asia, to say nothing of our Gallic neighbours, ask after Saleius Bassus! And
indeed, if any one does ask after him, having once seen him,
he passes on, and is satisfied, as if he had seen a picture or a
statue. I do not wish my remarks to be taken as implying
that I would deter from poetry those to whom nature has
denied the orator's talent, if only they can amuse their leisure and push themselves into fame by this branch of culture. For my part I hold all eloquence in its every variety
something sacred and venerable, and I regard as preferable
to all studies of other arts not merely your tragedian's
buskin or the measures of heroic verse, but even the sweetness of the lyric ode, the playfulness of the elegy, the satire
of the iambic, the wit of the epigram, and indeed any other
form of eloquence. But it is with you, Maternus, that I am
dealing; for, when your genius might carry you to the summit of eloquence, you prefer to wander from the path, and
though sure to win the highest prize you stop short at
meaner things. Just as, if you had been born in Greece,
where it is an honour to practise even the arts of the arena,
and if the gods had given you the vigour and strength of
Nicostratus, I should not suffer those giant arms meant by
nature for combat to waste themselves on the light javelin
or the throwing of the quoit, so now I summon you from
the lecture-room and the theatre to the law court with its
pleadings and its real battles. I do this the more because
you cannot even fall back on the refuge which shelters
many, the plea that the poet's pursuit is less liable to give
offence than that of the orator. In truth, with you the ardour
of a peculiarly noble nature bursts forth, and the offence
you give is not for the sake of a friend, but, what is more
dangerous, for the sake of Cato. Nor is this offending excused by the obligation of duty, or by the fidelity of an
advocate, or by the impulse of a casual and sudden speech

You have, it seems, prepared your part in having chosen a
character of note who would speak with authority. I foresee
your possible answer. Hence, you will say, came the decisive
approval; this is the style which the lecture-room chiefly
praises, and which next becomes the world's talk. Away then
with the excuse of quiet and safety, when you are deliberately choosing a more doughty adversary. For myself, let
it be enough to take a side in the private disputes of our
own time. In these, if at any time necessity has compelled
us on behalf of an imperilled friend to offend the ears of the
powerful, our loyalty must be approved, our liberty of speech
condoned.

11. Aper having said this with his usual spirit and with
vehemence of utterance, Maternus replied good-humouredly
with something of a smile. I was preparing to attack the
orators at as great length as Aper had praised them, for I
thought that he would leave his praises of them and go on
to demolish poets and the pursuit of poetry, but he appeased
me by a sort of stratagem, granting permission to those who
cannot plead causes, to make verses. For myself, though I
am perhaps able to accomplish and effect something in pleading causes, yet it was by the public reading of tragedies that
I first began to enter the path of fame, when in Nero's time
I broke the wicked power of Vatinius by which even the
sanctities of culture were profaned, and if at this moment I
possess any celebrity and distinction I maintain that it has
been acquired more by the renown of my poems than of my
speeches. And so now I have resolved to throw off the yoke
of my labours at the bar, and for trains of followers on my
way to and from the court and for crowded receptions I
crave no more than for the bronzes and busts which have
invaded my house even against my will. For hitherto I have
upheld my position and my safety better by integrity than
by eloquence, and I am not afraid of having ever to say a
word in the senate except to avert peril from another.

12. As to the woods and groves and that retirement which
Aper denounced, they bring such delight to me that I count
among the chief enjoyments of poetry the fact that it is composed not in the midst of bustle, or with a suitor sitting
before one's door, or amid the wretchedness and tears of

prisoners, but that the soul withdraws herself to abodes of purity and innocence, and enjoys her holy resting-place. Here eloquence had her earliest beginnings; here is her inmost shrine. In such guise and beauty did she first charm mortals, and steal into those virgin hearts which no vice had contaminated. Oracles spoke under these conditions. As for the present money-getting and blood-stained eloquence, its use is modern, its origin in corrupt manners, and, as you said, Aper, it is a device to serve as a weapon. But the happy golden age, to speak in our own poetic fashion, knew neither orators nor accusations, while it abounded in poets and bards, men who could sing of good deeds, but not defend evil actions. None enjoyed greater glory, or honours more august, first with the gods, whose answers they published, and at whose feasts they were present, as was commonly said, and then with the offspring of the gods and with sacred kings, among whom, so we have understood, was not a single pleader of causes, but an Orpheus, a Linus, and, if you care to dive into a remoter age, an Apollo himself. Or, if you think all this too fabulous and imaginary, at least you grant me that Homer has as much honour with posterity as Demosthenes, and that the fame of Euripides or Sophocles is bounded by a limit not narrower than that of Lysias or Hyperides. You will find in our own day more who disparage Cicero's than Virgil's glory. Nor is any production of Asinius or Messala so famous as Ovid's Medea or the Thyestes of Varius.

13. Look again at the poet's lot, with its delightful companionships. I should not be afraid of comparing it with the harassing and anxious life of the orator. Orators, it is true, have been raised to consulships by their contests and perils, but I prefer Virgil's serene, calm, and peaceful retirement, in which after all he was not without the favour of the divine Augustus, and fame among the people of Rome. We have the testimony of the letters of Augustus, the testimony too of the people themselves, who, on hearing in the theatre some of Virgil's verses, rose in a body and did homage to the poet, who happened to be present as a spectator, just as to Augustus himself. Even in our own day, Pomponius Secundus need not yield to Domitius Aper on the score of a

dignified life or an enduring reputation. As for your Crispus and Marcellus, whom you hold up to me as examples, what is there in their lot to be coveted? Is it that they are in fear themselves, or are a fear to others? Is it that, while every day something is asked from them, those to whom they grant it feel indignant? Is it that, bound as they are by the chain of flattery, they are never thought servile enough by those who rule, or free enough by us? What is their power at its highest? Why, the freedmen usually have as much. For myself, as Virgil says, let "the sweet muses" lead me to their sacred retreats, and to their fountains far away from anxieties and cares, and the necessity of doing every day something repugnant to my heart. Let me no longer tremblingly experience the madness and perils of the forum, and the pallors of fame. Let me not be aroused by a tumult of morning visitors, or a freedman's panting haste, or, anxious about the future, have to make a will to secure my wealth. Let me not possess more than what I can leave to whom I please, whenever the day appointed by my own fates shall come; and let the statue over my tomb be not gloomy and scowling, but bright and laurel-crowned. As for my memory, let there be no resolutions in the senate, or petitions to the emperor.

14. Excited and, I say say, full of enthusiasm, Maternus had hardly finished when Vipstanus Messala entered his room, and, from the earnest expression on each face, he con·jectured that their conversation was unusually serious. Have I, he asked, come among you unseasonably, while you are engaged in private deliberation, or the preparation of some case?

By no means, by no means, said Secundus. Indeed I could wish you had come sooner, for you would have been delighted with the very elaborate arguments of our friend Aper, in which he urged Maternus to apply all his ability and industry to the pleading of causes, and then too with Maternus's apology for his poems in a lively speech, which, as suited a poet's defence, was uncommonly spirited, and more like poetry than oratory.

For my part, he replied, I should have been infinitely charmed by the discourse, and I am delighted to find that you excellent men, the orators of our age, instead of exercising your talents simply on law-business and rhetorical studies, also engage in discussions which not only strengthen the intellect but also draw from learning and from letters a pleasure most exquisite both to you who discuss such subjects and to those too whose ears your words may reach. Hence the world, I see, is as much pleased with you, Secundus, for having by your life of Julius Asiaticus given it the promise of more such books, as it is with Aper for having not yet retired from the disputes of the schools, and for choosing to employ his leisure after the fashion of modern rhetoricians rather than of the old orators.

15. Upon this Aper replied, You still persist, Messala, in admiring only what is old and antique and in sneering at and disparaging the culture of our own day. I have often heard this sort of talk from you, when, forgetting the eloquence of yourself and your brother, you argued that nobody in this age is an orator. And you did this, I believe, with the more audacity because you were not afraid of a reputation for ill-nature, seeing that the glory which others concede to you, you deny to yourself. I feel no penitence, said Messala, for such talk, nor do I believe that Secundus or Maternus or you yourself, Aper, think differently, though now and then you argue for the opposite view. I could wish that one of you were prevailed on to investigate and describe to us the reasons of this vast difference. I often inquire into them by myself. That which consoles some minds, to me increases the difficulty. For I perceive that even with the Greeks it has happened that there is a greater distance between Aeschines and Demosthenes on the one hand, and your friend Nicetes or any other orator who shakes Ephesus or Mitylene with a chorus of rhetoricians and their noisy applause, on the other, than that which separates Afer, Africanus, or yourselves from Cicero or Asinius.

16. The question you have raised, said Secundus, is a great one and quite worthy of discussion. But who has a better claim to unravel it than yourself, you who to profound learning and transcendent ability have added reflection and study?

I will open my mind to you, replied Messala, if first I can

prevail on you to give me your assistance in our discussion. I can answer for two of us, said Maternus; Secundus and myself will take the part which we understand you have not so much omitted as left to us. Aper usually dissents, as you have just said, and he has clearly for some time been girding himself for the attack, and cannot bear with patience our union on behalf of the merits of the ancients.

Assuredly, said Aper, I will not allow our age to be condemned, unheard and undefended, by this conspiracy of yours. First, however, I will ask you whom you call ancients, or what period of orators you limit by your definition? When I hear of ancients, I understand men of the past, born ages ago; I have in my eye Ulysses and Nestor, whose time is about thirteen hundred years before our day. But you bring forward Demosthenes and Hyperides who flourished, as we know, in the period of Philip and Alexander, a period, however, which they both outlived. Hence we see that not much more than four hundred years has intervened between our own era and that of Demosthenes. If you measure this space of time by the frailty of human life, it perhaps seems long; if by the course of ages and by the thought of this boundless universe, it is extremely short and is very near us. For indeed, if, as Cicero says in his Hortensius, the great and the true year is that in which the position of the heavens and of the stars at any particular moment recurs, and if that year embraces twelve thousand nine hundred and ninety four of what we call years, then your Demosthenes, whom you represent as so old and ancient, began his existence not only in the same year, but almost in the same month as ourselves.

17. But I pass to the Latin orators. Among them, it is not, I imagine, Menenius Agrippa, who may seem ancient, whom you usually prefer to the speakers of our day, but Cicero, Caelius, Calvus, Brutus, Asinius, Messala. Why you assign them to antiquity rather than to our own times, I do not see. With respect to Cicero himself, it was in the consulship of Hirtius and Pansa, as his freedman Tiro has stated, on the 5th of December, that he was slain. In that same year the Divine Augustus elected himself and Quintus Pedius consuls in the room of Pansa and Hirtius. Fix at fifty-six years the

subsequent rule of the Divine Augustus over the state; add Tiberius's three-and-twenty years, the four years or less of Caius, the twenty-eight years of Claudius and Nero, the one memorable long year of Galba, Otho, and Vitellius, and the now six years of the present happy reign, during which Vespasian has been fostering the public weal, and the result is that from Cicero's death to our day is a hundred and twenty years, one man's life-time. For I saw myself an old man in Britain who declared that he was present at the battle in which they strove to drive and beat back from their shores the arms of Cæsar when he attacked their island. So, had this man who encountered Cæsar in the field, been brought to Rome either as a prisoner, or by his own choice or by some destiny, he might have heard Cæsar himself and Cicero, and also have been present at our own speeches. At the last largess of the Emperor you saw yourselves several old men who told you that they had actually shared once and again in the gifts of the divine Augustus. Hence we infer that they might have heard both Corvinus and Asinius. Corvinus indeed lived on to the middle of the reign of Augustus, Asinius almost to its close. You must not then divide the age, and habitually describe as old and ancient orators those with whom the ears of the self-same men might have made acquaintance, and whom they might, so to say, have linked and coupled together.

18. I have made these preliminary remarks to show that any credit reflected on the age by the fame and renown of these orators is common property, and is in fact more closely connected with us than with Servius Galba or Caius Carbo, and others whom we may rightly call "ancients." These indeed are rough, unpolished, awkward, and ungainly, and I wish that your favourite Calvus or Caelius or even Cicero had in no respect imitated them. I really mean now to deal with the subject more boldly and confidently, but I must first observe that the types and varieties of eloquence change with the age. Thus Caius Gracchus compared with the elder Cato is full and copious; Crassus compared with Gracchus is polished and ornate; Cicero compared with either is lucid, graceful, and lofty; Corvinus again is softer and sweeter and more finished in his phrases than Cicero. I do not ask

who is the best speaker. Meantime I am content to have proved that eloquence has more than one face, and even in those whom you call ancients several varieties are to be discovered. Nor does it at once follow that difference implies inferiority. It is the fault of envious human nature that the old is always the object of praise, the present of contempt. Can we doubt that there were found critics who admired Appius Caecus more than Cato? We know that even Cicero was not without his disparagers, who thought him inflated, turgid, not concise enough, but unduly diffuse and luxuriant, in short anything but Attic. You have read of course the letters of Calvus and Brutus to Cicero, and from these it is easy to perceive that in Cicero's opinion Calvus was bloodless and attenuated, Brutus slovenly and lax. Cicero again was slightingly spoken of by Calvus as loose and nerveless, and by Brutus, to use his own words, as "languid and effeminate." If you ask me, I think they all said what was true. But I shall come to them separately after a while; now I have to deal with them collectively.

19. While indeed the admirers of the ancients fix as the boundary, so to say, of antiquity, the period up to Cassius Severus who was the first, they assert, to deviate from the old and plain path of the speaker, I maintain that it was not from poverty of genius or ignorance of letters that he adopted his well known style, but from preference and intellectual conviction. He saw, in fact, that, as I was just now saying, the character and type of oratory must change with the circumstances of the age and an altered taste in the popular ear. The people of the past, ignorant and uncultured as they were, patiently endured the length of a very confused speech, and it was actually to the speaker's credit, if he took up one of their days by his speech-making. Then too they highly esteemed long preparatory introductions, narratives told from a remote beginning, a multitude of divisions ostentatiously paraded, proofs in a thousand links, and all the other directions prescribed in those driest of treatises by Hermagoras and Apollodorus. Any one who was supposed to have caught a scent of philosophy, and who introduced some philosophical commonplace into his speech, was praised up to the skies. And no wonder; for this was new

and unfamiliar, and even of the orators but very few had studied the rules of rhetoricians or the dogmas of philosophers. But now that all these are common property and that there is scarce a bystander in the throng who, if not fully instructed, has not at least been initiated into the rudiments of culture, eloquence must resort to new and skilfully chosen paths, in order that the orator may avoid offence to the fastidious ear, at any rate before judges who decide by power and authority, not by law and precedent, who fix the speaker's time, instead of leaving it to himself, and, so far from thinking that they ought to wait till he chooses to speak on the matter in question, continually remind him of it and recall him to it when he wanders, protesting that they are in a hurry.

20. Who will now tolerate an advocate who begins by speaking of the feebleness of his constitution, as is usual in the openings of Corvinus? Who will sit out the five books against Verres? Who will endure those huge volumes, on a legal plea or form, which we have read in the speeches for Marcus Tullius and Aulus Caecina? In our day the judge anticipates the speaker, and unless he is charmed and imposed on by the train of arguments, or the brilliancy of the thoughts, or the grace and elegance of the descriptive sketches, he is deaf to his eloquence. Even the mob of bystanders, and the chance listeners who flock in, now usually require brightness and beauty in a speech, and they no more endure in the law-court the harshness and roughness of antiquity, than they would an actor on the stage who chose to reproduce the gestures of Roscius or Ambivius. So again the young, those whose studies are on the anvil, who go after the orators with a view to their own progress, are anxious not merely to hear but also to carry back home some brilliant passage worthy of remembrance. They tell it one to another, and often mention it in letters to their colonies and provinces, whether it is a reflection lighted up by a neat and pithy phrase, or a passage bright with choice and poetic ornament. For we now expect from a speaker even poetic beauty, not indeed soiled with the old rust of Accius or Pacuvius, but such as is produced from the sacred treasures of Horace, Virgil, and Lucan. Thus the age of our orators,

in conforming itself to the ear and the taste of such a class, has advanced in beauty and ornateness. Nor does it follow that our speeches are less successful because they bring pleasure to the ears of those who have to decide. What if you were to assume that the temples of the present day are weaker, because, instead of being built of rough blocks and ill-shaped tiles, they shine with marble and glitter with gold?

21. I will frankly admit to you that I can hardly keep from laughing at some of the ancients, and from falling asleep at others. I do not single out any of the common herd, as Canutius, or Arrius, and others in the same sick-room, so to say, who are content with mere skin and bones. Even Calvus, although he has left, I think, one-and-twenty volumes, scarcely satisfies me in one or two short speeches. The rest of the world, I see, does not differ from my opinion about him; for how few read his speeches against Asitius or Drusus! Certainly his impeachment of Vatinius, as it is entitled, is in the hands of students, especially the second of the orations. This, indeed, has a finish about the phrases and the periods, and suits the ear of the critic, whence you may infer that even Calvus understood what a better style is, but that he lacked genius and power rather than the will to speak with more dignity and grace. What again from the speeches of Caelius do we admire? Why, we like of these the whole, or at least parts, in which we recognise the polish and elevation of our own day; but, as for those mean expressions, those gaps in the structure of the sentences, and uncouth sentiments, they savour of antiquity. No one, I suppose, is so thoroughly antique as to praise Caelius simply on the side of his antiqueness. We may, indeed, make allowance for Caius Julius Cæsar, on account of his vast schemes and many occupations, for having achieved less in eloquence than his divine genius demanded from him, and leave him indeed, just as we leave Brutus to his philosophy. Undoubtedly in his speeches he fell short of his reputation, even by the admission of his admirers. I hardly suppose that any one reads Cæsar's speech for Decius the Samnite, or that of Brutus for King Deiotarus, or other works equally dull and cold, unless it is some one who also admires their poems. For they did write poems, and sent them to libraries, with

no better success than Cicero, but with better luck, because fewer people know that they wrote them.

Asinius too, though born in a time nearer our own, seems to have studied with the Menenii and Appii. At any rate he imitated Pacuvius and Accius, not only in his tragedies but also in his speeches; he is so harsh and dry. Style, like the human body, is then specially beautiful when, so to say, the veins are not prominent, and the bones cannot be counted, but when a healthy and sound blood fills the limbs, and shows itself in the muscles, and the very sinews become beautiful under a ruddy glow and graceful outline. I will not attack Corvinus, for it was not indeed his own fault that he did not exhibit the luxuriance and brightness of our own day. Rather let us note how far the vigour of his intellect or of his imagination satisfied his critical faculty.

22. I come now to Cicero. He had the same battle with his contemporaries which I have with you. They admired the ancients; he preferred the eloquence of his own time. It was in taste more than anything else that he was superior to the orators of that age. In fact, he was the first who gave a finish to oratory, the first who applied a principle of selection to words, and art to composition. He tried his skill at beautiful passages, and invented certain arrangements of the sentence, at least in those speeches which he composed when old and near the close of life, that is when he had made more progress, and had learnt by practice and by many a trial, what was the best style of speaking. As for his early speeches, they are not free from the faults of antiquity. He is tedious in his introductions, lengthy in his narrations, careless about digressions; he is slow to rouse himself, and seldom warms to his subject, and only an idea here and there is brought to a fitting and a brilliant close. There is nothing which you can pick out or quote, and the style is like a rough building, the wall of which indeed is strong and lasting, but not particularly polished and bright. Now I would have an orator, like a rich and grand householder, not merely be sheltered by a roof sufficient to keep off rain and wind, but by one to delight the sight and the eye; not merely be provided with such furniture as is enough for necessary purposes, but also possess among his treasures gold and jewels, so that he may

find a frequent pleasure in handling them and gazing on them. On the other hand, some things should be kept at a distance as being now obsolete and ill-savoured. There should be no phrase stained, so to speak, with rust; no ideas should be expressed in halting and languid periods after the fashion of chronicles. The orator must shun an offensive and tasteless scurrility; he must vary the structure of his sentences and not end all his clauses in one and the same way.

23. Phrases like "Fortune's wheel" and "Verrine soup," I do not care to ridicule, or that stock ending of every third clause in all Cicero's speeches, "it would seem to be," brought in as the close of a period. I have mentioned them with reluctance, omitting several, although they are the sole peculiarities admired and imitated by those who call themselves orators of the old school. I will not name any one, as I think it enough to have pointed at a class. Still, you have before your eyes men who read Lucilius rather than Horace, and Lucretius rather than Virgil, who have a mean opinion of the eloquence of Aufidius Bassus, and Servilius Nonianus compared with that of Sisenna or Varro, and who despise and loathe the treatises of our modern rhetoricians, while those of Calvus are their admiration. When these men prose in the old style before the judges, they have neither select listeners nor a popular audience; in short the client himself hardly endures them. They are dismal and uncouth, and the very soundness of which they boast, is the result not so much of real vigour as of fasting. Even as to health of body, physicians are not satisfied with that which is attained at the cost of mental worry. It is a small matter not to be ill; I like a man to be robust and hearty and full of life. If soundness is all that you can praise him for, he is not very far from being an invalid. Be it yours, my eloquent friends, to grace our age to the best of your ability, as in fact you are doing, with the noblest style of oratory. You, Messala, imitate, I observe, the choicest beauties of the ancients. And you, Maternus and Secundus, combine charm and finish of expression with weight of thought. There is discrimination in the phrases you invent, order in the treatment of your subject, fullness, when the case demands it, conciseness, when it is possible, elegance in your style, and perspicuity in every

sentence. You can express passion, and yet control an orator's licence. And so, although ill-nature and envy may have
stood in the way of our good opinions, posterity will speak
the truth concerning you.

24. Aper having finished speaking, Maternus said, You
recognise, do you not, our friend Aper's force and passion?
With what a torrent, what a rush of eloquence has he been
defending our age? How full and varied was his tirade
against the ancients! What ability and spirit, what learning
and skill too did he show in borrowing from the very men
themselves the weapons with which he forthwith proceeded
to attack them! Still, as to your promise, Messala, there
must for all this be no change. We neither want a defence
of the ancients, nor do we compare any of ourselves, though
we have just heard our own praises, with those whom Aper
has denounced. Aper himself thinks otherwise; he merely
followed an old practice much in vogue with your philosophical school of assuming the part of an opponent. Giv
us then not a panegyric on the ancients (their own fame is
a sufficient panegyric) but tell us plainly the reasons why
with us there has been such a falling off from their eloquence, the more marked as dates have proved that from
the death of Cicero to this present day is but a hundred and
twenty years.

25. Messala replied, I will take the line you have prescribed for me. Certainly I need not argue long against
Aper, who began by raising what I think a controversy
about a name, implying that it is not correct to call ancients
those whom we all know to have lived a hundred years ago.
I am not fighting about a word. Let him call them ancients
or elders or any other name he prefers, provided only we
have the admission that the eloquence of that age exceeded
ours. If again he freely admits that even in the same, much
more in different periods, there were many varieties of oratory, against this part too of his argument I say nothing. I
maintain, however, that just as among Attic orators we give
the first place to Demosthenes and assign the next to Aeschines, Hyperides, Lysias and Lycurgus, while all agree in
regarding this as pre-eminently the age of speakers, so
among ourselves Cicero indeed was superior to all the elo-

quent men of his day, though Calvus, Asinius, Cæsar, Caelius, and Brutus may claim the right of being preferred to those who preceded and who followed them. It matters nothing that they differ in special points, seeing that they are generically alike. Calvus is the more terse, Asinius has the finer rhythm, Cæsar greater brilliancy, Caelius is the more caustic, Brutus the more earnest, Cicero the more impassioned, the richer and more forcible. Still about them all there is the same healthy tone of eloquence. Take into your hand the works of all alike and you see that amid wide differences of genius, there is a resemblance and affinity of intellect and moral purpose. Grant that they disparaged each other (and certainly there are some passages in their letters which show mutual ill-will), still this is the failing, not of the orator, but of the man. Calvus, Asinius, Cicero himself, I presume, were apt to be envious and ill-natured, and to have the other faults of human infirmity. Brutus alone of the number in my opinion laid open the convictions of his heart frankly and ingenuously, without ill-will or envy. Is it possible that he envied Cicero, when he seems not to have envied even Cæsar? As to Servius Galba, and Caius Laelius, and others of the ancients whom Aper has persistently assailed, he must not expect me to defend them, for I admit that their eloquence, being yet in its infancy and imperfectly developed, had certain defects.

26. After all, if I must put on one side the highest and most perfect type of eloquence and select a style, I should certainly prefer the vehemence of Caius Gracchus or the sobriety of Lucius Crassus to the curls of Maecenas or the jingles of Gallio: so much better is it for an orator to wear a rough dress than to glitter in many-coloured and meretricious attire. Indeed, neither for an orator or even a man is that style becoming which is adopted by many of the speakers of our age, and which, with its idle redundancy of words, its meaningless periods and licence of expression, imitates the art of the actor. Shocking as it ought to be to our ears, it is a fact that fame, glory, and genius are sacrificed by many to the boast that their compositions are given with the tones of the singer, the gestures of the dancer. Hence the exclamation, which, though often heard, is a shame and

an absurdity, that our orators speak prettily and our actors dance eloquently. For myself I would not deny that Cassius Severus, the only speaker whom Aper ventured to name, may, if compared with his successors, be called an orator, although in many of his works he shows more violence than vigour. The first to despise arrangement, to cast off propriety and delicacy of expression, confused by the very weapons he employs, and often stumbling in his eagerness to strike, he wrangles rather than fights. Still, as I have said, compared with his successors, he is far superior to all in the variety of his learning, the charm of his wit, and the solidity of his very strength. Not one of them has Aper had the courage to mention, and, so to say, to bring into the field. When he had censured Asinius, Caelius, and Calvus, I expected that he would show us a host of others, and name more, or at least as many who might be pitted man by man against Cicero, Cæsar, and the rest. As it is, he has contented himself with singling out for disparagement some ancient orators, and has not dared to praise any of their successors, except generally and in terms common to all, fearing, I suppose, that he would offend many, if he selected a few. For there is scarce one of our rhetoricians who does not rejoice in his conviction that he is to be ranked before Cicero, but unquestionably second to Gabinianus.

27. For my own part I shall not scruple to mention men by name, that, with examples before us, we may the more easily perceive the successive steps of the ruin and decay of eloquence.

Maternus here interrupted him. Rather prepare yourself to fulfil your promise. We do not want proof of the superior eloquence of the ancients; as far as I am concerned, it is admitted. We are inquiring into the causes, and these you told us but now you had been in the habit of discussing, when you were less excited and were not raving against the eloquence of our age, just before Aper offended you by attacking your ancestors.

I was not offended, replied Messala, by our friend Aper's argument, nor again will you have a right to be offended, if any remark of mine happens to grate on your ears, for you know that it is a rule in these discussions that we may speak out our convictions without impairing mutual good-will.

Proceed, said Maternus. As you are speaking of the ancients, avail yourself of ancient freedom, from which we have fallen away even yet more than from eloquence.

28. Messala continued. Far from obscure are the causes which you seek. Neither to yourself or to our friends, Secundus and Aper, are they unknown, though you assign me the part of speaking out before you what we all think. Who does not know that eloquence and all other arts have declined from their ancient glory, not from dearth of men, but from the indolence of the young, the carelessness of parents, the ignorance of teachers, and neglect of the old discipline? The evils which first began in Rome soon spread through Italy, and are now diffusing themselves into the provinces. But your provincial affairs are best known to yourselves. I shall speak of Rome, and of those native and home-bred vices which take hold of us as soon as we are born, and multiply with every stage of life, when I have first said a few words on the strict discipline of our ancestors in the education and training of children. Every citizen's son, the child of a chaste mother, was from the beginning reared, not in the chamber of a purchased nurse, but in that mother's bosom and embrace, and it was her special glory to study her home and devote herself to her children. It was usual to select an elderly kinswoman of approved and esteemed character to have the entire charge of all the children of the household. In her presence it was the last offence to utter an unseemly word or to do a disgraceful act. With scrupulous piety and modesty she regulated not only the boy's studies and occupations, but even his recreations and games. Thus it was, as tradition says, that the mothers of the Gracchi, of Cæsar, of Augustus, Cornelia, Aurelia, Atia, directed their children's education and reared the greatest of sons. The strictness of the discipline tended to form in each case a pure and virtuous nature which no vices could warp, and which would at once with the whole heart seize on every noble lesson. Whatever its bias, whether to the soldier's or the lawyer's art, or to the study of eloquence, it would make that its sole aim, and imbibe it in its fullness.

29. But in our day we entrust the infant to a little Greek servant-girl who is attended by one or two, commonly the worst of all the slaves, creatures utterly unfit for any important work. Their stories and their prejudices from the very first fill the child's tender and uninstructed mind. No one in the whole house cares what he says or does before his infant master. Even parents themselves familiarise their little ones, not with virtue and modesty, but with jesting and glib talk, which lead on by degrees to shamelessness and to contempt for themselves as well as for others. Really I think that the characteristic and peculiar vices of this city, a liking for actors and a passion for gladiators and horses, are all but conceived in the mother's womb. When these occupy and possess the mind, how little room has it left for worthy attainments! Few indeed are to be found who talk of any other subjects in their homes, and whenever we enter a classroom, what else is the conversation of the youths. Even with the teachers, these are the more frequent topics of talk with their scholars. In fact, they draw pupils, not by strictness of discipline or by giving proof of ability, but by assiduous court and cunning tricks of flattery.

30. I say nothing about the learners' first rudiments. Even with these little pains are taken, and on the reading of authors, on the study of antiquity and a knowledge of facts, of men and of periods, by no means enough labour is bestowed. It is rhetoricians, as they are called, who are in request. When this profession was first introduced into our city, and how little esteem it had among our ancestors, I am now about to explain; but I will first recall your attention to the training which we have been told was practised by those orators whose infinite industry, daily study and incessant application to every branch of learning are seen in the contents of their own books. You are doubtless familiar with Cicero's book, called Brutus. In the latter part of it (the first gives an account of the ancient orators) he relates his own beginnings, his progress, and the growth, so to say, of his eloquence. He tells us that he learnt the civil law under Quintus Mucius, and that he thoroughly imbibed every branch of philosophy under Philo of the Academy and under Diodotus the Stoic: that not content with the teachers under

whom he had had the opportunity of studying at Rome, he travelled through Achaia and Asia Minor so as to embrace every variety of every learned pursuit. Hence we really find in Cicero's works that he was not deficient in the knowledge of geometry, music, grammar, or, in short, any liberal accomplishment. The subtleties of logic, the useful lessons of ethical science, the movements and causes of the universe, were alike known to him. The truth indeed is this, my excellent friends, that Cicero's wonderful eloquence wells up and overflows out of a store of erudition, a multitude of accomplishments, and a knowledge that was universal. The strength and power of oratory, unlike all other arts, is not confined within narrow and straitened limits, but the orator is he who can speak on every question with grace, elegance, and persuasiveness, suitably to the dignity of his subject, the requirements of the occasion, and the taste of his audience.

31. Such was the conviction of the ancients, and to produce this result they were aware that it was necessary not only to declaim in the schools of rhetoricians, or to exercise the tongue and the voice in fictitious controversies quite remote from reality, but also to imbue the mind with those studies which treat of good and evil, of honour and dishonour, of right and wrong. All this, indeed, is the subject-matter of the orator's speeches. Equity in the law-court, honour in the council-chamber, are our usual topics of discussion. Still, these often pass into each other, and no one can speak on them with fulness, variety, and elegance but he who has studied human nature, the power of virtue, the depravity of vice, and the conception of those things which can be classed neither among virtues nor vices. These are the sources whence flows the greater ease with which he who knows what anger is, rouses or soothes the anger of a judge, the readier power with which he moves to pity who knows what pity is, and what emotions of the soul excite it. An orator practised in such arts and exercises, whether he has to address the angry, the biassed, the envious, the sorrowful, or the trembling, will understand different mental conditions, apply his skill, adapt his style, and have every instrument of his craft in readiness, or in reserve for every occasion. Some there are whose assent is more secured by

an incisive and terse style, in which each inference is rapidly drawn. With such, it will be an advantage to have studied logic. Others are more attracted by a diffuse and
smoothly flowing speech, appealing to the common sentiments of humanity. To impress such we must borrow from
the Peripatetics commonplaces suited and ready prepared
for every discussion. The Academy will give us combative-
ness, Plato, sublimity, Xenophon, sweetness. Nor will it be
unseemly in an orator to adopt even certain exclamations of
honest emotion, from Epicurus and Metrodorus, and to use
them as occasion requires. It is not a philosopher after the
Stoic school whom we are forming, but one who ought to
imbibe thoroughly some studies, and to have a taste of all.
Accordingly, knowledge of the civil law was included in the
training of the ancient orators, and they also imbued their
minds with grammar, music, and geometry. In truth, in very
many, I may say in all cases, acquaintance with law is de-
sirable, and in several this last-mentioned knowledge is a
necessity.

32. Let no one reply that it is enough for us to learn, as
occasion requires, some single and detached subject. In the
first place we use our own property in one way, a loan in
another, and there is evidently a wide difference between
possessing what one exhibits and borrowing it. Next, the
very knowledge of many subjects sits gracefully on us, even
when we are otherwise engaged, and makes itself visible
and conspicuous where you would least expect it. Even the
average citizen, and not only the learned and critical hearer,
perceives it, and forthwith showers his praises in the ac-
knowledgment that the man has been a genuine student,
has gone through every branch of eloquence, and is, in
short, an orator. And I maintain that the only orator is, and
ever has been, one who, like a soldier equipped at all points
going to the battle-field, enters the forum armed with every
learned accomplishment.

All this is so neglected by the speakers of our time that
we detect in their pleadings the style of every-day conversation, and unseemly and shameful deficiencies. They are
ignorant of the laws, they do not understand the senate's
decrees, they actually scoff at the civil law, while they quite

dread the study of philosophy, and the opinions of the learned; and eloquence, banished, so to say, from her proper realm, is dragged down by them into utter poverty of thought and constrained periods. Thus she who, once mistress of all the arts, held sway with a glorious retinue over our souls, now clipped and shorn, without state, without honour, I had almost said without her freedom, is studied as one of the meanest handicrafts. This then I believe to be the first and chief cause of so marked a falling off among us from the eloquence of the old orators. If witnesses are wanted, whom shall I name in preference to Demosthenes among the Greeks, who is said by tradition to have been a most attentive hearer of Plato? Cicero too tells us, I think, in these very words, that whatever he had achieved in eloquence he had gained, not from rhetoricians, but in the walks of the Academy. There are other causes, some of them great and important, which it is for you in fairness to explain, as I have now done my part, and, after my usual way, have offended pretty many persons who, if they happen to hear all this, will, I am sure, say that, in praising an acquaintance with law and philosophy as a necessity for an orator, I have been applauding my own follies.

33. For myself, replied Maternus, I do not think that you have completed the task which you undertook. Far from it. You have, I think, only made a beginning, and indicated, so to say, its traces and outlines. You have indeed described to us the usual equipment of the ancient orators, and pointed out the contrast presented by our idleness and ignorance to their very diligent and fruitful studies. I want to hear the rest. Having learnt from you what they knew, with which we are unacquainted, I wish also to be told the process of training by which, when mere lads, and when about to enter the forum, they used to strengthen and nourish their intellects. For you will not, I imagine, deny that eloquence depends much less on art and theory than on capacity and practice, and our friends here seem by their looks to think the same.

Aper and Secundus having assented, Messala, so to say, began afresh. As I have, it seems, explained to your satis-

faction the first elements and the germs of ancient eloquence in showing you the studies in which the orator of
antiquity was formed and educated, I will now discuss the
process of his training. However, even the studies themselves involve a training, and no one can acquire such profound and varied knowledge without adding practice to
theory, fluency to practice, and eloquence itself to fluency.
Hence we infer that the method of acquiring what you mean
to produce publicly, and of so producing what you have
acquired, is one and the same. Still, if any one thinks this
somewhat obscure, and distinguishes broadly between theory
and practice, he will at least allow that a mind thoroughly
furnished and imbued with such studies will enter with a
far better preparation on the kinds of practice which seem
specially appropriate to the orator.

34 It was accordingly usual with our ancestors, when a
lad was being prepared for public speaking, as soon as he
was fully trained by home discipline, and his mind was
stored with culture, to have him taken by his father, or his
relatives to the orator who held the highest rank in the
state. The boy used to accompany and attend him, and be
present at all his speeches, alike in the law-court and the
assembly, and thus he picked up the art of repartee, and
became habituated to the strife of words, and indeed, I may
almost say, learnt how to fight in battle. Thereby young
men acquired from the first great experience and confidence, and a very large stock of discrimination, for they
were studying in broad daylight, in the very thick of the
conflict, where no one can say anything foolish or self-
contradictory without its being refuted by the judge, or
ridiculed by the opponent, or, last of all, repudiated by the
very counsel with him. Thus from the beginning they were
imbued with true and genuine eloquence, and, although
they attached themselves to one pleader, still they became
acquainted with all advocates of their own standing in a
multitude of cases before the courts. They had too abundant experience of the popular ear in all its greatest varieties, and with this they could easily ascertain what was
liked or disapproved in each speaker. Thus they were not
in want of a teacher of the very best and choicest kind,

who could show them eloquence in her true features, not in a mere resemblance; nor did they lack opponents and rivals, who fought with actual steel, not with a wooden sword, and the audience too was always crowded, always changing, made up of unfriendly as well as of admiring critics, so that neither success nor failure could be disguised. You know, of course, that eloquence wins its great and enduring fame quite as much from the benches of our opponents as from those of our friends; nay, more, its rise from that quarter is steadier, and its growth surer. Undoubtedly it was under such teachers that the youth of whom I am speaking, the disciple of orators, the listener in the forum, the student in the law-courts, was trained and practised by the experiences of others. The laws he learnt by daily hearing; the faces of the judges were familiar to him; the ways of popular assemblies were continually before his eyes; he had frequent experience of the ear of the people, and whether he undertook a prosecution or a defence, he was at once singly and alone equal to any case. We still read with admiration the speeches in which Lucius Crassus in his nineteenth, Cæsar and Asinius Pollio in their twenty-first year, Calvus, when very little older, denounced, respectively, Carbo, Dolabella, Cato, and Vatinius.

35. But in these days we have our youths taken to the professors' theatre, the rhetoricians, as we call them. The class made its appearance a little before Cicero's time, and was not liked by our ancestors, as is evident from the fact that, when Crassus and Domitius were censors, they were ordered, as Cicero says, to close "the school of impudence." However, as I was just saying, the boys are taken to schools in which it is hard to tell whether the place itself, or their fellow-scholars, or the character of their studies, do their minds most harm. As for the place, there is no such thing as reverence, for no one enters it who is not as ignorant as the rest. As for the scholars, there can be no improvement, when boys and striplings with equal assurance address, and are addressed by, other boys and striplings. As for the mental exercises themselves, they are the reverse of beneficial. Two kinds of subject-matter are dealt with before

the rhetoricians, the persuasive and the controversial. The persuasive, as being comparatively easy and requiring less skill, is given to boys. The controversial is assigned to riper scholars, and, good heavens! what strange and astonishing productions are the result! It comes to pass that subjects remote from all reality are actually used for declamation. Thus the reward of a tyrannicide, or the choice of an outraged maiden, or a remedy for a pestilence, or a mother's incest, anything, in short, daily discussed in our schools, never, or but very rarely in the courts, is dwelt on in grand language.

[The rest of Messala's speech is lost. Maternus is now again the speaker.]

36. Great eloquence, like fire, grows with its material; it becomes fiercer with movement, and brighter as it burns. On this same principle was developed in our state too the eloquence of antiquity. Although even the modern orator has attained all that the circumstances of a settled, quiet, and prosperous community allow, still in the disorder and licence of the past more seemed to be within the reach of the speaker, when, amid a universal confusion that needed one guiding hand, he exactly adapted his wisdom to the bewildered people's capacity of conviction. Hence, laws without end and consequent popularity; hence, speeches of magistrates who, I may say, passed nights on the Rostra; hence, prosecutions of influential citizens brought to trial, and feuds transmitted to whole families; hence, factions among the nobles, and incessant strife between the senate and the people. In each case the state was torn asunder, but the eloquence of the age was exercised and, as it seemed, was loaded with great rewards. For the more powerful a man was as a speaker, the more easily did he obtain office, the more decisively superior was he to his colleagues in office, the more influence did he acquire with the leaders of the state, the more weight in the senate, the more notoriety and fame with the people. Such men had a host of clients, even among foreign nations; the magistrates, when leaving Rome for the provinces, showed them respect, and courted their favour as soon as they returned. The prætorship and the consulship seemed to offer themselves to them,

and even when they were out of office, they were not out
of power, for they swayed both people and senate with
their counsels and influence. Indeed, they had quite convinced themselves that without eloquence no one could
win or retain a distinguished and eminent position in the
state. And no wonder. Even against their own wish they
had to show themselves before the people. It was little good
for them to give a brief vote in the senate without supporting their opinion with ability and eloquence. If brought
into popular odium, or under some charge, they had to
reply in their own words. Again, they were under the necessity of giving evidence in the public courts, not in their
absence by affidavit, but of being present and of speaking
it openly. There was thus a strong stimulus to win the great
prizes of eloquence, and as the reputation of a good speaker
was considered an honour and a glory, so it was thought a
disgrace to seem mute and speechless. Shame therefore quite
as much as hope of reward prompted men not to take the
place of a pitiful client rather than that of a patron, or
to see hereditary connections transferred to others, or to
seem spiritless and incapable of office from either failing
to obtain it or from holding it weakly when obtained.

37. Perhaps you have had in your hands the old records,
still to be found in the libraries of antiquaries, which Mucianus is just now collecting, and which have already been
brought together and published in, I think, eleven books
of Transactions, and three of Letters. From these we may
gather that Cneius Pompeius and Marcus Crassus rose to
power as much by force of intellect and by speaking as by
their might in arms; that the Lentuli, Metelli, Luculli, and
Curios, and the rest of our nobles, bestowed great labour
and pains on these studies, and that, in fact, no one in
those days acquired much influence without some eloquence.
We must consider too the eminence of the men accused, and
the vast issues involved. These of themselves do very much
for eloquence. There is, indeed, a wide difference between
having to speak on a theft, a technical point, a judicial decision, and on bribery at elections, the plundering of the
allies, and the massacre of citizens. Though it is better that
these evils should not befall us, and the best condition of

the state is that in which we are spared such sufferings, still, when they did occur, they supplied a grand material for the orator. His mental powers rise with the dignity of his subject, and no one can produce a noble and brilliant speech unless he has got an adequate case. Demosthenes, I take it, does not owe his fame to his speeches against his guardians, and it is not his defence of Publius Quintius, or of Licinius Archias, which make Cicero a great orator; it is his Catiline, his Milo, his Verres, and Antonius, which have shed over him this lustre. Not indeed that it was worth the state's while to endure bad citizens that orators might have plenty of matter for their speeches, but, as I now and then remind you, we must remember the point, and understand that we are speaking of an art which arose more easily in stormy and unquiet times. Who knows not that it is better and more profitable to enjoy peace than to be harassed by war? Yet war produces more good soldiers than peace. Eloquence is on the same footing. The oftener she has stood, so to say, in the battle-field, the more wounds she has inflicted and received, the mightier her antagonist, the sharper the conflicts she has freely chosen, the higher and more splendid has been her rise, and ennobled by these contests she lives in the praises of mankind.

38. I pass now to the forms and character of procedure in the old courts. As they exist now, they are indeed more favourable to truth, but the forum in those days was a better training for eloquence. There no speaker was under the necessity of concluding within a very few hours; there was freedom of adjournment, and every one fixed for himself the limits of his speech, and there was no prescribed number of days or of counsel. It was Cneius Pompeius who, in his third consulship, first restricted all this, and put a bridle, so to say, on eloquence, intending, however, that all business should be transacted in the forum according to law, and before the prætors. Here is a stronger proof of the greater importance of the cases tried before these judges than in the fact that causes in the Court of the Hundred, causes which now hold the first place, were then so eclipsed by the fame of other trials that not a speech of Cicero, or Cæsar, or Brutus, or Caelius, or Calvus, or, in short, any

great orator is now read, that was delivered in that Court, except only the orations of Asinius Pollio for the heirs of Urbinia, as they are entitled, and even Pollio delivered these in the middle of the reign of Augustus, a period of long rest, of unbroken repose for the people and tranquillity for the senate, when the emperor's perfect discipline had put its restraints on eloquence as well as on all else.

39. Perhaps what I am going to say will be thought trifling and ridiculous; but I will say it even to be laughed at. What contempt (so I think at least) has been brought on eloquence by those little overcoats into which we squeeze, and, so to say, box ourselves up, when we chat with the judges! How much force may we suppose has been taken from our speeches by the little rooms and offices in which nearly all cases have to be set forth. Just as a spacious course tests a fine horse, so the orator has his field, and unless he can move in it freely and at ease, his eloquence grows feeble and breaks down. Nay more; we find the pains and labour of careful composition out of place, for the judge keeps asking when you are going to open the case, and you must begin from his question. Frequently he imposes silence on the advocate to hear proofs and witnesses. Meanwhile only one or two persons stand by you as you are speaking and the whole business is transacted almost in solitude. But the orator wants shouts and applause, and something like a theatre, all which and the like were the every day lot of the orators of antiquity, when both numbers and nobility pressed into the forum, when gatherings of clients and the people in their tribes and deputations from the towns and indeed a great part of Italy stood by the accused in his peril, and Rome's citizens felt in a multitude of trials that they themselves had an interest in the decision. We know that there was a universal rush of the people to hear the accusation and the defence of Cornelius, Scaurus, Milo, Bestia, and Vatinius, so that even the coldest speaker might have been stirred and kindled by the mere enthusiasm of the citizens in their strife. And therefore indeed such pleadings are still extant, and thus the men too who pleaded, owe their fame to no other speeches more than these.

40. Again, what stimulus to genius and what fire to the

orator was furnished by incessant popular assemblies, by
the privilege of attacking the most influential men, and by
the very glory of such feuds when most of the good speakers
did not spare even a Publius Scipio, or a Sulla, or a Cneius
Pompeius, and following the common impulse of envy
availed themselves of the popular ear for invective against
eminent citizens. I am not speaking of a quiet and peaceful
accomplishment, which delights in what is virtuous and
well regulated. No; the great and famous eloquence of old
is the nursling of the licence which fools called freedom;
it is the companion of sedition, the stimulant of an unruly
people, a stranger to obedience and subjection, a defiant,
reckless, presumptuous thing which does not show itself in
a well-governed state. What orator have we ever heard of
at Sparta or at Crete? A very strict discipline and very
strict laws prevailed, tradition says, in both those states.
Nor do we know of the existence of eloquence among the
Macedonians or Persians, or in any people content with
a settled government. There were some orators at Rhodes
and a host of them at Athens, but there the people, there
any ignorant fellow, anybody, in short, could do anything.
So too our own state, while it went astray and wore out
its strength in factious strife and discord, with neither peace
in the forum, unity in the senate, order in the courts, respect
for merit, or seemly behaviour in the magistrates, produced
beyond all question a more vigorous eloquence, just as an
untilled field yields certain herbage in special plenty. Still
the eloquence of the Gracchi was not an equivalent to Rome
for having to endure their legislation, and Cicero's fame as
an orator was a poor compensation for the death he died.

41. And so now the forum, which is all that our speakers
have left them of antiquity, is an evidence of a state not
thoroughly reformed or as orderly as we could wish. Who
but the guilty or unfortunate apply to us? What town puts
itself under our protection but one harassed by its neighbours or by strife at home? When we plead for a province,
is it not one that has been plundered and ill-treated? Surely
it would be better not to complain than to have to seek
redress. Could a community be found in which no one did
wrong, an orator would be as superfluous among its inno-

cent people as a physician among the healthy. As the healing art is of very little use and makes very little progress in nations which enjoy particularly robust constitutions and vigorous frames, so the orator gets an inferior and less splendid renown where a sound morality and willing obedience to authority prevail. What need there of long speeches in the senate, when the best men are soon of one mind, or of endless harangues to the people, when political questions are decided not by an ignorant multitude, but by one man of pre-eminent wisdom? What need of voluntary prosecutions, when crimes are so rare and slight, or of defences full of spiteful insinuation and exceeding proper bounds, when the clemency of the judge offers itself to the accused in his peril?

Be assured, my most excellent, and, as far as the age requires, most eloquent friends, that had you been born in the past, and the men we admire in our own day, had some god in fact suddenly changed your lives and your age, the highest fame and glory of eloquence would have been yours, and they too would not have lacked moderation and self-control. As it is, seeing that no one can at the same time enjoy great renown and great tranquillity, let everybody make the best of the blessings of his own age without disparaging other periods.

Maternus had now finished. There were, replied Messala, some points I should controvert, some on which I should like to hear more, if the day were not almost spent. It shall be, said Maternus, as you wish, on a future occasion, and anything you have thought obscure in my argument, we will again discuss. Then he rose and embraced Aper. I mean, he said, to accuse you before the poets, and so will Messala before the antiquarians. And I, rejoined Aper, will accuse you before the rhetoricians and professors.

They laughed good-humouredly, and we parted.

GLOSSARY OF PLACE NAMES

Names are not cited when identification is obvious, or the location is given in the text, or is inconsequential. For *tribes* the modern designation of the *territory* they occupied is given; these identifications are not in every case certain.

Abnoba: Black Forest
Addua, river: Adda
Adrana, river: Eder
Aenus, river: Inn
Aestii: Estonia
Agrippinensis, Colonia: Cologne
Albis, river: Elbe
Alieni, Forum: Ferrara
Allobroges: Savoy
Amisia, river: Ems
Amorgus, island: Morgo
Anglii: Schleswig-Holstein
Angrivarii: Westphalia
Antipolis: Antibes
Antium: Porto d'Anzo
Arar, river: Saône
Aravisci: S. W. Hungary
Aricia: La Riccia
Arnus, river: Arno
Asciburgium: Asburg
Ateste: Este
Augustodunum: Autun
Aventicum: Avenches
Avernus, lake: Lago d'Averno
Aviones: Mecklenburg

Barium: Bari
Bastarnae: Poland
Batavi: Holland
Berytus: Beyruth
Bingium: Bingen

Bodotria, estuary: Forth
Boiemum: Bohemia
Boii: E. Bavaria, part of Bohemia
Bonna: Bonn
Bononia: Bologna
Boresti: Scotland
Bovilla: Bojano (nr. Rome)
Brigantes: N. Britain
Brixellum: Brescello
Brixia: Brescia
Bructeri: bet. Rhine and Ems, on either side of Lippe
Brundisium: Brindisi
Buri: nr. Cracow
Byzantium: Constantinople

Camulodunum: Maldon
Capreae, island: Capri
Cercina, island: Karkenah, off Tunis
Chamavi: on Ems, nr. Osnabruck
Chasuarii: Oldenburg
Chatti: Hesse
Chauci: Oldenburg and parts of Hanover and Westphalia
Cherusci: Brunswick
Cimbri: Denmark
Clanis, river: Chiana
Clota, estuary: Clyde
Colonia Agrippinensis: Cologne

Corcyra: Corfu

Cusus, river: Waag

Dacia: S. Russia

Dulgubrii: Hanover

Elisii: Poland

Emerita: Merida

Endoses: Jutland

Fenni: Finland

Fidenae: Castel Giubileo (nr. Rome)

Flevum: Vlieland

Florentia: Florence

Forojulium, Forum Julium: Fréjus

Fortune, Temple of: Fano

Fosi: Hanover

Frisii: Friesland, N. E. Holland

Fucinus, lake: Lago di Celano

Gelduba: Gelb

Gothini: Silesia

Gothones: Pomerania, Prussia

Haemus, mountain: Great Balkan

Harii: Polish Prussia

Hellusii: Poland

Helvecones: Poland

Hercynian Forest: mountains of S. Germany, including Riesengebirge

Herminones: Hesse and Thuringia and Saxon Switzerland

Hermunduri: Bavaria

Hibernia: Ireland

Hispalis: Seville

Iazyges: Hungary

Idistavisus, plain: nr. Minden or Rinteln on Weser

Ingaevones: Danish peninsula

Intemelii: Vintimiglia

Istaevonii: between Rhine and Weser

Interamna: Terni

Langobardi: W. bank of Elbe, nr. Luneburg

Lemovii: Pomerania

Ligii, Lugii: Poland, perhaps Sclaves, ancestors of Vandals and Burgundians

Liris, river: Garigliano

Londinium: London

Lugdunum: Lyons

Marcodurum: Düren

Marcomanni: N. bank of Danube

Marsigni: borders of Silesia and Bohemia

Massilia: Marseilles

Mattiaci: Nassau

Mattium: Marburg or Maden

Mediolanum: Milan

Mevania: Bevagna

Misenum: Capo di Miseno

Moenus, river: Main

Moesia: Servia and Bulgaria

Mogontiacum: Mayence

Mona: Anglesea

Monoecus, Hercules: Monaco

Mosa, river: Meuse

Nar, river: Nera

Narnia: Narni on the Nera

Nauportus: Ober-Laybach in Carniola

Nava, river: Nahe

Neapolis: Naples

Nervii: Belgium

Novesium: Neuss

Nuceria: Nocera

Ocriculum: Otricoli

Old Camp (Castra Vetera): Xanten

Opitergium: Oderzo

Orcades, islands: Orkney and Shetland

Osi: Gallicia

Padus, river: Po

Pandataria, island: Vandotina

Pannonia: W. part of Hungary

Patavium: Padua

Petovio: Pettau

Placentia: Piacenza

Puteoli: Pozzuli

Pyramus, river: Jaihan

Quadi: Moravia

Raeti: E. Switzerland, Tyrol, S. Bavaria

Reate: Rieti

Regium Lepidum, Regini: Reggio

Rigodulum: Reol

Rugii: extreme N. of Pomerania

Sarmatae: S. Russia

Saxa Rubra: Prima Porta (nr. Rome)

Semnones: Brandenburg

Sena: Siena

Silures: S. Wales

Sinuessa: Mondragone

Sitones: Finland

Stoechades, islands: Isles d'Hières

Sublaqueum: Subiaco

Suebi: Serbia

Suines: Sweden

Tamesa, river: Thames

Tarentum: Taranto

Tarracina: Terracina

Taurini, Augusta of: Turin

Taus, estuary: unidentified; Tay. Forth, Tweed, N. Tyne, Solway Firth, and Clyde have all been suggested

Tencteri: E. bank of Rhine

Termestini: nr. Numantia

Thule: probably Mainland, largest of Shetlands; hardly Iceland

Ticinum: Pavia

Tolbiacum: Zülpich

Torone, bay: Gulf of Saloniki

Trapezus: Trebizond

Treveri: Trier, Trèves

Tungri: Belgium (Tongres)

Vahal, river: Waal

Venedi (not to be confused with Veneti): N. Germany (Wends)

Veline lake: Lago di pie di Lugo

Verulamium: St. Albans

Vicetia: Vicenza

Vienna: Vienne

Vindonissa: Windisch

Visurgis, river: Weser

Vocetius, mountain: Boetzburg, in Jura

Orcades islands; Orkney and
    Shetland
Oxi: Calisto

Padus river; Po
Pandataria island; Vandotena
Pannonia, W. part of Hungary
Patavium; Padua
Pelorào; Peloro
Placentia; Piacenza
Puteoli: Pozzuoli
Pyramus river; Jaihan

Oaseli; Morayia

Raeti, E. Switzerland, Tyrol, &c.
Ravenna
Reate; Rieti
Rhegium Lepidum, Reneli; Reggio
Rhaudium; Rud
Rugii: extrema N: of Venezuela

Sunnatae S. Russia
Saxa Rubrae Prima Porta (nr
    Rome)
Secitones; Brandenburg
Sena; Siena
Shurda &: Wales
Sinuessa; Montdragone
Sitoned: Finland
Stoechades islands; Iles d'Hieres
Sublaqueum; Subiaco

Squires; Sweden

Tamesa river; Thames
Tarentum; Taranto
Tarracina; Terracina
Taurini Augusta of; Turin
Tave, estuary
Perth, Tweed, N. Tyne. Solway, Forth and Clyde have all been suggested
Pandharis, E. bank of Rhine
Teutoburg; the Nunberg
Thiney probably Mainland larger of the Shetlands; hardly Iceland
Tibiscus river; Theiss
Tolbiacum; Zülpich
Tomoris: town, Gulf of Salonika
Thrasimene; Trasimend
Treveri; Trier, Treves
Tongri; Belgium (Tongres)

Vabali river; Waal
Veneti (not to be confused with Veneton N. Germany (Wendi)
Venta Iceno; Caistor nr St. Albans
Vicetia; Vicenza
Verona; Verona
Vindonissa; Windisch
Venetia, the river Wear
Vrulus; mountain, Mont'gura
In Jura